I MEANT TO DIVORCE MY WIFE NOT MY DAUGHTER

Zev Lewinson

SwordPen™
PUBLISHERS

SwordPen Publishers

The work of a memoir is often riddled by critics with contentions of the author's memory being flawed due to the caducity of old age. The traumatic events of my sixty-eight-year-old life and the agonizing details of my dystopian divorce negate any such allegations. They are not easily forgotten. Desperate accusations to discredit my work will surely arise from under many slimy judicial rocks and Abrahamic authoritative religious shrieking voices in an attempt to protest and diffuse the outrage my words will surely ignite. The louder the hisses and scorn, the more firmly I stand behind every letter of the approximately quarter-million words that comprise my story.

Mine is a non-fiction work. I make no apologies for refusing to change names to protect the innocent. Because the characters, from ancient times to present day, were not. Nor have I distorted any conversations. My quotes are verbatim emails that were entered into the court proceedings and are literal excerpts from the Rockland County Court System. I also source all scriptural and Masoretic traditional narratives. You can simply Google any fact that your conditioned mind finds too uncomfortable to digest. So although most books proclaim the protective proclamation of "to the best of my knowledge" to ward off possible lawsuits, I elaborate how this book was written, researched, and organized in the epilogue, and I believe that no such declaration is necessary when speaking the truth, the whole truth, and nothing but the truth.

Library of Congress Number: 2020937756
Title: I Meant To Divorce My Wife, Not My Daughter
ISBN-13: 978-1-940649-10-8
ISBN-10: 1-940649-10-2
ISBN-10: 1-940649-09-9 (ebook)
First edition 2020 / written by Zev Lewinson

SwordPenPublishers@gmail.com

Jacket design and layout by Dan Fernandez
Fernandez Design Group
danfdesign@gmail.com

"There is no crueler tyranny than that which is perpetuated under the shield of law and in the name of justice."

— Charles de Montesquieu

I sat on the edge of my bed as I watched my two sons trying to comfort my youngest daughter who had a slow stream of tears running down her cherubic face. I had barely opened my eyes, but I quickly understood that this latest spur-of-the-moment event my baby girl was crying over felt like a life-altering cataclysm in the imagination of her adorable two-year-old mind. And as I observed, through crusty morning eyes, the almost surreal scene unfolding in the dimly lit hallway beyond the half-opened door to my bedroom, both my boys, ages twelve and fourteen, who already had remarkable parenting skills, seemed to have the situation, and their sister's profuse crying, pretty much under control.

Josh, my older son, was using his mother's talent for psychological evaluation on his little sister, and in a gentle voice reassured her that she was merely experiencing her fears and that everything would be fine. Abraham then tried to double-team his brother's efforts by validating the soothing message as he gently stroked his baby sister's teary cheek. But Ester suddenly turned on him and snapped, "And you be quiet! You have stupid eyes!"

I knew I should have softly said something to my spirited cherub to the effect of, "Ester, we don't talk that way." But I instead burst out laughing. My son has beautiful rare emerald-green eyes, and the thought of a toddler attempting to insult the brother she so loved seemed adorably funny to me. I laughed so hard my body shook. I continued to laugh intensely, to the point where I could see the synapses in my brain lighting up, and I felt the bliss of my endorphins as they flowed, and exploded, erupting within my temporal lobes. How can I do that, I wondered as I experienced the tingling sensation of a cerebral orgasm-of-laughter as I shook uncontrollably — to the point of exhaustion — when my thoughts abruptly shifted as I wondered: whatever happened to Ester?

I suddenly realized I hadn't seen her in many years. And I couldn't remember why not. We were so close. As a wobbly-walking one-year-old she used to come crying to seek hugs and comfort from me over her own mother who still nursed her. My wife would laugh at how her once binge-drinking bad-boy-lover had become "a mommy." I remembered how ecstatic I felt walking on air for six miles through a light spring drizzle the Passover morning Ester was born, excited to share the joyous "It's a girl!" arrival of our newest family member with her four siblings.

It was at that very moment when I woke up so startled, from a dream created from scattered events which had taken place almost two decades earlier which felt so vividly real, that I found it difficult to reposition my mind and comprehend I had been asleep in the past only seconds before. Thoughts, images, and vivid memories of Ester as a baby continued to zap around my brain, as if they happened only moments ago, while I peed, brushed my teeth, and tried to sort the ancient from the present as I prepared my first of several cups of coffee I would drink that morning.

I recalled being called up to the Torah in the synagogue the first Shabbat of my newborn tabula-rasa's life where I publicly and proudly proclaimed my daughter's name. Ester bat Zev (Ester the daughter of Zev). She was named after my heroine, Queen Ester of Persian fame. I had only recently completed studying the tenth volume of the Talmud called Tractate Megillah, and I loved Queen Ester. And I loved Baby Ester. I took care of Princess Ester as a Mr. Mom for the first two years of her life while her mother wielded a scalpel to "take vein" and circumvent obstructed coronary arteries in the operating room at North Shore University Hospital.

I also reflected back to when I had written a daily log while Ester napped, from baby to mommy, called "My Day." Her mother loved that diary. I wrote, in Ester's voice, about the beautiful feelings of love a father felt for his daughter, and vice versa, and the fun he had raising her since birth. And I sketched out comedic routines about burping, pooping, and diapering wriggling babies that made her mother laugh hysterically, never imagining that the mother who gently held Princess Ester to her milk-swelled-breast would conjure up a crackbrained accusation ten years in the future about my being "obsessed with feces" and that I'd receive an instantaneous protection order to protect my wife and THE MINOR CHILD (protection order instructions are in screaming capital letters) from my humor.

Whatever happened to the diary, I wondered? What happened to Ester? Did she grow up? Did she die?

I had laughed so hard, experiencing an almost mild episode of brain fog, that I could not remember any of the missing details regarding the life of a child who I could have sworn I once loved more than any father on the planet ever loved his little girl. And my consciousness continued to hover between the universe in which we dream and the fantastical physical dimension in which we live and deceive ourselves by calling it reality.

I've always considered it rather ironic how you wake up from a dream, but go to sleep after living. And so, the dream becomes reality, like the dream I'm sharing right now, whereas a lifetime becomes nothing more than a lost and forgotten dream. Eventual stardust drifting eternally through the universe.

As I came to, emerging from an almost groggy-like stupor after having probably overdosed on an immense rush of exploding endorphins during my dream, I had to concentrate and focus as I scanned my memory to recall details of the precocious little girl's biography. I knew there was once a time I would have killed for her and, without the least bit of hesitancy, died for her. And now I couldn't remember her middle name — or if she had one.

The hazy missing details slowly returned. Vague recollections of what were once earth-shattering matters teasingly emerged and flickered in my mind. Like an apparition of a long-forgotten lover swimming desperately towards an island of shrinking grey matter in the dimming mind's eye beneath the cranium of her ninety-year-old dementia-stricken soul-mate, the phantom specter of my daughter's ghostlike existence continued to haunt and elude me. Whatever happened to Ester?

As the morning light, like the cute wife I once had, jarred me to wake up, the details of the past several years illuminated inside the approximately threescore old shrinking grey matter in my cranium with the same impartial observation as my having had to memorize the historical fact, as I sat in the first seat of row four in third grade, of the Revolutionary War having occurred before the Civil War. For some reason, like my future marriage, I couldn't understand what all the fighting was about. And so, like most good little schoolboys, I simply memorized the cold facts. I now recalled how after twenty-eight years of marriage, which consisted of too little love and too much therapy, I had finally filed for divorce.

Being an Orthodox Jew, and living in a closed mundane community in Monsey, New York, where personal family matters are handled by dozens of local rabbinical courts, it proved quite a scandal when, as a pillar of the community and a scholar with a Master's degree in Talmudical research, I filed my divorce papers through the secular court system instead of relying on a court of "Our Own." "Unzereh." Endless indoctrination warning Jews to never intermingle with outside people can be summed up with this single Yiddish word.

Unzereh is a deceptive divisive concept cloaked in a colloquial pleasantry, which, once uttered, makes it very clear that you'd have to be "A real, absolute Goy!" (Ah Rich'teh'ker Goy!) if you ever went to "one of their ________," and not one of ours. Fill in the blank. Use any noun (e.g. courts, schools, restaurants, etc. ...) except prostitutes.

It's a very exclusionary keyword which instantly segregates not only Jews from non-Jews, but even secular Jews from other segments of Orthodox and Modern-Orthodox Jews as well. It doesn't necessarily have any racist intent. It could simply mean something as innocuous as, "Don't eat in their (a modern Jew's) restaurant. He's not one of Unzereh." That simple statement implies a deep chasm in that the two groups don't share the same strict standards of keeping kosher.

Merely whispering the word "Unzereh" to a fellow Unzereh-Jew carries the instant dire warning of its opposite intended "Nisht foon Unzereh!" (They are not one of us!) cry of panic. It even works well between a Jewish Hasid in cahoots with a modern secular-atheist Jew against a Puerto Rican. Now it's the Puerto Rican who is not from "Unzereh." It's quite a versatile word in the Jewish lexicon.

Choosing to settle your differences with a fellow Jew in a gentile secular court is the ultimate "Nisht foon Unzereh!" transgression. After all, we have our own Torah! How dare a royal son of the "Chosen People" debase himself with traveling on a skateboard while his chauffeured Bentley awaits? The prohibition warning Jews to never seek justice in the courts of the "Goyim" has actual roots in the Talmud.

"Arkayos Akum" is a somewhat pejorative term used in the Talmud in the severe condemnation of a Jewish person who forsakes Talmudical Jurisprudence and instead seeks justice from the courts of Idol Worshipers. Its literal translation is Courts of those who Serve (worship) the Stars and Astrological Signs. Yes, I'm talking wood, stones, constellations, and totem poles in the year 2020.

To be precise, Arkayos Akum refers to a court whose judges are pagan worshipers. In truth, atheists and Christian deists are not idol worshipers. And so I admonished the amateur rabbinical court, chosen and hired by my wife, to stop trying to intimidate me with threats of excommunication if I went to the "Goy'esh'eh Courts." A modern-day secular court is not an Arkayos Akum, I logically debated. As a matter of fact, one of the seven Noahide Laws is for all nations — all of humanity — to establish fair courts of justice. Civilization cannot exist without honest courts.

Likewise, a group of arbitrators in yarmulkas, proclaiming they are a Beit Din does not make it so. It is a false statement. A true credentialed Beit Din, as described in the Talmud, must compensate its litigants to the penny for any losses incurred from an incorrect rendering of Halacha. And real Beit Din judges have no immunity. Meanwhile, the first document these do-it-yourself arbitration boards place before a divorcing couple is a consent form in which they agree to forgo any damages which might result from an incorrect Halachic decision on their part.

On top of that, the Jewish arbitration courts are using the very Arkayos Akum courts they deride to later enforce their own decisions. If the secular courts are truly pagan worshipers, why are they suddenly trusted to enforce the decisions rendered by the Jewish courts? I guess to these arbitration panels, the secular courts are like a shiksa to the rare Hasid who temporarily steps out of his cult. Prohibited technically, but well-tolerated when the need arises.

Also, the Talmud never forces one to go to arbitration. It offers two litigants the opportunity to work things out as gentlemen (or lady and gentleman) before heading to an actual Beit Din court of law where they will be coerced to solemnly swear, while holding a Torah scroll, their testimony. But if either litigant insists on going to a Beit Din, their request has to be honored.

In short, an arbitration board, according to the Talmud, is a way for two honest individuals to possibly compromise and sort out their differences amicably in order to avoid the intensity, drama, and severity of a full-blown court trial via a kosher Beit Din.

Allow me to say that my wife is not a lady. Nor is she honest. And she is awesome at playing the helpless wounded bird with a broken wing at the exact moment she plucks your eyes out with her beak. Her nose is kind of cute. My wife is a guppy that can instantly morph into the ancient female Megalodon shark (females were twice as large as males) faster than you can comprehend that your torso was separated from the bottom half of your body a split second ago. And like the above fauna, she'll find you on land or at sea. She is fierce.

Upon finally deciding to divorce my wife, I knew I needed a real Beit Din. And as a scholar who had studied the entire tractate of Ketuvot and Sanhedrin — detailing the minutiae of divorce rights and how Jewish courts are established and conducted — I was not going to be intimidated by three men who most likely had not.

Recalling the old saying, "Don't try to scare a whore with cash," I was not going to be intimidated by anyone trying to wield folios of the Talmud over my head. Certainly not by amateurs lacking any true Talmudical erudition. "How does a mere arbitration board suddenly find itself with the authority to excommunicate?" I asked the frustrated rabbis.

They responded with "letters of warning" along with an arrogant boorish ad hominem attack insisting I was a "troublemaker," merely because I defied their sham Beit Din. At the very least I wanted a real Beit Din or else a secular divorce court where there would be an actual record and some transparency of the proceedings.

I knew my wife would convincingly lie even while swearing to God Almighty as she held a Sefer Torah in a Beit Din. But at least I'd be allowed to counter swear. That would pose quite a dilemma to the court. And I would then settle the confusion because I had tape recordings with which I could prove what an unabashed, outrageous liar my wife is.

Swearing falsely in God's name while holding a Sefer Torah, wherein the commandment not to take God's name in vain is written, is considered an extremely grave sin. It's a blatant transgression of the third of the Ten Commandments. But in an arbitration proceeding (where no one swears because the goal is to compromise and not necessarily to seek truth), I knew my wife would mesmerize a panel of three amateurs who would easily be fooled by her genteel, Asperger savant mimicking voice coupled with unabashed flagrant lies. Besides, I already knew how the word 'compromise' was enunciated in my wife's lexicon. "Drop dead, Ze'ev!"

And even when caught lying, she would merely insist (repeatedly), "That's not what I meant! That's not what I meant!" She would easily wear them out. My wife is basically Dalia Dippolito in a sheitel. Like the trashy ex-escort who hired a wired undercover tough-looking cop (who posed as a hitman) to kill an unsuspecting husband who loved her (all infamously captured on now viral video), my Orthodox Jewish wife would utterly fucking exhaust anyone who proved she is a liar. She'd tire them out so badly they'd destroy their own evidence merely to get her to shut up and stop repeating herself.

The authors of the Talmud had enacted very detailed and methodical directions instructing litigants exactly how to swear while caressing the holy Sefer Torah in their arms as they called upon "Heaven and Earth" (God and the Earthly Sages) to bear witness to their declarations. They would never tolerate lies as some kind of joke or "misspoken" communication for some Spin Doctor to later obfuscate.

My wife would be as brazen as Bill Clinton when he stared into the cameras and — with an admonishing finger pointing right in the faces of the gullible masses to accentuate his lie — firmly and slowly insisted to the "American people" and the applause-clapping dolt crowd of congressional mutts and journalists that, "I did not have sexual relations with that woman." He then indignantly added, "These allegations are false! And I need to go back to work for the American people." Can't say I blame Bill for wanting to rush back to work so quickly. I'd also love to sit at my desk if I could get a blow job. I never realized Bill's acting ability rivaled that of my wife's.

The defendant in a Jewish court had to affirm their words in the positive and in the negative. Also, in the future tense and in the past tense. Under such conditions there would be no room for my meandering impish squiggly-wiggly wife to scream, "I don't want to talk about it anymore!" as she hung up the phone on me, or to repetitively insist, "That's not what I meant! That's not what I meant!"

Furthermore, an arbitration tribunal, falsely positing themselves as a Beit Din, renders a psak halacha (sort of like a fatwā) without having to explain how they arrived at their decision, whereas a legitimate Beit Din cites endless precedents and Talmudical sources to explain in almost blockchain transparency how they arrived at their legal conclusions. They are proud (not in an arrogant way) of their work. They encourage dissent and are thrilled to engage in serious Talmudical debate. It's "what they do."

Go ahead and challenge these eighty-year-old men on the Talmudical mat. You'd trip over the edge of the canvas in fear if you could even comprehend against whom you're inflating your chest.

Teach these lifetime scholars something they don't know, and they'll wash and kiss your feet in appreciation. There are no egos in a mighty Talmudical war of logic. Only a passionate desire for truth. Whereas an arbitration board basically hands back instructions which one is not even allowed to question (because, after all, you signed that you would blindly trust them), true Talmudical scholars welcome and insist on rendering flawless, pristine, legal decisions.

There are also no appeals to a higher court once an arbitration court rules since both parties agreed to abide by the decision of their specific panel as final. That is why even the procedure for choosing an arbitration threesome was always initiated by both litigants. One litigant chose one scholar of their choice. The other litigant chose the second scholar. And then the two scholars chose the third scholar to complete their panel as a fair-minded three-member body.

The final outcome would then be rendered unanimously even if the most erudite scholar disagreed with his two inferior peers. A judge is never allowed to later whisper to the litigant who lost, "I was on your side, but what could I do? I was outvoted." He is severely condemned in the Talmud for undermining respect for the Torah's judicial system were he to commit such an atrocity.

And that is why any three people can't plop down (although they often do) and excommunicate someone who refuses to come to their pre-chosen three-member arbitration team. It is also why only a rabbinically ordained Beit Din has the power, granted by the Talmud, to decree an excommunication. I have many religious-as-they-are-ignorant cousins who believe it's a huge mitzvah to shun me till the day I die for having refused to attend the "Beit Din" arbitration tribunal my wife ran to the minute I filed for divorce in the secular court of the Goyim.

No one less than the scholarly and exceptionally gifted Rabbi Nekritz — who received his precious ordination almost a half-century ago from the legendary genius Rabbi Yaakov Yitzchok Ruderman (the original dean of Ner Israel Rabbinical College) — agreed with me and backed my decision. But I had long ago discovered that the less someone knew about any subject, the more arrogant they were about the tiny morsel of knowledge they possessed. Couple gross arrogance with the insecurity of not ever having been truly ordained and it's no wonder my religious-as-they-are-ignorant cousins shunned me.

One of them serves as a "rabbi" in Malden, Massachusetts. He is a very nice guy (on the surface). The synagogue website speaks of his many "impressive credentials." He studied in a yeshiva high school followed by one year in Israel. Wow. Meanwhile, for the record, my cousin never came close to being legitimately ordained.

My cousin's ordination was like that of the disgraced convicted criminal and temporary owner of SunCruz Casinos, who emailed his request for ordination to Rabbi Daniel Lapin. Jack Abramoff sought to purchase his own quid pro quo Judaic degree after becoming a board member by meeting the single requirement for the "honor" through donating an annual ten-thousand-dollar persuasion-gift to Lapin's synagogue. Jack then suggested that Rabbi Lapin award him the title of "Scholar of Talmudic Studies," or some other "sufficiently academic title," adding the words "if you know what I mean" just in case the rabbi didn't quite grasp Jack's brilliant idea.

Abramoff met Rabbi Daniel Lapin through Daniel's brother, Rabbi David Lapin, who had become Jack's spiritual advisor (pardon my mirthless laughter) at the time the master-of-none Jack produced his one and only movie flop in South Africa, called Red Scorpion.

David introduced Jack to Daniel, who then introduced Abramoff to Congressman Tom DeLay at a Washington, DC dinner shortly after the Republican takeover of Congress in 1994. It was fellow Congressman Bob Ney who entered legalese into the Congressional Record that accused the SunCruz management of cheating passengers.

The corrupt political language sealed the deal for Jack Abramoff to manipulate and fraudulently purchase SunCruz Casinos which ultimately led to the cold-blooded murder of Gus Boulis. As the Mishnah states (ask Rabbi Abramoff!) in Sayings of our Fathers, "One good deed leads to another. One transgression leads to another." "Mitzvah Goreret Mitzvah. Averah Goreret Averah." One enabler leads to another.

Casino Jack unabashedly claimed he needed the completely undeserved honor to level the playing field as he tried to acquire membership in a very exclusive D.C. club whose accomplished members were Nobel Prize Laureates and winners of other prestigious prizes acknowledging and honoring their great achievements and enviable successes. Jack honestly explained; "Problem for me is that most prospective members have received awards and I have received none." *That's true Jack. Because it would be fifteen years before the UFC would create its BMF (Baddest Mother Fucker) championship title recently won by "gangster" Jorge Masvidal.*

Jack, who was clearly not one of-all-trades, let alone a master of any (unless "Liar" is a vocation), was a complete boorish arrogant jackass who could barely read and translate Hebrew, let alone Aramaic. But Casino Jack, a political conservative who decided to embrace Orthodox Judaism because he "valued the moral integrity of Judaic theology," made up for his illiteracy by the incredible amount of chutzpah he possessed.

His brass-balls aptitude was clearly off-the-charts when Jack then asked Lapin if he "wouldn't mind" retroactively awarding him for "several years past ... I think you see what I am trying to finagle here!" Nothing like making up for lost time. And since "time is money," it became a very easy thing for Jack to purchase. Or should I say, "finagle."

You would think a lawyer would have enough sense to pick up the phone to make such an obviously undeserved request. But then again, when said lawyer is willing to forge "cash-on-hand-assets" of twenty-three million dollars as "proof" that the claimed imaginary funds were sitting in his escrow account, in order to obtain a fraudulent bank loan of sixty million dollars — knowing how easily he would surely wind up in jail for committing wire-fraud, money laundering, and many other prosecutorial delights he would incur as quickly as he faxed over his whited-out asset sheet to the bank — why shy away from a little email "finagling" to acquire the distinction of being declared a Talmudical scholar? Besides, as in my cousin Yitzy's case, this was all to earn a better living. And anyway, who was going to test Jack's erudition? Or Yitzy's?

I now understand why Jack Abramoff and my brother-in-law Fred Mailman, and similarly their wives, were best of friends. They all prayed at the same Silver Spring synagogue. Both men were insane. Jack was obviously unbridled. Fred was more like his sister (my wife, Sharen Lewinson née Mailman). Sneaky and subtle. Quiet but deadly. Antifreeze surely runs in the veins of my wife and her brother Fred. And Jack. It's no wonder they rarely lost their cool. After all, it's easy to act mechanical when you're not human.

Fred donated his time and served as the synagogue president for many years. And his wife Jodi donated her time serving as its secretary. Everyone had only nice things to say about my wife and Fred and Jodi Mailman. And everyone spoke highly of Mr. Jack Abramoff. Or at least highly of his seemingly endless money.

Jack used some of the money to purchase, or should I say "bribe" (since that was how he conducted his professional and personal affairs), a lifetime membership at Woodside Synagogue Ahavas Torah for twenty-five thousand dollars. Mrs. Pam Abramoff, a cute blonde Christian Jack met in college who eventually converted to Jack's religion, nonchalantly walked into the place of worship one late morning and asked Jodi how much a lifetime membership cost upon filling out the family application for membership.

No one had ever asked that question before.

Because no one had ever purchased a lifetime membership in the history of the Ahavas Torah temple that was founded over a half-century ago.

Jodi quickly dialed Rabbi Kalman Winter who instantly calculated what he honestly believed was a fair price for a lifetime membership. Pam wrote the check easier and faster than a toddler, whose mother is desperately trying to wean off pacifiers, will pop one right back into his cute little face the second the cherubic little "addict" finds a stray one lying around that mommy forgot to hide. Rabbi Winter and Jodi, hardly suspecting the account it was drawn on was financed and devilishly crafted by Satan and a sixty-million dollar fraudulently obtained bank loan, probably thought the magical sorely-needed check that appeared out of nowhere was a miracle.

In truth, the only miracle is that Jack is still alive today. His partner, Konstantinos "Gus" Boulis, wound up with multiple bullets in his chest, delivered gangland style, as he was ambushed at a red light in his black convertible BMW. But it wasn't really the lead poisoning that killed poor Gus. It was the moment he signed a retainer agreement with the firm where Jack worked, eventually selling his SunCruz Casino enterprise to a Yarmulka-covered liar who never even passed the bar.

Abramoff was never solidly linked to the final crime. Mr. Google provides an incredible amount of circumstantial evidence and transparency that Jack was allegedly involved even if he never pulled the trigger, having paid the price of almost six Ahavas Torah lifetime memberships to his "caterer" who ordered the hit on Jack's partner, née client, Gus.

And although the Almighty (the favorite adjective Jack preferred whenever he evangelically described God) knew Abramoff was guilty, prosecutors decided not to fight "deep pockets." Their goal in life is typically to have a public record of all wins and minimal, if any, losses. Besides, they already had more than enough white-collar crimes audaciously committed by the dumb douchebag to put Jack away for centuries had it not been for extremely generous plea-bargaining reductions that allowed Abramoff an amazing amount of leniency along with a certain degree of immunity.

Jack didn't just 'sing like a canary.' He became the Pavarotti of Snitches. The prosecutors kept their word and rewarded Jack handsomely by requesting a fraction of the sentence that he deserved, as they explained to the judge that they want future informants to know how generous they had been to a man they could have probably put away for a thousand years. Casino quid pro quo Jack knew exactly "how to fold 'em."

Jack ate delicious, specially prepared kosher meals at his personal "Table 40" at *Signatures* while destroying people's lives. Kind of like Mengele politely telling the young patients he was about to murder, "this will only hurt a little." And kind of like my wife becoming insulted and screaming, "I would never do that!" when I gently warned her not to start up with protection orders as retribution for my filing for divorce. "This will only hurt a little, Zevie."

Why do I have such difficulty believing that an all-perfect God chooses to create not-all-there children like Abramoff, Sharen, and Mengele? Why can't I accept that the heavenly source of their maniacal DNA originates with God's Will? I hate to admit it, but I'd prefer Mr. Rogers sitting on the heavenly throne.

Like true narcissists, my wife and Jack could easily feel their own pain as their deepfake personalities (digitally-constructed by a perhaps bored God who simultaneously exists in the past, present, and future) begged for undeserved mercy and assistance while showing a complete and total lack of mercy, empathy or humanity towards anyone who got in their way — and even to those who didn't.

Like a selfish child, they seem unaware of anyone but themselves. Sixty-million-dollar fraudulent loan? "I need money." A wonderful husband of twenty-eight years? "Zev's obsessed with feces!" Court Order to pay maintenance? "Die, Ze'ev!" A little girl who needs her father? 'Horse therapy' distraction while sending said father off to the glue-factory.

For another sample of Psychopathy 101, simply trying to read the meshuggenah autobiographical Mein Kampf rant of Adolf Hitler, reveals how the minds of individuals like Abramoff and my wife works. The further mankind, historians, and neuroscientists step away from this Nazi lunatic, the more embarrassed they will feel at having wasted oceans of emotion, time, anger, shock, and ink to advance motives, logic, historical perspectives, and ultimately closure for this half-brained deformed-synapsed monster's actions.

Let's be honest. Most of the history written about Hitler fits the classic analogy of drawing circles around the target hole. The hole remains empty. Trying to rationalize the behavior of the demonic god called Hitler is as difficult as explaining the action of an all-loving Judeo-Christian "perfect" God that created him. Time will force us to realize and admit that not only was Hitler never anything more than totally insane, but that we were too — for trying to use logic where the priceless gift of rationality will sadly never work. It's like using logic to explain a loving God's merciless creation of a dimension called Hell, designated to administer excruciating pain to sinners — with many early arrivals born to suffer in this world. Good luck with that.

It's quite apparent that deranged personalities — God seemingly included — fail to distinguish between fantasy and reality. Even God keeps insisting, through his representatives in the Talmud, that our temporal world is not much more than a fictional illusion — and with a life expectancy of only six thousand years between the creation of Adam and the Messiah's imminent arrival, quite a short-lived one at that. Meanwhile, for the most trivial infraction committed in this temporary make-believe world — even for nothing more than an impure thought — one suffers hellish pain and eternal shame in the "real" one.

So let me get this straight: For merely thinking about some silicone-shell implanted zaftig blonde shiksa in this void and empty world, God will crush my testicles (punishment fitting the crime, as the Talmud explains, so that we "learn our lesson well") in the eternal, "real" world.

And although we all live in a three-dimensional world (and God surely in a multi-universe one), it is obviously partitioned into "me, myself, and I" coordinates for the self-Chosen deepfake fakers for whom the rules never seem to apply.

Those who are psychotic, deranged, and schizophrenic leave us endless discombobulated proof of their lunacies through messy financial trails, emails, government decrees, and court records. Sharen's emails are now on file in the storage unit of the Rockland County Court. No one kept better records than the Nazis. No one was more "organized" than the Germans and my Eishet Chayil hoarder. It merely takes a bit of time, or historical perspective, to piece the shards together. Kind of like gathering the body parts and bomb particles at a terrorist site. True, it's a bloody mess. But not if one patiently sorts through the endless evidence as they hold their noses while scratching their heads in dismay. It takes a detective. Or a real Talmudical Scholar.

And that's the problem of "doing business," or having a relationship with people like Jack, Mengele, and my Eishet Chayil. They'll destroy lives, reputations, and even their own children. Anything that stands in their way is instantly not in their way. Because it ceases to exist. It ceases to have ever existed.

The lives of those that circle around narcissists only exist to serve the self-centered egomaniac in the center. The narcissist will even destroy their own lives if it accomplishes destroying their perceived enemy. Like a worker-ant on fire, they will keep marching and "doing what they do" until they die or are behind bars. Or till they run out of money paying for divorce lawyers and then racing to bankruptcy court. But the one thing they never run out of is energy. Or anger.

They seem unable to fathom, as they unleash the destructive hurricanes that they imagine will allow them to achieve their "goals," that a time of reckoning will one day arrive.

And like the uncharted path of a blind hurricane, they are unable to see the course and eventual destruction that the winds of their feral actions will wreck. The miasma mayhem they inflict is easily smelled by anyone who patiently sorts through their crippling hurricane-wind-flung puzzle pieces of shit. One merely needs to put on a pair of latex gloves, do a little detective work, and then meticulously place the turds they uncover where the edges of their smelly shapes match.

Another film that portrays Abramoff, *Casino Jack,* vividly portrays the lives of those people who don't only "think outside of the box" but destroy it. It's what they do. In the film Jack is described as "smart," "charming," and "creative." But how much intelligence and creativity does it really take to wildly speed down a one-way road toward jail?

How difficult is it for a lawyer, who understands what the word perjury means two minutes after he sits down for his first law school class, to raise a ton of cash by committing fraud? And how "charming" do you really have to be to wrap your arm around the shoulder of your client as you lie to their face while stealing their wallet?

My wife is extremely charming. The bigger the lie, the gentler her voice. She is so believable that she could convince you she's performing heart surgery while carving your heart out of your chest while smiling innocently and assuring you that "everything is going to be alright."

Narcissistic personalities like Abramoff and my wife are insatiable. My wife admired Jack as much as I instinctively cringed whenever I saw him. I still recall Jodi salivating as she told us about the twenty-five-thousand-dollar check Pam scribbled, faster than a three-year-old coloring on canvas paper, for her and Jack's lifetime synagogue membership. "Why can't you write checks like that, Zev?" my wife teased me in front of my sister-in-law Jodi, while adding, "She didn't even have to call her husband." Ironically, I replied, "because I'm too busy studying the Talmud."

But for Sharen and the crook she so admired, it's all about that wobbly three-legged table. Money. Power. Glory. "It's all about them Benjamins." It's all about control. They were born with something you'll never have. Insane energy.

It's not that no one cares anymore about the mundane details regarding what constitutes a true Beit Din. It's a huge mitzvah to study the laws that allow justice to be served. There is an entire tome of the Talmud called Sanhedrin that details how Jewish courts are set up, and how rabbinical ordination is transferred from one aging scholar to his protégé.

Unfortunately, very few men have been blessed with the time or have the discipline and skills necessary to study the Talmud. And it's extremely rare to find, let alone study and debate, a scholar like Rabbi Israel Tzvi Nekritz. It's also an exhausting effort. Modern-day Jewish Orthodox men honestly don't have the time or energy.

And the real problem is that there is no such thing as "the short version." Especially when it comes to Jewish law. The short version soundbite is how most people vote for president. It's how most people decide about gun control and abortion and the women they bang.

People somehow understand they would never want "the short version" if they needed brain surgery. Yet they arrogantly insist that you not waste their time with details about major issues and events that affect their lives. They'll quickly swipe left or right and risk becoming infected with herpes, HIV or AIDS over a pair of silicone implants beneath some skin — never realizing that the "short version" is nothing more than what a Buddhist philosopher would describe as the "unskilled version." It is the path of the fool — the way of he who has a "Goyishe Kop" (the "brains" of a Gentile simpleton).

Sadly, nowadays, even most practicing Orthodox Jews are so busy with "being Jewish" that they've become very ignorant of their own religion and the legal rights and options that are allowed and completely permissible when practicing Judaism. The short version method of Orthodox Judaism has become a declaration of total prohibition. An ascetic is considered holy, when in truth, he's nothing more than OCD.

Many Orthodox Jews refuse to eat a wide variety of fruits and vegetables in fear of accidentally eating an insect. But they still smoke. Religiously. The Jewish religion has evolved into a flood of negativity and divisiveness where competing sects and schools attempt to prove their righteousness by the degree they distance themselves, as they stay far away, from every possible influence from "the contaminated Goyishe" outside world.

Even food is treacherously dangerous. Every piece of meat they place into their mouth is suspect to having been improperly slaughtered. Was the knife sharp enough? Was the Shochet rushed? Every possible microscopic bug-infested fruit and vegetable they hesitate to eat must be examined with a magnifying glass and "triple washed." Even the milk and wine they drink shouldn't be touched by "a Goy."

Teachers are severely warned they could be fired if they ever say the word "internet" or "Google." The newspapers they read, the thoughts that might enter their mind, or their child's mind, if they (God forbid!) see the opposite sex, all have to be edited and photoshopped to block the path of The Evil Inclination — the spooky Yetzer Hara. Otherwise known as The Satan (The Deceiver).

Famous pictures of great rabbis are now photoshopped to exclude the holy women who gave birth to the next generation of saints. Men are taught to say, "My House" (a euphemism for "wife") in order to avoid saying the four-letter word. "Wife" insinuates that a husband has a female counterpart. Gasp! Do you see the lengths I went to in order not to say the word "wife"? Somehow, in 1984 fashion, the community is terrified that a little boy will ejaculate because his mind might run wild if he sees a female that he imagines might be a w-i-f-e (who fucks her husband).

Professional Orthodox women no longer put their faces on business cards or in advertisements, terrified that the Taliban-Yentas will declare them to be "immodest." As in, "You wouldn't want your husband to take your Yossi to that whore for therapy, would you?" "Ta'ah'ruvos" (intermingling of the sexes) is considered an instant open door to Hell through which anyone can easily slip.

Even innocently entering a wedding hall through doors designated for women will instantly generate glaring stares armed with penetrating daggers of shameful scorn. The signs for "Men" and "Women" are in large letters, more clearly than any seen on bathroom doors. This childish obsessiveness with genitalia speaks volumes as to how sex is viewed in the community.

In Israel there are Jewish Haredi (Orthodox) women who wear a burka! One was accidentally shot by the police when she refused to stop at a checkpoint. She didn't want the men to hear her voice, fearing they might be sexually aroused, so she kept making her way to the Western Wall to pray. They thought she was an Arab wearing a bomb-vest, not realizing she was wearing a half-dozen layers of clothing under the outfit they saw (to hide her curves). Luckily, she survived, although I'm sure she probably preferred death over being stripped naked for surgery.

Some of these women refuse medical treatment at hospitals lest their uncovered arm (or even their mere presence) entice a doctor. Do I have to mention that they don't "believe" in vaccinations? (Maybe it's because they'd have to roll up their sleeve.) These women insist on wearing their multiple layers of clothing, with hems that extend to the ground, no matter how hot the weather. Meanwhile, they probably shave their pussies. (See what happens when you think about them! Lol). They even force their toddler girls to dress likewise because the ultimate sin is to reveal even a strand of hair, or a tiny patch of skin, that might cause a man to have "hir'hu'rim" (sinful thoughts).

Mainstream rabbis have fortunately condemned the behavior of these women as immodest (for drawing attention *to* themselves) and completely out of control. Yet, I often wonder how the very same rabbis know where to draw the line that separates lunatics from sincere devout God-fearing women. The line of separation they've decided upon nowadays is a very different boundary than the one drawn by their wiser predecessors a mere generation ago — who would never have tolerated famous images of the Chofetz Chaim's saintly wife, sitting next to her husband, to be photoshopped, 1984-style, out of existence.

The Talmud itself is much more tolerant of relationships than one would begin to imagine. There are amazing stories I've read in the Talmud between men and their wives. As a matter of fact, it's a good thing these "Orthodox" fanatically dressed OCD-modesty-obsessed women don't study the Talmud. I have no question they'd ban it as pornography based on some of the stories therein.

Yeshiva dinners honoring "Mr. and Mrs. Hymie Doe" only portray a picture of the man on the invitations mailed out to guests. Seating between men and women (even husbands and wives) is not only completely split at huge wedding hall ballrooms (I wonder when *that* word will be excised from Jewish life), but curtained-paneled dividers separate any possible eye contact between the sexes. In many Jewish towns men and women are compelled to walk on opposite sides of the street.

Soon they'll be wearing gas masks at weddings, so they don't intermingle sexually by breathing the same air while dancing separately. A particle of perfume might drift across the divide and enter the nasal passage of an unsuspecting youth causing him to experience a wet dream ... or worse yet, maybe a young girl will be forced into spending her life as a spinster, no longer a virgin deserving a Shidduch, because a subatomic particle of sperm from the boy's underpants entered her ... Oy vey!

Many Jews are not even sure about what they are allowed to believe anymore. Extremely repressed lives under a totalitarian God — backed by an army of controlling Yentas who constantly raise the bar for proper observance and flawless obedience by showing off and begging their rabbis for more stringent standards — has created a Matrix existence of doubtfulness and insecurity for those who choose to live in the iron cauldron called Monsey.

The Yenta-witches are constantly stirring the "can't be kosher enough!" brew as they add endless ingredients of prohibitions and control that poison and shame the innocent guilt-ridden minds of their indoctrinated offspring. By controlling the information and any shred of secular education their children receive, they have completely restricted their ability to think. It's maddening. Judaism was never like this a mere decade ago.

Young girls are being taught to walk from the knee down, lest they spread their thighs to take a larger step and, God forbid, appear promiscuous. These young ladies walk quickly and in tiny steps to keep both legs as close to each other as possible. I can easily imagine that eventually the Yentas will have them literally hopping to go anywhere. And the best of swimmers could drown in the one-piece turtle shell "shvimkleid" (bathing suit) they are forced to wear when they go swimming.

And when it comes to spring-cleaning for the Passover holidays, women share holier-than-thou bragging-rights stories of the fanatical lengths they go to scour, sandblast, and literally use blow torches to destroy any atom of wheat product from their midst. Some even get their teeth cleaned right before the holiday to scrape away any remnant of bread. I imagine in a few more years the OCD level of "searching for Chometz" among Yentas will reach a level of anxiety that will induce many of them to subject themselves to a D&C just in case their husbands licked their pussies the previous night (after eating a sandwich), or they'll stand outside their homes obsessively hunting for those last possible crumbs with a flame thrower!

Like when shopping for the most strictly slaughtered kosher meat or when choosing which school to "trust" for their child's 1984 indoctrination of "kosher" values (as if one school is somehow different than another), everyone in Monsey, NY plays the mindless children's game of "follow-the-(blind)-holiest-leader."

"Being Jewish" has evolved into living an obsessive life of apprehension as one tries to "cling to God," by foolishly adhering to the voice of their local holy ("the stricter the better") rabbi. Yet all that those "leaders" seem capable of doing is enacting more Unzereh-isolationist rules that has their flock constantly off-balance and trembling with anxiety. No movies. No internet. No smart phone. No mixed swimming. No eye contact with the opposite sex. No, no, and emphatically "No!" if it involves the opposite sex. And stoning (technically speaking) or meds if it's the same sex. Loyalty is defined by mindlessness.

Obsequiousness to one's leadership and mindlessly trusting their supposedly phronesis "Da'as Torah" fatwās is the ultimate proof of one's righteousness. *Emunas Chachomim.* Faith in the Wise. The only thing more valuable than blindly trusting their leaders is a congregant's willingness to consistently tithe funds to be used at the discretion of their rabbi.

But honestly, there are no leaders. The fringe-wearing skull-capped men and the women covered in stylish head-scarves and wigs pushing expensive baby strollers in the modern-day Dark Ages town all melt into one huge pulsating cult, with a thousand mini-cult-sect capillaries, flowing through the arteries of traffic-jammed streets, clogged with taxi cabs and yellow school buses painted in Yiddish and Hebraic letters that spell out names like 'Bais Rochel' and 'Yeshivas Beis Duvid' for the separate boys and girls centers of indoctrination and mind control.

I taught English for one year at the now infamous Beis Mikroh school for boys. There is a more gentle unaffiliated version for girls called Bas Mikroh. Girls never have to be hit. They really must be made out of sugar and spice. My oldest daughter Rachel taught there for several years while pursuing her online master's degree. As an afternoon ELA teacher at Beis Mikroh I rarely crossed paths with the now convicted principal, Rabbi Gabriel Bodenheimer. No one takes the afternoon secular studies seriously at the schools for boys and it's a quieter time of day. I took the job at the invitation of the English principal, the late Rabbi Mordechai Berg, a dear friend, and a wonderful person.

Enablers like the lively ever-friendly Rabbi Shamai Blobstein was quoted in the papers as responding, "They're laughing," when asked if the sexual molestation accusations against his boss were being taken seriously by the community. He claimed that Rabbi Bodenheimer was a "holy man," and that if he ever hit a child, it was "with love." I never saw him "love" a child. I would have instantly reported him to the authorities. But his yell was so loud that I would call the decibel level alone "emotional abuse."

I never cared for the man. And he brazenly lied to my face, never knowing that I knew he was lying. Still, I was shocked upon hearing that he was facing charges of oral and anal sex with a student. Maybe I'm naive, but it's hard for me to imagine that he sexually abused a child. Although I must add that I would sooner spend the rest of my life on death row before ever pleading guilty to "endangering the welfare of a child."

Why would an innocent wealthy person not value his priceless reputation? Bodenheimer came from a very wealthy family and could have fought for years. He was also close friends with his super wealthy neighbor, former diamond dealer Shimmy Glick, my former employer in the diamond business, who donated a huge portion of his abutting property for the modern new Beis Mikroh gulag that was built a decade ago.

And what about that horrific sin called "Publicly desecrating God's name," that the shameless admission of Bodenheimer, as he stood in front of Judge Thorson, left as an eternal stain (hopefully not the Bill Clinton kind) for the posterity of Monsey to recall every time they drive along Viola Road? *I think the real abusers are the medieval parents who send their kids to deplorable schools like Beis Mikroh and Beis Duvid.*

The cookie-cutter repetitive education these children receive is as divisive as it is numbingly boring. Many of them eventually rebel and leave the Shtetl. And the most amazing thing about a cult is realizing you were one of its most devoted lapidified members till the moment you finally escaped. But unlike the wife of Lot, you don't turn into salt upon looking back longingly at what you are leaving behind. You turn into yourself. You begin to look within as you search for your inner child. You learn what it means to be an individual. Worst of all for those *Da'as Torah* leaders — you start thinking for yourself.

The fast-growing God-fearing community you will miss the security of, as you head toward your own personal Exodus, oozes onto the lawns of its fleeing gentile neighbors, who are bought out of their tiny three-bedroom bungalows at hefty prices. Faster than the ten plagues were unleashed upon the ancient Egyptians, the seventy-five-year-old huts are quickly demolished as huge seven-bedroom mansions appear overnight, almost miraculously, on shrunken newly zoned parcels of land.

Prices soon soar because of the feverish demand for more housing resulting from exponential birth rates. "Be fruitful and multiply." (Genesis 1:28).

It's a reverse version of the biblical Exodus as the Gentiles complain about something called "quality of life" while escaping from neighbors they loathe, notwithstanding stuffing their pockets with the cash-spoils of the Jewish nation. No one is really at fault. In reality, it is nothing more miraculous than one ant colony devouring another.

Synagogues, religious private schools, and neighborhoods multiply and swell as quickly as the belly of a pregnant eighteen-year-old woman. Without the slightest concern for safety, noise pollution, zoning, water usage, traffic patterns, or fire hazards, the bursting growth multiplies like germs. "Zoning? Stop worrying! Hashem is watching over us!" Like an army of ants, and almost as robotically mindless, the zealous insects breed, work, build, carpool, and breed some more. Environmental concerns and global warming issues are of no concern to The Chosen — who believe they can already hear the footsteps of the Messiah and that they are the generation that will merit to greet him upon his arrival. *May it be speedily in our days.*

And with a Queen Bee Rebbe decreeing a "No *Yid* left behind" policy, endless inexpensive multi-unit Section 8 housing pops up as fast as the next generation of home buyers pop out of young eighteen-year-old mothers whose babies-first-words will be, "The Rebbe."

The well-intentioned parents, of the one-mind-fits-all-children sitting in those 'Bais Rochel' and 'Yeshivas Beis Duvid' prison buses driven by men with flowing sidelocks, all follow divergent customs of obscured traditions transmitted from the around-the-corner local "Da'as Torah" myopic minds of stringent control-freak unworldly black-bearded young rabbis who are completely convinced that using the internet or a smart phone is the equivalent of jumping directly into the flames of Hell.

And yet, Monsey, NY is still a beautiful Stepford-town place to live and raise obedient and robotic children. You rarely see a car on Shabbat or Jewish holidays (which easily accounts for a quarter of the year). Violent crime does not exist. White color crime is a different story — albeit a rare one. The modern-day 10952 zip code *Shtetl* is truly a warm and peaceful town that zaps its medieval devotees with a constant religious rhapsodic high. Surely needed in order to cope with the ever-increasing maddening congested traffic and endless lines of school buses, containing sardine-packed angelic uniformed puppets, that clogs its streets all day long and yet almost miraculously disappears the moment the sun sets on Friday night.

The impeccably trimmed lawns ensconce beautiful homes that match the immaculate souls of their inhabitants. And every house has one small section of sheet rock purposefully left rough and unpainted to recall the most tragic events in Jewish history — the two times our holy Temple in Jerusalem was destroyed. After all, how could our homes be complete when God's lies in ruins? *Don't trouble yourself with thoughts of why he chose to have it demolished.*

The kind people of the *Shtetl* are honest and constantly rushing to morning, noon, and nightly prayers, or to immerse themselves or their utensils in the *Mikvah*, or to perform one among hundreds of different *mitzvahs*. And there's plenty of Section 8 housing to pen the herded droves of look-alike think-alike Hasidim, along with tons of cheap Spanish labor to clean their homes, maintain their lawns, and watch their "chosen" children. And those who smoke too much or eat too much *cholent* can faithfully rely on an ambulance service that boasts the best care and fastest response times in the state. And they'll respond just as quickly *even* if you're not Jewish.

Go ahead and dial the local Hatzaloh number and 911 simultaneously and you will be quite impressed by the response time and professionalism of our *Unzereh* ambulance teams. Their *Hatzaloh* ambulance flashing lights and blaring sirens will already announce that the nicotine addicted patient inside is on his way to the hospital before the EMS wagon even arrives to get him. After all, they are not dealing with a mere mortal life. They are dealing with an eternal soul.

Should you need a favor or loan, there are endless societies that do charity and loan money without charging a penny of interest. And thanks to the crowds of stampeding power-walking prattling Yentas, everyone knows everyone else's business. And net worth. And their *Shidduch* problems in finding "a boy" for their twenty-one-year-old desperate old-maid depressed daughter.

Alongside the Yentas, there is the local 'Mikva lady' who eagle-eyes your naked wife, making sure she fully immerses herself in the gathered pure rain waters for her monthly ritual bath to cleanse the impurity of her menstrual blood, only declaring the meat "Kosher!" if a hair didn't float to the surface. Satmar Hasidic women go to extreme lengths of shaving their heads completely bald to avoid the problem of a wisp of hair becoming a "barrier" between their bodies and the purifying waters. *Do they also shave their pussies? I've eaten shaved pussy, but I never received a blow job while staring down at a bald head.*

The school system, whose principals know literally everything that goes on behind the closed doors of your home, along with your rabbi who knows every kinky Shalom Bayis issue that transpires between you and your wife behind the locked doors of your bedroom, also helps ensure your complete compliance as a member in good standing of the community. All in all, if you don't mind completely handing over your entire sense of self, I highly recommend moving to Monsey.

The inhabitants are as modest as they are nosey. The only threesome you'll ever see are the three men who stand over the open scroll of a Torah being read in the synagogue. And the closest thing you'll ever find comparable to an orgy in Monsey, NY are the throngs of naked young boys and old men bumping into each other as they immerse in the Mikvah before the start of their holy day. It's one-big-happy-family! *Just leave your mind behind.*

Upon relinquishing all sense of self, Modern-Orthodox Monsey parents must sign a school form in which they promise to never allow their pure *Yiddisheh* homes to become spiritually contaminated with "internet." *Feh!* Any refusal is immediately met with their quickly being shamed into submission. You might catch the occasional "off the *derech*" wayward husband with a hooker in Manhattan, but you will never catch him dialing for the escort service with a smart phone in his hand.

Major Hasidic sects do not allow their women to drive a car, and if mommy is caught in the driver's seat, her children will be suspended and eventually expelled from school. After all, one of the kids in carpool might see the *MILF-in-a-sheitel* in the sexy promiscuous act of spreading her heavily stockinged legs, as she moves her foot from the brakes to the gas pedal and wake up the following morning with cum in his little underpants. (Oy vey!)

Worse yet, having seen spread thighs, and imagining where the road to heaven might lead, the hormone-infused pre-Bar-Mitzvah pubescent religious-robot might become blind fantasizing about the naked *Mikvah-MILF* during her own immersions when he later masturbates.

Most of the local "Da'as Torah" rabbis receive their faux ordinations from the equivalent of those non-credentialed mail-order organizations that one finds on the back of matchbook covers. *Simply check off the vocation you are applying for.*

Our Lubavitcher *Unzereh's* custom of excessive drinking reveals its Russian roots because of their inability to stop imbibing vodka every time they gather for prayer or to celebrate some miraculous hyperbolic tale when "the sun stood still" for '*The Rebbe*' — pronounced with more awe and reverence when spoken by his followers than God's name.

One thing about Hasidim. They sure know how to party! Especially at a *Farbrengen*. I love the way Rebbe Schneerson used to vigorously, almost wildly, shake his head as he sped up and kept in synch with the *zemirot* enthusiastically sung by his followers. The Rebbe had soul. *Lechaim!*

So, come live in Monsey! A place where no one respects the privacy of the individual or understands the psychological concept of "boundaries." *We keep you in. While keeping Satan out!*

Orthodox Jews believe that all the wisdom in the universe, even future knowledge that will lead to medical and scientific discoveries centuries from now, is somehow miraculously contained and hidden (in a mystical, kabbalistic sort of way) deep within the Bible — the Five Books of Moses. The folios of the Talmud explain the very first Bible that was transcribed by the hand of Moses, as he clearly heard the voice of God in his prophetic mind's eye (that told him the *exact* words to write), three thousand and three hundred years ago.

There were many great prophets that followed Moses. They wrote the twenty-four holy *Tanach* texts (e.g. The book of Jonah, Lamentations, The Megillah of Ester, Ecclesiastes, etc. ...) and were imbued with the Holy Spirit and divine force of prophecy. But compared to Moses, they were in the minor leagues (with all due respect). Only 'Moses Our Teacher' is described (Deuteronomy 34:10) as the one "who knew God face to face," and he is the only seer whose prophetic declarations are accoladed throughout the Talmud with the proclamation that, "God spoke through the throat of Moses." Moses didn't just deliver God's message. When Moses spoke in the name of God, he even delivered the cadence of God's mighty voice.

So when Moses taught (Leviticus 20:10), "If a man commits adultery with the wife of his neighbor, both the adulterer and the adulteress shall surely be put to death," it was God talking. *"Uh-oh!"* And when Jesus spared the accused adulteress by challenging the scribes and daring them with the taunt of, "let he who is without sin cast the first stone," he was also defending his mother's reputation.

The Midrash relates stories of Moses debating the angels in heaven and besting even them. Proof again that the rabbinical student, ordained by God, understood the Torah better than any simpleton angel with an I.Q. of a trillion. Moses then taught the Oral Law to Joshua, who taught it to the Elders, whose disciples continued to relay the 'Masoretic tradition of Moses' (*Toras Moshe*) which was eventually recorded as The Talmud.

The roughly three thousand pages of centered-text Talmudic debates and instructions elucidating the commandments written in the Torah (Bible), spanned several centuries and were finalized approximately two thousand years ago. They are sandwiched by smaller text on the right and left sides, written by luminary commentators who lived roughly one thousand years ago, and explain in further detail, the commandments, history, and stories found in the Bible.

The Bible is the body of the Jewish nation. The Talmud its consciousness and soul. One sentence in the Bible can easily unfold as a dozen pages in the Talmud. And every one of those folios has hundreds of pages of commentary to explain the details of said page of Talmud. That is why it takes endless diligence and devotion to become a true Talmudical scholar.

And that is why we Jews reject other religious traditions. We know they have shamelessly "borrowed" the foundational tenants of Judaism and warped them into a newfangled nonsensical story about a "Son of God" and an insane "Messenger of Allah." (Please don't shoot, or decapitate, this messenger.) These distortions have continued for many millenniums, right down to Joseph Smith and his Book of Mormon, upon which his Church of Jesus Christ and Latter-Day Saints was founded as recently as (basically) yesterday. *Lots of cute shiksa's among their followers*. And I am not intolerant of other beliefs. I am happy that their followers espouse kindness and charity. *When they're not busy slaughtering us*.

The Talmudical commentaries are the source that reveal Muhammed was literally out of his mind. *I guess I won't be performing the hajj and walking around the Kaaba too soon*. And the Talmud emphatically portrays that Jesus was a man (or as Renee Castle passionately sang, "... he's just a man"), a budding Talmudical scholar whose young mother, like so many others, committed adultery. She gave birth to a Jew who sprouted a "new" Judaism that resulted in millions of his own *Unzereh* siblings being murdered, raped, crucified, mercilessly Jew-taxed, burned at the stake, exiled, gassed, and vilified for millenniums. With periods of respite for blood libels and horrific pogroms. Nothing like a long-standing family feud. *You can't make this shit up*.

And although the Jewish nation finally caught a break on a patch of desert land for which they fiercely fought to acquire that which was already theirs according to the Bible that everyone is killing each other over; they then created an incredible democratic country, while most of the world shared nothing but endless criticism for the remnant of PTSD holocaust survivors that reemerged, like a phoenix, as an enlightened oasis of tolerance and as a technologically advanced world power — a spectacular symbiotic combination of the pen and the sword — who is, to this day, constantly forced to defend her legitimate borders, while surrounded by medieval fanatical terrorist leaders who are hellbent on destroying her existence, even as those terrorists are sped in Magen David Adom (MDA) ambulances to Israeli hospitals whenever they need serious medical care. *And I thought divorce was painful*.

We quietly observe the silly foolish Christians who call our Testament "Old," as if the Word of God could ever become outdated and no longer pertinent. It's not that we privately ridicule or ever wanted to argue or force our beliefs on them. Jews never proselytize. All we ever wanted was a place to live. In peace.

After two thousand years of roaming four continents drenched in our blood, and miraculously surviving Romans, barbarians, Cossacks, The Inquisition, Nazis, and the indifference of the world to our near extinction, we miraculously wound up back home in Israel. Meanwhile in the year 2020 Israel was condemned by the United Nations as they adopted and passed seventeen resolutions against the "light unto the nations" country, while issuing only one against North Korea, Iran, and Syria. With a billion people on the planet relying on Al Jazeera for "truth and transparency" (their tag line), is it any wonder that peace still eludes us?

The Church has apologized for all the child molesters they've enabled, but it has yet to sincerely apologize for the persecution over the centuries during which they tortured, murdered, raped, burned, and taxed Jews mercilessly for no other reason than our understanding that their beliefs are a plagiarized version of our own. And false.

Yes, it needs repeating — especially for those wonderful Holocaust deniers. And for that knowledge, like the wild latecomer to the party, *Prophet* Muhammad, they resorted to the sword over debate. Church Inquisitors burned our bodies, while Nicholas Donin, enabled by Putz-Pope Gregory IX (and many other ecclesiastics spanning centuries) burned our precious soul (thousands of priceless handwritten scrolls of the Talmud).

It took seventeen years from the time Israel declared its independence for the Second Vatican Council (Vatican II) in 1965 to *finally* issue a half-assed reconciliation called the *Nostra aetate*, which basically stated that, although it *was* the Jews who killed Christ, Christians should not hold every living Jew alive today responsible. *Gee, thanks!* As we turn the other cheek, should we issue an edict to not punish a bastard simply because his mother spread her legs in a *love thy neighbor* act of *passion?* By the way, we never needed your forgiveness. *(So, shove it!)* Only your promise to stop murdering us. *Over nothing*.

And it took another twenty-eight years for the Vatican to formally recognize Israel as a state on the last day of the year in 1993. Forty-five fucking self-righteous years to proclaim what President Truman took several hours to declare on May 14, 1948. *Why do I like shiksas so much?*

For centuries we buried our mob-raped children and their butchered parents only to move on to the next place that would temporarily tolerate us while issuing the crushing Jew-Tax. We were expelled from every country we improved. We huddled in our wooden synagogues when there was nowhere else to go as throngs of drunken Goyim beat, chased and locked us inside after hearing the inspiring Sunday sermon rant, vilifying those who crucified their God, from their local ignorant priest. The Christian mob then proceeded to torch the silent Torah scrolls along with the screaming Jewish families who used their last breath to cry out the *Shema Yisrael* declaration of love to their deaf God.

Here is the one fucking sacred sentence issued by Vatican II that we waited for almost two thousand years to hear as our lives and pillaged shtetls were repeatedly destroyed: "Although the Church is the new people of God, the Jews should not be presented as rejected or accursed by God, as if this followed from the Holy Scriptures." *Mazel Tov!*

Thank God for democracy and science. I must admit I'd rather live in a modern-day society than in a medieval Jewish one. And I'd definitely choose the Jewish one over the other two major religions. Religion in general is extremely illogical. But Christianity is absolutely absurd. Sorry to burst your bubble. But the Church was basically founded by a sinner who has yet to repent.

And although *nice Jewish boys* are known for taking over the family business upon their father's retirement or demise, God has never collected social security or agreed to Nietzsche's observation of his having passed. There is only one God. And it is impossible to crucify him. (And obviously illogical.) He's out there "testing our faith" and punishing all of us (Christians, Jews, Muslims, and Atheists) no matter what we believe. And there is only one bible. Upon the death of Moses, God himself commands Joshua (Joshua 1:8) — and thereby all Jews for eternity — "Never allow *This Book* (The Old Testament and The Oral Laws of the Talmud taught to him by Moses) to cease departing from your mouth. Study it diligently day and night." There is no alternative *That Book*.

And for that reason, as The Sharks say to their quivering groveling obsequious guppy contestants, when it comes to believing any New Testament, *"I'm out." It's difficult enough for me to believe in the Old Testament. Don't bother tempting me with a new butchered version.*

And so, it's not only the first of the Ten Commandments, "I am the Lord thy God," that is still in force. The other six hundred and twelve are also in full swing as well. And notice the singular personal pronoun of "*I*" as opposed to the command beginning with the plural "*We*." There is no "One God in three Divine persons." #GetAMathLife! Orthodox Jews look at Christianity as one more wayward bastardized (no insult intended, Ahem!) offshoot of classical Judaism.

Like the dinosaur and the heretical now-defunct Sadducees and Boethusians, whose followers once outnumbered the original descendants of those who received the Torah on Mount Sinai almost three and a half millennia ago, we believe other beliefs are already extinct.

The real difference between Christians and Jews begins with our belief as to what exactly was revealed and transmitted by God at Mt. Sinai. Most religions believe that the Ten Commandments alone were entrusted to the Jewish nation and all mankind to follow. Jews, however, believe that in addition to the Ten Commandments, the entire Oral Law (which includes the entire Talmud and all of its commentaries) was taught to Moses in a miraculous crash-course when he went up to heaven for forty days and forty nights. On three different occasions!

Most Catholics don't even know that. And that is exactly what separates the Jewish *men* from the Catholic *goys*. Catholics didn't even exist, and they clearly had no oral tradition till Jesus the Orthodox Jew (who originally called himself a prophet — a false one to Jews and a real one to Muslims) came along one thousand and five hundred years *after* Moses studied the Talmud with God on Mount Sinai. Rabbi Jesus himself studied in a yeshiva during his youth before going, like many young men in our *Unzereh* community today, "Off the D," which means "Off the Derech." *Derech* means 'Path.' As in the pathway to heaven.

Jesus and the apostles later emerged with their perjured dogma fifteen-hundred years *after* the "old" Oral Laws given on Mount Sinai were transcribed into the corpus collection of 'all the wisdom and knowledge contained in God's brain' that we *Unzereh* Jews call "The Talmud." Or simply, "*Shas*" (an acronym for the six disciplines of knowledge necessary for the proper observance of Judaism and flawless devotion to God).

God's wisdom is endless. And so it becomes an eternal task to study God's word. Yet we are expected to "complete" it during one paltry lifespan. While being chased for millenniums by Babylonians, Romans, Crusaders, Muslims, and Nazis across several continents, and Ilhan Omar through the halls of Congress. And because there is no battle as bloody as the one waged in the name of God, we Jews have been totally fucked over ever since being declared God's Chosen People.

The followers of Christ arose from the ranks of ignorant Jews. Unable to study the Talmud, they simply followed the instructions of its glorious sages. It is of little wonder that they were easily manipulated into believing the lyrics of the Beatles that "all you need is love" when proclaimed by an aspiring prophet. *Kind of like many modern-day Hasidim.*

Upon his death, followers of the young thirty-three-year-old martyr (who barely lived out half his days) only possessed the Judaic Old Testament to plagiarize as they hastily wrote a sloppy New Testament that eventually introduced their new Trinity God, one of which was birthed by a virgin. And that literary outrageous hoax was topped by an even later scribbled convoluted book of misconstrued events that is nowadays revered by almost two billion Muslims. *Inshallah.*

Forget about the Jewish "two for the price of one." We'll give you three! The Talmud was way beyond their reach or intellectual grasp. That is why the Apostles constantly quote Jesus as deriding the scholars of the Talmud. Never happened. He wouldn't have had the nerve. Those Jewish priests, who Jesus supposedly scorned, were the saintly rabbinical scholars who chastised (not to be confused with the word "crucified") Jesus, who was an Orthodox Jew who wore the four-cornered tasseled garment known as *Tzitzit,* for falsely claiming to be a prophet of God.

It was only after the death of Jesus that the apostle Luke found the audacity to proclaim that the son of Mary shall be known as the "Son of God." They were already implementing Hitler's fantastical "Grobe Luge" advice two thousand years before he authored his *Mein Kampf* rant. And that is why Christian scholars are constantly forced to invent new dogma to reconcile historic events, or to magically turn sins into "miracles" and sinners into "saints."

Like the concept of Mary's own immaculate conception and her virgin birthing of Jesus (*Really?*), proclaimed in order to cover up the known fact that he was a bastard, and to then insist that Jesus was the Jewish Messiah who descended — in Christian la la reality, on his mother's side — from the House of David (i.e. the tribe of Judah), as prophesied by Isaiah, while completely refuting his having any DNA from his father Joseph, who they claim was also a descendant of the tribe of Judah. But the Church insists that Joseph was *not* the biological father. *No wonder Jesus got out of Dodge after three days. He didn't want to submit to a paternity test.*

In fact, it took almost two thousand years for Pope Pius IX, in his papal *Ineffabilis Deus* state, to finally muster his *ex cathedra* chutzpah in 1854 to proclaim the virginity of Mary, before, during and after the birth of Jesus. A biblical source for this madness does not exist anywhere in the Bible. It's all a result of sexual hang-ups having to do with the doctrine of original sin.

I can only imagine what lengthy convoluted dogma the Church would be forced to invent if the real shrouds of Jesus were ever discovered and a drop of his blood was tested for DNA. It took the Thomas Jefferson Foundation two decades to huffily admit that the Jefferson-Hemmings controversy is a "settled historical matter." How many centuries would have to pass before The Church would ever admit that Mary was fucked?

And one last thought, you stupid Pope. If you ever took the time to read *Our Bodies, Ourselves* you might learn something of value before you vomit your *ex cathedra* bullshit. The "Holy Hymen" of Mary that you are so OCD anal about was nothing more than a bit of tissue *surrounding* the vaginal opening. And even the presence of an intact hymen could never serve as proof that Mary was a virgin anyway.

The hymen does not stretch across the vagina. And it is not punctured by a penis the first time a woman has intercourse. They don't "break." And some women are born without one. Other women have flimsy flaps of tissue that would reveal nothing about their sexual activity. In truth, the hymen has no known function other than to reward "the virgin," whose wedding-night white sheets reveals blood, a bigger dowry according to those of us who believe in the Bible and study the Talmud. The *Ketuvah* of a virgin is two hundred *zuz* (ancient coin), where that of a divorcee or widow is one hundred *zuz*. *I'm feeling a little embarrassed right now.*

And the main purpose of the hymen, even in the twenty-first century, seems to serve no evolutionary purpose other than to slut-shame young women into being controlled by men. Many of them have never even come close to experiencing intercourse. *Please let me lick your wounds.*

This is all ancient scientific history. But I understand that the Pope would never look at a heavenly pussy or even a scientific diagram of one. He's too busy fantasizing about Mary's. So keep on speaking *ex cathedra* to your two and a half billion "blind" followers simply

Mr. Lewinson's
favorite
Student
Viagra for Women.
Rx
CyberDiamond.com
Our most precious gem is our word.
SUPREME COURT OF THE STATE OF NEW YORK
COUNTY OF ROCKLAND
ZEV LEWINSON,
Plaintiff,
- against -
SHAREN LEWINSON,
Defendant.
SIRS:
PLEASE TAKE NOTICE that the within is a copy of the
signed by the Hon. Victor J. Alfieri,
As usual, rock stars get all the attention.
CyberDiamond.com
Our most precious gem is our word.
STERLING LORD LITERISTIC, INC.
65 Bleecker Street • New York, N.Y. 10012 • (212) 780-6050 • FAX: (212) 780-6095
george@sll.com
George M. Nicholson
July 29, 2003
Zev Lewinson
19 Mariner Way
Monsey, New York 10952
Dear Mr. Lewinson:
I have recently reviewed HOW MICE BECOME SMALL, and though there are some lovely things in it, I am unable to represent it for I am limiting the number of picture books I represent. They are the least profitable and most costly type of book to publish, and my small staff and I cannot put in the time and effort required. I wish you success in your search for publication.
Sincerely,
George Nicholson

Love
TATY
TATY

because Matthew, Luke, and John bastardized our original verse from Isaiah 7:14 when they misinterpreted the original Hebrew word "maiden" as "virgin."

A similar botched and bastardized interpretation of scripture was committed when a putz name Jerome translated an original premodern Hebrew verse found in the Old Testament (Exodus 34:30) into Latin without having much of a clue as to what the authentic text was talking about.

The Hebraic verse in Exodus explained that when Moses descended Mount Sinai carrying the Ten Commandments, powerful beams of light (imagine a spotlight with the radiant power of our sun) emanated *from* his face. "Horns of light" ("Kohrahn Ohr") is how our holy Torah describes the miraculous light that resulted from Moses literally standing next to God. God is described as "light" by the Holy Kuzari, by the way. And because the illumination was so powerful, the radiant splendor looked like atomic antlers of sunlight protruding from the head of Moses.

Jerome, who was obviously more familiar with Latin than Hebrew, just focused on the word "horn." Just like the other schmucks focused on sex and translated "maiden" into "virgin." Forget about "lost in translation." Mary "found" her hymen in translation!

The resulting voluminous dogma, that was birthed by a mistranslated typo that omitted the word "light," would be comical — as is Sigmund Freud's evaluation of the sculpture of Moses, when he placed it under psychoanalysis to study its emotions, while he probably snorted cocaine, upon visiting the tomb of Pope Julius II for three weeks in 1913 — if not for the fact that the marvelous, but factually flawed, incredible sculpture of Michelangelo resulted in many people believing that Jews are devils and demons to this day. *So, we get a horny Moses and a Virgin Mary!*

I wonder what God thinks of all this as he constantly studies his holy book that has shed so much darkness (and blood) around the world.

Here is the short version of Christianity for Dummies. A silkworm made you a Christian. The Chinese discovered silk. The Far East kept it a secret from Western Civilization. But Romans were infatuated with the cloth and spent billions of dollars as they imported the magical material. They warred, conquered, and immediately built roads. Those roads (specifically The Silk Road) were for commerce. Meanwhile Paul (not the Jew named Jesus) started a brand new religion that became known as Christianity.

In the early days it was only the lowest, forsaken members of society (definitely not the Talmudical scholars) that embraced Paul's simple Jewish businessman guarantee. "All you need is love." Slaves, women, and the ignorant poor met in secret to hear the promise of a beautiful afterlife, after their miserable sojourn here on Earth, based on simply believing in the prophet Jesus. That's right. Prophet.

Eventually, Constantine himself felt the urge to be baptized. And now any Roman who wanted to be part of Roman high society and enjoy the rights and privileges of commerce and eventually iPhones, followed in the footsteps of Constantine and converted. Presto! Magic. Holy shit!

Flash forward a couple of centuries — as you sprinkle in some dogmatic fairy dust, a couple of Crusades, some paintings on a ceiling, and corporate meetings with a CEO voted in by the board and granted Ex Cathedra authority — and you have two billion people singing "Goin' to the Chapel" with the Dixie Cups and searching for Easter eggs with their adorable little shikses. When they're not killing Jews.

In the Jewish faith, one's Jewishness is based solely on his *mother* being Jewish. If Hitler and Queen Ester had a child, the baby would be a full-fledged, hundred percent, Jew. But when it comes to *tribal lineage*, which is determined by having descended from any of the twelve *sons* of Jacob, the descendant is considered a member of a tribe based *solely* on his *father's* tribe. All Jewish men have a Jewish mother. But they do not all share the same tribal ancestry. The child's father is the *only* factor that determines its tribal genealogy.

A Jewish woman can give birth to a son whose father descended from the tribe of Judah, and then divorce and marry a man from the tribe of Reuben and then birth another son with him. Her sons are *Jewish* brothers solely because of their mother, but they descended from any one of twelve different tribes based on their father's individual tribal lineage.

These two concepts are the Word of God recorded in the Talmud and even modern-day rabbis in Israel use them when determining who falls under the 'Right of return' law that grants Israeli citizenship to any Jew living in the Diaspora who chooses to immigrate. The person seeking to immigrate is considered to be a Jew based solely on his mother's lineage. The forms requesting citizenship only ask about the applicant's mommy.

Jon Gotti's wife was Jewish. The mother of Mrs. Victoria Gotti, née DiGiorgio was Jewish. Which means Jon and Victoria's daughter, Vicki, was an *Eishet Chayil Goombah* until she finally divorced Carmine "The Bull" Agnello (who was not exactly a *mensch*). And upon any of Vicki's own three sons marrying a Jewish woman who would give birth to a *Stugots*, *his* eight-day old penis would be circumcised based on the "Brit Milah" mitzvah commanded to Abraham in the Bible (Genesis 17:13).

If all three brothers marry a *shiksa,* then the Jewish lineage of the Gotti crime family will have ceased (*nebech, a shanda*) with Vicki, a *Yiddishe Mama,* who should have been home cooking chicken soup (and not baking homemade prosciutto bread with provolone cheese) and raising her three *Pisano* (#baseballbat #cementshoes) potential could-have-been Talmudical scholars (*nebach, ver vayst?*).

All these *Judaic* laws prove that Jesus did *not* descend from the tribe of Judah even if Mary did. On his "Father's side," Jesus could not possibly have descended from *any* of the twelve tribes — because he supposedly didn't have a flesh and blood daddy! And speaking *ex cathedra* or *ex toileta* does not entitle the spoken words of a flesh and blood *elected* (by bird-brain Cardinals) man to usurp the Word of God.

The Pope can't claim that Jesus possessed *paternal* lineage from God (and a Jewish woman He *didn't* have sex with) and in the same breath insist that Jesus descended from the tribe of Judah on the side of Joseph. God has no tribal ancestry. He is The Creator. He's an orphan! *No wonder he's so messed up! (lol)* I wonder what the Cardinals themselves are smoking when that white smoke comes billowing out of the tiny chimney of the Sistine Chapel that grants the Pope instant infallibility whenever he speaks *ex cathedra.*

As a matter of fact, it's really time we got that circular *illogical dogma* straightened out too. How can the Cardinals, who are fallible, grant infallibility merely because they're blowing some smoke? Let's face it. It's all smoke and dogma-mirrors. And a dash of potassium chlorate, lactose, and pine rosin to color the smoke white. But till the magicians revealed their tricks, millions of tear-stained cheeks faced the heavens as they marveled how black smoke billowed into white as the proclamation of a new Holy See was validated by nothing less than a miracle. *I'm getting all choked up.* From the smoke!

The entire immaculate conception tinselry has deluded millions of faithful worshipers into blindly worshiping an adulteress. Their entire devotion is based on the misinterpretation of the single Hebrew word 'maiden' as 'virgin.' *Every young maiden in the world is a virgin. Till she isn't.* And when the Pope immediately follows up his *ex cathedra* proclamation by ordering his soldiers to eviscerate the intestines of anyone who dares to question the veracity of the "miraculous" virgin birth of Jesus, you can rest assure that parents will teach their young kids that Mary was most definitely a hymen-intact hymn-singing virgin.

Besides, at a time when almost everyone believed that the Earth was flat and that the sun rotated around our planet, and only Christian clergy were allowed to interpret Scripture, how difficult do you think it was to pull off that Mary never committed any hanky-panky? The Talmud has so much more to say on this topic. And so do I. But I'd better stop before some Pontifical Swiss

Guards show up at my door to grab my Talmudical tomes and set them ablaze behind the Louvre at the command of The Holy Pontiff, as they did in 1242. Hopefully leaving me behind! I will leave a few lyrics from Billy Joel however: *The stained-glass curtain you're hiding behind never let in the sun.*

I'm actually very forgiving as I understand that everyone is simply trying to serve God in their own cultish way. But among all the third party historically verified recorded history I've read regarding Jews, Muslims, and Christians, it's only the Muslims and Christians that have been clearly identified as guilty of mercilessly slaughtering "Infidels" and those who refuse to accept Christ or the Prophet Muhammad as their savior.

The ancient Hebrews supposedly slaughtered Canaanites, but no one really knows the lineal descendants of those ancestral people or what those wars were about. Most historians consider biblical stories as too ancient to verify. And the followers of all three Abrahamic religions claim that they are the "true" pedigreed descendants of the Hebrews, which means that they insist on claiming credit for killing the Canaanites.

As a matter of fact, the Jewish religion is the only religion that not only never forces conversion, but vigorously refuses converts. We just want to be left alone. And even as an Orthodox Jew I would certainly abide by the "live and let live" philosophy of Hillel the Elder and hide gay men in my attic before ever allowing them to be stoned by some fanatical mob. Besides, most of the gay men I've met in literary circles are funny and witty. Often charming, if not occasionally bitchy. In other words, human. And as far as I am concerned, animal life is almost as precious. I would never harm an animal.

I'm already guilt-ridden for merely being a pescatarian, who finds the idea of slaughtering and *fressing* an innocent (sentient cow) hamburger utterly repulsive. I find it absurd to slaughter animals for sacrificial purposes. Please do not expect me to eat any. I cannot imagine murdering and eating a Pascal lamb when the Messiah arrives. I might heave if I did. On the other hand, being threatened with "Karet" ("cut off" as in "premature death") for not obeying the Passover precept might increase my appetite for eating rotting flesh.

Besides, why do we need to eat Matzohs and Pascal lamb to commemorate our hastily leaving ancient Egypt on (basically) eighteen minutes notice — not even allowing time for our dough to rise? After spending two-hundred and ten years in slavery, why were we forced to exit as cowards running away from their captors? After all those miraculous plagues, one would think we would have been allowed to leave at our leisure, and with pride. We Jews are still rushing like mad since the day we left Egypt.

When an Orthodox Jew says he's *studying* the *Torah* in a general sense, he means the whole nine yards (which includes the entire Talmud and its endless commentaries) and not merely the uncircumcised version made up by the plagiarizing Goyim. But if he says he's going to *read* the Torah to the congregation in the synagogue on the Sabbath, he would be referring only to the literal Five Books of Moses — what Catholics refer to as The Old Testament. "Old" to us means, "oldie but goodie." The foundation is the five books.

An Orthodox Jew believes that each word therein was literally spoken to Moses in crystal clear prophecy, who then transcribed God's message of 304,805 letters into one very long parchment scroll. Without any punctuation marks whatsoever, it could almost be called one long run-on sentence. *And you thought my run-on sentences were bad.*

Ancient Kabbalist teachings explain that God "gazed deeply into the Torah and created the entire World." Think of the Torah as a 'Creation for Dummies' handbook while simultaneously being a condensed mind-map of God's synapses and eternal brain-matter. God somehow confined his unlimited and eternal intelligence and authored his endless knowledge and wisdom into finite words that have infinite meaning. *He self-published The Bible!* And it's all miraculously truncated into a mere five books that contain an awful lot of bloody fatwās.

The Midrash says that God gazed into his self-published work and created the universe by following the "instructions" of the Five Books of Moses. Every Torah scroll that exists today is almost an exact duplicate of the one written by Moses. The only detail our tradition has a little confusion about are certain letters that were written one way and pronounced another — but we'll save that for another time.

Please don't ask how it's all possible. After all, God can do anything. And we're talking about the Kabbalah, so we'll pretend we understand. The unlettered CEO of the JCC I belong to once laughed as he confessed that simply adding the word 'Kabbalah' to the description of any program that was being offered at his community center instantly quadrupled attendance. "I can offer the course or lecture for free and very few people will show up, but if I add the magical word 'Kabbalah' I can charge for tickets and the event will be sold out." *And who knows ... maybe Madonna will show up. ("Papa don't preach. I'm in trouble deep.")*

Orthodox Jews believe that the more "Torah-knowledge" you obtain through decades of studying the Talmud, with all of its seemingly endless commentaries, while living a life ensconced in prayer and observance of endless detailed commandments and ancient rituals — while spending years of subservient squireship under the tutelage of a saintly angelic scholar as your brain shrinks due to years of lost REM sleep — the more godly you become.

You evolve a mini God-brain. Because you now think like God thinks. *(You now understand why it's okay to slaughter babies.)* All that "Torah-knowledge" and picayunish OCD observance, obtained through a lack of precious sleep, now entwines with every single now-holy neuron and your spiritually advanced manipulated brain now possesses "Da'as Torah."

I possess a great deal of Da'as Torah. I earned it. *But I still love shiksa's! And I would have loved banging Mary!* As a matter of fact, I love everyone. What I find most distasteful about religion (even with all my Da'as Torah) is the divisiveness caused by religious dogma. I find it utterly impossible to believe that God wants his own children to slaughter one another. Murder is the opposite of bringing life into the world. I am only able to worship a God of Life. I find it impossible to worship a petty, vengeful God of Death.

Even among my dysfunctional and destroyed family and extended family, I'd never want any of my children to kill each other or have them slaughter any of their many cousins. Refusing to speak with or acknowledge the living is painful enough. Excommunication and shaming are very nasty punishments. Hardly befitting true scholars. Or their God. Why does murdering family members sound so completely absurd and is totally unacceptable on a personal level to any rational person, and yet becomes a mitzvah and commendable act for which "heroes" are honored (usually posthumously) when one religious group attacks another?

When will mankind understand that all the brown, blue, and green-eyed Children of God received their hereditary eye color from the color of God's eyes and that we are one intimate family fighting during a Thanksgiving dinner meal? Why is everyone trying to gouge out their sibling's eyes? The eyes are the window to the soul. Why can't people see how horrific it is to hurt someone else? *God, why can't you see?*

Having Da'as Torah in Monsey, NY means people will sincerely flock to you in order to hear you dispense what they believe is your almost prophetic wisdom on matters not only pertaining to Jewish law, but regarding any and all personal matters of life. That is why I took my future *Vybie* to meet my "Da'as Torah" Rabbi Nekritz. I wanted to hear what "God" thought about the woman I chose to marry. *That's the last time I ever trust "God" again. Or God, for that matter.*

I still remember the first time I took Sharen to meet my Rabbi and his wife, "Batya," (whose name translates to "daughter of God"). We drove from Manhattan down the West Side Highway, romantically holding hands while driving, when all of a sudden my quiet cutie-pie, who was lost in her thoughts, burst out in tears, "What if he doesn't like me!" My Modern Orthodox Barnard babe knew the score and already understood how deeply Rabbi Nekritz's opinion could affect her fate. Never being one to lie or deny, I gently squeezed her hand as I smiled and assured her, with total confidence, "What's not to love?"

And sure enough, my Rabbi was ecstatic upon meeting my future bride. I almost thought my extremely religious Da'as Torah conduit to the Tetragrammaton was going to hug my fiancée at the door as he and Batyah said goodbye to us that night. "Sharen! Did you see how much he liked you! It was as if you were a folio of the Talmud!" *Thus sayeth The Lord.*

I was now committed to doing His Will. And although there were several panic attacks in the months ahead, sometimes when I was with the sweetest woman on the planet but usually when I was alone while driving or sitting on a rock after a ten-mile run and resting, I stubbornly ignored the pounding beats in my young, strong, seduced-by-Da'as Torah heart. The only guck clogging my arteries at that time was love for my future family, the blue eyes of my fiancée, and faith in my rabbi. *After all, how could I go against God's will?*

One of the first questions prospective in-laws of a future daughter-in-law asks the Shadchan before allowing her to meet their son is, "Who is her family's Da'as Torah?" The answer to that question is like a spiritual MRI of the family's mind and soul. "Rav Shmuel Kamenetsky," at age ninety-five, is still the most popular response. If he edifies anyone it's as if God has already guaranteed their entrance into heaven.

When people called Rav Shmuel to inquire about me as I arranged a possible marriage match for our oldest daughter through the Shadchan, he'd respond, "A Tzaddik! A Tzaddik!" *(A righteous man!)* When I was later made aware of such a beautiful accolade I jokingly quipped, "Maybe you shouldn't trust his *Da'as Torah*."

After Sharen visited Rabbi Nekritz several times, upon my filing for divorce, to request and then demand that he discontinue our relationship, Rabbi Kamenetsky was my *Bashert's* next mark. She played him as easily as she had played me for almost three decades. His *Da'as Torah* was no match for her thespian skills. *He should live and be well.*

Monsey, NY has as many *Da'as Torah* Rabbis nowadays as there are hookers in Tijuana, Mexico on payday. And you'll probably get better advice from the street-smart women. Funny thing is, the Monsey "Da'as Torah" inspired rabbinical hookers, like Rabbi Schabes and Rabbi Frank, are constantly calling Rabbi Kamenetsky in order to obfuscate the words of the elderly sage, as they then assure their followers that the leader of American Orthodox Jewry sanctioned and agreed with their views.

This is why so many of my fellow Jews are becoming fed up with the Beit Din system. The members of one of the lowest level quasi-judicial systems in Jewish scholarship are not *halachicly* deemed to have some divine level of inspiration. Any three circumcised Jewish dicks can sit down and convene an arbitration court. In fact, they don't even have to be circumcised. Or ordained. They can simply be a dick. *They can even be three chicks with dicks!* And one is not obligated to trust them no matter what their ultimate decision proclaims merely because they printed stationary with a scales of justice symbol in their letterhead design. In fact, little trust remains. The system was originally built upon saintliness and honesty. Those concepts have sadly become ancient.

I had also spent many years as a volunteer *Toen* (lawyer/consultant), refusing to bill the women I helped in order to never be tainted as favoring one side over the other. Working with an assortment of Beit Din's fighting for women's rights as a hero of sorts in helping *Agunot* escape from cruel husbands and an arcane set of unenforceable laws, I was all too familiar with the pockmarked terrain of the modern-day authoritarian Jewish court system that typically rules by the self-imposed blind-allegiance of an unsuspecting ignorant Jewish population that lives by the intimidation (how else does one describe 'religion?') of what their neighbors and Shadchanim (matchmaker yentas) might be (Oy vey!) thinking, rather than by intellectual honesty and logic.

When I took someone's side, the Beit Din involved could be damn sure it was the side that needed — and would receive — justice. I held the feet of the rabbis to the flame of our holy jurisprudence. Laws that worked flawlessly, I might add, but only when administered by saints, and not when executed by greedy sinners and ignoramuses — or circumcised holy pricks that were missing a pair of testicles. *Did the Mohel's knife slip?*

I didn't care if it was Rabbi Mordechai Willig in Riverdale, NY, Rabbi Mendel Epstein in Lakewood, NJ, Rabbi Pinchus Teitz in Elizabeth, NJ, or Rabbi Avrohom Union in Los Angeles, CA. I'd raise my voice and debate till my mouth was dry.

"Don't tell me to 'be patient' when you refuse to do what's right!" I'd yell. Rabbi Willig once hung up on me in the middle of our conversation.

I called right back and asked in a surprised voice, "Did you just hang up on me because I said you have no backbone?"

"I was exhausted," he responded, "and you were berating me."

"Well, don't call *me* a *hot-head* while yet another Agunah is told to be patient — for years! It only makes my head hotter! Do what you're supposed to do and you won't have to be so exhausted," I gently admonished the good rabbi, trying to use a little humor, as I apologized half-heartedly for my "lack of patience" and his lacking any testicles.

Rabbi Willig, who taught Talmud at the prestigious Yeshiva University, had been bending over backwards to give a recalcitrant young husband (who was refusing to divorce his wife) more time to tantrum so that he would then *hopefully* come to his senses. But the sinful shlepping of the recalcitrant rabbi came at the expense of yet another innocent young woman's biological clock ticking away.

I felt that having mercy on one side would be administering merciless cruelty to the other side and ORA (Organization for the Resolution of Agunot) agreed with me that it was time for a friendly phone call. Rabbi Willig had already made *that* mistake — of refusing to judge carefully and stubbornly delaying justice, and later, on February 19, 2003, *finally* publicly acknowledged his false conclusions and horrific "mistakes" — in the now infamous Baruch Lanner case over which he messily presided.

Four years earlier I had already insisted to Rabbi Willig that Rabbi Baruch Lanner was abusing and molesting young women *for decades*. I knew one of those women intimately (*a "natural" redhead*) from my heyday youth who was now a mom, and the very religious wife (who understandably wanted to remain anonymous) of a wonderful rabbi. And so I couldn't possibly relate her name as a witness. Nevertheless, I relayed the information about Lanner's having forcefully fondled this now forty-two-year-old woman decades ago.

"We (the young girls in the gatherings Lanner led) all knew to keep our distance. He felt me up more than once."

"Why didn't you tell your parents back then?" I asked her.

"Are you kidding me?! My parents would have never let me out of the house!" was her terse response.

Rabbi Willig's admission that his Beit Din (that earned very handsome fees) should "never have taken the case," as he later acknowledged their complete "lack of experience in adjudicating matters of abuse," came at the price of Lanner's abusive sexual molestations continuing unchecked for many more years. *There is often a history of abuse in many divorce cases, but somehow he supposedly understands how to settle those.*

The Jewish Orthodox Union, in order to save (its own) face, prepared its own "special commission" (vomit bag time) in 2003, critiquing the horrific complete "failure of taking action" and "profound errors of judgement" of the Beit Din case led by Rabbi Willig in 1989. The commission finally apologized to the physically, sexually, and emotionally abused victims of Rabbi Baruch Lanner for not acting sooner to stop the abuse. Rabbi Willig had been world-renowned for his divine *Da'as Torah*. Till the day it became obvious that he never had any.

So when it came time for my own divorce, I knew that even the most honest and decent Beit Din's (arbitration boards) were woefully behind the times and often unfair to men as well as women. Basically, they were pitifully inept and always very rushed, and I wanted the *real-deal* version of a true Beit Din convened to adjudicate my divorce. Many arbitration boards consisted of part-time wannabe scholars who are easily manipulated by emotion (and even more so by money — a lot of money!) and are incapable of applying the critical-thinking logic necessary to interpret the ancient complicated laws of the Talmud, and to then relate them to the scenario of a modern-day divorcing couple.

And if the accused Lanner could deceive the prestigious Yeshiva University panel for over a decade, my modest hard-working *Eishet Chayil* wife — with her beatific smile — would easily be able to hypnotize an arbitration wannabe Beit Din for an eternity. I could almost hear her calm angelic voice describing how she "stood on her feet in the O.R. for thirty years so that my husband Zev could study with Rabbi Nekritz."

The arbitration laymen themselves knew that endless mistakes were made. And that is why they insisted upon litigants absolving them of any financial responsibility. I refused to be judged by the amateurs my wife chose at the behest of some new non-ordained rabbi named Schabes she discovered through her deceitful therapist/rabbi (Dr. Donny Frank) after I filed for divorce.

Even an honest Beit Din like that of the snippy Rabbi Willig would never have taken the time to properly adjudicate my case — assuming they even had the ability to remain impartial. They'd quickly experience cognitive bias and decide within seconds of meeting my Ms. Perfect (on the outside, deeply flawed on the inside) wife that I'm the crazy one to divorce such a gem. Go ahead and call me old-fashioned (you would be too if you spent a lifetime slowly studying our ancient tomes), but I knew I needed wise and patient scholars to preside over my divorce.

Especially going up against the Oscar-worthy performances of my thespian talented wife who had no peer or competitor among the entire Hollywood community when it came to playing the dramatic role of the "woe is me" Jewish-wife. No one sported a halo like the one worn by my crafty wife.

Sharen could easily have been the poster girl for the "halo effect" named by psychologist Edward Thorndike. Anyone introduced to my wife would be instantly influenced by her genteel charm, tiny body, and angelic soft-spoken voice that immediately left them with the overall impression of their having met the reincarnation of Florence Nightingale.

Never could they imagine the character flaws in the grey matter behind her radiant royal-blue eyes that seemed to sparkle as if they reflected the light of a full-moon. Legend claims that the light of a full moon made people act crazy. You try staring into her eyes. *Did she make me crazy?*

My wife reminded me of the Roman goddess, *Luna*, whose name is the prefix for the word that best describes her verbal-violent episodic tantrums. My wife wasn't only crazy when people said, "must be a full moon out there." She could erupt at the birth of even a pitch-black new moon or on the sunniest of days. She was a lunatic even when kissing a mezuzah on a typical early Sabbath morning as she entered the synagogue to pray.

Rabbi Bernard S. Lanner was finally convicted in 2002 of sexually abusing two teenage girls who attended the Jewish religious private school where he had been principal. He was sentenced to seven years in prison for one out of (probably) hundreds of molestations over the decades he interacted with children. Willig's crude Beit Din could have curtailed Lanner's sexual assault career by a full decade had it acted responsibly and listened humbly instead of deciding arrogantly. Lanner assured them that it had all been a "misunderstanding." *So much for Da'as Torah.*

I knew it would take a near eternity before even our burgeoning neuroscience could begin to fathom the mentally ill mind of my wife, let alone her being understood by an arbitration board of three tired old men whose greatest concern was mumbling the exact same thrice-daily silent *Amidah* prayer with a minyan during which they begged an all-merciful God to find a *Shidduch* for their old-maid daughters who had already turned the ripe old age of twenty-one (*Oy vey! Vat's gonna be!*) and have not yet found their *Bashert* among our *Unzereh* cult. By age twenty-two these poor girls know it will take a miracle like the parting of the waters at The Crossing of the Red Sea to find a husband.

My wife would sigh that she works so hard, raises children, and "makes Shabbos," while allowing me to constantly study the Talmud. She makes an awesome impression. Calm. Quiet. Composed. At a minimum, I needed a *real* Beit-Din. And even then I knew trouble loomed on the horizon. But at least I'd be playing on a level field.

I called the world-renowned Rabbi Shmuel Kamenetsky (whose father was an extremely close friend of my grandfather) and asked him to serve on my Beit Din. "*Oy, Ich hob nisht keyn koach" (Woe, I don't have the strength),* the ninety-two-year-old saint apologetically replied.

I didn't have the strength either. What I did have was too much firsthand experience with Jewish arbitration courts. The local arbitration boards rarely followed the amazing protocols of the Talmud, such as administering the proper execution of a woman's *Ketuvah* (her cash-laden whole-life insurance policy paid upon divorce or becoming widowed). And more than I believed in an afterlife, I knew that my wife would never honor any decision they rendered anyway. It has always been, and will forever be, her way or the "Go to Hell!" highway. *Thy will be done.*

If things didn't go her way, she'd dismiss them faster than the way she cutely passed gas. "Zev outsmarted them with all his Talmudical knowledge," she'd state in a voice that would sound more believable than the one you heard when your mother told you she loves you. I also knew through firsthand experience that the board would never enforce their own decisions. The worst thing they would ever do is excommunicate my wife. She'd laugh within. At God and at me.

Even batty wife aside, I understood that I'd never find justice in our own *Unzereh-zany* courts. Most of the self-declared judges didn't know the basic laws of a woman's *Ketuvah*, and viewed everything as good versus evil in simple amateur black and white logic, so how could I expect them to comprehend a devilish mind like that of my possessed wife?

Like a Cold Case file, it would take many years for the best of detectives with skills of forensic profiling to even suspect, let alone understand, how utterly ruthless this adorably cute mother-of-five could be. It took me twenty-seven. And no one saw her mind or pussy more up-close than I did. Both were cold enough to make your teeth chatter. At the very least I needed a *"Nisht foon Unzereh!"* court that kept full and transparent documentation of proceedings and held liars accountable. *Or so I thought.*

The *Ketuvah* document has always been a Jewish woman's guarantee of funds in case her husband chose to divorce her, or upon his death. Children, basically, inherit their father according to biblical law, and they (or trustees if they are minors) provide for their mother's needs through her Ketuvah rights. It is an ingenious system and there is a huge tome in the Talmud dedicated entirely to the *Ketuvah* process that "kicks in" upon divorce or a husband's death. The "alimony" payment of the payout stopped upon remarrying and being supported by her new husband.

It's amazing how detailed and clever the ancient procedural elements of the Jewish courts meshed with all possible scenarios — both probable and highly irregular and unlikely — of daily Jewish life. From verification of witnesses and meticulously executing documents that were folded and wax-sealed in ways that were almost impossible to replicate, down to severe punishments for testifying falsely or committing plagiarism, the system worked almost flawlessly. Especially compared to the slipshod butchery conducted in our modern-day criminal, divorce, and probate courts. And we're talking two millennia ago.

The systems invented by the Talmudical scholars were used in Ancient Rome. Emperors had Jewish advisors. Half a millennium later Abarbanel was running the most civilized country on the planet for King Ferdinand and Bitch Isabella. The Jews didn't originally "own all the banks." They *became* bankers because it was one of the few fields they were allowed to pursue. They simply used the documentation procedures of the Talmud and their flawless reputations to keep track of Europe's wealth.

The Jews were trusted by the very same gentiles who often killed them (to get out of debt!). And even our modern-day democracy is hardly a new invention. It's based on European parliamentary procedures that trace back to the way Jewish courts were run during the half millennia that the Talmud was formally debated, codified, and edited. All while being decimated by *The Goyim. You're welcome World.*

Nowadays unfortunately, a Jewish man can not only divorce a wife against her will, but he can also keep her married *to* him against her will. The expense of having to pay a *Ketuvah* made a man think twice before frivolously divorcing his wife in a moment of anger in Talmudical times. But hardly anyone pays a *Ketuvah* nowadays — or it's estimated at some minimum value or paid in lieu of some marital savings. The entire divorce code *Ketuvah* procedure has become nothing more than a custom and tradition.

Unfortunately, in a Jewish divorce, it's a man's world. *He* divorces *her*. Period. (Trust me, I know and agree it's "not fair." Please don't shoot the messenger.) A woman's willingness to forgo her *Ketuvah* money was the only way she could reverse the status quo and exit her marriage *against* the will of her husband in the era of the Talmud.

By declaring her total disdain for her marriage and proclaiming the words *"Nim'as Li"* ("It is disgusting to me") — to the extent of willingly forfeiting her *Ketuvah* payout — the ancient Beit Din's, at that point, would literally force the man to give his wife a Jewish Get (divorce). They would even physically whip him till he agreed to free her from the marriage through his delivering the divorce decree document and releasing it into her eagerly awaiting cupped hands.

That option no longer exists because modern-day Jewish husbands are protected by the separation of church and state. It's illegal to beat up a recalcitrant asshole. And it's impossible to beat up an intractable God. All a wife can do is cup her empty hands in prayer (often for years) as she waits for the father of her children to drop her Get into her outstretched palms. Like a few coins to a beggar. The mere threat of a man withholding a Get cowers a woman into an almost fetal position of defenselessness. She is stranded and, like a child, forced to depend on the Jewish courts to defend her — even when she is willing to forgo her *Ketuvah*. But even then, too many husbands refuse to relent.

An All-Seeing God apparently failed to look far enough into the future and left this issue up to his modern-day "Da'as Torah" rabbis to figure out. Unfortunately, they have completely failed to resolve the problem. The only thing accomplished has been Yeshiva University's birthing of ORA which requests that engaged couples sign a prenup of sorts that would obligate a man to give the Get immediately if divorce statistics caught up with their lives in the future. But even the prenup is a weak attempt (although certainly better than nothing).

Not only do the Jewish courts fail in regard to equitable distribution, but they tolerate the men who refuse to give their wives a Get, thus allowing the blackmailing of these completely innocent women who are then forced to pay huge fortunes to "buy" their freedom from their "Orthodox" husbands. Women quickly discharge the financial obligation by "forgiving" the debt. They relinquish their valuable *Ketuvah* rights merely to get on with their lives. Enablers like Willig, Teitz and too many other sincere "gentlemanly scholars" continue to tolerate, to this very day, the abusive and outrageous implementation of our holy Torah to be used by recalcitrant husbands as a Dark Ages spiked chastity belt upon the pussies of far too many Jewish Orthodox women.

Instead of insisting that issuing the Get is a prerequisite for initiating a Beit Din to process a Jewish divorce (so that it does not become the main issue of the court proceedings), the Get becomes the final issue the Beit-Din deals with. I am almost in tears when I think about how obvious the solution is. I worked out the actual details to quickly undermine men who refuse to immediately give their wives a Get, but it seems that, similar to our systemic Criminal Justice System, the Beit Din courts are profiting from the mess and have no real desire to improve what I could fix within a month. This is exactly how the secular courts deal with an Order of Protection flung against an innocent father during a divorce.

Instead of judges asking, "Why the sudden orders?" (that they *know* destroys paternal bonds), the Protection Order becomes the last issue the divorce court judges worry about. Instead of nipping the obvious "oldest trick in a dirty divorce lawyer's book" in the bud, they instantly treat the innocent father like a dangerous wild beast. In fact, the orders are never even questioned during the entire divorce proceedings. They simply eventually expire. Just like daddy's relationship with his little girl.

The Jewish courts also rarely divide money equitably because they don't ask for 401K statements or tax returns. Money is easily hidden. The "moneyed spouse" easily retains that title post-divorce. And if a man, such as myself, allowed his wife to place *their* life savings into *her* work retirement account (because her employer matched a quarter of the savings as an employee benefit) for twenty-eight years, he would very likely not see a penny of those funds upon divorce in a Jewish court of law. For this reason alone, most Jewish courts are basically not kosher. They are not much better than the *Arkayos Akum* out-of-control courts they despise.

Knowing my empathy for the many defenseless women I represented through ORA, coupled with hearing how angry I got at men that withheld giving the Jewish Get to their wives, my wife knew that I would never in a trillion years withhold a Get for a nanosecond and was dying to go to a Jewish court. My liberal Barnard-educated spouse could care less about ancient *Unzereh* courts and Jewish Divorce procedures. Like when she shopped, all my *Eishet Chayil* cared about was getting the best deal.

It didn't matter if the goods "fell off a truck," my wife was an eager shopper. Rules meant nothing to her. Religion and God meant less. I merely wanted to split everything down the middle — even though she was the moneyed spouse during the third decade of our marriage. What I saw as a fifty-fifty split was viewed according to her math as "Drop dead! Ze'ev. It's all mine!"

As a matter of fact, I was quite shocked to discover — three months into our divorce, during our second day of sworn depositions as we sat with our attorneys — that "we" had saved up four-hundred thousand dollars in retirement monies and not the mere two-hundred thousand amount that my wife had been lying to me about for the past twenty-eight years of our match-made-in-heaven marriage. I was so surprised that I just blurted out, "So that's where all the cash I gave you went!" right in front of our lawyers and the stenographer.

"*I* saved that money Ze'eh'ev!" my wife shot back during our lively deposition, as she turned my one syllable name into three.

"*Yes Dear*, after I gave you a thousand dollars in cash every week for seventeen years."

Typically, my wife's cadence was to enunciate my name with two syllables when she was upset (i.e. Ze'ev), only reserving her three-syllable syntax for when she held me in utter "Die Zev. Die now!" contempt that she would soon enough be teaching Ester.

The three-syllable enunciation of my name was usually pronounced when it came to monetary matters like lifetime savings or paying maintenance and child support. My wife is an extremist when it comes to money. Because money means control. And with a narcissist, it's always about "them Benjamins." It's always about control. Money is power. I had allowed my wife to take complete financial control over my life. *You would too*. Even my car and EZ Pass were in her name. So were my testicles. But a narcissist can never have enough control. I filed for my own divorce with my superhuman last ounce of strength. I had lost my self-esteem and confidence years earlier. I was now penniless, emotionless, and numb. I'd soon be "Esterless." *And then Godless.*

I remember asking her why we have so little in savings with all the money I gave her. "You don't trust me?" she angrily responded as she showed me her 401K containing a tad under two-hundred thousand. I never realized that she had another plan with almost matching funds! I figured she'd outlive me anyway. So why would I care to know the exact amount? I honestly wanted my wife to have more savings when I'd be gone. Now I understand why she kept badgering me to give her more money to save. Like a whore, even her gentle pillow talk would be about *our* "having to save more money, Zevie." *It's all about control.*

Most men give the Get immediately. But the Beit Din's understand the complications resulting from the rare rotten-apple man who refuses to give one. They try to remedy the potential nightmare by showing the bully how eager his wife is willing to "compromise." Sort of like Chamberlain handing over Czechoslovakia to Hitler. But that works about as well as Hitler being satisfied with acquiring thousands of square miles with a simple signature on perhaps one of the most shameful treaties in world history. And that is why Putin can brazenly "offer Russian citizenship" to the civilian population of the Ukraine in the year 2019.

An ungodly Jewish man can keep his wife "anchored" to him indefinitely. The term *Agunah* means *anchor* in Aramaic. It's an incredibly accurate term because the wife isn't going anywhere. She can travel the world or hide on a different planet. But she knows God is watching her. And it's extremely rare for an observant Jewish woman — especially a Hasidic one — to defy everything she's been taught and indoctrinated to believe since nursery school. Basically, "assume an eternally-unconscious subservient mental-missionary position as a wife."

This is especially true because any child born of a union outside of her marriage is considered a *mamzer* (bastard) and tainted for life. Even if she would dare to attempt any clandestine trysts, she is surely using at least a half dozen methods of birth control. Most likely, she has been forced to obey Hamlet's command of "Get thee to a nunnery." Either way she is screwed. Or not.

Don't even try to imagine the emotional stress of a young twenty-three-year-old mother of three (an age at which a never-yet-married *old* lassie would be crying over her prayer book and considered a virtual old-maid by Monsey Yenta standards) who probably rushed into her first marriage as a seventeen year old virgin (ironically in the hopes of avoiding becoming a twenty-three year old, old-maid) and now hopes to remarry and start a fresh life for herself with *a nice man* this time around, and have many more children of course. God willing!

Even with an immediate *Get* she has a long haul ahead of her. And she's no longer a virgin — *Oy vey!* She certainly does not want to spend years as an *Agunah*. The ringing of her biological clock is deafening — surely much louder than her blackmailing defiant husband's cash-register. And if the young divorcee has not yet birthed children — having not fulfilled the ultimate purpose for which she believes she was created — the stress level multiplies exponentially.

The best scholars in the world are busy studying and refuse to waste time sitting on a mundane Beit Din earning outrageous fees. They are too enlightened to trade their Eternal Life accumulated through a lifetime of detailed study and habitual prayer for something as temporal as hoarding money. Like their enlightened Far East neighbors, they understand that the man who dies with the most toys is *not* the winner.

Unfortunately, the mediocre scholars are the ones you will typically find sitting on an arbitration Beit Din tribunal or certifying food products as Kosher. It becomes a livelihood for them. They rush through case after case believing they've "heard it all before." Hearings often erupt into a disorderly he said–she said shouting match. The rabbis are not calmly judging each case *on an individual basis* as they are instructed and severely admonished to do by the saints, mystics, and miracle workers who set forth the laws and procedures in the holy Talmud and Torah.

And the corrupt Jewish courts are another entirely different, disgusting and shameful, story. Tripe-trash men of the integrity-frayed cloth, like Rabbi Aryeh Ralbag and Rabbi Zushe Blech, who quickly, shabbily and disrespectfully cobble together a sinfully counterfeit *Heter Mei'ah Rabbanim* (*Dispensation by a Hundred Rabbis*) upon request (and envelopes stuffed with lots of cash) — falsely permitting any recalcitrant husband to remarry without giving a Get to his first wife (in essence forcing said *real* wife to spend her remaining years of life as an *Agunah*) — is the ultimate disgrace of God and abuse of His Holy Torah that one can imagine.

Ironically enough, Rabbi Ralbag's own niece, Lonna Kin, was granted fifteen minutes of fame — one minute representing each year her vagina has been anchored by an invisible chastity belt — when she was featured on the front-page of the *NY Times* (March 21, 2014) as an *Agunah* victim whose husband, Meir Kin, took a second wife by catching a wild *Heter Mei'ah Hail Mary divorce pass* thrown by bribed profane rabbis.

As they used to say in journalism school, "Jews are news." We receive disproportionate coverage, perhaps due to the world's fascination with those who observe history's oldest monotheistic religion. And the ongoing Kin saga will probably continue through the year 2074 when the announcement "with heavy hearts" of the passing of Lonna Kin, having held the record as the oldest living Agunah, will finally jump from the front-page of the *NY Times* to the back-page obituary section.

Lonna Kin, who had her own troubles, took the time to write a letter to my judge during my early divorce proceedings in which she profusely praised my kindness and integrity and validated my helping her and many other women for over a decade in their plight as *Agunot.* I had been on an informal layperson think-tank for ORA at Yeshiva University for ideas on dealing with fractious husbands regarding how to coax or ultimately publicly pressure them into giving a Get — quickly. I illustrated how the longer it took, the longer it was going to take. Give an inch, and you gave a yard. And, No! ORA does not beat men up (although at times I certainly wish they did).

I discovered that the "time and patience" methods prescribed by old and insensitive rabbis were definitively not divinely intentioned. They were cruel and squandered the future of many young Jewish women whose childbearing years (her net worth statement of "nest eggs" to be fertilized) were fleeting. Most men made demands that were overboard but could be dealt with. I had one Israeli who insisted on, and received, his green card before he'd free his wife. But tyrants like Meir and my wife only dug in deeper. Meir's idea of negotiation was like Arafat's, "Okay, and *now* I want ...." And my wife's was a total incendiary intifada of, "Die Zev! Die now!"

I had written many responses to men like Meir Kin. Some of the lawyers at ORA laughingly nicknamed me *The Punisher* (after the Marvel Comics character) because of how scathing my comments were. They apologized for obstructing my first amendment rights on more than one occasion, fearing lawsuits by litigious angry and bitter husbands.

I also spoke at length and debated with many famous rabbinical leaders on behalf of many innocent victims of religious abuse who were clueless of the protection and rights that the Saints of the Talmud granted them two thousand years ago. Not all Jews are as backward as too many of us appear to be. And I was soon to discover that too many modern-day bombastic local judges aren't exactly as *modern* and enlightened as they should be.

It seems that for thirty pieces of silver coin these maniacal husbands were always able to find a Jewish-Judas P.O.S. *Toen* (lawyer) like Ralbag to obfuscate and defend their client's dastardly withholding of a Get. As if there could ever be a reason — other than control. It's sinful and shameful that young Hasid men are taught by their *Toen* and elders, *"Loiftnisht, tzu gebben dem Get"* (Don't run to give her the Get). In other words, let her sweat it out. *Enablers!* As if their young, clueless breeding-machine girls haven't been fucked enough already. It seems the less a *rabbi* respected and understood the profound laws of the Talmud, the more readily the charlatan rushed to distort and falsify it.

These felons (in God's eyes) who perpetrated nothing short of *Kosher* Domestic Violence would then concoct a perverted bogus *Heter Meiah,* allowing the young horny husband to remarry, while the young bride wept in her parents' house, baking braided *challos* for Shabbos as she'd daydream about nursing one day, while her father was being extorted for "wasting the *scholarly* young groom's best-years" that said father's daughter "*took away*" from him. Seems that divorce lawyers are uniformly scum no matter which religion they profess to observe. How God watches all this without flooding the planet again amazes me.

Many times, an angry young man could easily be coaxed to unlock the anchor chains he had wrapped around his wife's neck by my persuading him to simply look into the future. "Come on dude ... give her the *Get* already! Don't you realize what your next wife will think of you if she finds out you did this?" was always an effective final blow (after patiently giving the shithead hours upon hours of my time on the phone or in meetings) in convincing a man of the utter foolishness of being mean, vengeful and spiteful.

Like an old and tired detective, I had spent many hours playing both roles of good cop/bad cop, while allowing a husband to blow off some steam, knowing that he was going to roll. I got so good at it that I could almost predict an *Agunah's* future. And sadly, I could predict when she wasn't going to have one.

And that was, when I ran into men like Meir Kin who would literally continue to self-immolate if it meant yanking his wife to combust within his own pyre. "I'll tie up your fucking cunt forever!" Meir screamed at Lonna upon her evicting him from *her* house (only her parents are on the deed) with an Order of Protection (after he shot a ground hog in their backyard and grabbed her checkbook and car keys).

It's been fifteen years and this remarried, tantrum throwing, daily attender of synagogue morning services, who painstakingly makes sure to fervently pray with a minyan of ten men, is keeping his word. Meir Kin is still in total control of the vaginal orifice of Lonna Ralbag's body. If he can't have her, no one will. She is now post menopause. Unless Meir dies from some form of cancer or catches Covid, I sadly predict that Lonna will die an *Agunah*. I know this because I have seen my wife's stubborn eyes as I stared into Meir's.

Meir theoretically killed the children Lonna would have very likely given birth to had she been allowed to remarry. She's quite the sweet eye candy and very intelligent "catch" that most men would die for. Like a textbook abusive spouse, Meir (unlike O.J.) destroyed Lonna without having to slit her throat. He locked Lonna into solitary confinement. And sadistically melted the key. I imagine that the hair under her sheitel is now mostly grey. I also imagine her beautiful bright-hazel eyes, a few decades from now, bookended by century old crow's feet as Meir commits bigamy with his third wife while insisting he wants custody of sixty-eight-year-old Moshe and millions of Bitcoin as payment for all his "suffering" in denying Lonna a simple Get.

Lonna used to joke that my wife and her husband were a true match. I laughed, not knowing how not funny her prophetic words would one day prove to be. My wife and Meir even work at the same job. They both share the often-misunderstood title of Physician Assistant. And they are both very insistent on getting their way. Lonna and I were the easygoing artsy type. She wrote poetry and lyrics, and I wrote children's stories. The four of us shared many Shabbat lunches laughing and talking as our small children played together nearly twenty years ago. And Meir and I were good friends and he often asked me about the "outside world" as he told me he admired my secular and Talmudical knowledge. He was, as they say in Monsey, "a nice *Heimishe* (down-to-earth) guy."

So it was quite a shock when Lonna called me (because married women don't usually call married men in Monsey, NY), and gently asked if I could "perhaps speak with Meir" because they were having some "mild marital issues." Both Meir and Lonna completely confided in me, and I patiently listened to both sides, doing my best to remain fair and impartial, as the Talmud insists, because I was a closer friend to Meir.

But eventually, after speaking with husband and wife in dozens of "he said-she said" conversations, one runs out of words. I saw that Lonna was the more innocent of the two, but I understood (actually, the three of us understood) that the marriage had come to an end. It was over. It was a second marriage for both, and all they had to do was part like two adults. Lonna wanted an amicable divorce. After all, she and Meir shared a newborn one-year-old son together.

But "divorce" is where a person reveals who (and what) they truly are. And Meir's response to Lonna's request for a divorce displayed his affinity for the political philosophy of Machiavelli. He was a no-holds-barred bat out of hell. Definitely a silver-medalist divorcing beast. Only to eventually have his record demolished by my gold-medalist wife.

Screaming his initial war cry of "I'll tie up your cunt forever!" as he slammed the front door in Lonna's face, Meir ran to a loony Hasidic Beit Din (*Kedushas Levi*) that had been declared non-kosher by all the major Beit Din's in the tri-state area and insisted on full custody of his then one-year-old nursing son with no alimony or child support for Lonna. He also demanded an immediate $250 thousand dollar payment (eventually doubling the extortion) from Lonna's financially comfortable parents, threatening to withhold the Jewish Get from Lonna. It wasn't the money that caused Lonna to refuse giving into his extortion. She knew it was common for lowlife husbands to blackmail their wives.

But Lonna already lost one son before embarking on her second marriage to Meir Kin, by trusting the horrific Hasid female-hating Rabbi Chaim Rottenberg. Yes, his name says it all. And yes, the same Rottenberg who was in the news on December 28, 2019 when a machete wielding mentally-ill African American stormed into his house and stabbed five Jews (one eventually passed away as a result of his wounds) as they celebrated Hanukkah. Knowing Rottenberg, I could almost swear, while holding a Torah scroll, that there's much more going on regarding that harrowing event than meets the eye. The maniac is ruthless behind the scenes.

As a very young and innocent (i.e. clueless) Modern-Orthodox Jewess, Mrs. Lonna Presser signed an arbitration agreement trusting the *Da'as Torah* of the homophobic, Goyim-xenophobic, Hasid-Ape Rabbi Rottenberg when her first husband, Dr. Steven Presser, insisted that they go to the Beit Din of his choice to settle their custodial and financial issues.

As a top-producing real estate agent in Monsey-Yenta, NY, Lonna did not even hesitate to consider refusing her husband's "invitation" to attend the Beit-Din of the misogynist Rottenberg. Chaim Rottenberg's worldview stank worse than the odor he exuded due to his constant chain-smoking. He perceived a woman as nothing more than a cum-dumpster created by God, whose sole purpose of existence was to quickly produce a dozen children while lying flat on her back for three minutes at a time, cooking and cleaning as she repeatedly mumbles Psalms ad nauseam like some Buddhist monk during her running-wheel lifetime.

Adorable toddlers are quickly taught to "help Mommy make Shabbos" and nothing changes for the next nine decades of their simpleton lives. Rottenberg would probably literally run through a wall before ever allowing a female to touch him, never knowing when Aunt Flo might arrive. *I wonder if the lactating cows are fed more supplements to increase their milk production upon giving birth to new cute little future Hasid misogynists.*

Rottenberg decided to give full custody of the boy to the father and the three girls to the mother. And that was that. Lonna rarely saw her son after that (one man) Beit Din experience. This time she absolutely refused to relinquish full custody to Meir. I tried every possible argument with Meir to convince him to give Lonna her *Get* in the interim. "Come on Meir! What's your son Moshe going to say when he grows up and discovers how you treated his mother?" But Meir ignored my phone calls. Like I'd discover upon divorcing my own wife ten years in the future — confront a narcissist head on and you become a persona non grata.

I even contacted Rabbi Irving (Yitzchak) Breitowitz, a wonderful Talmudical scholar and professor of law — who graduated from Harvard Law School while studying folio after folio of the Talmud. Rabbi Breitowitz and I were roommates back in high school. Our principal at Ner Israel Rabbinical College, Rabbi Yosef Tendler, always referred to us as his "two pieces of gold" (it's a much bigger compliment when spoken in the original Yiddish). "Don't worry Yitz, I'm fool's gold compared to you," I quipped fifty years ago.

I now sought the sagacious *Da'as Torah* advice of my brilliant friend. "You're not going to like what I say," he warned me, "but my advice is that she pay, relinquish custody, and get on with her life." I couldn't believe it.

"But that's blackmail — it's so unfair!" I yelled.

But he was right. And I was right. But the real truth was that even if Lonna had paid *and* given full custody of her nursing baby son to Meir, he still would not have given her the Get. It's all about control.

Meir then contacted Dr. Presser, Lonna's first husband to enlist his "your enemy is my enemy" help. Spinning a web of outrageously insane entangled lies (almost as sticky and messy as those my wife would spin in the future) along with accusations of Lonna instantly having wild trysts with any rabbi who defended his wife, Meir then hired some crazy porn-movie-reviewer (which tells us how Meir was spending his time — I guess he missed Lonna!) to voluminously blog Lonna's name and ruin her pristine realtor reputation online. Only on Monsey, NY reality TV! You would have thought this Modern-Orthodox mother of five was a porn star.

To this day, poor little Meir Kin is still posting YouTube videos where he continues to rant, completely out-of-control, against "Lonna The Phony Agunah." Their son Moshe is now approaching his twenty-first birthday.

This exact outrageous *Grobe luge* Nazi tactic was what my wife would also use, as she would accuse me of being a violent pedophile, a decade in the future — going right for the jugular of a grade school teacher that wrote and published books for children. Meir was instantly screaming that Lonna was a whore, who was fucking anyone that spoke in her defense. I wish, lol. Lonna would have had to twist through all sixty-four positions of the Kama Sutra for how hard I fought for her. Many Yentas, by the way, have added an additional sixty-fifth pose. It's known by their frustrated husbands as the "no-sex" position, or the "hand job."

All this shameless nonsense by Meir in a sexually repressed town that prohibits women from wearing short sleeves that might reveal their elbow (guess it rhymes with "blow" job) or leaving a single button of their blouse unbuttoned (God forbid!), which might reveal a clavicle bone (guess it rhymes with "boner"). Worse yet, heaven help us, if a wisp of hair were to be uncovered in public (guess if rhymes with "pubic hair").

Meir even played a tape during court of Lonna orgasming "to prove" that he'd "never hurt her," and that the Order of Protection was uncalled for. *What about that gun, Meir?* Lonna, who is extremely ladylike and flawlessly charming, sat in court red-faced and in shock that her husband tapped her during intimacy as the judge looked at her pretty face — and dabbed his perspiring head with his handkerchief, I imagine — as he probably wondered how Meir could give up such a stunning beauty.

Lonna's first ex-husband than provided some kind of "personal opinion" about Lonna's character. It's amazing how two previously-bickering dogs will unite to fight off a ferocious mama-bear protecting her newborn cub. Meanwhile I was paying twenty-five thousand dollars in local taxes a year, escrowed into my mortgage, to finance the judge having all the time in the world (overtime too!) to listen to this bullshit.

I did my best to reason with Meir, pleading with him, leaving message after message, almost begging him to give Lonna her *Get*. He had angrily hung up the phone after yelling at me, "And I thought you were so intelligent!" Meir now refused to return my calls, and then attacked me by accusing me of having an affair with his pretty wife. He then took the time to print up flyers in the name of some fictitious Jewish grass-roots organization — yes, angry individuals have no embarrassment at revealing how kooky they certifiably are — and stuffed the seventy-one mailboxes of the gated seventy-two-home clique in which I lived, with urgent news that the entire community should immediately be aware of!

The flyers warned my seventy-one neighbors that Zev Lewinson is having a torrid affair with Lonna Kin. And like Jimmy Carter, the worst I had ever done was "sin in my heart." The Yenta's tongues wetted more quickly than their pussies ever did, and instantly started wagging, faster than their pussies ever moved, as they *innocently* wondered, "What did Lonna do to make her husband so angry? She can't possibly be having an affair with the gentle scholar Zev Lewinson!"

And my own wife, knowing how outlandish Meir's lies were, nevertheless screamed at me for getting involved when, "We have daughters that are going to need a Shidduch one day, Ze'ev!" *I guess she wasn't that concerned about the future of our daughters once she herself was served divorce papers.*

Once again, the best defense a psycho can come up with is to destroy the reputation of the innocent. Meir bullied Lonna 24/7 all over Monsey and the Internet. His vicious online assault to destroy her career as a top realtor in an Ultra-Orthodox Jewish town was a mild portrayal of how my wife would treat me, and my capacity to earn a living, in the future.

Lonna had become merely a whore based upon the whining of her husband. I was destined to become a violent and dangerous pedophile based upon the maniacal treachery of my wife, her lawyer, and her hypocritical army of Yapping Yentas who, like the aliens in *Invasion of the Body Snatchers*, pointed and emitted loud shrill shrieks as they screeched while describing the lecherous *Tatie* to everyone in their midst.

I wasn't insulted by Meir's tactics. After all, I was in world-renowned company. Meir carried out the exact reputation maligning perverted assault upon the reputation of Rabbi Union (the very intellectual Chief Rabbi of Los Angeles) and many other prestigious rabbis that sided with Lonna Kin. He even did it to the Dean of Yeshiva University, Rabbi Hershel Schachter. The deranged never stop to think how ridiculous they look or sound. They simply fling the next round of turds dumped from their feces diseased brain tissue.

Flash forward a decade and a half and I now understood that my gently asking Meir Kin to give Lonna a Jewish Get, as I calmly explained how destructive his actions would one day appear to his baby son, was the exact waste of time as my explaining to my wife how damaging alienation would be to Ester as I patiently warned her not to take out an Order of Protection merely because I was filing for divorce.

"I would never do that! I'm not like that, Ze'eh'ev!" my wife yelled into the recording app of my phone. I was no longer laughing at Lonna's almost prophetic observation that her husband and my wife were a true match. It wasn't funny anymore. It was scary. Because I knew that the louder my wife screamed that she *wouldn't*, the more she sure as hell *fucking would*. I was beginning to comprehend that psychotic, unhinged, pathological beings are truly unable to hear a word of what you are saying. The most articulate person in the world becomes a mute to the eardrums of a narcissist. They are not wired to be moved by the empathy or logic you express. It is *only* about them. And isn't it amazing how they go right after the personal reputation of the spouse they once swore to cherish?

Pathological liars feel no shame or guilt. That's how they easily pass lie detector tests. They don't sweat it. Because the disturbed believe their own words. In truth, they don't even care what they spew, or if they contradict themselves in the same sentence. Their mouth immediately ejaculates the craziest shit which the sheeple instantly accept as truth because they believe that "no one just makes up 'that kind' of accusation out of thin air." *What a wonderful display of Socratic logic.*

The complete lack of truth in their words is compensated for by the volume of their voice and the repetition of their message. Scream and repeat. And then enlist a pack of gossipmongers to spread the news.

And so the sweet Ulta-Orthodox Mrs. Kin, mother of five children, instantly became a whore and insatiable nymphomaniac upon filing for divorce. And fifteen years later, also upon filing for divorce, the soft-spoken scholar, writer, teacher, Mister Mom/father of five, grandfather of two, Zev Lewinson, suddenly transformed into a dangerous, angry and violent pedophile who was obsessed with feces.

I'm always amazed at how frigid personalities can suddenly turn into nuclear fission the moment they begin to lose their narcissistic control of spouses who only want a simple equitable divorce. They explode in an eruption of anger, as they dispense shit in a cackle of chatter, emails, and malicious prosecution to exhaust their shocked and outraged spouses by keeping them busy wiping the shit off their heretofore spotless reputations. And, in my case, fighting for my life in three different court systems simultaneously as I faced the very real possibility of being placed in jail and forced to register as a child molester.

The unhinged don't have to bother emotionally distancing themselves from the lover they shared their bed with only last night (or the past *thirty years* of nights) because they were obviously never capable of true intimacy from the start. And they all love using whatever little pittance of psychology they've picked up from magazines and news reports. In fact, they love psychological babble and constantly use the terminology created to explain their certifiable minds to describe your sane one. They know how to use whatever society respects.

"I get nervous and anxious when it comes to money, Zev," my wife would explain, as she'd "apologize" after snapping and yelling at me for buying takeout or forgetting to save a five-dollar receipt. "There's food in the fridge Ze'ev! Use it!" I guess her thriftiness forced her to limit herself to a quarter million-dollar divorce budget. Don't try to defend your actions or apologize for the sake of peace, because every sincere request that you beg of a narcissist to stop their unrelenting onslaught is, in reality, another feather (and tar, for you) in their control-cap.

And each deaf response and frozen refusal to even acknowledge your fervid emotions morphs your heartfelt spoken words into a silenced icy brick, which they use to build a tomb to further control your life as they continue to belittle you while they bury you alive. And every tear you shed falls right into their cement trough. And the more you talk and plead, the more you emotionally bleed, and the more bricks you *silently* and obsequiously hand them to build an even stronger impenetrable wall, as they use the receiver of the phone, that they constantly slam down on you at the exact moment you thought they were *finally* listening, as a trowel to firmly pat down the stone slab of the living tomb in which you, relying on exhausted red blood cells, gasp and choke for air.

And if you appreciate and comprehend the thoughts I'm sharing, you had better file for divorce faster than you can say the Mourner's Kaddish at a late Monsey minyan of Hasidim. Or it will be recited in remembrance of your sojourn on Earth after you stroke out and drop dead in frustration.

As a man, I was fortunate to escape the tomb my wife (and my talking) walled me into. My jailer fought viciously to cover my grave with tons of Yenta-gossip-dirt, as tricky in her tactics and as instinctively clever and cunning as the Blue Paul Terrier fighting dog. She was relentless at flawlessly mimicking that dog breed. Similarly, my bitch would willingly suffer great pain in order to inflict death on her opponent. Sharen enlisted anyone who fell for her desperate yelps, as she cried about trying to survive a green monster named Zev. If you don't believe me, try not responding to a child suddenly screaming "Fire!" at the top of her smoke-filled lungs gasping for air.

My eventual freedom was only attained after *years* of crawling on my knees, singeing myself on figuratively hot coals, through an emotionally exhausting gauntlet of merciless outrageous lies, false accusations, manipulations, and malicious prosecution. Lonna remains buried alive, as age lines slowly branch out along her beautiful face, and will probably remain that way till Meyer is gently lowered into his deserved grave.

Lonna's letter was very beautiful and emotional. I had merely asked Ms. Kin to write a few words in response to my wife's claim in the affidavit my *Eishet Chayil* wrote to our judge (under an oath affirmation) that I was "violent," and that she "fears my wrath." For a little added spice and drama, my wife included that the man who sat in court, wearing his black yarmulke and fringes, constantly called her "a cunt." She also enlisted Rachel, our oldest daughter, to add her own lying screed in which she validated (also under oath) her mother's lie as she claimed that I also constantly called her the "C" word.

It would take another book to explain how I felt reading that sentence written by the very first child I brought into this world. I'll only say that from the moment I held my newborn baby girl in my arms, I never imagined one human capable of feeling so much love for another. The first word my future betrayal-baby ever spoke was "Zev." Oh my God! I can still hear her saying it. She was so adorable! My wife and I laughed as we realized that Rachel had never heard the word "daddy," or "Tatie." *How did such a cute baby morph into such a lying beast,* I wondered, as I stared at my daughters "testimony."

So many beautiful memories were instantly shredded as Rachel's treacherous sentence, launched simultaneously in an opening double-barrel shotgun blast adding firepower to her mother's wild allegation, ripped my heart out of my chest. Forget about my wife, but to have my own first-born child join the fray was ghastly. At that point I would have still bet my life that they'd never be able to convince Ester to join them in a billion years. And I don't bet.

I finally understood that my wife was not playing. I also realized that not only did I make the right decision to divorce her, but that I should have never stared into her eyes twenty-eight years ago. And I sadly realized that Rachel had inherited the cold-hearted DNA of her mother.

I was literally nauseous as I read the outrageously perfidious letters of the two women I would have gladly died for, not so long ago, that were attached to the very first motion my wife's pompous kapo, overpriced mouthpiece, submitted to The Honorable Victor Alfieri in which Daniel Schwartz Esquire, the last man on the planet that deserves any honorary title, insisted that I was an abusive husband who should receive zero maintenance. I never expected such a touching response from Lonna, who had her own portion of pain to deal with.

My wife incessantly called Lonna to rescind that letter so that she could have it expunged from the court proceedings. She cried. She cajoled. She screamed about her also being an abused woman that would surely soon be forced to suffer the life of an *Agunah*. "We're *sisters*, Lonna! We were best friends! How could you do this to me!" the mother of our five children yelled. Lonna told my wife that I was an amazing man who had been incredibly kind to her. My wife never spoke to her *sister* again. Lonna instantly became persona non grata. To this day my wife hasn't spoken to her "sister" because her "best friend" refused to lie for her.

Thank you Lonna. I know in Monsey it's considered improper for men to address a married woman by her given personal name. I'd respectfully address you as "Mrs. Kin," but it's too painful a reminder.

Understanding the sad modern-day inner workings of too many of my own Jewish courts of law, I refused to allow my future to be decided by the ineptitude, corruption and ignorance of imposters who didn't even attempt to emulate what had once been an exceptional system of justice in earlier Talmudical times. I was extremely frustrated but equally brainwashed, or at least thoroughly conditioned, and I was torn to attend one of our *Unzereh* half decent cult-courts, and I would have still avoided even the semblance of *Arkayos* courts and met my wife at some of the more reputable Beit Din's had she been amenable to any compromise.

But her new bad-boy Rabbi Schabes, acquired through a five-thousand-dollar tax deductible wire transfer "donation" — hired and paid for by my "wealthy as she is morally ugly" sister-in-law Elyce Smedresman — told my wife exactly which Beit Din to use. And I knew they would be exactly like Scumbag Schabes. Easily purchased for a few silver coin biscuits. If you think congressional staff is corruptible you should check out the plaques adorning too many of the synagogues in Monsey. Many of their generous, honored, "Buy a Rabbi" patrons have paid their debt to society while eating kosher and praying with a *minyan*. Behind bars.

Typically, they "only" stole from "the government," or other *non-Unzereh* enterprises (*"It's not so terrible to steal from a Goy")*. Besides, they are immediately granted forgiveness upon kosher-laundering the money by tithing a generous portion which they donate to the community. All is quickly forgiven. Especially by the rabbinical recipients of the loot. *"He vas framed by deh goyisheh prosecutor!"*

If their jail sentence is a long one (i.e. a lot of stolen *goyish* money) there's always a trustworthy politician like Crooked Hillary Clinton to ensure that the thieves will be pardoned — another ancient ritual that everyone blindly accepts since the days of yore when divinely inspired kings forgave prisoners on a whim — if their community can deliver a huge block of voters. And so the

Rebbe merely had to whisper Hillary's name while giving her a *Bracha* (a blessing), and a cult of four thousand sheeple-Hasidim instantly thought the blessed bitch was an angel.

And miraculously — surely due to the Rebbeh's *Da'as Torah* and prophetic vision that the former FLOTUS was destined for greatness — Hillary morphed into *Senator* Clinton.

Never has a weirder political coupling between strange bedfellows been more scandalous, or more obvious, than an Arkansas "Senator from New York" climbing into bed with the spiritual leader of the Skverer Hasidim bedecked in his black-silk "bekishe" frock coat while crowned with his very expensive "shtreimel" fur hat.

The newly elected Democratic junior senator — insisting she was never anything more than "a bystander," because she was obviously busy packing up historical priceless White House furniture (that the staff kept reminding her belonged to the American people) while her husband granted executive clemency to four Skverer Hasid crooks from the Village of New Square in Rockland County, on January 20, 2001, as he walked out the White House door on his last day in office — was now well on her way to being elected the first female President of the United States. And had Donald Trump's big mouth, thick skin, and honed marketing skills been a smidgeon less miraculous than the "blessing" of the spiritual leader of the Skverer Hasidim, Senator Hillary Clinton surely would have been our first "Madam President." *Mazel Tov!* Well, almost.

The men had bilked the state Senator Clinton now represented out of tens of millions of dollars. Her first (quid pro quo) political act as senator was to acquit those four thieves. God bless America! A white trash (morally speaking) woman from Arkansas acquitted the "black is the new black" New York white trash (spiritually speaking) Hassidim for delivering fourteen hundred votes while her opponent, Republican Rick Lazio, received seven votes (*probably from seven farsighted Skverer Hasidim*).

The four wealthy men traded their orange jumpsuits for their black Hasidic garb and celebrated their *"Pidyan Shvuyim"* redemption as heroes "freed from the captivity of the Goyishe jails." What a miracle! Grand Rabbi David Twersky shook hands with Bill Clinton, and "Crooked Hillary" was well on her way towards becoming the first female presidential candidate of a major party in American History. U.S. attorney Mary Jo White, another legendary white trash enabler, investigated the rancid stench but, of course, smelled nothing. *In God We Trust.*

I made one last attempt and asked some of the very famous rabbis I knew for decades to sit as a judge my case. The gentle scholars, Kamenetsky, Breitowitz, Nekrtiz, and even a few rabbis from Yeshiva University, never sat on divorce courts. And none of them wanted to judge me. Rabbi Nekritz and several of the other rabbis felt they might be accused by my wife of not being impartial. Or perhaps they didn't want to debate me. Who knows? Probably not. It's what we all absolutely love to do.

I took a deep breath and called my lawyer, telling him to proceed and file the paperwork I had prepared at his office months ago.

"You sure?" he asked. "This is the third time you're telling me to do this."

"No, I'm not sure," I replied, "but I'm sure I can't live like this anymore. Please file the fucking papers."

Innocently jumping out of the frying pan into the fire, I naively proceeded to the transparent secular courts that I believed had clear-cut guidelines and transparent procedures for divorcing couples along with the ability to enforce their legal decisions. I was hastily excommunicated by three Jewish Court Jesters who decreed that I be shunned and ostracized by the entire Monsey community. Some of the synagogues instantly honored the arbitrator's requests. Others, like the Lubavitcher sect, didn't care.

The largest nearby synagogue, Kehilas Bais Avrohom, was led by the renowned Rabbi Yitzchok Lichtenstein who lectured at the yeshiva founded by Rabbi Nekritz. Needless to say, it took two phone calls (mine to Rabbi Nekritz and his to Rabbi Lichtenstein) for me to be allowed to attend the main synagogue where I had named Ester eleven years ago. But, to be honest, at this point I was already beginning to question the value of constantly praying the exact same monotonous daily words to a God that seemed as deaf as my wife.

Besides, almost overnight, half of the minyan praying there already ignored me. The other half kept their safe, polite distance. I was still the very popular teacher that taught their sons English Language Arts at the local *Unzereh* Yeshiva of Spring Valley grade school, but I was amazed at how quickly their parents, who praised me effusively at PTA meetings and had wished me a hearty Mazel Tov when Ester was named, now turned away from me more energetically than a Hasid from a prostitute once he ejaculates and can only think about getting to a *Mikvah* before the unholy invisible aura of her body further contaminated his spiritual, albeit occasionally wayward, cock.

The Yenta grapevine had whispered the word "pedophile." The lightning results were much more powerful than any front-page headlines printed by The New York Times. Yenta's voices defy science and somehow travel much faster than the speed of sound. *Do demons exist?*

The Beit Din board's medieval edict traveled quickly, as my wife and her mischief swarm of Yentas scurried around town, like little rats, hanging up copies on the bulletin boards of any Beit-Midrash that I frequented or synagogue where I might pray, as the pack tried to enforce the cultish decree that declared I was to be blackballed by the entire Jewish community and warned that I am "no longer shielded by God's Glory and that doing business with me would not be blessed with entrepreneurial success, let alone yield any profits."

The decree also prophesied my eventual descent into purgatory (What do you think my marriage was, Gentlemen?) if I continued to "stubbornly refuse" to heed their invitation to attend their court. It's very embarrassing to be shunned. I'm a pretty confident person but being denied human contact is a very emotionally draining experience. You quickly become lonely. My wife got everyone to stop talking to me and convinced them to block my phone number. Even Ester ignored me. The only upside was that for the first time in thirty years I finally had some quiet in my life. *I had forgotten how beautiful quiet sounds*.

Ironically, I was also taking my first baby steps and leaving the Monsey purgatory of societal conditioning and manipulation. The arbitration board's backward dark-ages angry proclamation turned out to be one of the most enlightening documents of my life. It opened my eyes as to how *backwards* I had been living. Like the Hasidim, I was even wearing white shirts every day of the week to please the Yentas who might be suggesting a future match for my three daughters. I was beginning my escape from the most supermax prison of all — the one with thick invisible bars.

But not till I first descended into the purgatory fires of our secular divorce and family court system of law.

The *writ of shit* of my wife's arbitration board (who called me a *troublemaker* as if I was defying the authority of God Himself) was a childish tantrum response based on intimidation by which they undercut their own self-proclaimed credentials to judge. They wanted to make an example of me to protect their own little arbitration business. And all that had been requested of them was to at least allow me the Talmudical option of my choosing one of the three rabbis that would sit on the tribunal. But how could I expect them to know any laws from the Talmud? I recorded their conversations with me. Their logic was embarrassing and flawed.

Little did I realize that I was leaving the toilet and heading straight into the septic tank. The kind that decomposes an already decayed and disintegrated family.

Emergency police visits at all hours of the day and night, amid a cacophony of my wife's shrieking Yenta friend's constantly calling my school principal, insisting that their children were in mortal danger because I'm a pedophile and violent, along with summonses to appear (and face trial) simultaneously in family, criminal, and divorce court, served in tandem with over a half-dozen rubber-stamped protection orders along with dozens of subpoenas to Barnes and Noble, Amazon, and any distributor or publisher that was carrying my stories for children, were all vindictively and brazenly unleashed in a fifteen-month avalanche that buried me alive under the sheer weight of outrageous fictitious accusations that took many more months and many hardened arteries to reveal as delusional attempts of pathological, psychological and emotional torture by my *Blitzkreig* war-machine wife and her pants-on-fire lawyer to crucify me on the cross of yenta-grapevine public opinion.

And if you feel that the previous paragraph was a bit of a run-on, as you catch your breath while imagining what I endured, it doesn't begin to describe the deluge of malicious prosecution and heart-constricting torrential stress that suddenly rained down upon my existence as I tried to catch my own breath. My wife howled and cried wolf with more intense tears and shrieks than Aesop could ever have imagined. *I honestly thought she had to be snorting crystal meth to keep up such a blistering pace of 24/7 round-the-clock relentless attacks.*

I was suddenly taking more phone calls and drop-in visits from relatives, friends, parents, neighbors, and my principal, at all hours, than the CDC upon the public first hearing about Coronavirus or their fraudulently tampering trial studies regarding the MMR vaccine and its link to autism.

My wife had them convinced that I lost my mind, proven by my decision to file for divorce in a secular "Goyish" court, and that it would be a mitzvah for them to *reason* with me to go to her Beit Din of choice. My wife never gives up. And I can't blame her. Almost thirty years of marriage taught her that my rarely declared "no" never meant more than "not yet." She always got her way. And as the Passover Haggadah asks, "Why is this night different from other nights?"

"Gotta give the car gas to make it go!" her pissant attorney kept hissing in venomous emails to my wife. And my wife generously poured in the most expensive highly explosive race-car propellant she could find — fueling a law firm that was as sleazy as she was hebephrenic. They laughed together senselessly in their online correspondence about "giving zev a heart attack," reveling in their regressive behavior as they revealed their infantile minds about my being obsessed with feces. Ha-ha.

Even before the ringing of the bell in Round One, Mrs. Lewinson raced out of her corner and mercilessly started pummeling me to death. A flyweight was killing a light-heavyweight. *Wow! She doesn't even have to come up for air or use any head and foot movement,* I marveled at my relentless Asperger cyborg killing machine.

All this in advance of the eventual weirdly platonic "Dear Mr. Lewinson," email sent directly to me by my wife's attorney that stated, "This can all stop the moment you agree to forgo any maintenance."

I definitely understood what "this" meant, but I had never come across the word *maintenance* as a legal term. All I knew was that women get alimony and child support like my mother did a half century ago.

"Oh no! What's good for the goose is good for the gander," my lawyer explained. "It's like alimony, but they started calling it maintenance when men started to get it. Political correctness. Welcome to the twenty-first century. I think I may be able to get you some," he informed me. Meanwhile my wife was slaughtering me for something that I had not even requested as part of my divorce petition.

I gained thirty pounds of cortisol induced weight and my doctor had to triple my dosage of Amlodipine during the years of my divorce. My raging fight or flight hormones were destroying my body. Constantly on high alert as I was being chased 24/7 by wild animal's whose constant stalking and surprise attacks were relentless, while I was focused only on protecting Ester, nearly caused me to experience a mental breakdown. I don't know who scared me more, the armed police or the Yentas.

I'm an extremely cool and calm guy. My wife, who was amazed that I never got upset, often described me as, "The nicest guy in the world." But upon serving her with divorce papers she put me to the test. I couldn't process how quickly my life was suddenly unraveling, along with my emotions and mental well-being, due to the long-term stress. I slowly began to suffer from PTSD long before I knew what the initials stood for.

I felt like Winston in the scene where he is being tortured by O'Brian in *1984* as the rat cage was placed over the head and face of the broken protagonist. My wife and her attorney are the two starving rats scrambling inside the trap-door cage excited and anxious to bore through my blue eyes which they would ravenously devour with their razor-sharp harder-than-iron teeth.

The seemingly endless carefully-laid landmines dispersed by my wife and her lawyer were always positioned to inflict the most carnage possible to constrict my arteries, while stalking me with protection orders that they hoped would cause me to figuratively and literally explode.

Like most Jewish Orthodox wives, the Sabbath was surely my bride's favorite day. Cell phones are shut off. Car keys are tossed into a drawer. All preparations are completed the day before, and the seventh day of the week is truly a day of rest. A day set aside to profane and urgently call the police on an early Saturday morning in a desperate panicked voice, begging them to "Come now! He's dangerous! He burst through my bedroom door!" as I sat peacefully sipping a coffee, engrossed in a complicated folio of the Talmud at 6:45 AM. In under three minutes there were two huge handsome Aryan-looking policemen, dressed in full body armor, stepping inside my front door as my heart raced faster than the blaring patrol car they arrived in, almost instantaneously.

This frantic "emergency" call by an Ultra-Orthodox Jewess, who understood that the *only* time it is permitted to desecrate the Sabbath according to Jewish law is if one's physical life is in danger, had been carefully and strategically planned well in advance. Only one day earlier the double-protection order that my wife obtained to "protect" herself and our minor daughter from my "wrath" came through after being urgently signed by Judge Mendelson in Family Court.

My wife was figuratively bursting in her anticipation of my *violating* the conditions set forth in the one-day-old protection order. She certainly did not stop to think that perhaps the police might be needed for some *real* emergency. In her pathological mind, the possibility of paying me a penny of maintenance had become the ultimate apocalyptic event, definitely an obvious case of *Pikuach Nefesh* (the preservation of *her* life), and worthy of the rare dispensation to profane the Sabbath according to Jewish Talmudical law guidelines.

My wife honestly believed that her life was in danger. She interpreted my lawyers petition for temporary maintenance as a threat that she spend part of her life to support me. In her crazed cranium she viewed "supporting zev" as assisted suicide. She saw the "danger" as the equivalent of my holding a loaded revolver to her head. My wife repeats phrases to others, and thoughts to herself, incessantly. She can easily wear down normal people. But she herself never tires.
Like an ant.

"Zev is trying to kill me! Zev is trying to kill me!" In her mind it was not only permissible to desecrate the Sabbath, it was a mitzvah! To be honest, I'm lucky she didn't see herself as being held hostage by my lawyer's motion for maintenance. She would have deployed a SWAT team.

The stage had been set the previous night. It began in a very ominous way by the sudden disappearance of my favorite picture of Rabbi Israel Zvi Nekritz when he was a young man. I later discovered it had been torn to shreds by my laughing lunatic wife and my daughters, Sara and Ester.

Rabbi Nekritz, who is now 74 years old, is a world-renowned Talmudical scholar. He is the grandson of the legendary Alter of Novardok. He and I have been studying the Talmud together unceasingly and religiously (literally *and* figuratively) for the past thirty-eight years.

Rabbi Nekritz was the first person with whom I shared the news of my imminent engagement to my future wife on a Saturday night thirty-six years ago. I had surprised my future ex-wife by telling her that we had been *invited* to the Nekritz's for a quiet post-Sabbath *Melava Malka* (Escorting the Sabbath Queen) dinner celebration. My Rabbi and his wife were the only two people on the planet who knew that Sharen and I would be newly engaged upon our arrival at their home. Meanwhile my future bride had no idea that I was about to propose.

I deceived my wife with the excuse that the handmade platinum and 18K yellow gold mounting (with two long perfectly matching baguettes) that I had ordered would have to be hand-casted to flawlessly fit around the gem I had chosen for her. "It would take a few more weeks before it was ready," I apologized. She had no clue that the tad-under-two-carat white color, bursting with light, sparkling gem was resting impatiently in my pocket, almost vibrating in excited anticipation of ensconcing the ring finger of my captivating size-two bride-to-be.

My wife knew I was terrible at keeping secrets. Especially from her. I always wanted to make the women in my life happy (a psychological vestige of my basically motherless childhood coupled with my desire to always satisfy and please any female in my life — including those little girls back in kindergarten who included me in their games) and, unable to contain myself, I would usually surprise her that I'm *going* to surprise her. But this time I somehow reined in my impetuous instant-gratification nature and Sharen really had no idea that she was about to become the happiest woman in the world (her words).

I had lovingly orchestrated the entire evening well in advance. Just as my wife now responded in kind by planning *this* wonderful social function with the police and all our neighbors on the Sabbath — a special occasion that she surely planned to joyously celebrate in emails with all her Yenta friends and relatives the moment the Sabbath ended as I'd be eating and choking on *my Melava Malka* meal behind iron bars at the Rockland County Correctional Facility.

On the way to their house that evening many decades ago I acted impulsively and said, "Wanna see where Rabbi Nekritz and I study?" I explained to my imminent fiancée that we were early anyway, and she agreed to make a quick stop at the House of Study so that she could see where I studied three times a week. It was there in the quiet and gentle darkness of the dim Eternal Light (the Ner Tamid) that hung above the Sanctuary Ark of the study hall, studded with endless tomes, that I romantically proposed to the sweetest woman I had ever known.

I gently removed a huge volume (Tractate Kiddushin — the laws of betrothal and marriage) from one of the many old wooden shelves and discreetly placed the diamond ring, that was still trembling with as much emotion as I was, between its worn thumbed pages. I then explained to my future wife that the endless wisdom of our nation is contained within the three thousand pages of these books.

"Look inside!" I gently insisted. "Anything you'll ever desire or want to understand is written within *these* pages. The entire conversation that God spoke to Moses for forty days and forty nights on Mount Sinai is right here! And if there is ever a time that we disagree about something, or can't figure out what we should do, we'll always be able to ask Rabbi Nekritz," I delicately explained.

"I can't read Aramaic," my future bride responded sweetly.

"No, look!" I insisted, "Everything you could *ever want* is in these pages. Just look!"

Merely to be polite my sweet fiancée finally glanced inside the open pages of the tome I was holding and lost her breath. She began crying as I gently put the ring on her finger. Her gorgeous adoring moist eyes radiated with as much scintillation as the diamond she was now wearing.

"God willing we'll merit to raise a beautiful family together," I softly whispered. "Mazel Tov, Honey."

"Mazel Tov," her barely moving lips whispered as they headed toward mine.

We hugged each other as we cried. I held my sweet-smelling fiancée so tightly that I had to loosen my hug if only to allow her to inhale. I continued to embrace my trembling lover *forever* in those few moments. I felt as if we were standing in the Garden of Eden. And I was beyond exhilarated at the thought of imminently bringing a life into the world. It could possibly have been the most romantic moment in human history as far as we knew. We were both completely overwhelmed with emotion.

"Mazel Tov! Mazel Tov!" the Nekritz's greeted us after we composed ourselves and gently knocked on their door thirty-six years ago.

Rabbi Nekritz blessed us under our wedding canopy. He and his wife attended all our family affairs. And we attended theirs. We spent Shabbos with them, and they honored us by spending Shabbos with us. My kids knew that their father was constantly studying with the famous Rabbi Nekritz. I drove to Brooklyn three times a week for three decades to travel thousands of years into the past, joining the brilliant sage who never left ancient Babylon, as we sat among the saints and scholars in the archaic study halls of the academies of Pumbedita and Nehardea.

My family revered Rabbi Nekritz, and his priceless saintly image sat by the holy Sabbath lamp, undisturbed, for a quarter century. The kids would even kiss it, like a holy object, when they were young, because I constantly edified the man for his saintliness, erudition, and integrity. I instantly knew trouble was lurking the moment I saw the picture was missing. I called my lawyer anticipating a sinister situation. "I *know* they're up to something … they're probably trying to get me angry after the protection orders she just took out."

"Okay, sit tight," was all my lawyer could advise, "It's the weekend already … we'll deal with this bullshit on Monday." Meanwhile I had no clue that evil never rests. Not even on the Sabbath.

I greeted the two policemen at the door. "Officers, I can explain …." "You wait there, Sir!" one officer barked as he motioned for me to sit in my study. They then turned to my damsel-in-distress wife, who was holding the protection orders in her hand as she jumped into her role as an award-winning actress to appear shaken-up and nervous.

"Officer! He just barged into our room this morning while we were sleeping and demanded some picture of his Rabbi! He was so angry and kept yelling for the picture! Thank you for coming so quickly!" She then proceeded to display the *proof* of my tendency for violence as indicated by the protection orders that she obtained because she *fears my wrath*.

I watched her in the distance spanning our dining and living rooms, as she frantically spoke to our Shabbos guests, thinking how could I possibly even begin to describe my wife's deranged behavior to the two policemen standing sixty feet away, as I sat at the desk in my office waiting for my turn to try and explain the staged perfidy she concocted. There was no question I'd soon be taken away.

My heart felt like it was pounding louder than the ringing of the bells at the Notre Dame Cathedral. I knew that I had been royally screwed and that I'd be spending the Sabbath in jail. My wife is an incredible liar. She earnestly believes anything that comes out of her cute little mouth. How could a listener *not* believe her flawless acting skills coupled with her pathetically sweet siren voice?

I understood that I was minutes away from being handcuffed and driven away on the Holy Sabbath in front of all the neighbors in our gated "Jews only" community who instantly believed that the patient teacher they raved about for years was suddenly a very dangerous man upon his filing for a divorce. I'd soon be staring out the back window of the patrol car at Ester, who would be watching her gentle handcuffed Tatie from the second-floor window in the bedroom where she was conceived. I'd watch her shrink in the distance along with my reputation and belief in God.

I imagined myself being strip-searched and then forced to sit in a tiny cell at the local jail for the next fifty-four hours where I would feel dehumanized as I thought about my children, grandchildren, neighbors, and principal (*"Sorry I missed school ..."*). My blood pressure would rise while waiting till Monday morning (*Officers, we forgot to take my medications as you rushed me out the door ... I really need the Amlodipine*) to appear disheveled and half-asleep in front of Judge Mendelson — who would surely now side with my wife and his earlier mindless rubber-stamped decision to sign a now obviously necessary Order of Protection.

I wondered if the movie scenes I watched as a child, where the prisoner gets one free call in jail, were true — as I imagined myself trying to explain to Rabbi Nekritz why I couldn't study with him on Sunday afternoon and the indefinite future.

My present appearance in shackles would surely validate the urgency, in the eyes of Mendelson, to continue my being held in custody as his only logical option. I could be held in jail indefinitely. At best I'd be reporting weekly to some parole officer and accounting for my daily whereabouts — while not even being able to answer the first simple question ("And where do you live?") she was likely to ask (having been booted out of my house). My teaching position was obviously ancient history. To say my sixty-two-year-old antiquated heart and shocked mind were racing, as the two policemen now approached me to drive me away on the holy Sabbath, would be quite an understatement.

I stood up behind my desk as they asked me to step outside. "Don't listen to anything he says!" my wife warned the officer as he asked her to close the door. "He's very convincing!" she added as she slowly closed the front door and continued to watch the reality show she produced through our huge living room window. The three of us stepped out onto my front lawn as my Yenta neighbors were probably experiencing their first multiple orgasm ever as they voyeuristically watched the thriller they'd be sharing with all their friends the second Shabbat was over.

The policemen did not stand directly in front of me. One officer stood out of my reach to the right and the other stood to my far left. I had studied enough karate to understand what their stance was about. I knew I was about to be tackled on my manicured front lawn in front of a dozen Yentas that were standing at their windows enjoying the spectacular Shabbat presentation taking place at 19 Mariner Yenta Way in Rockland County, NY. I could see myself seconds into the future with grass stains on my knees and my shirt half pulled out after being subdued and handcuffed in front of Ester.

"When are you leaving your house?!" one of the officers suddenly asked. "I don't know," my pounding heart and dry mouth innocently replied. "When my lawyer tells me to?" I guessed (in order to keep the conversation alive).

"You don't understand! We're trying to tell you somethin' ... when are you getting the fuck out of your house?!" the policeman repeated.

"I don't know," I honestly and nervously replied, my voice almost shaking at the thought of driving on Shabbos, to his aggressive repetition of the same question.

"I'm waiting for the maintenance the judge ordered my wife to give me so that I can leave," I added in the hope that every word spoken would delay their handcuffing my hands behind my back (*Why is my mouth so dry?*) and placing me into the police car on the Sabbath as they placed their hand on my yarmulka to make sure I didn't bang my head on the rooftop.

"Listen to me," the older of the team now explained in a tone of voice that seemed to indicate that I was somehow supposed to know all this stuff after leading the life of a henpecked Jewish husband.

"If your wife had claimed you hit her, or if the order had been a 'stay away,' we'd have no choice other than to take you down to the station right now. We'd have to protect ourselves because if anything happened after we left, we'd be in hot water for not removing you from the premises. You'd be cuffed, finger-printed, and placed in a holding cell till the judge could see you at noon on Monday. You'd be entered into the prison system and your life would be a mess."

I just stared at him in disbelief and meekly asked, "You're not taking me?"

"No! We've been doin' this long enough to see your wife is crazy. The ink didn't even dry on the order and she's calling us already. She's just takin' out orders in all the kids' names and then calling us the next day. We can tell the kind of person you are. We're not takin' ya. But you're lucky it wasn't a 'stay-away' or we'd a' had no choice but to bring you in."

"Get out of the house!" he added in a bit friendlier voice, "You're sitting on a time bomb!"

The officers must have thought that I'm the one who's crazy, but I just looked up at the sky and said, "Thank you Hashem." The officers then headed back to their car and I turned to walk back into my house. But I suddenly found myself bolting back to their car and I gently rapped on the fender not wanting to startle them. The officer lowered his window and I politely asked, "Aren't you guys supposed to fill out some sort of report about all this?"

"Yes," he answered, "call the station on Monday after lunch and you can pick up a copy."

"And get outta the house," he smiled as he drove off.

I literally saw a dozen silhouettes move away from their windows at that very moment. I took a deep breath and walked back into the jungle I once called home. My wife glared at me. I ignored her stare — afraid she might justify such a *brazen* act as reason to call the police right back to our home — and sat down at my desk. I couldn't see one word of the Hieroglyphics in front of me.

By now it was almost time for prayer anyway and so I walked to the synagogue, ensconced myself in my prayer shawl, and began to tremble as I prayed. Not out of trepidation for the God of The Chosen. I feared the Devil. Fifteen minutes later the door opened, and Satan appeared. Once again, she had morphed back into *Eishet Chayil* form.

I will never forget the modest entry of my cunning assailant as my muse daintily stepped through the door of the House of Worship. Demurely tucking away any straggler wisp of hair beneath her snood, my saintly wife gently raised the hand with which she had only moments ago desecrated the Holy Sabbath, frantically screaming "Come now!" after dialing the police, to now righteously touch the Mezuzah on the doorpost. She then delicately tapped her fingertips to her lips, connoting a kiss of the holy object that contained the *Shema* "Adonai Echad" prayer.

My sanctimonious Shylock, who invented her own genre of medieval blood libel accusations against this completely innocent Jew during our divorce, unpretentiously made her way to her seat in the women's section of the synagogue where she opened her prayer book in the most ladylike manner you could imagine. She then began to silently chirp the Shabbat liturgy as her thin lips probably prayed, to a God that seemed to have been manipulated by her emails and prayers, that *"Ze'ev fucking drops dead next time."*

Next time wasn't too far in the future. Her Orthodox Jewish lawyer perfectly timed another order of protection he drafted, signed by my twenty-year-old learning-disabled daughter, Sara, who had been duped and enlisted by her mother, to be delivered precisely as the sun set on Friday afternoon, surely praying fervently to disturb my day of rest, knowing that I couldn't drive or pick up a phone on the Sabbath, and hoping that I'd be spending my sacred day of rest on the street or in a comfortable jail cell.

My wife lit the Sabbath candles, surely praying for a peaceful day as she delicately waved her hands three times in a circular motion over the flickering flames as a sign of purification of her body, soul, and savage mind, and with her next breath called the police, once again profaning the Holy Sabbath, to tell them that I was "still in the house!" — as she explained that I was violating an order of protection. "He's here! Come *now*, please!"

The only ritual she forgot to do that day, as she had done for the previous quarter of a century of Sabbaths, was to give me a warm hug and gentle kiss upon her completion of lighting the candles. *With all the outrageous bullshit she accused me of, I'm almost surprised that she didn't add, "Hurry, he wants to use Ester and Sara's blood to bake matzah!"*

The order had been issued that very afternoon and served upon me only minutes before Shabbat, ordering me to distance myself from Sara and to vacate the premises immediately. I grabbed a bag, stuffed it with my meds and some clothes, and explained to the arriving police, *in front of Ester* and her mother, that I had only received the notice moments ago and that I was leaving immediately. Sara, probably too embarrassed to look into my eyes, hid in her room. "O.K. Just make sure you don't go back in there!" they warned the dangerous looking man that had been paying their salary for over fifteen years.

Like an embarrassed homeless beggar, I walked to a distant surprised neighbor to ask if I could spend the Sabbath with them as I watched the ever-staring blatherskites, Hannah Fonfedder, Vittie Blech, and Devorah Radzik, perched like yenta-vultures at the sides of their windows, shrink in the distance — along with the many happy memories of my once-upon-a-time-there-was-a-loving-family-that-lived at 19 Mariner Way in Monsey, NY. Seems that upon filing for divorce a scholar can fall from grace faster than Adam and Eve being expelled from the Garden of Eden.

All these overt and insidious time-bomb traps were mere firecrackers compared to the atomic explosion of withdrawal-pain I experienced as Princess Ester slowly withdrew her scepter of laughter and love from me.

As in the science fiction horror film, *The Body Snatchers*, it seemed that my wife had placed a pod next to my daughter and "taken over" Ester while she slept. An emotionless, almost inhuman being was sprouting before my very eyes and I was not even allowed to speak to it. Ester was acting more like her mother every day. It was quite scary. The *Alien* suffering from alienation refused to acknowledge my existence, let alone that I was once her father. *Oh God! Please don't tell me You afflicted Ester with my wife's denuded-of-empathy DNA.*

My wife always had the power and work ethic of a worker ant who will continue, robotic-like, to build a colony even as it is being roasted alive in a forest fire. She will even self-detonate (spending a fortune of money and wasted years), like the recently studied Colobopsis Explodens specie that commits actual suicide, like a WW2 Japanese kamikaze pilot, by exploding and releasing a toxic sticky liquid that entangles their enemy. Throughout her attacks during our divorce, my wife used her extremely powerful Yenta-mandibles to crush my reputation while entwining me in three court systems of law.

I understood how savant-focused my insect-wife was capable of being and I braved the storm of daring to divorce her. Yet even I underestimated the treachery of my five-foot, ninety pound, beautifully sculpted Medusa because I retained fond memories of her as my bride. And "for better, for worse," with five children that we'd continue to raise, sharing in their future milestone celebrations, I was imagining a post-divorce future and still trying to settle our divorce amicably while my praying mantis mate was gung-ho on removing my testicles with her spiked forelegs and feasting on them with her voracious appetite for money.

I was still blinded by her once gorgeous long black mane and steely blue eyes, and the way she used to rest her head on my forty-four-inch chest as she cuddled me while we slept. "My teddy-bear *Vybie* with a gorgeous *tush*," I teased the woman I loved as I wrapped my arm across her slender beautiful backside. In Yiddish the word *wife* translates to "vyb," pronounced as in "good vibes." I affectionately called my wife, "Vybie." As in "cute little wife."

I still cherished memories of my future bride shedding tears of joy upon discovering that a single thornless red rose (which symbolizes love at first sight) wrapped in light-pink paper, that I discretely placed on her white dinner plate as we were being seated for an intimate dinner for two, was entwined with an eighteen-inch strand of perfectly matched pink pearls wrapped around the stem. She understood that a ring would soon follow. I was a young diamond dealer, and money was no object. I never believed money could buy love, but I loved spending it on someone I loved.

Perhaps money can't buy love, but it sure can end whatever love once existed. Especially when flung at a vile slob of a divorce lawyer at four-hundred and fifty dollars an hour. And my once-frugal cute wife was now spending money faster than our government prints it.

It was difficult for me to grasp that the mother of our five children, the woman who delicately held my hand as we took walks in the summer rain together, the woman who moaned that she loved me as she christened my new car parked in the Jewish Community Center parking lot while making love to me in its back seat, the woman with whom I shed tears of joy with each child, and ultimately grandchildren, that we brought into the world … *that woman* was now celebrating what would have been our 28th wedding anniversary by blasting toxic emails with her savage attorney, exerting the immense rage of a fire ant, squirting poison from her abdomen, that once ensconced our children as their tiny souls serenely waited for their bodies to form, to scourge my reputation and life. It's hard for me to comprehend evil, insanity, and stupidity.

The queen ant quickly telegraphed and embroiled an army of angry-yenta-red-warrior ants, furiously led by The Three Little Pigs (Mmes. Blech, Fonfedder and Radzik), to scurry to and fro all over the Monsey, NY colony of mindless Jewish inhabitants to inject venomous deceit onto my reputation. Like an ant, my wife also has an extremely high tolerance for pain. And she was willing to endure any amount, including spending a quarter of a million dollars, to inflict as much of it as possible on me.

I also didn't grasp the absolute and supreme authoritarian power given to a halfwit local Supreme Court judge. Victor Alfieri, a good-looking guy who spent too much time drinking at one bar and not enough time studying for another, barely made it through law school. Vic then stayed semi-sober long enough to tend bar at his father's watering hole called the *Deer Head Inn* (the name could easily have been describing the intellect of its bartender) where he sat schmoozing and drinking with the patrons who helped him win the quiet local election that granted him a job in his courtroom hellhole for the next forty years.

Vic started out as a village justice whose part time position in a fledgling Rockland County town was granted by a mere week of attending legal procedure and ethics classes (*Really*?) followed by a true-or-false exam that any simpleton could pass. Nothing more than a burgeoning population boom can be attributed as the reason for Alfieri's status and longevity as a judge. His second-rate career can be attributed to his good fortune at remaining half-sober as he landed a job thanks to his brilliant marketing skills of saying "this one's on me." A karma no different than my horrible one of being at the wrong place at the wrong time, and losing my daughter to the village idiot, the minute I walked into Alfieri's courtroom.

Judge Alfieri, who would prove too lazy and dimwitted to read and comprehend the motions that kept piling up in his "incredibly congested calendar," landed a job that possibly took more effort for him to simply don his black robe without red eyes every morning than to display any legal logic. And surely not any compassion. Alfieri, in his judicial attire, dispensed justice the way a gorilla in blue scrubs might perform brain surgery. The only comparison this beast displayed to our Lady Justice was that he was blind when it came to reading any of the motions submitted, and stubbornly obtuse when it came to "seeing" the obvious truths revealed by the criminal emails between my wife and her lawyer. At sixty-seven years old Alfieri was hellbent on sucking this case dry as he looked forward to his retirement stuffed with overtime hours.

This divorced notorious womanizer, who I imagine sorely needed to attend AA meetings (he probably passed his father's bar with flying hazy colors), suddenly had absolute and total control over my freedom, finances, and — worst of all — my innocent daughter. The ill-bred and uncouth boorish Alfieri became the father of Princess Ester while enjoying the protection of complete "absolute judicial immunity from liability for judicial acts, no matter how erroneous the act or how evil the motive, unless the act is performed in the clear absence of all jurisdiction." All based upon the Medieval English common law precedent of "The King (and hence, their delegates) can do no wrong" belief that still shockingly prevails in our twenty-first century courtrooms.

As my lawyer, Robert Lewis, who interned for Alfieri after graduating from law school, once said regarding Oscar (my lawyer's Old English bulldog), "he's got a higher I.Q. than Alfieri." And the real problem with "The Alf" was, that you were better off being judged by him when he *was* slightly inebriated. He was a real Pit Bull beast when he was sober. To describe Alfieri's courtroom as a nightmarish legally sanctioned PTSD gulag where "anything goes," would be a gross understatement.

According to the Code of Conduct for U.S. Judges, they are entrusted upon being sworn into office, to be fair, impartial, respectful, dignified, and courteous to all litigants who appear in their courtroom to be judged.

You could have dressed Koko the gorilla in Alfieri's black robe and receive more empathy, and surely more logical decrees and fair jurisprudence, than any ruling issued by The Alf himself.

Thirty years ago, I believed I had chosen the ultimate girl next door — the kind you proudly bring home to mama — as my fiancée. But the sweet girl-next-door I adored would have shocked the most experienced FBI Agent-Profiler. The woman my rabbi and I admired as the ultimate to-die-for Jewish trophy wife turned out to be a Svengali *Eishet Chayil* spouse. The woman I was once willing to literally die for tested my earlier conviction as she went all-out to turn my willingness to sacrifice my life for hers into a reality.

Like Katherine Heigl in the drama thriller *Unforgettable*, my wife masterminded a response to my divorce papers that made Heigl's ruthless, yet forever flawlessly ladylike, character look like an amateur. She flouted all rules as if we were back in the Paleolithic era before any existed.

My wife would have been a natural portraying the role of Tessa in that film. Like Tessa, the girl of my dreams had her own stubborn "blue steel" stare that meshed a ladylike Mona-Lisa modest smile with a blazy-eyed intensity that hinted "just try me." Her gaze pierced through any opposition while seemingly saying "we'll see about that" in a hundred different ways. Most people are intimidated by eyes that stare into theirs. Not me.

It was my fatal attraction to my future wife's bland-like relentlessly penetrating stare that was one of the many opposites-attract ingredients that induced me to agree to marry her over a quarter century ago. My wife always made eye contact. She never blinked. I thought it was because she was honest. I didn't realize it was because she was crazy. The future mother of our half-dozen children could outstare God. I thought she was cool. My wife has gorgeous dark hazel-blue eyes. They're mesmerizing. Next time I'll rely upon the reflection of my polished shield instead of staring directly into those batty eyes.

And like Tessa, who accidentally-on-purpose got pregnant in order to land the man of her dreams in the movie, my Touro College valedictorian fiancée got pregnant (whoops!) while she dated the man of *her* dreams. As she coyly explained, "... seeing how we're discussing marriage quite often anyway, let's get married!"

Couple that siren proposal with soft spoken promises of "nothing's gonna change if you marry me, Zevie" that she whispered to me upon our waking up and making love in the mornings, I figured, *I certainly sowed my wild oats; maybe it really is time to settle down and have kids.* Aside for her proclivity to display thanatosis in bed, Sharen was the perfect wife. On paper. Not on a mattress.

I completely shut off my amygdala and ignored my emotions and gut feelings. It's so easy to do when you are an Orthodox Jew. I relied on my left-brain as I addled through the mental list of pros and cons I created to convince myself that I met my *Bashert.* Sharen's eyes and mesmerizing voice tipped the scales in her favor. Ester, in the far future, would turn out to be my Achilles' heel. So painful at times that I wish my mother had simply drowned me in the River Styx.

And like the uppish Tessa who almost pulls off the perfect crime while never experiencing a single blond hair of her flawlessly coiffed tresses falling out of place — it was an engagement ring that Tessa forgot to remove from her finger that instantly proved her guilt in this thrilling almost-got-away-with-it caper — my own impeccable wife spun a heart-stopping thriller drama financed by a quarter-million-dollar web of malicious prosecution that was completely unraveled and instantly proved *her* guilt, upon my vestal *Eishet Chayil* forgetting to change a simple password. You really must watch the movie if you want to see a brilliant synonymous portrayal of my wife during our divorce.

"Can't we be amicable foes?" I gently asked my wife at the start of our divorce.

"After all, we have five children, two grandchildren, and we've been married for twenty-eight years. Remember all the times we made love?"

"We'll be amicable foes when you go to Hell!" she assured me.

Insisting behind closed doors that she'd kill me by poisoning my wine with the potassium medication used in the operating room to stop a patient's heart in order to connect it to the heart-lung bypass machine, the emails of my wife and her rapscallion attorney soon revealed that they were the ones who were truly obsessed with feces.

Faster than a detonating bolide, Thing One and Thing Two jumped right out of the pages of a Dr. Seuss crime story for adults and created a calculated mess of deception as they wildly flung shit in every direction possible without any hesitation as to where it would land, not remembering that a decade ago, in my role as Mr. Mom, my wife had given me her email password (Tatie5521).

She assured me that it was a romantic password. "Because I love you," she said. She combined my name with her birthday. "Tatie" means "Daddy" in Yiddish. Our kids always called me "Tatie." And my wife was born on June 21, 1955. My wife, at that time, shared an office with six surgeons who constantly pulled rank on her for use of its one computer. "Zevie, can you check my email," she'd call several times a day while I lovingly watched our precious princess.

The Mr. Mom that my wife laughingly admired as the best mother in the world was instantly transformed into Mr. Monster upon my filing for divorce. And my relationship with my daughter went from "I want to live with you!" to one of eerie silence. Meanwhile all I could do was collect the endless emails of my "till death do us part" bride to show my attorney, along with opening a fresh new bottle of wine whenever I poured myself a sorely needed drink to calm my nerves.

I was beginning to comprehend that the "Till death do us part" wedding vows proclaiming endless devotion could also be declared as a war cry by a marauding wife who, upon being served divorce papers, launched a blitzkrieg that seemed to run on perpetual motion. Göring would have been proud.

Tatie5521 probably saved my life. And it definitely saved my priceless reputation. I still recall holding my breath as I sat down at the computer in our kitchen and typed the decade old password into my robotic wife's email account. Twelve years later and she's still with Yahoo. *So her.* Oh my God! It worked! In her mad rush to destroy me, my ex forgot her own cardinal-rule to the new surgical assistants that she constantly trained: PAY ATTENTION TO DETAIL.

My wife's enthusiasm to get down to business and shoot five-page emails (later submitted to Alfieri) to all her friends and relatives about her husband's "kissing his daughters with a bit too much love," eclipsed the few seconds that it would have taken her to create a new password. Her time was better spent banging out the next ludicrous email chain letter that warned the world that I "spent too much time in Ester's room."

My wife especially homed in on Vittie Blech, completely and easily manipulating her best friend to go ballistic because, sadly, Vittie was severely sexually assaulted for many years as a young girl. It basically drove her off the deep end. Vittie is a pitiful five-foot tall, nasty, two-hundred-pound train-wreck that can't stop eating or gossiping. Her late ill-tempered husband, Zushe, was also extremely obese. They honestly reminded me of Tweedledee and Tweedledum.

But the "prosperous looking" chunky couple wasn't that cute the moment I served my wife divorce papers. Zushe instantly told me not to come to his synagogue anymore because he needed to "keep the wife happy." So much for a man of the commodious cloth. And Vittie moved quickly for the first time in her life.

A simple well-placed instigation sparked by my wife that I "spent too much time in Ester's room" ignited an email chit-chat that quickly spun into a conflagration with a frenzied Vittie Blech urgently emailing and contacting her psychiatrist cousin asking "for a friend" how to deal with a "pedophile father." Notice the math. Time in Ester's room equates to instantly being labeled as a pedophile.

I watched wide-eyed as the email chain quickly evolved into immediate demands to "contact the police to save Ester!!!" I never use more than one exclamation point. I always taught my students that an exclamation point is "a screamer." "Do you think using three exclamation points will increase the sound of your voice to be heard louder by your reader?" I'd ask rhetorically.

Vittie writes the way her mind, and the ground she stomps upon, thunders. My Wife could probably burn down the Amazon merely by staring at a few twigs. And her soft-spoken words are even more flammable. Her ability to mimic urgency is seen as sincere. She can win your trust in the blink of an eye.

The incendiary vulgar diatribe instantly escalated from the initial few flakes sprinkled by my "concerned for Ester's welfare" wife, quickly gaining momentum and snowballing into an avalanche as it rolled along to Vittie, Jodie, and a psychiatrist who never even met me. I could almost imagine myself on death row, with an execution team inserting a catheter into my vein, had the email assault continued.

My wife, realizing that she outdid herself, had to actually calm Vittie down by claiming in her follow up email that she "didn't really think zev would physically do anything to Ester. This was the only time he ever went into her room."

Please notice the lower-case letter "z" as Sharen spells my name. She purposefully sends a subliminal message that implies that I don't deserve the effort of her quickly tapping the 'Shift' key to capitalize my name since that might lead to someone thinking of me as a proper noun and somewhat special. Sharen did the same thing to Rabbi Nekritz, as she denuded his title and name to "nekritz," the moment he no longer served any purpose in her life. Do not think of her demotion as a typo. For thirty years she always referred to him as "Rabbi Nekritz" or "Rebbi" in any note or email correspondence regarding our rabbi. My wife leaves nothing to chance. She makes the most consummate spy in the world look like a bungler. Except for her inability to update email passwords.

Vittie then writes back to her psychiatrist that she overreacted because of "her situation." Again, notice the math of my wife. It was the "only time" I went into Ester's room. It most definitely was not the only time I went into Ester's room! I gently woke Ester up every morning to get her ready for school. And I spoke to Ester about her school-day, the world, and life-in-general every night before she went to bed. *For years!*

But what my wife meant was that it was "the *only time* I went into Ester's room" *with the intention of molesting her.* My wife is awesome at dropping subtle lies that hints danger and elicits an "Oh my God!" hit nerve that causes the listener to infer the subliminal message of pure shit as if it were truer than a prophecy whispered by God.

Notice also how my wife tosses in — even upon retreat — that I wouldn't "physically" do anything to Ester. She subliminally leaves Vittie with the message that I would *emotionally* harm my child. The horridly vile emails drenched in lies and imbecilic plans to destroy my life were clearly concocted by a mind that can only be described as deranged.

My A.I. wife and her Orthodox Jewish pet-pig-esquire revealed that they were incapable of understanding or even recognizing the concept called truth. Their shabbily written lunacy, full of typos in their rush to fling shit, spewing lascivious yearnings between a father and his daughter, reveals a side of humanity that can only be categorized as demoniacal.

My wife would soon move on to my learning-disabled daughter to insist that Sara file charges that included my "being under the covers" with her nineteen-year-old body and ten-year-old mind. Science hasn't yet caught up with describing this grey area of distorted grey matter. "Sociopathic" is the most academic scientific description they could probably state at the present time.

There is a famous quote attributed to an unknown source: *A single lie discovered is enough to create doubt in every truth exposed.* With my wife and her modestly dressed serpentine-tongued bitches it had become impossible to discover a grain of truth to even doubt. Her Jewish Pussy-Posse, armed with tongues that never tired, kept validating and forwarding the emails started by my wife as they added lie upon lie for God to observe and hopefully record comments of his own, such as, *I can't believe I breathed the breath of life into these crazy bitches!*

Meanwhile her Nazi trained, barbarous *shvine-hund* voyeur attorney gleefully laughed at the endlessly long vapid narcissistic rants, composed during the wee hours during which my wife should have been resting her sleep-deprived brain, as he quipped, "I can't believe I'm getting paid to read all of this." Ha-ha. Very funny indeed.

I later entered her attorney-client protected screed into the court documentation. They were deadly. The emails should have sent both of them to jail, or at the very least, shamefully scurrying for cover. But exhibiting the exact narcissistic talents as my wife, her lawyer did not blink. He stormed into court the day of our next appearance totally outraged and on the offensive. Hazan Dan Schwartz (her attorney was also a cantor) yelled and bellowed in his trained baritone voice that my attorney, Robert Lewis, "should be disbarred!" It was quite a solo performance.

Alfieri, without even expressing outrage at the criminal web of malicious prosecution woven by the pernicious words of two ruthless lunatics — their vile frame-up clearly proven beyond a shadow of a doubt — chose instead to berate my lawyer and insisted that he explain how the protected correspondence wound up in his court submission. "How did you dare allow Plaintiff to enter Defendant's emails with her attorney into your motion!" Alfieri roared. *I could almost hear the Nazi SS concentration camp guard, that could have easily stumbled upon my emaciated father "stealing" potato peel scraps from the garbage, barking, "Thief! How dare you steal food!" as he shot my dad.*

My attorney responded that, "Plaintiff is a writer who does not need editing and my paralegal stapled his statement to the back of my own submission." "I didn't realize he entered the *criminal* communication emails between your client and you," my lawyer calmly continued to explain as he stared at Schwartz. "Go ahead and disbar my client," he added.

My wife's attorney — hypocritically livid at our "not playing by the rules" — continued to roar and bark about the constitutional protection of attorney-client communication and its guarantee of confidentiality while angrily insisting that I had "hacked" my wife's computer, and pompously demanded, while stomping to and fro in front of the judge's raised bench, that the court immediately delete all of the emails from the court records. Alfieri, gazing down at Schwartz's antics, and annoyed as usual at having to do anything, let alone being lectured to, finally shouted, "Enough already! Just leave it in! I don't care!"

Alfieri then reprimanded me for hacking my wife's computer. I explained that I barely know how to fully use email, let alone understand how to "hack" a computer, and that my wife had *given* her password to me. Alfieri then warned that I had better not use "that password!" anymore. I assured him that I would not.

Those emails proved the mendacious prosecution that my wife and her attorney sadistically wove around my reputation. It was a miracle that "The Alf" didn't order them expunged from the record and that I was able to shovel the trail of their squirrelly-shit and smear it into their faces. Unfortunately, The Alf really didn't care. In fact, he didn't give a shit. Once again, Alfieri chose to totally ignore what would have outraged any jurist with a semblance of integrity.

The emails portrayed a high functioning Asperger woman that had no shame, regrets, or any fear of being discovered at some future date as a blatant liar. The woman to whom I once gently whispered, "What are you dreaming, Honey?" as I heard her moaning in her sleep; who sweetly responded, "about you eating me" as I gently removed her panties while whispering, "You don't have to dream anymore," had now transformed into a hideous Mrs. Hyde whose inner demon was casting a deplorable assault of bogus accusations in an endless delirious effort to defame my reputation.

Those gentle hands that once took my yearly blood sample, while landing on my veins more delicately than a mosquito (to spare me the bruise marks of rushed technicians), were now banging away on their keyboard like some acid-rock drummer tripped out on anger. The sterile hands of Dr. Jekyll that stitched new pathways for clogged hearts by day became the malformed claws of a wild and slanderous beast that could not wait to feast on my heart upon ripping it out of my chest by night.

Mrs. Hyde made phone calls and sent emails to every rabbi, friend, work associate and relative that shared the sphere of our silver anniversary marriage. The emails exhibited how my wife had even contacted my previous employers, crying for help, as she explained that I refused to go to Beit-Din, begging them to compose any kind of negative statement that she might submit to our judge as "evidence" that I was trying to evade working at a higher-paying job so that he might impute more salary to offset the maintenance he had ordered her to pay me.

Mrs. Hyde was desperately trying to get Alfieri to impute additional "earnings" to my meager teacher's salary in order to close the 150K gap between our W-2 earnings statements so that she would be responsible for less maintenance. Mrs. Lewinson and her attorney were desperate to "prove" that I had "planned this all along" and that I was deliberately avoiding work so that I could receive substantial monthly maintenance.

Her only problem was that she had outearned me for more than a decade by the time I filed for divorce. Divorce guidelines instruct a judge to declare a "moneyed spouse" based on the preceding five-year income of any couple filing for divorce. Sometimes it's a close call. My wife earned seven times what I earned. For the past ten years.

While simultaneously trying to prove that I was capable of earning more money, my wife was giving her best Oscar performance to get me fired from the low-paying part-time teachers salary that I was receiving. She was trying to starve me to death while refusing to pay a penny of the temporary maintenance that Alfieri had court-ordered *for a third time*.

Like a female spider that eats its mate, my cutthroat bride injected poison into anyone who knew me, as she warned them that I was a pedophile who should not be allowed to teach children or share custody of our daughter. "And don't loan him any money! He's a bamboozler who will never pay you back!" Nothing reveals a person's personality like money.

It's an amazing coincidence how all these accusations coincided with my filing for divorce after twenty-eight years of sitting at the Shabbat table where I expounded new insights of the week's Torah portion to my children and adoring wife, who proclaimed week after week that I should publish my enrapturing concepts.

The stranger I shared a bed with for over thirty-five years now laughed, through e-mail correspondence with her attorney, relatives, and friends, to "give Zev a heart attack." Ha-ha. I marveled at how heartless they were as her lawyer explained, "It's a long shot Sharen ... but it's time to kick Zev outta the house," even as he expressed doubt in their ability to accomplish their plan because I was such a "goody-two-shoes."

"He boxes! Say that he hit you!" her POS esquire brother, Fred Mailman, whose marriage I saved a decade earlier, chimed in as he CC'd everyone in the email chain. Like his friend Jack Abramoff, Fred was another dumb lawyer that failed to comprehend that emails reveal brain matter — and criminal intent!

"But he'd never hit me," my wife — who knew I was the only boy in kindergarten that the girls allowed to play with them — matter-of-factly responds to Jack Abramoff's best friend as she proceeded the following day to cleverly alter her brothers blatant lie to now be inferred as a constant looming physical threat, instead of an act everyone knew I was completely incapable of committing, as she gave a statement to our local police that she "fears my wrath." Throwing in that I'm "obsessed with feces," for good measure. *Sorry, even I can't even begin to imagine what she was thinking*.

I observed all this chatter online as I wondered how hominids could not be embarrassed to carry on like this in front of each other. I was almost tempted to jump in on their email chain to ask, "How can all of you be doing this? *To me!*" I realized, however, that it would be like requesting manners from a pack of frenzied wild dogs ripping muscle off a dying gazelle. The only difference between the two species is that dogs eventually become sated.

Like true psychopaths whose MRI's show weak electrical activation in those regions of the brain that decipher moral dilemmas, my pretty but amoral sheitel-clad wife proceeded to create a hellish existence from which it took me almost three years to escape. This is not said in anger. I loved my wife. She's sweet. On the surface. I still had fond memories of walking on the beach with her as she picked up a huge branch and shyly wrote *I LOVE YOU!* in the sand.

But the sands of time now revealed that our relationship had always been much less than merely incompatible. You can't treat someone you once truly loved with such unbounded savagery. The behavior of my wife was as violent as a Middle Eastern Muslim man throwing acid into the blue eyes and face of the gorgeous Viking descendant he gently made love to the previous night.

It was obvious to me that my wife's etched *I LOVE YOU!* declaration was as ephemeral as it was short-lived, disintegrating in the sand from which it was quickly washed away by the next few waves.

Yes, like that message in the sand, it's the little things lovers do and say that go a long way. Tiny thoughtful acts leave lasting impressions when a lover goes out of their way to tenderly share that you're on their mind. Like shutting off my phone and causing me to lose what my wife knew was a highly valued 800 toll-free number (to me only) that's been part of my businesses for two decades.

And that was *after* forcing me to unnecessarily spend a few grand merely to have the judge in our divorce proceedings finally warn her, as he ultimately threatened to hold her in contempt of court if she didn't release my number by the 27th day of March. Sure enough, at sunset on that final day, my wife, fearing neither God nor Alfieri, contemptuously shut off my service minutes before the Sabbath began. *She loved getting into my head right at the start of the Day of Rest.* After claiming the number should be treated as 'marital property,' and insisting that I pay her for "her half" of the number's value, she was happy to lose (destroy) the number as long as I wouldn't get it.

What spiteful message were you sending me, Sharen? Or were you merely trying to show God what a humane and compassionate individual you are? Wasn't dumping me off your North Shore University Hospital medical insurance policy and forcing me to spend $1,364.00 a month for a COBRA policy enough of a message? North Shore's policy is to carry a spouse even post-divorce at no cost to the divorced employee spouse. But being the kind, caring, Jewish Orthodox woman that you are, you fiendishly chose to force me to spend over sixteen thousand dollars a year.

I wonder which box you checked faster than you blink your eyes. The one on the protection order where you affirmed under oath that we were not contesting each other in any other court during our divorce, or the one that asked if you would like your divorced spouse to remain on your North Shore policy?

I won't even ask if it ever occurred to you (who can't resist a great bargain) to suggest that you wouldn't sign me off of your policy in exchange for my giving you an additional five or seven hundred a month towards Ester's child support. After all, I understand that in your sick mind, I no longer existed.

Everything with you has always been an eviscerating till the-final-broken-straw gut-wrenching moment. And then some. Months of effort fighting over a number that I used for SwordPen Publishers — a company you agreed had no value in your hands and willingly relinquished in lieu of keeping the 100K (wholesale) in jewelry I gave you throughout our marriage — and you then shut off my phone knowing Alfieri could hold you in contempt, only to say, *Fuck you, Ze'ev!*

Thank you Sharen. I'll always remember your affectionate Orders of Protection and the thoughtful little things you so kindly went out of your way to do for me, to display what a wonderful *Eishet Chayil* I was married to for twenty-eight years. I realize that to your meshuggenah-mind I was never anything more than a circumcised Jewish Orthodox dildo. And please don't think I'm upset. You have no idea how much I appreciate the lonely island of peace upon which your deranged mind washed me ashore, baptized by your fiery brain.

I share all the above to explain that of all the weapons included in my wife's cache of acrimonious and sadistic tactics during our divorce, her merciless and brazen alienation of our daughter Ester would prove to be the most brutal torture device of all. Protection Orders, Family court trials, Criminal court trials, excommunication, shunning from the Monsey community, silence from all the relatives for whom I had been the go-to person for decades, malicious prosecution by Alfieri and Schwartz — all paled into insignificance compared to the alienation-death of my precious late-in-life miracle baby.

There is nothing my wife would not destroy, including Ester's physical health, merely to avoid maintenance payments. Money means control. Money buys everything — but love. And the lovingly warm, emotionally healthy, father-daughter relationship Ester shared with her *Tatie* for over a decade was completely worthless in the decoded thought processes of my wife's brain tissue when compared to her losing control over my life while being held legally obligated to pay partial support for its existence.

So after spending twenty-five years being edified as an incredibly wonderful Mr. Mom by my *Eishet Chayil,* upon being served with divorce papers, she immediately ran around to our own children and anyone with a snood or a yarmulka, screaming that I am a dangerous pedophile who is obsessed with feces. My wife, my two older daughters, and sadly even Ester, continue to refuse to speak with me nine years since the day I filed for divorce. It's all about control.

Like a mind afflicted with the mental illness of Munchausen syndrome by proxy, my ex factitiously faked symptoms of my being abusive to our daughter with such intense ferocity, that Ester began to suffer actual angst and depression. My wife virtually kidnapped Ester by taking out an order of protection that instantly allowed her to change Ester's school while keeping Ester completely shielded from any possible contact with me. She then convincingly persuaded Ester that my going to court is destroying "the family" and that my refusal to go to Beit Din would cause our family to become homeless.

My wife also invited Ester to sleep in my bed every night for a fitful night's sleep with the lights on till all hours, locked "safely" behind the master bedroom door, so that she could hear my wife's endless soliloquy of being the poor mother trying to hold it all together.

Ester became a frantic nervous wreck as my wife relentlessly stressed her about not having any money because of my going to court. My wife is unstinting in getting her way. She badgers without mercy. She repeats. She insists. She interrupts. She scolds. She cajoles. She cries. She nags. She whips you with a frenzy of ferocious energy till she corrals you and breaks you like an old, tired horse. She can have the proudest stallion on the planet praying and whinnying to become pet food or glue.

A mother suffering from Munchausen by proxy syndrome will poison her own child while outwardly appearing as the most loving and caring parent in the world. She will stroke her daughter's forehead while gently holding the hand of the victim she is murdering. Said mother will have her child undergo excruciating and totally unwarranted medical procedures while acting like the most grieving person on the planet. And that is why it is so difficult to catch them and why their disease is rarely discovered.

After all, who would suspect a woman who carried a baby for nine months in her womb, capable of using doctors to torture said baby upon birth? And who would suddenly claim that a loving father would harm his little girl? Like my marriage, these things will never add up.

I have no scientific evidence that my wife truly suffers from Munchausen by proxy syndrome. It is an extremely difficult disease to diagnose. Partly because it's so unbelievable. Fortunately, because it's so rare. But my wife's actions during our divorce certainly fit the mold of a ruthlessly unsympathetic mind. Upon my serving her with divorce papers, she instantly proclaimed "You're never taking Ester to fucking school again!" as she transformed into a father-daughter relationship destroying Alienation-Terminator on steroids that would have made Arnold Schwarzenegger cower at her presence.

Alienation is a very common occurrence in many divorces. An angry parent merely needs to allege that their spouse is harming their child — or might harm their child — and the divorce becomes an instant drawn-out nightmare. Ester was used as a disposable Pawn in a terrifying game of chess where the deranged Queen could move anytime, in any direction or pattern she chose, in a game without rules, in order to avoid paying maintenance to a King who only sought an amicable draw.

In the early 1980's, Dr. Richard Gardner diagnosed another maternal evil and gave the horrifically diseased femme-fatale mommy-mind upon divorce a clinical name. He called it, "Malicious Mother Syndrome, where-by vengeful mothers employ child abuse allegations as a 'powerful weapon' to punish the ex and ensure custody to themselves." (He should have replaced the word 'punish' with 'torture.') Gardner claimed that MMS was *rampant* (italics are my own) and existed in 90 percent of custody cases and although he originally called the abuse "Malicious Mother Syndrome," he claimed that fathers were also capable of such tactics. And they were.

Political correctness forced Gardner to change the name from its 90 percent "Malicious Mother" description to the more all-inclusive "Parental Alienation Syndrome" term the world has come to know as PAS. Gardner couldn't prove his ninety percent claim and therefore switched from the malicious mother designation to the all-inclusive parental one. A description that is quite fair because there are many women who have been destroyed by powerful and abusive husbands who employed the horrific tactics of a scheming alienating parent.

Amazingly enough, major studies completed two decades later substantiated Gardner's original numbers as true. And more incredibly outrageous is the pitifully sad fact that another two decades have flown by and *nothing* has changed. The ninety percent Malicious Mother Syndrome is *very* alive and well, as 96.90 percent of divorced mothers continue to gain custody of children during a divorce.

I do not suggest that we stop being politically correct and use the original name. That would be completely unfair to the minority of mothers who suffer beyond belief, because no one expects a woman to lose her child during divorce proceedings, and when she does, people assume she must be an unfit mother. But a more accurate understanding of the sheer number of mothers who will effortlessly inflict alienation upon their children during a divorce, would very likely spare a lot of kids from losing their relationship with the most important man in their lives.

Gardner further theorized (according to Professor Joan Meier at George Washington University in her 2009 paper describing PAS) that mothers enlist the children in the obsessive 'campaign of denigration' and 'vilification' of the father, and that they often 'brainwash' or 'program' the children into believing untrue claims of abuse by the father." "Obsessed with feces," and "you could say Tatie is a pedophile," are flawless examples of the irrational extremes an unhinged spouse will shamelessly exhibit to inflict alienation and pain without pausing to breathe, eat, or sleep. "Call him Zev. He's not your father anymore," is another example of the reptilian behavior of my *Bashert*.

And programing Ester to draw a captioned "Die Zev!" picture of her father as a green monster while emailing the mentally unstable, sexually assaulted *little girl* (she never got past her trauma) named Vittie Blech that "Zev spent too much time in Ester's room" is another heart-rendering example of an unhinged malicious mother's diseased mind. And haranguing Ester to the point that she turned to scream at me that I'm "killing Mommy!" is proof of how powerfully well alienation tactics work.

And please don't try and explain my wife's behavior as somehow normal but merely "stressed-out." Nietzsche brilliantly expressed the psyche of my Jekyll-Hyde wife when he wrote: The irrationality of a thing is not an argument against its existence, rather a condition of it.

Sending your daughters on a spiritually suicidal mission to incessantly scream and call the saintly Rabbi Nekritz "a piece of shit" to his face is the irrational reality of a woman who was obviously never normal during one day of her entire existence. Thirty years of speaking *modestly* to a saint were revealed as a total farce by one brazen spoken-with-sincerity proclamation by my wife, in her desperate carefully calculated pre-meditated plan to anger me by denigrating the angelic rabbi that lovingly wished her a heartfelt "Mazel Tov!" thirty-five years ago.

My wife would never call a bum on the street "a piece of shit." Yet she sent her two adult daughters on a four-hour round-trip drive for the sole purpose of delivering that lovely message to the seventy-two-year-old soft-spoken utterly brilliant Rabbi Yisroel Tzvi Nekritz in front of his lovely wife and quiet Borough Park neighbors. Gardner's study describes my wife as clearly as the Talmud explains the Five Books of Moses.

My wife became obsessed and preoccupied 24/7 (and I mean "including Shabbat") with destroying my role as a parent (the main parent, actually) in Ester's life. It's rare to see the rage that this cute ninety-pound woman can exhibit. But I have. And I can honestly say I'd rather fight Khabib Nurmagomedov in an octagon cage than my wife in court. At least there I have a chance (albeit minuscule) of winning. At the very least, Khabib would allow me to tap out quickly.

And although Alienation Syndrome is now considered to be one of the most destructive manifestations of child abuse, nothing has changed in forty years.

The Jerusalem Family Court System has tackled the problem aggressively with a system called Therapeutic Jurisprudence (which does exactly what its name implies). They use endless prudence monitoring both parents and severely punish a parent that *abuses* their child during a divorce. Israel is as progressive as the United States is ancient regarding children of divorced parents. Israeli courts honestly care and seriously focus on the child's "best interests."

But the United States is still as backward as Alfieri is wild. And getting rid of carnivores like The Alf will only effect minor change. The Court System itself has to change. Trouble is, granting the courts the power to fix itself would be like asking a thief to chop off his own hand. Or like asking my wife to encourage Ester to give me a phone call. The Messiah will surely arrive before that ever happens.

I have friends who are still in divorce court proceedings after an entire decade of endless trials, hearings, appeals, and re-trials. I know fathers who are waiting for over ten years for the courts to enforce their already granted court ordered visitation while their wives disdainfully claim, "It's the kids' fault. They don't want to see their Father."

World Wars have begun and ended more quickly than many divorce cases. Especially when those divorce cases are conducted by Perverts of Justice like the Honorable Victor Alfieri. And there are many of them infesting our entire criminal and family court systems.

In the end my wife never claimed that I hit her or even threatened to hit her. She didn't have to, thanks to our family court system that can't wait to maul a father. The worst thing Sharen avowed under threat of perjury was simply that she "fears my wrath," and that I was "obsessed with feces, as evidenced by my publishing a children's story called *When You Gotta Go!*"

Kirkus Reviews loved the book and proclaimed: *Family members find relief in the bathroom in this humorous children's picture book.* They gave it their "suggested by our critics" accolade. And among the six hundred thousand Indie books published in 2017, "*When You Gotta Go!*" won an award and was proclaimed among the one hundred "Best Books of 2017" by Kirkus Reviews.

But my wife's terrifyingly dreadful claim, that I was *obsessed with feces,* was solid enough "evidence" for Family Court Judge Dean Richardson-Mendelson to immediately grant and rubber-stamp an order of protection that, combined with Alfieri's imbecility and direction-of-the-wind-blowing-that-day skewed jurisprudence, threw my life and pristine reputation into a witch's cauldron whose brew made me feel as if I were being boiled alive.

Four months later, I wound up submitting a copy of the actual book to a laughing and apologetic Judge *Rubber-Stamp* Mendelson as *real* evidence in a Family Court trial battling yet a *third* protection order that my wife had coerced our twenty-year-old daughter, Sara, to file. My wife and Schwartz instructed Sara to mimic my wife's own "obsessed with feces" allegation (again displaying her robotic lack of any real creativity) along with additional charges that I had been "under the covers" with Sara and had threatened to "mush her head in the wall." In other words, she was claiming that I was a violent, incestuous, feces-loving pervert. *Just another day in court.*

My children's intelligence quotient's range from very high to quite low. I can't begin to describe the love, patience, humor, and effort I exerted to instill self-esteem into my challenged mildly-learning-disabled young daughter's personality as she grew up. My wife, once again, destroyed a two-decade wonderfully close (I'm almost afraid to say so!) father-daughter relationship with a talent for slander that even Joseph Goebbels would have envied.

Once the trial started, my daughter Sara's lawyer, Martin Gotkin, wanted to suddenly enter an additional charge of my having been "inappropriate under the covers." Said lawyer, in a plea bargain deal, was disbarred from practicing law for seven years and had only recently been reinstated. A forced seven-year hiatus (as a shady detective) and he was as sleazy as the day he was indicted for fraud. The judge responded that it was too late to add any new claims. "Why didn't your client make that claim when she took out her original protection order?" he asked. At least some judges make the effort to use a little logic.

Goblin Gotkin's first question as I took the stand was: "Mr. Lewinson! Did you ever go to a Hooker?" I stared in shock at the heap of feces reeking in front of me, thinking of what I could possibly answer to such a wild question, and responded: "No, I never had the pleasure of being intimate with your Mother!" The judge went wild, banging his gavel repetitively, and told me to behave as he admonished the lawyer to ask pertinent questions. Gotkin knew my daughter was lying but he didn't care. All he cared about was earning a few dollars and perhaps trying to double-dip if he could once again find a way to do so without getting disbarred.

This time-consuming legal circus is all the result of protection orders being issued to any female that takes the few minutes necessary to request one. It costs the state tens of millions of taxpayer dollars a year in judicial and auxiliary salaries and overtime to investigate, track, and monitor these obviously blatantly repetitive bogus allegations, chirped by birdbrain wives, that are as common during divorces as a 'cup of joe' being called out to a waitress at a truck stop. And it costs spouses their energy, health, money, and ultimately, their children.

Fighting the systemic system is the equivalent of throwing dry branches onto your own funeral pyre. In my divorce case, I was fortunate to read all the heartfelt eulogies of my friends and relatives by signing into the email account of my wife, as my relationship with Ester went up in smoke. Before I died. *None of them ever imagined I'd rise from the dead to write a bestseller.*

It is hard to envisage the stress and constraints of living under the shame and frustration of a single bogus order of protection. And here I was — living under *the same roof* with my wife and two daughters, each of whom held their own personal and individual lethal order of protection against me. Do the math. One maniac plus two manipulated daughters, equals three little ladies who could dial 911 whenever they were in the mood for some fun.

A simple dialing of three digits by any one of them, or my wife accidentally tripping in the dark and banging her head while getting up to pee in the middle of the night and deciding she received a propitious godsend moment to incarcerate me, would have the police rushing over with their sirens blaring faster than my ex could enunciate the word she most dreaded: maintenance. The police would then see the other two females in the house waving their own protection orders against their monstrous father. Try falling asleep with those thoughts on your mind.

Fortunately, I taped my daughter admitting that I never so much as yelled at her in her entire life. I also had her admitting that I was the best father in the world. Sara even explained how badly she wanted to attend the BEA book show at the Javits Center with me, where we had a booth for my publishing company, but her mother and older sister, Rachel, explained to my daughter that if she attended "and drove all the way to Manhattan with Tatie," it would show that she's not "really" afraid of me, and that her protection order would lose credibility.

"Sara," I pleaded into my cell phone, "How could you do this to me?!" "Who taught you how to read? Who taught you how to drive? How could you take out an order of protection against your own *father!*" I gently, but desperately asked.

"I ... I ... but you divorced mommy," she replied in a childlike voice. "Are you mad at me?" she added. "No. I still love you," I whispered in a weak exhausted voice as I hung up because of actual pain in my chest.

The judge screamed at my daughter and asked, "How can a wife and daughter do this to such a fine gentleman?" He was livid as he highlighted the many inconsistencies in my daughter's testimony while basically calling her an outright liar. He also questioned how she was able to consistently laugh and giggle at my humor in court if I was truly a man that had harmed her.

Without needing a day or even a minute to deliberate before issuing a final judgement, Judge Mendelson (from the bench) immediately ruled completely in my favor and dismissed the entire case. Mendelson informed Gotkin and my daughter of her right to appeal his decision, while adding, "Although I highly doubt it!" The incredible stress and embarrassment of six months had ended as quickly and suddenly as the Jewish exodus from Egypt.

But the stress and trauma had taken its pound of flesh from my soul and wrapped it around my midsection. I suffered badly from PTSD after the Family Court trial that was bogusly initiated by a daughter for whom I would have donated two kidneys *and* my soul. But it seems that all anyone wanted was my broken heart. Long term stress is truly a form of torture. And God was fucking torturing me. I tried to remain cool, and I thought I had managed pretty well, but my weight and blood pressure bore witness against my being nothing tougher than a wimpy old scholar as they both continued to soar mercilessly.

My wife had originally taken out two protection orders. One for herself and one in the name of our minor child, Ester. My wife *loves* twofers. Without ever contacting me, pulling up my social security number, or even bothering to Google my name, the court system immediately, and with grave urgency, trusted the drama-queen wife against whom I had filed for divorce after having been married to her for twenty-eight very long and emotionally arduous years.

Our for-profit court system is primed to instantly assume that any father filing for divorce is a faceless stranger who suddenly evolves into a beast and morphs as an imminent threatening monster that might harm his own child. In my case, a very happy daughter that I had been Mr. Mom to for her entire eleven-year-old life. Not one judge, supervisory appellate judge, court official, lawyer (including my own), or court-appointed attorney or professional during my entire divorce case gave a flying fuck. Neither did her mother. Once again, "It's all about them Benjamins."

On the flip side, try missing one or two child support payments and you'll see how fast the court revokes your professional license, freezes your passport, and pulls up your social security number and credit report to get your attention while garnishing your wages and bank accounts.

Two imbecilic jurists, Mendelson and Alfieri could not figure out (or simply refused to trouble themselves) what two policemen easily deduced after speaking a mere five minutes with my *Eishet Chayil* and myself. On the other hand, perhaps I should be thankful that the two cops weren't the judges, and that Alfieri and Mendelson weren't the cops who showed up that Saturday morning. I'd probably have been tasered and shot.

A grand jury needs to be convened to examine the validity of an *accusation* before handing down an indictment. And even an actual indictment (with mounds of evidence) is not allowed to be used against the indicted party until he has stood trial — even for murder. It's merely an indictment. It is a *formal accusation*. But nothing more.

You can google this if you're interested in understanding the legal details of our Sixth Amendment rights. They are amazingly protective. As they should be. But those Sixth Amendment rights cease to exist in divorce court, where any loving father can instantly be "convicted" by a simple whispered *accusation* as his crazed wife gently sighs, "I'm afraid of his wrath." Five falsely uttered words, and his right to a public trial without unnecessary delay, his right to a lawyer, his right to know the evidence, and his right to an impartial jury of his peers, are instantly trampled upon by wild horses that whisk him back to the Dark Ages. The only thing he gets to know, as he is booted in the balls and into the street, is who his accuser is. Big surprise.

A man can lovingly embrace and kiss his wife and kids as he heads out to work in the morning, and upon arriving home at night discover that he'll be arrested if he walks on his lawn. *In God We Trust.*

The "dangerous man" in Ester's life, aka, her father, was immediately ordered to: STAY AWAY FROM MINOR CHILD. DO NOT TALK TO MINOR CHILD.

I'm still amazed, in shock actually, that this happened to *me*. I'm still triggered by the event even as I compose this sentence, five years after the fact. And it's still happening every day to thousands of wonderful "I can't believe it!" dads across our entire supposedly "innocent till proven guilty" country.

Judge Mendelson stamped my wife's double order, and three days later stamped my other daughter's order, without ever so much as cross referencing the credentials of the father of five, married for twenty-eight years, teacher, writer, publisher, Talmudical scholar, and conscientious payer of outrageous Rockland County property taxes (i.e. Mendelson's salary) for the past two decades, whose name was suddenly popping up in protection order requests and all three Rockland County court systems faster than quantum mechanics quarks popping in and out of existence.

Upon the dismissal of my case in Family Court, this white-privileged Jewish male delicately reminded Judge Mendelson that he was the one who rubber-stamped the original three orders and I asked if he could at least speak to Judge Alfieri on my behalf and explain the relentless hellfire with which my wife and her lawyer had engulfed my life through fictitious protection orders obtained through perjury. "You can help me now," I obsequiously entreated the judge. Mendelson confided that "the system was far from perfect," and apologized for his haste in urgently signing all orders, while explaining that he was not allowed to communicate ex parte regarding my case with Alfieri.

Try and imagine my frustration upon being told that the orders of protection that had been proven as an outright frame-up in Family Court, urgently served upon me ex parte (without requiring my presence, and hastily issued through secrecy in order *to protect* the issuer from her *abuser)*, could now not be exposed and revealed ex parte (without notice to the issuer of said *false* protection orders) to Judge Alfieri.

"I'm going to have to trust that Judge Alfieri will figure this out for himself," a shoulder-shrugging Judge Mendelson woefully responded. I really don't know how these people sleep at night.

Cherie Blair is quoted as having said that the cornerstone of any society is a well-functioning legal system. Sad to say, I, and *millions* of other spouses, never experienced anything as dysfunctional as our protection-order-driven divorce-family court system.

Even David Letterman (television host) had an order of protection issued against him in 2005. The crazed fan, Colleen Nestler, told Judge Daniel Sanchez that Mr. Letterman used code words during his monologue (taped live earlier in the day) that "inflicted mental cruelty and sleep deprivation." Nestler had also accused Regis Philbin and other television personalities of mind control through "code." The Sante Fe lunatic insisted that the talk show icon wanted to marry her and train her to be his co-host on the show.

The restraining order application, urgently requested by Ms. Nutsy Nestler, contained six pages of neatly typed total *meshugaas* that should have had her institutionalized. Claiming that Letterman was using "eye expressions" and hand gestures (through *her* T.V. set) to convey his desire to marry her, Colleen had her lunacy notarized and sent to Judge Sanchez. Ms. Colleen Nestler also wrote that she had responded to David Letterman and sent *him* "thoughts of love" telepathically. How she accomplished sending telepathic thoughts to a talk show host who appeared on her screen in a show he recorded *in the past* escapes me. But hey! We're talking about Orders of Protection, so who said anything has to make sense?

I guess Sanchez also didn't trouble his legal, supposedly logically trained mind to consider that telepathic assault should count as mental cruelty when the waves travel from the female brain to a male brain as well. But then again, we're observing evolution at the state court level and it is admittedly difficult for reptilian minds to grasp anything other than a moving life form that might reveal itself as a potential next meal (aka a man filing for divorce). Reptiles can only shuffle paper, and they move slowly. And so the government sloth dropped the application on Sanchez's desk and waited for the signature of the cold-blooded judge.

Crazier than Colleen signing her surely-hallucinogenic-inspired request was Judge Sanchez's *immediate and urgent* actual signing and granting her Order of Protection petition! And that is because they are rarely denied. The details of Protection Order requests are also rarely read. They're granted instantly. Almost telepathically!

Letterman and CBS quickly hired top white-shoe law firm attorneys to undo the damage. David could afford lawyers who earn $500 thousand dollars a year compared to a loser prehistoric once-dominant-land-animal judge that earns a mere $100 thousand. Letterman had the financial wherewithal necessary to immediately challenge, appeal, and instantly expunge the ludicrous order issued by yet another idiotic loose-cannon judge in our State Court System of Stupidity. *Imagine if Letterman was a blue-collar worker who couldn't afford a lawyer. His life could have easily spun out of control.*

The material it gave him for his show was easily worth the price David paid his lawyers. The wheels of justice move quickly when you can grease them with a lot of money, and almost in reverse when you can't. Letterman's attorneys were not playing games. But typical sleazy divorce lawyers have a financial interest in keeping your case in court for as long as possible. They are not your friend. In fact, there is probably no life form on the planet as heartless as a divorce lawyer. I have many close friends who are lawyers, and they all tell me that one already knew in law school which losers would choose to become divorce attorneys in the future. "You could smell them a mile away," one friend told me.

Judge Sanchez later admitted that he granted the restraining order *not on the merits of the case* (italics are my own), but because the petitioner had completely filled out the required paperwork. Notice Sanchez's admission that the incoherent gibberish of telepathic assault that the petitioner proclaimed (under threat of perjury) against Letterman was considered *evidence beyond a reasonable doubt* and hastily stamped because the meshuggenah *had completely filled out the required paperwork* requesting, in essence, that David stop thinking. *Lettermen should be happy that Sanchez did not order a lobotomy.*

Nothing more clearly portrays how easy it is for a woman to obtain an Order of Protection. She merely has to *completely fill out the required paperwork*. Said "paperwork" is nothing more than a simple form. But I imagine that to a reptilian brain it would take a lot of cerebral effort and mental concentration to check off a few boxes.

The Letterman saga was all very comical for the comedian (not that I'm belittling his stress or expense), but during a divorce — and especially where children are involved — there is absolutely nothing to laugh about.

Judge Sanchez faced no negative recriminations for his wanton stupidity that wasted Letterman's time and money. Not even a sanction by Appellate judges. And Sanchez suffered no financial penalty for costing David Letterman a hefty tab to quickly defend himself. Judges can't be sued. Once again, that good old medieval common law precedent, "The King can do no wrong."

Most divorcing dads don't have a white-shoe law firm at their instant beck and call. And far too many judges have little or no integrity. Their fear of that one-in-a-million lunatic that will kill his wife (which he'll do with or without an order) during a divorce justifies an instant stamp of approval on every single protection order that lands on their desk. Stamp first (protect yourself from possible public outrage). Ask questions later.

Meanwhile, the sucker-punch dropping and detonation of an Atom Bomb Protection Order on the head of an unsuspecting innocent spouse instantly places him in the epicenter of a fireball whose shock waves fling him out of the house while incinerating his soul through endless Court Ordered measures that will poison and ultimately vaporize his relationship with his young child.

Endless Alienation Radiation will continue to be inflicted by the child's mother while the taxpayer finances court appointed bottom-feeders who feign a mantra of "protect the poor child" as malicious prosecution drains the fallout-life of a loving father. Even the symptoms of Alienation Radiation are the same as radioactive radiation: nausea, vomiting, headaches, and endless fatigue. And enough exposure *will* kill you. But hey! We must "protect" our children.

My wife's restraining order was as ludicrous as the one issued by Ms. Nestler. Transcribing her wildly-disordered thoughts on a legal court document for the entire world to see, Mrs. Nutsy Lewinson *completely filled out the required paperwork* and committed perjury by swearing (in writing) that we were not engaged in any other court system (e.g. divorce court) while stating that I "was obsessed with feces — *proven* (italics are my own) by the fact that I wrote and published a book called *When You Gotta Go!*" Guilty, Your Honor! I'm so fucking guilty! Yes, I penned that hysterical children's book. How much time do you think I'll spend on death row?

This completely mad scheme was bantered about in her late-night emails with her lawyer, rabbi, psychologist, siblings, and Yenta friends — all supposedly God-fearing, Sabbath observing, kind Orthodox Jews who are wonderful upstanding *fucking hypocritical* members of their communities.

By the way, Your Honor, that book was featured in KIRKUS REVIEWS and received recognition in their annual *The Best Books of 2017* magazine. Do I now receive a life sentence for having a great sense of humor and making children laugh? Are you going to give me Hemlock to drink because I corrupted the youth of our society when I did library readings and instilled within our children a lifelong passion to read great books? Will you be sending out police on Shabbat to taser and arrest me?

RADAR (Respecting Accuracy in Domestic Abuse Reporting) is a Maryland Think Tank that gathers information and statistics to expose excesses of the "domestic violence" bureaucracy. They wrote that Letterman's case was "not a judicial anomaly but the logical culmination of years of *ever-expanding* (italics are my own) definitions of domestic violence."

It's gotten to the point where serving divorce papers is considered domestic violence by our divorce court system. It's a simple four step process. 1) Serve your wife divorce papers. 2) Receive an Order of Protection. 3) Say goodbye to your child. 4) Forever.

My wife and her attorney further expanded the definition of domestic violence by classifying my possibly receiving a single rusted penny of maintenance as pure unadulterated domestic violence on my part — proven by the email sent to me directly from her lawyer that stated, "This can all stop the moment you agree to forgo any maintenance."

I shared the coercion-laced email, that threatened me with endless malicious prosecution for merely continuing to request the temporary maintenance that had already been "Court Ordered!" many times, with Alfieri himself, who, being the judge from Sodom, screamed at me not to hack my wife's emails. "But Your Honor, this one is directly from her attorney to me. It's a regular email. It's not hacked, Sir." "Stop being argumentative!" the beastly judge growled like an angry dog. Like the German guards that screamed at my father, Alfieri glared and continued to bark, "I'll hold you in contempt!"

Basically, judges shoot first and ask questions later. *All* requests are deemed urgent — as if an imminent threat of danger exists. Judges are terrified at the possibility of refusing any order because of that rare instance where the husband does eventually prove to be violent. And so a million innocent men are instantly punished. Judges insist that "no harm will be done" if the man receiving the order is innocent. (Man up! You still have a penis. We're only removing your balls.) Judges also know that they receive time-and-a-half-pay for slowly unravelling their "overburdened" court calendars.

Even if society agreed that any protection order by any woman against any man needs to be instantly stamped, would it not make sense to deal with the reason for the request immediately? Why take years to obliterate a parental relationship that prohibits a father from seeing his child and destroys said child while exploiting the life of a loving parent?

Meanwhile a man can be refused employment years after his *harmless* order of protection has been dismissed as frivolous. Companies do a quick background check and they also don't want to deal with any possible consequences of an employee that once had an Order of Protection issued against him (frivolous or not) who might go postal at some future date. Try going down to your local court to get it expunged. Then be sure to go back again. And again. And be patient upon your fourth or fifth request. Or they'll reinstate it before you can say ... anything.

This situation has to change. Men are refusing to get married. Women are hurting themselves. Mothers are destroying their children. It's all as blatantly obvious as it is outrageously unfair. Many fathers fought for their daughters to have every possible chance to succeed in society — whether it was sports, voting, college, or the workplace. Fathers stood up for their little girls. Men want women to be safe. Protection orders *are* necessary. But 85 percent of all Orders of Protection are unleashed during a divorce. Read that again. Men are tired of it all. Even as women complain that they can't find a date — let alone a husband.

Here are some facts regarding orphaned-by-protection-order girls who live with their single moms. Unlike the adorable little girls, these facts are not very pretty. The alienated young women are twice as likely to have a child out of wedlock. They are three times more likely to wind up in jail. They are fifty percent more likely to experience poverty. The young woman's need for treatment for behavioral and emotional issues also doubles when only one parent (almost always a mother) is involved in her life. Their grades will plummet, and they are more likely to drop out of school.

The fatherless young ladies are also twice as likely to now give birth to a child without getting married. Let's not even discuss the diseases and STD's they will become riddled with for life because they were searching for a kind and gentle man to replace the one that their mother raped out of theirs. Speaking of rape, the odds for experiencing sexual assault also sadly soar. Are you sure you want to drop that Alienation Atom Bomb on your spouse during a divorce?

It's urgent that society, legislators, appellate courts, and women themselves seriously work to change the system. Protection Orders do far more damage than good. The simplest act of not rubber-stamping orders without seriously examining why they are (obviously) being requested at the outset of a divorce would spare a lot of unnecessary destruction in the lives of so many children and their parents. It's a problem that is almost too easy to fix. Don't even worry about the men. Do it for the innocent children.

Study after study has proven the importance of even incarcerated fathers (even those guilty of violent crimes) having a relationship with their children. Even a ten-minute phone call a week is priceless and powerful in maintaining the parent-child bond. If it's so important for the child of a convicted criminal to have a relationship with their dad, how much more so for the child of a loving innocent intellectual father? *It's been almost ten years since I heard Ester's voice. I'd happily pay a thousand dollars a minute for a ten-minute phone call.*

A mother has to be beyond vile, actually demoniacally possessed, to harm her own daughter this way. But criminal narcissistic minds work that way. If something is in their way, they simply kill it or serve it an Order of Protection — which also has the potential to kill, albeit slowly.

The American Heart Association clearly states that divorce is a significant risk factor for heart attack. Throw in a few Protection Orders, police visits on Shabbat, family and criminal court appearances, all bundled with the alienation of the daughter you raised from birth, and it is surely a miracle that I didn't suffer a heart attack or stroke during my divorce.

The only thing worse than the unbalanced behavior of divorcing *Wives Gone Wild* is our criminal court system which has the highest rate of incarceration in the world. File for a divorce and you'll begin to understand how quickly you can be sucked into the belly of *that* beast.

If they could do this to me — a White, Jewish, Johns Hopkins graduate with a Master's degree from the Ner Israel Rabbinical College, publisher, author, teacher, diamond dealer, father of five — then imagine what they can do to a poor young Black eighteen-year-old whose hoodie is pulled over his head while driving a car.

He doesn't even have to be poor. I have African-American friends earning seven figures a year that cried when they shared with me how they had to explain to their ("I just got my permit Dad!") kid to never *ever* question a cop if they are pulled over. "Move *slowly* and do *exactly* what the man says." Blacks have this whole method for dealing with a mere traffic stop. They are forced to dehumanize themselves and act like Uncle Tom subservient castrated bootlicking slaves. It's pitiful. And appalling.

But most of all, it's sad that a Black mother is forced to hold her breath when she hears her happy and excited young man mouth those famous lyrics from Harry Chapin's song upon requesting the car keys from his father. "See you later ... can I have them please?" Her heart palpitates and skips a beat as she warns her child to "Drive safely!" because she knows "later" could easily mean *at the morgue*.

I thought it was tough enough seeking a divorce as a White man. Try driving a car for a while as a Black one. Drive slowly.

Get in touch with
AN WHO
OUGHT
ASHINGTON

ACTION FOR A DIVORCE
Jnwilling to
llow His Wife a
ivorce, He
larries Another
eir Kin, right, married Daniela
arbosa on Thursday night,
ough he has refused Lonna Kin
Orthodox Jewish divorce. Isaac
ekken for The New York Times

A new study from Cornell University and FWD.us claims that one in two U.S. adults have had an immediate family member (parent, child, sibling, or spouse) incarcerated overnight (or longer) in the land of the Stars and Stripes. Read that again. Studies have shown that even *a single night in jail* can be devastating and traumatic for the families involved. I can't recall one court date with Alfieri not growling while threatening to put me in jail for thirty days for contempt of court. For trying to explain the truth. The "truth" to The Alf was "interference with the administration of justice." It is at the sole discretion of the judge to decide if a defendant (or lawyer) is being disrespectful or if his ability to administer justice is being hampered in any way.

I have an old diamond dealer friend (nicest guy, and someone I trusted with millions) whose ogre wife threw him into Rikers on a Friday. Luckily, his father bailed him out the following Monday. But it was surely the longest weekend of Alex's life.

Alex's ex mother-in-law is a very wealthy established realtor who knows *everyone* in Westchester County. And I mean *all* the judges and politicians. Alex was mauled by the system. An exclamation point in a single text that followed a frustrated third attempt to see his children (after their mother purposefully planned their *not being home* on scheduled visitation days) was considered "aggressive contact" and a violation of yet another *urgent* Protection Order that was mindlessly stamped by Judge Bruce Tolbert in White Plains. Not understanding that *texting* is considered *contacting* almost landed Alex in jail. Asking his ex to see his children for scheduled court-ordered visitation was a crime in our *fuck-you-Daddy-Dearest* court system.

Alex had to spend the next *three years* on probation upon Judge Regina Kelly (who also practices real estate law and knew the local realtors) gaveling his egregious exclamation point as a threat. Twelve years have gone by and his ex-wife continues to blatantly defy Court Ordered visitation as brazenly as my ex defied her orders to pay temporary maintenance while alienating Ester. At this point his children, who begged to see *Daddy* when they were young, refuse to see or even speak with their father on the phone. *It's all about them Protection Orders.*

My friend Alex hasn't seen his two young children since they were three and six. They are now seventeen and twenty years old. His ordeal, like so many others, was very similar to mine. But unfortunately, Alex didn't have any passwords. No *Alex5521* for him. I spent hours begging, crying, and finally convincing him not to blow his or his wife's brains out. Eventually he got help. And a wonderful new girlfriend.

But Alex still lives in constant pain. His elderly parents, also jewelers, can no longer afford to retire. Alex's parents are also not able to spend time with the grandchildren they love because their daughter-in-law will not allow them to visit — punishment for their spending over four hundred thousand dollars on lawyers fighting for their son's visitation rights (that he was finally granted after a two year battle). Alex lost his million-dollar house and his priceless kids. He is now in arrears on his child-support and is in court where he faces going to jail. Pain is permanently etched on his once-young-looking face.

Alex refused to share the details of his Rikers experience with me. But his moist eyes betrayed that it was not pleasant. He also swore that he'd kill himself before ever going back to jail. Alex has given up on ever seeing his kids. My handsome, white-privileged, six foot, two inches tall, blonde friend easily aged thirty years during the last fifteen. It especially shows around his eyes. Their bags, unlike his empty pockets, are full of the memories of when he was a father with two beautiful young kids.

The crushing consequences of even a short stint in jail exacerbates the daily existence of the entire family of an incarcerated victim the longer the *innocent till proven guilty* person remains there. And the people who least belong there are treated the most harshly by the ones that do. The jungle is a place you never express fear. The other animals will instantly smell weakness and pounce. Onto your ass.

There is an incarceration crises in the U.S. today. The *epidemic* disease of being born poor and dark-skinned has grown to *pandemic* proportion in recent years and is now affecting our entire U.S. population. Our prison population has quadrupled since the 1980's. Forty years of political stupidity, imbecilic and antiquated three-strike laws, judicial *baboonism* (yes, I just coined a new word) and civilian ignorance has filled our prisons to overcapacity because of woefully deplorable judges like Victor Alfieri. He is, unfortunately, not an anomaly.

In the State of New York, two-thirds of the *inmates locked away from their families* are sitting in jail having *never* been convicted of a crime. Read my lips: In the Empire State, two out of every three people in jail, have *not* been convicted of any crime whatsoever. They are merely waiting for their trial date to be entered onto an overwhelmingly crowded court calendar. Their senseless pretrial jailing (waiting *months* for their *day* in court) *simply because they are poor* and cannot afford the minimum amount of bail, set by a judge that *knows* they don't have two nickels to rub together, decimates their already wretched and miserable existence and snaps the thin thread that held their minimum-waged uneducated-lives together and results in a free fall that sends them spiraling into an abyss of unfair plea deals, divorce, unemployment, drug addiction, illness, depression and even death.

Forty percent of Americans can't cover a sudden four-hundred-dollar expense without selling something or borrowing the money. That means that almost one out of two people would not be able to meet the typical standard minimum five-hundred-dollar bail amount suggested and set by most judges *for misdemeanor charges that quickly evolve into criminal records for life*. Not being able to post bail means being instantly detained until a lawyer can file a motion to review their bond, which can *easily* take a week or two.

And a judge can quickly gavel "Thirty days!" (if you're not obsequious while patiently allowing authority to pulverize your life) and still be in full compliance of your legal rights. He might even gavel sixty days, according to an amazing 2011 Israeli parole board study, that found that a cranky judge who didn't eat breakfast, or skipped lunch, would be more likely to dole out a much harsher sentence. The judge's education, the crime of the defendant, were less of an ingredient in sentencing guidelines than a missed meal. Talk about remaining impartial.

By the time a month passes by a father will surely have learned never to ever roll his eyes again when standing before a black robed life-coach and, in order to avoid those nasty rectal exams, quickly plead guilty if only to get out of jail and back home to talk to his little girl again, and to explain what happened to daddy. He also now has a record for life. And he now *knows* things that you can't even *imagine* to be true. And he will never talk about it. Not with his probation officer for the next two years. Not even with his wife. And certainly not with the authorities.

He will try, however, to explain "why he was in jail" on his next job interview. Good luck on even landing the interview — let alone the position you so desperately need.

At sixty-eight years of age, I trust most judges about as much as the average African American trusts most police officers. Every judge that has ever slammed his gavel as he declared "defendant is indigent and unable to post bail ..." should be incarcerated himself for inflicting such undeserved barbarous punishment upon some of the most helpless people in society. But unlike the angry young men, I understand that hate and frustration lead nowhere, and I quickly reflect that it is our entire judicial system that sorely needs *major* reformation.

We mock the disgustingly and outrageously inhumane Philippine President Rodrigo Duterte's war on drugs when there is endless work to do right here in the Land of Liberty. Let's face it. We are also an embarrassingly savage society of barbarians. And although our police aren't popping lead into the heads of suspected criminals, our criminal system is popping heads into jail for minor crimes. Robert Sapolsky has conducted incredible studies on baboons in the wild when he could have headed right over to the White House and Congress for his research. On a positive note, there are many wonderful humanists, organizations (e.g. RepresentUs), and powerful wealthy laypeople trying to affect change.

Speaking of Sapolsky, who considers our prison system prehistoric, I'm always amazed how this fascinating genius constantly shows up for major events to lecture in nothing more than washed-out denims and a blue jean shirt, delivering articulate words that are far more important to humanity than any "Peace on Earth" drivel ever delivered by any Pope dressed up in fancy thousand-year-old stylish *holy* vestments.

It's an innocuous observation, but worthy of taking note, that quite often, the less important or more deceitful a message is, the more dressed up the individual delivering said proclamation will adorn themselves to deliver the news. Bill Clinton is a phenomenally well-dressed man. Bill Cosby makes Bill Clinton look homeless by comparison.

"Clothes make the man," explains why obfuscating lawyers dress so professionally, and why doctors wear *white* coats. (*Think about that one.*) It explains the necessity for the leeching fairy-tale fabricated Royal Family of England — whose reigning monarchs *only* duty is to sire heirs to perpetuate its reality-show existence — to perform so many worthless, vacuous, and totally insignificant protocols, while wearing silly outfits for every historic *majestic* event since that first wild bastard Saxon probably grabbed a huge goblet and inverted it into a crown as he slammed it on his drunken head declaring himself 'King!' *Thanks for lecturing us peasants to give charity.*

"Apparel oft proclaims the man," as Shakespeare wrote, explains why Alfieri always wore a black robe, as the deceiving psychologically manipulative firm voice of the bailiff announced the idiot jurist's grand entrance by commanding, "All rise," as the buffoon entered the courtroom as we stood and waited obediently for further instructions to "be seated." *And society's dress code equation of "the less important, the more you dress up," probably explains why a writer like me sits around in pajama bottoms all day typing the truth.*

Give me one Robert Sapolsky (*I'm begging you!*) in worn-out jeans and I'll happily trade the entire lineage of England's good-for-nothing royalty along with every pompous pope, bishop, cardinal, and priest that ever lived, in exchange. And I'll throw in most judges for free! The world will be better served with this one scientist running the show.

If the likes of a Sapolsky ran our criminal justice system, the instant humane and scientific methods he'd very likely implement to deal with prisoners would result in astounding results. Sapolsky's science would also serve to map out the deranged minds of many of our elected leaders — many of whom belong with our incarcerated population. And truth be told, Sapolsky is one among thousands of brilliant men and women who could change the world overnight.

But it's all a day late and a dollar short for millions of innocent souls and depressed recreational smokers of marijuana that languish behind bars as they wait and wait and wait ... and it's too late for Ester and millions of young children whose loving relationship with their father came to a screeching halt the day their mothers decided all's fair in love, war, and divorce, as they took out an Order of Protection.

There are a half-million people that go to sleep every night in the United States in a six by eight-foot prison cell *simply because they are guilty of being poor*. The measly $350-500 dollar bail amount, rubber-stamped by a mechanical judge in an attempt to prevent a flight-risk (*Really? Were their Louis Vuitton bags packed for a jet-setting holiday excursion to Monte Carlo*?) immediately incarcerates someone merely accused of a misdemeanor and detains them with the same severity as if they were a serial killer.

Real rapists and murderers can easily become the "sleepover friend" of someone who merely jaywalked or momentarily rode his bicycle on the sidewalk to avoid a traffic light but then had the *audacity* to ask the cop why he needs to write a summons for something so trivial.

A quick escalation results with the prison-fodder being flung to the ground, and that good old reliable "he was trying to resist arrest" bullshit charge added to the original allegation to pad the *seriousness* of the arrest, followed by a likely literal date-rape by a gang of tattooed Crips twelve hours later as a reminder to "cross at the green, not in between." Meanwhile, count your blessings that you weren't suffocated to death in a chokehold by some steroid-enraged cop from Long Island for selling a couple of "loosies" (individual cigarettes, also known as a "cancer-stick" sold on the street at a slight premium from a freshly opened pack).

That initiation is followed by more rapes in the days to come once you've been "turned out." After all, you wanted it, or you would have fought it off. Meanwhile, as you try to make sense of the rapist's logic and adjust to prison culture while staring into a stainless-steel mirror at your black eye, you suddenly realize that the guards aren't there to protect you. They were placing bets on how long you'd last before being raped. You went from being the man of the house to the new *fish* bitch as you wonder how to escape becoming a *gump* now that you fell through a warp hole into a new dimension called hell.

Because you failed to show up at work, your boss already hired someone else to do your minimum wage job. But don't worry about that right now because you're about to lose your wife and kids. Kids, by the way, that are very likely on their way to foster care and becoming, in a few years, like the violent angry men who raped you last night. And the odds of your fatherless daughter becoming a victim of the sex-trafficking trade has increased seven-fold. On a positive note, the pension of the judge you'll eventually meet is getting fatter every minute he delays seeing you due to his over-scheduled busy court calendar. *So many important cases to hear. So little time.*

Think any of this is exaggeration? Then please Google "incarcerated dads." They should honestly be called "serrated dads," by the time they (and their children) are hacked and butchered by our deplorable divorce and family court system. A system through which the Alfieri's of the land fatten their pensions by pitilessly legal trafficking in completely innocent human lives.

It is shocking how quickly a poor person's threadbare life and family can unravel. You'll accept any plea-bargain deal offered in order to escape the system that legally enslaved your ass (feeding you on $5.00 a day while taxing the public $100.00 to *protect* them from you) as politicians complain about overcrowded jails. Your parting gift, by the way, is your recently HIV tainted blood. No medical insurance? We're so sorry.

Judges that remand poor people who can't post bail, while bemoaning, "It's the system," are evil and spineless pencil-pushers at best. They know damn well it's all about *'them Benjamins.' Their* own salaries, full hour and a half lunchtime, overtime, and fat pensions, all depend on their ability to over-schedule their *overburdened* 9:30 AM to 4:00 PM court calendar day. *It's amazing how badly they can bungle and butcher people's lives merely putting in five hours a day.*

Alfieri constantly asked his peers if they had any cases for him. The Alf was not lazy. He loved arriving to court and seeing a jammed-up calendar day. A *busy* day like so many others, containing the cases he repeatedly manipulated back onto his court calendar by rehashing easily understood issues ad nauseam, and by his complete failure to resolve the mundane matters of a divorcing couple according to state-imposed guidelines, procedures, and deadlines. Alfieri would merely scribble off an extension request that was instantly rubber-stamped by his black-robed superiors.

I politely mentioned several times that Alfieri's endless tolerance of my wife's attorney filing frivolous motion after motion to delay my urgently needed maintenance payments (that he himself had finally "so ordered!" thirteen months ago) was stretching our divorce out to years instead of the maximum twelve month "standards and procedure guidelines" proposed by the legislature.

Vic the bartender yelled at me to stop being *argumentative* (his favorite word every time I nervously opened my mouth) and told me he already filed for extensions because of how acrimonious this case (like all his cases) was turning out. You really can't fight the system. The punctual "time for a coffee-break and lunch" mindset of 'us versus them' shiftless state employees, guarantees their upper hand prowess in moving the wheels of justice very slowly. *It's easier to fight God.*

The Alf simply scribbled off his need for time extensions to the Appellate division that oversaw his caseload. You think they cared? They covered their asses by instantly trusting the integrity of a sitting judge and rubber-stamped his requests for extensions. Alfieri constantly blamed the lawyers and divorcing couples for *complicating* things. All requests were immediately granted without even questioning the coincidence of *all* of Alfieri's cases being endlessly drawn-out nightmares. So much for state-imposed deadlines. No one gives a damn. Taxpayers be damned.

Meanwhile the lawyers who got Alfieri assigned as their judge were thrilled. Alfieri's MO was to schlepp. Alfieri would even schedule a court date only to show up and forget what he wanted to discuss (i.e. waste time on). And so, he'd mumble while shuffling a few papers, gavel to see the lawyers privately in chambers (for an update and more wasted time), and then ask for earnings statements a *third* time. Anything to look busy. Or he'd extend yet another "urgently-needed" Protection Order. Anything to delay. Everyone would then shrug their shoulders and go home till the next PTSD court date.

I felt like the protagonist narrator in Edgar Allan Poe's *The Pit and Pendulum* story every PTSD second that I sat in Alfieri's courtroom. It was as sickening as it was stressful. I too experienced the dreadful torture of Poe's character in my fearful anticipation of "What was my inquisitor going to suddenly do next?"

Like my wife, Alfieri would grab every second of (time and a half) overtime possible. As a backup, The Alf simply created his own overtime. He always made sure to turn a three-month case into a three-year overtime case by grumbling at divorcing spouses in court to "figure it out for yourselves!" Or he'd yell "I'll decide all that after the trial," because his divorce cases always wound up needing a trial. The one deadline Alfieri vigorously adhered to was making sure that morning court ended by 12:30 sharp so that he could enjoy his one-and-a-half-hour lunch before resuming to further torture his victims at 2:00 in the afternoon. Court adjourns at 4:00. Why are you surprised that state budgets are always bursting at their seams?

Meanwhile, this country has roughly a half million untested rape-kits that are sitting in warehouses for decades awaiting funding to test the DNA of rapists and murderers who continue to perpetrate further acts of violent rape and unimaginable crimes. And don't forget that for every reported rape, there are roughly seven to eight more women who choose to remain silent. They know that the lawyers who will help them file an instant protection order in the future will unsparingly slut-shame them into oblivion for having a drink or two before they were raped. *So, Honey, what outfit were you wearing that night? Were you wearing a bra? Panties?*

Why not use some of the money wasted on two armed policemen delivering totally bullshit protection orders to harmless Orthodox Jewish men — and on paychecks for vile judges that have total immunity no matter how ineptly they stupidly dispense injustice — to instead test a few hundred-thousand rape kits? Society allows the divorce court system to spend hundreds of millions of wasted dollars a year judiciously-raping victimized fathers while allowing serial rapists of innocent young women to remain free while their female victims suffer endless PTSD for many decades or even a lifetime. And they are the "lucky" ones.

You would cry if you knew the actual amount of rape victims that could have easily been spared from a lifetime of emotionally-freezing upon the gentle touch of a man that they love, or from staring over their shoulder in a panic while their hand trembles as they try to turn a key to unlock their car door, because of a lousy thousand-dollar fee to test some semen on a rape kit. The money needed for testing those kits was set aside for Alfieri's overtime and future pension. Priorities? Most courts have direct control over their own budgets. The fox is not only guarding the henhouse. It's gorging itself like a gluttonous ancient Roman emperor.

Our state court system could not be more ludicrous or Sodom-like if it tried. Screaming headlines of blistering state audits which reveal mind-boggling waste are of little interest to the average distracted-by-Facebook mind. Federal courts have much higher caliber credentialed and experienced judges that are nominated by the President and confirmed by the Senate, whereas most lowly state court judges simply land their position by the appointment of their legislators or they are voted into office.

Federal judges hear complicated intellectual property, corporate, copyright and patent cases, and they rule on violations of constitutional rights. They are serious jurists and rarely issue a warning for contempt. Most are refined and dignified and their presence commands respect. Not their gavels.

A state court judge like Alfieri, by comparison, shuffles paper, issues Court Ordered scribbled decrees that are sloppy and confusing and often need to be redone, while rushing to intimidate with angry threats of contempt and bullying screams, while shuffling more files that he refuses to complete. Alfieri then complains about over-scheduled court calendars that are stuffed like some disgusting overflowing toilet because of his own shitty jurisprudence.

He then adjourns after accomplishing nothing and reschedules court dates. Six weeks later he returns to violently bang his toy gavel once again like a tantrum throwing two-year-old as he threatens to hold in contempt anyone who speaks logically for their being "argumentative." And the writing level of his almost infantile ca-ca correspondence full of typos smells as foul as his dispensed justice.

And municipal courts, with their endless nuisance laws, sneaky speed-traps, and plea-bargain "deals" that allow for no points against your driving record while shamelessly charging more for the pay-to-play coercion (that fills local coffers to the brim) are the most outrageous of all.

Unfortunately, the vast majority of criminal cases, and all divorce and family court cases in the United States, are heard by too many sloppy and inept state court judges — who attained their powerful positions by simply winning a local election or getting their appointment through the state legislature. Often, their election or appointment was funded by donations from the very law firms whose well-connected lawyers will now appear before them.

Throw in the way too many prosecutors that are completely out of control and care only about winning and their own future political careers and it's the perfect recipe for judiciary purgatory for defendants. The prosecutors constantly throw in ridiculous kitchen-sink 'conspiracy to commit wire fraud and money laundering' charges (on top of a parking ticket if they could get away with it), that threaten extremely long jail sentences, in an effort to intimidate and bully the accused into pretrial settlements.

Prosecutors constantly intimidate innocent people (who would have easily won had their case gone to trial) into accepting plea-bargain "so here's the deal" sentences. They stack on obviously ridiculous charges that threaten cruel long-term stints in jail. They contrast those potential decades of jail with an "extremely-reduced generous offer" sentence of a mere six months (with two months off for good behavior) if an admission of guilt is conceded. And most defendants can't afford to pay for the half-decent lawyer that would have easily won their case had they chosen to go to trial. The reverse occurs when a huge corporation goes to trial. It took a full two decades to settle the Exxon Valdez oil spill case.

My own "trial" to "prove my innocence" as a father who loves his daughter and would never harm her, after experiencing endless malicious prosecution that Alfieri absolutely understood and gleefully contributed to, would have cost me over a hundred and fifty thousand dollars. Abe Konstam, my horrifically nasty final divorce lawyer (who deserves to go to jail and then hell) refused to even address the issue in court. "Add an additional fifty-thousand to your twenty-five-thousand-dollar retainer and we'll talk about split custody of your daughter. I'm not going through a trial. You can't afford me." The beast was as heartless as Alfieri.

"So, what's it gonna be? Are you really going to roll the dice?" the prosecutor asks the poor defendant. Yet these traffickers in human misery can never be prosecuted for their own ineptitude or careless "mistakes" — like not handing over *all* their evidence to a defense attorney that results in an innocent man spending two decades on death row.

I was also given a plea-bargain offer reducing the potential one-year jail sentence I faced for "computer hacking" my wife's laptop. The baby-faced prosecutor fresh out of law school offered me "no time in jail and six months' probation" if I "promised not to do it again." Facing much more serious charges if my wife merely brought the exact same fake allegations again any time in the future, I interrupted him and responded in a tired and bored voice, "The judge sitting over there is more guilty of this 'crime' than I am."

Is it any wonder that the United States has the highest incarceration rate in the world? Higher than El Salvador and Cuba! That outrageously barbaric statistic should have all Americans hanging their heads in shame.

Does it surprise you that the majority of *profits* (aka, inmates) are held in state prisons and local jails, and *not* in Federal prisons? The only thing that runs smoothly on the state level is that everyone gets paid on time. And that includes all their overtime for wreaking havoc. And the taxpayer foolishly foots the bill while the "tough on crime!" politician raises local taxes for budgets that are bursting at the seams. I'm thinking of moving to Israel.

This year (2019-2020) will witness 24,229 marijuana criminal convictions fully pardoned with most of those cases expunged and cleared from the NY State court system. And this is merely the tip of the iceberg regarding the necessary reform that further needs to take place to melt the corporate fat of the belly of the beast.

It took literally billions of dollars of taxpayers hard earned money to arrest, prosecute, and jail all those *criminals*. Private corporations that pay politicians like Senator Biden (yes, *that* wonderfully progressive Biden) to write three-strike laws that will house innocent slaves, build, staff, and feed millions of modern-day slaves with "fighting crime" tax dollars while earning billions of dollars by providing cheap "prison labor" to dozens of major corporations like Walmart (owned by the Walton family), McDonald's, and JC Penny.

They all earn a pretty penny at the expense of too many innocent men and hoodwinked hardworking *Make America Great Again* taxpayers. Those heavily taxed citizens are then forced to eat dollar burgers while purchasing cheaply produced clothing by monsters like Abramoff. *God bless The Land of Opportunity.*

Wasted money and wasted lives is what most of our Criminal Justice System is about. Wasted money and wasted husbands is what most of our Divorce Court System is about. I only fail to mention the wasted children of those husbands because their priceless lives will be devastated and altered in ways that are impossible to completely calculate.

Much of our rehabilitation system still exists in the Dark Ages. Solitary confinement is still used punitively to crush the existence of roughly eighty thousand prisoners in America on any given day to the point of insanity or suicide. Many men in long term isolation cut themselves merely to feel anything. They will smear themselves in their own feces to break the maniacal boredom. They'll trap and befriend an insect merely to have someone to talk to.

For any minuscule human interaction and connection, they will lie on their cold concrete cell floor, for hours, simply to catch a glance of the approaching footsteps of the guard who will push a tray of food into their tiny steel cage — where they'll eat their meal next to the toilet in their windowless concrete closet. Prisoners will scream into the pipes of their sink hoping to be heard by another prisoner.

Thomas Silverstein spent thirty-six years in solitary confinement till he died (no cause was ever given) in May of 2019. It cost taxpayers $2,232,000.00 to throw away the key. He was first sent to prison in 1978 for robbery. Silverstein (no, he was not Jewish) then killed an inmate but that murder conviction was overturned. He then killed two inmates and fatally stabbed a prison guard several dozen times.

Even assuming total guilt for those murders, it is beyond cruel to bury a man alive in a six by seven-foot cell with bright lights that were left on continuously. Try solitary for two days (knowing you'll be out in forty-eight hours) and you will still be crying and begging for anyone to talk to within twenty-four hours. You'll probably go cuckoo without Facebook within minutes of your confinement. *If I could only post a selfie.*

"It's almost more humane to kill someone immediately than to intentionally bury a man alive," Silverstein wrote to a friend ten years before he died *(of boredom, probably)* at the Supermax prison in Colorado. Studies show that one twenty-second hug releases the powerful brain hormone oxytocin which immediately reduces the harmful effects of stress. I understand it's difficult to respond to a cold-blooded murderer who says, "I need a hug," but there are more humane methods of dealing with living beings than burying them alive.

And although the public can watch a trial whose details are transparent, the moment the prisoner enters the prison system, he turns invisible. To quote law professor Laura Rovner, "What happens behind prison walls, stays behind prison walls." And we're not talking about a trip to Vegas.

Forget about what psychologists term "skin hunger" (the need for physical human contact that is as important as food and water) that prisoners starve for. Simple human interaction — like a "Good morning!" greeting — reduces aggression and cortisol levels. Prisoners have shared that they were happy when the guards came to move them simply because they were touched by someone (even guards they loathed) when placed into handcuffs.

The blindfolded Lady of Justice, with her modern-day unbalanced scales and blunted sword, has been revealed as a naked, shameless, amoral, drunken, lying slut when it comes to our criminal, family, and divorce court systems of law. Sentencing guidelines vary greatly from state to state while the Federal guidelines are extremely complex. Oversight and accountability barely exist in a "Who will guard the guards themselves?" legal system. *Alfieri squeezed my balls for almost three years while threatening me with contempt if I so much as whimpered.*

Sorry Ms. Justice, but your pussy has been ravaged by so many litigious sleazy herpes-ridden divorce lawyers and Cro-Magnon judges that it stinks! Your once tight pussy has been fist-fucked beyond recognition. And your measuring scales have only served as chamber pots for the defecating-spewing mouths of attorneys like Schwartz and shitty "Court Ordered!" decisions by maniacal judges like Alfieri.

The only worse smells emanating from any orifice in our twenty-first century judicial system is from the bruised and infected torn anuses of gang-raped young men who landed on a factory assembly line that creates poverty-stricken children through a lifelong prison experience, created by society at large. The only *crime* the majority of these wretched souls are guilty of is being born into a life of poverty that moved them along a conveyor belt towards their "first time," when they finally understood what "Bend over, Bitch!" meant.

Judges like Alfieri who remand innocent husbands into jail for contempt for "crimes" as minimal as not being able to keep current with the outrageously padded invoices of their spouses' legal bills (whose hours they are not allowed to question) are worse than the angry rapist's and uneducated criminals already behind bars.

I say "worse" in the sense that there is no authority to supervise the judges and declare their actions as unfair other than a sign hanging in the asylum proclaiming *In God We Trust.* Fathers are disparaged and treated like criminals. Miss paying a child support payment and your driver's license and passport will be revoked. Wait till you see what you'll go through to be reinstated.

You'll also find your FICO scores dropping more quickly than your pants because, as of recently, the child enforcement agency is now reporting late payments to the credit bureaus. This is actually forcing suddenly unemployed fathers to disappear and live off the grid. The good news is that mommy is no longer lying when she tells *her* child that daddy is a criminal. The moment our criminal and divorce court system goon-squad gets their fingers up a man's butt they roll them into a fist.

I contacted Alfieri's supervising judge and wrote a wonderfully polite letter detailing my own trying ordeal to the Honorable Alan D. Scheinkman during my divorce. The man wrote back that he merely schedule's Alfieri's cases and that I would have to use the appeals process for any complaints about Alfieri's competence or judicial decisions. He was as heartless as Alfieri. He punted the problem right back to me, knowing that the appeals process is a very long and arduous journey and that judges favor their own. He could have done so much more. But most judges just cover their own ass. *While uncovering the defendant's.*

Like most government pencil-pushers, too many judges and prosecutors want to look good on paper. They could care less about what they are sworn to dispense and rarely bother reading most of the documents submitted to them. The only document they care about is their resume.

Incarcerating a father that loses his job during a divorce as a deadbeat dad while holding him responsible for *continued* child support payments, after revoking his driver's license, is clearly cruel and unusual punishment. It instantly turns a man who legitimately loses his job into a criminal. Actually, cruel and unusual punishment is when the punishment is too severe for the *crime* committed. Losing your job is not a crime. It's a sad part of the economic climate that millions of Americans are facing in today's market. And stopping dad from driving to job interviews is yet another example of our modern-day Divorce Court Inquisition system. The system is more than happy to lump all fathers with the rare one who is purposefully refusing to pay child support.

The added insult to injury comes when daddy tries to call his little child from jail. Perhaps hearing the sweet voice of his daughter or son will give dad something to live for. But in a for-profit prison and family court system that charges $11.80 for clicking "send" to pay your monthly child support payment online, and where a mere ten minute local call between a father and child can easily cost twenty dollars (it has to be recorded in case his three-year-old daughter is planning a prison escape for daddy), it should come as no surprise that the over one and a half million children who would love to speak to their fathers, whose prison wage earnings run anywhere from 86 cents to $3.45 *a day,* are unable to do so.

After all, soap in prison is very expensive and daddy needs to wash last night's ejaculate out of his anus. The system would turn daddy into glue if it could. *What century are we in?* Meanwhile the modern-day slaves earn the Walton family the accolade of being named the richest family in America with an estimated fortune of a quarter *trillion* dollars.

The only reason the prisoners and fathers aren't converted into glue is because they're worth more alive than dead. They generate a lot of profit that winds up lining the pockets of people whose names you will never read. Because they only appear on invitations to lavish charity ball events that take place at geographical locations you can't even create in your dreams, and at Yacht Clubs they would never be hired simply as a servant, that are attended by elitists whose wealth the prisoners can't begin to fathom with their malnourished brain that subsists on a five-dollar-a-day diet.

Alfieri roared his weapon-of-choice "You're being argumentative! I'll hold you in contempt!" charge to constantly bully me in an almost mindless psittacism of unremitting threats of incarceration. Vic never began with thirty or sixty days, always jumping to flagellate with an immediate ninety-day threat. And he enjoyed following through. It was sickening. His face looked angry in its natural pose. This man tortured me by allowing the ancillary court jesters destruction of Ester while starving me as he gripped my testicles through protection orders. Logic would claim it was merely to earn overtime pay. But the face of my inquisitor displayed that he enjoyed his work. Alfieri was the captain of the ship. And he steered it straight into an iceberg as cold as his heart.

And yes, man to man, I must admit that I would enjoy using his sourpuss mug as my heavy bag for one ten-minute round. I earned it. And Vic deserves it for destroying my baby girl's life. God could then reward me for doing a mitzvah. Then I would give Schwartz and Ferro a turn. I like doing mitzvahs. My ex could just sit and watch while waving and throwing a sweet kiss in my direction between rounds.

As my fiancée, Sharen loved watching me work out. She would hang in there and run my warm-up mile with me when we were engaged. My future wife tired quickly — just like in the bedroom. It wasn't like she couldn't orgasm. But it was more like a *whoregasm*. Business-like and professional. She'd then sit nearby when she was done, like she'd lay-there in bed at home, as she watched me for the next hour or so while I ran my next six to eight miles.

I had no idea that she was reserving her energy for our divorce three decades in the future. My *Bashert Vybie* would throw me a kiss every time I circled the quarter-mile track and ran past her. I'd throw one right back to her. She was so bewitching. *I still can't believe we're divorced.*

Maybe I could also put God's sourpuss face on the bag. Too bad the first commandment prohibits one from portraying any likeness or graven image of The Almighty.

I'm amazed that we're living in the twenty-first century in an incredibly scientific and technologically advanced era while our entire court system still creeps along in the Dark Ages, hunkered down in an "us versus them" mentality the moment a "belligerent" citizen who has "issues accepting authority" dares to challenge them.

Catholic dogma takes centuries for the slightest rays of enlightenment to shine through. But even the Church has stopped burning witches and Jews. Our donnybrook courts, stocked with aboriginal judges whose erratic and uncivilized behavior are destroying and virtually incinerating so many lives, must catch up to the miraculous science we now possess. Yes, miraculous! A slow evolution is taking place, but sadly, it is moving at an even slower pace than our "wheels of injustice."

It really is all about "them Benjamins." It's a racket that nets billions of dollars to those that are employed by our *In Our White Homophobic WASP God We Trust* judicial court and correctional penal systems that grabs minor children from their parents, incarcerates the poor for minor offenses, and shackles divorcing fathers into indentured servitude.

Perhaps we need to start paying more attention to *real* people like Shon Hopwood and Neil deGrasse Tyson instead of staring at the *artificial* behinds and forced-voluptuous silicon-filled breasts and lips of a few shallow drama-queen reality-show Kardashian sisters. At the very least, stare at both Shon *and* Kim. What we seriously need for our justice system are many more people like Robin Steinberg and Brian Stevenson. We need a little less *booty* and a lot more *brains*.

And the same holds for our plastic-political-parrot "leaders." Political parties must start offering voters brilliant minds instead of artificial smiles that reveal veneer brightly colored teeth inside of filthy lying mouths. I can instantly rattle off a dozen names of CEO's and intellectuals who could change the world. The solutions are already out there. Meanwhile, we citizens continue to eat Middle Ages shit when we could easily be feasting on Age of Enlightenment cake.

It's incomprehensible that we are still living in a time where *one out of every three* (I'm holding back on the exclamation points because the words are already screaming) black men between the age of eighteen and thirty is in prison, on probation, or on parole. And in urban communities the figure stands at over fifty percent. Blacks are *four times* (I'm still holding back) more likely to be arrested for possession of marijuana than whites, even though both groups use the substance at the same rate.

And non-whites are arrested way out of proportion for misdemeanor crimes like jaywalking, disorderly conduct, driving slightly over the speed limit, and that old reliable "resisting arrest" classic 'oldie but goodie' add-on. Because they are only being accused of a misdemeanor, they often receive a shoddy lawyer who rushes them through the system. The young men, accused of minor crimes, wind up digging their own graves. Just like many of their ancestors.

These "defendants," most of whom are completely ignorant of the law, often suffer from low intelligence after snacking on lead as toddlers or getting high on crack cocaine in utero. A childhood of being raised by a single working mother (if they are lucky and have only one incarcerated parent) who feeds them Fruit Loops and Wacky Mac that barely nourishes their undeveloped minds, leaves them unable to resist the intense pressure of a cruel social and criminal justice system that forces them to quickly plead guilty to minor offenses they were destined to be charged with upon birth.

They quickly plead out, trusting in their underpaid public defender sporting a five-dollar K-Mart tie, to get back to flipping hamburgers or stocking shelves — or to hustling petty crimes on the street for the gang that's become the only *family* they've ever known. Their barely legible illiterate signature locks them into a lifetime struggle for survival. They are treated far worse than wild animals, which is what they are perceived to be, by a punitive society that believes in "justice being served." Prison. Probation. Parole. *Ka-ching*! Let's face it. Not much has changed since The Temptations sang, "run, run, run, but you sho' can't hide," back in 1970. *Rap on, Brother, rap on*.

Unlike the three R's that they never stood a chance of learning, the three "P's" keep rotating young black lives like a scary horror movie popping-heads-toy, over and over again, through our criminally systemic criminal court system. Neuropsychologist Kim Gorgens explains — after shocking us with the statistic that fifty to eighty-percent of the people in our criminal justice system in the United States have suffered a traumatic brain injury severe enough to require hospitalization — that most prisoners are basically serving a rotating prison-probation-parole "popping-head" bashed-in-the-head life sentence, in thirty-day-plus incremental prison terms, due to their inability to fit into society.

It's hard to "fit in" when you are constantly being slammed in the head while eating lead paint and mountains of sugary foods coated in syrup. And you're only way out is more brain damage as you play football to win a sports scholarship to pay for college. And fucking hillbillies are still yelling, "No! *All* lives matter!"

Among the general public only five percent of society suffers from traumatic brain injury (TBI), typically athletes (high school football players), soldiers, and car accident victims. Poor judgement and impulsivity is one of the most common symptoms of TBI.

Try remembering to meet with your probation officer every other Tuesday and every third Thursday while suffering endless headaches, dizziness, fatigue, and poor concentration. *Why didn't you enter the appointment into your calendar?! Why did you lose your calendar?!* Display the irritability you have a sixty-six percent chance of suffering while responding to those questions due to your head being slammed on the concrete during the illegal stop-and-frisk search that you had an eighty-four percent chance of experiencing because you are Black or Latino, and you'll have to keep visiting your probation officer for eternity.

And don't forget to sign the dotted line (if you can see it with your blurry vision) of the rushed plea-bargain "great deal" offered to you by your court-appointed public *defender* that you are too illiterate to read. Oh! And by the way, we'll be adding six more months of probation to teach you to never miss appointments. *Numbers are fun!*

But don't worry about any of this, because with your poor cognitive skills it will be years before you even begin to fathom, let alone figure out, how badly you were screwed! *Just like your mama and grandma likely were*. Feel like smashing your head into the concrete wall while you sit in solitary confinement, yearning for human contact and the touch of a woman's gentle hand to remind you that you once mattered, while locked away by prison guards (who are not that much more intelligent than you) in their effort to *treat and manage* your anger? I wouldn't do that if I were you, my friend. You've already suffered enough brain damage.

A gentle huge forty-three-year-old black man can sell a couple of loose cigarettes and wind-up dead within minutes due to a sneaky cheap-shot chokehold — delivered by a pig who was previously sanctioned and disciplined seven times in the past for administering illegal chokeholds.

One can only wonder how many illegal chokeholds the Staten Island pig was not sanctioned and disciplined for by the time he decided to escalate matters and execute the "dangerous black man," surrounded by a pack of hyenas who were foraging for an easy kill to substantiate the hours of their time-clock card the morning they all murdered Eric Garner. *Does a person's skin pigmentation make them more dangerous?*

Calmly standing there and merely pleading and begging the near-minyan of cops not to take him (as a quota-filler) to jail, yet again, for his "just trying to feed my family" — as Officer Daniel Pantaleo slowly snuck up on his unsuspecting prey while stealthily loosening his left arm, with which he was about to choke his victim, from its shirt sleeve — cost the passive Eric Garner, who never fought back even as he was strangled by an illegal "weapon" that mercilessly cut off his air supply, his worthless-to-society life. The video was heartbreaking.

"I can't breathe! I can't breathe!" Mr. Garner gasped almost a dozen times as the clan (as in Ku Klux as far as I'm concerned) of blue uniformed hyenas fell on top of his beached whale-like prone body, pushing his head into the pavement, as they handcuffed their "suspect," while preparing to feast on their paid-for-by-overtime prey.

I couldn't breathe either as I watched the video, because I couldn't stop crying and mourning the completely senseless death that unfolded in front of my eyes. *They killed him! I can't believe it. They just killed a harmless, innocent man!* I was so upset, that I immediately called the police in a very professional and "concerned citizen" voice to express my consternation and was directed to a website where I was instructed to voice my concerns. And indeed, I did.

My diatribe and run-on sentences must have blown out the lights and circuitry at the police station. No one ever got back to me. I doubt that anyone ever bothered to even read my message. I even wonder if it was just automatically deleted into cyberspace. *Like so many black lives.*

The first official police reports claimed that Garner died of a heart attack on the way to the hospital. A decade ago that is where the story would have ended. But cell phones have done more to wake up privileged la-la land White folk (yes, myself included) to the lives Black people live than any investigative news article ever did. And so an autopsy was performed and Eric Garner morphed into a deceased guru whose senseless death would now awaken many sleeping minds.

I admire and appreciate honest and heroic police officers as much as I despise Staten Island *bacon* (police slang) like Pantaleo, who had quite a reputation for dehumanizing Black men upon ordering them to drop their pants while they stood on their neighborhood street. Daniel then dug his fingers up the rectum of Black spread buttocks in an "Your ass is mine!" rectal-search-for-drugs display in front of the protesting gathered crowd. Emulating Justin Volpe, who infamously sodomized Abner Louima in 1997, Pantaleo administered the all-too-common station-house bathroom-payback right on the public streets of NYC.

In fact, it isn't the deranged behavior of Volpe that shocks me. It's the dozens of enabler men in blue that stood around or sat at their desks while completely ignoring the horrific screams coming from the bathroom in which Abner was raped by a plunger — almost murdered as his intestines were ripped apart.

The police knew atrocious crimes were being committed as Louima moaned and begged for mercy, but not one single "Finest" officer came to his aid. They did nothing to help the handcuffed victim that was being held down by several of *New York's Finest.* As far as I'm concerned, any policeman that is part of the Blue Wall of Silence is, in fact, a Dirty Cop. One thing they completely share with the gangs they are supposed to be arresting is their complete aversion to snitching. "*Who? Me? I didn't hear nothin' at all.*"

Loudmouth white-trash enablers like Patrick Lynch are as sleazy as most divorce attorneys. Police Union officials jump to protect their own without even questioning possible guilt. These men bring shame and scorn to the rest of New York's Finest. Sad to say, but even the honest cops instantly back their own *Unzereh* men in blue no matter how loud the videos and evidence screams their guilt. The blue wall of silence might as well be a concrete one for the heads of people of color.

The city of NY settled the murder case pretrial with a taxpayer payment of 5.9 million dollars along with a lot of bad publicity for the police department. Four years after Eric Garner's death, Lynch, the head of the Patrolmen's Benevolent Association, is still using every tactic possible to delay Officer Pantaleo's day in court. I find it more than ironic that this hypocrite carries the perfect surname to match his bigotry.

Patrick Lynch described Pantaleo as "the model of what we want a police officer to be." He wasn't lying. The Staten Island bigot thinks that police sticking their fingers up the anus of stop-and-frisk minorities in public is a great way to control them.

Pantaleo used his degrading trick on anyone who *got in his face.* Guards use it in prison all the time. Pantaleo saw no difference in where his victims were standing. Behind bars or in front of them didn't really matter. He probably believes "those peoples" all belong behind bars anyway. Panteleo had shoved his fingers up Garner's rectum in the past. They were *intimate* friends. In fact, Pantaleo's fingers are probably the most fragrant part of his body. And surely his soul. He is a piece of shit. Feces probably comes *off* his hand when he shoves it up a human butt.

Pantaleo merely used his entire arm on July 17, 2014 to kill Eric Garner mindlessly and mercilessly — who was (you guessed it!) "resisting arrest." I imagine the *Policy and Procedure Manual for the NYPD* surely instructs police with the following policy and course of action permitting chokeholds: "any person of color calmly speaking with officers, while holding their hands up in the air as they are earnestly pleading their innocence, while gently trying to explain they were not committing any crime, but had actually just stopped a fight, constitutes, resisting arrest."

Lynch shouts that Mayor de Blasio has hands dripping with blood, while ignoring the cesspool of innocent blood that policemen like Pantaleo have spilled for nearly a century. Every court or grand jury that a policeman has to face is instantly labeled by Loud-Mouth-Lynch as a kangaroo court. His friendship with the NY prosecutor is closer than Adam and Eve's. Did I forget to mention that Pantaleo is earning more money and more overtime than ever before as he sits at a desk job waiting for this entire debacle to blow over (as it surely will)?

I would love to write the biography (Cigarettes *Will* Kill You, *2023, etc.)* of this man who was a father, husband, and "just trying to feed [his] my family" when a pack of stealthy attack dogs suffocated him as he repeatedly begged for air. Pantaleo then, for good measure, used both of his hands to push Garner's face into the sidewalk. An unarmed father of a three-month-old daughter (his youngest of six children) named Legacy was executed over the *alleged* resale, at a minuscule markup, of a few loose cigarettes without a tax stamp while *trying to feed his baby*. All that remains of his literally doing so is a beautiful picture on the internet of this giant man tenderly bottle-feeding his ten-week-old daughter.

Baby formula is very expensive. It cost Eric Garner his life. How ironic that Legacy will inherit a small fortune at the cost of her father's life. Her name could not be more prophetic. And her legacy could not come at a price more pathetic than watching her daddy begging for air. Can you blame minorities for hating police?

Imagine if society had spent the nearly six-million-dollar settlement on educating the gentle giant (and many other young men who are rotting in jail for smoking pot and other non-violent petty crimes) so that he didn't have to sell loose cigarettes. Those men would all be *paying* taxes instead of our being taxed to *protect* us from them. This is simple math. And it's very simple human decency. Black lives have to start mattering as much as White ones.

Add this to our math equation. Taxpayers coughed up almost six million dollars for "The City" to settle the Garner suit. Add in several million dollars of wasted payroll for the police gang that roamed the streets of NY that day searching for a body to fill their arrest quota, and for Officer Pantaleo's "desk job" while awaiting trial, along with the salaries of lawyers, prosecutors, and judges till "The City" finally settled the wrongful death lawsuit brought by Garner's family.

Do not for a moment fall for the Orwellian catchphrase of "The City" into tricking you into believing the "Us versus Them" mentality. In truth it's "Us" paying dearly for our being foolish in trusting *them.* Our politicians and leaders are the real "Them." And *they* are the ones who should be held responsible when police brutality and malicious prosecution occurs.

Police Union dues should go toward paying victims of *their* crimes. Our modern-day court system is the most flawless example of "The blind leading the blind" imaginable. And our politicians are as mindless as the people they serve. And here is the proof: Politicians constantly poll their ignorant citizens political views before deciding the platform upon which they will run for office. *God bless America. Land of dumb and dumber.*

According to the Department of Housing and Urban Development (HUD) it would cost a mere twenty billion dollars to permanently end homelessness in America. It would cost approximately fifty billion a year to pay for a free undergrad college education for those who graduate high school. Meanwhile we spend a hundred billion a year on police. Half of their efforts are a complete waste of time. Especially delivering protection orders during a divorce. And they have this real knack for racking up overtime hours. It wouldn't take more than a forensic accountant and a few strokes of legislative pens to instantly change the lives of millions of people. The solutions are as obvious as a police unit at a Dunkin' Donuts.

"The City's" prosecutor was smart to settle with Garner's family than to go to trial and pay a fortune later. He was right in having "The City" offer a plea deal, that, in essence allowed the taxpayer to pay for the senseless murder without admitting they (The People) *hired* the hitman Pantaleo to murder Garner. We (The People) got away with murder.

The city pays millions a year for nuisance tripped-on-the-pavement cases. Garner was nothing more than a nuisance. His family should have never settled. But their lawyer explained that it would take years to get to trial. And by then Garner's sons might get killed for selling "loosies." They were advised to take the bird in the hand. *Justice served?*

Life goes on in Gotham City. Great policemen, dedicated and heroic, get killed in the line of duty. Horrible policemen kill innocent people and get away with murder. Yin-Yang. I know there will always be both. I respect and love the good cops. I admire them immensely and feel they can't be paid enough for risking their lives every scary day of their career. Black ones. White ones. Hispanic ones. And my favorite, female ones!

But the Police Academy allows too many steroid-infused wise-guys, and emotionally unskilled idiot's, onto the force. And once they are part of their local police union, they are instantly part of the *Unzereh* Blue Wall. The sad truth is, as a society, all of us are quite barbaric. The sooner we admit it, the better. It's the twenty-first century and we are still dealing with social problems by locking men away in cages that zoos are no longer allowed to place wild animals. Think about that. *Keep thinking*.

Uniforms quickly transform Homo sapiens into the cogs of society. A black robe turned Alfieri into a God. A red tie turned Trump into a president. A blue outfit turns individual men into a police force. I suppose it's due to the same mentality that has us believing in, and dying for, imaginary lines on the earth called borders. Invisible lines that divide humanity into warring cultures willing to die for invisible gods. It's as silly as a bar-fight over sport teams wearing different color shirts. We think we live "in" Iran, or "in" New York, when we simply live "on" some latitude-longitude location of land on our planet. Wake up in Jerusalem or Sydney and all you can think about is peeing. And die anywhere in the world and Mother Earth will warmly welcome your body.

Meanwhile, while Garner was choked to death for *allegedly* selling a few tax-evaded "loosies" in Gotham-Sodom, the CEO's of all the major cigarette companies — who have mercilessly slaughtered millions of smokers, while earning billions of dollars, in total denial of a later acknowledged *premeditated* effort of adding nicotine to further addict smokers to their *lethal* product — arrived in Washington, D.C. in their individual jets (*couldn't these serial killers carpool?*) and stood in front of *our* congress, whose reelection campaigns are subsidized by *their* major stockholders, and falsely swore, while solemnly declaring with their right hands raised high in front of all the news cameras, that they are not adding nicotine to their addiction-enhanced products.

They were then compensated for their integrity with a multi-million-dollar bonus at the end of their illustrious careers. And I won't even begin to discuss the Wall Street CEO whose right hand never knows what his left is doing as he pummels the housing market with derivative contracts that are *too sophisticated* (i.e. legal obfuscated brazen theft) for the average mind to understand. And they weren't "too big to fail." They were "too lawyered up to fail."

Prosecutors (to whom the word 'justice' is as foreign as an interplanetary visitor) and lazy roid-raged policemen (under pressure to statistically show they are "tough on crime" before Election Day) prey upon the poor and ignorant lowest strata of society while shitting in their pants at the mere thought of indicting a lawyered-up CEO.

It's so much easier to later declare victory against someone with empty pockets than to dare indict an obviously guilty, but extremely wealthy, Jeffery Epstein, Bill Cosby, or Harvey Weinstein, whose pockets are stuffed deep with cash, and are able to reach powerful best friends like William Jefferson Clinton faster than you can order a latte at Starbucks. It has taken decades for justice to be served in their cases. Weinstein paid a king's ransom to none other than Ben Brafman till he hired another team. *Maybe being a nice Jewish boy and praying with a minyan really does help one to earn a living.*

This is why prosecutors have the easiest job in the world. They get to hand-pick the cases that enable their scoring an easy win. Of the 70,301 federal criminal cases charged in 2016, Preet Bahara self-indulgently gloats a 99.6 percent conviction rate during his *illustrious career* in his memoir (*Doing Justice*, 2016, etc.). What he fails to mention is that much of what was accomplished was unceremoniously achieved by pressuring defendants and strong-arming them into accepting a plea bargain. He is nothing more than a stuffed shirt — full of shit!

Prosecutors use the oldest trick shown on every television crime show as they bully the unsuspecting poor minority-colored pot smoker by "throwing the book" (charging ten statutes in the hope that one might stick) at the uneducated Hispanic or Black "criminal" who understands enough to know that he does not want to face a trial by a middle-class jury of his *peers*.

Meanwhile assholes like Alexander Acosta deliver non-prosecution agreements to privileged pedophile serial-rapists like Jeffery Epstein (close friend of Bill Clinton, Harvey Weinstein, and Alan Dershowitz) who raped and sexually assaulted over eighty young *minor* girls. FBI agents handed the ugly Acosta beast a thick file that they claimed could have *easily* put Epstein away for life.

Acosta barely slapped little Jeffery on the wrist, and he even granted immunity to all co-conspirators, and even to any *future* co-conspirators of Epstein. This enabled years of countless rapes and the continued sex trafficking of minors to be flown around the world as Jeffery dazzled the young girls with his seemingly endless homes, and the famous and powerful friends he rubbed shoulders with, as they rubbed him down, before he assaulted them.

Promises of an education and a future free of white-trash poverty were never delivered to these naive, unsuspecting, gullible as they were poor, young women who saw Jeffery, and his socialite sidekick, Ghislaine Maxwell, as their caring meal-ticket for a future life. And "all they had to do," according to Ghislaine, "was give Jeffrey a message." Often, they were raped before they even realized what happened.

Epstein could afford a legal dream-team that O.J. Simpson would have been jealous of. They were so good, in fact, that Jeffery's case never even proceeded to trial — utterly shocking the team of frustrated FBI agents who claimed they had amassed enough evidence over two years to "easily put Epstein away for life." Acosta basically tossed their file and years of hard painstaking work into the trash can, defending his actions in bullshit legalese obfuscation. You get what you pay for. *Especially from those you reward with a payoff.*

But for those who consider a McDonald's family meal "a night out on the town," cheap, hastily performed forensic science lab tests are often not all they are cracked up to be — especially when carried out by sloppy labs and lazy technicians. Seldom are results tested by other fellow scientists as commonly done during true rigorous lab experimentation. And so after being represented by overburdened Public Defenders who are friends of the aggressive prosecutor that promised a reduced sentence to his single incentivized "eye-witness" jailhouse snitch felon, many innocent men are rushed off to jail, wondering for many *years* about lab results that they could have sworn would prove their innocence in a matter of *days*.

In fact, of the 11,788 *homicide* charges by the FBI in 2016, *only a handful* were fully prosecuted by Bahara's office. The vast majority were withdrawn or settled as plea-bargained "deals." Surprisingly, even with all the technological advances of modern-day society, it's still not that difficult to "get away" with murder. And even upon getting caught the penalty for killing someone rarely exceeds two decades in jail. Typical stints range at approximately a dozen years behind bars.

But why aim at a target that stands a hundred yards in the distance when you can hit the low hanging fruit right in front of you? And so, most of Bahara's team's time was better spent, wasting time and resources, prosecuting 1,640 cases of narcotics possession — cases that will soon not even be considered criminal as our drug laws become more tolerant. Marijuana will eventually be legal in all fifty states. This country is "going green" as far as weed is concerned.

I'm really impressed that my tax dollars are being wisely spent on delivering Protection Orders to divorcing fathers and putting young men in jail for smoking pot instead of testing thousands upon thousands of rape kits. I can't be part of it all and I have refused to vote for almost two decades. I'm so tired of voting for the "lesser of two shitty evils."

Worst of all is the immoral prosecutorial game of using the second most common trick portrayed in crime dramas. The jailhouse snitch. Part of our lovely Secret Justice Criminal System. Criminal informants (even murderers) make off-the-record deals that remain totally invisible to the public, while allowing guilty suspects (while still in their "alleged" legally protected status of "innocent") to avoid prosecution in exchange for information or for their agreeing to be a witness against their partner in crime (who might be the more innocent of the two perpetrators).

The "evidence" they provide is notoriously unreliable. There are no rules to follow and basically no oversight. Detectives constantly use "The Prisoner's Dilemma" to hand prosecutors an easy win. Jack Abramoff never even faced any dilemma as he placed over two dozen constituents behind bars. He snitched faster than he acquired his bribed degree for Talmudical scholarship.

We are living in a time where scientists are producing artificial DNA. Most people can't even imagine what that means! Genetic engineering and gene editing are already producing banana vaccines, glow-in-the-dark cats, and fast-growing salmon. We are printing body parts and growing human muscle for patients who experienced half of one of their limbs being blown off their body in Afghanistan.

Science has become so advanced, that the only limit now is basically the imagination of researchers. And a wild bunch they are! They are certainly not afraid to ask, "What's next?" They are only limited by a moral (*how moral really?*) majority whose religious beliefs in a merciful God, a god who invented the very childhood diseases that the scientists are begging permission to cure, forces their representatives in Congress to mumble idiotic vote-seeking catch-phrases of, "No stem cell research that destroys human embryos!"

The politicians worry about the opinions of their anti-abortion and homophobic constituents who ardently follow the same Church that threatened to torture Galileo, but later found it more expedient to simply keep him imprisoned under house arrest for the remainder of his life. It took many more lifetimes (359 years) for the Vatican to finally admit it made a mistake (Surprise! The Earth *does* move around the Sun!) and to *finally* state that Galileo was not a heretic. I wonder if Galileo *finally* ascended to heaven in 1992. Surely, he orbited the sun on his way up!

We are supposed to be a country with a complete separation of Church and State, but much of our American law is based upon the "values" and often contradictory commandments found in The Bible (that contains an awful lot of assumptions). Many of those commandments became common-law precedents upon which most world governments base their legal systems to this day. That is why homosexuality and pornography were considered a crime in this country until recently. Love thy neighbor, but stone him if he is gay. Do not kill, but slaughter your son, Isaac. Innocent till proven guilty upon eyewitness testimony. But not if you are a father in divorce court enduring a systemic dysfunctional legal castration of your fatherhood while facing the authority of an idiot in a black robe.

Meanwhile "lifelong bachelor" J. Edgar Hoover had the world's biggest stash of porn — culled from his investigations into this "horrid" crime. It would be comical if we ignored the monster that Hoover was. Arafat was another closet homosexual who claimed he never had time to marry because he was already wedded to the revolution: the slaughter of innocent

Jews to complete the work of Hitler and make Palestine, "Judenrein" ('cleansed, of those dirty Jews').

The average citizen is still screaming for more guns, proud of themselves for knowing only one amendment among the twenty-seven ratified by the states, while our leaders express (nothing more than) their hot-air condolences to parents who cry over the shot-up fresh remains of their school children. I could almost go postal myself every time I hear those selfless "servants" of the public heartlessly politically-placating bereaving young parents with their "thoughts and prayers" bullshit while probably thinking, "I hope I'm not upsetting the NRA."

I'm always amazed at how the more shamelessly ignorant people are, the more they are supremely confident that *their* way is the obvious and absolute correct way — rushing in their unworldly arrogance to share their political, religious, and philosophical opinions while demanding that everyone instantly accept their views. "Lock them up! Execute them! Justice needs to be served! The court system — along with our tiny nanosecond-existing speck of minerals and water hurtling through space — cannot possibly continue this way.

I like to imagine that most people are probably dizzy because they are spinning at roughly a thousand miles an hour while hurtling forward in our Milky Way Galaxy at 1.3 million miles per hour. Heading nowhere. Exactly like the crawling ants moving aimlessly on the surface of our planet. Worker ants are females and typically live for a year as they run around serving orders of protection and spreading gossip. The life expectancy of a male ant is approximately one week. Their only function is to mate (*bye-bye!*). Seen from the distance we look exactly like our arthropod relatives. Our minds are moving even faster. In truth, there is no need to rush. We. Are. Slowly. Dying.

Speaking of dying, I had just endured six very long months facing possible criminal prosecution for "threatening to physically assault" my twenty-year-old daughter and for "being under the covers" with her. There is no statute that declares *being under the covers* as a crime. But one way or another, thanks to divorce court procedures and their failure to insist on some kind of detailed description as to what exactly happened "under those covers," my daughter's vague accusation instantly morphed into a criminal act for which I was now expected to defend myself in criminal court and somehow prove that I was not *under the covers*. It was a hazy allegation which directed one to assume that something abominable and odious surely must have occurred while "my daughter and her drunken-Lot-father" were under those covers committing some abhorrent sinful act of lust.

Neither accusation was even remotely true of course, but my life and emotions were in knots for the four full months that it took for me to finally be allowed to take the stand and set the record straight. My wife and her lawyer used those four months to destroy my reputation more painstakingly than a young female cancer patient planning her family's future after being sadly informed that she has less than six months to live. They portrayed me not as someone who was losing his mind, but as a pedophile who had always been a deviant. Seems that my wife of twenty-eight years never suspected a thing till the issue of *maintenance* triggered the control center of her out-of-control brain.

My principal was called by dozens of parents to *fire the dangerous pedophile!* To his credit, he put his career on the line and refused to terminate my contract in the middle of the year knowing the kind of person I am. Parents were insisting that even as a precautionary safety measure I had to be fired. But Rabbi Beller assured them the accusations were all based upon my filing for divorce from an angry, vengeful wife.

Rabbi Beller did not understand that Sharen was not "angry." She was literally mentally ill. Her entire life. And that is why, aside from being human once in a while, I am not angry at the wife God gifted me in his supposedly infinite wisdom. I mostly view my wife as someone who is "away with the fairies," for lack of an exact scientific term.

I'm not even certain that psychiatry has yet coined an exact name for what ails my wife. But the parallel dimension full of elves and Scottish goblins, that bewitch people while wreaking havoc with their lives, works. I am much more upset at God for being short-sighted and designating my wife as Ester's mother.

As an Orthodox Jew I am supposed to accept that God, with his all-knowing omniscient power, "knows" what he is doing. But in all honesty, God looks more like a bumbling Alfieri, in a robe of fire, as he delays and pushes off every case file that lands at the feet of his throne as he reincarnates soul after soul, repeatedly raping them into futile existence to fulfill their "purpose in life" as he refuses to face retirement.

From the moment Cain killed his twin toddler Abel in the original world war, where half of humanity slaughtered the other half over nothing more than a desire that sought being granted God's favor, the world has been one train wreck ride on derailed tracks.

Meanwhile, God hides in chambers, as he assures us through his holy prophets that he will eventually render a decision and deliver a just settlement for all mankind, at some future Day of Judgement, after one very long trial where he will take into evidence and carefully weigh, on a miraculous flawlessly-balanced scale, every act and thought of every individual ejaculated into existence since the creation of Adam.

Like Alfieri mumbling in response to my protest at his illegally dividing our retirement monies *before* signing our divorce decree, merely because my wife defiantly refused to pay the temporary maintenance that he ordered in court, God also seems to stutter, "I'll deal with the monies and any adjustments Mrs. Lewinson owes Mr. Lewinson after the (Day of Judgement) trial."

In all honesty, on a day-to-day basis, once again, the world looks more like it's being run by Koko the gorilla on steroids, than by a flawless, eternal God.

Through my wife, God put incredible pressure on me. His scandalmonger messenger instantly took out an order of protection to "protect" Ester. The grandmother of our two grandchildren then displayed her crocodile tears in a 911 call to have me tasered and jailed on the Sabbath. Then she tried to starve me (no job or maintenance) after forcing me into the streets. I was literally homeless overnight, kicked from a six-bedroom mini mansion into the gutter.

Without even stopping to catch her breath, my wife then filed *criminal* charges for computer hacking while simultaneously enlisting our twenty-year-old gullible and slow-witted daughter Sara to sign another order of protection that threw me into family court and necessitated an actual trial that could have easily resulted in my being labeled a violent child molester, resulting in my being labeled and registered as a sex-offender for life. I guess she was being honest when we dated, and she promised, "Nothing's gonna change, if you marry me, Zevie."

My relationship-destroyer wife used our sweet, but mildly gormless daughter to put me through hell as I sat through a trial, wearing a black yarmulke that professed my devoutness as a God-fearing Jew, with a false accuser-daughter for whom I emotionally and financially exhausted myself for two decades merely to keep her mainstreamed in school so that she would have some self-esteem.

A timorous daughter over whom I constantly worried and prayed that she might one day meet a similar sweet boy that she could marry, turned on me, like an attack dog, upon the command of her mother. I would surely have labeled God as a homophobic misogynist before imagining the possibility that my cheerful daughter would one day agree to publicly embarrass and defame me. To this day I wonder if my simpleminded twenty-year-old daughter fully comprehended what she almost did to me.

All this chicanery was launched the moment Sharen was served by a female processor who was instructed to wear kid-gloves upon serving her with divorce papers. And in case the damage of my being condemned as a sex-offender was not effective, my wife, once again, took the time to include branding me as a "violent man who was obsessed with feces," as she executed this follow up Order of Protection through Sara to augment the pressure she was already inflicting on me through her first protection order. *And I licked this stranger's pussy for thirty-five years.*

If I somehow survived all the above, and had a few minutes remaining in my day to pray for help, my wife made sure I was excommunicated so that I had nowhere to attend minyan. And in case I had a few seconds left to inhale, she found the time to patiently break Ester while turning her into a Tatie-hater as she destroyed that father-daughter relationship while decimating the one between Sara and myself. And, in a final coup de grâce act to impede my catching one last nanosecond of time to exhale, as my chest ached in anxiousness, God's Angel of Death manipulated our learning-disabled daughter Sara into accusing me of sexual molestation along with a threat of physical violence.

Knowing that God had the Tatie5521 password, even before my wife chose it as her own, caused my relationship with him to slowly dissipate. But that had already begun when my ten-year-old curiosity forced me to open that huge musty smelling Pandora's box that revealed his dark side on my birthday a long time ago.

It still scares me to recall how tightly my heart constricted when I first read the allegations of "being under the covers" and "threatening to mush my [daughters] head," in yet a third bizarre order of protection, initiated by my wife and signed (with the penmanship of a five-year-old) by my daughter Sara, delivered by two armed police at 11:10 P.M. on a Monday night, while they rubbed salt in my wound as they firmly asked if I ever hit my daughter or if I had any weapons in my house. As I closed the front door I felt a sudden anxious need to catch my breath, as if I was going to pass out, and I sat down on the hallway stairs on the exact spot Sara sat laughing when I allegedly "threatened to mush her head" according to the papers I now held in my hand.

The constriction continued sporadically over the next few weeks and further tightened when I again heard the words "under the covers" at the start of a criminal trial in Family Court in which I found myself appearing as the *(fucking!)* defendant facing the learning-disabled daughter, that I still loved, in her role — as the plaintiff!

I knew I could easily make Sara look like a liar and a fool. But I still didn't want to embarrass her or cause my daughter to lose the self-esteem I had spent two patient decades fostering. The child I lovingly taught to read, when her mom and Special Ed. teachers all gave up, sat across the small courtroom to the left of a judge who had the sole authority of deciding if her father, sitting at his right, was a potentially violent sexual predator.

I still can't believe this happened to me. I'm even more in shock that Sara's heart turned out to be as empty as her brain. I know that sounds cruel. But she's not "that stupid." I know. Because I'm the one who sat every night, on the edge of her bed, patiently sharing and explaining the major headline current event news occurring around the world, before she fell asleep at around eleven-thirty. That kindnesses, the "sitting on the edge of her bed," turned into, "being under the covers," in the cruel and dangerously manipulative brilliant brain of my Barnard wife.

Sara would hear my opening the electric garage door as I arrived back to Monsey. Utterly exhausted after studying and debating a folio of the Talmud in Brooklyn with Rabbi Nekritz for several hours, and then driving an hour and a half back home, I'd slowly climb the twenty steps leading up from our basement door as I entered the kitchen. "Tatie! Tatie! Please come up!" I'd hear my sweet Sara call over and over like an excited four-year-old. I'd ask for, "Just a minute!" so that I could go to the bathroom so that my kidneys would stop screaming.

No matter how long my day (my wife's alarm started shrieking like its taskmaster at 4:45 AM), I'd sit and patiently explain astronomy, religion, and events in the Middle East, Africa, and Europe. I explained our system of law and the presidential election, and what each political party stood for, as I sat on the edge of Sarah's bed till she fell asleep when I'd kiss her on her forehead and whisper, "Good night, Honey."

That fatherly sitting on the edge of Sarah's bed, and patiently teaching a learning-disabled child all about the world, flipped into an accusation of who-knows-what "under the covers" that somersaulted me, through a rubber-stamped Order of Protection, into Family Court for a criminal trial for violent sexual molestation. *And you think I'm a privileged Whitey?*

Those nefarious "under the cover" words, conjured up by my depraved *Eishet Chayil* wife who advised the impressionable gullible daughter we raised together for two decades, to now brazenly lie, will ring, like the never-ending faint tinnitus in my right ear, forever. "You *could say* he's a pedophile ..." my *Bashert* advised our daughter Sara, while her cowardly, always behind the scenes (like Rabbi Frank), older sister Rachel teased her with, "You're not gonna chicken-out, are you?" My cortisol levels must have skyrocketed to a level that would have even shocked that nice Jewish boy who grew up to become the famous Dr. Robert Sapolsky.

The one Shabbat morning of the year that I overslept (God sure punished me for *that* one) found me alone in my own house with my daughter Sara and a special (severely-retarded) child, for whom an all-merciful God decreed a lifetime wheelchair existence, who Sara often cared for. I spoke to my daughter for a few rushed minutes before I left for the synagogue.

Sara sat on the hallway stairs and I stood next to the front door through which I was in a hurry to exit. I can't recall the details of our conversation that morning, but I do remember my daughter still laughing when I said, "Good Shabbos, Honey, I don't want to miss the reading of the Torah," as I dashed off to pray.

That momentary conversation cost me unimaginable stress, angst, and my permanently damaged reputation, thanks to the very ungodly Yentas of Monsey. That very Saturday night, right after Shabbat, there was a hushed frenzy as my wife, her tag-team partner Rachel, and Sara kept whispering between themselves as they drove off together.

I went to play ping-pong with Mrs. Swaticky to exercise her ninety-two-year-old heart and then to the gym to exercise my own, figuring the three women for whom I would have once offered my body parts for a transplant operation were seeing Dr. Frank, never imagining that their eventual destination was a place our compassionate God calls Hell.

I had no idea that they went to the police and filled out a form together (my daughter is only capable of writing on the level of an average third grader) in which my impressionable lass claimed I had threatened to "mush her head" against the wall and stairs that she sat on (while laughing) during a conversation we had approximately eight hours earlier.

From that day forward my wife used the next four months to email and constantly update all her relatives and friends — including mothers whose children I taught ELA — about my being in Family Court facing accusations of molestation from "his own daughter!" Even though Mendelson was later outraged by the charge, and berated my daughter as a liar in court, my wife continued to work hard, spreading her initial lie and its accompanying Order of Protection. Sara's lawyer knew it was a lie all along.

Upon news of my having revealed the machinations of my daughter and defeating her in court, my wife smugly explained my "shocking victory" to all her friends by simply stating that, "Zev's a great talker. He won the judge over with his charming fast-talking personality." My wife is incredibly quick on the draw, pumping and blasting her next double-barrel outrageous "Grobe Luge" lie of psychological bullshit, milliseconds after you just spent many excruciating months in a trial surviving and unraveling her last blast. *I'm amazed that I don't weigh three-hundred pounds.*

It's been years since my divorce, and the Yenta's tongues are still wagging about my being "under the covers" and "threatening" to hit my daughter. Hannah, Vittie, and Devorah Radzik (a mindless, as she is loud, constantly cackling headache-inducing, witless Yenta) combined could easily weigh in to win a Blue-Ribbon Hog trophy — for virulent slander.

Their lips, that would never so much as press against a piece of pork, are still squealing pure unadulterated gossip with mouths dirtier than the snouts of the raunchiest bottom-feeding hogs in the muddiest pigsty you could ever imagine — somehow believing that their mantra-induced repetition of a lie turns it into the truth. The Talmud explains that evil people are called "dead" even during their lifetimes. The Yentas are surely the walking-oinking dead.

Meanwhile, four words ("I fear his wrath") continued to destroy one of the most loving and tender relationships that ever existed between a father and his daughter. *It was also destroying the relationship between God and myself.* Precious time had now been wasted because my wife's lawyer told Alfieri that I was busy with a Family Court trial facing charges of assault and molestation from "another daughter" (surprise!).

Schwartz and my wife had been insisting during our divorce court proceedings that I should be evicted from my home based upon the accusations of Sara. After all, there was a minor at home and Mr. Lewinson was "a very dangerous man." But because my daughter Sara's lawyer already made the request to evict me part of *her* petition, the decision to "toss Zev outta the house" now rested with Judge Mendelson. The Honorable Alfieri — as much as he would have loved to — could not decide my fate from his kangaroo-courtroom. The Divorce Court Judge was forced to wait for the results of the Family Court trial.

My wife and Schwartz had been praying fervently for a victory in Family Court so that they could claim that a convicted sex-offender father should not be allowed visitation, let alone full-custodial guardianship of his minor daughter. They were doing their best to kill two birds (father and husband) with one stone. This way there would be no maintenance and no child-support payments that my wife would have been forced to pay had I received full custody of Ester. As dense as Alfieri was, he fully understood the game they were playing. *Psst! God, are you paying any attention to all of this?*

My lawyer and I had originally requested full legal custody of Ester, based upon the relentless alienation she was being subjected to by her mother, for which I had too much solid evidence for anyone to bother reading or examining. My wife was in a complete panic. Not at my being the legal guardian of Ester (she constantly told everyone what a great father I was before I filed), but the thought of her having to now pay child support *and* maintenance forced her to reveal her true personality.

But both Margaret Smith, the Court appointed shiftless attorney that I petitioned the court to hire to represent the interests of the minor child Ester, and Margaret's eventual requesting a forensic psychiatrist, as Alfieri plucked a landsman from hell named Dominic Ferro (after Smith lazily chose to punt rather than running with the ball) as her successor, did not bother to read one word of all the emails or listen to one tape of all the recordings that I had amassed.

Like government contracts that are awarded to the lowest bidder in which the resulting work is often inferior and not delivered according to specifications (all too often a bridge will later collapse because of inferior cement or a million prison sheets will be a few inches shorter or of lighter fabric than promised), the court system also pays minuscule flat fees to the lawyers in suits pulled off-the-rack and bottom-feeder psychiatrists who have their own issues and can't find clients in the real world.

Dr. Dominic Ferro made a living dispensing drugs in the basement of his shoddy home to recovering addicts by overcharging them for his shabby evaluations (paid for in cash, like all drug deals) before prescribing whatever they desperately wanted. An alleyway would have been a more apropos setting to portray the quality of his professional care. Ferro was the perfect quid pro quo 'legitimate' drug dealer.

The *drug dealer* then supplemented this shady income by evaluating prisoners for the state and prescribing their medication regime, and by interviewing divorcing parents and then "recommending" to the court (i.e. the judge) which parent should receive custody. The judge, especially a lazy one, is going to trust the "opinion" of his credentialed professional friend as if it were etched in stone. Meanwhile the psychiatrist protects himself by stating his evaluation is merely his professional "opinion." An opinion that is so powerful that a trial after an evaluation in which the psychiatrist already recommends one parent over another is basically a hopeless scenario and a complete waste of time. The only way to even attempt to counter it is to pay for a second evaluation by another psychiatrist.

Our society foolishly places an amazing amount of trust on any lunatic that has the title of "Forensic Psychiatrist." We are watching way too much television and we're convinced by great shows like *Criminal Minds,* whose awesome actors have us believing that their forensic skills quickly resolve that the serial killer torturing young moms had a crushed left testicle, and walks with a slight limp, because his mother was careless when she diapered him as a baby.

Enough lawyers and politicians sit behind bars to curtail our gullible trust in those "professionals." But it is almost impossible to complain against someone who can instantly label you as a "psychotic narcissist who has no respect for medical authority" if you dare question them. The more you complain, the tighter you pull his "opinion" around your neck.

Even a forensic psychiatrist like Dr. Aruna Khilanani did not have her medical license revoked upon addressing an audience at Yale that, "talking to white people about race was a waste of our breath." In her *brilliant* expletive filled rant, she shared her fantasies of "unloading" her revolver in the heads of any white person who got in her way and then walking away with "a bounce in her step." Yale cringed and weighed their grave concern about the imagery of violence and profanity expressed by the forensic "expert." Then they compromised and posted her video as a commitment to freedom of expression, while simultaneously limiting access to members of the Yale community. *The rest of us dumb Whitey folk who attended Johns Hopkins wouldn't understand. So much for Yale's phony commitment to free speech.*

Dr. Khilanani describes all white people as "demented violent predators." Columbia University educated this angry demon. Yale University invited this hellhound bitch to share her wisdom. We, as a society, trust this fiend to treat our PTSD and preconscious fears and anxieties. And we trust her looney evaluations in any court proceeding more effusively than we believe in actual evidence.

Remove her soiled toilet paper medical degree, however, and Khilanani is instantly revealed as nothing more than an angry madwoman ranting her hate for any human being with less melanin than the other half of mankind on our planet. Although, in a broad sense, I believe that "art is anything we call art," we should not have the same "artsy" opinion when it comes to mental health and psychiatry. We are the ones who are crazy for placing so much trust in the nameless "governing bodies" who sign medical diplomas with ecumenical papal infallibility. It's a farce when a pope claims he cannot err in matters of faith. It's catastrophic when we place such faith in individuals like Khilanani.

Dr. Dominic Ferro — another licensed maniacal manipulator — yelled at me that he "wasn't getting paid enough" and that he didn't need to listen to phone recordings or read the email evidence I provided. Insisting that he was more than capable of "drawing his own conclusions" (a constant favorite term of Dr. Rabbi Frank), Ferro labeled reviewing actual evidence as a waste of his precious professional time. *Was he already talking to Rabbi Frank?*

It is of little wonder that Innocence Project is working hard to dismiss much of what is called "forensic evidence" in court trials. They have repeatedly proven how dental matchups and psychological "evaluations" were never anything more than an exaggeration of fabricated hyperbole spewed by an unreliable mind. (*On a good day.*)

A simple mitochondrial match (petitioned and paid for by the Innocence Project) instantly blew away many of the sloppy, credentialed, overstated, "medical opinions" that were often based on sloppier contaminated specimens, fabricated results, and ignored exculpatory proof that "just didn't match up" with the circle the so-called "experts" had already decided to draw around the bullseye hole.

The NAS (National Academy of Sciences) has much to say on this topic. But suffice it to say that television shows like NCIS, Law & Order, and Criminal Minds — that have handsome actors and gorgeous young women solving decades-long (in real life) cases in forty-eight minutes — have jurors completely convinced that any jerky kid who barely made it through med school is suddenly some kind of prophet of God merely because the descriptive title of "Forensic" was added to his undeserved medical license. *Might as well change their title to "Kabbalist."*

There have been over three-hundred and sixty DNA exonerations. And the Innocence Project can only afford to take on one percent of all the handwritten, tear-jerking letters they receive from prisoners all over the country who are begging for representation. Many of those prisoners fall asleep at night with ejaculate in their anus. They are as much a prisoner as Ferro and Khilanani are doctors.

Now that I had been completely vindicated in Family Court from the false accusations of my older daughter, I was back in Divorce Court where I was still paying my lawyer to petition for me to receive temporary visitation rights with Ester. I was literally (if we count rising blood pressure) dying for a few minutes to talk to her. Even a few seconds. Anything! I was fucking plotzing! I really missed her. She is so cute! And funny!

Alfieri agreed and said "it's way past time that we gave Mr. Lewinson some visitation" as he began to *finally* dictate an order for said visitation to the court stenographer. As I heard, "Every Sunday and every other Wednesday night," which sounded like angels singing from heaven above, the music was suddenly interrupted by my wife's attorney as he bellowed in his cantor trained, powerful Chazan voice. "There's a protection order for the minor child!"

"Oh my God!" Alfieri squealed from the bench, "Erase that!"

I'm hardly exaggerating when I say that I felt like grabbing one of the bailiff's guns and shooting myself in the head. I couldn't take much more of this bullshit drama. My heart was exploding.

Eventually my lawyer worked out a deal where I could see Ester, but "only" at her therapist's office, and "only" if Ester was accompanied by a court-appointed "Big Sister" that I would have to pay for.

"I'm sorry Zev. It's the best I could do while they have the protection orders on you," my lawyer explained.

"And off the record, you'd be nuts to sit there with Ester's therapist who can use anything you say to Ester *against you* in the upcoming trial. She can use any reaction of Ester or even interpret your kid's body language as 'fear' or 'anxiousness' at having to sit in the same room with you. And if Ester cries, for whatever reason, you're finished. The bitch can even say you're intimidating because you have a big head," he added trying to elicit a smile while warning me not to dig my own grave.

My heart sank to the point where I thought that I should perhaps take the well-intentioned advice of a female psychologist I visited a few times. A wonderful woman I had once helped with her own Jewish divorce in Riverdale, NY, who, at the time, tried to seduce me as she escaped from being the trophy-wife of a wealthy thyroid doctor in a sexually-frustrating marriage, some twenty years prior to mine. She almost succeeded. The doctor offered some meds for my emotional exhaustion (i.e. depression) after disclosing that I suffered from CPSTD. She honestly told me that I had, "lost my balls." Adding, "You're nothing like the Zev I remember."

It was a correct evaluation. They had been squeezed by a manipulative wife and God for twenty-eight years, and by Alfieri for almost three more. You'd lose yours too. But I chose the heavy bag instead of meds. I had some great workouts while imagining the faces of Schwartz and Alfieri imprinted on the bag. It's amazing how I could almost feel the endorphins freeing my mind from the dark clouds of threatening depression-laden storms and court trials.

I understood that I had to last one round at a time. I knew I would be pummeled. You can't hit a wife. And you can't slug a white-trash judge. I never imagined how many rounds I'd have to endure while dancing around the ring, but I knew I would survive. My own superpower is my ability to adapt and move on. *I'm still a child.*

My childhood discovery of flowing endorphins while playing basketball four hours a day, as I sprinted endless full-court miles, had prepared me well for dealing with a lifetime of stress. I was never going to allow my wife, or my God, to force me to kill myself.

Beads of sweat ran down my face mixed with the tears I shed as I realized that I wouldn't be seeing Princess Ester for quite some time. My wife really fucked me, I realized. Way better than in any bed we ever shared. *What's next*, I wondered, *death row?*

Death row was not such an idle thought after all, because for my wife's next act, I suddenly found myself appearing in yet another *criminal* court trial for computer hacking. Seriously! I was facing *a year in jail* because of the Tatie5521 password my wife had voluntarily given me over a decade ago. My eyes were popping out of their sockets as I read the summons that warned me in stern bold letters that I faced a warrant for my arrest if I did not respond immediately. Even after admitting in her deposition, under oath, that she had *given* me her password, my wife filed a criminal complaint that I had hacked her computer. And guess what? Judge Simon immediately stamped it! No one reads a single document on the state level.

I contacted Ben Brafman, who was a close friend of Rabbi Nekritz and yes, Harvey Weinstein's original attorney, who advised me to let my lawyer handle this for me. "You don't need me for this bullshit," he explained as he assuaged my fears in a calm and confident voice, assuring me that I'm not going to jail. "Judges know that crazy wives and sleazy divorce lawyers do this all the time," he added.

Sure enough, Judge Simon immediately dismissed the case upon my telling him that I'm going through an acrimonious divorce. "I'm not dealing with your meshuggenah wife," he added in his own high-pitched, annoyed Jewish-wife voice, mimicking exactly what Ben had foretold. Their filing wound up in the bureaucracy of Rockland's court system and landed on the prosecutor's desk who robotically filed it as some type of "State of New York vs. Zev Lewinson" criminal action. With the silent pressing of a rubber stamp against a single piece of paper filed by my wife,

I instantly became a defendant fighting the entire State of New York. If they can do this to Whitey, imagine what they do to people with a lot of melanin.

My wife and her attorney didn't even bother showing up in court to follow through and litigate her computer-hacking charges. It was obvious that she and her rabid Nazi German Shepard dog were busily chirping and barking, and filing more motions, simply to keep my blood pressure elevated. Obvious to everyone but Alfieri.

The immediate gaveled dismissal by Judge Simon, and his unwillingness "to waste valuable court time" (Alfieri's forté) in dealing with my wife, only came after two months of wasting my own valuable time racing to respond on three separate court dates to answer questions, and to refuse a plea-bargain "generous offer" by the prosecutor before a trial would even begin. All that time and stress merely to refuse the plea deal and finally explain to Judge Simon that I was in the midst of learning the ropes during a divorce on the arrival of the twenty-first century in America. Mission accomplished, Sharen.

I can't express how quickly I rejected the plea bargain deal when I heard the words "for good behavior." I wonder how many young, uneducated people of color are sitting in jail because they accepted "generous" offers by prosecutors, when all they had to do was wait ten more minutes for the judge to simply dismiss their case as groundless.

Thing One and Thing Two were brutal in administering nonstop trauma and drama. Between running back and forth breathlessly to three different judges in curtain call after curtain call court appearances, in response to my wife's awesome acting talents, I also jumped over hurdle after hurdle of protection orders acquired through perjury.

All the above was endured while living under the relentless continuous twenty-four hour a day pressure of sharing a kitchen and sleeping under the same roof with three females who all had their own individual protection orders against me and could call the police any hour of the day or night if they suddenly "feared my wrath." Yes, my life was a terrifyingly unnecessarily prolonged distressful run-on sentence. I'm amazed that I did not suffer a stroke. Mission accomplished, Alfieri. Almost.

Judge Alan Simon was eventually stripped of his judicial robes and even disbarred as an attorney for his court antics and angry ranting. The system finally caught up with the raging maniac at age seventy-five. A day late and a dollar short. He retired in disgrace. Big deal. Alfieri entered forced retirement at age seventy, one month after I settled into an uncontested divorce just to escape his cruel courtroom.

Alfieri was somehow able to finalize his career as "The Honorable" even though he was twice as bad a judge as Simon. I think Simon just screamed louder. If anyone ever wanted to write a book reviewing the cases of state judges, I suspect that Alfieri — as stupid as he was nasty and mean — would not stand out among the crowd of shit. For some reason, society honors these pencil pushers. I'm sure many of them barely made it through law school. They really are not that bright.

Monsey and Spring Valley are known for their dysfunctional government that grew more corrupt during the two decades that I lived there. The politicians are constantly going to jail. The judicial conduct is outrageous. Inept, cruel, sloppy, shameful, shocking, and vindictive are just the first of many descriptions that come to mind when I think of Monsey, New York. But in truth, our entire nation is rife with political criminals and mendacious state judges who have literal blood on their hands.

Groups like Civil Rights Corps are just beginning to barely dent the "old boys" systemic court system as they fight fire with fire by litigating the likes of monsters like Alfieri and Simon. They are also a day late and a dollar short, but hopefully they will receive the funds to help change and revamp our American legal system. "We the People" are woefully ignorant as we wait for a worthless check during the pandemic while our politicians spend trillions of our future dollars that our grandchildren won't be able to repay. Our country is financially bankrupt. Our currency will soon be worth less than toilet paper during a pandemic.

Meanwhile, the feds are constantly showing up early in the morning to raid a "nice Jewish home" in Monsey. There is always some scandal that results in a very big disgrace of God's name while delivering multiple orgasms to the Yenta's tongues. "The nicest people you ever met," are constantly doing the perp walk. "They were probably framed by the Goyim! And they give money to people to buy food for Shabbos." Sure! Why not? It's easy to give a few hundred dollars to 'Tomche Shabbos' when you're stealing fucking millions!

A Jew is supposed to die, if necessary, to sanctify God's name. But too many "Unzereh" Jews are only out to sanctify their own names with a nice dedication plaque at the synagogue upon their release from jail. A recent offense included seven defendants who defrauded a federal program that provided funding for schools. My old "friend," Judge Karas sentenced all of them a little more than a year ago.

I sometimes don't know who is worse — the Jews or the judges! Meanwhile, I'm the schmuck who paid the bill yearly to finance the theft committed by my wonderful Unzereh neighbors, along with financing the salaries of Alfieri and Simon for their role of playing God in their "In God We Trust" kangaroo courtrooms. Twenty-five thousand dollars a year on my house for two decades just to live in a corrupt Jewish ghetto while reading the LoHud morning newspaper in shock. Never imagining that one day I'd also be part of the local news.

Ester was becoming more alienated every day. A child that used to bounce up laughing the moment I entered a room she was in, was now sneaking into the guest room where I slept to toss dirt on my *deathbed* (as far as her mother was concerned). It wasn't enough earth to bury me. But the metaphor was obvious to my writer's mind.

Ester was also playing into her mother's portrayal of me by drawing childish pictures of monsters named Zev, while writing "I hate Zev" beneath the drawings. Her mother commended and encouraged the "art-therapy." "*It's alright Ester. It's good to express your feelings. Let it out, Honey. You'll feel better if you let all the anger out. I'm angry too.*" And trust me, my *Eishet Chayil* was letting hers out in her own twisted version of "Torture-Zev Therapy."

This all conclusively proved, of course, the "need" for Ester's being treated immediately for her anger at an "abusive father" by yet another screwy Hasidic psychologist with an online degree that had a reputation for hating men. "*It's in the best interest of the child not to have visitation with a father she views as a monster, Your Honor.*" Even the "big-sister" visitation option was now immediately withdrawn and off the table till a trial assessing my paternal behavior would take place.

At least I understood what was being done to me. Poor, eleven-year-old, Ester must have been so confused and angry. What she knew as an absolute truth in her little heart — *Tatie loves his precious Princess* — now sadly etched in alienated stone, was being chipped and pounded away through her gullible brain by her mother. "*Zev's destroying our family. He's dangerous. I can barely pay the mortgage and he expects me to support him. He won't even go to a Beit Din. With all his learning! He's going to make us homeless!*" My wife could easily make the Buddha suffer from anxiety.

Alfieri loved all this bullshit. He was happier than a pig in mud. After all, the messier his cases became, the more retirement he'd collect one day. It's barbaric to earn money at the expense of someone else's hard life. Mega Billionaire Bezos — who earns over three thousand dollars every *second* of every twenty-four-hour day — should be ashamed to look in the mirror after forcing his part-time (thus avoiding paying employee benefits) serfs to wear digital wristbands to prove they are moving fast enough while repetitiously boxing up online orders. I'm not a socialist. I merely feel it's obscene to earn money at almost the speed of light while forcing your workers to live on diets of cat food and Wacky-Mac.

But, unlike the selfish Bezos, what was truly sickening about the Honorable Victor Alfieri was that he couldn't wipe that constant smirk, which revealed his sadistic enjoyment at destroying people's lives, off his face. Bezos wasn't forcing people to work for him. He merely lacked empathy and took advantage of cheap labor. The Alf, however, would sit in court relishing the power of control he had over so many innocent lives. *It's all about control.* I must admit, that at that unenlightened time of my life, I would have paid five thousand dollars to slap that smirk off his face just one time. *How much would it cost to slap God?*

I'm still incredulous at my wife's ability to find the perfect lawyer and therapist to match her own bitter personality. In truth, she paid a consult fee to at least a half-dozen scumbags before choosing the sleaziest one she could find. She also constantly switched psychologists the moment one dared making the mistake of disagreeing with her. It was never *her* personality that needed evaluation, it was always a therapy session about "how to deal with" (i.e. control) the other personalities in her life.

I'm honestly amazed my wife went to any therapist. Because she sincerely believes she's the most gifted analyst of all. My wife had total confidence with any interpretation she threw onto anyone she evaluated. Like "nekritz" being "radicalized by zev." *"That was easy!"* She is unable to pause and read her own emails to comprehend and "hear" how foolish she sounds before hurriedly clicking "send" to spur her mindless email chain of henchmen to chatter "the latest" all over Monsey.

My ex was a reverse sniper. She'd take any action you did, or any statement you expressed, and then draw circle after circle of nonsensical psychological babble around the bullseye she drew, *after* blasting your reputation by pumping her double-barreled blast of ammunition filled with shit instead of gunpowder, while insisting her fabricated evaluation made absolute perfect sense.

"It's so obvious, Ze'ev! You deny! You deny!" And the more you disagreed with her, the more circles she quickly drew. With less logic but more creative license and inspiration than the hermit-like often-volatile Jackson Pollock flinging and splashing household paints onto a canvas, my wife was a flawless practitioner of Mr. Hyde forensic psychology.

When my wife liked you, you were God's gift to the world, and mentally stable and psychologically sound. But the moment you questioned her, you became a pedophile and a narcissist. Or you were stripped of your rabbinical credentials. And it was always a perfectly logical assessment on her part. After all, like Meir Kin's snippy remark of, "And I thought you were so intelligent!" when I urged him to give Lonna her Jewish divorce papers, how dare you challenge her?

I think my cyborg mainly enjoyed psychology because it gave her the language and ability to interpret people's feelings any way she decided they needed interpretation. She loved telling me

I'm passive-aggressive, selfish, angry, delusional, emotionally challenged, narcissistic, and two dozen other random ad hoc descriptions, that often included my relationship with my mother, or accusations of "defending my father," the moment I said anything other than, "Yes Dear."

In truth, my wife always had this ability to describe me any way she liked because she herself has the ability to instantly alter into any personality she chooses. She's a human chameleon that can take on the demeanor, emotions, psychological profile, and traits of any being on our planet.

It's so natural for her to morph. *Because she doesn't have a personality of her own to replace.* My wife has a brain that can gently soothe a crying baby she's carrying on her right arm, while simultaneously turning her head to scream into the cell in her left hand with the same single breath of air, begging the police in her most urgent and anxious voice to, "Come now! He's dangerous!"

Far too often, and justifiably so, psychiatry has often been generalized, documented, and fairly perceived as a "draw your own conclusion" pseudo-science of sorts, with the resulting evaluation frequently depending on whether the hired gun analyzing the subject being diagnosed was paid for by the prosecutor or the defense.

There was a famous 1973 groundbreaking study by David Rosenhan, titled, *On Being Insane*, that questioned psychiatrists' ability to properly diagnose patients with mental illness. He figuratively threw psychiatry on its own head. It's taken almost fifty years, and the addition of *real* doctors armed with neuroscience and technology, to make psychiatry and psychology a respectable medical vocation. It's no longer simply an *art*. Only now, in the early part of the twenty-first century, is psychiatry becoming a true science.

The more educated and intelligent among us are only beginning to understand that quite often what people once referred to as an "evil" mind, was never anything scarier than a "deranged" one. Just as eclipses are no longer seen as evil omens portending imminent disasters by an angry God, neuroscientists are using MRI scans, meds, and surgery to prove that the very people society once called *heartless* are, in truth, *emotionless*. Or they have other issues with emotions (or a lack of them), such as their inability to regulate their response when challenged (*or upon being served with divorce papers*).

Their serial-killing sprees were never the result of some evil demon whispering in their ear, but rather the product of a deformed mind from birth that *hears voices*. I'm still incredulous that almost half of all Americans still believe in real demons.

Depression is no longer attributed to laziness. And alcoholism, along with other addictions, is seen as a physical and emotional-crutch disease that often begins with a painful childhood or occurs because of a prolonged traumatic event. I certainly *drank* to that! And gay sex has become a lifestyle choice and is no longer portrayed as a deviant and disgusting perverted act that warrants being stoned to death or medically castrated to prevent its repetition. And interracial marriage hasn't been a crime in this country since 1967. Mazel Tov!

Whatever makes consenting adults happy is fine by me. And it's fine with any logical human being. It's time that we understood all those "ungodly" people who are not heterosexual while honestly admitting that it's impossible to comprehend a God who hates so many of the "perverted" lives he created as he lovingly breathed the breath of life into their nostrils.

Even as an Orthodox Jew I figured the commandment was always about making sure lots of babies are born. *After all, we need to keep replenishing all the children that God only recently allowed to go up as smoke through the chimneys of Auschwitz.* Stoning gay men was "one of those things" in the Bible that never made sense to me and that I told myself "will never happen anyway." Especially because you need two witnesses admonishing the gay perpetrators during their actual act of transgression, as they respond, "We don't care." Good luck with that. The whole concept is clearly not logical. Like getting forty lashes (minus one, showing the mercy of God) for wearing wool and linen when woven together. My bad. But honestly, I don't need to defend God. He needs to explain himself. I'm not the one who told Moses what to write in the Old Testament.

Violent minds are now understood as what they often are. Faulty-wired from birth — or damaged from playing football and competing in boxing and the martial arts. Or from being slammed in the head for not moving fast enough during a simple lineup at the police station or a surprise prison roll call in the middle of the night.

Only now are scientists clearly able to literally see the devastation and shriveled brain tissue caused by CTE, or even one well-placed shin-kick to the temple of an opponent during an MMA match. Sadly, most athletes laugh-off their headaches, mood swings, and memory loss. One of the side-effects of testosterone is that it makes young fighters feel their bodies are invincible even as their I.Q.'s are pummeled into mush.

And that is why I can't hate my wife. That is why I chose not to sue her for perjury. It's why I refused to play the divorce game that rewards litigious lawyers and amoral underhanded judges. I only feel compassion (most of the time) for the woman that gave me five gorgeous children. I must admit that, as crazy as she is, I still adore her potential post-surgical *"if only she were normal"* side. God, how I wish she was. Then Ester would have had two wonderful parents.

The overly empathetic, positive side of me, that sees condensation in an empty water glass as a tidal wave, insisted for too long on seeing the Dr. Jekyll maternal side of my sweet wife as she soothed and nursed our crying babies, rather than staring into the eyes of the Mrs. Hyde potential-wine-tampering lying psycho who was taking out protection orders and arrest warrants against a "pedophile." *Now I just have to stop viewing a full glass of dry red wine as empty.*

I'd probably still be with her if not for the fact that I ran out of width in my now hardened arteries while waiting for the eon during which neuroscience will advance to the point where it will treat the likes of the beguiling woman I married for whatever it is exactly that ails her. I'm all for "in sickness and in health." But you try hanging in there with "in deranged and in bi-polar."

In short, it's easy to prove a wacko serial killer like Ted Bundy was insane. Fornicating with the post-mortem bodies of the lovely women whose heads he bashed in meets the lowest of standards obviating any further proof of his sanity. Positing proof that Charles Cullen — a quiet unassuming wisp-of-a-male nurse who enjoyed some kind of deep control "gratification" while gently knocking off patient *after several hundred patients* — is completely out of his mind sets the bar only slightly higher.

And finally, labeling a soft spoken, cute Physician Assistant as a psychotic meshuggenah (as opposed to an angry divorcee) takes an awful lot of medical, psychological, neurological, and neurophysiological credentials. Or you can simply study the Cliff-Notes by reading her emails and protection orders.

I only get upset at my wife when I take the religious approach to assess her "disgustingly evil" behavior. Jumping with a religious mind causes me to quickly respond with thoughts of, *I can't believe what she did!* Not a lot of leeway when everything is simplistic black and white 'good versus evil' repetitious rhetoric. When I use science, and my enlightened meditative mind, all I can honestly feel is a deep sadness for Ester, and genuine compassion and pity towards her sick mother. I've become my own independent self-reliant *Burning Man*. A man who no longer fears burning in Hell. After all, we all eventually succumb to a "leave no trace" life. Who needs to fly out to the Black Rock Desert in Nevada? *Guess I'm no longer that religious. Thank God!*

I must admit that making love to my wife almost places me in a league with Bundy. Her emotionless soul made it feel as if I was guilty of practicing necrophilia when I slept with her. Her hands were skilled in the O.R., but my wife was awkward at playing sports. And she was worse when it came to being in synch in bed. Mechanical. Like the warped A.I. computer that controlled her frontal lobes. She basically imitated a woman having sex during sex. My wife's body was there, but *she* never appeared. Only now am I able to put two and two together.

That is why it took me so long to understand my wife. I had to become calm in order to hear my own inner voice above her anxious shrieking one. It's hard to be introspective when someone is yelling at you while calling you selfish. It's impossible to focus and write beautiful children's stories, and surely not a book like this one, when the two most important beings in your life are nagging and whining that you don't measure up.

I was harangued by my devoted belief in a pestering voyeuristic God whose penetrating stare could read the promiscuous thoughts in my mind, while he insisted that I had to even put on my shoes and tie their laces in a correct order and pattern every day, while never holding my penis in my hand when I pee in order not to be aroused, while studying the Talmud six to eight hours a day, while being married to a wild harem of pell-mell personalities out of bed, and an uncreative, immobile piece of deranged-dead-meat in bed. *No wonder I'm a vegan.*

Alienated children suffer the most and they typically lose precious guidance from the parent that truly loves them and would never dream of using them as a pawn or tool of revenge. Divorce is already a major upheaval in their lives. Forced to side with an angry or morally corrupt parent confuses a young mind and further exacerbates an already upended family life. And restricting a child from a loving parent adds an explosive amount of emotional and psychological trauma to an already tumultuous situation. Their life is already changing at warp speed in a *good* divorce. To then change their school, or last name, is akin to skinning off another layer of their now-bloodied and scorched childhood.

I know this from firsthand experience. Faster than my wife took out Orders of Protection, my own narcissist mother divorced my father and, as the ink dried on her divorce decree, married the married guy (with two little kids) she was fucking from across the street, and the next thing I knew we were having a "family meeting" in which she and Skip quickly convinced my two brothers to allow their last name to be legally changed from "Lewinson" to "Zarra." "Skip is making a lot of money now, and it would be easier legally if he adopted the three of you," my mother matter-of-factly explained. "If anything ever happened to us, the three of you boys would be as much Skip's kids as Sharon and Larry."

At twelve years old, I just looked up at Skip and innocently asked, "How would you feel if your ex-wife Hannah remarried, and her new husband was suddenly making a lot of money, and then wanted to change Sharon and Larry's (his two kids) last name?" My stepdad glanced over to my mom as if to say that there was nothing more to say.

That thought popped out of my mouth because an image of my stressed-out father, biting his pursed lip, jumped into my head at the thought of my Dad learning that I no longer shared his murdered father's surname. Aside from my brothers and myself, there were no other male "Lewinson" descendants to pass along the name. The Nazis almost made the name extinct. I have two sons and one grandson to pass the name onto the next generation. My brothers have four sons between the two of them that now carry the name.

No problem with racing back to your "Mailman" maiden name upon receiving your divorce papers, Sharen. Don't worry, I had it inscribed that way on Chezkie's monument. But bellowing, "He's not your father anymore!" was a horrific thing to say to our youngest miracle child. Like the Nazis, you took everything from me that you could possibly steal, and you destroyed every relationship you could destroy. *It's a good thing that I have no gold fillings for you to yank out of my deceased gaping mouth.*

I knew what a twelve-year-old child of divorcing parents experiences, and I sadly understood that my alienated daughter's pain and confusion had to be much worse than my own adult version. I had promised Ester, and myself, upon explaining that I was going to separate from her mother, that her life wasn't going to change by my filing for divorce. And although I was obviously unable to keep my word, I still felt very guilty for letting my princess down and not protecting her from undergoing the depressing and traumatic childhood experiences that I sadly knew would scar her beautiful facial expressions forever.

As worldly as I thought I was, I knew absolutely nothing about the unbridled power given to local uncircumcised putrid-putz smegma-riddled-brain judges, nor the level of scandalous incompetence of our Divorce and Family court systems. I knew my wife was ill, but it took divorcing her to realize how severely.

Like my father, I always acquiesced to any of my wife's demands in an effort to avoid conflict during our marriage. So it was only upon divorce that she displayed the lengths she would go to destroy anyone that challenged her. Only now did I finally understand that her exoskeleton emotions were made out of chromium. My skeleton was very soft and pliable. It was made out of empathy and love. Not the best armor to wear battling in divorce court.

The last thing my sweet daughter ever said to me was "Don't worry, I believe you Tatie." Ester had been taken to visit her cousins in Philadelphia for the weekend to celebrate Hanukkah. My wife and all of Ester's aunts and uncles were sitting around the table discussing "Zev's issues" and my refusal to go to Beit Din, right in front of her. Ester called me later that day and shared their "subtle" harmful comments with me. She then sweetly added, "Don't worry, I believe *you* Tatie." She never saw my eyes tear up as she said goodbye.

Those haunting words, spoken at the start of her alienation makeover, will remain with me till the day I die. But the adults surrounding her life — Ester's aunts, uncles, mother, sisters, therapist, my wife's new "go-fetch!" rabbi, and even her new teachers — were all expressing their sympathy for the "poor child" whose father "refused to go to Beit Din and was hell-bent on destroying his family." As I explained, upon being rewarded temporary full custody for perjuring herself on her Orders of Protection, my wife immediately withdrew Ester from the grade school she attended for the past nine years (her entire school career) and enrolled her in a new one.

My wife knew that my daughter's principal and his wife were outraged at the way she was abusing me. Rabbi and Mrs. Zaks even wrote a beautiful letter to Alfieri explaining what a wonderful and caring parent I was. They described how I lovingly dropped Ester off at school every day (for nine years), how I attended all the PTA meetings as Mr. Mom and helped Ester with her homework every night. They even described the face of joy that Ester displayed as she greeted me when I picked her up from school every afternoon.

In her typical Asperger *1984* payback fashion, my wife "unpersoned" them, along with all of Ester's prior teachers and school friends. Ester didn't understand any of this. My wife bribed and distracted Ester with endless riding lessons (my daughter's passion) and an explanation that the new school is "easier" and that she would have more time for her "Horse therapy sessions." Nothing my wife did surprised me. The only thing that would possibly surprise me at this point of my life would be that Ester and I still share the same surname.

My wife, by the way, in her constant assumed role of "World's best psychiatrist," labeled anything needed to improve emotional well-being as "therapy." She is more intimate with the mental disorders described in the DSM than the comprehension displayed by Pope Francis as he studies the New Testament, and she is immediately able to evaluate the psychosis of any individual upon whom she wishes to disembowel and castrate in one fell swoop. I tried "Divorce Therapy" to escape an Orwellian marriage. I then went through a lot of "Protection Order Therapy" with my wonderful *Eishet Chayil* during our divorce.

My wife can razzle-dazzle the foremost criminal-mind profilers in the world with her "deep understanding" of the human psyche. And she diagnoses with such articulate confidence that they'd believe she is one of them. She has no formal training and no credentials in the field. But her confidence can instantly melt away any formulating thoughts that might possibly question her narrative more quickly than a Hasid ejaculating on his wedding night. In short, she can roll her eyes without blinking. Case closed. No need for any other opinions. Especially in Yenta-Monsey.

Dr. Sharen Lewinson Psy.D. has this almost instinctive well-worn method of babbling generic general psychiatric evaluations of her subjects with such complete self-assurance that one is almost mesmerized into believing her and to then immediately question the mental health of any *patient* or ex-husband she chooses to analyze.

I still remember my wife's response when I delicately asked what caused her first marriage (to a neurosurgeon) to fall apart. "My ex was a narcissist," she sadly whispered as she lowered her gorgeous lying eyes. "He was very opinionated and kept getting fired from every hospital that hired him," the gentle voice of my Asperger goddess assured me.

Forty years ago, I didn't exactly understand what a narcissist was. But I knew I'd look cool if I pretended that I knew. I wasn't that interested in the new-craze pseudo-science everyone talked about that enabled them to control other people, other than to leave the most recent copy of *Psychology Today* on my coffee table to increase my odds of getting laid by the women I brought back to my apartment after a date. "Are you interested in psychology?" my Columbia or Barnard date would ask. "Only to the degree that it'll help me remove your panties," I jokingly responded.

I knew that psychiatrists were the only medical specialists that never examined the organ they treated. It's only due to neuroendocrinology researchers like Robert Sapolsky that psychiatry has evolved — from violent insulin-shock coma-inducing therapy, merciless ice pick lobotomies, shock therapy (the electroconvulsive kind, not the protection-order vomiting-inducing kind), and suicidal-causing pill-popping trial guessing-games upon a patient — into a true modern day science.

Speaking of lobotomies, more than 50,000 brain castrations were performed in the United States between 1949 and 1952. This wildly popular severing of the frontal lobe denuded the id portion of a personality and was a great method for controlling defiant children. Thank God I was born in 1953. I have no question my mother would have been tempted to use the procedure to deal with my "anger" (i.e. my knowledge of Rabbi Tellem's daughter fucking Skip Zarra while she mistreated my father).

But even forty years ago I knew that narcissism, especially the way it was confidently diagnosed by my future surgeon wife, was a serious enough mental disorder that necessitated no further questions on my behalf. So, trusting her, I nodded my head, as if I knowingly understood, and instantly believed the woman I was going to marry. With a mere five words she exited one marriage and was about to begin a second.

Guess which exact seven syllables my wife is now calmly enunciating, four decades later, as she sadly whispers to all our neighbors and friends, while lowering her gorgeous lying crow-footed eyes, to explain the reason for the dissolution of our marriage upon my serving Mrs. Hyde her latest divorce papers.

I still recall, and can't believe, the sincere wedding vows I once whispered to you under our wedding canopy Sharen, swearing that I would even die for you, as I stared at you intently, while you stood frail and whimpering like a beautiful innocent child.

I remember how you held a white kerchief to your mascara outlined eyes in order not to let the makeup run down your cheeks thirty-six years ago. Five children. Intimacy. Pillow talk. Pregnancies. Trust. Endless Sabbaths. So many holidays. Nursing so many babies in bed in the middle of the night, and my whispering little jokes to be careful that they don't roll over and suffocate you. Juggling a big family together. What happened, my sweet love? Didn't anything that we once shared have any meaning or sanctity at all? Talk to me! Where did we go wrong, Sharen? Were you always this certifiable? How were you able to bamboozle a streetwise diamond dealer and a worldly Talmudical scholar? Was I really the one who "made you crazy? Or was it God who created you that way?"

My *Eishet Chayil* psychiatrist has her own (obvious to all but herself) very serious mental disorder. She labels her illness under the accolade of being the "World's most organized person." She buys plastic containers and organizers to organize her last Herculean attempt to organize her previous five decades of "getting organized."

My wife still has shoes, clothing, accessories, textbooks, and boxes of things she purchased as a college student and newlywed. She is saving thirty-five-year-old toys from the childhood of our oldest child for our future great-grandchildren.

My wife also hoarded piles of magazines dating back three decades containing medical articles she plans "to read one day, Ze'ev!" (Pronounced with two syllables at my slightest suggestion that she toss them because the articles are outdated, and we now live in an online world where we can scan six drawers full of magazines onto a flash drive.) We even shlepped a dozen heavy boxes of *Physician Assistant* magazines when we moved from Riverdale to Monsey twenty years ago.

My *Vybie* still hoards files upon files of receipts and itemized expenditures (and emotional baggage) from decades immemorial with which she peppered our accountant for permissible deductions every year as April approached. Statutes of limitations have expired, but my wife still saved her paperwork "just in case." I have no question that she left a notation on her quarter-million-dollar divorce bill receipts as "therapy" for which she'll be asking our accountant for a deduction. Despite our home constantly looking as if a hurricane had just swept through, she always hung onto garage-sale junk and old clothing and she'd get angry at the slightest suggestion to throw something out or give it away.

“Horse therapy sessions” aside, Ester was utterly confused, frustrated, and angry. So was I. But at least I understood what was happening. How much can an eleven-year-old kid deal with? The sweet trust that Ester assured me would never be lost faded away as her combined Yenta-psychologist and “horse therapy” lobotomy sessions multiplied.

Ester was approaching her Bat-Mitzvah and puberty as a living orphan, estranged from the dad with whom she used to play her own version of the trust-fall game as she laughed hysterically while jumping into my arms from the tenth step of our hallway staircase. She knew I’d die before ever letting her fall. And now, not knowing who to trust, she was ensconced and surrounded by my enemies, whose tongues, like sharp swords (as King David proclaims in Psalms), were hungry for my flesh and thirsty for my blood (pressure to increase).

It is said that upon fully trusting someone with your life, you will either get a true friend for life, or the lesson of your life. The woman that I had once trusted with my life was now busy, full throttle, teaching me the lesson of my life. And the little woman in my life, for whom I would have sacrificed my life, slowly relinquished her trust in me. Ester was constantly being harangued with stories about my refusal to go to Beit Din, surely wondering why Rabbi Nekritz never insisted that I attend. And she was barraged with instructions to express “her true feelings” by a mother and therapist that had full rein over her impressionable young life.

Respect for my daughter’s privacy precludes me from saying much more. Suffice it to say that alienation is so easy to see, but only after the damage is done. The before and after picture of Ester, separated by an almost two-foot-tall stack of malicious prosecution perpetrated by my wife and her attorney to derail my life in a blizzard of motions, subpoenas, and protection orders, vividly portrays the horrendous about-face change in my sweet daughter’s once-adorable personality. The emotional issues she’s been forced to cope with have also taken their toll on her health. Perhaps it’s best that I do not see her. We both suffered through more than our fair share of pain. I doubt that I’d recognize her anyway.

All these scattered thoughts crystalized as I woke up from my laughing bout. The endorphins were medicinal. But once awake, the reality of my “orphaned daughter from a living dad” kicked in. With subdued sadness, and a calm deep breath, I poured my first cup of freshly brewed coffee as I vividly comprehended for the first time that alienation festers in both directions. Ester is becoming a distant memory, I sadly realized.

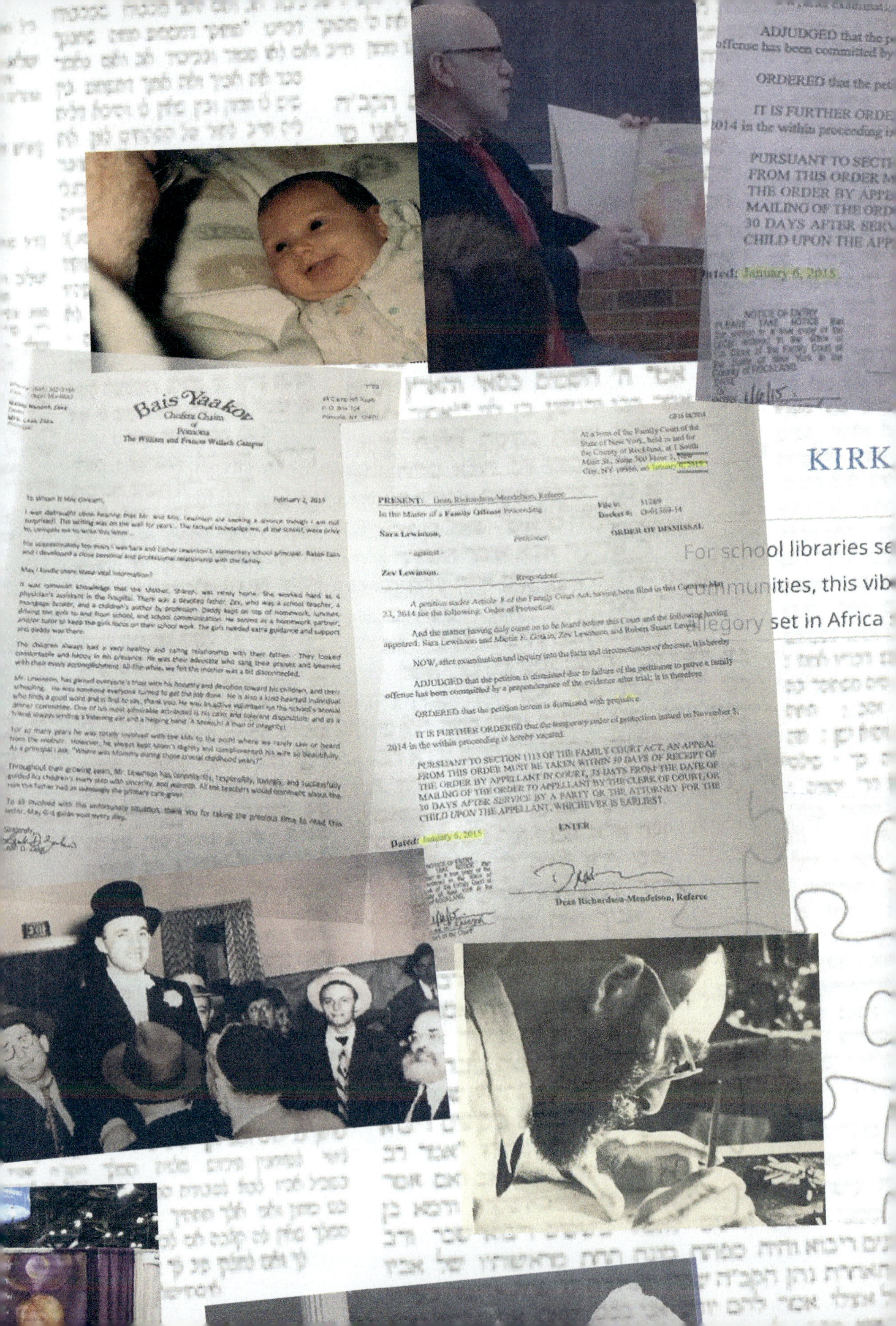

Bais Yaakov
Chofetz Chaim
of
Pomona
The William and Frances Wallach Campus
February 2, 2015
PRESENT:
In the Matter of a Family Offense Proceeding
File #: 51289
ORDER OF DISMISSAL
Sara Lewinson,
Petitioner
- against -
Zev Lewinson.
Respondent
23, 2014 for the following: Order of Protection;
NOW, after examination and inquiry into the facts and circumstances of the case, it is hereby
ADJUDGED that the petition is dismissed due to failure of the petitioner to prove a family offense has been committed by a preponderance of the evidence after trial; it is therefore
ORDERED that the petition herein is dismissed with prejudice
IT IS FURTHER ORDERED that the temporary order of protection issued on November 5, 2014 in the within proceeding is hereby vacated.
PURSUANT TO SECTION 1113 OF THE FAMILY COURT ACT, AN APPEAL FROM THIS ORDER MUST BE TAKEN WITHIN 30 DAYS OF RECEIPT OF THE ORDER BY APPELLANT IN COURT, 35 DAYS FROM THE DATE OF MAILING OF THE ORDER TO APPELLANT BY THE CLERK OF COURT, OR 30 DAYS AFTER SERVICE BY A PARTY OR THE ATTORNEY FOR THE CHILD UPON THE APPELLANT, WHICHEVER IS EARLIEST.
ENTER
Dated: January 6, 2015
Dean Richardson-Mendelson, Referee
KIRK
For school libraries se
communities, this vib
allegory set in Africa

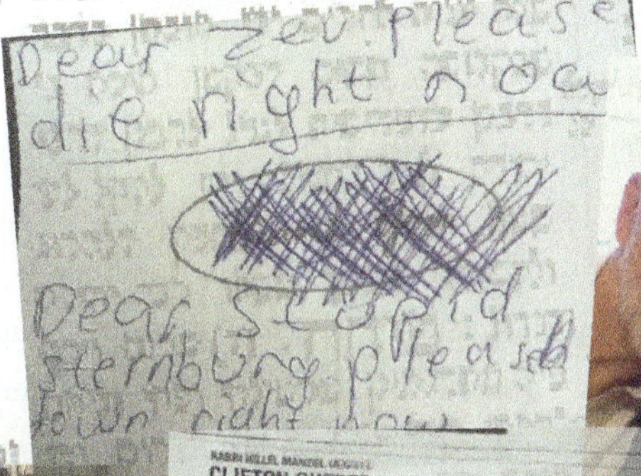

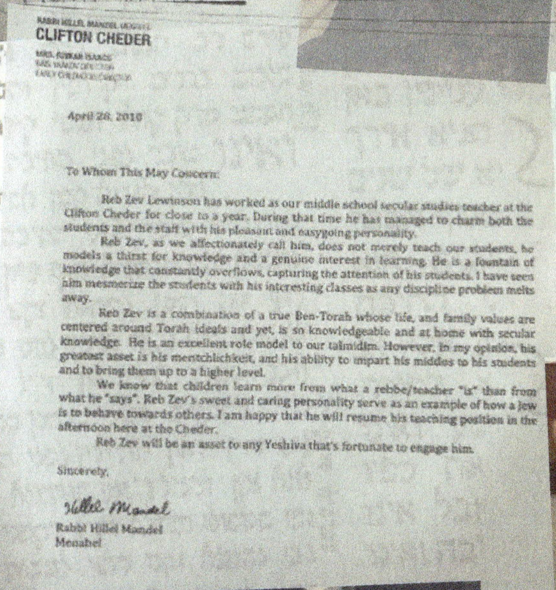

CLIFTON CHEDER

April 26, 2010

To Whom This May Concern:

Reb Zev Lewinson has worked as our middle school secular studies teacher at the Clifton Cheder for close to a year. During that time he has managed to charm both the students and the staff with his pleasant and easygoing personality.

Reb Zev, as we affectionately call him, does not merely teach our students, he models a thirst for knowledge and a genuine interest in learning. He is a fountain of knowledge that constantly overflows, capturing the attention of his students. I have seen him mesmerize the students with his interesting classes as any discipline problem melts away.

Reb Zev is a combination of a true Ben-Torah whose life, and family values are centered around Torah ideals and yet, is so knowledgeable and at home with secular knowledge. He is an excellent role model to our talmidim. However, in my opinion, his greatest asset is his mentchlichkeit, and his ability to impart his middos to his students and to bring them up to a higher level.

We know that children learn more from what a rebbe/teacher "is" than from what he "says". Reb Zev's sweet and caring personality serve as an example of how a Jew is to behave towards others. I am happy that he will resume his teaching position in the afternoon here at the Cheder.

Reb Zev will be an asset to any Yeshiva that's fortunate to engage him.

Sincerely,

Hillel Mandel

Rabbi Hillel Mandel
Menahel

I had originally asked my lawyer to use a female process server so as not to be accused of intimidation tactics by my atom-weight Barnard educated wife. Upon slamming the door in the female's face, my wife's second reaction was to turn around, motion for divorce (dated November 15th, 2013) in hand, and scream at her heavyweight husband in front of our child, "You're never taking Ester to fucking school again!"

Ester cringed as I calmly said, "It's O.K. Honey, I'll take you tomorrow."

But my wife was right.

I would never get to take Ester to school ever again. Because my wife's third reaction was to file a double order of protection that included "DO NOT TALK TO MINOR CHILD [Ester]" that abruptly neutralized the loving father-daughter relationship with the little angel I raised, as a Mr. Mom, from birth. I delicately wiped the newborn angelic shit from Ester's baby vagina, and I tenderly kissed the reddish-purple port-wine stains on her Buddha tummy while telling her she's so breathtaking beautiful as I reassured her that they would disappear before her wedding night.

I warmed up the milk, expressed from her mother's icy breasts, to perfect room temperature to feed my royal baby as I held her and sang songs while dancing around the room with her for the few minutes that it took to heat up her bottle. And I gently burped my cherub and then rubbed Ester's tiny forehead as she dozed off to nap. And while she dreamt whatever babies dream about, I described Ester's day from her hysterical and baby-philosopher point of view in a diary called, "My Day."

I carried Ester in a light-blue baby carrier on my hard chest, a chest that would have once served as a shield to protect her from anything that might possibly harm her. I took Ester on long walks and smiled at her as I told her to, "Look up at the birdies, Esti! They're singing just for you!" And I eventually took Ester to nursery school, promising her that, "Tatie is coming back soon, after you finish playing and coloring with your little friends." Then I'd be the (fifty-two-year-old) baby who cried after dropping her off as I got back into my car and stared at her empty car seat.

For eleven years my miraculously conceived, late in life, beautiful girl had been the apple of my eye. And now, in one second, Sharen and society gouged out both of my eyes with a fucking piece of inquisition paper.

I had no idea, not even the slightest clue, that my wife had instantly won a war in which she barely uttered her first insane battle cry.

I even anticipated my wife's imminent Oscar for her performance of "wife acting hysterical upon receiving divorce papers." I drove to the police station several days before the process server handed my wife her justification to destroy my life and explained that after twenty-eight years of an incident-free marriage, five kids and two grandchildren, that I was about to serve my wife divorce papers and that I was positive she would show up immediately to file a bogus order of protection.

The police laughed and told me it happens all the time. I even played one of the many tete-a-tete TapeACall (awesome app!) conversations I recorded, in which my wife admitted that I was a great father and gentle husband.

"Please don't run and take out one of those orders of protection," I gently urged her, "it will blow up in your face. Everyone knows the type of person I am."

"I'm not like that!" she screamed into her phone, "I don't think that way! I'd never do that!"

The policeman laughed at the recording. "Jesus! Good luck, man."

My *Vybie* kept her word. She didn't file one. She filed two! I still recall the shock I felt as I read the spurious legal document that I once believed was only served upon white-trash Trump supporters who beat up their women. I naively thought that I had headed my wife off at the pass by anticipating her psycho personality and warning the police about her knee-jerk reaction to being served. I didn't understand that the police just "follow orders." I couldn't believe this was happening. To me! I don't get parking tickets, let alone orders of protection.

I was literally traumatized as I read the fraudulent flaming letters, in bold upper-case commands, that seared my blue eyes: VACATE MARITAL RESIDENCE; STAY AWAY FROM THE PETITIONER AND THE CHILD WHEREVER THEY MAY BE; DO NOT TALK TO MOTHER OR TO MINOR CHILD; REFRAIN FROM ANY TYPE OF CONTACT WITH THE PETITIONER AND THE CHILD.

Meanwhile, I could not comply with the court order to vacate the marital residence because my wife refused to pay a penny of the court-ordered temporary maintenance, so my lawyer told me to "stay put" till he wrote to the judge. The judge understood the impossible paradoxical cross on which I hung, but chose to mercilessly spew my blood in his courtroom while banging the nails through my flesh as he yelled at me for being "argumentative" whenever I respectfully explained the legal quagmire I was enduring because of his "In God We Trust" *justice*.

Meanwhile, THE CHILD continued to sneak downstairs early in the morning to meet me in the kitchen to talk and laugh and discuss current events, but her mother would run in with her catch-22 protection orders minutes later, screaming, "Stop talking to her! I'll call the police!"

The order could just as well have read: HERE LIES PRINCESS ESTER. ALIENATED, BUT NOT FORGOTTEN.

Ester would sulk and slowly walk away. Eventually she stopped coming down to meet me in the morning. By the time the protection orders expired, so did my relationship with Ester. The huge hoarder-infested master bedroom containing two queen-size beds, where Ester was conceived, was now full of divorce paperwork and archaic excommunication fatwa papers. My wife had Ester sleeping in my bed from the day I filed for divorce.

I could easily hear the vitriol Ester heard late at night through the thin sheetrock that separated our bedrooms. That bedroom was the worst place for a young innocent child of a divorcing angry mother to sleep. It was a true alienation chamber of horrors.

I wish I could take out an Order of Protection against God: VACATE PLANET EARTH; STAY AWAY FROM PETITIONER AND HUMANKIND WHEREVER THEY MAY BE; DO NOT TORTURE OR KILL ANY OF THE INHABITANTS THEREIN; NO MORE GENOCIDE, POGROMS, OR HOLOCAUSTS; REFRAIN FROM ANY TYPE OF CONTACT OR INTIMIDATION TACTICS THREATENING HELL WITH PETITIONER AND THE CHILDREN OF THE PLANET.

It took approximately sixteen months, but by March 11, 2015 Ester would no longer respond to any of my morning conversation. She completely refused to speak. She would not make eye contact with me. She even controlled herself not to laugh at anything I said. The reason I know the date is because I was still taping Ester to show my lawyer the alienation that was taking place.

On the tape you can hear a pitiful father, in his typical soft-spoken voice, trying to engage his daughter in some topic that he knew she'd find interesting. But it seems that Ester's mother had taught her the sadistic torture of dehumanizing and turning someone you once loved into an *Unperson*. That was the day the music died for me.

The bed in which Ester was brought to life was now the coffin of her alienation from a father that stuck-out the dull-throbbing pain of a mirage marriage in exchange for the honor of being Mr. Mom to Her Royal Cuteness. I have no regrets. Her laughter was worth the pain. Sadly, I hear she's not laughing too much anymore.

Ester eventually forgot, or perhaps it was too painful for her to remember, how much she used to laugh with her Tatie. We used to jog together and then cool down and have "deep and meaningful conversations" (Ester's description) when we finally sat down to rest. She was growing up quickly and the day Ester could probably have beaten me in a short sprint seemed not too far away. But that day never arrived.

I had also been teaching Ester how to play basketball and she would get the hiccups from laughing hysterically when I would do my best to imitate the Harlem Globetrotters. "Come on, Ester! Steal the ball from me!" I'd lovingly tease her while warning her not to jam her fingers. God, how I miss her funny facial expressions. The protection orders protected my sweet princess from any future hiccups. They also stole her from my love and fatherly attention and stalemated any chance of visitation for a full year and a half till a trial ascertaining my worthiness as a father could be determined. And even if I won, it would still take years before Alfieri would allow me more than an hour or two a week, under strict conditions and supervision, to speak with my own daughter. After all, she had been severely traumatized, and we wouldn't want to harm "THE MINOR CHILD."

Alfieri had this knack to keep delaying, stalling, and pushing off every single issue (temporary maintenance, visitation, alienation charges, perjured protection orders, my lawyers fees, etc...) of our divorce file into some distant messianic future, at which time he would prophetically reveal his jaundiced wisdom and what he would finally decree upon the lives he was destroying by procrastinating and yelling "Figure it out yourselves!" All while calculating the overtime pay he was earning. The only thing Victor Alfieri did "correctly" was his division of our life savings. But he did it prematurely, enabling my wife not to pay the maintenance and legal fees he "So ordered!" (five prior times) during our divorce before he signed off on our final divorce decree. It was a completely illegal act. I could have easily won an appeal. But a defendant can only appeal one decision at a time. And each one costs anywhere from twelve to fifteen thousand dollars to contest.

Like God, Alfieri could issue illogical catch-22 edicts full of wrath that one would be held in contempt and threatened with "ninety days!" for even questioning, while greedily enjoying the forcefully tithed monetary fruits and the sacrificed bloodied childhoods of his defendant's parenting labor and physical toil, as he kept pushing off his final Day of Judgement, when The Savior Idiot promised to finally give a reckoning of my divorce and reveal how destroying a child and her dad made sense after all.

Till that revelation would occur, "Figure it out yourselves!" was the only sagacious advice constantly hollered by the angry baboon as he complained about his heavy overload of file cases for which he would one day collect a royal pension in a Garden of Eden full of bananas.

Even after insisting that I was to receive temporary maintenance, admitting with complete disdain to my face (and all he knew about me at that time was that I wore a yarmulke on my big head), in open court, that he had "no other choice" based on the numbers of our five-year tax return schedules, His Honor refused to enforce his own "So Ordered" court directives. I don't know if it was the yarmulke on my head or the cruelness in his heart, but Victor Alfieri continued to give my wife over nine months of chances and warnings to start paying the maintenance that he had calculated and ordered her to pay as the "moneyed spouse" within four months of our first court appearance. And at four months he was already three months late in response to an "urgent request for temporary maintenance" filed by my lawyer.

Thirteen months into proceedings His Honorable Brute finally vociferously demanded that my wife "Stop playing games and pay Mr. Lewinson!" the temporary maintenance of $3400.00 a month, which by now had accumulated to almost forty-five thousand dollars, along with an immediate $7,500.00 payment toward my legal fees. The true amount was $3,800.00 a month. But when my sloppy lawyer requested to amend his mistake, The Alf just snapped, "Your client signed off on $3,400.00 a month, so that's all he's getting!" I, of course, signed the paper my lawyer placed in front of me. No second chances for my lawyer to correct his mistakes. But a year of precious time for my wife to pay her lawyer to file endless frivolous motions to delay paying me a penny of temporary maintenance.

I'm hardly exaggerating when I write that I was not that far from emulating my father and searching for potato peals in garbage cans. But now it seemed as if Alfieri had run out of excuses to delay any longer. "If Mr. Lewinson was a *Mrs*. Lewinson and *you* were the husband, you would have been in jail months ago!" Alfieri fumed at my wife in open court. You could almost see the flames exiting the mouth of the dragon. *Who would have imagined that they were nothing more than hot air?*

Amazingly undaunted by Alfieri's screaming, my fearless cyborg (organic body, mechanical mind) stared at The Alf completely unintimidated and chirped, "I don't have it. I just don't have it!" Meanwhile she was writing out checks for over ten thousand dollars a month to the nightmarish dream-team law firm of Kantrowitz, Goldhamer, and Graifman, whose tag line was "The Fine Art of Practicing Law." Dan Schwartz, a low-ranking member of said firm who was on the verge of being dismissed due to his inability to bring in clients (I can't imagine why), took that tag line and perfected it into "The Fine Art of Throwing Shit" as he insisted that his client [my wife] "was the moneyed spouse only because Zev was lazy and never worked a day in his life."

My wife's lawyer delayed her having to pay any of the urgent maintenance Alfieri ordered by filing motion after bullshit motion, in an obvious wasted effort of pure obfuscation, as Kapo Schwartz repetitively implored and insisted that the judge dismiss all of his prior directives to pay me any temporary maintenance.

Dan Schwartz claimed that my wife's "generosity" had allowed me to stay home as "a lazy good-for-nothing Mr. Mom." He further claimed that a full twenty-five percent of my wife's salary over the past five years had been due to her working overtime at the hospital while I "ate sushi and drank saké all day," and that her overtime pay should not be included in the temporary maintenance support, since upon divorce she'd have to be home earlier to take care of the minor child.

I listened red-faced to the well-rehearsed lines composed by my wife in her early morning emails to Schwartz that were now flawlessly bellowed as they poured through the throat (deserving cancer) of her cantor lawyer, and I whispered to Robert Lewis, my lame lawyer, "Don't just sit there! Say something!" But Lazy Lewis just sat there like a doofus dolt and whispered back to me, "Sit tight! Alfieri knows that Schwartz is just a clown." A clown that I didn't find very entertaining.

Having to suffer a loafing mute mouthpiece for a lawyer I decided to call out Schwartz's feeble logic to Alfieri: "How can Dan Schwartz call me a "lazy good-for-nothing," Your Honor, and yet admit that without me in the picture, my wife would have to work less hours? Doesn't that prove that I helped her during the marriage? Furthermore, even if the court subtracted the twenty-five percent amount for overtime, my wife would still have to pay approximately $2800.00 a month and I have not yet received one red cent." I also pointed out that my wife had been paying her lawyer ten thousand dollars a month to delay paying me a penny.

"I would have left the house ten months ago, Your Honor, if she would have begun paying maintenance when you first ordered her to do so. On top of that," I explained, "I am still Ester's father and would gladly take her to school and do her homework with her as I did for a decade before I filed for divorce and suddenly found myself holding a fistful of perjured protection orders. My wife could work all the overtime she wants."

"Not you! Let your lawyer speak for you!" Alfieri's voice blazed in anger in response to my honest rebuttal to Schwartz's vomit. I honestly think that it's painful for Alfieri to follow more than one or two ideas at once. I had so much more to say, but I was terrified that the rabid dog would break free from its leash. Meanwhile, Alfieri just stared blankly for a few moments, but then suddenly, amazingly, erupted again.

"I'll put you in jail Ma'am! Do you hear me! I'll throw you in jail!" Alfieri yelled and roared in a scorched voice as he stared at my calm frost-covered wife. The fire in Alfieri's voice didn't melt a single atom of the icy armor she wears at will. It was nothing more than a pleasant "Have a nice day!" greeting by the time his searing threat reached the signaling auditory nerves inside her brain.

My wife simply stared back at our judge. She showed zero emotion. Here I was, worrying about my wife being thrown into jail, while she calmly and politely continued to stare right into Alfieri's face with that indescribable subliminal "I dare you" Mona-Lisa smile. My ninety-pound wife surely possesses two testicles that weigh forty-five pounds apiece. Like a three-hundred-pound bouncer, with a martial arts background, she never even blinked as she squared off with The Alf. *Conner McGregor could throw a fast jab a millimeter away from my Eishet Chayil's nose in a UFC face off and my wife would continue to stare him down.*

Upon leaving court that day, my lawyer looked at me, as he proudly put his hand around my shoulder, as if we had experienced some great victory, and said, "At least now she'll *finally* pay you maintenance."

I slowly turned to face my lawyer and looked at him full-face as I haltingly responded, "When. Hell. Freezes. Over."

I can't describe the look on my own face, or the conviction in my voice, when I calmly stated what I knew was truer than God's creation of the world in a mere six days. But my lawyer's simple and deflated shocked response of "Wow," showed me that he was finally beginning to comprehend that fire ants are incapable of backing down.

My wife would destroy our daughter, flagrantly ignore Alfieri's court orders, and spend endless all-nighters composing outrageous accusations as Mrs. Hyde to demolish my reputation, while spending a quarter-of-a-million dollars to legitimize her protection-order treachery, without ever missing a beat in her senseless robotic goose-stepping march to victory.

She did all this while standing on her feet eight to ten hours a day "taking vein" and working the very busy cardiac units containing the remains of quintuple-bypass wealthy WASPs and Jews at North Shore University Hospital. *You don't want to mess with my wife.*

Alfieri, however, did back down and, instead of holding my wife in contempt of court, rewarded her three months later by accepting the outrageous illegal suggestion of her lawyer to immediately divide our life savings in order not to allow my "delaying" the divorce court proceedings any longer — as if I was the one filing motion after frivolous motion against myself that landed me into the family and criminal courts facing trials for computer hacking and child molestation.

"It's time for Mr. Lewinson to put some skin in the game!" Schwartz bellowed as his voice farted as loud as the stench of his antics smelled. Judge Alfieri then unleashed an incredibly illegal Court Ordered maneuver demanding the division (*before* signing our actual divorce decree) of our 401K savings and pensions in order to "get Mr. Lewinson some money to pay for his own lawyer!" The *Deer Head Inn* bartender then yelled at me for firing Lewis and forced me to lie and sign that I was a divorced man (401K funds and pensions are always separated *after* a divorce) or else he would hold me in contempt and put me in jail. I asked if what I was doing was legal, and SS Alfieri fumed, "I am the law!" I still trigger myself as I write about what I endured in Alfieri's hellhole.

I'm the kind of guy that would stubbornly sit in jail before doing anything wrong. I am not easily intimidated. But after enduring literal poverty and homelessness; as I drove around with my meds, toiletry kit, a few books, and a third of my wardrobe in the trunk of my car; showering at the nearby JCC every morning after sleeping in the filthy basement of a building in which I rented a tiny office for SwordPen Publishers (where the landlord was threatening to evict me for falling behind on the rent); along with the constant stress of the police banging on my door at home, work, or the synagogue to deliver yet one more embarrassing protection order or summons to court; while dealing with three court systems simultaneously as I watched my sweet Ester slip away; I caved.

I thought I hit bottom when I was starving late one afternoon and stopped to get a tuna sandwich at a diner. I looked up their menu on my phone, and I calculated exactly what the sandwich, a coffee, and a twenty percent tip would cost as I scrounged the ashtray of my car for loose change. I would have also ordered a salad and fries, but my cards were all maxed-out months ago and my FICO scores were plummeting as fast as my blood pressure was soaring. I realized that I had no leftover change for the parking meter. Teaneck is a quiet town and I figured I'd be fine.

"You're welcome," I smiled at the young waitress as I exited the diner only to discover a seventy-five-dollar parking ticket on my windshield. I calmly opened my car door and slid behind the wheel. *That was the moment I completely fucking lost it.* I think I literally had a nervous breakdown. I cried so hard that I couldn't catch my breath. I think everything just hit me at once.

But I still hadn't imagined how far down one could free fall as they tried to avoid hitting "bottom" while flailing their arms like a dodo bird trying to fly. I think I reached as far as I ever want to go when the lights suddenly shut off in my house long after the sun had settled down for the night. I knew it wasn't a circuit breaker. Orange & Rockland Utilities had been threatening me for months. They had finally put me on some payment plan for the elderly (it's more difficult to shut off the electricity of some old geezer who might trip in the dark or uses oxygen tanks).

But between ducking Orders of Protection and playing pro se lawyer (a lot less fun than playing "house" in Kindergarten) I couldn't even keep up with the modified plan. I will never be able to describe how mortified I felt as I pulled up to the Rockland County Department of Social Services, in an orange-flame six-speed stick-shift BMW, to sign a Confession of Judgment for a paltry $548.23 that they wired to the electric company to turn my lights back on.

I prayed that I wouldn't be seen by the many Hasidim I knew, or the scholarly life-of-poverty rabbis that I was friends with. I had given charity to many of them in the past, even paying for some of their kid's weddings, and now I was standing in a line waiting to see my caseworker and being asked if I wanted a Spanish interpreter. *Gracias. Habla Inglesia.*

Knowing that Alfieri's maneuver was blatantly illegal, but having reached the end of my rope, I reached for my pen to sign away half my life savings. I was physically and emotionally exhausted. The massive amount of stress, PTSD, alienation from almost everyone I knew, and the sheer lack of finances was dominating my life. I was once a man that had several million dollars of diamond inventory, huge credit lines, and fifty thousand in cash in my deposit boxes. I dropped fifteen thousand on Blackjack "double or nothing" bets while drunk. *When fifteen thousand was money.* And now I was reduced to scrounging my car ashtray for loose change.

I was no longer playing rope-a-dope. I was happy to take a ten-count. I had been so furiously flipped, pummeled, and kicked in the balls in that dirty motherfucker's divorce-dojo, that I would have been happy if someone put a bullet in my skull. Why would I care if some official later challenged my signature? I would simply claim that Alfieri insisted that I sign. It's all recorded in the court proceedings. So, I signed. I understood that I immediately lost well over a hundred and fifty-thousand dollars but, after being tortured, you would also sign any paper they put in front of you. It's not like the way they portray tough guys in the movies. Everyone eventually breaks. *Or they die.*

Mumbling something to the effect of, "I'll deal with the monies and any adjustments Mrs. Lewinson owes Mr. Lewinson after the trial," in order to avoid a showdown with my wife and the contempt she displayed toward anyone who dared butt heads with her, Victor Alfieri skipped past his earlier multiple "So Ordered!" court directives and threats of "I'll put you in jail!" and stone-heartedly pushed aside the entire idea behind the legal concept of "temporary maintenance and legal fees" that a "moneyed spouse" pays the stay-at-home parent throughout the proceedings of divorce court (based on mathematical divorce court formulas and milestone guidelines) till the judge signs their final divorce decree.

So after requesting (and receiving) our same exact net worth statements on three separate occasions (with several months passing between each request as Ester became further alienated); after declaring Mrs. Lewinson the moneyed spouse party of my Motion for Divorce at least a half-dozen times; after refusing visitation because of obvious perjured protection orders that were proven false by defendants own emails with her lawyer; after allowing Schwartz nine months to file motion after frivolous motion merely to delay and quash any payments to me; and after threatening to hold my wife in contempt of court and screaming that he would place her in jail for adamantly refusing to pay maintenance; it was quite obvious that I wasn't going to be receiving any.

A full-term pregnancy of nine wasted litigious months in divorce court, and four extremely anxious months running back and forth between family and criminal court, had produced an alienated minor child and a PTSD nerve-racked and exhausted husband who had been mercilessly flung through three court systems. And basically, it was as if I had just filed for divorce. We were literally back to square one. And I'm a highly educated privileged Orthodox Jewish White male. Believe me when I tell you #BlackLivesMatter.

A simple filing for divorce had somehow warped into a battle for visitation rights, in which a loving Mr. Mom father, who was forced into appearing pro se due to lack of receiving court ordered legal fees, would now have to attend and finance an extremely expensive trial (paid for with his "post-divorce" life savings) to prove that he was not violent or obsessed with feces and that he deserved visitation rights with his minor daughter. And the harder I fought, and the longer I survived, the more our systemic court system inflicted pain and punished me while emptying my pockets. Worse than all the above was my being scolded by Ester back home.

"You're killing Mommy!" screamed the angel for whose life I was sacrificing my own. "And Mommy already has to pay the mortgage!" As if she understood what was going on in court. *Or in her head.*

This all happened in an American court of law in the 21st century. And it continues to happen every day in family and divorce courts all around our country. I know there are some astounding judges out there. Such as the Honorable Kenneth M. Karas, in front of whom I had the pleasure to appear pro se, as the plaintiff in a plagiarism suit (SwordPen vs. Holt) which I brought against the publisher Henry Holt.

Kenneth Karas was personally familiar with every filing I submitted in my case against Henry Holt. He read every single word that I carefully wrote and edited. Judge Karas admired me in open court as "more intelligent, erudite and honest" than most of the licensed lawyers who appear in front of him. "You should consider becoming a lawyer," he quipped from his bench in Federal court.

And I admired Judge Karas for the intelligent, compassionate, articulate, and humorous jurist that he was. I enjoyed his intellect and looked forward to every next court appearance against Robert Bailin, the lead litigator from the white-shoe firm of Davis Wright Tremaine, along with his accompanying defense team, in a year-long epic battle, which was fairly and calmly judged by The Honorable Kenneth Karas.

In a forty-two-page long dissertation (typically a judge issues a few sentences in a plagiarism case, but the judge was completely fascinated by this case), Judge Karas dismissed my case apologetically on the simple grounds that I had not updated my copyright on a story that I had later reworked before submitting to Holt. But Karas then allowed me to refile.

Judge Karas even outlined eight more striking similarities (on top of the twelve for which I took Holt to court) between the two books being represented and then patiently explained that he was not allowed to judge those eight similarities (or the twelve I outlined) on the technicality of their not having been properly copyrighted.

Judge Karas then set an actual legal precedent (this was wild!) that allowed me to update my copyright retroactively — since the defendant (Henry Holt) admitted to having received my updated version based on the date they stamped my submission, which was two years prior to the publication of their forged version of my manuscript. I could then properly refile my lawsuit and bring Holt back into the courtroom where I would then sue based upon the (now twenty) similarities between the SwordPen Publishers book (*What Do You Call It?*) and the Henry Holt plagiarized version (*Can You Say Peace?*). "It" in the SwordPen title, by the way, is cleverly revealed as the word "Peace" at the end of the story. It is then that the true title conveying the message of the story is understood (*What Do You Call Peace?*).

Henry Holt wasted $120 thousand dollars in defense attorney fees because of the immorality of their children's editor, Laura Godwin, who *allegedly* passed my manuscript along to, Karen Katz, the author of *Can You Say Peace*. "Just write from your heart!" Laura responded to Karen, an illustrator, when she protested, "But I'm not a writer. I'm an illustrator." Godwin probably answered, "If you can't write from your own heart, just use this manuscript and write from Zev's heart."

If Holt would have simply settled with me out of court (without an admission of guilt) and given me the money they wasted in court, coupled with the $250 thousand my looney wife threw away on her worthless attorney, I'd be able to produce the next twenty-five incredible manuscripts in our SwordPen Publishers pipeline. But Holt would spend five million before ever settling. They are a Goliath that saw me as an ant, and not even a David. And my wife was an ant who would prefer to torch our children and her three-decade relationship with a "David," before slowing down long enough to allow the following simple four word question to formulate in her mind: "What am I doing?"

Imagine how many happy children would be reading over two-dozen great new books instead of one exhausted father mourning the loss of his alienated daughter. So much dishonesty. So much wasted time and resources. And contrast the sadness of a tired old writer compared to the happiness so many children could have experienced. Thanks, Holt! Thanks, Sharen!

Appearing before the professional Judge Kenneth Karas was a unique and enjoyable experience. I have a very warm and fond place in my heart whenever I see the name Karas in the news. The pleasant memory of this wise gentleman releases endorphins in my brain. I would vote for Kenneth Karas as POTUS in an excited heartbeat.

Comparing a brilliant Federal Judge like Karas to a boorish State drunkard like Alfieri, would be like comparing a Lamborghini to a broken-down rusted jalopy. The one and only similarity that the Lambo and The Alf share is that they both roar.

My initial mistake (assuming honesty, logic, and unbiased justice from a judge) upon Alfieri entering the courtroom in a black robe the first time we met, was because the image of the stately Kenneth Karas, and my experience with his impartiality, integrity, and compassion, had already conditioned my mind to trust our legal system.

Boy did I get a chillingly shrill wake-up call.

The problem with our judicial system is that inept and horrific judges like Alfieri are rarely removed from office. It's extremely rare to merely overturn one of their decisions, let alone have them impeached. In their courtrooms they have the power of the tyrant Caligula.

Alan Dershowitz is quoted as having said, "Judges are the weakest link in our system of justice, and they are also the most protected." Alfieri is surely one of the weakest links in our already dysfunctional State Court system. A system that established him as the Almighty during my divorce and reminded me of the chasm of power between a czar and a serf.

A married judge can grab a quickie with his secretary in chambers during working hours (while being paid to bang his gavel, not said secretary) or masturbate with a penis pump during a trial (it's not *that* boring) and receive nothing more than a reprimand. He can snippily claim contempt charges and toss any defendant or even their lawyer into jail simply because he feels they are being "argumentative." Everything a judge does is at his own discretion. And like a king, a judge "can do no wrong." And like a king, a judge can drain the state treasury and glom as much overtime he feels is necessary to rule the belligerent rabble. It's a cushy job.

At worse, even after horrific outrageous jurisprudence, the most a shoddy or mendacious judge will face (short of his engaging in blatant criminal perjury) is the "public humiliation" of an informal reprimand for violating the Code of Judicial Conduct. And that can only happen upon appeal. And very few individuals dare challenge their judge in the appellate division. It's prohibitively expensive and tantamount to challenging a wolf in an Appellate Court convened by wolves.

The reprimanded judges obviously feel no embarrassment, or they would never have found themselves mired in such scandalous behavior. It's all merely a display for John Q. Public, not to lose faith in the system, and to assure them that justice will always (eventually) be served. Besides, the working class is quickly placated that they can always fall back on their day late and dollar short, extremely expensive, right to appeal.

Good luck with that! Like I explained, it's like a sheep going to the wolves to ask for protection. Similar to the Blue Wall of silence among CYA ("Cover your ass!") policemen, judges ban together and hide behind a Black Robe Wall of deafening unethical silence as they favor their colleagues upon rendering their decisions. A fellow judge has to be grossly irresponsible to lose in the Appellate Division. And appeals are very costly. Especially emergency appeals that demand immediate intervention.

Alfieri constantly snapped, "Ya don't like it? Appeal!" knowing full well that the process is an expensive and arduous one that rarely results in a positive outcome for the poor plebeian who dares to criticize one of their own *Unzereh* judges. My lawyer advised me not to waste my money. I insisted that it was way past time to appeal this motherfucker gangster bully with a switchblade gavel.

Meanwhile, more menacing than all the abuse I stomached with The Alf; the latest, excruciatingly painful, looming Sword of Damocles suddenly hovered over my head by defendant's lawyer. Daniel Schwartz was now requesting permission to be granted for the minor child, Ester Lewinson, to take the stand at our upcoming trial.

Schwartz confidently, and with total feigned concern for my daughter's welfare in the tone of his voice, explained to Alfieri — while throwing a mockingly slow, completely-overkill, threatening, paused-glance in my direction — that, if allowed to take the stand, Princess Ester would be expressing her "complete hate" for her father (good job Sharen).

Included in her testimony, SS Schwartz promised, Ester would describe "the many times that her father had been *inappropriate* with her." (Italics are my own in order to emphasize a newspeak word connoting sexual deviancy if ever there was one.) I am still amazed how low a sleazy Kapo

Jewish lawyer can slither for a dollar. *May he be rewarded with spending the ill-begotten gains on expensive throat-cancer treatments.*

All their "evidence" was, of course, concocted in emails by my wife, her attorney, and her mad mob of yenta-pack hyenas. The emails proved my wife's mendacious manipulation and alienation of Ester for the past year-and-a-half. They didn't know that I was planning to reintroduce the emails at our trial. I'm still trying to comprehend how filing for a divorce lands a father as the defendant in a trial.

My plan was that my wife's emails had already become part of the court proceedings and I would merely add more documentation to support my case. I did fear Alfieri holding me in contempt, but I never went back into her email account after he said not to. These additional ones were all from the same original batch.

But I understood, by now, that Alfieri would never allow them to be entered. My wife's lawyer would scream bloody murder that they were "attorney-client protected." My own lawyer was terrified to push our luck, insisting that I'd be crazy to add more emails and that Alfieri would very likely expunge the first round of communications that I had already been lucky enough to enter. He would also surely hold me in contempt this time and most probably punish me with ninety days in jail.

I understood that I was desperately thrashing around in quicksand. Alfieri could enjoy torturing me for another five years without blinking. And he loved his job. He was a sadistic bacterium. Like some fictional anti-hero monster, the more I fought, the more Alfieri infected my blood and drained my powers and money. It was time to quit while I was behind.

Ester became a lost cause. The cherub I was willing to die for was now willing to hammer the nails into her father's coffin. My wife used her primeval skills to destroy what I loved most. In truth, I no longer had a daughter to fight for. And I no longer had any willpower. My fight-or-flight involuntary sympathetic nervous stress system had been activated since the day I filed for divorce and there was no way I could shut it off.

I couldn't fight, because no matter what I did Alfieri favored my wife and would not enforce his own court-ordered directives. And I couldn't take flight, because my wife kept spending a fortune on a lawyer that kept filing bullshit motions. His latest outrageous "Final Solution of the Zev Lewinson Question" was a motion that the court impute double of what my salary had been for the past five years and then base my child support payments on that completely fictitious amount. All I could do was lean on the ropes, barely able to hold my pro se arms up, to deflect my being slowly pummeled to death as I put on pound after pound of stress inducing-death. I was on the opposite program of the Dachau Diet Plan.

Alfieri liked Schwartz's idea and, in an offhanded compliment in which he proclaimed that I'm a "very intelligent man," then bellowed in dragon breath, as if he were speaking to a bum on the street, that I had better "Get a job already!" I understood that I was stuck in a medieval court system that burned fathers at the stake. And the weight I was gaining would only provide more fat to roast as I remained strapped to Alfieri's hellish courtroom pyre.

Schwartz insisted that I didn't deserve a red cent of maintenance and that "Mrs. Lewinson's kindness and patience had allowed her loser-husband to stay home all-day eating sushi and drinking saké for the past twenty-eight years." (I must admit that Schwartz flawlessly delivered the lines my wife wrote for him in her email diatribes.) And to make sure I died red-faced *and* penniless, Schwartz then ordered a bogus appraisal of our home and had its value lowered by $200,000 dollars. He then insisted that my wife receive ownership of the house (because she'd obviously be getting custody) by paying me "half" of the remaining tiny amount of equity ($7,500.00) which she would then deduct from my share of an obligation on a loan we had both signed for.

Alfieri patiently listened to all of Schwartz's fantastical grotesque antics as he formally sat at the bench, draped in black judicial cloth, with his chin resting on the palm of his hand, with curled knuckles pressed against his jowly cheek, attentively paying serious attention for hours on end to every word oinked by the most unkosher pig I've ever seen. The Alf seemed to have all the time in the world at his disposal and he clearly enjoyed burning up my life and father-daughter relationship at his leisure, while allowing his courtroom circus and the grievous alienation of Ester to continue for years, as he fattened his pension while balancing his "terribly congested" calendar. *May he merit to spend his ill-begotten gains on stroke medication and extended hospice care.*

But The Alf's patience came to an abrupt halt every time I tried to open my mouth, as he'd yell, "Not you! Let your lawyer speak for you!" Meanwhile, my lawyer refused to work till Alfieri enforced his own decision that ordered my wife to pay a paltry $7,500 dollars towards my legal fees, even as she continued to spend $250,000 dollars on her lawyer.

My bargain-basement lawyer would simply sit there and repeat that, "defendant has not complied with the court's orders." Alfieri would then insist that my wife, "had better pay," and he'd call it a day, as my cardiologist expressed shock at my systolic blood pressure number inflating faster than my wife's legal tab.

My ever-increasing blood pressure and thirty pounds of cortisol induced weight was literally causing me to walk around looking flushed. My cardiologist, Dr. Joel Goldberg, tripled my

Amlodipine blood pressure medication during the past year, while yelling at me to lose weight, and he now wanted to increase the dosage again.

"I'm not supposed to get in the middle of you guys (my wife and I shared the same cardiologist), but she's going to kill you," he warned. "I can't just keep increasing your meds like this. You're gonna die if you continue on like this!" Joel wasn't informing me of anything that my body wasn't already constantly screaming at me.

Upon requesting that the minor child herself appear at my trial in which I was contesting my wife's protection order, my wife's attorney continued to explain that Ester would close her statement by stating that she did not want to see her father anymore. Ester would state that she did not want any visitation arrangements made as part of the divorce settlement between my wife and myself.

The man-hating, angry Hasidic new therapist, a social worker with an online degree and a heavy Yiddish accent — hired by my wife in her newfound position as "temporary sole-guardian" of Ester's well-being and mental health — had primed Ester well. My wife followed the email instructions of Dr. Frank perfectly as she quickly hired Rabbi Shithead Schabes while arranging therapy sessions for Ester with the social worker.

Goldie Unger was the miserably married go-to *meshuggenah*-turned-therapist that every angry wife in Monsey turned to for the "therapy" of destroying their husbands. My wife knows how to pick attorneys, therapists, new rabbis, and new husbands. She paid more in mere consultation fees to over a half-dozen attorneys before choosing the sleaziest one she could find, than I paid Robert Lewis ($2,500.00) for the entire ten months that he represented me. And with Robert, I clearly overpaid.

I was, to say the least, beyond devastated. Not by their deranged, black-hearted malevolent plot to destroy me. Not by my experiencing the exhaustive constant angst by the gaveling threats of a fucking lunatic who was backed by all the invested powers of The State of New York. Not even by the pussy-pious Yentas who constantly called my principal, or the pain of my lost reputation and being shunned by the entire community. I'm used to being lonely anyway, and it's a wonderfully quiet place for a writer to exist and constantly philosophize, imagine, and dream. *I'm awesome company.*

But the clear realization that Ester was going to be raised by her mother caused me to almost pray that the sword that hung over my relationship with the child I raised from birth would just fall already. It's hard for a man to admit. They broke me.

Again, like Winston in *1984*, I was meekly asking Brian in a whimpering, innocent, childlike voice, "When ... will ... you ... shoot me?" I just wanted it to end. I no longer cared how. I knew the kind of control my wife could exert over anyone. The situation was going downhill faster than any slope ever skied by Lindsey Vonn for any of her Olympic gold. A trial that would cost a near-penniless dad a hundred-thousand dollars and only enrich a sordid divorce lawyer and corrupt judge hadn't even begun, but I clearly understood that my wife already won from the moment her first Order of Protection was hastily stamped.

"Might take a long time. Don't give up hope," I could almost hear my wife calmly responding in Brian's role, with the soothing cadence of Richard Burton's patient voice, in the movie released during the Common Era year that shared the same date as the title of the book by George Orwell that portrayed a world almost as dystopian as my Jewish one. "Everyone is cured sooner or later. And in the end, we shall shoot you, Zevie," my Asperger thespian *Bashert* muse promisingly-purrs as she assures me with her twinkling eyes that "nothing's gonna change" when I marry her.

My blood pressure continued to soar. Hydra heads were appearing everywhere. I could see them swirling in every direction. Policemen, Yentas, Sharen, Margaret Smith, sheriffs, Rabbi Schabes, Dr. Frank, Alfieri, Dan Schwartz, bailiffs, Goldie Unger, Robert Lewis, Judge Mendelson, Martin Gotkin, Judge Simon, Appellate judges, Dr. Ferro, Beit Din notices, my principal, next-door neighbors and my own close family of betraying braying relatives shunning me for my refusal to attend Beit Din ... the list of demons went on and on. I was dizzy. I was broke. I was homeless. I was anxious and riddled with PTSD. Worst of all, I was Ester-less. Like my doctor said, I really was "gonna die." *Or maybe I'd just kill myself.*

I no longer even had a lawyer of my own to add to the aforementioned list of tormentors, because Robert Lewis refused to work a minute more in response to my wife's refusing to pay the court ordered legal fees — which Alfieri refused to enforce.

I was eventually forced to appear pro se, even representing myself when Dan Schwartz subpoenaed to interview Gary Barnett, a New York real estate mogul who had invested $150,000 dollars into my company, SwordPen Publishers. My wife went after anyone in my life that might possibly be a source of love, friendship — and especially, money.

Even countries at war have temporary truces of détente. But my wife was a War Machine. And it seemed that she had God as an ally. Her lawyer subpoenaed my school, Amazon (we sold our books online), Skyhorse Publishers, with whom I had been in negotiations to become an imprint. And now, Gary Barnett. I'm sure she and Schwartz subpoenaed God. I imagine the summons demanded an "immediate list of any and all sins ever committed by Zev," as an excuse for more Orders of Protection.

I sat alone with Gary in the conference room of his NY Extell office while we waited for Schwartz to arrive, as he suddenly began yelling at me for my "refusing to give my wife a Get."

"I see my wife got to your mother," I calmly responded. "It's all lies Gary. You know me better than that," I added. "Then why won't you move out of your house!" he quickly snapped and shouted (Gary always spoke as fast as he made money) as he accused me of being a recalcitrant husband. My wife knew how much I hated pedophiles and men who sent their wives to the Jewish nunnery as an Aguna. And so she instantly slammed me with those labels the second I filed for divorce.

"I don't have any money, Gary. Why do you think I've been asking you if you want to take the next step you mentioned about putting another 250K into SwordPen? Our savings are in Sharen's credit union because she has great 401K plans at the hospital where she works and she won't pay me a penny of the court ordered temporary maintenance," I responded. "I don't even have money for an apartment."

"No one doesn't have *any* money!" Gary snapped back moments before Schwartz walked into the room.

I realized that Gary couldn't even imagine a person not having a few million lying around for an emergency, let alone being overdrawn for weeks at a time in his checking account.

But it was true. My account was constantly overdrawn. My bank would cover a negative balance in my business account up to (minus) $5,000 dollars. Having no money in my account was bad enough, but I would be charged a $35 dollar fee every time a new charge hit my card. Then I had to cover the charge *and* the fee. I tapped every source available for food and the basic necessities of life as I waited (like a schmuck) for maintenance. My wife was surely wondering how I managed to stay alive.

I remember exercising at the JCC and I was starving after working out for two hours. I needed to eat something. I dropped by my older brother's office to say "Hi!" (The brother who kept emailing me, at the instruction of my wife, to meet him for lunch.)

"Avi, can you loan me twenty bucks, please," I asked my sibling (who was earning a quarter million a year as CEO) after a few minutes of small talk. The sibling that I once purchased a house for a quarter century earlier responded, "Sorry Zev, I don't have it."

I saw the emails between Avi and my wife, but I still couldn't believe he'd refuse such a simple request. I guess he never read any of the speeches I wrote for him about Jewish kindness, *Chessed,* and *Tikkun Olam.* I should have charged him. He did a great job delivering them. Too bad he never comprehended one fucking word.

I handed my debit card to the cashier and paid $9.00 dollars for a salad and cup of soup that I knew would cost me $44.00 dollars. *It was worth every penny of the lesson I learned.*

My life was a nightmare. Kind of hard to explain to a guy that was selling sheetrock in Manhattan for millions of dollars by merely buying airspace property rights, erecting penises made of steel, and adding the word "penthouse" to the head of the dick.

It was obvious that Gary was no longer going to invest in SwordPen. But I figured I had nothing to lose by asking.

"What about your investment," I asked.

"Keep it!"

Gary was a very aggressive investor who was fearless in grabbing financial opportunities by the horns. Losing him as an investor was quite painful, but a mere scratch when compared to having Ester denuded from my life. Gary often trumped Trump (aka 'The Donald,' before he became the POTUS) in several landmark Manhattan projects. There is no question that Gary's I.Q. surpasses Trump's by at least twenty-five points. But I.Q. has nothing to do with E.Q. and it seems that although our "measure for measure" God had been generous with a dozen or so extra points in the I.Q. department, he subtracted the same amount from Gary's E.Q. score.

As smart as Gary was, he instantly believed everything his mommy related to him (via Sharen) and he never spoke to me again. Gary did everything super-fast. Almost as fast as he threw up nauseating buildings across Manhattan that could make anyone throw up. Some of it seems to have been financed by the blood money of desperate despots who needed to launder their ill-begotten gains. But Gary always did everything right. Barnett was also a speed reader. Perhaps that explains why he was unable to read between the lines. Geniuses are often like that. Gary snippily and honestly answered my questions at his deposition, although we had a few tense moments between us as I insisted that he clarify our partnership.

I did my best to keep it civil, but Gary never even responded to my thanks and goodbye salutation after our meeting that day. I walked myself out of the offices of Extell Development. Like everyone else who knew "Sharen and Zev," Mr. Barnett never spoke to me again.

Without Gary, or the temporary maintenance my wife had been ordered to pay me, I was down to living off the tolerance of my compassionate bank charging me $35.00 every time I swiped my card. I was also forced into representing myself in court. Being forced to appear pro se didn't matter anyway, because all Robert Lewis did was mumble "sit tight" in response to Schwartz's grandiose baritone performances about my being "a lazy bum" every time we appeared in court. Lewis wouldn't even notify the court that my wife refused to pay him. He would even forget to show up for scheduled court dates! I remember speeding one morning to pick him up and take him to court. I literally helped him get dressed quickly and I even tied his shoelaces for him because he was too chubby to tie them himself. I finally fired him.

Alfieri tried to strong-arm me "not to start with a new lawyer," but finally agreed, unable to refuse my request, because I had complied with every rule regarding notifying my lawyer (who tried to lie) and the court. Alfieri then ordered my wife to "pay $15,000 dollars in legal fees already!" for the new lawyer I chose that would now have to catch up with the case.

My wife never blinked. And she never paid.

Obviously, she continued to refuse to comply with the directive — which Alfieri continued to refuse to enforce. I wrote to chambers (The Honorable Victor Alfieri) on three different occasions to explain my predicament and that I still was not able to retain a lawyer. And Alfieri kept showing up in court, having to cancel again and again, violently screaming at me for "not hiring a lawyer," while I continued to explain that His Honor had obviously not read my hand-delivered and stamped letters to the court explaining that I would not have representation because my wife refused to obey the "So orderered!" directives of the judge. If that was not a Catch-22, please tell me what is. Finally, The Honorable Alfieri just screamed at me in court, "I don't care! We're starting the trial! Today!"

My heart is pretty fearless, but it was weakening physically and emotionally. I hadn't seen Ester in over ten months. I was a mess. I didn't want to imagine what she must be like. It was then that my wife's lawyer asked Alfieri to split our retirement savings, forcing me to pay for my own lawyer from my retirement funds. "Let's have Mr. Lewinson put some skin in the game!" he bellowed in court. And in a totally illegal maneuver — and in total defiance of temporary maintenance guidelines established by the NY State Court Matrimonial Law Committee — Alfieri granted the outrageous request!

I could have easily appealed Alfieri's decision, and I would have won, but I was literally scrounging for food (read that again slowly: I literally had no money for food) and could certainly not afford the ten to fifteen thousand dollars it would take to win an appeal. Meanwhile my wife and Schwartz couldn't wait to begin the trial. They were blaming me for Ester's poor psychological state of mind and, letter in hand from Ester's quack therapist, insisting that it was "urgent" to proceed with a trial to "protect" poor Ester from her father. Like Job, my patience was wearing thin as I questioned God in whom I still had (very little remaining) trust.

After ineffectually begging stone-hearted Alfieri for mercy and pleading for food and shelter, I was forced to beg some more as I borrowed a small fortune from a now very wealthy friend that I once helped get through a Talmud class in high school. I should have saved the money for food and rent for the next few months of my court-riddled miserable life, but I knew I'd vomit out the food in disgust because I constantly felt nauseous and couldn't stomach the shame and smearing of my reputation with yet one more fucking order of protection! I also knew that I somehow had to escape Alfieri.

And so choosing between eating or defending my reputation and untangling my testicles from Alfieri's shredding claws, I retained an appellate lawyer who charged me over twelve thousand dollars — not to fight and easily win the illegal court-ordered division of our retirement monies that Alfieri had just forced me to sign. That would simply keep me in the same status of Alfieri yelling at my wife to pay temporary maintenance, while she stared at him. Rather, I decided to challenge the latest brand-new protection order issued by our divorce court judge — despite my wife and her attorney refusing the judge's out of the blue offer to issue said order against me.

That's correct. My own wife repeatedly declined the totally unexpected gift-horse severe Stay-Away Order of Protection "against Mr. Lewinson" generously proffered by a black-robed braying donkey in open court. I was shocked! And so was The Alf.

Alfieri looked at Mrs. Lewinson incredulously and asked, "You sure? Maybe speak it over with your lawyer, Ma'am?"

Thing One and Thing Two whispered to each other and then her lawyer boisterously responded, in his animated booming voice, "Yes, Your Honor, Mr. Lewinson has been behaving himself (as if I ever hadn't) and it isn't necessary. There have been no incidents."

Schwartz had this natural, almost instinctive talent for speaking pejoratively, even when saying something positive. The disdain in his voice at my mere existence was always loud and clear from his opening statement the moment he first stood up to address the court, when he described me as a "bum who leeches off his wife," as he introduced me to the Honorable Victor Alfieri. I was always amazed at how loud this Orthodox Jewish pig, wrapped in a yarmulka, could squeal and debase himself for a dollar. *Against a human being he never even met.*

Like a reincarnation of the charming and seductive satanic bipedal serpent that walked upright in the Garden of Eden, who caused the downfall of mankind, Schwartz also walked on his hind legs as he hissed his respite response in a baritone voice through a flickering forked tongue and throat that surely deserves to be smitten with cancer one day for all the vicious lies that have passed through its hellish chamber of darkness.

Yet I could not believe that Schwartz's brain was as thick as his voice and that he wasn't able to comprehend Alfieri's not-too-subtle hint. I was beyond shocked that Schwartz didn't accept the judge's offer and that he refused to jump at the opportunity to finally "toss Zev outta the house."

But not as shocked as when I heard Alfieri's appallingly dreadful response to SS Swine Schwartz that increased the voltage in my rapidly beating heart and nearly jolted me out of my chair.

"Well, I'm gonna issue it myself!" the judge cried out. "Today!"

Here I was, observing an unbelievable scene in which my two most savage carnivorous enemies, who had been stalking like Bengal tigers to tear Ester out of my life while ripping the jugular vein out of my throat for the past eighteen months, were suddenly calmly insisting — in open court (where every word is recorded and documented for posterity) — that a protection order against me was totally unnecessary. I was pinching myself to check if I was dreaming.

To state that I was startled, stunned, and as incredulous as Alfieri had been only moments ago, at my sudden reprieve, would have been an understatement. But the endorphin-like high was quickly crashed by Alfieri's sudden monstrously-irrational "Today!" declaration.

But what happened next was even more astounding.

Upon Alfieri insisting that he was going to immediately implement a Stay-Away (much more severe than a regular one) Order of Protection, I literally begged for my existence.

"But Your Honor," I groveled for mercy, "I have nowhere to go! I have no money! I have no lawyer! You are literally throwing me into the street!"

"Not my problem!" Alfieri roared with a heartless, ghastly Führer growl. "You're outta the house today, Sir!" he snarled.

"Do you have any weapons, Sir!?" the commandant barked as he proceeded to check off his protection order list with his right paw and extended sharp claws …

"He can stay ..." an angelic, soothing but bold, voice that sounded like a cross between Florence Nightingale and Amelia Earhart suddenly emanated from la-la heaven above, as my divinely inspired out-of-the-Twilight-Zone wife interrupted the proceedings to declare my reprieve.

"Mrs. Lewinson …?" Alfieri queried. His voice was a third part shock, a third stunned curiosity, and a third betraying his sheer amusement.

"Are you sure? Talk to your lawyer, Ma'am."

Thing One and Thing Two huddled for a few moments, whispering back-and-forth, as a huge heavily-jowled face and meaty head covered by a small yarmulka leaned over to decide my fate with a tiny head draped in an oversized sheitel ...

"Yes, Your Honor, I don't mind if he stays. Ester and I are going away for Passover in four days and then we'll be away for two weeks. He can stay in the house till we return," my *Eishet Chayil* calmly explained as if she were commenting on the lovely spring weather we were experiencing at the start of April that day. The scene was so bizarre that I was almost waiting for her to cry out to Alfieri, "April Fools'!"

If I had smelling salts in my pocket I would have inhaled deeply if only to assure myself that I was truly conscious at that moment. Even God can't pull off miracles like my batshit crazy wife.

"Are you positive, Mrs. Lewinson? I'm advising you to speak to your lawyer."

More whispering between Thing One and Thing Two.

"Yes, Your Honor, in a magnanimous gesture Mrs. Lewinson is fine with Mr. Lewinson remaining in the house till after the Passover holiday." Her pompous lawyer always spoke as if he were on stage.

Alfieri seemed lost for a moment. Suddenly frozen in time, he didn't know what to do or say. With a confused expression on his eternally sourpuss once chiseled but now jowly face, Alfieri stared blankly at my wife and then down at his papers. Then he stared at me and back at my wife. She, as usual, did not blink. Then he stared at his trusted court stenographer in her lopsided sheitel. It almost seemed as if The Alf was searching for someone to advise him.

My own mind was experiencing its own brain-freeze of sorts as I held my breath, gripped by fear. Actually, the entire courtroom sat frozen in silence, like the plaster casts of the citizens of ancient Pompeii, as everyone waited anxiously, trying to anticipate the response of The Alf to all this reality-show drama.

"Okay! I'm gonna date this order twenty-one days from today! You Sir, had better be out of the house by the 22nd of April!" Alfieri breathed with fire and disgust, as he once again took control and warmed up the frigid courtroom atmosphere with his malignant dragon breath.

Alfieri then issued an immediate "urgent" stay-away emergency Order of Protection that he post-dated three weeks into the fucking future! I would have been marveling at the stupidity of such an illogical, obviously bullshit, directive had my heart not just undergone defibrillation while being constricted due to the court proceedings that morning.

Once again, the commandant barked, "Do you have any weapons, Sir!?"

In actuality, Alfieri was asking me if I "would have" any weapons starting three weeks forward from the day he was post-dating his decree. This kangaroo court sham would have been almost comical had I not had to worry about a roof over my head in the next few weeks. I could have, in reality, legally purchased an arsenal during the next twenty-one days.

The devil is absurdly prophesying that I'm "going to become dangerous" in three weeks from today ... what a complete and total fucking idiot wearing a black robe when he should be dressed in shrouds like the angel of death, I mused to myself.

I looked over to where my wife was sitting. Even I could not believe what she had just done. Here my *Eishet Chayil* had tortured me for over a year with multiple protection orders, eight police visits (with more to come), and hundreds of venomous emails and phone calls to anyone who even remotely knew me, to warn them of my narcissistic and violent pedophilic personality. All that love and attention from a devoted wife while she flung me through three court systems while simultaneously serving twelve subpoenas to Amazon, Gary Barnett, YSV (Yeshiva of Spring Valley) grade school, previous employers, and an assortment of publishers and distributors to disclose every single dollar they paid me in royalties.

That was aside from unleashing a wolf-pack of Yentas sniffing my crotch to see if I cared about their son's education a bit too much ("*Vee all know that pedophiles like to become teachers and boy scout leaders"),* and a "Cherry on Top" for alienating Ester from her loving father. All executed while constantly visiting the Ramapo Police Department to conjure up more fictitious crimes with which to charge me for my true crime of having filed for a divorce to escape a lunatic stranger that I was manipulated into impregnating six times. *I'm a little embarrassed.*

I accidentally discovered that Coercion and Blackmail were her most recent and final two attempts, which the Ramapo officers, finally tiring of her repetitive acting, refused to accept. I had seen a pamphlet in one of the many files she constantly shlepped around that she accidentally left behind on the kitchen counter one morning as she flew out the door. I couldn't imagine "what she was up to now" as I almost laughed at my "once upon a time" cute wife. One officer bumped into me at the gym.

"You don't recognize me?" the big guy now sporting an incognito sweatshirt asked, "I've been out to your house a couple of times. Your wife's fuckin' crazy!" he laughed.

"How do you know?" I teasingly jested in response to his laughter.

"Because she's comin' down to the station every week tryin' to charge you with somethin' or other," he replied. "Good luck, man!"

"Thanks for refusing," I half-smiled.

I now understand why Ramapo Police Chief Brad Weidel reported scandalous earnings of $369,412 dollars that year. He earned over a thousand dollars a day while my wife spent almost the same as his base salary to keep Brad and his department busy.

Weidel's base pay of $266,663 dollars, partially paid for by my taxes, was surely augmented by the overtime he worked as the part-time lackey of Mrs. Hyde, filling out forms and filing oh-so-important paperwork as he hurriedly sent out officers on nine different "emergency" calls to our home (that had a long dangerous history of twenty-eight years of *Shalom* Bayit) at 19 Mariner Way, to deliver protection orders and family court notices, and to investigate my "barging into my wife's bedroom" as I searched for a picture of "some rabbi."

And now her alter-ego Dr. Jekyll persona suddenly appeared, almost pleading with Alfieri for a reprieve on my behalf, persisting to the point of insisting, as Ester's mother pleasantly invited me for a four-day childhood sleepover of sorts with her and Ester under the same roof as if we were, once again, one big happy family.

I glanced over at my wife, wanting to thank her (*maybe she'll even allow me to drive Ester to school for the next four days*), but quickly looked away, afraid to stare for more than a second lest she instantly transform back into Mrs. Hyde. After twenty-eight years of this type of behavior I knew how quickly things could change. I knew to keep my distance. You never want to startle a tigress. I no longer trusted her sweetly purring, "I'm your best friend, Zevie."

What is amazing about this outwardly beneficent gesture by my wife, is that one would be inclined to say that she had finally shown some mercy and compassion. But this is what people fail to understand.

You don't shoot someone through the heart and then run over to administer mouth-to-mouth resuscitation to try and save their life. You don't cut someone's carotid artery and then heroically compress the vein spurting blood with two fingers. And you don't worship the famous Rabbi Nekritz as your rabbi for twenty-eight years and have him recite the blessings at your wedding as you dabbed your tearing eyes, and then send your two adult daughters to verbally assault him and repetitively scream that he is a "piece of shit" in front of his wife and neighbors. But then again, he was no longer my wife's rabbi. So he became feces.

"Rebbi is *your* rabbi, Ze'ev! And Rabbi Schabes is *mine*!" my ex angrily informed me after I calmly relayed the respectful message of her *Da'as Torah* Rabbi to please stop calling him. This from a woman who often sweetly replied, "Why don't you just call Rebbi?" whenever we faced any major decision as a family. From choosing schools for our children, Ritalin for Sarah (I was against medicating my child, and it was a rare occasion where I firmly stood my ground), or deciding upon any sort of medical procedure, my wife immediately suggested that we seek the wisdom of the Oracle she first met the night I "put a ring on it." Emphasis on the personal pronoun, "it." As in, "it" was never really a human. Or humane.

You don't take out Orders of Protection to "toss Zev outta the house," feigning to protect yourself AND THE MINOR CHILD from the "wrath and obsession with feces" of a husband with whom you endlessly orgasmed for twenty-eight years as we brought five children into the world — six if you include our three-month old fetus Ezekiel who I held in the palm of my hand as his tiny heart stopped beating — and then invite him for a four-day sleepover with you AND THE MINOR CHILD.

That would be like the serial killer, Charles Cullen (*The Good Nurse*, 2013, etc.), who intravenously administered lethal doses of assorted medicines for years (murdering hundreds of patients), followed by his running heroically into the patient's rooms upon their alarms and beepers going off as he frantically jumped on their beds and pounded on their chests in an Oscar winning compassionate performance attempt to resuscitate them, all the while knowing the exact lethal cocktail dosage that caused their heartbeat to flatline. My wife exhibited Cullen-like behavior throughout our entire marriage. And her acting put his to shame.

I am not calling my wife a serial killer, although she unflinchingly exhibits the heartless personality it takes to be one. Sharen's total disdain for Ester's well-being, and for our two other daughters ever finding a spouse in Monsey, coupled with her complete lack of shame at being exposed as the audacious liar that she has always been — whether stealing plastic cutlery, buying "kosher" chicken that "fell off the truck," or having an abortion or an affair with her best friend's future husband — clearly portrays her total lack of humanity. This is said without malice. Because I don't believe my wife is evil. Her limbic system simply doesn't spark empathy.

My wife is cold. She can act warm. But the closer I got, the more distant I felt. And I sensed this going into the marriage. I can only blame myself and my own issues. And therefore, even after all she put Ester through, it's hard for me to be angry at Dr. Jekyll. She is what she is. Adorably heartless. I can only say that I was foolish for not listening to my own heart. I allowed my rabbi, my God, and the Jewish Orthodox society in which I lived, to make the final decision regarding who I married.

My wife often related the sad news of a patient dying on the table with less emotion than saying we need to order out because dinner got burnt. She emotes feelings on demand (except anger, which comes naturally). But it's all artificial intelligence. I attributed her lack of compassion and emotion regarding "the patient" the result of surgeons being trained to remain impartial in order not to get emotionally involved with their patients.

But with my wife they didn't have to bother. She was a natural at being unnatural. I chalked up her robotic inadequacy in the bedroom to her being inexperienced and unskilled. In truth, I was miserable. But for better or for worse I was married. And so, I accepted a mechanical sex life with my *Eishet Chayil* robot as part of my penance for having sown my wild oats throughout my twenties when I should have been bringing little Jewish souls into the world instead of aborting them.

I'm embarrassed to admit that I was so religious at the time, that I accepted my sexual frustration as retribution from God for all the wild times I had experienced during the decadent decade of my life preceding my marriage. Jewish theology teaches that it's better to suffer in this temporal world than in the eternal one. I certainly was experiencing pussy-pain. Compared to what I was used to, it was excruciating. *I'll never understand how men make love to blow-up dolls.*

I still recall some small talk from decades in the past, while we drove somewhere, in which I was admiring my future wife's surgical skills and complimenting her for saving people's lives. "What do you like most about being a surgeon?" I asked my cute date to stir up the conversation.

"I like giving good stitch," she robotically responded. "Good stitch" meant matching up and sewing two flaps of skin like a skilled tailor after removing the sectioned-off vein. "And I like surgery because I prefer my patients knocked out cold," she added. "This way I have control and don't have to deal with them."

I thought she was being sarcastic.

But her brain was sharing the truth with me. The irony of people who are out of control (sadistic killers, spouses like O.J. Simpson, etc.) needing to have total control over others has not escaped my writer's mind.

In contrast to my constantly complimenting her surgical skills, my wife would never tell me I'm good at anything. If I had great success, I was "lucky." If I failed, I was "an idiot." And I now understand. Complimenting someone means giving them confidence. And control.

People think the professional title of an individual defines who they are. As if all doctors are caring. Or all priests and nuns are angelic. My deviant physicians-assistant wife still looks like a cute, professional workingwoman to me. After all, work is the main part of our day. It often does define who we are.

I often looked at my wife's erratic behavior as her being "out of control." In reality "out of control" is what she was all the time. When my gestalt shifted, I was able to see that she merely looked "in control" when she did surgery at work, looking absolutely lovable "playing doctor" in her oversized, size small scrubs, when not displaying her true "out of control" behavior. Meanwhile, her completely "out of control" behavior during our divorce was as normal, natural, and mundane as her "taking vein" at work for thirty-five years.

You may be thinking that I am exaggerating. But many times people have no idea of what it's like to be in a narcissistic relationship, because from the outside it looks idyllic. Inside, it's a nightmare. It took me decades to understand that I was living with a ladylike bi-polar individual.

My A.I. robotic wife constantly displayed this deranged 180-degree instant turnaround behavior behind closed doors throughout our marriage. I never knew what comment or act might trigger her schizotypal contradictory behavior. It could be for something as minor as forgetting to take out the garbage. On some days she might say nothing and schlep the cans to the street by herself, leaving me a gentle note reminding me that Monday and Wednesday are garbage day. Or she might wind up yelling at me.

At other times, she could literally scream at me for something inconsequential over the phone while I drove to Brooklyn to study, and five hours later upon my arrival home late at night I'd find her all showered and perfumed in bed as she'd wink at me to join her. "Come here. I want to check your plumbing," she'd romantically-robotically tease as I'd wonder if she was watching porn at work. "We good?" I'd ask the stranger in my wife's bed as she teasingly flashed her cute little breasts.

My wife could even orgasm in ecstasy and minutes later bring up a diamond loss I had that week, and literally seethe over nothing that was my fault while berating me at having lost $25,000 dollars because a jeweler went bankrupt on me. It didn't matter that I knew him for over a decade and that he never bounced a check. It didn't matter that he took many other large firms for much larger amounts. It was still my fault. As if I wanted to lose money. *I guess she never experienced doing business with Trump.* The torment of her anger was worse than the money I lost.

I remember one time, after an hour-long torturous session of nasty comments behind closed doors, how I went to the bathroom for a minute and came out to a snoring wife in a deep sleep. *How can she instantly fall asleep like that?* I wondered, as my heart raced all night while I stared out the window, waiting for the sun to come up, as I worried about my kids while weighing my divorce options.

My wife harangued me with a constant barrage of Gish-gallop disjointed accusations for which she incessantly insisted that I, "take ownership Ze'ev!" She had me pleading mea culpa for things that were totally beyond my control, such as screaming at me for not trying hard enough to find a husband for my oldest daughter Rachel who finally admitted that she wanted to take an indefinite "break" from dating.

I suffered endless sessions of yelling because of my daughter's natural desires. "She's turning twenty-two, Ze'ev!" my wife yelped after Rachel broke off an engagement to an incredible young man. My daughter panicked at the realization of her becoming a fiancée. Then she almost had a nervous breakdown upon imagining her fiancé putting a ring on it. I realized that the odds of her sleeping with a boy were less than the likelihood of my sashaying into Rikers Island dressed up as a drag queen in a sheitel.

I was completely comfortable with my daughter's decision. Sure, I wanted grandchildren, but if there is one lesson my life has taught me, it is that life is best lived if one can adapt. Many Orthodox families have young women that would probably puke at the thought of "being fruitful" with a "Bashert," and are easily hidden and excused among the thousands of desperate lasses who simply can't find a mate in the Jewish Orthodox world (due to Yenta mothers rushing to marry off their daughters by the time they turn eighteen, whereas boys get engaged at twenty-three).

An Ultra Orthodox Jewish girl's potential for marriage shelf-life is thirty-six months from the day she graduates from seminary a year after high school. Any older than twenty-two and any larger than a size four, and she can cry over her book of Psalms for eternity.

My wife continued to torture me. "Email blast the Shadchonim, Ze'ev!" she would scream at me. "I don't think she wants to get married, Sharen. Rabbi Nekritz and Batyah set her up with dates from among the best young men in his yeshiva. She nitpicked and found something wrong with all of them. Let her be *Aunt Rachel*," I delicately suggested.

My wife then insisted that I go to therapy with my daughter Rachel because she decided that it was my fault that she was utterly grossed out by the thought of sleeping with a man. "You need to improve your relationship with her, Ze'ev!" I had hoped Rachel was bisexual. But God refused to listen to my prayers. *God never even had sex in his entire eternal life. I wonder why he's so hung up about a bodily function.*

Little spoiler alert here: There is no prohibition decrying "gay women" as sinful in the Bible or Talmud. And I don't care how hot Rachel Weisz and Rachel McAdams were as they embraced and passionately kissed each other in the movie *Disobedience*. The Bible only discusses stoning two *men*. And even that makes no sense. People assume the prohibition also applies to two women. Sorry ladies. Seems that lacking a penis is a blessing. Certainly nothing to envy. The rabbis of the Talmud actually look at frolicking (emphasis on "licking") between two women as nothing more sinful than their distraction from tending their children or completing their household chores. Or from supporting their husbands who are "sitting and learning." #JewishWomanSmashGlassCeiling

For some reason God seemingly gets upset only when a man sticks his penis into the rear of another man. Even oral sex between two men would not warrant Biblical stoning. Two women enjoying a clitoral kissing orgasm certainly doesn't do the trick and is not a sin. And as far as I'm concerned, it's a mitzvah!

Rachel will soon be celebrating her thirty-sixth birthday. I'm sure my ex-wife is still blaming my daughter's being single on my being her father. It must be true. Because my wife is never wrong. Just ask her. Or get a second opinion from Vittie Blech. Vittie instantly believes, validates, and email blasts anything my wife tells her.

I could never explain my wife's erratic behavior. My wife mimicked perfect manners among friends and displayed almost flawless professional conduct at work. Except for the time she finally got caught stealing boxes of plastic cutlery from the hospital. She used to bring home these huge boxes from North Shore. "But it's for the staff, and I'm staff!" she insisted, through tears that she could turn on faster than your mind could ever comprehend were totally crocodile.

Besides her self-defense explanation of being part of the surgical staff, and taking boxes of two thousand forks, knives, and spoons, instead of one at a time, she was outraged at being accused of "stealing" by security who worked at minimum wage. Who were they to judge her?

My wife was used to the other side's temperature dropping. As in our marriage, it was always only a matter of time till her opponents figured out that "it just wasn't worth it." Besides, what's a pair of two-hundred-pound hospital security officers compared to my ninety-pound wife?

The only person I ever saw not give into my wife was my genius Asperger (literally a computer) demented daughter-in-law. It was an incredible standoff between an angry Alpha Zero daughter-in-law versus the older version Deep Blue incensed mother-in-law. There was no chance of a draw and I remember my wife storming out of the room after the confrontation with my son's wife. I ran up to our bedroom where my wife was seething, lava-like, in anger.

Even I had never seen her like this. My *Vybie* was physically shaking, as if volcanically smoking with trembling rage. It was scary. She looked like she was going to explode and rain down as molten lava as in some special-effects scene in a sci-fi movie. I held my wife tightly to keep her tiny pubescent body from erupting all over the room and I gently pleaded with her to calm down as she fumed and cursed like a sailor.

So "out of control" for my cute wife, I sadly observed at the time. "I know you're right Honey," I soothingly said, "but you have to let go." At that time of my life I was fully immersed in my Talmudical pursuit of turning folio after folio in order to complete another tractate with Rabbi Nekritz. I was completely unaware of mental health issues and that the violent outburst of anger that I had witnessed a moment earlier was a flawless example of what psychiatry defines as "narcissistic rage." *It's not really all that cute*.

The security guard was not backing down either. The sign clearly said, "for hospital staff only" he insisted, "and that didn't mean taking boxes out of the storeroom closet to take home with you."

Eventually the Chief of Surgery had to intervene with security, and he saved my wife's cute butt by writing up something to the effect of her working long hours and not having time to shop. He made a joke out of the entire situation, insisting that the guards just drop it already, and he diffused her sticky-fingers pilfering to a mere write up by security where her insanity was filed away forever. Just like her insane emails, Orders of Protection, perjured accusations of sexual molestation, and criminal accusations of computer hacking are now filed and sitting in the basement of the Rockland County Courthouse. I can only imagine what the Chief of Surgery would write to make a joke out of all the long-term PTSD trauma I'm still suffering from.

American society counts anyone that can drive, pay their bills, and hold down a job as "normal." A good credit rating, even achieved through corporate stock manipulation and deception, is much more valuable in our economically driven coarse culture than the high E.Q. score of an honest, kind, intelligent man. And paying for your bar tab with a Dubai Royale Black Card while sporting the Paul Newman Rolex Daytona on your wrist is going to swoon your date off her feet, and right into your bed, much more quickly than having healthy clean oxygenated blood flowing through your veins as opposed to the herpes tainted blood of the Black Card holder. Figure out the odds for that statistic yourself.

If not for his propensity for rape, murder, decapitation, and necrophilia with putrefying corpses, the charming Ted Bundy, with his high I.Q. and gorgeous blue eyes, along with his always being dressed to kill, literally, picked up chicks faster and with greater efficiency than a hungry lioness executing a kill. Ted's prey, however, suffered an excruciatingly worse death than merely being quickly torn apart by a lion.

And with his degree in psychology — because crackbrained lunatics love the discipline that gives them the labels to describe and profile others along with the language to control them — and then attending law school while achieving success as a burgeoning politician, Ted, like my wife, was certainly considered a very wonderful person by everyone who met the polite young student that later confessed to thirty-six murders.

Detectives estimate there were more than one hundred. Either way, let's quote Ted, who quipped, while honestly displaying his complete disdain for the lives of others, "What's one less person on the face of the earth, anyway?" Or one less dad? Right, Sharen? Bundy also claimed that, "Murder is not just a crime of lust or violence. It becomes a possession." It's always about control. Even after death. Even after divorce.

Physicians and surgeons have always been admired as society's elite. It's a well-deserved accolade. Driving to North Shore University Hospital and standing in an operating room for over thirty years certainly qualified my responsible, polite, yet ruthlessly and chillingly evil-upon-divorce, wife as "very normal." But drill beneath the quarter inch thickness of her cranium and you will quickly discover she's not. Again, I'm not saying my wife is Ted Bundy, but the pathological and deviant behavior which my wife exhibited during our divorce easily portrays the profile of a sociopath. Even I still find it hard to believe all the evidence I accumulated during our divorce. And I was married to her.

Hitler described the concept of the "Grobe Luge" (i.e. the big, fat lie) in *Mein Kampf*. Herr Wolf explained that when a colossal fabrication was proclaimed ("I fear Zev's wrath! Zev's obsessed with feces! Zev keeps going into Ester's room!") and firmly repeated enough times ("I didn't do it! I didn't do it!"), it would be believed because no one would imagine a person capable of having the impudence to so brazenly distort reality.

Joseph Goebbels used the Grobe Luge propaganda technique, inciting and repeating a hostile anti-Semitic narrative of an "international Jewry" that held the financial reins of power in a "war of extermination against the German people," starting with their losses during the first World War, that justified Germany's "self-defense" annihilation of every single Jewish man, woman, and child on the planet. It's nothing short of, dare I say, a miracle that there are living Jews in this day and age. What's even more amazing is that you can drop many of them over two-thousand years into the past and they'd feel right at home. Try that with a modern-day German, Italian, or Frenchman. They're all a long way from Valhalla.

Goebbels never bothered to mention that one of the few jobs Jews were permitted to pursue during the Middle Ages was as money lenders, because Christians are not allowed to charge interest. So just like Jews use Gentiles as a "Shabbos Goy" to turn on lights on the Sabbath, the Goyim used "Those Jews" to charge interest.

Hence the incredible "Our Crowd" Jewish banking families of Marcus Goldman and Joseph Sachs, and the Kuhns and the Loebs (Lehman), along with the legendary Rothschilds. Like my wife turning a loving Mr. Mom into a sexual deviant who molested "his own daughters," Gobbles almost destroyed banking royalty that funded governments and built roads and railroads, and awarded them an accolade still whispered by so many people to this day: "Jews love money."

The Grobe Luge worked as simple as the masses behave when it comes to believing anything they read in the press: The bigger the lie, the better. So, when an Orthodox woman in a sheitel started screaming and frantically emailing every Yentabitch (yes, I coined a new word) in town that her husband is a violent pedophile who is obsessed with feces, the "Grobe Luge" concept worked flawlessly.

And when a Yiddishe Mama brazenly took out a Grobe Luge Order of Protection and repeatedly told her instantly legally-orphaned daughter that "Tatie's going to make us homeless and he's using his Talmudical knowledge to avoid going to Bais Din," the endless repetition drilled itself into sweet Ester's pliable young mind.

Not one individual from our entire systemic judicial system that is primed to greedily choose to automatically believe any "Grobe Luge" request for an Order of Protection, nor any of the Orthodox Beit Din Rabbis that are cautioned to be extremely cautious before rendering decisions of Halacha, gave a damn. And that's besides the extreme prohibition not to accept or speak evil speech. I'll take a humanist atheist over a shitty sanctimonious Monsey "Rabbi" any day of the week.

Herr Vybie took a page right out of Hitler's psychological profile: Never allow the public (the police or Yentabitches) time to cool off; never admit to a fault or a wrong; never concede there may be an iota of good in your enemy (even if you slept with him for three decades); never accept blame; blame your enemy for everything that goes wrong (including your own decision to waste a quarter million dollars on a slob divorce lawyer); and remember that people will always believe a big lie much sooner than a little lie. *Especially if you scream and act shocked.* One good momentary firm scream can instantly wipe away three decades of a flawless paternal history. Especially with feeble-minded propaganda-spouting Yenta neighbors like Radzik, Fonfedder, and Blech.

For twenty-eight years I could never really explain my wife to myself. I often felt my marriage was reminiscent of the Chinese "Death by a Thousand cuts" experience. But my spouse would often kiss the wounds. Or I'd place a rationalization-Band-aid on the emotional cut to keep my marriage from hemorrhaging, and "... even as I lay dying," as Agamemnon told Ulysses, "the woman with the dog's eyes would not close my eyes as I descended into Hades." How could I have ever imagined that my divorce would be a "Death by a thousand Yentas" experience?

If I could believe God orchestrated the murder of his six million children as an act of kindness (so we are taught), then I could easily rationalize my wife's bi-polar behavior. I really must thank her for the complete clarification and "Tatie 5521" revelation of "what" (as in WTF!) I had been married to upon my serving her divorce papers. Better late than never. Now I'm just waiting for God's email password revelation so that I can clarify his irrational bi-polar behavior.

With the speed of two imploding white-dwarf stars dancing around each other at unfathomable speed, my wife's Yin-Yang behavior was torture for a logical mind like my own. Modern-day neuroscience has yet to define how or why my wife's brain sparks the way it does. She is able to frugally save pennies for decades, drive ten miles to save eleven cents per gallon on gas, hoard receipts and the boxes of items she bought so that she can proudly return some five-dollar item three years after it was purchased for a full refund ... and then fling all those savings on a scuzzy lawyer who accomplished nothing for a full two and a half years.

Many experts found Ted Bundy to be an elusive patient to diagnose properly. They correctly labeled him as psychopathic based on his behavior. Bundy had outward charm and charisma, they claimed, but very little true personality or genuine insight beneath his façade. So like my wife. Great façade, and not much beneath the surface. And that is why she always insisted that I carry the conversation when we went out to dinner with another couple.

"You do the talking, Zevie," my wife would remind me as we drove to meet our friends. "I'm not fast on my feet like you. I'm not a talker," she'd honestly add. It's amazing how A.I. has the ability to define itself. My wife, however, was a "very fast talker" when it came to spewing lies. Like her brother Dead (even when he was alive) Fred, she'd just make things up and instantly believe what she said. "He boxes. Say he hit you!" Abracadabra, "I fear his wrath." Bundy's psychoanalyst claimed that although he could differentiate between right and wrong, it had minimal effect on his behavior or his ability to feel guilt or remorse.

I honestly think Ted was my wife's true twin *Bashert.* I believe she is merely sociopathic compared to his being psychopathic. But they certainly would have been a match made in Hell. I think God plucked the wrong blue-eyed baby when sending my wife her future second husband.

The Chinese philosopher Mo Ti, also known as Mozi, (fourth century B.C.) shared the following insight many years ago: "When one man kills another man it is considered unrighteous and he is punished by a quick death. By the same token if a man kills ten men, he is punished more severely, with a more torturous death, as if he would be punished ten times. Also, if a man commits a small crime it's considered as a mere misdemeanor, but if his crime becomes huge, such as attacking another country and stripping it of its wealth and killing hundreds of thousands of people (like Putin attacking Ukraine), it is somehow considered that he is to be hailed as a conquering hero."

Mo Ti goes on to explain that we are able to comprehend the horrible violence of one death, but Six Million tortured and murdered innocent Jews during the twentieth century, for example, becomes a mere number. Most people don't even know how many zeros to add to numerically display the amount of one trillion. It's too much for the mind to grasp. Our minds are still very primitive. Fortunately, we are biped. Our brains, however, are still quite Neanderthal. Large numbers become abstract concepts.

I believe the above also holds true in reverse. Small emotionally-draining crimes and immeasurably minuscule amounts of theft become too tiny to grasp. But, subliminally speaking, they can be just as violent.

I became an excellent basketball player because I experienced being chosen last in a simple neighborhood game. At age eleven I didn't know how to play, and I had no father to teach me, as I stood anxiously waiting to be picked. I almost started crying when I finally heard, "Okay, you're stuck with Zev." The thirteen-year old kid wasn't even trying to be mean. But I was so embarrassed to be chosen last. I spent the next ten weeks practicing dribbling and shooting by myself, for many hours a day, before I showed up back at Weequahic Park in Newark to play basketball again.

And speaking of tiny infractions that add up, some Wall Street companies have "earned millions the old-fashioned way" by simply grabbing an eighth of a penny off of billions of trades till they were caught. Merely being rude or snippy to someone is "violence" to a certain degree. Hanging up on your spouse is marriage-murder.

Purposefully ignoring someone and tormenting them with the silent treatment (the narcissist's weapon of choice) is a punitive act, carried out by inflicting emotional violence. It is difficult to measure because the abuser is not being overtly unkind or aggressive in any visible way. They are not breaking any laws. After all, they're not "doing" anything. Yet their assault is nothing less than the constant pummeling of your mental health. They are silently killing you. Slowly. Methodically. Mercilessly.

Even a brief period of exposure to the silent treatment instantly activates the anterior cingulate cortex — where not only pain perception occurs, but where a variety of neurobehavioral damage (such as memory loss and depression) will now take place. That's why my wife refused to meet me to receive her Jewish divorce papers. She knew there was never a risk that she would wind up as a permanently anchored Agunah "for the rest of my [her] life," as she described her faux fears in her emails.

Preferring to never hear my voice one last time, which would have allowed me to have the last words in our marriage ("You are divorced from me") as I would have dropped the "anxiously" awaited for Jewish Get into her hands; my wife called in last minute as the scribe, rabbis, witnesses, and I all stood waiting for her to show up, and claimed to be stuck at work. As if she didn't have dozens of accumulated vacation days that she could have used. Or perhaps she refused to show because she was afraid that I'd "hit her."

MRI research has proven that an ignored individual's brain, even by an almost subliminal act as innocuous as not being tossed a ball while standing in a circle of participants during a study on the brain's response to isolation, immediately responds to the insult and activates in the exact same area where they experience pain. And stress. We are sensitive children. Solitary confinement is torture. And deadly. Studies show that social isolation increases the risk of dementia by approximately fifty percent. Old people die of loneliness. Confined prisoners go insane.

Speaking of pain and loneliness, many men suffer heart attacks or commit suicide during, or as a result of their divorce and losing their house and kids. Almost all of them "fall apart." I'm one of the lucky ones to land on my feet. I guess one's ability to survive pain is like the training of great athletes. Start 'em when they're young.

My first childhood memory is one of severe loneliness. I was two years old and approaching my third birthday. I only remember waking up in a room full of strange kids and a lot of beds and I started to cry that I wanted my father. I was so scared. I was almost hyperventilating that, "I want to go home." Finally a "big boy" said to me, "Don't worry. Your dad is coming soon." I believed him and sat on my hospital bed waiting. Finally a nurse came and I got dressed and then my father handed me my little grey coat and matching cap. I had no clue that my tonsils had been removed that day. Just like I had no clue sixty years in the future that they remove men's testicles in divorce court.

And that is why the childish, infamous "silent treatment" is so effective. The weapon of choice used by spoiled brats and manipulative narcissists, that is easily seen as nothing more than the obvious immature behavior of a toddler throwing a tantrum, works. The rabbis of the Talmud understood its power upon the manipulated masses. Excommunication works. Shunning is abuse. In fact, it is slow torture. Try finding a *Shidduch* for your child in Monsey in the first quarter of this twenty-first century if you are excommunicated. Good luck with that. Saying Pslams won't help.

It should come as no surprise that the risk of death due to loneliness and social isolation is twice more likely to occur than succumbing to the Grim Reaper because of obesity. Loneliness has the same effect on one's mortality as smoking fifteen cigarettes a day. *I've probably been smoking a full carton a day since my first protection order.* Isn't science fun!

In modern-day terms, we would say that stealing a dollar means you're a "bit of a thief." But pocketing four billion dollars into your personal account as the butcher-terrorist Arafat did while posing as a "freedom fighter" for the Palestinian (i.e. Jordanian) people gets a wreath placed on his grave by Mandela. Power and fame blur reality. When a government drops a second atom bomb on innocent civilians before their government can even comprehend the devastation of the first one, the merciless overkill that we tolerate as simply a part of "waging war" barely emotes a sigh from Americans on the other side of the ocean. And when a cruel, imbecilic state judge issues an Order of Protection, people automatically believe it must have been warranted.

The greatest transference of wealth has always been through politics, war, and acts of violence. The Inquisition brought incredible wealth to The Church. The threat of jail forces the individual to pay inordinate amounts of taxes on every dollar he earns, spends, saves, inherits, or bequeaths to his heirs — even though he knows more than half the money will be wasted. If government is so good, why does everyone hate it? If politicians are our representatives, why are we filled with dread and contemptuous disgust by the time we vote a new liar into office?

Despots are constantly emptying the coffers of their treasuries. Democratic leaders vote to raise their own salaries and secure excellent health benefits for themselves while taking decades to raise the minimum wage of their constituents to a still-unlivable rate. A house is something you buy on credit, and spend your life paying off, as you pay for it a second time in local taxes and amortization schedules that you don't begin to even pretend you comprehend. You're too busy trying to "catch up on your bills" to even understand what it is exactly that you are paying.

You have no clue that if states would lower local taxes, they could probably cure half the issues of their homeless population. But you barely have time to grumble about another yearly tax increase as you catch your breath from the one levied last year. In truth, so much time, money, and lives are wasted because of short term greed. Yes, "lives," because you are spending over a third of yours for the privilege of being called an "American." You'll live an average of seventy-eight years, watch football on Sunday, and MMA on Saturday, but you're highly unlikely to ask, even once in your life, "What if there was no such thing as countries?" Your brain only comprehends Socialism vs. Democracy. And so we all "eat a small piece of cake" and we tolerate all of the bullshit we're fed because trillion dollar budgets are incomprehensible to the average Joe.

I paid a very heavy emotional marriage tax. My wife stole one PTSD-dollar at a time till my soul declared bankruptcy. I almost broke down by the time I finally filed for divorce and a fresh start late in life. But with my wife, that's when the fun started. One might be inclined to think that a little Protection Order or six that followed during our divorce might not seem like a big deal. But losing your daughter because of how easily orders are issued is a major earth-shattering destructive event. And the lie of being labeled a violent pedophile is still being whispered among the droopy double-chinned blabbermouths of Rockland County.

My wife will keep repeating her delusional accusations forever. Even after she is laid to rest. Because my wife will never rest. My super-focused wife is as unstable as Hitler (not said in anger). She did not kill one. She did not kill many. She only "almost" killed me. One emotional cut at a time. One protection order at a time. One elevated blood pressure digit at a time. One lonely Ester-less minute at a time. One summons to appear in criminal court at a time. One summons to appear in family court at a time. One sirens-wailing urgent police visit on Shabbat at a time. One call to my principal at a time. One discussion with Ester (after it became a "crime" for me to speak with her) at a time.

I am merely fortunate to have a physically strong heart. Even if it is a lonely and broken one. That's what happens when you exercise, play sports, and run thirty miles a week for decades. Your body becomes strong. But scientists now know that stress will distend and literally break even a powerful heart. It's all just a matter of time. But ants don't tell time. They keep marching. One step at a time.

My wife did her best to strip away my passion for life, my self-esteem, my reputation, and my paternal love for Ester. Her emails completely exposed her. And Alfieri, Ferro, and Schwartz were obviously cut from the same mold as my wife, Putin, Hitler, and Bundy. They simply present their mental illnesses in various, but obvious, ways.

What they share is a complete lack of humanity. Like red ants, who are relentless warriors, they will continue to march — foraging for one more overtime dollar while warring with their perceived enemies as they squirt tittle-tattle venomous "Grobe Luge" falsehoods and issue manipulative court-ordered toxic directives achieved through perjury, while spiking their enemies drinks with plutonium or their husband's wine with potassium — beheading the heads of their enemies as they suck the lifeblood out of their helpless squirming victims who are firmly entangled in the gossip-spewing Jew-jaws of their "over nourished" Yenta armies.

Alfieri handed the bailiff what was probably the only "urgent" Stay-Away Protection Order ever stamped in a United States courtroom dated three weeks in the future! The bailiff, wearing his firm gun belt that holstered and snuggled a shiny automatic 9mm pistol, taser, and mace, walked the order over to the "future" dangerous, life-threatening, treacherous "pedophile" who was "obsessed with feces," that had only moments ago been invited to spend some quality time with his wife and minor daughter — with whom it would become a criminal act to even approach "within a hundred yards" of wherever said wife and daughter stood in a dangerous future, envisioned by the Poop Prophet Alfieri in a mere twenty-one days.

According to the state court guidelines regarding issuing an order of protection, Alfieri deemed it "more likely than not" that I was "going to become dangerous" at the end of the next few weeks. The deranged devil had suddenly morphed into a holy prophet.

I could have slept with my cute blow-up doll who "feared my wrath," swinging with her from the proverbial chandelier for the next four nights in a row, cuddling her before she left for Silver Spring where we always spent the Passover holiday with my sleazy brother-in-law and the notorious Jack Abramoff, and no one would have been the wiser.

I could have even left a money-shot evidence of my DNA all over her cute face and gossip-spewing tongue, and sexual assault would have been the furthest thought on anyone's mind. I could have even slapped the shit out of her and claimed she liked rough sex. Nice fantasy there. (Please don't take out a protection order, Sharen. It's a joke.) Four full nights of pre-pedophilic marital coitus. All sanctioned by the Honorable Village Idiot, Victor J. Alfieri.

And then I had been granted an additional two weeks to spend alone in a house that my wife had earlier insisted in open court that I should be evicted from because she claimed that I had, "hacked the computers and wired the entire home for sound and bugged all the rooms with hidden cameras." My wife and her lawyer had even filed a criminal complaint against me in criminal court for computer hacking her email account for which I had faced a year in jail.

And now Thing One and Thing Two were suddenly allowing me free access to our marital abode for a full two weeks and three days. My wife and Schwartz had graciously given me enough time to even assemble my entire Mission Impossible team to wire the entire perimeter at 19 Mariner Way with the latest satellite surveillance technology and even explosives! And Alfieri now agreed, for the next few weeks, at least, that THE MINOR CHILD was the safest kid in the world. And she was.

Alfieri also once again displayed what an imbecilic fucking moron he was. This man was beyond impulsive. He could have simply said, "Sorry Ma'am, I'm issuing the order today. It's for your and the minor child's protection." Trust me, it was not an act of mercy that pushed his hand to post-date the order. His actions could only be attributed to one of three factors. Stupidity. Insanity. Or, God. I'm going with "door number one." I'm not even sure if there is a door number three anymore. If there is, all I have to say is, "Shut the door!"

It really is difficult to explain the combined wickedness, ineptitude, and slovenly judicial oversight in the divorce-family court system that wreaks havoc upon countless families. There are an army of detestable miscreant-judges scattered throughout our entire judicial system that are permanently destroying the lives of millions of innocent, hardworking, tax-paying citizens daily. Every facet of our judicial system has spiraled out of control in the last fifty years.

The family, divorce, and foster care systems are nothing more than a cash-cow bank for those in power who earn millions while tormenting anyone who steps into their oppressive hellhole. Civil forfeiture is another outrageous piggy bank for local governments to instantly strip away the wealth of its citizens. And the criminal court system is bursting in its need to be reformed.

One merely has to experience any of the inferno chambers of our court system to recognize how badly Lady Justice has been gang-raped by lawyers, judges, and court-appointed bottom-feeders. Her blindfold sits over her gouged-out eye sockets as the puffy blackened-eyes of the helpless citizens she was supposed to serve and protect cry for her to execute justice. Meanwhile, an army of lazy leeches are hacking-away with her sword, sacrificing countless innocent men, women, and, worst of all, children, on their profit-altar dripping in high-blood-pressure blood.

Here I had been suddenly tossed out of my house, while miraculously being granted three weeks to find a place to live by the very woman I was desperately trying to divorce. I didn't have enough money in my account for a week's worth of groceries, let alone two month's deposit for an apartment. Perhaps I'm the one who is crazy, but my back was so against the wall that I decided to do what any warrior would do the moment he saw there was no escape route. I chose to visit the enemy's camp. If Alfieri was going to kill me, I might as well expose his judicial viciousness and include him in my execution.

I decided Alfieri's decision had to be challenged in the Appellate Courts. Surely those experienced gentlemen would agree that The Alf's behavior had been beyond egregious, wantonly abusive, irrational, cruel, and judiciously primitive. *Maybe they'd even demand that he retire.*

Divorce court is a well-greased cremation machine that incinerates whatever is left of a broken family and sends the remains up in smoke. It is designed to empty the pockets of those who are wildly enraged, or foolish enough to fight it out in court. And it only takes one spouse to yell "Flame on!" Or one capricious judge. Trouble is, there are so many of them. Like rats infesting New York City.

As Kelly Rutherford told *Vanity Fair* regarding her own $1.5 million legal tab, "Divorce is a total racket." The felled forests of appeals, criminal complaints, subpoenas, depositions, protection orders, trial transcripts, motions and cross-motions, and scores of other frivolous legalese filed (and rarely read) during the course of a typical divorce all attest to the wasted monies and wasted years spent wasting the lives of a parting couple as they bid each other a final "Fuck-you-adieu!"

At this point, I knew that Judge Alfieri was going to destroy my life, and so I figured I'd finally incur the expense of proving how inept and cruel this drunkard was by appealing just one of his endless deranged "So ordered!" directives. I had many decisions to choose from, such as his taking the illegal advice of my wife's lawyer to split our retirement monies — instead of freezing my wife's paycheck with the stroke of his pen and instantly enforcing temporary maintenance — when I finally decided to take my case to the appellate division. I merely chose The Alf's most recent protection order because I was so bloody tired of the immense stress and destruction they caused in my life ... and Ester's.

There were over two dozen directives I could have chosen to challenge. Each one costs a minimum of $10,000 dollars to appeal. I knew I lost Ester. I really had nothing to fight for anymore. I understood that appellate judges rarely vote against their own. *But surely I'm not living in North Korea. How could they possibly agree with Alfieri,* I reasoned. Against the advice of my friends that I might anger Alfieri even more (are you kidding me?), I figured I had nothing to lose but the money that I borrowed to battle the beast.

After all, I was dying anyway. I figured I might as well have something to show for my efforts. The appellate lawyer I retained prepared the appeal and had to spend a day (at $450 dollars an hour) waiting his turn to serve an *emergency request.* The court read his four pages of legalese and summarily issued an immediate response (within 24 hours) that was found to be completely in my favor.

The only faster legal decision is a governor's stay of execution which can instantly block a death warrant even if the prisoner has already been strapped down to the execution table with an intravenous tube inserted in his arm whose prepped veins are ready to receive a lethal injection of phenobarbital. James Autry gets dishonorable mention as the recipient of such a last-second stay. Sharen would have made an excellent Executioner. She was all for law and order, and great at "finding vein."

The Appellate Court issued an immediate decision that was not merely a temporary injunction, but a naked revelation of the brazen error in basic law bumbled by The Alf that would have been embarrassing, along with being registered as a failing grade, to any first-year law student in a mock court trial. Alfieri had denied me my most rudimentary legal rights protected under the law. He was finally tagged for doing what he had been doing since day one — being his "own law" (literally making shit up) and keeping his barbaric intravenous tube open in my stress clogged vein while dispensing illegal "court ordered" *In God We Trust* directives full of lethal stress.

In short, the higher court ruled that no reasonable judge with an iota of logic or decency would have ever done the bullying from the bench that Alfieri illegally did to me. The latest protection order was instantly vacated by the appellate jurisdiction where it abruptly vanished almost as magically as the warlock Alfieri made it appear.

My lawyer wrote a quick four-page brief which outlined and explained how I was railroaded out of my house. Without the least bit of concern for due process, and along with my wife's attorney proclaiming and admitting in open court that there had "never been any incidents" during our entire riddled-with-protection-orders-divorce ... The Honorable Victor Alfieri, on a capricious whim, after forcing me to appear pro se, after refusing to enforce the maintenance and legal fees payments he had ordered my moneyed-spouse wife to pay numerous times so that I could rent a place to live, issued an outrageous *Stay-Away* order of protection.

The Appellate court must have thought Alfieri was crazy. Or on drugs and medications. Or simply embarrassingly foolish. I imagine they must have fallen off their bench while reading the transcripts that revealed the stench of Alfieri's courtroom proceedings. They had to be shocked at what transpired in a court under their jurisdiction. Yet, they did nothing more than respond to the one single issue brought before them.

I did have the right to appeal my entire discombobulated case. But it would have cost me a minimum of ten times the amount I had just spent on this single simple no-brainer appeal that I won on borrowed money and borrowed time. Because there is no reimbursement for proving that a judge has treated you mendaciously — just a shitty piece of Appellate toilet paper to prove what an asshole you've been dealing with and then more anal-like torture when you land back in the lap of a furious judge.

In truth, most litigants rarely bother to even question the decisions of their judge. They are conditioned to be impressed by a judge's judicial black robe and pedestal seating. As a scholar, I've been trained to question, attack, and debate every word in the Talmud uttered by our holy sages. Credentials mean nothing. We are taught to speak logically and truthfully or remain humbly silent.

On a level playing field I would have destroyed the unlettered and uncircumcised smelly smegma dickhead mind of Alfieri — whose response to evidence and logic was never anything more intelligent than, "I'll hold you in contempt!" And the more you respectfully tried to explain your honest and clever position, the louder Alfieri's roaring threats of contempt reverberated in his churlish courtroom.

The truth is that this man's judicial chamber should not have displayed gleaming polished wooden walls, but padded cushion protective panels. What it resembled most was Purgatory. And Alfieri flawlessly played the role of the fire-breathing prosecutor known as The Satan.

Most people just do as they are told, figuring the "professional judge" surely knows what he is doing. And so they rarely protest (except for an angry Facebook post that is forgotten faster than it was typed). Litigant's rarely file appeals. Besides, aside from their cost being prohibitive, the outcome almost always favors the decision of the judge.

Appellate judges lead very calm, pontifical lives ignoring the shenanigans of their peers while flowing with the status quo. And furthermore, our entire judicial court system, that includes Appellate judges getting paid to bury their heads in the sand, is moving at the perfect snail pace for pension-fortunes to be made.

I'm literally a one among one-hundred statistic that found the finances and nerve (frayed ones, actually) to appeal the decision of his judge. It's prohibitively expensive because you are daring to move the wheels of justice faster than the pace of a shifting tectonic plate. Judges get away with issuing whatever their mood-swing emotions instructs them to do the day they fuck up your life. After all, they're wearing a black robe. And the sign does say, "In God We Trust." So how can a judge possibly be wrong when he yells out, "Well, I'm gonna issue it myself! Today!"

Robert Sapolsky cites a famous Israeli scientific study which proved that a hungry judge is much more likely to issue a harsh prison sentence than a judge that enjoyed a recent gratifying lunch. The mild stress of one missed meal could easily cost a man many extra years in jail. And Sapolsky is talking about rational judges. Now imagine waiting for justice to be dispensed by someone as wild and incorrigible as Alfieri whose every meal nourishes a Last Supper "So ordered!" betrayal. The recipient of a decision rendered by The Alf could wind up ordering their last meal on death row.

I easily won my appeal (and now historically-documented decision) in an incredibly deserved slap-in-the-fucking-face by three appellate division judges against Alfieri — who suffered not the slightest downside at my having to spend $12,000 dollars merely to contest just one of his maniacal decisions. There is no such thing as a split decision or a close call in the Appellate Court. It's a cold day in hell when an appellate court overturns the ruling of a presiding "Unzereh" judge. But then again, every day in The Alf's courtroom was hell. Might as well enjoy a cold one.

A local legal-analyst journalist named Michael Volpe came across the newsworthy, extremely rare appellate turnover decision and politely contacted me for details. He'd been writing for years about judges like Alfieri that pop up like herpes cold sores in hundreds of US cities.

My case eventually made it into our local paper, *The Rockland Times* in an article titled *Complaints Against Judge Alfieri Rack up*. I wasn't the only person to experience the inebriated, illogical, empathy-challenged, shriveled brain of "The Alf." I still remember the shock of the jaded and experienced journalist who interviewed me for the article.

"Do you have proof of that Mr. Lewinson?" he'd gently ask over a dozen times in a somewhat stunned state of mind as we spoke for hours over the phone.

I shot over document after document so that Volpe could verify facts, along with the court proceedings of what transpired in Alfieri's kangaroo-court room. Michael Volpe couldn't even use everything I gave him. "I'd have to write a book," he explained. I'm now writing "that book," and even I am forced to leave out endless material because the tempestuous tsunami-onslaught of the mendacious malicious prosecution I experienced would be too overwhelming for any reader to ingest.

I had been praying that the article, upon being published, might have Alfieri removed from the bench. *If the authorities only knew what a tyrant this thug was* ... I imagined. What I did not realize was that a story about yet another pathetically incompetent, arrogant judge is less newsworthy than yesterday's weather report. The Catholic Church merely takes a century to change its mind on some dogmatic issue like divorce or gay rights. But defrocking a judge takes forever. The article did enjoy its own fifteen minutes of fame in Rockland County, but winning my appeal accomplished nothing more than that day's paper being sold out by mid-morning. Zip-a-dee-doodah!

Returning home from her Passover holiday, my wife was shocked to find me in the house. Faster than she could grab a bargain kosher chicken that fell off a truck, and without even asking me if I dropped by merely to pick up a few last things, the angel who only a few weeks earlier proclaimed in open court that I "can stay," now acted as if there was a burglar in the house and, in a desperately dire voice, immediately dialed an extremely urgent emergency call to the police to explain that although she had "a Stay Away Order of Protection" that, "... he's still here! Come now!" The fastest sports car in the world can't go from zero to sixty as fast as my *Vybie*.

Sure enough, Dr. Jekyll had transformed back into Mrs. Hyde mode. I listened from behind my guest room door as they placed a "frantic" Mrs. Hyde on hold, even as she insisted that the world was on fire, and then told her that there was no order of protection. "No!" I could hear her shout. "No! You're making a big mistake! There's an Order of Protection!" Her immediate next call was to her lawyer. Ants never stop marching.

When we appeared again in court, my wife's attorney, who admitted in his emails that tossing me out of the house was a "long shot" because I was such a "goody-two-shoes," informed our judge that I "went behind his [Alfieri's] back" to the appellate division — insinuating that I had committed a dastardly crime of sorts by exercising my constitutional rights in filing a costly motion to the appellate division in order to contest his illegal, issued without any due process, protection order.

The judge, always jumping like a trained dog to idiotically follow any lead suggested by Schwartz, looked at me savagely, and in a growl filled with a combination of outrage and disgust, scowled as he barked, "And ...?!" as he stared at me intently.

"... and we won, your honor," I respectfully whispered.

Alfieri's face turned crimson as he roared at me in a voice that combined furious hate and fiery wrath as he threatened to hold me in contempt and to "put you [me] in jail if you [I] ever try that again!"

I wasn't exactly expecting a contrite apology for his having issued a ridiculous and totally uncalled for order of protection that cost me a small fortune to easily defeat upon appeal. But I had hoped The Alf might be embarrassed or somewhat evasive about what the higher courts thought of his dimwit decisions and ignore that it ever happened.

Instead, I found myself imagining that I was standing in some medieval court of inquisition during the Dark Ages, as the Honorable Victor Alfieri, sitting in front of a sign that said *In God We Trust*, growled like a madman, heating up his implements of torture over glowing hot coals as he stared at me with utter contempt ...

I remember the first time I learned about the concentration camps of the Nazi era. Ironically it was a very happy day, as I was celebrating my turning ten years old at my own birthday party. Among the many gifts I received that day was a pair of clip-on roller-skates. My father was always overprotective (probably because he was too aware of how fragile life can be) and nervous about my possibly hurting myself if I would learn to skate. He wanted to take away the skates, but Dad never forced me to do anything, and I refused to relinquish them.

The Jewish people survived for many millenniums through bribing the authorities in exchange for their lives. And now, my father bribed me. Twenty-five cents could buy a lot of baseball cards (five packs — with gum!) back in 1963, and I smiled at my father as I handed over the skates while admiring my shiny new quarter.

Little did Dad realize just how entrepreneurial I already was as I celebrated my first decade of existence. I stealthily followed my father as he descended the basement stairs to see where he would hide my skates. Very shortly I'd have a shiny quarter *and* a shiny new pair of clip-on skates to match.

I was making "money moves" thirty years before Cardi B. would even exist. Dad walked back upstairs, and I snuck out from my hiding spot and carefully pulled down a dusty, musty-smelling, old leather valise. I undid the two huge tan colored belt buckles and scanned the contents to retrieve my skates.

Little did I realize that I was unwrapping another lifetime gift of sorts that would haunt me for the rest of my life as I opened a Pandora's Box that revealed a dark side of humanity that, like the little woman I once cuddled, I find impossible to comprehend to this day.

A picture of half-naked skeletal people staring at the camera that immortalized their short lives suddenly caught my eye. I lifted the rubber-banded pile of postcard-size pictures and slowly rotated picture after shocking picture. Many were gruesome as they displayed mounds of dead skeletons-with-skin whose emaciated limbs protruded and dangled from the rotting heaps of God's Chosen.

There were also pictures of smiling handsome young men and vibrant pretty women who had become ghosts. Years later I would discover that some were my murdered relatives and others were nameless friends of my father that had joined the resistance and were never seen again. The pictures Dad saved was all that remained of their existence.

Having absolutely no fear of a father who never raised his voice to me in my entire life, let alone hit me, my curiosity forced me to immediately return to the only source I knew that could answer questions that I was too young to articulate. My father laughed as he saw me holding the boxed-up skates, and gently explained that we have to keep our word. I handed him the pictures, and in Yiddish (German, too) I asked, "Vos es dos, Tatie?"

My father sat me down as he tried to explain the impossible to a ten-year-old precocious little boy. He told me that there were once some very bad people that killed most of his family and many other people.

"Why?" I innocently asked.

"Because they were evil," he answered without a hint of hate or anger (or science). My dad explained that there was an evil man named Hitler who killed many Jews, and that he was one of the lucky ones that survived a prison camp called Dachau. I suddenly understood why I had only one set of grandparents.

My Dad told me how his mother cried her heart out as she insisted that he leave home as the Germans quickly advanced. "Run Yankeleh, run!" his mother lovingly advised as she gently kissed her sixteen-year-old son for the last time. "Maybe you'll live," she wept, as she desperately prayed to an angry God to have mercy, begging that her youngest of eight children might possibly survive the German blitzkrieg engulfing country after European country, seventeen years before I was destined to be born.

My father showed me his blue-stripped prison jacket — that he was forced to wear for the crime of being a direct descendant of the Holy Patriarchs — made from some rag material that felt like cardboard. He explained that it was the only thing he had to wear in the freezing cold weather and that he would stuff newspapers inside the jacket to act as a lining of sorts to protect him from the bitter cold as he walked barefoot on frozen ground, working himself to death for the price of a piece of stale bread and some warm broth-water called soup.

But the labor of my father's emaciated life was totally worthless to the German's whose pleasure in physically and verbally abusing their "pig-dog!" prisoners was the only value they placed on the shaved pistol-practice heads of their starving Jewish targets.

"A dog in the street had more legal rights than a Jew," my father calmly explained in Yiddish to his ever-curious young son. He was being literal — not sarcastic.

My father told me how he stumbled upon a garbage can that had slices of peeled potato skins from the kitchen where the SS concentration camp guards' meals were prepared. He explained that starvation was so painful that he risked his life as he ate what felt like a banquet meal, knowing that he'd be shot before he could even swallow if a German citizen in uniform caught him "stealing."

"Weren't you scared, Tatie?"

"I vos [was] dead already," my dad (who spoke fluently in four other languages) tried to explain in his Yiddish accent and Lithuanian lisp, "So how could I be scared? Vonce you're dead, 'der is nothing more vat to fear."

The Dachau Diet Plan, by the way, guaranteed a weight loss within a mere forty-five days that would slowly starve a prisoner to death if an unmerciful bullet didn't end the dieters' life first. In other words, one's life expectancy in Dachau was anywhere from one to forty-five days, starting from the day they arrived, already half-starved, upon their first-class cattle-car accommodation to death. One thing for sure. By six weeks they were going to be skin and bones. Or ash.

If a prisoner lived a long life at Dachau, his emaciated remains would be cremated and the ashes of a being "created in the image of God" would then be used as fertilizer for the flower and vegetable gardens of the SS devils. If you truly are what you eat, then ironically, the Germans monsters became Jewish. Lieutenant Colonel Walter Fellenz, upon being informed that dead Jewish parents and their children were fertilizing his gardens, politely quipped in his report to the Commanding General, as he marveled "… no wonder the flowers were so beautiful!"

The man surely must have been as charming as Kapo Dan Schwartz, Esq. I attach the accolade of 'Kapo' to Mr. Schwartz — not intended in any way as a barb, but as a true description of the role of a heartless kapo in the concentration camps. A Kapo was a Jew that would turn on his fellow Jew for money. It is the most horrific name one Jew would ever call another Jew. But I don't consider Schwartz a Jew. Or even human. Posting pictures of yourself wearing a Cantor's Yarmulka on Facebook doesn't disguise the fact that you are a Kapo-Cantor.

I don't know exactly why, perhaps it was the curious child in me, but I impulsively tried on my father's jacket. It was a perfectly tailored fit. For a ten-year-old little boy. Without the lining. It occurred to me that my father might have been one of those skeletons standing in the pictures I had just handed him. But I was so young, that I didn't know how to ask him. At that age all I could do was to constantly think about things that I didn't know how to express.

My donning the jacket caught Dad by surprise. He stared at me with an almost blank look in his rare grayish-green colored eyes when he suddenly began to whimper. I had never seen him cry. I stared back and wondered how they (whoever "they" were) could be so inhumane to such a nice man. I continued to stare at the gentlest man on the planet … a man whose survival of the Dachau

1.03 carat, Fancy Vivid Yellow,
DECISION AND ORDER
WITH NOTICE OF ENTRY
- against -
Index No.: 2129/2013
SHAREN LEWINSON,
Defendant.
SIRS:
PLEASE TAKE NOTICE that the within is a copy of the DECISION AND
signed by the Hon. Victor J. Alfieri, Jr., JSC. on September 11, 2015; and duly
the office of the Clerk of the within Court on the 11th day of September, 2015.
Dated: Chestnut Ridge, New York
September 11, 2015
DANIEL B. SCHWARTZ, ESQ.
KANTROWITZ, GOLDHAMER,
& GRAIFMAN, P.C.
Attorneys for Defendant
747 Chestnut Ridge Road
Chestnut Ridge, New York 10977
(845) 356-2570
TO: ZEV LEWINSON
Plaintiff Pro Se
19 Marner Way
New York 10952
request the honour of your presence
at the marriage of their children
Sharon Faith
and
Zev
Tuesday, the second of July
Nineteen hundred and eighty-five
at half after six o'clock
Chupah at eight o'clock
Manhattan Beach Jewish Center
Sixty West End Avenue
Brooklyn, New York
Get
in touch
with
your
feminine
side.

Re: Swordpen.com, Inc. v. Henry Holt and Co., et al.
S.D.N.Y. Civil Action No. 07 Civ. 10955 (KMK)
Dear Judge Karas:
As your Honor is aware, we represent the defendants in the above-captioned action. I am writing to inform the Court that the defendants have decided not to pursue their motion for attorneys' fees, filed on October 8, 2009, and have notified Mr. Lewinson of that decision.
Respectfully,
Robert D. Balin
call ms. Smith and tell her this and whats in the other notebook
Rabbinical Court
Ezer Mishpat
Rabbi Pinchus Rabinowitz
בית דין צדק
עזר משפט
109 Park Ln. • Monsey • NY • 10952 • Tel. (845) 641-4345
כתב סירוב
זאת למודעי בשער בת רבים שהוזמן ר' זאב לעווינסאן לדי"ת על פי
בקשת התובע אשתו מרת שעראן לעווינסאן, בביד"צ עזר משפט ,
ומשתמט מלהתדיין.
ע"כ אנו מוצאים חובה לנפשנו להכריז על ר' זאב לעווינסאן שנקרא
מסרב
ודינו מבואר בשו"ע חו"מ סימן י"א סעיף א' וביו"ד סימן
של"ד, עד שיחזור בו ויציית לדין כדת, ואז ושב ורפא
לו. חובה מוטלת על כל מי שיש בידו להשפיע על הנ"ל
שיהא ציית דינא, מחויב לעשות כן ויהא בכלל המעמידים
הדת על תילה.
8. RF-ins.
9. Cheeky Cup Ore
Call Rachel Skjoell
call meany
Best of luck today! ... great year! ... especially ... that book by Levy!

death camp was more rare than the color of his eyes, and I asked, almost in a whisper, "How could they do this … to you?"

It was a question I will ask as long as I live. And I'll then continue to ask it after I die.

I became obsessed with the history of the Jews during the decade from 1940 to 1950. Eventually I became a student of Jewish history, and then of world history, and I majored in history and philosophy at Johns Hopkins. I read *The Nazi Doctors* and Solzhenitsyn. I read *Night* by Elie Wiesel and *The Diary of a Young Girl* by Anne Frank. I read *Mein Kampf.* I researched and I spoke delicately to survivors at the synagogue who shared their incredibly powerful, yet pitifully sorrowful, stories with me.

As I got older, my father shared sad stories and nightmarish details about his own experiences during the war. Shouted out of bed by two-legged barking dogs and huge German Shepherds that weighed as much as the human-remains lining up for roll call at 4 A.M. each morning, the "prisoners" were forced to stand in line for hours on end in the bitter cold while never knowing when they would suddenly be forced to "play" *Tzenter* (every tenth man shot) with the guards. *Tzenter* was a terrifyingly dreadful ritual that the bored half-drunk guards frequently forced the prisoners to survive in their thrice-daily attendance routine.

"Tzenter! Tzenter!" was originally a common cry for a "Tenth man!" in European Jewish Ghettos to assemble a quorum of the ten men (a *minyan*) needed to recite the *Kaddish* (a prayer for universal peace — that didn't seem to be working out too well for the Jewish reciters) at the synagogue. A town crier would often walk about the shanty shops shouting *"Tzenter! Tzenter!"* as if to say, "We have nine already, we need just one more man to complete the mitzvah! Please come join us!" It was considered an added mitzvah — a merit God would add to the positive side of one's 'good deeds versus bad deeds scale' — to be the final worshiper who walked in to complete the minyan.

In their typical deranged fashion, there was nothing the Nazis could not diabolically pervert to psychologically torment their prisoners. The German guards took the lovely concept of *Tzenter!* and invented a new version of Russian-Roulette as they asked, "Who wants to be the tenth? Who wants to be the tenth?" Then a few guards slowly walked behind the lines of emaciated souls, and one never knew when they'd suddenly pump a bullet into the shaved bald head of a Jew. That bullet could arrive in a second or in sixty seconds. No one breathed.

The Nazi's absolutely treasured the suspense. And it didn't help if you were first in line. Oftentimes, the count would begin from prisoner number two or three. And to keep the "game" really interesting and exciting, the guards further modified their Nazi-Roulette pastime as they occasionally let loose with a surprise burst of rapid fire, killing a bunch of prisoners at once.

They'd laugh hysterically as they had the other skeletons pile up a dead *minyan*. Ha-ha.

King David proclaims in Psalm 121:4, "Behold! The Protector of Israel will not slumber or sleep." I wouldn't be able to sleep either.

We foolish Jews still sincerely believe that God, and the world, plays by the rules. Joke's on us. We are a cuckolded nation that keeps apologizing to its *spouse*, begging to be forgiven for our "sins." The more I read, and the more I learned of the senseless and barbaric atrocities of the Holocaust, the less I understood.

The knowledge I accumulated only became more propellant to feed the flames of burning unanswerable questions. In my naive quest for truth, I was searching for closure to something which could never be defined by a rational mind or an irrational "It was God's will" insulting explanation. I was emotionally exhausting myself to explain the unfathomable. It was beyond painful. It was more debilitating than trying to frantically swim out of quicksand. And it was a terrible conditioning fortelling how I would deal with my future marriage. I would talk my parched heart out before finally serving papers.

Victor Alfieri helped me comprehend the type of men who callously and inhumanly dispensed death without the least bit of logic, shame, or remorse. Trust me, I understand that my experience in a Rockland County courtroom was not Dachau, and I am not rushing to invoke "Godwin's law" to compare Alfieri to Hitler. But I will certainly say that experiencing the heartless and completely unnecessary "Court Ordered!" base-brutishness of a smirking Alfieri — as a sickening half-smile appeared on his icy face revealing his lust for power in a shitty county courtroom — helped me to comprehend the type of men that incarcerated my saintly father for the crime of simply being a Jew.

The complete and total disdain with which the Honorable Victor Alfieri invoked his powers granted and empowered by the state against such an innocent man as myself was a very enlightening first-hand lesson in experiencing a fraction of what my father endured. And a fraction was more than enough of a lesson for me to comprehend how mindlessly evil, heartless, and cold-blooded damaged DNA and misfiring synapses can be. "I'm the law!" Alfieri would constantly scream from the bench. And even respectfully trying to state the truth would only deliver a quick sadistic slap of, "You're being argumentative! I'll hold you in contempt!"

The Alf, who viciously remarked, "Not my problem!" when I pleaded and begged that I had no money for food and nowhere to go as he threw me out of my house with a "stay away" Order of

Protection, could easily have been a reincarnation of the inhuman SS beasts that taunted my then ninety-pound emaciated father by calling him a "muselmann" after starving him to literal near-death weakness. And the cold fury with which The Alf rushed like a madman to dispense his heartless judicial decisions and "So Ordered!" decrees could as easily have been his stamping my papers, while barking at me in German to board a cattle car to Dachau.

I am not Nazi-phobic. I have a phobia against all evil. But between the wanton degeneracy of Heer Doktor Mengele Ferro, Amtsrichter Victor Alfieri, and Kapo Dan Schwartz, "Yimakh shemo v zikhro" ("May his name and memory be erased"), I continued to suffer my way through the Fourth Fucking Reich.

The Rockland Times story hit the newsstands several days later and all hell broke loose. My first amendment rights were protected, but Alfieri had issued a gag order because of the minor child and now wanted to hold me in contempt for "discussing the case in public," screaming at my having "gone to the press" while threatening to immediately incarcerate me for at least ninety days.

I argued that I had not spoken about the child and only related facts that were "out there" for anyone who Googled our names. I was so exhausted at this point that I no longer cared if I lived or died. I'm amazed at what many other men tolerate, and sadly, what many men do to themselves when they no longer can. Alfieri finally settled down and satisfied himself with roaring at me as he warned me to "Shut up!"

I then asked His Honor if he would recuse himself from my case since it was obvious that he could no longer remain impartial, and that Ester's future hung in the balance. Alfieri once again fumed at me, "Ya think ya know the law! Well here's the law Mr. Lewinson! In Rockland County the *judge* gets to decide if the case warrants reclusion! And I'm not stepping aside! I *know* this case! I've got a stack of papers reaching to the ceiling," as he intimated a huge stack with his clawed hand that amazingly possessed a prehensile thumb, "and if you dare ask me again, I'll hold you in contempt!"

I had finally publicly chopped off the head of this Hydra monster, who barely read any of his ceiling-high stack, only to watch the serpentine Alfieri instantly regrow two in its place. I continued to stare at the monstrous creature sitting in front of the *In God We Trust* sign, as I wondered where God was right now when Ester really needed Him.

"Ya won the battle Mr. Lewinson, but ya lost the war!" it roared. "Maybe I can't issue a protection order, but I'm immediately granting sole usage of the house to Mrs. Lewinson! You had better be outta the house by tonight!"

Just to rub salt into the wound, Alfieri then rescinded an earlier court order that demanded my wife pay $15,000 dollars to the new attorney I had chosen to represent me in our upcoming trial. Alfieri was now forcing me to appear pro se as payback for my having borrowed money to appeal his order of protection. "How did you pay the attorney you hired to appeal! You must have hidden money!" After completely ignoring that my wife was spending ten thousand dollars a month while refusing to pay a penny of temporary Court Ordered maintenance, The Alf "decided" that I had a hidden stash of cash. Alfieri was no longer out of control. He was out for blood.

The $12,000 dollars I had just begged and finally borrowed from my wealthy high-school friend to win my appeal accomplished nothing. I explained to Alfieri that I could source the money I borrowed, but I was fighting a Nazi bully surrounded by bailiff German Shepherds in a war that I was not allowed to finish. Evidence and truth meant absolutely nothing to SS Alfieri. He basically looked at me as an irritating annoyance.

Jewish prisoners were finally allowed to leave Auschwitz through its chimneys or by throwing themselves against the electrified barbed wire gates. But I could not release my testicles from the claws and vise-like grip of The Honorable Alfieri.

Every time I somehow miraculously outplayed the hand I was dealt from a stacked deck, the outlaw Alfieri calmly reshuffled the cards till he held all the aces and then once again proceeded to slowly deal them with that knowing smirk on his obnoxious sourpuss face. I never saw such an ugly handsome face in my life. *You really can't fight city hall*, I realized. I also understood that although divorce court was wilder than the old Wild West, I could not pull out a six-shooter to blast that creepy cheatin' critter between his eyes. Whether I shot him or not, I understood that I was never going to see Ester again. I knew it was over.

Ester used to cajole and teasingly beg me to drive past her school every morning because she found our conversations so interesting that she wanted me to continue talking.

"But you'll be late to school Honey," I'd warn, As I made believe I was about to turn into the school driveway but then continued straight ahead.

"I don't care! I want to talk to you! I'll get a note," she'd laugh.

DO NOT TALK TO MINOR CHILD.

Now Ester would not even look at me. I knew my divorce would have gone on for at least another two years and I wouldn't be seeing Ester anyway during that entire time. I couldn't take any more stress. The late Kenny Rogers wisely advised, as he emotionally sang in his rich tenor voice, "You gotta know when to fold 'em." At this point I knew that the most I could hope for was to die in my sleep.

I now understood how men languished in jail for an additional five years even after Innocence Project had clearly proven their innocence. It only took one vile prosecutor (and there are so many) to dangle many future years of continued incarceration over the head of a guiltless man, who was suffering a now obvious-to-all undeserved jail sentence, merely to force and barter the exchange of a time-served "victory" in place of an immediate long overdue pardon that will cost the state a few million dollars. What's an innocent man's life worth compared to not tarnishing the prosecutor's perfect record of "being tough on crime?" Backed by a heartless judge eager to cover his own behind at having rushed an innocent victim off to jail, it is easy to comprehend why the wheels of justice move so tortuously slow.

I knew I lost my daughter. I also knew that Alfieri was out to bury me. And I knew he would relish taking his time. He'd drag this on for years. Because "Vicious Vic" loved money as much as he hated me. What could be more pleasurable to this Nazi than to continue torturing me while getting paid overtime? Talk about a win-win windfall.

Victor Alfieri also had a thing for the ladies. Especially when they weren't married to him. And he showed it in court. The black-robed abhorrent cacodemon spoke gently to women, barely managing to feign interest as to how "their" children were faring, while simultaneously speaking angrily at the fathers of those often-alienated youngsters who no longer saw the most important man in their lives (thanks to The Alf's own maniacal malfeasance).

The wasted tax dollars, disowned children, and broken relationships were all a result of his endless court proceedings and wack-job jurisprudence. Alfieri simply filed for extensions while blaming the fathers who refused to roll over and die and foolishly chose to continue to fight to see their kids. For an amoral judge, defecating a shitty mess in his courtroom only added more "time and a half" funds to his pension. The shameless shaman alchemist turned shit into gold.

And although Vile Vic shouted at my wife during several court hearings, warning her that he'd hold her in contempt, admitting to the court stenographer for posterity that theoretically, "If *Missus* Lewinson were a *Mister* Lewinson she would have been in jail a long time ago" (that much was true), it was never more than a playacting front, because his actions completely tolerated her brazen contumacy.

The "Honorable" Victor Alfieri spoke to me with utter contempt from the very first day he met me in court. And his scorn and disdain only increased exponentially every time I opened my "argumentative" mouth.

Alfieri hated me even before I went to the Appellate division but was now angrily doubling down as he threatened to impose an additional $50,000 dollar salary to my teacher's salary. Imputing salary is only done when someone was earning a lot of money and then quits their job right before filing for divorce to lower their eventual alimony and child support payments. I pointed out to The Honorable Victor Alfieri that I had been earning the same salary for the past six years. His growling response was a nasty and vindictive, "Ya don't like it?! Appeal!"

Here I had been receiving the same W-2's as a part time afternoon teacher for the past six years. But Alfieri suddenly decided, in an underhanded compliment, that I'm very intelligent and could "easily" find better paying work (at age 63). "Get a job!" he snarled in contemptuous disgust in open court as if he were speaking to some bum on the street.

More than doubling my salary out of thin air would automatically halve any maintenance my wife would have to pay me while automatically doubling my child support payments to her. The vengefully vindictive and punitive Monopoly-money imputation of additional salary that Alfieri was now threatening to add to my base salary would obligate me to make payments in real dollars that would far exceed what I was actually earning. I'd be labeled a deadbeat dad faster than receiving my first illusionary paycheck and jailed as quickly as Alfieri could growl, "You're in contempt! Ninety days!"

A landmine field does not begin to describe the quagmire terrain of Herculean tasks that I had somehow overcome and survived for the past two and a half years. But I now found myself entangled in the hot serpentine coils of Alfieri's judicial opportunism as he deliberately manipulated the divorce codes to strangle me to death. I was no longer being asked to walk through the minefield. I was being forced to step on the explosives. It was very clear that Alfieri was set on destroying me and turning me into a deadbeat dad for my having revealed his egregious courtroom antics in the press.

Appealing merely one decision by this judiciously skanky judge cost me twelve thousand dollars. Appealing an entire court case containing all the files and transcripts of over two years of tangled motions and unenforced wishy-washy court-ordered decrees would easily cost over $150,000 dollars. That was basically half my life savings. And it would take at least a year to appeal.

I honestly didn't even know if the Appellate judges would be able to follow the illogicality of what had ensued under Alfieri's watch. And I was afraid they might simply toss their hands up and let the final divorce decree with Alfieri's imputation of my salary at $90,000 dollars stand. I wasn't between a rock and a hard spot. I was inside the rock.

I would also have to order a $25,000-dollar second opinion to totally negate the fifth-grade level rant submitted by the court appointed forensic psychiatrist, Dr. Dominic Ferro. But I knew Alfieri would simply repeat what he had already promised if I tried. "I know Dr. Ferro a long time, and between opposing evaluations, I'm going to trust his opinion." I could hire the most famous psychiatrist in the world, and it wouldn't matter. The Alf already "knew" that the pathological practitioner, who was his longtime Italian American goombah, was the best science had to offer.

Meanwhile, one merely needs to Google this harebrained demon's name to see how this Family Court bottom-feeder is described in reviews by his clients. As bad as Alfieri was as a judge, this total unprofessional quack was worse in his role as "doctor." His having graduated med school reminded me of the old joke: "What do you call the dumbest guy who graduates med school? A doctor." But there was nothing humorous about Ferro. This man was so diabolical, that even Alfieri, by contrast, would be eligible for sainthood.

Ferro's vindictiveness at my refusing to sign permission granting him the legal right to speak with my wife's therapist regarding Dr. Frank's "professional" opinion of my personality was capped with Ferro's continued and relentless shouting at me and vindictively promising, "I'm going to bury you when I write my report!" Like my wife, Ferro was obsessed with being in control. He really lost it. And I lost Ester.

I had seen the very criminal personal emails between my wife and her therapist in which Dr. Frank sneakily suggested that Sharen accuse me of alienation (fight fire with fire strategy). I understood that Rabbi Dr. Frank was a flagrant liar. After giving his word that if Sharen or I filed for divorce he would not see either of us as his patient, he quickly joined her dream-team of evildoers.

Two sessions a week at a hundred and fifty dollars each was hard for the shithead in a yarmulke to refuse. Meanwhile, Ferro contacted Alfieri to demand that I sign permission for Dr. Frank to evaluate and give his opinion of me. I didn't have to use much creative imagination to fathom the "professional" opinion the two villains would construct regarding any visitation with Ester. Fortunately, the very form that Ferro screamed at me to sign, also stated my RIGHT TO REFUSE in large bold letters.

"Hold me in contempt, Your Honor," I calmly replied as I finally stood up to all the bullies that were destroying my daughter's life, "I know my rights." I reached the point that I was willing to sit in jail. My blood pressure was surely off the charts. Exasperated, Alfieri told Ferro that he could not force me. My heart is racing even as I type these words five years after the experience.

And after all that stress in standing up to Ferro and Alfieri, Ferro contemptuously called my wife's therapist anyway. These wack-jobs will stop at nothing. Ferro confesses to breaking the law and incriminated himself in his own forensic report in which he took the time to write page upon page to chronicle my "arrogant defiance towards authority." Ferro obviously viewed himself as "authority," and in his professional opinion decided I'm an "arrogant" narcissist because of my "defiance" in refusing to relinquish my personal rights. Those rights were guaranteed by the same legal system that stamped his Nazi medical license.

The report reads as if it were written by an angry ten-year-old child on Ritalin. My wife's therapist refused to take Ferro's call (knowing the severity of the laws involving patient privacy). It didn't matter. Ferro's report was a psychoanalysis-rape. He inserted things I never even intimated, let alone spoke. He insinuated I was "weird" (a very scientific term surely listed in the DSM) for having taken a beautiful picture of Ester while she slept. I had entered her room to gently wake her up for her first day of school and, admiring how gorgeous my sleeping beauty looked, I snapped a picture with my cellphone that I showed her while gently waking her up to get ready for her big day.

There is nothing this screwball didn't invent or pervert to accomplish exactly what he said he would do. I even requested permission to tape our meeting for transparency purposes knowing that he would carry out his *Mein Kampf* plan to destroy me. He yelled at me to shut off my phone and insisted that I place it on his desk, leaving it lying in front of him during our session.

Like my wife and Schwartz, Ferro played by the rules till the rules didn't fit his vendetta to bury me. In truth, these soulless creatures have no fear of breaking the law. They wreak havoc and destruction till they are jailed (Abramoff) or exposed (Sharen), or till they get a brain tumor (Fred Mailman), heart attack (Gotkin), or stroke (Alfieri).

When I hear about a patient going berserk and physically assaulting or killing their therapist, the image of Dr. Ferro as their manipulating tormentor immediately comes to mind. I'm amazed at how our courts attract prehistoric levels of lazy mammalian bottom-feeders like Ferro to serve as court appointed professionals.

It's obvious that they seek employment as government workers because they can't find clients in the real world. Their own personalities expose them. Ferro literally worked out of his basement office. Low overhead — keeping in line with his low pay scale wages to cobble together ranting incoherent reports with endless typos that a sixth grader would never make, and psychological babble that a third grader would never spew. You get what you pay for.

Had The Honorable Kenneth M. Karas served as our judge on the Federal Court level, I have no doubt that my wife would have been placed in jail. Schwartz would have been disbarred. Ferro would have lost his medical license. And Ester would be the happiest child on the planet, laughing and giggling while having "deep and meaningful" conversations with her Tatie about everything under the sun as he drove right past her Bais Yaakov Chofetz Chaim school.

Meanwhile, the thought of my little girl testifying against me, after having just survived my daughter Sara's machinations, was too much for my frayed nerves to sustain. I could easily bear the public shame of obese Monsey Yentas lying about me. I could also survive Shabbat visits by policemen based upon perjured Orders of Protection (*Thank you Officers, for easily seeing the truth*). I could even survive Princess Ester banishing her Tatie from her life, because at that point I still felt the damage was only temporary. "If only I could talk to her," I still imagined.

But the thought of sitting in court while staring at my gorgeous miracle-baby as she testified against the father she once loved snapped my heart. I couldn't imagine what my wife and Rachel might have brainwashed Princess Ester to repeat at this point, but I knew for certain that the mendacious Alfieri had already pre-determined that any words my severely alienated child would disgorge against her father would be considered completely credible — as if spoken with *ex cathedra* infallibility.

If my wife could get Sara to take out an Order of Protection against the person she trusted most in the entire world, and use her again upon convincing her to allow Rachel to drive her to Brooklyn several days later to call the saintly Rabbi Nekritz, "a piece of shit," then I could only imagine what power my manipulative wife now exerted over Ester and what vile incendiary Grobe Luge accusations she was surely grooming her impressionable eleven-year-old mind to repeat when she would testify in court. I could easily envision a two-hundred-pound shackled pedophile Orthodox Jewish father being taken into custody by the time Ester's innocent and adorable voice reverberated throughout the courtroom.

I imagined that even if Ester broke down in court and began crying that she loved me, Alfieri and my wife's lawyer would instantly start screaming at me for causing Ester to cry. I could almost hear Alfieri shouting, "Stop staring at her!" No matter what happened, I understood that I couldn't possibly win with Alfieri as the judge. I could see Goldie Unger rushing over to comfort her client, scornfully staring at me with contempt, while Sharen whispered in Ester's ear to calm down, adding that she'd take her for a long therapeutic riding lesson as soon as court closed for the day.

I was still in shock after the experience of Ester yelling at me that "You're killing Mommy!" And I still would not have believed it possible for her mother to turn Ester against me had I not seen the many ugly green-monster pictures titled "Zev" that Ester drew — under which she would now caption "I hate Zev" or "Die Zev! Die now!"

Ester made it very clear that I was no longer her "Tatie." A voice that giggled for eleven years upon pronouncing my paternal name now refused to even write down the first word she ever spoke as a baby.

I was sure her "therapist" had saved plenty of those wonderful expressions of emotional dysfunction for my "trial," as I imagined Goldie Unger encouraging Ester to keep expressing her anger at the father she once loved. "Uh, I see … so your father took a *weird* picture of you on your first day of school right before he woke you up to get dressed and have breakfast … and he *kissed* you a second too long on your cheek … so you now realize your father never *really* loved you after all …" as they practiced for when Ester would take the stand and sweetly demolish the man who refused to nap while she did over a decade ago because he wanted to make sure his newborn baby girl was breathing comfortably. "If only I could talk to her" now became greater odds than my winning the lottery.

Upon Schwartz requesting permission from Alfieri to allow Ester to take the stand "against her father," and adamantly insisting that Ester would testify that she "hates" me, I took a bathroom break and stoically walked out of the courtroom. Everyone stared as I left without permission as I walked out of the septic tank to get some air.

Contrasting the exciting six miles I briskly walked eleven years ago to announce, "It's a girl!" to Ester's four siblings, I now took the gloomiest walk of my life to allow Schwartz's next callous tactic to sink in. I slowly made my way down the court hallway which stretched and meandered as it wrapped itself around the rear of the building, where I then turned left, which led me into the timeless, older, and magnificent Art Deco style section of the Rockland County Courthouse that was under renovation and presently not being used. This original section was constructed in 1928. It's a lovely three-story edifice that displays an ornate three-level open interior that features a grand marble-floored lobby that extends across the entire front of the building.

It was as serene there in its figurative past as the other starkly efficient, modern side of the building was swarmed in hustle and bustle court proceedings. I imagined how a time traveler could walk from the frenzied endlessly crazy-busy present, to the quieter, peaceful good-old-days past merely by walking through the entire building. I pushed the old heavy wooden door whose frosted glass panel read GENTLEMEN, as I imagined that Alfieri and Schwartz should never be allowed to use this olden-day men's-room, and I walked along the black and white diamond-tiled floor where I entered the last stall.

It was there that a sixty-three-year-old man, who could still do thirty-five push-ups after hitting the heavy bag for twenty minutes straight, cried his heart out. I lost it. I absolutely and completely, totally fucking lost it.

My body was heaving, and I thought I was having what people call a nervous breakdown. Maybe I was. I honestly don't know. I cried so hard that I could not catch my breath. Ester is going to be raised by the insane, I realized. Sharen and Rachel will make a basket-case out of her. My Princess is ironically now also going to grow up without a father at the same age I lost mine, and nothing I do can protect the child I sacrificed ten years of my life to protect.

I slowly pushed open the door, that now read GENTLEMEN backwards and in reverse letters on frosted glass, that led back to Hell. A silly random thought entered my mind as I mused that there would be no confusion with the word being spelled backwards as one left a room full of urinals.

I was an emotional wreck. I almost felt like jumping over the third floor beautifully polished wooden railing as I rested my elbows on the dark wood while staring into the expansive lobby below. I imagined the peacefulness my soul might find as my bloody body would be discovered lying broken and twisted in the grandeur of the splendid vestibule. "Don't even think of letting a bad day destroy your entire life. Tomorrow will be a better one," a faint voice barely whispered inside my head.

That act would be my final protest against a heartless God and a sinful Sodomite Court system of cruel jurisprudence. But as painful as my life was at that moment, I refused the momentary inclination of splattering the wonderful memories of my sweet daughter onto the century-old lobby floor. I had so many priceless recollections of Ester as a baby and toddler. No kid every made me laugh as much as she did.

If I kill myself, we'll surely never get to see each other again. This isn't the first time I've been in pain and it's probably not the last. I raised my ribs, inhaled deeply, held my breath, pulled in my diaphragm ("Tighter! Tighter!" as I imagined Sijo barking at me like a drill sergeant), and then slowly released the flurry of thoughts that swirled in my mind. Again and again till I felt my head perspiring. Thank you Sijo Mims for teaching me how to use the "breath of life" whenever I feel anxious.

I returned to the courtroom and found myself fantasizing about grabbing the bailiff's gun and shooting Alfieri and Schwartz. I imagined the best angle as I'd quickly shoot Alfieri and then turn and point the 9mm automatic at Schwartz. I could see the coward grabbing my petite wife as a shield to protect his huge belly. Her head barely comes up to his chest.

My gun is pointing at my *Vybie's* head and Schwartz's heart. One bullet is all it would take to permanently lobotomize two muddled minds and end so much pain and the destruction of Ester's life. My wife stares at me with that steel-blue stare … daring me to shoot. But as she wrote in her email, "Zev would never hit me." She knows. And so I raise the gun a barely visible amount and shoot Schwartz right in his evil, deranged, fat, inexorable, yarmulka covered, kapo head.

The half-dozen protection orders never prohibited my going to the range to practice, and so in my fantasy I was still quite an accurate marksman. The tiny yarmulka flies off what remains of Schwartz's head as his rotund body deflates and drops like a flip-flopping balloon after all its hot air has been released upon popping, and the frightened herd of people stampede out of the courtroom while my calm wife smiles demurely at me as I pop the magazine out of the gun that I slide a second later toward the heavy glass court doors for the outside policemen to retrieve. I get down on my knees and raise my hands above my head as the court police come rushing in — hurling me to the floor to cuff me.

"They pushed me over the deep end," I can barely hear myself explaining to my attorney, Ben Brafman, because of the still ringing sound in my right ear, as I try to logically rationalize how a nice Jewish scholar just executed two people in cold blood.

"Don't worry," Ben calmly reassures me, "It's not as bad as it looks. I'm going to plead severe long-term intense Complex PTSD combined with temporary insanity," Brafman explains in his plan to defend my actions to the jury. "Thank God you had her password with which I can prove an incredibly vicious case of malicious prosecution. And I wouldn't be surprised if Alfieri was being paid off. I've already subpoenaed his and Schwartz's records. It wasn't premeditated, but you're still going to have to serve at least ten to fifteen years. Had you merely killed a divorce attorney it would probably have been perceived as a mitzvah by the jury. But you just killed a sitting judge. Unfortunately, that's going to cost you. But don't worry. I'll make sure you're sent upstate to Otisville and you can give the Daf-Yomi Talmud class to my other clients. It's a religious haven. Their commissary even has gefilte fish and matzo ball soup. You'll hardly notice you're in jail. The time will pass quickly for a scholar like you."

"When can I see Ester?" I reply.

With thoughts like these, no matter how fantastical they were, I knew I had reached the limit of what a gentlemanly, loving father could possibly put up with. As much as I believed in the sweet quote attributed to Michael Ratnadeepak which beautifully proclaims that, "*No one in the world can love a girl more than her father*," I also knew that love has to move freely in both directions. Unfortunately, the direction from Ester to her father had been blocked by an impenetrable wall.

That "wall" was the willpower of my little wife who, in spite of her *love* of psychology and her understanding the importance of a father's presence in the life of a child, determined that her alienation of Ester was fully justified. "Ze'ev! It's your fault! Call off the divorce and this will all stop! It's your filing for divorce that brought this on our family." Like the Nazis who blamed the Jews for all that was wrong in pre-war Germany, after being the first country to attack her neighbors in both World Wars, my wife blamed me for serving her papers and then "stealing" her password and exposing her malicious prosecution.

This was the exact logic she used after snatching my EZ Pass off my car windshield while I sat in the driver's seat, as I calmly handed her "bricks" while explaining that I was sincerely sorry it had come to this, but that I planned to continue with my divorce action. Grabbing the tan plastic contraption off the inside glass pane, she yelled, in response to my calm request that she return the device so that I could go study already, "I didn't take your EZ Pass, Ze'ev! Your filing for divorce took your EZ Pass!"

My heart was still beating rapidly as I sat in the long line to pay cash at the George Washington Bridge toll. I turned on the radio, trying to clear my head, so that I could debate in Talmudical discourse with Rabbi Nekritz by the time I reached Brooklyn.

I understood that I had no choice but to walk out of the saloon-court where the drunkard Alfieri tended bar and dealt the cards. It. Was. Over. I rolled. I took the first offer my wife put on the table the day she was to sit in the witness stand and swear under oath that she would not lie in response to the questions my lawyer and I had prepared. I managed to wear a great diamond-dealer poker face during the literal twenty-eight minutes it took for us to settle into an *Uncontested* Divorce after running in circles while being lashed by Alfieri for two and a half years.

I instantly acquired my ex's share of the house in lieu of any long-term maintenance as I pathetically abdicated custody, in a pained voice, as the once proud and loving father of Princess Ester — thus avoiding an expensive, year-long, $100,000-dollar trial, that would have included my staring at Ester on the witness stand with tears running down my face. Besides, I knew the verdict The Alf had already decided the first day I stepped into his Ninth Circle of Hell Court.

I went from seeking justified full custody to voluntarily allowing my capricious assaulter to have total control over the baby I loved. This was the most difficult moment in my entire divorce. I literally handed Ester over to her maniacal mother and consented to being the Non-Custodial Parent. Like my grandmother, I was forced to say goodbye to my child in the knowledge that I could do absolutely nothing to protect her from the advancing army of lunatics. *"Run Esterlah, run! Maybe you'll live."*

Through our uncontested divorce I avoided any child-support payments and the looming devastating imputation of a higher salary by Alfieri. I then shocked Alfieri as I volunteered to pay two hundred dollars a month in child support, and two thousand a year towards Ester's tuition, in the hope of keeping in touch with her. "I offer this as a goodwill gesture in anticipation of Ester's mother encouraging her to speak to me." My wife nodded in agreement. Visitation was not imposed or denied. I didn't exactly expect Ester to text back anytime soon. But at least I could wish.

Any time I tried to talk, Alfieri screamed at me abusively to be quiet, while adding in disgust, "You have zero credibility with me! Let your lawyer speak for you!" Alfieri no longer even tried to pretend that he was an impartial and ethical administrator. He was hell-bent on destroying my life and making me pay for loving my daughter and for exposing him in the *Rockland Times*. But I would now have the last word.

Here are the literal final transcribed court stenographer's "For the Record" nails as they were hammered into the crucified body of a living Mr. Mom Orthodox Jew on the cross of alienation, administered by a corrupt court system (words in parentheses are my own, added for clarification):

The Court (Alfieri to me): You enter into this stipulation? (i.e. my agreeing to an UNCONTESTED DIVORCE and that mother has full custody.)

Mr. Lewinson: Very unhappily after two years of my daughter being —

The Court (Alfieri interrupting me in a tone of disgust): Just answer the question!

Mr. Lewinson: Very unhappily after not seeing my daughter for two years because of the court (i.e. Alfieri) system, Sir. (I didn't back down.)

The Court: And you entered in this stipulation freely and voluntarily, sir?

Mr. Lewinson: Not freely and voluntarily. I don't have the funds to fight what's been done to me, so I have to enter into it.

The judge then angrily called me "obstinate" and told me to "Stop it!" He then shouted that my "modus operandi throughout the entire divorce" has constantly been to be "argumentative." Appealing mendacious Protection Orders, and wining, is "argumentative." Fighting with everything you have with your hands tied behind your back to save your daughter is being "obstinate."

I'm amazed that Alfieri did not yell out "strike that!" to the court stenographer, as he had done with so many other statements I made in the past two and a half years, or threaten to hold me in contempt, leaving my final declaration of the system, and essentially of Alfieri himself, in the documentation of the closing moments of my divorce case for posterity.

I think the mad dog simply finally exhausted himself with sinking his teeth into the now many pounds of my flesh. Or maybe there was simply nothing more that he could do to collect additional padded inflated overtime. On the record it looks like my wife and I had the most amicable divorce settlement one could ever hope for. A mere twenty-eight minutes of negotiations. After wasting almost three years in fucking hell and twenty-seven years on a match made in fucking heaven.

Did you enjoy the show, God? Watching six million of Your Chosen suffer incredible torture wasn't enough of a cheap thrill? Was it really necessary for my blood-boiling saga and Ester's alienation to be added as a footnote in the history of human misery? Was vaporizing her father from her life part of your "Tikun Olam" plan to save humanity? Wasn't the pleasure of taking my father away from me enough titillation? Can't Ester have anyone nice and normal to relate to?

I still get embarrassed and upset at myself as I recall how I relinquished my rights, six years ago, to being the father of the baby girl I had crowned at birth and once loved with all my heart. I had hoped that once the divorce was over that I would be able to see Ester. When will I learn? If you could glance inside my heart for even a second you would certainly understand. You would also very likely burst out in tears. I know my daughter is facing incredible odds for living a truly fulfilled future life. I can't imagine what the inside of Ester's heart might look like. Not sure I want to see. I can only pray. I'm just no longer sure who to pray to.

I'm now rested, and I can't believe I did it. I'm the kind of guy who never gives up. But at the time, I had been pummeled beyond recognition. I had no access to my money. My heart was black and blue. My emotions were fried. Both my eyes and reputation were blackened. My vision was blurry. My mind was in a fog. I hadn't slept through an entire night in over two years. My brains felt as if they were swelling up inside my cranium due to constant headaches. And I had no one in my corner. My ex saw to that.

I fought more rounds than a human can possibly fight. And I knew the referee in the ring was as cruel and unscrupulous as my opponent. And the ringside judges were also corrupt. I also understood that The Alf would never let me collect my purse even if I fought to the death — having already declared in open court that he would impute my salary to more than double the amount of the meager teacher's salary I had been earning for the past six years.

And so, after being pummeled while playing rope-a-dope to buy time that only unleashed more beatdowns, I was too winded to even bother taking a slowly enunciated ten-count. I stood in my lonely corner and threw in my tear-stained towel. Along with my fatuous belief in a merciful God.

Mine is merely one case among tens of thousands of cases a year that are much more severe than my (comparatively speaking) walk in the park. I know I'm one of the lucky ones. Because despite the emotional scars, I not only survived; I became enlightened. I realize there are many stoic fathers who abandon their children, wind up incarcerated, or commit suicide by the time the system heartlessly churns out their case.

And there are many wonderful mothers, among those fifteen percent of women who receive orders of protection, who cry a nightly flood of hot tears as they doze off to a fitful sleep wondering about their children who have been placed in foster care: another profit center emulating our penal system into which many of those children will surely be granted access to for a higher education one day.

It's appalling how quickly a model citizen can become a convict, royally screwed, and then screwed-in as one more cog into the U.S. penal system, literally overnight, upon divorcing their spouse. A decent man, a loving father, can instantly become a vagrant pariah.

Men know that the court system is old fashioned and generally considers a mother to be the more "natural" parent to raise a child. I always feel a micro insensitive display of ignorance is committed when people sound surprised, as if they are witnessing a rare individual, when they compliment a man as a "Great Dad." No one compliments a woman as a "Great Mom." That would be redundant.

Everyone assumes that the parent who birthed the child is surely the *natural* primary caretaker. Especially if the minor child is a girl. Even in a "good" divorce the mother almost always gets the child. It's a societal given. As natural as opening a car door for a female. And who do most men trust more than their own mother? So when a mother claims to need a protection order, to protect herself and *her* child, that "Grobe Luge" is assumed to be the absolute truth. *It's so fucking easy.*

Without reading one word of all the email evidence I prepared for Alfieri regarding my daughter's alienation, which was presented along with my request for full custody early on in our divorce court proceedings, the gowned beast yelled, "Unless you want to claim that your wife is a drug addict and beating your daughter, you are *not* getting full custody!"

Unlike my wife I would never lie. Alfieri then gave us equal custody. My wife's attorney immediately petitioned for "final say" rights which Alfieri instantly granted, "because *someone* has to have the final say," while yelling at me to stop being "argumentative" at a mere "temporary" court decree. I never saw Ester again.

What amazed me in my case was the lesson I learned *after* serving divorce papers. I was astonished at how easy it is to brand a loving father, who certainly was the primary caretaker and loving Mr. Mom in my child's life before I filed for divorce, into a dangerous *violent criminal* based on a totally fictitious lie. Experiencing our divorce court system knowing that I was an innocent husband and caring father who suddenly had to prove that he wasn't a pedophile and violent brute, was like overdosing on a fistful of red pills in the sci-fi movie, *The Matrix*. Needless to say, I am now woke.

I quickly learned not to even think of expressing outrage or indignation against my wife or the court system that allowed her to legally assault me while alienating my daughter. That would only retroactively prove that she was right all along.

You angry Bro? Well you had better calm down. It takes less than a moment's display of anger to get a pair of handcuffs snapped around your wrists during a divorce. Keep your frustrations to yourself. And keep popping that Amlodipine into your bloodstream. "Die Zev! Die now!"

A spouse merely needs to claim that her husband yelled at her, as she holds a protection order in hand, to have him whisked away in a patrol car in front of their child. It then takes dad years to get out of the mess that it took his wife seconds to throw him into.

The lowered and dejected face of their handcuffed dad in the back seat of a cop cruiser is often the last image that many children will ever see of their father. The estranged child often winds up as lost and lonely as the look on Dad's face. They also exhibit a lot of anger, confusion, and anxiety. Moms are supposed to teach their kids to get back up after falling. They are not supposed to trip them.

The ease with which a spouse can use a protection order with total impunity during a divorce has completely reversed their original purpose. Instead of shielding a woman from being assaulted, many women are using the document to violate men. The protection order has transformed from a means of protecting women into a wildly flung corybantic weapon that horrifically abuses parting spouses and their children.

It is the modern-day legal version of figuratively being drawn and quartered. It breaks a father down and tears him apart. It's a character assassination that ruthlessly declares a man, "guilty till proven innocent." Dad quickly becomes marginalized and vilified, and the more he protests and rants about his innocence, the less he is believed. Especially if there is a hint of anger or trace of bitterness in his voice.

Instead of his pain being understood as blistering frustration, it instantly becomes solid proof that the Protection Order was justified from the get-go, surely necessary to protect the minor child from the tirades of a raging lunatic. And the right of a loving parent to see or merely speak to their child is instantly declared an illegal act, punishable by jail and a criminal record. You can't even send a text. Wish your little girl a "Happy Birthday!" and get arrested. It. Is. Hell.

Judges clearly understand its brazen and wanton misuse during a divorce. It's not that difficult to assess the situation before trampling the reputation of a man and launching an all-out attack on the life of an innocent person trying to get a simple divorce. It is also extremely cruel for a child to be torn away from their parent under the guise of "protecting" them from some suddenly dangerous "creepy stranger." Does society really believe that millions of fathers instantly morph into dangerous stalking violent beasts upon divorce?

In truth, the separation of assets and visitation schedule with the minor child in my divorce case could have been figured out in an hour or two. Leave it to government sloths to take almost three years and still not come to any conclusion in my (amazingly enough) *uncontested* divorce.

In a divorce, men have become a social group of sorts that will likely experience a protection order at the outset of the filing. According to the U.S. Department of Justice, there are between two to three million restraining orders issued every year. If you are a man and have not received one during your divorce, consider yourself very fortunate. You beat the odds by a landslide.

Most people instantly believe that the recipient of an order surely must have carried out a horrific act against his own family for a judge to issue such an urgent directive. After all, the fourteenth amendment clearly declares a presumption of innocence until proven guilty. Surely there are laws in place, they assume, that guarantee a father's unalienable rights to life, liberty, and the pursuit of happiness till the completion of a public trial wherein an individual is promised all the rights of a fair defense.

Most men have no idea, no clue, till they are shocked (or tasered) upon being slapped with one, that a protection order is easier to obtain than a driver's license or a gun. Or even a cup of coffee. That's right! Coffee costs a buck and a half. But protection orders are free. And they are rubber stamped more nimbly than a Barista filling up an empty paper cup and snapping on a lid, and the simple automated process to issue the dastardly document is more organized than iPhones rolling off an assembly line in China. No fees. No fuss. No questions asked. *Welcome back to the fifteenth century.*

Actually, a protection order is very similar to a gun in that it's always loaded, cocked, and pointed at your head — while threateningly held in the very hand of the woman you are trying to divorce. It's constantly aimed at your existence, and with a mere phone call, can be launched like a heat-seeking missile to instantly vaporize your life, career, and parent-child relationship. All accomplished faster than a speeding bullet, while said wife legally holds your child hostage.

Your wife, in her new role of instantly-granted sole-guardianship, is automatically backed by a legal system that then forces you to walk on eggshells and somehow prove in a family court trial that her witless accusations are *untrue* (a 1984 newspeak-word in the divorce court lexicon).

In other words, based on the ludicrous claims stated in my wife's Order of Protection, I had to prove that my wife doesn't really "fear my wrath" or believe that I'm "obsessed with feces." Just like I had to prove that I was never "under the covers" with my daughter Sara, and that I never threatened to "mush her head."

Think about that logically and you'll acquire a vivid understanding of how The Inquisition made The Church fabulously wealthy as it rewarded itself for investigating the "crime" of heresy. Mercilessly torturing innocent converted citizens, and incinerating them with a crackling dose of very real fiery flames, in order to spare the dissident and stubbornly Jewish soul from a fantastical hell — while earning a quick buck in an effort to combat the fictitious thought regarding which Abrahamic God the victim *really* believed in — yielded incredible profits. Absurdly, this was all instituted in the name of God. Because after all, who do we trust?

This exact inquisition continues in the twenty-first century with Orders of Protection, as a heartless baboon inquisitor, dressed in a black frock, sits in front of a proclamation that he is serving God by dispensing justice.

Our modern-day criminal and divorce court systems emotionally and financially rapes men while holding them upside down by the ankles, as they shake the last coins of loose change out of the inverted dad's pockets, while *The Church Court* creates immense wealth for itself in the guise of protecting his children. *In God We Trust*.

Meanwhile Spain — after committing the atrocities of torturing and executing tens of thousands of Jews who had finally converted, after fifteen hundred years of bloodletting by God, choosing to give up their souls in order to save their bodies and children — ultimately divorced itself in 1492 from their entire remaining Orthodox Jewish population who still clung to their Monotheistic God and refused to convert.

The Stiff-necked Jews were then exiled to the dark and unknown far corners of the earth to be raped, murdered, and sold as slaves by pirates and other messengers of God, while Church officials raced to grab the homes, businesses, and edifices of their expelled victims. Just like many Germans and Polish citizens later did in WWII.

Let's not forget those wonderfully "impartial" Switzerland bankers who earned billions while politely explaining "bank policy" that insisted on a death certificate from descendants of relatives incinerated in Auschwitz in order to prove their next of kin didn't just disappear like smoke. *And*

I'm supposed to remain calm while Mel Gibson and Abbas claim that the numbers of Jewish victims in the Holocaust were grossly exaggerated. And let's not forget the ranting anti-Semitic maniacal history-distorting Louis Farrakhan. Google "ADL Farrakhan."

Mighty Spain was then reduced, within a few short decades, to a crumbling has-been ex-superpower with a minuscule economy. Look at modern-day Israel and look at fifteen-hundred-year-old Spain. *#Think twice before dumping your Jews.*

To this very day over ten percent of Spain's GNP is generated through nothing more creative than tourism, her main source of income, which largely consists of drunk revelers watching grown men in bright-colored tights sticking daggers into the necks of anxious charging bulls. The poor beasts are first starved and held in confused isolation away from their herd for many hours, and then speared for good measure by human beasts, before the Alfieri-matador thug even begins to bang his dagger-gavel at the start of the "fight."

And I don't care how artistically or metaphorically whimsical Hemingway idolizes the *descabellar* moment of death. That coup-de-grâce is nothing more than a cowardly finish after the slow-torture bullying of a terrified and exhausted sentient mammal in an unfair "sport" where it is surrounded, in a circular stadium from which it has no escape, by a pack of mindless macho hyenas, who are idol worshipped by throngs of idol worshipping descendants of those who once jeered the flaming Jewish sinners who were tied to a pyre as penance for their possibly having worshipped the Jewish God as opposed to the Christian one.

Cruelty to animals is never an art form no matter how daintily the athletes prance about the ring. And although I'm very sorry that the gifted Hemingway shot himself, I'd still feel empathy and sadness for Ernest had karma dictated his demise by being gored to death as a warning to other unskillful minds for romanticizing this backward "beastly matador versus gladiator bovine" culture to the Western world as something to admire in *A Sun Also Rises*. There is nothing glamorous about being fatally gored as you are about to thrust a sword into a living being for entertainment.

Olé? No way! I embarrassingly admit that I often find myself rooting for the confused and cornered innocent bull. I don't think it would be in bad taste to see a downed matador dragged out of the stadium by horses as the bull trots a victory lap around the ring.

Thank God Spain has evolved a trifle and no longer kills and tortures Jews. It seems that their culture and lust for blood is now satisfied by throwing tomatoes at each other in the festival of *La Tomatina* and the mindless mistreatment of animals in the sport of *Corrida de Toros*. In truth, no one wins in a bullfight in which the observers self-castrate their own humanity and empathy. For this you exiled your Jews? Estúpido!

I laugh at the thought of Alfieri and Schwartz chasing me while wearing tight toreador pants. But there was nothing humorous in my playing the role of the terrified and exhausted wounded bull in Lewinson vs. Lewinson while Ester and my testicles were castrated out of my life.

Divorce is truly comparable to the auto-de-fé experience of The Spanish Inquisition. Those lovely public celebrations, at which the nobility married off their wonderful Christian children as they listened to the excruciating screams of Jews whose skin broiled, while they sipped wine and observed their version of a well-done roasted "marrano on a spit," were initiated by nothing more than one single witness, whose identity was always kept secret, accusing a Jewish Converso of secretly adhering to their original Jewish faith.

The proceedings of the trial that followed were also kept secret. The accused were stripped naked by "holy" church officials for a "confession" that would only be accepted through torture that often included sadistically placing a barbed item inside a potential confessors anal or vaginal orifice, not wanting to mar their victim's external facade because, after all, "man was created in God's image." *How fucking righteous.*

The "confession" was followed with being burned alive in a merciful act that spared the wayward convert from an eternal sentence in a fiery Hell. The apostate's wealth was then confiscated by Church authorities, on his behalf of course, in an act of charitable generosity that further guaranteed, along with the redemptive cleansing flames, the crypto-Jew's path to Heaven.

After all, what dying sinner wouldn't yearn to pave their entrance into the Kingdom of God by donating all their money to Our Savior the moment before they died? A real win-win for The Jewish Lord who loves money as much as he craves blood and was able to cash-in on the horrific Massacre of Spanish Jewry in 1391 and the roughly 32,000 executions across the two centuries that the Office of the Inquisition ruled in Spain.

Incredibly, it was the pressure of many earlier pogroms and the bloody Massacre of 1391, inspired by years of fiery sermons by the Archdeacon Ferrand Martinez depicting how the Jews crucified Jesus, that led to the murder and plundering of the Jews of Seville and many Jewish communities in Spain. The church did what they always do when *their* "Unzereh" kills Jews or molests little boys. They sinned mercilessly.

After all, the Jews crucified Jesus (who "chose" to die for our sins). Like the cruel Alfieri, Martinez also made sure that a Jew lost whenever they came to court. All this, of course, was seen by Jews as collective punishment for not being devoted to their God who was now testing his Chosen as he burned them alive, along with their Torah scrolls, in the synagogue.

Many Jews failed the test and a majority of Spanish Jews converted to Christianity. And then upon conversion, many converso's, after publicly recanting the faith of their forefathers, were executed for being a crypto-Jew. I hate to imagine what our lives would have been like if we weren't The Chosen.

The Converso's steadfast loyalty to Christ; his swearing devotion as he attended weekly services where he fervently prayed to Jesus; his raising children to be good Catholics; and his donating huge sums to the Church, all meant nothing in the face of one anonymous witness. It could have been a business competitor or a jealous neighbor who couldn't keep up with the incognito "Goldbergs." Once a Converso was accused of being a crypto-Jew, they were instantly assumed guilty.

Likewise, a man can receive a well-deserved "World's Greatest Dad" Father's Day card, lovingly signed by his adoring wife and children, and hours later find himself holding a protection order that will incinerate his emotional and financial life to ashes.

The only difference between the secular modern-day heathen Divorce Inquisition and the spiritual Middle Ages Christian version, is that the latter-day accusing witness is obviously someone who should not be trusted, and yet she is treated as if her villainous words were the gospel truth. The court system instantly believes any woman who initiates a protection order as part of her divorce proceedings, granting an instant "Hail Mary" for the wife, coupled with a "Go to Hell!" blessing to the husband. The court then strips the man of his wealth, children, and reputation as the inquisitor judge shoves a barbed Order of Protection up his anus. All without evidence, or a shred of human compassion. *In God We Trust.*

I am still incredulous that a sixty-three-year-old man, an Orthodox Jewish grandfather with a sterling reputation, who spent his life as a scholar, publisher, writer, and teacher — a man who was a devoted husband for twenty-eight years while raising five wonderful children as a part time Mr. Mom — was figuratively burned at the stake by nothing more than a perjured piece of paper filled out by an amoral diabolical wife who was served divorce papers. Our systemic court system instantly did what it does best. It destroys innocent lives. Only now, after seven years, am I finally stepping away from the idiots, fools, and paper shufflers that have shaken any remaining loose coins from my pocket while wasting my time.

A mere assertion of "I'm afraid of his wrath," gave my wife immediate state-granted protection-orders upon-request, backed up by the full power of the police and a judicial system that instantly accepted her asinine drivel as solid evidence, thereby incinerating the parent-child loving bonds of what had once been an incredible father-daughter relationship.

My life would have been completely destroyed in both the Jewish and secular worlds in which my eclectic existence crisscrossed had I not been able to recall the decade old password of my *Eishet Chayil* assailant. *"Tatie5521. Because I love you, Zevie."* I love you too, Sharen.

Here are the incredibly outrageous facts surrounding the abusive misuse of protection orders published by SAVE (Stop Abusive and Violent Environment): "Eighty-five percent of all orders of protection are issued against men. Ninety percent of those orders are strategically used in divorce proceedings without cause merely for the benefits instantly gained by putting the husband/father on the defensive." Please read that again.

They are issued ex parte (secretly and without any warning to the recipient), and the order instantly throws a man out of his home. They are supposed to be temporary, but the wheels of justice come to a screeching halt once they are stamped. It is rare for the restrained recipient to get a full hearing for at least a month. By that time the damage is done.

It was over two months before we met in Alfieri's courtroom after my first order was stamped. He immediately left the order in place and, like everything else that landed on his plate, ineptly pushed off the issue till after the family trial with Sarah would be settled. By the time I won the Family Court trial that Sara initiated, The Alf, on a whim, felt, "no harm will be done," and left the Divorce Court protection order in place till we had another trial that would have included an alienated-modified manipulated Ester testifying against the father she wanted to live with when I gently told her that her mother and I haven't been getting along for quite some time. So much for "temporary" restraining orders. *Goodbye, my sweet child.*

Being thrown out of one's house is an incredibly difficult experience. It's like being the victim of a fire or hurricane. Yet those are natural disasters where kind neighbors quickly step in, volunteering to help. But being suddenly shunned at the synagogue by neighbors and friends that "don't want to get involved" because they believe you might be dangerous, makes it excruciating for a vagrant father to go about his daily business.

Couple the stress of sudden exile from an insular Jewish community for not attending Beit Din, along with being accused in the secular family court of being a deviant and violent danger to your daughters, while simultaneously attending divorce court under the aegis of a Neanderthal loutish judge who is forcing you to appear pro se, and it's easily understood why the average man gains twenty pounds during a divorce. Throw in an additional ten pounds for having to run to criminal court to simultaneously face false charges of computer hacking during my divorce saga.

A loving father whose children are suddenly torn from his life is analogous to the nipple of a nursing mother, still squirting milk to feed the baby it was created to nurture, the moment the hungry baby's suctioned mouth is snatched off her mother's engorged breast. Try playing with *that* nipple. See what mood it's in.

And a severed dad, whose alienated daughter is suddenly snatched away, finds himself choking on a tidal wave of repressed love that he is forced to withhold because of a Protection Order dam. With nowhere to release the ocean of his swelling emotions, the PTSD stress causes his own blood pressure to rise precipitously. Try fixing him up with a date. See what mood he's in.

Like a samurai warrior with no cause to fight for in a time of peace, dad's life, like the body of the assassin, turns to mush. He doesn't know anything other than the frustration of feeling worthless and lonely. He suddenly has nothing to do. One man has no one to fight. The other man has no one to love. Both men will put on weight. The two men who used to jump out of bed every morning, willing to fight to the death for what they once lived for, no longer desire to even wake up. *It took me years to get out of bed.*

Mommy's milk, and daddy's blood (father's willingness to do anything for his kids), are the two major ingredients necessary for a future adult to experience a happy and productive childhood in which they feel both safe and loved. I'm not a Muslim. But if I were, I just might pray, "May Allah chop off the arm of any judge who knowingly issues an unnecessary Order of Protection." *And may he toss Alfieri into a woodchipper.*

At the eventual "full hearing" one discovers that it's anything but complete. The recipient is set upon by a system that forces him to survive a tortuous trek that would make any Ninja Warrior course look like a walk in the park. The journey begins with court appointed attorneys for the children, court appointed therapists, forensic examinations, probation officers, temporary maintenance, instantly frozen bank accounts, frozen professional licenses (your regular driver's license can easily be revoked by the child support agency computer system), and an endless gauntlet of almost-rectal penetration into one's life.

Miss a few child-support payments and those rectal exam penetrations become embarrassingly real. You can try to slip out of the country, but you're likely to discover that your passport has been revoked. The experience almost feels like an emotional version of medieval Coffin Torture where the victim was hung in a prison cell that was only large enough for a body to fit inside without any space to move around.

Bump into your wife at the local fast-food joint and, faster than a flipping hamburger, she can claim you threatened to hit her. Merely unfolding her protection order to the arriving police, who are mindlessly forced to assume that you "once again" must have lost your temper, will have you searched, cuffed, and entered into the criminal court system.

Protesting your innocence too angrily will only serve as further "evidence" that you are indeed in dire need of anger management classes. It's like being carted off by the KGB to an insane asylum. Try screaming "I'm not crazy!" once you've been entered into that notorious system. The doctors and staff will only increase your mind-altering medications. Protest too loudly and you'll quickly be scheduled for a lobotomy. Divorce Court conducted by nightmarish characters like Ferro and Alfieri is the judicial equivalent of being a patient in a Stalin-era mental hospital.

Fingerprints, photo-op mug shot, pleasantries of a rectal strip-search exam, an appearance in an orange jumpsuit and shackles before a stern judge, anger management classes, and a probable criminal trial — resulting in a multi-year probation necessitating your need to report biweekly to a probation officer — are the results of your simply trying to buy a shitty (possibly Jacob Creutzfeldt diseased), cheap, antibiotic-infused adulterated hamburger so that you could stay afloat with your child support payments. *Bon Appétit!*

This mangled and bizarre scenario, and similar stories of fathers who were figuratively buried alive by a cruel and inhuman chain of divorce-related events, are a commonly recurring everyday theme upon trying to terminate even a mundane, uncomplicated, normal marriage in our dysfunctional divorce court system in this first trimester of the 21st century.

We are creating artificial intelligence, quark computers, conducting bioengineering miracles on DNA that boggles the mind, as we explore the outer reaches of our universe with miniature cameras that will soon travel at a fourth of the speed of light, while allowing bi-polar orangutan judges to shuffle paper in our systemic criminal, divorce, and family court systems. The difference between an ignorant state judge like Alfieri and a research scientist, is similar to contrasting the lifestyle of Melania Trump to a sex slave living in a slum in the Philippines.

Combine an early-stage hominid inept judge with a sleazy divorce lawyer (pardon the redundancy) and a pathologically angry wife, and why wouldn't the alienation of your child ensue along with a half-dozen protection orders being issued during a simple divorce?

I'm super impressed with all those wonderful mothers who well understood the weapon of choice that was available to them during their divorce proceedings and yet refused the opportunity to destroy their husbands because they wanted their children to maintain a healthy relationship with their father. Kudos to all those incredible women! And there are many of them. Their divorce proceeds with restrained anger because these mothers understand that they "will always be married" to their spouse through the children they brought into this world together.

Many parents remain amicable post-divorce. They understand that the one last notion they can still agree on is that their marriage was "worth it" even if only for the beautiful children they conceived. But there are far too many women that resort to this horrendously malicious tactic that only a self-centered narcissist would use to wantonly strike and destroy their own family.

Men's lives are being devastated at an alarming rate through our intentionally bureaucratic criminal and divorce court systems. There could easily be a new movement in this country with a huge following of lonely fathers and shattered men: #METOOPROTECTIONORDER

Protection orders are dynamiting the fabric of family life. And a slew of judges like Alfieri, augmented by bottom-feeding "court appointed officials" (a serious sounding title for losers that can't find legal or psychiatric work in the real world), are throwing fuel onto the systematic legal pyre that incinerates any remaining delicate already-frayed bonds between members of what was once a loving family.

Roughly half of all Western culture marriages wind up in divorce. The damage of a simple *piece of paper* destroys the life and reputation of any man who receives even only one. Imagine surviving six while still living at home with your *three* false accusers. Now imagine being summoned to a Criminal Court trial for computer hacking.

For added fun, visualize doing all that while facing the learning-disabled daughter you love — a daughter you exhausted yourself teaching her how to read in order to mainstream her into society — in a Family Court trial in which she is suddenly accusing you of having molested her (not that she even understands what "molested" means). Yes, "*What the Fuck!*" would be quite the appropriate, healthy, proper response.

Any divorcing woman in this country is instantly trusted and believed the moment she accuses her husband of having anger issues. It's astonishing how this psychological ailment always presents itself upon a husband's filing for divorce. In rare instances the roles are reversed, but it's much more difficult for a man to obtain an order of protection. He needs a minimum amount of evidence. When a woman files one, the judge doesn't even bother giving the document a cursory glance.

All a wife needs to do is simply fill out a one-page form while allowing a tiny tear to well up in her right or left eye while muffling the erupting celebratory laughter from within. She had better sign quickly!

What's more astonishing than the bubonic-protection-order-plague psychopathy is society's mindless enabling of this father-flagellating scourge. It amazes me how quickly the average person believes anything declared emphatically, or printed on a piece of paper, as the absolute truth. Stamp it with an official seal and it might as well have floated down from God. Kind of a far cry from a modicum of skepticism and critical thinking.

That calm logical request to provide even a snippet of evidence, normally needed upon making allegations against an upright citizen, has vanished. A man's legal rights, the "self-evident truths" guaranteed by our constitution, have been completely silenced and erased by the false urgent cries of hysterical angry and vindictive wives during a divorce.

No one bothers to even check if the issuer of an order of protection is a felon, has issued prior orders that proved to be a sham (as in my case), or if they recently walked out of an asylum for the mentally ill. No witnesses are necessary. No taped phone calls. No emails or texts. No evidence. All that's needed is a vagina. It doesn't even have to be shaved or trimmed. Statistically speaking, three of the following four men — Moses, Gandhi, Jesus, and the Buddha — would have easily been slapped with a protection order had they decided to divorce their wives in the 21st century in the United States.

A wife can even blatantly perjure herself upon issuing her protection order in Family Court, as my wife did, by signing — under the threat of perjury and a jail sentence — that they are not litigating in any other court system (e.g. Divorce Court) and never face prosecution. Why? Because judges are loathe to inhibit or intimidate any young woman who may feel the need to file one. They don't want women to fear any possible recrimination upon filing a protection order. And the judges themselves are intimidated by any potential bad press that may occur as a result of their not having instantly granted any requested "protection."

And so approximately four months after we were in the throes of divorce court, my thespian wife of twenty-eight years just moseyed-on-in to Family court, following the instructions of the email she received from her kapo attorney that, "it's time to toss Zev outta the house."

In truth, I was surprised it took so long. I remember telling my original lawyer, on the day he called to say he's leaving his office to file my divorce papers, that my wife will instantly respond with an order of protection. I was amazed at not having received one. "I know my wife! Why hasn't she taken out an order of protection?!"

My Vybie was plotting and plotzing to take out an order from the moment I shared with her that I intended to file for divorce, as I knew she would when I went down to our local police station a few days earlier to notify them of my intention. The delay was only due to her lawyer's advice that she wait awhile to make her request "look more realistic." Her yarmulke-bedecked devil was earning $10,000 dollars a month for sharing his wonderfully strategic legal advice.

Many women are protected by such orders, as they surely should be. But the wanton assault upon a man's reputation initiated by a false protection order, and the resulting severed paternal bond from their child upon any brazen bitch that signs this sinister document to gain the upper hand in a divorce, almost outweighs the original purpose for which legitimate orders of protection were created.

My solution is not to suggest that we ban protection orders. Not at all! I am only pointing out that they should be issued with at least as much caution as a parking violation citation. We laugh at the thought of a woman being allowed to simply point at any man who has a perfect driving record as he sits in a parked car, screaming that she fears being hit by him if he is permitted to drive, and a policeman suddenly running over and hastily issuing a ticket while grabbing the car keys and hauling the driver off to jail!

But that is exactly how easy it is for any wife, anywhere in this country, to issue a restraining order against her husband, no matter what his credentials are and irrespective of how pristine his prior decades of behavior as a father testifies, the moment he files for divorce. *He doesn't even have to be sitting in his car!*

Society sees these sociopaths as "Mommy." It is a title that allows them to instantly eviscerate father-daughter relationships. I can easily imagine my wife holding my Motion for Divorce in her left hand as she signed her responding Order for Protection with her right hand. She could have written, "divorce and probable child-support and maintenance payments," as her reason for taking out her Order of Protection and I have no doubt that it would still have been instantly stamped.

I'm not saying to abandon the original purpose for which Orders of Protection were intended. Nor am I denying the absolute need for protection orders in everyday life. I know protection orders help save lives. They are a great invention. I personally have advised many *Agunot* women to take out a protection order against their recalcitrant husbands.

One of the earliest questions I'd gently ask a crying young woman seeking a Jewish divorce was, "Has he ever hit, shoved, or even intimidated you?" *I get it.* I know there are stunning beauties like Evan Rachel Wood who have survived domestic violence and would probably be outraged at the slightest suggestion that the effectiveness of protection orders be even mildly diminished.

And I have three gorgeous daughters — and I'm on their side! I am also on the side of many women like Evan Rachel Wood. I don't want to diminish or abolish Orders of Protection. So please, ladies, fold your claws back into your palms. I'm the guy who jumps and somersaults the second you call. As high and as fast as I can!

I understand that the #MeToo movement was long overdue and that women have been screwed over, not merely for the last couple of millenniums by the likes of men like Cosby and Weinstein, but even by God since the moment he created Eve. And so I totally comprehend the urgent necessity for an order of protection. I would merely like to amend the previous sentence with two little words: *"When needed."*

I'm simply saying that "Do you want a protection order?" should not be the first hot-air question an overblown pretentious cannibal sporting a tiny yarmulka, strapped in Brooks Brothers lawyer-suspenders, blathers while winking at his bonkers client. And our judicial system needs to punish lawyers and anyone who abuses the system. Judges included. Everyone agrees that a woman who is proven to have falsely accused a man of rape deserves the jail sentence she will likely receive. But a woman who takes out false protection orders during a divorce is seen as "having caused no actual harm." She will never spend a day in jail.

And even granting that the protection order should be instantly stamped to be on the safe side of the woman requesting protection, we should then immediately examine the "crime scene" before chasing a man out of his house. And definitely before severing his relationship with his minor children! Especially when everyone knows that orders are constantly being used in a divorce to gain the upper hand. Does this take any special intelligence to understand? Also, women who commit perjury should be held accountable and punished under the law. Isn't this obvious? The laws are basically already in place. They just need to be enforced.

Women who cry wolf by issuing false protection orders are only harming their "sisters" who desperately need such orders to be as protective as Israel's Iron Dome Shield. Far too often the ease and speed with which the orders are issued, as part of the assembly line process of divorce, leads to the orders not being taken seriously when they should be.

It's gotten to the point where they have sadly become completely ineffective when most needed and flawlessly efficient when they should have never been launched in the first place. Beasts who stalk and murder their defenseless wives and girlfriends, who are trying to exit an abusive and violent relationship, are not threatened by a piece of paper. They patently don't give a shit. Meanwhile, gentle, loving fathers suffer immensely upon receiving one.

The incidence of spousal (including romantic partners) homicide in the United States, according to FBI data, found that for every one-hundred husbands who killed their wives, about seventy-five women killed their husbands. And although eighty percent of all murders are against men, more women are killed when they preliminarily suffer physical and emotional abuse from an aggressive male partner. *It's obvious they are heading to their grave.* Women need all the help they can get.

But sadly, when a spouse is willing to kill, a piece of paper does not shield the victim from a fist, knife, or bullet. Gun ownership by a male greatly increases the risk of the female being murdered. This is one more reason for much stricter gun control laws. Especially when a man wants a permit! There is no question that males are much more aggressive and physically violent than females.

That said, the protection order, at a minimum, also establishes a history against an abusive partner which can then help to incarcerate the ruthless companion. They are definitely a necessary part of our legal system and needed to protect the innocent. Women should never tolerate the slightest physical aggression from any male in their lives. But they need much more help than a piece of ineffectual paper. Despots, thugs, and brutish men don't respect peace treaties or Orders of Protection.

Sadly, the weak ineffectual cure of a Protection Order has become the dreaded deadly Ebola virus explosive disease when it comes to a common good man seeking a divorce. And although I don't expect anything less from sleazy blood-sucking toxic divorce attorneys, our court system should never have allowed — and for all practical purposes, continues to flagrantly encourage — this kind of tactic to be maliciously used to destroy family after family during a divorce. Fathers are instantly stripped of their Sixth Amendment rights upon filing for divorce and are injected with the merciless septic contagion caused by malicious prosecution.

Like bad mortgage lending, "they" (legislators and appellate judges) could stop all this bullshit yesterday if they really wanted to. But like the Wall Street thieves that destroyed so many lives, and figuratively demolished millions of homes, most judges have little if any humanity. There was simply too much money to be made by creating knowingly high-risk bad-credit derivatives based on the inflated value of homes created by the housing bubble.

And our divorce and family court system, obfuscated by unscrupulous lawyers, inept stone-hearted judges and their paper-pushing staff, is also bereft of any humanity as they earn fortunes in overtime pay and undeserved pensions, created by prolonging the simple process of a divorce (division of money, property, and setting minimum visitation rights with your own child), while treating every father served with a protection order as a "criminal-till-proven-innocent" schmuck. All under the guise of protecting the poor defenseless children of wire-monkey moms.

Let's admit it. Who wants to slaughter a cash-cow when you can cash-out by slaughtering Daddy? It's so much easier to take your time shuffling files while torturing Daddy. After all, he's paying for it. What a racket.

So please, give us a break. Besides, it's not easy being a man. We spend the first half of our lives walking around with a painful erection and the second half trying to pee. And somewhere in the middle we give you a house, child-support, and alimony. What else do you want? A new car every three years so you can "feel safer" when you drive the kids? Sure! A nice wardrobe and nine-tenths of the closet for all the outfits you wear just one time? Help yourself! A bathroom and shower full of exfoliates, shampoos, moisturizers, and perfumes as you complain about our one bar of soap being in your way? No problem! Freedom to fling instant protection orders upon receiving divorce papers? We gave you that too. *Did you have to take the kids?*

Think about how easy it is for a woman to sign a document, a piece of fantastical toilet tissue paper, that becomes an instant electrified iron gate that immediately awards her "temporary" full legal custody of any minor children during her divorce while simultaneously ejecting the "allegedly abusive" father and husband from the marital abode.

More quickly than a shocked heartbeat, the loving dad is barricaded from any further visitation until a trial can ascertain his worthiness and competency as a father. Years can now pass by without him ever seeing his kids. Ester turned twenty on April 6, 2021. I have barely seen her face since I filed for divorce when she was eleven years old.

And although a judge is supposed to decide custodial issues after careful deliberation, a protection order does all that for him instantly. Mom gets the house and kids, and Dad gets the bills and the hope of eventually being granted some visitation with his kids. Throw in alienation tactics and a Nazi donning a black robe, and you can kiss those children goodbye. Actually, you had better throw them a last kiss or you'll be accused of being a pedophile and a rapist. In truth, you'd be better off doing nothing. Walk away quietly.

Because "throwing a kiss" might be construed as *initiating contact*. And that simple gesture could turn you into a felon. Back away slowly. Because any quick movements on your part will very likely be interpreted as "aggression."

Thank you *Vybie*. Trust me, I never expected anything less. Your raw and naked emails revealed the real you. A man could never ask for a more transparent revelation of his spouse. They clearly removed any remaining doubts and explain why I had to divorce you. Thank you for liberating me from any remaining guilt that I needed to possibly hang in there *Tzu lib der kinder* (for the children's sake). And thank you for sparing me from the wrath of God, who surely won't punish me for sleeping with you since it was unknowingly that I made love to a ferocious beast (Exodus 22:19).

Even the guidelines for signing off on a protection order are incredibly inquisition-like. A petitioner who takes out an order of protection is never asked for evidence. A judge has to simply "feel" an inclination (very scientific) that "there is a preponderance of veracity to the allegations being made." In simple terms that means "more likely than not." In mathematical terms, we'd call that fifty-one percent.

And so the mere filing of a protection order becomes the one percent of necessary "evidence" that tips the scale which then allows any divorce court judge to instantly rationalize that there is "a preponderance of veracity" to every order of protection ever filed in this country. He instantly signs off on the order the moment it descends like "overtime" manna from divorce-attorney-heaven and alights on his desk. *In God We Trust*.

Translated over to my case, Judge Mendelson, who never met me or Googled my name, instantly believed "more likely than not" that my wife "feared my wrath," and that I was an individual "obsessed with feces" because I had authored a very funny children's book that won a coveted Kirkus award.

The fact that I had been married for twenty-eight years, had never been issued a parking ticket, let alone had any familial incident remotely necessitating the police or authorities being dispatched to my home, meant nothing to the judge.

Forty-five seconds spent Googling my name, or the name of my company, SwordPen Publishers, would have yielded over thirty pages of my "violent" life story as a boring five-star mortgage advisor and Small Press publisher of children's literature. Two more seconds would have revealed video and pictures of a gentle author doing library readings for a crowd of adoring children and their parents. An obviously very dangerous man. But who has forty-five seconds when you can just rubber-stamp a document in a nanosecond and then collect years of overtime?

The fact that I was the plaintiff who had issued the divorce papers and that we were now in our fourth month of litigation meant nothing. In truth, my wife could have written "refuses to take out the garbage" or "doesn't like the Yankees," or even "he once ejaculated before I came," and her orders would still have been signed faster than you can say, "Bye Kids!"

And that is because judges rarely read the details of any protection order. Like most of their robotic pension-driven jurisprudence-jaded peers, they stamp it faster than a mohel runs his scalpel across the clamped Mogen-shield flattened-foreskin of an eight-day-old Jewish future #MeTooProtectionOrder recipient. *Mazel Tov!*

In truth, most documents received by the divorce court are never read. Alfieri constantly began our proceedings by hastily calling both attorneys into chambers (i.e. off the record) to get a "short version" update of all the motions that were filed. I once scotch-taped a twenty-dollar bill onto page eighteen of one of the submissions with a note that said, "Please keep this for having finally read a submission. Tell me you read this and I'll donate $100 dollars to your favorite charity." Never heard a word from the court. I could have written, "Alfieri is a drunken, fucking-stupid, nasty, white-trash POS," and the safest place to do so would have been in a submission to the court.

I also scotch-taped a twenty-dollar bill with a similar note of thanks onto page eighteen of a box of documentation detailing my wife's alienation of Ester. I am the one who originally requested a court appointed lawyer for the minor upon seeking full custody of Ester. My lawyer explained the endless alienation tactics of my wife upon Ester in full detail to the court. He even showed an email from her therapist, Rabbi Donny Frank, in which he sent her links on the topic after promising (during marital therapy) that he would no longer see or advise either of us if one or both of us chose to go the divorce route. So much for a "rabbi," or "therapist," keeping their word.

My wife has continued seeing Donny Frank for eight years since the day I filed for divorce. That's a lot of Benjamin's. *So much for keeping your word "Rabbi" Frank.* I imagine my ex still needs his professional help to "deal with Zev." But most likely, my ex, according to the last emails I saw, is dealing with "boundaries" and still trying to convince her Asperger daughter-in-law to allow her to see our grandchildren. *Good luck with that, Sharen! She's as likely to let you see them as you are inclined to encourage Ester to see me.*

Frank is the Monsey go-to *Unzereh* source for help in destroying lives through controlling frustrated young boys by allegedly engaging in Conversion Therapy — drugging them with anti-psychotic drugs and other medications commonly used to treat sex-addiction — whenever they express "feelings" for other boys. This treatment will supposedly make them feel better (i.e. *feel nothing*) so they won't *misbehave* anymore, the clueless young Yeshiva boys are assured.

After all, surely their "condition" is temporary and merely the Evil Inclination (the *Yetzer Hara* spreading perversion, *Feh!*) at work. "Don't worry Mommy and Tatie, we'll find Yossie a nice *Shidduch* one day." All the Monsey school principals highly recommend this "trusted" therapist to control the "urges" of little boys. "And who knows," the trusted therapist assures the parents, "Perhaps Yossie will be able to better focus on his studies now that he's not thinking about his classmates. Maybe we'll be able to lower his Ritalin dosage."

Forget about athletes and enhanced performance. These little saints are being *fucking drugged* for enhanced devotion to God! Another little known, and never openly discussed, family secret in the quaint Yentasville, NY, suburb.

I remember how carefully I prepared every single piece of paper in the box my lawyer and I were delivering to the law offices of Margaret Smith. I literally laid out the timeline, in an almost forensic display, of my wife's psychological manipulation of my sweet daughter's now lobotomized love for her Tatie alongside the history of how I loved Ester and cared for her as a Mr. Mom from the day she was born till the day I filed for divorce.

A prosecutor in a murder trial could not have organized a more meticulously prepared play-by-play portrayal of my case. With so many emails and transcribed voice recordings (painstakingly typed and signed under the threat of perjury as to their originality), I innocently believed that I would be granted immediate full custody of Ester upon Margaret's mere perusal of its contents.

I was already deciding where I'd take Ester on our first outing. Perhaps some basketball and then a restaurant for some "deep and meaningful conversation." *Or perhaps we'd go to …* as I considered so many wonderful things we might do together to catch up on so much lost time.

Meanwhile, Margaret shows up in court three months later, slightly tipping her bleach-blond white-roots, lazy head as if to indicate confusion, and reports to the judge that she "just can't figure out what exactly is going on," and then adds, "I think I'm going to have to recommend a forensic psychiatric examination." I. Was. Shocked. I felt as if Mike Tyson just stunned me with a liver punch.

The court had allowed a full twelve weeks for Margaret Smith to carefully investigate the very serious charge of alienation. It pained me that it would be three more months during which Ester would be further brainwashed to hate the father she once loved. *But at least now I had someone in my corner who would clearly see what's going on.* Someone who would finally read the vile emails and publicize the horrific efforts of my wife to rape Ester out of my life after labeling me as an angry and dangerous pedophile. I was so excited at the thought of hearing Ester's laughter again as I counted down the days to our next court appearance.

Margaret's sole role was to protect Ester and ascertain if any alienation was taking place. The proof of my Mr. Mom credentials being validated and then instantly being granted sole custody now seemed inevitable. I could almost see twelve weeks into the future as I envisioned a movie scene of Margaret Smith bursting out in incredulous anger and indignation when we reconvened to discuss Ester's fate, angrily pointing an accusatory finger across the courtroom at my wife.

I was positive I'd be granted immediate custody of Ester by an apologetic judge based upon the mountain of irrefutable evidence I had provided (ruthless emails devilishly concocted by my wife and her attorney that depicted their diabolical behavior).

Instead, the reality of the family court system slammed into me like a three-hundred-pound blitzing linebacker as it occurred to me that Margaret never made the effort to even open the meticulously prepared box that my lawyer and I organized for her. I was thunderstruck and could barely mouth my next few words as I tried to regain my air: "She never read a fucking word of what we sent her!" I whispered in a devastated-beyond-belief wounded voice to my lawyer.

My lawyer (who knew Margaret well) later approached Ms. Smith in the hallway and said, "You never read one paper in that box."

"How do you know?" she defensively asked.

"Because I taped a $20 dollar bill onto page eighteen," I responded. "You never even bothered opening the box we delivered to you."

Margaret stared at me for the next few moments with an expression as empty as her brain — an eternity, compared to the amount of time she spent reviewing the evidence I had prepared for her — and then apologized, adding, "I'm so sorry Mr. Lewinson, but alienation is very commonplace in a divorce. I hope things work out for you."

"Of course it's commonplace in a divorce you lazy white-trash trailer-bred bitch!" I felt like screaming. But I didn't. Because that kind of response would only fuel more protection orders to muzzle an "angry" father. It would prove that I'm human. The loudest scream would never be seen as even one percent of the pain I felt as I endured my new tortured life. And so I blankly stared back at Margaret, with an expression as empty as my heart, and said nothing. Zero. *Nada.* Like my future relationship with Ester from that moment on.

I wonder if Margaret ever went back to that box to fleece her twenty-dollar bill. If she did, it would mean she earned three months' pay as a special "court-appointed attorney for the minor child" merely to hustle an additional twenty-dollar bill while squandering my chances of receiving guardianship and being granted immediate visitation.

A moral individual would have returned to that box to read all its contents. Doing so would surely have prompted anyone with a conscience, and a minuscule of empathy, to reconvene the court. But I have yet to meet one court appointed lazy bottom-feeder who gives a shit about that courtroom sign that proclaims: *In God We Trust.* They are so slothful I'm amazed they even bother to pick up their checks.

And this is the family-divorce court system. Lawyers, judges, and ancillary court appointed "specialists" financially drain the taxpayer and divorcing couple while rewarding themselves for stretching out the divorce file for years. Like Alfieri, they develop this talent to bill the court while pushing off any decision regarding their file for as long as possible.

Yes. A family is nothing more than "a file."

A simple thirty-second search of the names on a protection order (typically issued in family court) would display if either party involved had already been in litigation in another court system (e.g. divorce court). This could be treated as a red flag. It does not mean that the protection order should be denied, but it would at least allow the court to be notified immediately and to then examine if the order is being issued as a tactical ploy to destroy a spouse instead of mindlessly jumping to rubber-stamp #METOOPROTECTIONORDER in crimson-red screaming bold letters onto the forehead of yet another victimized dad.

A destroyed man typically includes a much-damaged child. The father-child relationship will be obliterated upon dad receiving that screeching order from two armed policemen stating: DO NOT TALK TO MINOR CHILD.

Said child almost always winds up in the custody of the heartless parent who issued the orders. The probability of that alienated minor child eventually using drugs, having unprotected sex, getting poor grades in school, and engaging in a host of endless "stupid behavior" while painfully subliminally-searching for lost fatherly love — all carried out in place of the quality time they should have been spending with their father — greatly increases as an outcome of mommy dearest issuing an order of protection. The gentle male figure that was once the most protective source in their life is suddenly the most dangerous one. *Dad is vaporized.*

I was a gentle middle-aged father who wanted nothing more than to parent the late in life child that was born, almost miraculously, as I concluded my fifth decade of life. Upon trying to exit my marriage, as I began my seventh decade of existence, I was sentenced to judicial vaporization and suddenly found myself living in a dystopian divorce-netherworld. I was labeled as a deviant who needed to be supervised merely to speak to the little girl I once gently diapered, patiently fed, and tenderly burped.

The lovely cherub whose mind I stimulated with laughter, reading, and love; the excited toddler that screeched in delight as she heard my key turning the lock of the front door upon my arrival home; the trusting young girl who jumped into my arms from the top step, now believed that I was a green monster that deserved death.

Like the fast-turning blades of a wood-chipper, God, my wife, and the State Court system shredded the strongest bond of love I ever felt for any human on this planet. I am not angry. In fact, I no longer feel. Anything.

I know what *Vaporized Father Syndrome* feels like firsthand, having grown up with an abusive mother who grossly maltreated, tormented, and then divorced my incredibly kind and long-suffering father to shamelessly marry the already-married neighbor across the street who never got past his "glory days" as a muscular ripped football player for Rutgers University. Yes, like the prior run-on sentence, Mom wasted no time. And as a lithe sinewy cornerback, neither did my stepdad.

My stepdad, Arnold "Skip" Zarra, was as hard-hearted as my mother. Theirs was a rocky marriage but it lasted even when their hormones and money dissipated, because my mother didn't want to get divorced at forty-five. People toughed it out in the late sixties and early seventies.

My life spiraled out of control once my dad was out of the house.

The Holocaust was difficult for a ten-year-old to comprehend. But I clearly understood that my cuckolded father had been "tossed outta the house" by the passionate newlyweds, Skip and Esther, in as cruel and ugly a fashion as I would one day be ejected from mine. I only saw my father sporadically after his escape from a second holocaust. And once he remarried, I rarely saw him at all. And as I now look back decades later, the saddest part of all this is that it felt normal to me.

My mother was honeymooning with Skip in Niagara Falls before the ink dried on her Jewish divorce papers, and the five of us (my two brothers, new chiseled-father, and wire-monkey-mommy) immediately moved six blocks away from Skip's ex-wife and his two small kids to 256 Goldsmith Avenue in Newark, New Jersey. Skip then did well selling mutual funds for a new company called Dreyfus and two years later we moved to 48 Korwel Circle in West Orange, NJ.

Mom still cooked a traditional Friday night Shabbat dinner and things seemed quieter, but I understood that the two monsters, who had brutalized the nicest man I ever knew, were now in complete control of my life. I wanted to live with my father, but the judge instantly ruled that my mother would have full control of my life. (Don't forget we are talking about the year 1965.)

Fortunately, with a busy school schedule that included secular and Jewish studies, along with hours upon hours of basketball practice ("basketball therapy," just like Ester's future horse therapy), I spent very little time with them. With their newfound financial comfort, they were busy with each other. They weren't mean to me. Like my future wife, they just "weren't."

My immigrant mom must have been a great lay at thirty-seven to land a USA Eagle Scout with a chiseled abdomen who was two years younger than herself. But you don't have to subject me to psychoanalysis, Mr. Freud. I don't think of my mother "that way." Even subliminally. Trust me. All I ever wanted from her as a child was a warm hug. And maybe her taking the time to read a bedtime story to me before running out to fuck and suck some policeman's cock. But it's okay. Like Mick always reminded me, "You can't always get what you want." Even without her, I certainly learned how to read. And I certainly made up for my lost share of warm childhood hugs. *Or did I?*

Mom shlepped her three sons into the now sanctioned-by-money adulterous relationship that her paid-off Ultra-Orthodox sisters celebrated with her because my mother imitated Sammy Davis Jr. by generously spreading the wealth around — although her own parents refused her largess, along with her invitation to attend her second wedding. Mom even insisted that my older brother and I hold two of the four poles of her wedding canopy.

I had just turned bar-mitzvah and I watched my mother sip the wine after the marital blessings were sung. And even though I loved her, I felt like congratulating her with a salutation of, "Mazel Tov, you cruel Bitch!" as my step-dad stomped the crystal glass in memory of the two times our Temple in Jerusalem was destroyed by the Babylonians and then the Romans. *Along with the two sets of children he and my mom demolished.*

By some miracle, I wound up going to boarding school at age fifteen, flying from Newark airport to what is now known as Thurgood Marshall airport, upon my mother handing me a one-way first-class ticket while scrimping on a goodbye hug. I basically stayed away from "home bitter home" for a half-dozen years, including a year that I studied abroad in Jerusalem. I'd come home for summers, but I did my own thing. I was happier that way. So were my mom and stepfather.

My real dad was the gentlest man on the planet. He made Gandhi look like Genghis Khan. But I rarely saw him. Even when he was married to my mom. Dad, who smuggled diamonds for chump change after graduating from Dachau and before being allowed entry into America, was out the door to the factory where he robotically cut patterns for women's clothing before I even woke up most mornings, and he arrived home after I fell asleep most nights. I typically saw him on Shabbos and Sundays.

While his other two sons watched *The Addams Family* on Friday night, I'd polish my shoes, dress up for the Sabbath Queen, comb my hair after messaging my scalp with some Brylcreem as I stared into the mirror while wishing I looked like Ricky Nelson, and dash off to the synagogue.

Although my favorite show was *Bewitched*, which aired on Thursdays, and aside from being madly infatuated with Elizabeth Montgomery at eleven years of age, *The Addams Family* was more bizarre than my own mad mishpacha and certainly a show I did not want to miss. But I had so much empathy for a very sad, wonderfully kind man whose forlorn expression only changed when he saw that I was already sitting — like a loyal puppy — next to his empty chair as he arrived late to prayers, having rushed back from work to finally rest on the Sabbath.

It was the only time I saw a happy countenance and full-blown smile replace the constantly worried and anxious-looking face with pursed lips — which dad often bit out of pure anxiety. I wanted my father to be happy. Even if it meant missing out on *The Addams Family*. But Dad's happy facial expression never lasted long. Neither did his fulfillment of the commandment, "On the seventh day you shall rest" (Exodus 34:21).

Because a typical Friday night Shabbat dinner would often result with my mother screaming and literally throwing plates at my Tatie. My brothers and I would duck and run out of the room while I, once again, like the Revolutionary and Civil Wars I once pondered, tried to figure out what all the fighting was about.

I often hid behind an open door, because I'd get slapped right in the face if I defended my father. I guess you could say that I received my self-esteem from my father and my future ability to dodge a punch from my mother. I watched my unhinged mother, through the crack of the hinged door, as she screamed and threw things at the gentlest man on the planet while he tried to reason with her to calm down.

By age eleven, I was advising Tatie to get a divorce. It took me about a year to convince him. Dad knew how to deal with Nazi's and was willing to stay married to his narcissist for the sake of his three sons. No one (especially religious Jews and Catholics) got divorced in the "olden days." I was the only kid who attended the Hebrew Youth Academy in Newark during the year of 1965 that came from a "broken home," as if my parents' divorce shattered what had once been a safe haven. It was extremely embarrassing to have divorced parents during *The Age of Aquarius*. Adults would give me these pitiful stares as if I was missing a limb. I was. But I was willing to suffer and limp without a father. "Run Yankeleh! Run!"

My logical advice was great for my dad. He laughed in admission when I simply pointed out that he was already obviously divorced. Like Ester in the future, I told my father that I wanted to live with him. He told me that the judge wouldn't let me. I still insisted that he divorce my mother. Dad escaped Dachau a second time and, after several very lonely years, eventually married a nice quiet widow.

"She's not as pretty as your *Muhder*," he explained in his Yiddish accent, "but she's so nice to me." Mom wound up marrying her paramour. Juxtaposed to my dad, mom was already obviously married to Skip. And at eleven years of age I didn't get any mate. I got fucked. Thankfully, not literally. But that's another story.

The wise and sincere advice I gave my dad was horrific for me. I now had no one. The one man who constantly told me that I was, "so smart and funny and could even be president if I *vanted* to be," was now someone I'd rarely see. The man I completely confided in, and fully trusted from my brain's earliest ability to form memories — the father I called out for when I woke up in a strange room full of kids in hospital beds or when I wet my own bed as a toddler — was basically out of my life. Ironically, at the same age that Ester's father was maligned out of hers.

"Tatie, swear to me I won't die while I'm sleeping!" a very precocious three-year-old, who had only recently learned that people die and was passing through a phase fearing death while sleeping, would demand nightly of an angelic man whose words, he knew, God would never allow to be broken.

"You're not allowed to swear," my father would gently respond (as per Jewish Halacha).

"Then I'm never falling asleep!" I stubbornly insisted.

"Okay, I swear," my father assured me as he chuckled, instantly giving in to the love he felt for his child (who didn't understand or care what was so humorous) over the fear he felt for his God.

I remember dreaming that I needed to pee so badly. I lifted the toilet seat and felt so relieved as a powerful stream sprayed out of my body (at sixty-eight I wish I could do that now). Suddenly I woke up and called out to my father that I "made pishy." Unlike Rabbi Tratner a few years later, dad changed my sheets and put nice warm pajama pants on me. Then he tucked me in and kissed my head. Bye, Dad.

All I knew was that my father was a good man. And good men didn't lie. So I knew I'd wake up. Flawless three-year-old logic. I had already caught my mom lying many times. But not Tatie. Never, ever. I don't think he even knew how. Eight years later, at eleven years of age, my father was almost completely out of my life.

I eventually became a kid who technically had four parents, but zero parenting. And even less love. Amazingly enough, the warmest caregiver that consistently gave me attention as a young child was an old Russian Jewish lady born in the last decade of the nineteenth century named Gussie. She was an old woman about whom I knew virtually nothing. But I did know the most important thing I needed to know. Gussie loved me. She was as warm and loving as my mother and future wife were cold.

Like a Russian peasant who survived to reach old age, Gussie probably lived an extremely harsh, uneventful life. The kind of life that history is seldom aware of to recognize individually, let alone take the time to chronicle personally. Gussie lived with us for several years during the five-day work week. I think she stayed with a married niece on weekends. I instinctively knew that I could trust this woman, who was basically a stranger, with my life. She earned my certitude by the way she rejoiced and laughed while sitting and watching television with me, while squishing me with loving hugs and drowning me with "disgusting" sloppy wet kisses as she squealed, "I love you!"

Knowing some Russian history about what Jews in Russia endured during the first half of the twentieth century I can only imagine how interesting a biography of her life would have read. But I knew absolutely nothing about Gussie. I only remember asking, "Mommy, is she Jewish?" Her affirmative response was the only detail I knew about Gussie. My mother, who spoke seven languages, spoke to Gussie in Russian. Like a true peasant, Gussie did exactly as she was told. And like a peasant, she never wasted anything. Nor did she ever complain.

I never asked Gussie if she had ever been married or had kids of her own. She barely spoke Yiddish so I couldn't communicate with her. She simply agreed with anything I said. Even with staying up late to watch television. I can't recall when Gussie stopped being a part of my life. Did she die and no one told me because I was so young? Anyone I could ask is gone. Soon I'll be joining them.

It's been about a hundred and thirty years since an affectionate and kindhearted sweet baby girl was born. If not for these few nostalgic reminiscent memories, no one would know that she lived to a ripe old age. She did many *mitzvot* (kind deeds) during her lifetime by hugging a lonely future writer. One who would only become lonelier with age.

Thoughts of Gussie as a young woman occasionally formed in my juvenile mind like water vapor attempting to condense into droplets or ice crystals in a cloud. But the curious musings vaporized as quickly as a sudden burst of sunlight evaporating a hazy sky because we didn't share a common language that allowed me to articulate my childhood curiosity. So I left those thoughts for some future date, like a million other questions that five-year-old minds wonder about for a quick moment as they attempt to formulate what they are trying to comprehend before quickly jumping to their next query.

I was told, "You'll know when you're older" so often in my ingenue preadolescent youth, that I simply figured God somehow eventually dumps a bunch of information into one's head at a certain age before they get married. I still wonder why he didn't share what narcissists were till after I got married.

Gussie barely spoke Yiddish and understood very little English. She could hardly enunciate more than the three "America" words that she constantly repeated as she chuckled with delight. But they were all the "America" I needed to hear. Gussie loved me.

Gussie squeezed me tightly while we watched *Father Knows Best, The Invisible Man, Topper, My Little Margie,* and *Zorro*. I was amazed at the swordsmanship of Don Diego de la Vega and his ability to slash the coolest "Z" into the clothing of his shocked opponent, who realized that Zorro had chosen to spare his life. I liked to imagine that I was the handsome man slashing "Zev" into the clothing of the "bad guys."

I sat squished between Gussie's huge bosom and her encircling arm, that flapped loose skin when extended, and the arm of the old big upholstered yellow-leather chair whose skin was also distended. The oversized leather chair was meant for one person but could accommodate one-and-a-half not too uncomfortably. Watching television with her Mr. Magoo huge eyes through extremely thick glasses, I knew Gussie couldn't understand the plot or storyline of any of the shows we watched together. I tried my best, but it was too much to explain to someone who only spoke Russian. Gussie enjoyed herself anyway as she laughed whenever I laughed.

As a five-year-old I understood much more than I was able to articulate. I was the epitome of the English proverb, "Children should be seen, not heard." I was so shy, that I didn't even want to be seen. It didn't seem to matter. Gussie was so happy to just sit with me, like a loyal puppy, while I watched television. My mother would order me to be in bed by eight as she walked out the door (looking, as much as possible, like Ava Gardner) to party, but Gussie always let me stay up as late as I wanted. She would laugh while hugging me, as she effusively repeated the simple three "America" words I never heard my mother say.

It really is wonderful to be told you are loved. A man needs to hear that. And surely a little boy. Gussie bathed me in endless declarations of "I love you!" and lots of hot water because she wanted to make sure I was squeaky clean. And her "America" words helped to cleanse the lonely lachrymose decay left by a mother who took the time to abuse my father, but never found the time to kiss me, cuddle me, or read a book to me. And when I woke up in the middle of the night Gussie was the one who was there for me. So quickly, in fact, that I often wondered if she slept.

"What time is it?" I'd ask.

"It's a quarter to four," she'd answer in her very weak Yiddish, "Go to sleep kitten."

"But first I want to check!" as I'd scamper out of my bed.

I was amazed at how Gussie always knew the exact time without having to look at a clock. Perhaps it was because she was a calm peasant who never rushed and could always sense if it was time to milk the cows or feed the chickens. I thought she had magical powers. I'd race into the kitchen to check the clock at all hours of the night or day just to test her. As a five-year-old I could barely tell time myself. But I was smart enough to figure out the big hand and the little hand if I took my time and used my fingers.

Right again! It was exactly 3:44 A.M. I was so used to Gussie taking care of me that I didn't even question where mommy was in the middle of the night. All I knew was that Mommy worked, so it didn't occur to me that she wasn't working in the middle of the night. Unless you call a blowjob a job. You don't know how to miss something you never had. Kids just flow. Till they discover they're completely fucked-up adults suffering as a result of the traumatic childhood they have yet to learn to survive.

I didn't ask questions. I had food and a roof over my head. And lots of television. I obediently did whatever I was told to do. Exactly like my peasant friend. And exactly like I was destined to do in the future as the manipulated husband of an ex machina wife.

Thank you Gussie. Wherever you are. Thank you for loving me. I don't remember if I ever told you. But I loved you too. I hope you're with my dad now. After all, the two of you have so much in common.

I grew up quickly after I convinced my father not to tolerate being treated like a *schweinehund* by his abusive wife. "Vat ken I do?" he would wonder in response, "I don't vant to leave you." Even as a ten-year-old I couldn't stand the injustice of the way my mother treated the anxious-looking man she was married to, and I constantly got cursed-out in Russian (*Yahpt Fa Ya Maht!*) or slapped right in the face for speaking the truth. As I mentioned, Mom spoke seven languages and could curse fluently in any of them.

Getting slapped when I knew I was speaking the truth was the perfect preparation for my future marriage and divorce court experience. Simply substitute the word "slapped" with a nagging "Your family, Ze'eh'ev!" or a roaring "I'll hold you in contempt!" I knew from experience what happens when things escalate. And with having been well-conditioned by my father to back down, I constantly found myself apologizing to my wife, writing beautiful letters to her, to try and restore peace.

Upon mom remarrying I was now threatened, and sometimes slapped, by my etched-in-stone-physique stepdad, to "Be respectful!" and not talk back to my mother — as if the sins they executed against my father were somehow expunged by a marriage license from the Gentile *Arkayos Akum* courthouse. A license, by the way, for a marriage that Jewish Orthodox biblical law would never sanction in a billion years.

The Bible forbids an adulteress from ever marrying her paramour. It is one of the three-hundred and sixty-five negative (as in "Do not!") commandments in the Old Testament. And according to the Talmudical saint, Rabbi Akiva, any child resulting from such a marital union would be a *mamzer* (bastard) according to Jewish law. (Like Jesus was, because his mother had the affair while still married to Joseph.) But hey! As the daughter of the famous Rabbi Ya'akov Eliezer Tellem of Newark, New Jersey, my mother surely felt protected by her father's spiritual merit.

The entire Newark Jewish community gossiped about the Rabbi's daughter. *Host du geh'hert dem nayis?* (*Did you hear the news?*) But like her future daughter-in-law, my mother felt no shame for her parent's reputation or her own. And she certainly felt no guilt or empathy. Mom wore her Hester Prynne scarlet *Aleph* with a confidence that only money (or true narcissism) can buy.

Mom got pregnant when I was fifteen. My *Zaydeh* must have been mortified in front of his synagogue congregants. But he always walked with what can only be described as a humble self-confident stride. He seemed to know that he was marching on the path of righteousness. I wonder how he felt knowing the halachic ruling of Rabbi Akiva.

As it turned out, *Zaydeh* was spared from embarrassment and Mamzer-Mazal *Tov's* because his daughter's pregnancy, and my future mamzer Rutgers University cornerback half-brother's life, had to be terminated when doctors saw cysts on mom's thirty-nine-year-old ovaries. A half century ago, decades before laparoscopic surgery became a commonplace procedure, doctors immediately chose to perform a hysterectomy.

Interestingly enough, the final Talmudical Halachic decision regarding the legal status of a child birthed by a Scarlet-lettered Jewish woman, after marrying her paramour, was decided in favor of the more lenient majority who debated against the restrictive minority opinion of Rabbi Akiva. Turns out, my half-brother would have been kosher. I would have loved him either way. Kosher or not. Jewish or not. I. Love. Babies.

I would have loved raising my baby brother, Mommy. You would never have had to lift a finger. God must have been quite angry to punish you so severely that he completely ignored my innocent brother and I as mere collateral damage. But his "eye for an eye" removal of your ovaries certainly proclaimed the exact lesson he was trying to teach you. She who lives by the pussy, dies by the pussy.

And although I, and probably even God, can forgive the sin of adultery, I suspect your punishment was meted out, not because of your passionate adulterous relationship with Skip, but in retribution for heartlessly smearing your pussy juice mixed with Skip's cum into the nervous pressed-lips and twisted-in-pain face of your cuckolded husband. I'll never forget Skip telling Dad, laughing in his face, while you stood smiling with pride at your smirking future husband's side, that you give a great blowjob.

I was too young to understand the entire conversation I overheard, having woken up early because of the tenseness in the air, as I stood in my pajamas, a practiced expert at hiding behind an open door and spying through the crack. Dad rushed home from the bus stop to get the brown-bag lunch he forgot to grab as he hurried out the door to go to work that morning (Dad was never late for anything in his life except for divorcing mom). It was there in the kitchen that he found his cheating wife sitting and laughing boisterously with her paramour while they enjoyed an intimate early cup of coffee together.

"Leave my vife alone!" my father insisted.

"I can't! She gives too good a blow job!" the muscular Rutgers football player kindly responded.

I didn't know what a "blowjob" was, and, thank God, I don't recall this scene from my childhood when I get one. But I understood by my future stepdad's insulting tone of voice, and the severe pained expression on my father's sad face, that it was some kind of viciously nasty taunt. My father bit his lip so hard, that he squinted his effaced image-of-God countenance into such a deformed, nervous guise, that my own mouth hurt.

I continued to spy as the broken, silent, *schweinehund* slowly fetched his brown paper bag of dog biscuits and scurried away with his tail behind his legs. The dehumanizing psychological tactics of the Nazis was a class in self-esteem by comparison.

I didn't understand the details of the serrating words I had witnessed only moments ago, but I could easily imagine the visible trail of my father's daggered-heart dripping the sacrificed blood of a saint, spotting the sidewalk, had I chosen to follow his path to the bus stop to tell him to, "Divorce mommy already!" But I had to get ready for school. I'd save my instructions and loving advice for when we'd walk back from the synagogue on Friday night. *Guess what I thought about all day in school?*

I started to whimper silently behind the door at the callous ("preordained by God") onslaught my father had just endured for forgetting his lunch. His painfully contorted face, as he kept biting down on his bottom lip, as if that physical pain could distract him from the more severe inhumane agony he was suffering at that moment while being laughed at, is as vivid today as when I first heard the sharp words stabbing into his heart almost sixty years ago.

As a skinny nine-year-old I was almost as helpless as my father and I also slunk away, choking on my tears, as the happy cruel couple sipped coffee while smearing their lungs with tar. I loved my father. And I loved the crazy self-centered bitch I had called "Mommy" my entire life. My father, unfortunately, taught me to tolerate abuse. He's the opposite of a man who beats his wife and sets a horrific example for his son. No wonder I stayed married for twenty-eight years.

Like a confused young rape victim, I couldn't even begin to understand, let alone compartmentalize, my feelings. Kind of like the way I still deal with God. I could literally feel my father's pain and debased ego as he ran to catch a bus to pay the bills for a wife that was balling the football player who lived seventy-five yards from our front door. Skip could sprint that distance in seconds. And he often did whenever my father wasn't home. You'd run too for a blowjob from my mother.

I imagine that my father playing *Tzenter* with laughing Nazi soldiers had to be less painful than standing already dead while my mother and her vile paramour mocked and jeered him.

I guess Skip got his etiquette lessons and that heartless "What are you gonna do about it?" expression from you, Mom. Did you have to laugh, Mommy? Was Skip's cruel and crass joke really that funny? I'll never understand why God put Dad through Dachau while allowing you to safely escape to America. But then again, for someone who can watch nursing babies and their older toddler siblings being mowed down by soldiers with machine guns, what's a little verbal abuse?

I pretty much lost touch with my stepdad after my mom died on my birthday in 1996. Was that supposed to be a present, God? Discovering what the world thought of Jews on my tenth birthday, and losing Malcom X on my twelfth one wasn't enough gifts? Amazingly enough, I Googled Skip's name out of the blue the day after he died on the first day of June in 2017. I was shocked to discover that Arnold H. "Skip" Zarra was a Megan's law registrant who had been sentenced to lifetime parole in 2013! As a convicted felon he was obviously not allowed to have weapons, but bizarrely chose to walk into his senior center housing complex with a loaded rifle draped onto his walker.

Skip wound up spending a year in Southwoods State Prison. He died shortly afterwards at age eighty-four following complications from leukemia. As cruel as he was to my father, I can only feel ... well, nothing.

Another conversation I was too young to understand was the time you picked me up from school for a doctor's appointment. I can still see you Mommy, as I sat in the backseat of your brand-new baby-blue Pontiac.

The year was 1958, way before seatbelts were standard features of the automobile, let alone any laws and advertising jingles decreeing and conditioning the masses to "Buckle-up-for-safety, buckle-up! Buckle-up-for-safety. Everybody-buckle-up!" I remember as you stealthily pulled up behind a police car at a red light. And I recall the devilish, playful gleam in your man-eater eyes as you "accidentally-on-purpose" inched forward and gently bumped into the police car in front of you. Their probable spouses and children never had a chance.

At age five I had no understanding of what you were initiating, and I jumped up and said, "Mommy! Mommy! What are you doing?!" You simply laughed your earthy laugh and snapped, "It's okay Zev. Sit down!" I looked up into your mirror to watch you. I can still see the confident glint in your hungry tigress eyes as you hunted down the two cops looking up at you through their rearview mirror. They were laughing. And so were you. And then you calmly, carefully, bumped them again. You were so smooth. The cop looked up into his mirror again. He wore a "this is a wild one" expression on his brow, but I was too young to comprehend the emotion of sexual hunger behind his half-squinted eyes.

The light turned green. The policeman calmly turned on his rotating red gumball light as if he had all the time in the world. That really impressed me because I was faintly beginning to understand what technology, what everyone called "gadgets" in those days, was. I watched the cop exude his best James Dean aura as he carefully opened his door, got out of his seat, and slowly approached your car. I had no idea as to what was happening. But like most of my childhood (and eventual marriage), I saw and was not heard.

I knew you were pretty, but as a little boy how could I begin to imagine, let alone describe, how alluringly you were able to smile at twenty-nine years of age, or what you were seductively inviting. You were my mommy. How could I fathom that you were also a clone of Tura Satana in *Faster, Pussycat! Kill! Kill!* You rolled down your window as the cop playfully rolled his eyes, continuing his routine that imitated the handsome star who died three years before he would have been eligible to join the 27 Club, and asked, "Ma'am, are we having a problem with the breaks?"

You looked up at him with a half suggestive — half apologetic voice, coupled with a "let's get it on" wink, and soothingly purred, "I'm so sorry Officer. Would you like my phone number?"

He then took out his black ticket book and jotted down our home number (I can easily imagine you group messaging the entire police force had cell phones been invented) while politely advising you to "Please drive more carefully in the future, Ma'am," as he smiled charmingly while winking back at you. I wonder if he wore his uniform and handcuffed you for foreplay. Did he share you with his partner? Did he write "for a good time, call the daughter of Rabbi Tellem" in the bathroom stalls back at the precinct?

I had no clue as to what had just transpired. I was a little boy. And, like all little kids, the incident that made no sense disappeared from my thoughts the moment we drove away. But little boys have big memories. And that childhood scene came back to me, in the future, as an adult who now clearly understood that your husband meant nothing to you. Zero. Nada. Like the narcissist that you were — it was all about you. Even in front of your little son.

You threw plates and knives and forks at Dad. You screamed at him. You cheated on him. And I'm not complaining about an affair. Adults are free to make their own choices. But I feel it was cruel and inhumane to constantly, blatantly, rub your friendly-neighbor-pussy in the face of the gentlest man on the planet. Oh yeah! I almost forgot. Did it ever occur to you how painful it was for me to watch it all?

I also remember how I wanted to run away from home. Away from you. I was only five, but sad beyond my years. I still remember packing some clothes and books as you, trying to hold back your laughter, asked me if I wanted any pictures to remember you by. Glad I entertained you as I chocked on my tears. Did it ever occur to you to stop manipulating me? And all you had to do,

Mommy, was get on your knees (a position you were probably very comfortable assuming) and give me a big hug. And a gentle kiss while whispering "I love you" would have been ... beyond even my wildest, innocent-childhood imagination.

I wasn't articulate yet. But I told you that "I hate living here." You understood why. But you had nothing to say. And I couldn't express my feelings. I didn't hate you Mommy. But I detested living with you. Being forced to relate to you was, unfortunately, great practice for my future marriage. It was also a perfectly flawless preparation for coping with the God I'd worship so devotedly in the future. We didn't even say goodbye. And in my mind, I was really leaving.

I walked out the front door and up the long hill to the corner of West Runyon Street and Osborne Terrace. It was there that I suddenly realized I had nowhere to go. The world looked as big to me then as the universe now appears tiny. For many minutes I watched the cars drive by in both directions. I started to cry. Not because I was scared. But I realized I had to go back home. Back to you. Back to Friday night Shabbat dinners. I realized how young I was and that I knew nothing about working or renting an apartment. I stood there. Trapped. I continued to watch the cars. I continued to stand and stare. I didn't know what to do. I was so young. So alone. So unhappy.

I thought of running straight into the traffic I had watched for so many minutes. I estimated the exact moment to launch myself so that the driver wouldn't have time to break. But I didn't want to die. Even though I felt dead inside. I still preferred being alive. I wanted to read more books. I wanted to watch more television. I wanted a wife and children one day. And so I turned around and walked, not into your loving arms, but back into our smoke-filled apartment and our sick and dysfunctional suffocating relationship. Back to your telling Dad, "I'm going out, Yankel. Watch the boys." Again, more practice at being miserable so that I could endure my future marriage.

And so I headed back to your constant screaming, back to the Friday night plate-pitching Shabbat dinners, back to our apartment filled with your choking second-hand smoke, dirty ashtrays, and crushed stubs and spirits. And worst of all — back to watching you assault my Tatie. You laughed as your defeated and broken little boy slowly walked back into the house. Like father, like son. I must have looked adorable. It would have taken empathy on your part to understand that I certainly didn't feel precious. Or loved. Watching my father's meek acceptance of your outbursts taught me well. He didn't just take shit. He feasted on feces. And Dad would never hit his wife. He just bit his lip.

It was bad enough that the entire city of Newark knew that the daughter of the famous Rabbi Yaakov Eliezer Tellem ran out on Friday nights to party and fuck, but did you have to rub it in the face of your parents and children? I still remember my little four-year-old brother reaching out to grab you, crying, "Mommy! Mommy! Don't go! It's Shabbos!" while you laughed like a drunken

H.L. GROSS & BRO. Inc.
Jewelers since 1910
840 FRANKLIN AVENUE, GARDEN CITY, NEW YORK 11530 / (516) 747-6666

March 12, 2015

Whom It May Concern:

business and personal relationship with Zev Lewinson began approximately in 1985. Over course of the next sixteen years we transacted many of millions of dollars in wholesale mond trading together. The items ranged from as little as a thousand dollars to estates valued ver a hundred thousand dollars. Mr. Lewinson was always a pleasure to work with and ays very professional, honest and reliable. He possessed remarkable people skills which gave the confidence to allow him to work with my clients directly. I was also going to be a partner is internet company CyberDiamond which we planned to develop into a major internet start- in the jewelry industry at the time. Mr. Lewinson left the business after the "internet bubble" st in 2001. My sons have now replaced what was a very valuable asset in my five-generation ily business.

cerely,

hael Gross
ident.

whore, and said to Dad, "Hold him, Yankel!" as you walked out the door and jumped into the car of Annette, your cute French alcoholic best friend.

Sometimes Annette would climb the stairs in her high heels and skin-tight pants to our second-floor apartment — right above the first level unit of your holy parents — to avoid honking her horn and alerting them. I'd open the door, and Annette would lean down to me and say, "Zevie, geeyve me a kiss," as I'd shyly kiss your pretty, but amazingly skinny, vodka-nourished girlfriend on her heavily blushed cheek as I wondered why she smelled like perfumed Shabbos Kiddush schnapps.

I also remember walking in on another friend of yours after I scraped my knee while playing outside. You were embracing Rabbi Tratner while he fondled you. I had no idea why my friend's father was visiting you on Shabbos. And I didn't understand what you two were doing. Because I was too young to comprehend what fondling each other meant. You were startled and yelled at me to go to my room.

And when I protested, as any innocent seven-year-old surely would, at having to go to my room — when "I didn't do anything!" — Rabbi Tratner asked your permission "to discipline me," which you granted. Tratner just threw me into my room and flung me onto my bed while yanking my pants off, holding me hostage and dehumanized, as he told me not to "dare come out till your mother gives you permission!" No warnings. No talking. Just violence and shame. The complete opposite of the man you married. Did you enjoy fucking the compassionate rabbi? At least I read a good book. After I finished crying.

Rabbi Tratner was much meaner to his own son who developed a serious nervous twitch and literally jumped when his father said anything. His dad pulled off his pants, and even underpants, in front of all the kids in our classroom (even the girls!) and hit him with a belt. I don't want to imagine what kind of train wreck Aaron must have grown up to become.

I hope he didn't evolve into a serial killer. If he did, I hope his father was his first victim. I wouldn't be the least bit surprised if Aaron cannibalized him afterwards. The blessing on human flesh, by the way, if you're ever stranded on the Andes Mountain as the result of a plane crash, is as follows: "Blessed art Thou, Adonai our God, King of the universe, Who by His mere word, caused all things to exist." And if you're disgusted by that thought, why do you still eat animal flesh?

What did you see in such a handsome monster, Mommy? Did his great looks excite you that much? Did your young thirty-three-year-old body have a multiple orgasm as you observed God's fourth commandment to "Honor the Sabbath" with the *Neshama Yesayra* (additional soul) that a Jew receives every Shabbat — described in the Talmud as a day of "double-delight" because of the double portion of manna that gently descended from the skies above in its honor?

Your cuckolded husband constantly forgave everything you did. *Tzu lib der kinder* (for the sake of the children). He even forgave you when you got pregnant and aborted a Black fetus into the toilet. At least you weren't prejudice, Mommy. #NoLivesMatter

And after you served (or should I say "pitched?") your Friday night dinner and walked out the door with Annette, I'd always be "the good one" and clean up, and put everything away, to "surprise Mommy" and make you proud of me when you found a clean house upon your arrival home as the sun rose. You'd sleep a few hours while we prayed in the synagogue and then we'd once again have a nice Shabbos lunch while you yelled and flung more cutlery at the gentlest man on the planet. Yes Mommy, you were definitely a great cook. Too bad the ambiance was fucking Hell.

I knew other friends who had quiet, gentle moms. But you were the only mom I knew, and so you seemed "normal" to me — a hyena mommy that shared her teats with many strangers but never with her own young. It would be years before psychology would coin the word dysfunctional. And many more years before Robert Sapolsky would describe a variant of the gene MAOA called MAO-L. And it will probably be centuries before I understand why my seemingly bi-polar God subjected me to so many cruel people and heartless relatives throughout my life.

An amazing new study (January 2019) was recently published from Dr. Patrick Hill, associate professor at Washington University in St. Lewis, which found that a child's early troubled relationship with their (specifically) mother predicts their inability to find purpose in their adult lives. One of the biggest takeaway messages from the research was that the path to a purposeful life starts very early, way before a child even begins to imagine or set any future "What do you want to be when you grow up?" expectations and goals. A loving and nurturing mother is an extremely crucial factor in determining a child's later success in life.

The more conflict and marginalization between said mother and child, the greater the likelihood of the unloved child living a troubled life. I now understand why I'm the epitome of a "been there, done that" personality. I could easily have been the poster boy for that study. The miracle of my mother handing me a one-way ticket out of her life at age fifteen spared me from further conflict. But the damage was done.

Like the planting of one's own seeds of sorrow in Buddhist philosophy in order to nourish one's personal growth and eventual enlightenment, the conflict-from-birth dry seeds of my emotionally malnourished childhood, parched by an apathetic and abusive mother, eventually sprouted loneliness and grew self-destructive weeds that strangled my earliest development and almost buried me (literally) in my twenties. Forget about complaining that my mother never nursed me because she didn't want to be "tied down." I'm happy someone took a few moments to bottle-feed me!

And the domestic violence and in-your-face adulterous abuse suffered by my father that I witnessed as a young child, along with being slapped in my face upon defending him, certainly conditioned me to tolerate and condone my own future abuse by my emotionally frigid pathological wife.

As I look back at my childhood, I feel as if I never had a mother or father. I wasn't an orphan, but I have no warm memories of my mom interacting with me. She basically appears in my life, after I got married, as a sickly rapidly aged "old" woman to enjoy her grandchildren for a few years as she suffered through many different health issues, operations, a heart attack that doctors predicted she would not survive, and an eventual early demise due to a rare form of leukemia. I remember once thinking, as I watched her playing and laughing with my oldest child, "I guess mom loves me, after all."

Mom's smoking addiction hacked off twenty years of her lifespan and forced her to live her final ten as if she was two decades older than her chronological age. Mom used to joke that having so many internal parts of herself removed through surgery was the sure-fire way to lose weight. She was forced to poison herself on dozens of medications and took fistfuls of pills at all hours of the day to eke out a few more years of doctor visits and hospital stays.

And the rare memories of my father are of a gentle man, that I saw only occasionally, who always looked so sad, that I never complained about not seeing him more often. Dad never saw how well I played basketball. He never threw a ball to me. Obviously, I don't blame him. They didn't shoot hoops in Dachau. They shot Jews. I spent more time with a friend of my mother, named Joe Levine, than I ever did with my own father.

As I now look back, I cannot comprehend how I was able to remain silent throughout my almost three decades of marriage. I can only attribute my tolerance for the derision I endured, to a conditioned and stultified mind that never questioned God (too harshly) and the manipulative machinations and numbing years of devotedly serving said God despite his having mercilessly slaughtered six million of my relatives. My mother prepared me to accept abuse from a spouse. God taught me to keep my mouth shut no matter how ferociously cruel my tormentor treated me.

A devoted Orthodox Jew learns to completely ignore his own feelings and thoughts. We strive to emulate our holy ancestor Abraham, who is eternally commended for conquering his emotions and the intense love he felt for Isaac, as he bound his thirty-seven-year-old son tightly to be slaughtered on an altar. In an almost delirious desire to serve the Creator of the Universe, Abraham never bothered questioning the logic of a Jewish Aztec God who suddenly requested a desire for human flesh to be sacrificed to himself and immolated as a total burnt offering, and to then scatter the remains of Isaac as holy ash.

It took the voice of an angel to stay the mighty hand of the servant of God from slashing a clean cut across the trachea of his son, as Abraham requested permission to display his devotion to the All-merciful Creator. "Shall I nevertheless cut his flesh to spill some blood on the altar?" our greatest patriarch implored (there is a sacrificial mitzvah to catch some of the pulsating blood into a bowl and spill the animal's blood on the altar) as the sharp blade was still in position to slice the extended neck of a son that God granted Abraham and Sarah to miraculously conceive after eighty years of listening to their tearful prayers for a child.

The sages of the Talmud teach that God loves the prayers of the righteous. So I just want to ask the Jewish Nation, "How's that workin' out for ya?" And please don't even think of debating me with your protestations of "but Abraham didn't do it." The Midrash clearly states that upon slaughtering the ram in place of his son, Abraham uttered prayers that professed his complete dedication that every aspect of his service was "in place of what he would have done to Isaac."

Make no mistake. Abraham was not only willing to sacrifice Isaac. He was excited to hastily carry out God's request. A request that was uttered as nothing more insistent than a, "Please, if you wouldn't mind ... slaughter your son as a sacrifice to me," suggestion. Abraham would have then entered Olam Ha'Ba [Eternal Life] when he died at the ripe old age of a hundred and seventy-five, to be remembered for eternity as the devoted Patriarch who slaughtered his beloved son. What a lovely legacy. Sounds a bit Christian. Church officials have passed around the joint for centuries while blowing parallels of smoke as they compare Jesus to Isaac.

It is Abraham's unwavering commitment to serve God — no matter what the cost — that bestows upon him God's incredible blessing that Abraham would now have descendants as numerous as the stars in the heavens and the sands of the sea. Because Abraham was willing to slaughter one child, God promised him a reward of billions (Genesis 22:17). I suppose Abraham would have been promised a harem had God commanded him to sacrifice the prophetess Sara.

But God, didn't you teach us that one life is as precious as a trillion? And besides, why all the fucking drama?

I have no doubt that Abraham would have cannibalized Isaac had God suggested that he be brought as a regular sacrifice (a *Shlamim*, from which the donating patron eats parts of the meat) and not as a total burnt offering (an *Olah*, which is completely immolated on the altar as the fragrance of sizzling flesh ascends to heaven where God then finds spiritual pleasure from the aroma of roasted meat). I have enough expertise to paraphrase the probable blessing: Blessed art Thou, O' Lord: King of The Universe, who has sanctified us in his commandments and ordered us to slaughter and cannibalize our beautiful child. Amen.

Logically speaking, a God might want mortal man to infer, "What is one short-lived human relationship worth compared to having an eternally spiritual one with God?" But love is not logical, my dear God. It's not quantifiable. So please understand that Ester was not my sacrifice to you. Know that she was not offered willingly. You are the one that allowed her to be slaughtered by the mother you decreed as her future sole custodian forty days before Ester was conceived. You are the one who placed her on the altar of alienation and bound her in custody to a deranged woman. I feel no shame in admitting that I would have bound you on that altar before ever placing Ester there. In fact, I have.

Isaac would have been quickly slaughtered. But you tortured me with three generations of absent female love. You are the source that forced me to begin my life with a mother who had the maternal warmth of a cuckoo bird who lay their eggs in foreign nests, sparing themselves from having to raise their young.

Then, in fulfillment of your matchmaker announcement, I married a cuckoo zombie that could morph into any character type on the planet. Except her own. And after all that suffering, at an age where most men finally relax and are called grandpa, you granted me a miraculous third-generation beautiful little girl who you then raped out of my life after a mere decade. Be glad that I don't worship Jesus or Muhammad. I can't. But only because I know how fake and unworthy of worship they are. Almost as artificial and undeserving as serving the real God.

I have no memory of my mother ever hugging or kissing me. No memory of her sharing laughter or songs with me. Aside from the cigarette smoke I inhaled in utero for nine months, we were never connected. Thank God mom hated alcohol. I have no doubt that I would have looked like Annette if she didn't. I do have one picture of my mother in a bathing suit holding me as a baby. In all honesty, I almost feel it had to be photoshopped. I don't recall one night where she read a bedtime story or cuddled me. I would say it's sad. But because I never experienced any maternal love, it's impossible for me to feel something was missing.

Yet I must say that it was my grandparent's great example of how a truly wonderful couple should live together that prompted me, as a very young boy, to desire a marriage that would emulate their love and respect for each other. But my father's marriage was a horrific example as to how much a man should tolerate before divorcing a crazy bitch. I can forgive my father. He stayed with my mom for the sake of his kids. I can even forgive my mom. Because I now understand that she never knew how to love. I understand that, like my wife, she was incapable.

Like my future wife, mom had no empathy. No warmth. No long talks like I had with Tatie. She was certainly a piece of work. And she had a funny sense of black humor. But she was never maternal. And although I did my best to avoid taking someone like her for a spouse by marrying a nice quiet Ivy League schooled young lady, I still somehow wound up marrying her narcissistic twin. I only wish I knew as much about recently discovered science and neuropsychology then as I do now. What's God's excuse for not sharing that information with mankind sooner?

My Dad was the original Mr. Mom — decades before that maternal surname was ever introduced to society. My mom was the man of the house who did as she pleased (and whomever she pleased). I learned how to open my mouth from my mom. I guess I'm finally using the skill she bequeathed me as I describe the experiences of my own bricolage life. Unfortunately, Dad taught me how to keep it shut during a bad marriage.

Emulating the eponymous protagonist in the Bontche Schweig tale by Sholem Aleichem (known as the Jewish Mark Twain), my father had the patience of a saint. Not the bullshit beatified kind of those who supposedly performed miracles while they lived or were declared, through canonization, to have posthumously performed them. My father was a real saint. And he didn't need any pope to pop him into heaven.

Anyone who met Dad knew he didn't have a bad bone in his body. (And anyone who met Mom knew they could jump on her bones! Sorry, Mom.) After surviving Dachau and the mass execution pit his parents tumbled into, as they were sprayed with machine gun fire for the crime of carrying the holy DNA of the three patriarchs of the original Israelites in their genes, the only thing Dad wanted was a wife and children. But even that was too much to ask for as my father stepped out of the frying pan and into the fire upon marrying the pretty, second to youngest daughter of Rabbi Tellem's eight children.

In the Yiddish yarn, Bontche, who never once complained about his domineering wife and bitter life, arrives to be judged before the heavenly tribunal upon death and is immediately granted anything he requests — for eternity! Bontche is informed that he died without sin and anything in the entire universe will instantly be rewarded upon his mere behest.

But Bontche, a broken man who never dared to tame his shrew and was hardly a man of words since birth, is pathetically unable to fathom anything to ask for as the angels calmly anticipate what they suspect will surely be a long list solicitation for eternal life, fame, riches, knowledge, and blissful happiness.

"Nu! Nu!" (Yiddish for "So? So?" but much is lost in translation.)

The divine beings gently try to encourage Bontche as they prod and urge him to, "ask for anything in the entire universe!"

Bontche timidly looks up at the Beit-Din composed of three angels and meekly tries to assure himself that he really, for the first time in his life, has permission to speak.

"Anything?" he bashfully asks.

"Yes, Bontche! Anything! Anything!" the center seated angel responds as he coaxes the shy Bontche to simply make a wish already.

Bontche, timidly, slightly raises his head, mawkishly holding his peasant cap in his hand, and finally, haltingly, makes his request.

"Efsher [maybe] a piece of bread … and perhaps a bissle [little] butter?"

The angels lower their heads in sadness and utter defeat.

I'm certain that when my beat-up-by-life father died and appeared before the heavenly tribunal, that he was also instantly granted anything his heart desired. I can see him standing nervously, biting his lower lip as he carries his Dachau jacket draped over his arm along with the brown lunch bag that ultimately caused his face to flush in embarrassment, shy upon being the center of attention, as he haltingly looks up at the heavenly tribunal, as they promise him anything he desires. "Nu! Nu!" I can hear the angels coaxing my father to request his eternal desires.

After being hugged and kissed by his compassionate mother, with a scar in her temple marking where the bullet that ended her young life entered, and assured and reassured by my grandmother and the other angels that anything my dad desires is his for the asking, I can almost hear my father as he finally responds, "Efsher a family … and perhaps a bissle time vit my son Zev ven he arrives here?"

The only way my mother and stepdad could deal with my knowing how horridly they treated my father, aside from eventually sending me away to a great boarding school, was to constantly order me to, "Go to your room!" And I did.

My great escape was reading. Endless biographies of great women and men. Fredrick Douglass. Helen Keller. Madam Curie and Malcolm X. Sammy Davis Jr. and Winston Churchill. I read the works of Isaac Bashevis Singer, Mark Twain, Florence Nightingale, Upton Sinclair, and George Orwell. I read voraciously to escape a world that was devouring me.

I also played a lot of basketball. Four hours a day. What an escape from my constant sadness! I survived the tryouts and made it onto the West Orange YMYWHA junior varsity basketball team as the youngest and shortest (babies that are not cuddled and hugged often do not grow to their full capacity) member at that time. I was number 22. Which worked since I was about half the size of our (number 44) center.

My cold-hearted, backstabbing till the day he gets his final stroke, one year and eight months older brother "Avi" (as much an insensitive DNA replication of our mother as I was of our empathetic father) got cut at tryouts and decided that I needed to be punished for his never practicing. Without warning he adamantly refused to speak to me for a full year. Nothing I pleaded could melt his almost-autistic silent anger. He never yelled. Never said a word. I simply didn't exist. It seemed as if his heart was molded from the same iceberg as my wife's. I suppose he was warming me up for the shunning and silent treatment I'd experience upon filing for divorce.

Unknowingly, between the endless hours I spent reading in my room and constantly playing basketball, I developed a thirst for knowledge while releasing endorphins (having no clue that such a chemical even existed) that helped stave off my constant depression. If my soul was starving for affection, at least my mind and body were being nourished.

Mom couldn't wait to get rid of the last troublesome vestigial organ from her prior marriage and was quite thrilled to hand her fifteen-year-old fetus a one-way first-class ticket to fly out of her life. Escaping the trauma of an adverse childhood with haunting emotional issues that would last a lifetime, I politely waved to mom as I boarded the front of the plane. She probably forgot to kiss and hug me goodbye. At least she never said that she hates me.

I was happy in boarding school among the scholars and saints, but I had no intention of emulating them till much later in life. I was at peace for the first time in my life and glad to have the physical distance of three-hundred miles between myself and the dysfunctional relationship of my mother and

Skip. It was nothing compared to the emotional distance between us. I remember walking by a student who was crying profusely in one of the dorm phone booths we used for making calls back home.

"Why was Yosi crying?" I asked one of my roommates.

"He's homesick," the kid who slept in the bunk bed above me replied.

"Why?" I asked. Because I honestly did not understand how someone could be "homesick." The only thing I understood was being sick of home.

It felt great to be cared for — even if the rabbis were strict about the long daily schedule. The genuine warmth of the soft-spoken saints and the kind attention of their holy wives, that replaced the emotionally distant wire-monkey-mom and threatening muscular bully in my life, was heavenly. And best of all, no more flying dishes on Friday night. Only beautiful soulful Zemirot (Jewish hymns) whose lyrics were sung from poems written by different Kabbalist sages during the Middle Ages.

I often began crying during the heartfelt Zemirot and, pretending to need some religious book from my dorm room for the weekly bible lesson immediately following the meal (delivered during desert so that we'd be conditioned to equate the sweet words of Torah with something delicious), I'd rush out of the dining hall till I composed myself by swallowing the pain of watching my father getting screamed at on Friday nights while ducking dishes as I pushed those daunting memories to the back of my scarred mind.

Always trying to please the adults in my life, I wanted to impress my teachers and I studied complex Talmudical debates ten hours a day. After a few months I began to enjoy the boring logical flawless arguments of the ancient sages. And after a year of mild torture, it was all I wanted to do for the rest of my entire life. I wanted to become a *Talmid Chacham*.

The only painful memory I recall from my boarding school days was the extreme guilt I suffered whenever I masturbated. One of the many tenets we learned in our ethics class was that every single sperm was an actual potential life. You basically became a serial killer every time you committed the sin that cost Onan, the son of Judah, his life. The commentaries explain that Onan pulled out upon ejaculation. He didn't want to mar the beauty of his gorgeous wife, Tamar, by having her carry a child for nine months and disfigure her flawless skin with a few stretch marks. I'd get horny merely reading the story.

"God delivers the perfect punishment to fit the crime," we were taught. "Since Onan 'murdered,' God took his soul." Great lesson for a fifteen-year-old on fire with testosterone. I felt as if I was going to suddenly die, besides feeling spiritually filthy and guilt-ridden any time I masturbated after thinking about Lynn and the few sweet girls in my life that I had kissed while playing Spin the Bottle before I left for boarding school.

I wanted to ask my saintly teachers if Onan died instantly upon ejaculation. That way the punishment would really fit the crime, I reasoned. But my instructors were as clever as they were smart, and I doubted they'd believe that I was just "asking for a friend."

There was, of course, nowhere to hide from an all-seeing eye, and I could envision God as an angry voyeur staring at me intently as he recorded every drop of my semen into an eternal book of sinful shame right in the middle of his enrapturing lectures to the great scholars of the Talmudical era as they sat in the Garden of Eden — while I embarrassingly ejaculated in front of the entire crowd, relieving myself into some tissue paper knowing full-well that God, and millenniums of deceased saints, could easily see me through the blue-tiled bathroom walls and insulated foam-cardboard ceilings in the dormitory of Ner Israel.

I could imagine Rabbi Akiva, Ravina, and Rav Ashi, along with thousands of famous scholars, as they looked up from their heavenly tomes to watch an out-of-control testosterone fueled kid jerking off. I almost became OCD with having to shower immediately afterwards, and peeing at least one time, to make sure all the dead bodies were off me and that none remained inside my urethra tube to bear witness against a father who slaughtered them. At least I didn't send them to Auschwitz.

I took hotter showers than the baths Gussie gave me ten years earlier. I was like a rape victim that wanted to wash away the sexual abuse and shame I committed against myself. I hated myself for what I did to myself. (Caution: Do not try this at home.) When you're a Jew, everything is your fault. And God and the world keep reminding you. And your many hours of daily prayers have you constantly admitting and bemoaning your sins while begging God for forgiveness.

The demeaning guilt I suffered was as excruciating painful as the erect penis in my hand was hard. I know I sound crazy. But try being a young scholar full of testosterone. I doubt God could pass the test. And surely, in an earthly body, Jesus Jerked Off. Great name for a reality-television show!

I even had this repetitive repentance-purification protocol that I followed. *Religiously*. I had this OCD urge, stemming from extreme guilt, to review the entire chapter of the tractate of Talmud I was studying, all over again, from the very beginning, every time I masturbated. I imagined that the self-inflicted sinful ejaculation spiritual wound might have made my mind impure and unable to comprehend the holy words of the sages. So I reviewed them again. And again. I guess it was my own version of *Talmud for Dummies*.

It should come as no surprise that during the final trimester session of the 1968 Ner Israel school year I memorized the third chapter (*Hamafkid*) of Tractate Bava Metzia in its entirety. I could even recite the chapter's entire commentary of Rashi verbatim. I had two different rabbis test me as they peppered me with questions as to the logicality of the sages, and they spoke two or three words anywhere in the chapter as I'd recite the next ten or twenty lines to validate my scholarship. They were quite impressed and praised me effusively for being such a brilliant and diligent young scholar. But I shamefully knew what I really was. Horny as fuck.

Upon graduating high school, I attended the Ner Israel college while attending Johns Hopkins at night. After a year of studying the Talmud in Jerusalem where I met and became close friends with Meir Kahana (who wanted me to run his Jerusalem campaign for the Knesset), I went off the deep end. Fast cars. Faster women. I lost the viridity of attending a strict all-boys yeshiva faster than my virginity. My little black book (yes, we're back in the early seventies) had an assortment of women along a large spectrum, from unhappy or bored wives, dancers and strippers, to honor students from Johns Hopkins, Barnard, and Columbia.

I always believed in diversity. I was an equal opportunity love machine. And I really did love every individual woman. Each one was truly unique and beautiful. It was very painful for me to remain monogamous during my entire marriage. I could have never done it without God staring at me every fucking without-any-boundaries second.

I then earned a lot of money as a young diamond dealer and treated my clients well. Wine, women, and drugs was how this perfect gentleman by day rewarded many jewelers for selling me the estates they purchased from the public. Maître d's would greet me at the finest restaurants as if Sammy Davis Jr. suddenly walked in with a wad of cash. Madams would hug me as if I was their son whenever I arrived with a few clients.

I knew it was all bullshit, but my rabbis taught me that the entire existence of this world is false, ephemeral, and nothing more than a fleeting dream. It is a short-lived walk through an empty long corridor that leads to an eternal palace. Do you waste time working to furnish a hallway, or do you decorate the mansion? Do you waste your life accumulating worthless gold coins or priceless heavenly brownie points? I believed them. So if I was no longer hoarding good deeds and *mitzvahs* for the Eternal life, I might as well eat, drink, and be merry in this fleeting, transient one.

And so I'd slip the maître d a "Benjamin" as if I was the most suave gentleman on the planet as they gushingly shook my generous hand while obsequiously sitting me at their best table. And I whispered, "Whatever my clients want," into my loving mother-madam's ear. And I treated the women I dated even better.

That is, until the one I spent the most time with would coyly ask me, "Zevie, when am I going to meet your mother?" I loved all of them, and several were "a keeper," but quite honestly, I understood that I was not marriage material.

The gentile girls were willing to convert, and the Jewish ones promised to keep the Sabbath. But I didn't even know who I was, and so how could I possibly choose the woman I wanted to "spend my life" with? That still sounds like a jail sentence to me. So I kept busy accumulating more diamonds during my refractory period by day and medicated and drank away my repressed emotions by night — typically after a four-hour intense workout at the gym.

I doused my childhood depression of living with "divorced parents" and lack of a mother's love, with pussy and alcohol and anything that could kick in my endorphins — like driving my orange-flame stick-shift Corvette like a demon at 140 MPH on route 280 in Livingston, NJ at the witching hour of 3 A.M. after drinking for several hours.

One girlfriend, a gorgeous dental hygienist with perfect teeth, who was definitely a keeper had she not been Italian, upon waking up with me one morning and staring at my body, gently ran her fingers across the chiseled squares of my abdomen and sweetly pointed out the illogicality and absurdity of my working out like crazy to maintain a ripped body that looked like Michelangelo's *David,* and then snorting endless lines of cocaine while drinking to the point of passing out most nights. I smiled, and quipped, "You want me to stop working out?" I was in pain. Drugs and booze work wonders. Pussy is miraculous.

The old-time diamond dealers closed a sale with a "Lechayim!" and a shot of schnapps, but I was more like Tony Montana and sealed my deals with a "Mazal!" followed by a few white lines. I even tipped my Sassoon hairstylist that way along with letting her keep the rolled-up bill. Olga would giggle as I'd whisper in her ear, "Meet me in my changing room and we'll powder our noses together." I watched the pretty single mom politely snort the white powder into her perfectly pinched nostrils.

I merely had to walk into a room or restaurant to meet friends or greet clients for dinner and everyone instantly knew the party had just begun. The drugs, booze, and laughter were sure to follow. Exactly like Ester laughing three decades in the future whenever her Tatie scholar walked into a room she was in. *Calm down Sharen. I never cut any lines of cocaine for our daughter.*

My "Cogito, ergo sum" existence, often expressed as "I drink; therefore I am not," dangled from my neck as I sported three gold chains (herring-bone, lace, and snakeskin) whose pendants advertised my beliefs. A Magen David, engraved with the word JUDE in pavé flawless melee, a Ten Commandments tablet, that kept bumping into the chest of my neighbor's wife reminding me not to covet her whenever we made love, and a tricolored coke-spoon twisted in yellow, white, and pink gold, topped with a 24-karat golden nugget, succinctly portrayed my entire life story. Especially the "twisted" stem of the coke spoon. I personally designed all three pieces which were handmade and cast in 18-karat gold and set with flawless melee that sparkled to the world outside while my corroded soul rusted within.

I shopped at the most expensive boutiques in Manhattan, and I dressed to kill, always leaving half the buttons of my silk shirts open to reveal my marble six-pack. My lean and muscular body played A-level racquetball for hours at a time and I easily won any B-level contest I entered. And I still played a lot of basketball. I also studied karate, but realized early-on that I'm a lover, not a fighter.

To relax, I lifted weights and ran over fifty miles a week. I was running alright. Running wild. But no matter how fast I moved, I couldn't get away from myself. My thighs looked like I did a thousand squats a day, but my slovenly soul was fucking aching. I removed the letter 'Y' from the word "Yid," and the two remaining letters then described my personality perfectly.

I was dating a gorgeous French Canadian who wore a gold cross that hung smack between her firm athletic breasts. I am probably the only Orthodox Jew that gazed at a cross a million times. The Passion of Zev. It would be worth suffering crucifixion if the reward was Lauren. If stolen waters are sweet, as proclaimed by the wisest of all men, then you could have drowned me in the tidal wave of passion I felt for this alluring sex goddess. I even enrolled my shiksa-gem to attend the GIA and study gemology. "Sure," Lauren replied, after I suggested she get her certification, "but I already own these," as she playfully, gently cupped my testicles in her hand.

Oy gevalt! She was hotter than anywhere God might be threatening to send me. And forget about urgently showering immediately after ejaculating into tissues. We'd fall asleep in each other's embrace after making love for hours. No guilt-driven shameful anguish to hurriedly wash off the thrilling sensation of Lauren's skin pressing against mine. My testosterone driven brain believed it was worth paying the price for the head she gave no matter where I myself might be heading.

The passion I once felt for a folio of the Talmud was now replaced by Lauren's sweet warm flesh and eternally wet pussy. She'd teasingly seduce me with suggestive thoughts that had me salivating faster than Pavlov's dog while having dinner at some swanky restaurant — taunting me with scenes of, "I'm getting wet watching your mouth while you're talking, and I can't focus on one word of the interesting things you're saying, because I'm imagining you eating me."

"Waiter! Check please!"

Lauren's bite marks were constantly incised upon my shoulders and neck, and her scratches were etched on my back. I looked more beat up after making love to this seductive Aphrodite than returning home after the rare times I sparred at the gym. And making love to her, sometimes thrice daily (there went my prayers), definitely used up more energy than any wild workout I invented. Forget about writing insightful concepts on the Talmud with my pen that was mightier than the sword. Because pussy is mightier than the pen!

But incredibly awesome sex aside, the best thing about Lauren was how she instinctively reached for my hand whenever we walked on the street together. It could be ensconced deep within my leather coat jacket pocket on a cold and slightly windy fall day, as we briskly tapped the East Side pavement in Manhattan walking to brunch on a Sunday morning, but like a magical magnet, Lauren's hand somehow materialized and found its way into being snugly held by mine.

Almost as if by sign language, her angelic touch professed unconditional love. The tender way she caressed my hand quickly aroused me, and she understood the gaze in my eyes as she'd laugh and inquire, "Already?!"

After brunch I'd usually have Lauren half undressed with one hand, by the time we ascended twenty-two stairs, as I unlocked our apartment door with the other. I whispered the details of my imminent plans to make her speak French, and she giggled and moaned, as we stood and kissed on every step. I couldn't stop jumping on her bones. And she got under my skin. Lauren pierced my soul deeper than I penetrated her pussy. I never lost my air hitting the speed bag or playing racquetball. But Lauren left me breathless. We ran together. We laughed together. We made love as one. I really loved her. But I didn't love myself.

Lauren certainly thawed my frozen first decade and a half of existence, but it would take many more years and endless introspection to discover my inner beautiful self before the dysfunctional past of my early years would dissipate into nothingness. It would take the fiery destruction of an even colder frigid marriage, and a divorce litigated in hell while my relationship with Ester went up in smoke, to finally evaporate the lonely memories of the relationship I never had with my wire-monkey mother. I now realize that I shared that exact same relationship with my wife. And my God.

Meanwhile my relationship with Lauren was primal and instinctively animalistic. It was pure, true, and free. It was open, adventurous, honest, and fun. I hoped it could stay that way. Forever. (If such a word truly exists.) Sure enough, Lauren eventually wondered about "our future" and softly requested, "Zevie, when am I going to meet your mother?"

The classic relationship-killer question.

"But you said you love me!" Lauren logically argued. "I am going to have your baby!" she insisted, half-threatening not to use birth control (after sadly aborting one baby conceived with me, while using birth control, a year earlier).

"I do love you," I responded. "But I hate marriage," I jokingly added.

"Go ahead and have my child," I bluffed, "I'll play with the baby and support it," I seriously added. "But I can't possibly get married. What's a piece of paper anyway?"

Frustration turned to slight anger as she teasingly threatened that she'd tell her two strapping hockey-playing brothers back in Quebec to "box me." Which in translation from her French to English brain meant "beat the shit out of me." I laughed and said that I would tell them throughout the pummeling that she was worth every fist they'd throw at me.

"I don't even care if they shoot me," I joked, "... a bullet is nothing compared to the pain of walking around with a hard-on."

Lauren wasn't simply a well-mannered lady. She. Was. Woman. Pure salt of the Earth. She was honest and warned me that if she couldn't have me, she'd "find someone else and settle for second best." At twenty-three years of age, she yearned for a baby. "I'm never having an abortion again," she warned me. Her soul and biological clock pined for a family. Meanwhile (speaking of clocks), at twenty-six I had to admit that I told time more precisely back when I counted on my fingers to test Gussie in the middle of the night. I no longer had a fucking clue what time it was. All I knew was that it wasn't time to settle down.

Lauren rarely wore underwear. But even when she did, I'd unhook her bra and slip off her panties more deftly than a magician to embrace heaven on earth. I couldn't get enough of her. And I learned a lot of French. Because Lauren only spoke in her native tongue when she gave tongue while French-kissing and climaxing. I listened in tortured ecstasy to this epitome of womanhood and her primal guttural cries as she orgasmed.

"I want a baby … I want your baby!" she'd moan in French as she came again and again. I didn't want to lose her. But I couldn't work out all my shit. Not enough cocaine in the world at that time of my life. I couldn't commit. And so I lost a gorgeous gem on the wheel of life.

I still get aroused forty years later as I hear her voice in my memory. I hope Lauren is happy today. I'm sure she didn't settle. And I pray she's a mother. Lucky children if she is. Very lucky husband.

We remained friends and addicted to each other even after she got engaged to a jet-setting guy from some very wealthy land-owning family in Jamaica. She showed me a picture of her fiancé when she came to New York for a visit.

"He's so handsome!" I observed, "Why do you still sleep with me?"

"Only till I'm married. There is no one like you Zevie," she purred in her lightly accented French-Canadian accent. She always buckled my knees faster than any body-punch I ever took. And I took some hard ones.

As a religious Jew, I'm somehow supposed to make believe that I regret this heavenly relationship and repent for dating a shiksa. But how can I possibly dismiss a two-year love affair with a fiery passionate woman who was more internally beautiful than she was externally gorgeous? Lauren made Isaac Singer's protagonist Wanda (The Slave, 1962, etc.) look frigid by comparison, and any single day (and certainly any night) I spent with Lauren was more real than my twenty-eight-year marriage to an emotionally crippled A.I. cute Bashert.

Meanwhile my Hasidic diamond brokers, who would have sworn that I was "Nisht foon Unzereh," had no hint that I spoke fluent Hebrew and a more nuanced and proper Yiddish (unadulterated by English words) than they did, as they called their sellers from my 47th street office, assuming that I didn't understand one word of the prices they were negotiating. "Ken I use your phone?" they'd ask. "Sure! Help yourself!"

I felt like Joseph in Egypt whose brothers could not envision that the viceroy goy in Egyptian garb, in front of whom they bowed, was their Jewish kid brother who spoke fluent Hebrew and was their father's favorite son. In the eyes of my brokers, I was nothing more than "ah goyish'eh Yid (a lost Jew, in name only, who shares the values, beliefs, and dress codes of the gentile nations). They saw a muscular suave and sophisticated diamond dealer, sporting a curly Afro, bedecked in gold jewelry and Italian silk shirts. How could they possibly see the shy scholar buried beneath my skin?

The Hasidic diamond brokers believed they were speaking a foreign language as they unknowingly disclosed their prices to "ah goy" that could have recited the entire chapter of Hamafkid to them from memory.

Coincidently, like Joseph, I was also my fathers' favorite. Tatie gave me his Dachau Coat of Bloody Colors. I decided to share it with my jealous brothers and, not wanting to cause any envy, said the jacket belongs to the three of us (haven't seen it since). My brothers instantly joined my wife upon my filing for divorce, feigning concern and constantly inviting me to lunch or dinner

— only to immediately email and report the details of our conversations that I wanted my wife to "discover." Tatie5521.

Like Joseph, my deceitful brothers threw me into a pit full of vipers upon my filing for divorce. They called everyone who knew me, including incessantly phoning Rabbi Nekritz, who refused to take their calls. "Please tell Leon to stop calling me!" Rabbi Nekritz implored, as he got into the habit of listening to his answering machine before picking up the phone. I was eventually forced to take out an order of protection against my own younger brother Leon, who literally stalked me during my divorce. Sharen was hoping that I'd slug him.

If there was ever anyone who needed anger management therapy, sadly, it's my kid brother. Leon has a heart of gold that is raging on fire. That's what happens when your mother runs out on Friday night when you are a little boy. Leon is still throwing tantrums to this day. And like our mother, my brother (who was a high school track star till he got kicked off the team for smoking) continued his smelly habit most of his life and can barely walk up a flight of stairs. I'm still running ten miles a week. Like Shakira wildly proclaims, "My hips don't lie." (Mi casa, su casa ...)

Boys are seven times more likely to smoke when their mother smokes. Girls, who are even more influenced by the behavior of their mothers, even more so. Smoking is not cool.

I learned the gem business quickly — especially after a two-year stint working for Louis Glick Diamonds. I decided to go out on my own and the money started to pour in. I honestly had no long-term goals other than to acquire more inventory during my refractory periods.

I also began to specialize in colored diamonds. Life was good. Not that I was happy. But I certainly wasn't exactly miserable. I was so busy. Always on the move. The phone never stopped ringing.

Inventory increased rapidly. I was almost printing money. I'd trade twenty gems in a week and simply jot down a single new diamond in my inventory that represented the weeks entire trading and ultimate hidden profit in one final stone. I would never tally a weekly $8,000 dollars as profit. I merely added a 2.54 carat brilliant on my inventory list and tossed the bundle of memos and transactions that evolved into that final gem. My diamond wallets bulged as quickly as the package in my pants.

The ever-taller Manhattan skyline was thrown into existence by developers like former diamond dealer Gary Barnett (who invested 150K into my publishing company). Why do you think Gary is incapable of imagining someone running out of money?

But at twenty-seven years of age, I wasn't thinking too far into the future real estate market of Manhattan. I was moving way too fast to wait for prices to rise. I didn't even have the patience to spend time with myself. I didn't want to exhaust myself anymore thinking about why bad things happen to six million good people. The pain had become too much for me to bear. So, I drank it, snorted it, fucked it, and vomited it. But for some reason it kept regurgitating on me.

I was tired of asking, "Where the hell were you, God!? How could you watch the lines of naked mothers trying to nurse and comfort their crying babies, while soothing their whiny hungry toddlers, as they were mercilessly cut in half by machine-gun fire, falling piecemeal into open mass graves on top of each other's bodies?

And I no longer cared to revisit my missing-matriarch meshuggenah childhood. What was, was. It's so much easier to exercise, party, and fuck for a couple of hours. Like mother, like son. At least I never smoked.

And what twenty-five-year-old is going to choose studying the Talmud over a sexual relationship? Mommy taught me well. And so, I became the life of the party. I almost lost my life doing so. The more you refilled my glass, the more the hysterical opinions on politics, life, sex, and love poured out of my mouth. If I wasn't the smartest person in the room (and often I was), I was definitely the most outrageous. Laughing feels better than crying.

I never had to write my material. Endless humor originated from the embers of my burnt-out soul and somehow ignited into a conflagration of hysterical comedy. Like a great stand-up comic, I always got a laugh. And flashing the cash, I always got laid.

I banged up more cars and more women while driving drunk than I can or want to remember. My body-shop guy would call me laughing as he inquired "How-the-fuck did you do that?!" while trying to figure out how the orange-flame stick-shift Corvette he was towing for the fourth time in as many months was dented on three sides. I couldn't remember leaving the bar, let alone what I crashed into. Another time he questioned how the hood was dented from underneath that it popped outwards, wondering how my engine got lifted off its block and pushed upwards — while I was driving! I laughed as I explained that I had driven onto the median divider while "napping" at the wheel.

Money meant nothing. I laughed at the $2,000 dollar invoice I'd be billed shortly. As Biggie Smalls famously sang, "No need to worry, my accountant handles that." I feared nothing. Everything was a joke. Every date was a party. And every party was a vomiting celebration of my loneliness. I laughed inwardly at the idea that I might overdose, often singing the lyrics, "Room 714, I'll be waiting," written by Rick James, as I entered a hotel with a girlfriend, "Super freak ... that girl is pretty kinky ... I'd really like to taste her," as the party often turned into a blackout by the following morning when I tried to recall the details of the previous night with a mind that felt as if it were hit with a sledge-hammer.

I can't begin to compute the number of times I painfully puked and wretched my guts out into a toilet or bathroom sink or woke up covered in my expensive four-star restaurant meal after ingesting lethal doses of Black Russian's and Bill Cosby's favorite blue pill of seduction.

There are many studies whose research proves that a traumatic and abusive childhood leads to alcohol and drug abuse as an adult. In the largest study ever conducted on obesity by the brilliant Dr. Vincent Feliti and the CDC, they amazingly (accidentally) discovered that children who suffered from ACE [adverse childhood experiences] had a 4600 percent future likelihood of becoming an intravenous drug user as an adult.

Childhood memories don't fade away with time. Unfortunately, they typically become the grooved pathways of an adult brain. Far too often the emotionally stunted mind that has been traumatized in its youth finds it difficult to live a normal adult life.

The "in the moment" impressions of an ACE childhood, the occasional smack by a threatening stepdad or having your pants pulled off by some insane rabbi who is fucking your mother, or ducking flying dishes at Friday night Shabbat dinners, are all similar to the "karmic seeds" discussed in Buddhist philosophy that are planted in our preconscious minds that later sprout so much suffering.

During my twenties I could easily have been the poster boy for the CDC study. I could afford any addiction I wanted, and my athletic heart kept me in the game. I climbed the instant-gratification addiction ladder faster than I scaled the ropes hanging from the high gym ceilings where I exercised, decades before any studies of drug tolerance and dependency were published, and I was very curious to experience what heroin felt like. Surprisingly, it was one of my drug dealers that talked me out of reaching the 4600 percent destiny of my using intravenous drugs. "You're killing yourself already," he joked, "why rush things? Besides, I'm not losing my best customer."

Blasting Sly Stone's lyrics on my car radio I certainly wanted to be taken higher and, feeling invincible, I figured the worst thing that could happen is that I'd vomit my guts out. Besides, I had the cure for nausea and vomiting in my little blue diamond papers. I was always amazed how a few lines instantly brought me back to life. "Melee" was my secret code-word for cocaine. I specialized in large stones (as they're called in the diamond trade), but my clients were always asking me if I had any fine quality *melee* in stock.

"Seriously," my best supplier warned me, "you don't want to mess with that shit." It's a sad situation when your drug dealer is more responsible than you. The wisdom of the sages that I had studied for years was of little help to me now. I didn't really care if I'd wake up in the morning — think I worried about living for eternity?

And so I convinced myself that I was nothing more than a recreational (as in a complete wreck) user of alcohol, powder and pills. I'd pass out in the fanciest restaurants in Manhattan and upon my date subtly reviving me, rush into the men's room to vomit, snort a few lines, and "refreshed," start all over again. My dealer was right. Why rush things?

There were many nights where I could not remember what I ate, or who I ate, before passing out nearly comatose from whopping amounts of drugs and booze. And like the lyrics sung by the super cool Tone Loc, I had my own real-life Funky Cold Medina experience when I picked up a gorgeous "Black is Beautiful" light-skinned hooker in my two-year-old orange-flame 1975 Corvette, who I quickly threw out of my car, as my Talmudical mind, restrained and unprepared by a silver-spoon Jewish upbringing, raced to grasp and conceptualize something it had never seen anything the likes of before — a beautiful woman with full breasts and a long hard cock.

I still recall a very scary long night at The Pierre during which I called a close friend at three in the morning because my other friend's wife was barely breathing. "I think I might have accidentally killed her," I nervously half-joked to the family doctor on the phone. "What did you give her?" he asked. "Everything!" I replied, "Whatever she wanted. And a lot of pink champagne."

I had an antique 18K yellow-gold pillbox, beautifully engraved with my name, that was always well-stocked with a nice seduction-supply of rainbow-colored mood-swinging treats that could send daring, mindless chimpanzees in any direction their young hearts desired, while launching those rapidly-pounding strong beating hearts in a zigzag route they could never imagine traveling while still pumping blood — before needing possible defibrillation.

I had zero comprehension about dosage being dispensed according to weight and so I figured a pharmaceutical 714 wouldn't harm my ninety-pound temp-wife any more than it would hurt me at one-hundred and fifty-pounds. And we already enjoyed a nice romantic dinner, so I figured it was a safe dosage when she asked for one. Besides, it was "prescribed" by a real medical doctor that seemed to have hundreds of patients that, wink-wink, suffered from insomnia. I honestly figured they couldn't be *that* dangerous.

I granted any desire requested by the women I dated. They'd laugh as I responded with "Your wish is my command," as I playfully pretended to magically cause some pills or cocaine to appear. I'm glad my sleepover-wife playmate was too wasted to ask for a second one. I knew a lot of vocabulary words, but "no" was an unimaginative word I had long forgotten how to pronounce without the inflection of a question mark in my voice.

"Stand her up! Now!" my friend shouted into his end of the phone. "I can't! She's totally limp!" It was almost comical as I stood there drunk and naked (sounds like a reality show), trying to lift this cute birthday-suited woman, who had recently sworn her marriage vows, out of a potential grave. "Get her on her feet! Now! And into a cold shower!" It worked. She came to. And then she came. And came. Eventually she puked her guts out. And we lived happily ever after. That night. Life was shallow. But even shallow was too deep for me.

Another time I recall using up one of my nine lives was upon waking up, or to be more accurate, "coming to," on the sofa of a wonderful girlfriend named Jan. I was stark naked and could only recall having woken up in the middle of the night, after a cocaine fueled evening of sex and vodka martinis, to stagger into the bathroom and vomit what felt like three gallons of my dysfunctional childhood into the toilet only to discover that the bedroom door was locked upon my return. I figured I locked myself out and didn't want to wake up my exhausted partner. Hardly able to wobble, let alone walk another step, I stumbled and passed out spread-eagle on her sofa.

I woke up a few hours later when sunrise rays hit my eyes and initiated a throbbing morning headache that had almost become routine in my daily life. I was freezing and wanted to get back under the covers with Jan. Faintly knocking on her bedroom door, I heard a timid, "Are you okay?" on the other side. "Yeah, I'm fine," I laughed, "I think I accidentally locked myself out in the middle of the night."

Jan opened the door and told me she locked it when I got up to pray to the porcelain god. "Why?" I laughed. "Your eyes were so glazed over that *you* weren't in your body. I looked at your muscles and thought 'he could kill me so easily,' so I locked the door and went to sleep." I smiled at her "fears" and said, "let me show you how gentle I am ..."

Jan eventually told me she loved me. But unlike the others she never asked me to introduce her to my mother. "I'm breaking up with you," she whispered seriously one night over a surprise romantic dinner, after attending a Broadway show starring Sammy Davis Jr., on my birthday. "Why?" I nervously whispered back. "Because I love you too much and I know I don't have enough class for you to ever marry me. I couldn't take the hurt. So I'm ending it tonight."

I didn't know what to say. So I dealt with my sudden loss and future *erection-dysfunction* pain (and it wasn't the testosterone in my body — I really loved Jan) the only way I knew how. "Not even a mercy fuck," I smiled. "One last blowjob and that's it. We can still be friends but I'm too addicted to you. I have to move on with my life," she maturely insisted. "I'm a-dick-ted to you too!" I immaturely responded. But jokes weren't going to work this time. Jan had made up her mind. She was right about my unwillingness to marry. But wrong about her opinion of herself. In my heart I'll always remember how much class she had.

The blowjob was great, but back at the ranch this stallion had to seek out new mares and sort out the emotions of having lost such a beautiful relationship for another day. My body was in incredible shape and my athletic heart often raced to process the poisons with which I medicated my feelings as I dozed off to a sleep from which many others would have rested eternally. I don't want to imagine how I taxed my liver. I certainly don't want to think about how I fried my brain along with many wagonloads of "scorched" folios of the Talmud. I was galloping so fast that the only way I knew how to stop was by passing out.

I experienced endless mornings waking up with a whopping-headache-hangover, that made me almost wish I had not woken up, where I still retained an abundance of alcohol in my system that incentivized me to go out for my morning run in order to get high again. Often it took me an entire day to recuperate. But by dinner I was already ordering my first Vodka martini or Black Russian of the night. I could easily have been a member of the Forever 27 Club — my actual age at that time.

I now realize that people don't overdose on drugs, alcohol and pills. They overdose on pain. I was just luckier than most. My strong athletic heart allowed me to vomit the lethal doses of sadness and pain that an all-loving God mercilessly injected into my soul.

I surely could have been entered into the Guinness Book of World Records for "farthest vomited projectiles" for the time I propelled gin-laced Percocet-pink vomit, while lying on my circular bed, with such anti-gravity force that it splattered onto my bedroom ceiling. The color-splashed ceiling reminded me of the abstract expressionist artwork of Jackson Pollack. But I created my work of art even more quickly. It looked rather beautiful when it dried. It even smelled sweet. And at the speed I was living it easily could have quickly become a valuable posthumous collector's item.

The natural-blonde cute pussy I was dining on that night, whose flung bra was now hanging on the edge of a dusty tome of Talmud that sat on my bookshelf (as my Jewish guilt-ridden brain imagined the sages inside staring at me wide-eyed), was an adorable dancer and ditzy artist who was begging me to allow her to call an ambulance. I was more intrigued with her inverted nipples (first time I ever saw a pair) than my life, and I pleaded with her not to call.

"I'm fine," I promised as I jokingly lifted the blanket to reveal the hard evidence of my being alive and well, as I explained that she was quite capable of administering the life support between her legs that I needed to fully recuperate. "Just looking at your beautiful body is already resuscitating me," I assured her. "Besides," I quipped with a mouthful of delicious firm breast, "I really need to study these."

I buried my lonely and traumatized childhood beneath a mountain of coke and vodka. I'm lucky to be alive. I surely lived nine lives. I think I used up the final three surviving the gauntlet my wife and Schwartz made me pass through during my divorce. And like dad, all I ever wanted was a family. A son needs a healthy relationship with his mother.

It's not only little boys who need a healthy relationship with their mother. Young girls need their daddy. In fact, according to a recent study published in the Journal of Family Psychology, daughter's benefit greatly from having a healthy relationship with their father. Young ladies are more likely to garner a better self-image from a father, and they are more likely to develop their own fulfilling relationships and healthy sexuality with other men in their future, by forming a deep, trusting bond with their dad. *Daddy's Little Girl* is more than a cute image and quip on a Father's Day greeting card. It's the essence of a young lady's life.

Daddy knows what boys are like, and he'll teach his daughter what not to tolerate in the opposite sex. He'll teach his baby-girl what he teaches his young sons. "Open your mouth, and close your fists if you have to, but never let anyone bully or intimidate you." And the sincere affection and absolute love until death that daddy devotedly showers on his little angel is what she learns to expect — and feel — from any future man in her life.

A mother who issues a groundless protection order during a divorce is literally shortening her own daughter's quality and quantity of life. Treating her father like shit only teaches said child, who will surely emulate her parent, to treat the future man in her life the same way.

A Mother who loves her daughter would never teach her child to hate the man who gave her life (unless said mother hates the father more than she loves her daughter). A man who would sacrifice his own life for her. Is it any wonder that children who experience parental divorce are much more likely to experience divorce themselves? Dissolution of a marriage is a very high-risk factor for intergenerational marital instability. Aside from the obvious observation that their parents were not committed to a lifelong marriage, a child who witnesses a parent who abuses their own spouse (911 calls, protection orders, alienation, allegations of violence) is at risk of repeating such behavior when they dissolve their own marriage.

Ester already began imitating and practicing her mother's behavior when she started screaming,

"Call the police!" when her older brother (and her favorite sibling), who adores her and was the junior Mr. Mom in her life, refused to do some menial things she wanted done.

If you're lucky enough to evade jail time, as I was when the police refused to take me away on that Saturday morning as my wife fearfully warned that I'm "dangerous," you will still feel the constantly clanging heavily weighted shackles of an order of protection. The slightest outburst — even a sternly placed exclamation point in a text — could easily necessitate immediate further measures to keep you in line. Think I'm exaggerating? Then you have obviously never been through a divorce.

Court-ordered anger management classes, psychological evaluations, and visitation only when accompanied by a social worker will quickly be ordered and billed to you for the most minute negative reaction on your part against your Stalinist wife's Great Purge. These additional "protective measures" will be added to your child support payments, along with horse riding lessons, tutors, sleep away camp, medical insurance, and a host of other "add-on" responsibilities that will fade away any memory of your "marriage made in heaven." The people hired to keep you in line will surely find something to justify the need to defend their ridiculously unnecessary jobs.

My wife taunted me with professional spread sheets of detailed forensic accounting for every single expenditure on Ester's behalf — from gas and car mileage spent driving her to school, down to half the cost of an eighty-cent Slurpee that she purchased for Ester after a riding lesson (copies of receipts included). This was then deducted from the court-ordered maintenance that she adamantly refused to pay me.

A woman that earns over one hundred dollars an hour was spending endless hours accounting for items that cost pennies. And what purpose did it serve to deduct anything if she refused to pay me anyway? I imagine my wife thought it was funny as she expressed her humor while bantering with Schwartz about wishing to see my expression when I received her spread sheets. Perhaps it was her way of saying, "Fuck you, Ze'ev!" My reaction, by the way, was nothing more than a deep sigh. Whatever floats your boat, Sharen.

Upon filing for divorce your life will resemble what it's like to live in a gulag. You become a wounded zebra in a river of alligators. Missing a few child support payments, losing your job, or even communicating with your wife or child via texting, can easily land you in jail. And unlike an indigent criminal, you will not receive a court appointed attorney. You'll have to appear pro se. DO NOT TALK includes any kind of contact. Try finding a new job upon your release.

Nothing in my divorce added up. Nothing made sense. Lifetime relationships melted away faster and more sloppily than a child's chocolate ice cream cone on a hot August day. I try to assuage my own guilt, my failure to protect Ester, with the thought that I certainly did my best and that at least my daughter is alive.

But it doesn't work. I miss Princess Ester. I miss her laughter. I miss her royal ditziness. And I miss her funny faces. Marriage is buying a house for someone you hate; the old joke goes. Marriage is also having a child you will likely never see once you file for divorce, I might add.

"Don't worry," everyone tells me, "alienation is a common product of divorce. That's life. She'll come back to you one day. Get over it." But they don't seem to understand that you can't just "get over" someone you brought into the world. Ten irreplaceable years just flew by. Tell me again that she's coming back and that I should "get over it."

Whatever happened to Ester? I continued to muse as I poured my second cup of coffee that morning. My dream had been so emotionally intense that I still had difficulty waking up from its almost hypnotic effect.

Looking back, I recalled how delicately I had broached the topic of divorce with my wife a full year before she became pregnant with Ester, our fifth child. My wife agreed to go to couples therapy (which should, grammatically speaking, be called "couple" therapy). I was very hesitant to even suggest marital counseling, never knowing if her response would be one of furious anger or received as a great idea to "work on our marriage, Zevie." As miserable as things were, I was still hopeful that perhaps a professional could help us work things out for the sake of our four children. In truth, I was unenlightened (blinded actually) by my desperate panicked thoughts of not being around during the childhood of my magnificent munchkins.

I knew how lonely it felt to play on a basketball team with kids whose dads encouraged and enthusiastically cheered them on. I remember watching my friends as they enjoyed a post-game ice cream outing while their fathers gazed at them in admiration across the glass-covered restaurant table with that so-proud-of-you stare. I became the tag-along shy "orphan" that listlessly responded "Yes, thank you," to the merciful, "Wanna' join us?" invitations after a game. I still remember how I drew happy faces with my finger on the frosted glass-top table to try and cheer myself up as I sat quietly waiting for my cherry soda.

I knew what it felt like to grow up without a father. I wanted to spare my children the sorrowful experience. Reluctantly, I committed myself to a few more years of marriage determined that my kids would never have to grow up without their Tatie.

But, to be totally honest, I felt more like committing myself into an asylum, because the marital Imago mirroring therapy sessions "designed to turn conflict into healing and growth" only exacerbated the situation because of my wife's inability to follow even the ground rule: letting your spouse speak without interrupting. My wife felt therapy was about how she could better manage "Ze'ev." The frustration on our therapists face further proved to me just how "over" the marriage truly was.

Besides, anything even temporarily accomplished in an hour-long session was quickly undone during the short five-minute ride back home. I was torn to overstretched stressed-out shreds between knowing the marriage was over and not wanting to be reduced to a visitation-scheduled-dad that only saw his four kids on alternate Tuesdays and Thursdays and every other Shabbos. I already heard enough horror stories from divorced male friends who were five minutes late dropping off their kids only to be greeted by the police. I knew what my wife would be like. In reality, I had no clue.

I couldn't pull the trigger on my kids, but I also couldn't deal with the post-mortem marriage anymore. I then recused myself (not because of a conflict of interest, but because I had no interest) from our huge master bedroom, with a fourteen-foot-high ceiling that led to where our marriage had gone, and blamed my need for a quiet night of sleep on my age and my wife's snoring. I felt lonelier when I slept in a room with my wife than by myself in our guest bedroom, where I wound up spending most nights. I was miserable. Washed-out. And beyond depressed.

There's a saying that you never stop loving someone. You either never did or you always will. I realized that I never did. It's always been over, I finally admitted to myself. "I'll call my lawyer in the morning," I finally decided. After fifteen years of sexual frustration and exhaustive emotional whiplashing, I was only beginning to live my life by the 1989 haunting ballad sung by the gorgeous Marie Fredriksson as she desperately pleaded with me to "listen to your [my] heart." I had no idea that I was about to put off that morning call for another twelve years.

By approximately age thirty-five most women are already in their declining years of fertility. While their six-pack Homo-erectus potential hunter-gatherer mate swipes left or right on Tinder with a mindless erection in his pants that inflates his cranium, their biological clock starts ticking louder with every desperate one-night stand as they search for Mr. Right.

"But we had such a beautiful sextlationship!" she cries, the morning after sucking his cock after riding it for an hour while faking orgasm, when he doesn't even bother to text back a "Thank you," or to even tap and send a heart emoji. "Because he has none," it suddenly occurs to her — not understanding that her own hormones control her poor choices as much as her chimpanzee Tinder-boy is controlled by his.

Meanwhile, her maternal evolutionary instincts sense the paltry amount of time remaining for her to produce offspring as she regretfully releases yet another rare egg from her ovaries every month while that white picket "happily forever after" fence, ensconcing two kids playing on a manicured suburban lawn, recedes further into the distance — along with her memories of being the "mommy" when she played "house" in kindergarten with that gentle boy named Zev who the girls grabbed by his sleeve to play the role of "daddy."

It was such an easy role for the little boy to play. He simply imitated his own father and did whatever he was ordered to do by the "mommy." "Hold him, Yankel!" I wonder why I never asked one of the little girls to play the role of Annette while sipping some vodka from a teacup.

Add five years to the math and a woman's chances of getting pregnant drop to about five percent. Add another five years and the odds of her getting pregnant hover at a mere one percent.

My wife no longer used any kind of birth control by age forty-five when she became a representative of that one percent statistic. Her period, which once flowed and angrily exploded with a punctuality by which you could set an atomic clock, and my worst day of the month, now arrived about as often as Santa Claus coming down the chimney of a Jewish home on Yom Kippur. But what my wife's vagina lacked in passion; her ovaries overcompensated for and produced eggs in abundance.

I must have sleepwalked from the guest room to our decomposing marital bed one evening after finishing off the nightly bottle of wine that I drank to "celebrate" my marriage and childhood. As a result of an almost immaculate occurrence of necrophilic intimacy with the remains of my *Bashert,* my wife gave premature birth to Princess Ester two months shy of her forty-sixth birthday. It was the love and mercy I had on this newborn "miracle-baby" from the moment she was conceived that kept me incarcerated in solitary matrimony confinement for another eleven years.

The thought of my not being around for Ester's childhood was more painful than the loneliness of my loveless marriage. I love babies. I had to make it work. And anyway, I was used to pain. Like any young athlete who hopes to win a gold medal in their sport, the secret to success is to start 'em when they're young.

It's been ten years since I filed for divorce. I remember how I did my best to sound upbeat and natural when I sat down with an endearing eleven-year-old gregarious Ester to explain that mommy and daddy are going to get a divorce. It had been eleven years since I moved back upstairs from our guest room determined to make my marriage work for my miracle baby's sake. I pointed out that five of her ten best friends had parents who were getting a divorce and that mommy and daddy would always remain the very best of friends.

I had Ester laughing about an experience that was about to drastically change her life. Almost a half century older than my late-in-life daughter, I was twice as naïve about how radically both of our lives were about to become unhinged. How could I possibly imagine, upon serving my wife with divorce papers, that I was also giving my daughter the proverbial kiss goodbye?

"I want to live with you!" Ester giggled. I laughed as I explained that I was going to rent a small house nearby and would always be around. "Sometimes you'll live with me. Sometimes with mommy. You'll still live in our big house (Ester loved her room with the huge circular window and cathedral ceiling) and I'll continue to take you to school. Your life's not gonna change," I assured her, clueless as I was, as Ester skipped away from her once-happy childhood to play with her friends outside.

I have not seen Ester in ten years. In another ten I'll be seventy-eight years old. She will be thirty-one. I probably won't even know if Ester has children or if she's married. Should I "get over it?"

Ester is now almost twenty-one years old. The tidbits I receive about her life are scant. I often Google her name, hoping to find a picture of what she looks like, but as an Orthodox Jewish young lady Esther stays away from the Internet and I can't retrieve any information about her. I look up our relatives on Facebook, but I'm blocked. As a man whose funeral, at one time, would have been attended by hundreds of people, I now wonder if there will even be a minyan to say Kaddish.

Ester was instructed years ago by her mother, somewhere around protection order number two, to refer to me as "Zev," because, "He's not your father anymore!" I'm still in shock. Not at my wife. Insanity has no filter and no foresight. But I still can't believe Ester complied.

I was sitting one night, unnoticed, meditating in the quiet and darkness of our sunroom, which happened to be the darkest room in the house at night because the rear of our home sat adjacent to a forest, as my wife spoke to our daughter in the kitchen. In Jewish law and custom it's considered a huge act of disrespect to utter a parent's first name. Even when not in their presence. Ester knew this. But my tiny wife is much more powerful than any invisible God's commandment to *Honor Thy Parent*.

In truth, I'm not that old fashioned, and it was the least of my problems, but my wife's angry directive to Ester to, "Call him Zev! He's not your father anymore!" was indicative of the endless *Scorch the Earth Zev Walks On* policy of my wife.

With my wife, when it's over, it's so over, that it never began. Like Big Brother in 1984, my *Bashert* has a knack for deleting people, denying their ever having existed. Even as a form of light element or energy somewhere in the far universe. They are never to be mentioned and forever to be ignored. Any documentation or pictures portraying their having been married to her or proof of their ever having lived, will be erased retroactively. *He-Who-Must-Not-Be-Named* is no longer Ester's father. Even I believe it. Ester certainly does.

Thanks for not being a hoarder once in your life, and leaving behind my surname and our wedding album, my dear Vybie. It contains many beautiful thirty-five-year-old priceless pictures of Rabbi Nekritz, Rabbi Kaplan, and Rabbi Breitowitz. We could have used them as our Beit Din. Or does "nekritz" no longer qualify to satisfy your high moral standards? A junky album to my wife. Priceless pictures to her empath husband. One wacko's trash is another man's treasure.

Amazingly similar to my wife's nostalgic feelings for our match made in heaven wedding album, and the many beautiful images of her standing in a flowing white gown while staring at me with adoring eyes as we were blessed by Rabbi Naftali Kaplan (who is now approaching his ninetieth birthday) and Rabbi Nekritz, was my mother's tossing away the seventy-year-old wedding album of her having never been married to my father.

I literally picked the 1949 ancient-ruins off-white satin covered album out of the garbage. The priceless black and white photographs of famous rabbis, scholars and guests, whose families, towns, and yeshivas were razed by the Nazis, were hours away from being driven off to some landfill to decompose — like the match made in heaven joyous occasion their static stills portrayed. Worthless garbage to my wire-monkey Mommy. Priceless gems to her empath son and to the progeny of many of the famous long-departed scholars portrayed therein — whose descendants were thrilled to receive copies of photographs of their holy ancestors.

I rescued many treasured pictures of some of the most famous rabbis of that era, who had only recently survived The Holocaust and were guests of my esteemed grandfather. Among those guests was a middle-aged scholar whose name the Jewish Orthodox world would come to revere as the saintly Rabbi Yaakov Kamenetsky (father of Rabbi Shmuel Kamenetsky who I requested to serve as a judge in my divorce case) who was an extremely close friend of my grandfather.

One mother's trash is another son's treasure. Rav Shmuel, as he is fondly known by every Orthodox Jew in the world, couldn't stop hugging and thanking me when I surprised him with the pictures of his father. As with her life, Mom didn't have a clue as to what she was tossing away. Like mother-in-law, like daughter-in-law.

Once my wife is done with you, you can stand at her side as both of you stare into a mirror and you will no longer see your own reflection. You have been erased from society. *Vaporized.* My wife refused to even sit in the same room with me when she finally came to my lawyer to sign her name off our house.

She only showed up because a threat of contempt had finally been issued by Judge Alfieri, after my lawyer wrote to the court about her refusal to abide by the divorce decree, warning her that she would be incarcerated if she continued to brazenly defy the uncontested divorce decree she initiated and swore to abide by in court.

Even in defeat, my terminator ex will force her enemy to expend energy as she twists the blade, even if it's also inside of her, if it will further damage and exhaust her adversary for one more second. Like a cruel UFC fighter, who knows he'll be suspended for hitting his opponent after the bell rings, my ex will keep sledgehammering her defeated warrior's sleeping brain till the referee rushes over and physically throws her off her opponent. After all, what's a lousy fifty-thousand dollar fine when you can mash your enemy's brain for three more seconds? And of what value is two-hundred and fifty-thousand dollars if it brings you the pleasure of torturing your ex-husband for three full years?

It cost me an additional completely wasted three-thousand dollars (and two months of precious life) to formally challenge, and instantly win, my wife's "I changed my mind!" declaration. My ex-Bashert then had my lawyer run up and down the hallway of his office several times, fetching our signatures on the documents we had to sign. She quietly whispered, in her genteel voice, that she doesn't want to sit in the same room with "*him.*" Pronounced with as many syllables as *Voldemort*. My ex refused to even utter my name, acting as if there were disastrously dark and dire consequences upon doing so.

In truth, my wife could easily put the Dementors of J.K. Rowling's series to shame. Her ability to consume human happiness, while inflicting anxiety and depression, makes those creatures look more like a trained PTSD service dog by comparison. Like the flash-heated-to-death lava-sealed suspended-in-action victims of ancient Pompeii, those who are vaporized by my wife are instantly suffocated and entombed in the ancient past.

I have tried many times in the past few years to initiate contact with Ester through her mother — who still refuses to utter one word to me. I have no doubt that if Ester died tomorrow my wife would not inform me where funeral services were being held. My wife will also walk down the wedding aisle with some other male family member, as if she is a widow, when Ester marries one day. Like she most probably did for my daughter Sara's wedding two years ago. I don't know for certain since I wasn't invited. I only heard about the marriage a week later, when someone I knew peripherally in the neighborhood mumbled a brief "Mazel Tov!" as he walked by me on a Shabbos afternoon.

Actually, the term "widow" would indicate that I once existed. More likely, my ex will walk down the aisle as if she had never been married. I wonder if they even wrote my name in Sara's *Ketuva.* According to Jewish law they would have been obligated to write *Sara bāt Zev* (Sarah the daughter of Zev) in the Jewish marriage contract. But I'm sure my ex insisted that the officiating rabbi inscribe *Sara bāt He-Who-Must-Not-Be-Named* instead. Either way, I still wish my misguided, duped daughter Sara a wonderful life.

My wife, who was always meticulous in her typing, also arrogantly vaporized and "unpersoned" our mutual rabbi of thirty-two years. Sharen instantly laicized Rabbi Israel Tzvi Nekritz, as "nekritz." Declaring, with a few strokes of her dastardly keyboard, the swift removal of his rabbinical title along with a lower-case letter "n" that expeditiously morphed one of the most brilliant Talmudical scholars on the planet into an instant mononymous nobody.

Rabbi Nekritz, who was one of the few individuals ever fully ordained (even most Jews don't know the levels of ordination) by the original Dean of Ner Israel Rabbinical College, became "nekritz" as fast as Tatie became "zev." A lifetime of intensely studying the Talmud, lecturing to thousands of students, and writing priceless Aramaic rare and insightful Talmudical discourses on every chapter of the Talmud, was instantly vaporized by the Orwellian dystopian mind of my wife. After all, she was typing to Vittie.

A narcissist will never relinquish control over anyone. Not talking, in their angry mind, is their final act of controlling the person they once manipulated mercilessly. They will always have the last word by no longer allowing you to have any.

Mrs. Hyde then ripped the picture of "nekritz," and sent our two oldest daughters on a mission of self-immolation to call the man in the picture they used to kiss as toddlers (while running around the house in excitement because Rebbi is coming for Shabbos!) "a piece of shit." Faster than Haman's ten son's necks snapped on the gallows in ancient Persia, Rachel and Sara drove an hour and a half to Brooklyn to carry out Mrs. Haman's insane plan.

My wife took a whore's bath and instantly wiped away the closest two male relationships that she had cherished for over a quarter of a century. Rabbi? Swish. Husband? Swash. Sorry, Sharen, but it still smells raunchy down there. Sin stinks.

Chop-chop! A mere issuance of psychiatric claptrap proclaiming her latest profound forensic evaluation upon the dazzling mind of Rabbi Israel Tzvi Nekritz having been "radicalized by Zev" via her email chain of overfed and undersexed Yenta howler monkeys meant it had to be true.

And who needs "nekritz" anyway? After all, she now had the well-bribed Rabbi Chaim Schabes slut as her Seeing Eye bitch. Let the Jew with an oversized beard and ego sniff some money and he'll fetch whatever boned-up rabbinical decision his "followers" want to hear. Like a leashed dog that "leads" his master, Schabes barked like a bitch upon receiving a five-thousand-dollar wire from Sharen's grotesque witch sister Elyce. I'm sure she's cackling like one as she reads this.

My wife did the same thing to *He-Who-Must-Not-Be-Named* when she refused to come to the RCA (Rabbinical Council of America) to receive her Jewish Get from me. Cancelling the morning of our scheduled meeting with the rabbis, she explained, surely in her Florence Nightingale voice, that she was "stuck in the O.R. again."

My ex knew that I would instantly recognize her famous excuse for getting out of any meeting on a moment's notice if she did not want to attend. I doubt she was even on the O.R. schedule that day. The schedules are planned weeks in advance. Not that there weren't a dozen hands on deck that could have easily covered for her had she wanted to receive her Jewish Get in person.

So after frantically and hysterically crying wolf to Gary Barnet's mother, and screaming in her emails to her entire extended family upon my serving her divorce papers that I was a recalcitrant husband who would surely withhold her Jewish Get, forcing her to remain a lifelong Agunah; my wife didn't even bother to show up to receive hers. Sharen knows three things about me (not much else). I would never hit her. I would never withhold a Get. I would die to save a child. Upon serving her papers I instantly became an angry violent pedophile recalcitrant husband. I'm actually rather surprised she didn't add, "who hates studying the Talmud."

To this day, all my neighbors believe "Zev got the house" because I withheld delivering my wife's Get until she signed the deed over to me. The fact that her Get is dated four months earlier than her dated signature transferring her fifty-percent ownership of the property to my name meant nothing to the Yentas. They also let all the Yenta Jewish Realtors know that whoever bought the house would be cursed because "the divorced husband had a better lawyer and stole the house from his poor wife by going to the Goyishe courts." Lonna Kin was the one who found a buyer that was willing to suffer the "curse" of buying my house at a seventy-five thousand dollar discount.

But in truth, not showing up to receive her Get was my wife's way of informing me that I had been vaporized and would never be allowed to speak with her again.

"Please tell Zev to use a *shaliach*," my suddenly scholarly wife insisted as she asked the Beit Din to appoint a Power of Attorney of sorts on her behalf, "I'll come tomorrow to pick it up."

I could have left and returned the following day. But I knew the late day updated version of my *NY Times* online subscription would be shouting, 'ZEV LEWINSON WITHHOLDS JEWISH GET!' with the sub headline declaration of: 'Fearless advocate for Orthodox Jewish women's rights maliciously withholds his own wife's Jewish divorce papers in a recalcitrant about-face after thirty-year marriage.' If you ever heard my wife's voice, you'd understand why fact-checking is a total waste of time. Her voice is more believable than the truth.

I appointed one of the young scholars at the RCA Beit Din as my messenger to deliver the Get to my wife. It is totally permissible to do so according to Jewish Halacha.

In reality, my wife believed she didn't even need a *shaliach*, or a Jewish Get. You see, according to Jewish law, a wife is instantly considered a single woman again upon the death of her husband. My widowed wife assumed full guardianship over an orphaned Ester the moment that female processor came to our front door seven years ago. Here lies Zev Lewinson, February 21, 1953 — November 15, 2013.

Turns out my wife was right. I'm no longer Ester's father. My wife wore Ester out. Then she wore me out. Like any aggressive third-world interrogator, my ex wears you down. It doesn't matter how tough you are. That just gives her more pleasure. She will still make you tap-out faster than an arm-bar locked in by Rhonda Rousey. But even upon tapping, she will never release your arm. Or your child. My wife's reputation-crushing mandibles are still spewing anger, contempt, and deceit to this very day. And tomorrow. And forever. Even after this book sells twenty-five million copies. Ant's never stop marching.

Ester recently got her learners permit a few years ago. I've always driven a stick shift and would have loved to teach her how to drive one. I can hear her impish laughter as I daydream how cool Ester would have looked with her light brown hair and huge blue eyes, sitting behind the wheel of my orange-flame, six-speed BMW. I can see her smiling with her beautifully straightened teeth (not seen since she sported alternating pink and purple rubber bands to hold her wires in place so long ago) as I'd teasingly dare her to go over the limit. She was such an amusing and quick-witted child. I can barely imagine what she looks like as a woman.

There's a certain peacefulness in dying. Many people who have survived near-death experiences describe it as a time of total serenity, tranquility, and an almost in-utero place of security and warmth. Accounts of individuals who have died on the operating table or survived the long drop of a parachute that failed to open, all share a similar tale of having reached in Buddhism terminology, what can only be called that highest of all states, Nirvana — a total freedom from suffering.

It seems that once a person knows they're about to die, the fear of impending death no longer exists. They are no longer attached to life, and hence have no fear of being detached. "*Vonce* you're dead, *'der* is nothing more *vat* to fear."

I had this near-death experience as a five-year-old child when I dove into the deep end of a swimming pool at Sunshine Victory Bungalow Colony in the late 1950's. I didn't know how to swim yet, but a group of teenagers promised to fish me out of the water and all I had to do was run over and tell them I'm about to dive in again. I trusted them, and they kept their word all summer long. But the testosterone-synapsed minds of young men are easily distracted when the scent of females clad in colorful short-shorts and skimpy bathing suits arrive giggling at a swimming pool.

I remember walking along the bottom of the pool desperately trying to find a way out. I recall looking up at the bottom rung of the ladder, a mere few inches above my outstretched arm and extended shoulder as I jumped upwards in the deep end of the pool, and the frustration I felt as I ran out of air when I couldn't grasp the curved piece of metal that held that bottom step in place because I was too short to reach it. I understood that I was going to die.

I can still feel my lungs bursting for air, as if they were being scratched, burned, and torn apart from within, as I frantically, instinctively, began to gulp the pool water to cool the searing pain. And I recall the calm sensation that suddenly overcame me as I marveled at how I immediately felt so much better now that I was breathing water. Just like a fish!

It amazed me that lungs could feel satiated by replacing air with water. The bursting pain in my chest eased with each gigantic gulp of chlorinated water. I felt as if I was breathing, and I wondered if scientists knew how good it felt for a drowning kid to breathe water. I remember feeling completely calm and relaxed, as my brain began to shut down, but also very sad that my father would soon learn that one of his three sons (the one who could even be the President if he "vanted" to) had died, when hands, it seemed, suddenly yanked me out of my dream state while snatching me out of the water.

In actual fact, I had been unconscious and was waking up poolside, coughing up water and crying after too many minutes underwater. I had no idea that had my dream continued for a few more minutes that I would have been one more summer statistic regarding a child left unattended who drowned in a pool. A million of me (Jewish children) didn't drown during the Holocaust. The world left those Jewish children unattended and watched as they went up in smoke. Where was the angel you sent to stop Abraham from slaughtering Isaac, Dear God?

Kind of similar to that childhood experience was my falling into the cesspool of Alfieri's courtroom where I suddenly found myself drowning in stress and gasping for air. My divorce was also a near-death experience. Literally. It had all the angst, PTSD, excitement, and drama that most men, half my age, would be unable to handle without going ballistic. More than once I had the ambulance come to my house because my heart painfully constricted to the point where I was convinced I was suffering an actual heart attack.

I remember the right side of my brain thinking, "I can't really be dying," as my left hemisphere logically insisted that I "prepare for the worst," as I desperately popped an aspirin into my mouth in the hopes of curtailing a stroke. "Is this how I finally pass from the world?" I wondered as my chest seemed to collapse from within. "Death by divorce?"

Those wonderful responders gave me oxygen and watched my systolic numbers slowly return to somewhat normal, begging me, like that ditzy beautiful artist forty years earlier, to allow them to take me to the hospital, while this embarrassed old man cracked jokes to diffuse the situation and avoid spending an overnight, getting poked from all directions, at Good Samaritan Hospital in Suffern, New York.

"Why do Jewish men die seven years before their wives?" I asked the small crowd of heroes. "Because they want to!"

The plan of my wife and her attorney to "give Zev a heart attack" almost succeeded. It took me a long time to free myself from the manipulations of Jewish theology and Monsey-Yenta-Culture along with the conditionings of behavioral therapists who kept chirping about mirroring the other person's perspective "no matter what they said" in my effort to avoid a divorce at all costs.

I married a woman who I believed was the opposite of my own mother. A sweet woman who assured me that she shared my desire to raise children in a happy home. And so I explained away deranged behavior till I, who believes a thesaurus is more holy than a bible, ran out of words. I should probably kiss my thesaurus after looking up a word.

But the day arrived when the pain of loneliness, blistering frustrations, and physically impairing stress, that I endured throughout twenty-eight years of talking to a wall of ice, forced me to walk over and simply pull upon the bars of the jail cell door. I was shocked at how easily it yanked open. It was never even locked, I realized. *Why didn't I walk out sooner?*

I knew my wife would torture me, but I finally decided that my dementor could shoot me in the back and I would not turn around. *I'm safe as long as she doesn't penetrate a vital organ.* And I knew there was no vital organ to hit because I never committed one single act of any of the charges for which I was being chased throughout the traffic-clogged streets of Monsey, as I raced back and forth between three *Arkayos Akum* secular court systems of law.

The sharp cracks of bullet-words and the whistle of feathered-arrow emails — digital binary byte fangs of gossiped poison bullshit, typed by stay-at-home Yentas with too much time on their pudgy hands — flew past me at all hours and from all directions devouring my relationship with Ester while she slept. Patiently executed client-lawyer protected traps, wildly concocted by two lunatics in the middle of the night to deliver their latest Order of Protection grenade, were always rocket-launched from Schwartz's round shoulder late on Friday afternoons, perfectly aimed to desecrate my Sabbath. Forget about a day of rest. Thing One and Thing Two wouldn't give me a minute to breathe.

My wife and her dumpy cronies orchestrated constant drive-by senseless Yenta gossip-shootings that disrupted our "Jews Only" neighborhood non-stop for two and a half years. In heaven the value of their future homes surely decreased.

"So ordered!" machinated malicious Protection Order land mines placed between father and daughter by SS Alfierinsane. Frivolous Zyklon B motions and subpoena stun-grenades. Bang! Bang! Court Ordered visitation denied among shouts of, "There's an Order of Protection!" Pop! Pop! Criminal court. Family court. Divorce court. Ping! Ping! Wailing police sirens heralding urgent visits by Aryan-looking weapon-clad muscular young men on the holy Sabbath. Bam! Bam! I get anxious merely describing all that I somehow survived.

My wife's arsenal of insanity, that seemed to run on perpetual motion, was stockpiled with an endless brazen onslaught of manipulation and deceit without concern or regard for any of the collateral damage that might occur as the result of her deviant behavior.

The missiles whizzed by. I was certainly scathed by them. But none of them hit the bullseye on my back. Like the falsehoods they represented, they all faded or dissolved upon impact. There had literally been nothing to fear but fear itself. But in contrast to Churchill's sagacious advice, I never imagined that Ester would become the center of that bullseye. Ester was the one target I couldn't foresee my wife aiming at. My wife and Daniel Schwartz (who always wore that tiny yarmulka on his gigantic head) shot my vital organ right through her innocent heart that once pulsed with endless laughter. Mine will never beat the same.

I spent many years of my life as a diamond dealer. Like the discovery of many famous gems, the profession I stumbled into for over three decades occurred totally by accident. While contemplating a career as a criminal defense attorney while repeatedly complaining that "I don't know what to do with my life" as if I suffered from palilalia, I accidentally stubbed my way into the diamond business. I knew someone who knew someone. Just like I tumbled into a career as the spouse of a lunatic for three decades because my aunt, who was a kindergarten teacher, knew Sharen's entire family. Boy, did I waste my life. At least I compensated by writing a great book.

As luck would have it, I had a real eye for seeing the varying nuanced shades of color in natural-colored diamonds. Coupled with a charming smooth-talking personality, it was of little wonder that I amassed quite a beautiful stash of rainbow-colored diamonds by the time I was twenty-seven years old. But mine was a paltry million-dollar selection compared to the unique priceless collections of men that had been trading these rarest of all gems their entire wasted lives.

Pinks, blues, canaries (as the vivid-yellow ones are called) were constantly shown to me by old-world gentlemanly super-wealthy cutters, querying my opinion regarding recutting their exquisite stones into different shapes that would reduce their brilliancy but dramatically enhance their worth many times over by increasing the depth of the stone's color.

Vivid-grade natural color diamonds are a uniquely rare gemological event.

Extremely scarce and only occasionally found in nature, these superb jewels are a magnificent anomaly of Mother Nature's diamond hoard and are much more valuable than the rough diamonds that yield perfectly shaped D-color-Flawless white gems of similar weight.

They are, choosing an accolade from the thesaurus of the late Rick James, a Super Freak. "She's a very kinky diamond ... the kind you sell for lots of money .... She's super freaky!"

These holy grail gems are a remarkable fluke of the mineral family. They truly are in short supply — unlike the manipulative and controlled syndicated release of white diamonds, whose rarity was created by the most clever Madison Avenue minds in history and are far more abundant than any engaged woman could ever imagine as she screeches in joy over her "He put a ring on it!" finger (right next to the one she'll be extending upon divorce). I bought a small pink diamond for each of my daughters when they were born and set them aside as a Bat Mitzvah present. I never got to give Ester the one I put away for her. DO NOT CELEBRATE WITH MINOR CHILD.

The cutters would press a few-hundred folded bucks into my hand as they thanked me for my precious opinion before cutting their natural-color diamonds from their rough octahedron predominant shape or before recutting already-polished gems that they purchased from heirs who wanted to cash out of their family heirlooms and memories.

Meanwhile I would have paid them if only to sneak a peek at these rarest of all gems — ravaged, almost stolen, when one tallies the price of human misery required to mine them from deep within the dissected body of Mother Nature, to be cut and then hoarded, as a bragging-rights accomplishment, in the deposit box of some wealthy real estate mogul or oil sheik's safe.

Keep in mind that natural occurring color in a diamond is a much rarer gemological event than a white (clear) diamond that lacks any color at all. Ironically it is the opposite of how too many people sadly view skin color. A one carat flawless white diamond is drastically less valuable than a one carat flawless blue, pink, or red diamond. And the deeper the color, the more valuable the gem. The financial reward is greatly increased if a cutter can even slightly improve the vividness of a stone's yellow, blue, or pinkish hues by cleverly reshaping its facets.

White diamonds are cut to reflect light off of the stone's facets, which causes the scintillation and flashing cacophonous lightning display that appears and teases the greedy "mine's-bigger-than-yours" consumer's eye as light bounces off the mirror-facets of a perfectly cut stone. As a woman gently moves her hand, causing the stone to slightly shift, said stone "sparkles."

Colored diamonds, however, are not perfectly cut. On purpose. They are cut asymmetrically to control the amount of light that passes through the stone, and they are typically faceted into a deeper shaped stone to enhance ("bring out" in cutter's jargon) and intensify their natural color. Scintillation is purposefully and methodically sacrificed in exchange for the deeper color that the omission of light allows to surface. This is caused by an intentional improper ratio of the stone's table and pavilion facets, thus limiting the reflection of light.

A cutter of a natural-colored diamond wants to keep the light (color) in and not let it bounce out. Too much light and scintillation will mask and dim the natural color rarely found in diamonds. The diamond cutter actually "cheats" (and here is where fortunes are made) as he intentionally skimps on the proper mathematical proportions, refusing to facet the stone as sharply as he could. Natural white light shooting through the stone will dull and weaken the natural yellow, green, or pink color by flooding the colored-by-nature stone with white light.

Unlike this honest artistic maneuver to increase the vividness of a diamond's color, is a nasty trick used by some jewelers to deceive wealthy buyers. The jeweler sets a low-scale "piss-yellow" diamond into a gold setting mixed with copper alloy that turns the metal pink. Presto! The stone now reflects the color of the pink gold! It's all legal because the gold and diamond are natural. Please don't ever try to outsmart a diamond dealer at their trade. Don't try to find too much of a bargain. Because you'll get what you pay for.

One day a certain dealer called to ask if I could run up to his office to "look at a stone." Refusing to even tell me what it was only increased my curiosity. "Give me twenty minutes. I'll be right over."

I was almost blinded as I delicately unfolded the shiny-blue origami shaped diamond paper. The naked beauty was truly breathtaking.

"It's gorgeous," I breathed like a woman near climax. "This has to be an Intense-Vivid-Yellow if there ever was one," I gasped as I stared at a deeply shaped, stunningly gorgeous sixteen-carat cushion-cut coruscant gem. I was so smitten by her elegance that I could barely talk as I asked, "Is it certified yet?"

The dealer, quite impressed with my hitting the color on the nose, took out a GIA (Gemological Institute of America) certificate which described the alluring feminine stone's color exactly as I had adored her with only my bare eyes, sans microscope or a GIA laboratory Master Set of natural-yellow comparison stones, only moments before. *Intense Vivid-Yellow* the paper emphatically read.

"So what do you want to know?" I asked, surprised at being asked advice on a completely polished and already certified stone. *What more could he possibly want to know?* I wondered.

"I'm thinking of recutting it into an emerald cut shape," he seriously replied.

"You're totally crazy!" I responded, "You're gonna lose so much weight, and you'll never get the *Intense*-Vivid again. It doesn't exist in an open faceted emerald shape! It's unheard of! You'll flood the stone with light! You're gonna kill the color!" I warned, almost begging him, with a flurry of gemological supplications, to spare the life of this one-of-a-kind gem and not slaughter a ten-million-dollar Super Freak into a mere one-million-dollar has-been. And it wasn't about the money.

I was in love.

"No," he calmly insisted, "I think I can get it. It'll be worth fifteen million easily."

I looked at him and asked, "Are you paying off some of the gemologists at the lab?"

The dealer ignored my remark and laughed with a deep confidence. The kind of confidence that warns a gunslinger to leave his six-shooter in its holster. "I'll make a killing on one of my Middle East Arab customers that thinks they're a connoisseur just because they can buy whatever I show them," he mockingly laughed.

"But why don't you simply sell it to your Arab client for the fifteen and tell him the truth — that it's a spectacular gem that's even more precious than the certificate is able to describe?"

"You don't get it!" the dealer barked. "People don't understand beauty like you do. They're buying the GIA paper, not the stone!"

"But you're destroying something so beautiful!" I mercifully begged on behalf of an inanimate stone that was about to be sacrificed on the altar of profits.

"I'm here to make money!" was the dealer's response. I understood he couldn't hear a word I was saying. He was more deaf than the rock I still lovingly held in my hand. His ears were stuffed with cash.

I continued to stare at the stone that had more heart than the dealer who stood in front of me, memorizing her sheer beauty for a few more moments, as I gently shrouded the gem, ensconcing it back into its blue body-bag, and reluctantly handed her over to my greedy friend. I felt like a sex-trafficker co-conspirator knowing she'd never be the same.

"Do me a favor," I asked in an almost depressed last-meal-wish of sorts. "I'll bet you a hundred bucks you don't get the 'Intense' again. Promise me you'll show me the stone when it's done," I beseeched my "my-word-is-my-bond" friend.

"Promise," he answered as he squeezed several hundred into my palm as we shook hands.

"Good luck," I wished him in a sad tone of voice as if I were witnessing ten thousand scribe-written priceless Torah scrolls in wooden wagons about to be incinerated in Paris in the year 1242. What a waste.

Several weeks later I got the call.

"Did you get it?!" I asked.

"Come up," my never-to-speak-much over the phone friend replied. The buzzer and three-hundred-pound guard allowed me in and once again I unwrapped the diamond tissue paper. I looked at the beautiful twelve carat emerald shaped vivid-yellow diamond. She was most definitely still a head-turner. But as I had foreseen, a mere shadow of its youthful vividness and vitality was all that remained.

The vitiated reincarnation, forcefully birthed through a negative desire of corrupted passion (otherwise known as "greed"), was pale by comparison against the original conceived-in-love by Mother Nature gem that still existed in my mind's eye. The virginal Intense-Vivid innocence of her youth had been raped and ravaged by an old cutter who was rushing in his voracious desire to satiate his mindless obscure goal of accumulating more inventory and endless wealth. Talk about a self-indulging money-shot.

I knew I should not have expected any other possible action from my boorish entrepreneurial sixty-year-old colleague. He'd been exchanging his own life for money for decades. How could he possibly understand true intrinsic beauty or feel any remorse for destroying something so rare and aesthetically pleasing, and then bartering the counterfeit remains for the few extra digits that would appear on his monthly bank statement? He'd have to see outside of himself to accomplish that.

So "unskilled and unawakened," as Gautama Buddha would have surely observed. Not that I was exactly enlightened at twenty-six years of age while I bartered my own life for vodka and pussy. But at least I knew I was shallow. And at least I knew a gorgeous gem when I saw one.

My friend teased me as he held up the new GIA certificate a few feet from me and slowly waved it in front of my inquisitive face.

"No way," I chuckled nervously, "There's no way you got the 'Intense' again." He handed me the certificate. "Yes, way," he laughed in an almost demonic voice that gloated that he had not only won our hundred-dollar bet but would easily net an additional five million dollars on what I felt was a traumatized Zircon compared to the fetching gem that once existed in its place.

"Mazel Tov," I said as I handed him a hundred-dollar bill.

"Keep it," my friend chuckled with a celebratory laugh. Like Harry in Chapin's song *Taxi*, I stashed the bill in my shirt.

Now another man might have been angry at such destruction. The pale emerald cut descendant of her cushion-cut ruddy-complexioned predecessor looked like a strung-out hooker doing flat-back twenty-five-dollar quickies compared to a well-refined sophisticated jet-setting breathtaking beauty, educated at Oxford, who receives lavish gifts in exchange for merely jotting down her cellphone number on a serving napkin.

But I understood that human personalities are as diverse as the diamonds they admire out of appreciation or greed. Where I saw incomparable beauty, the cutter blindly saw, "Profit!" The cutter's brain was only capable of acquiring more money and more inventory. That is all that his consciousness was able to fathom till the day its activity ceased, and his greedy neurons died, leaving his vast inventory to his son. And guess what the heir conditioned-grandchild, whose cold-hearted DNA probably has icy desire-for-profit strands entwined in its sequencing, will be doing for a living till the day he dies?

I would have found a way to allow the diamond to exist. There are many ways to achieve success without killing or rushing to our deaths. To quote Benjamin Franklin: "Haste makes waste."

The seductive siren call for "more profits" aroused a sick passion that blinded the cutter from being able to see the true value of the original truly *Intense-Vivid* gem. Its natural beauty, in and of itself, was all the reward one could possibly ask or hope for.

My personal belief is that destroying anything natural on our planet for the sole outcome of stashing away yet one more artificially inflated dollar can only lead to a negative outcome. Egrets, flamingos, and many other prodigiously colored bird species were nearly wiped out of existence by plume hunters who shot the birds during mating season, when their feathers were most colorful to attract a spouse, for no other reason than a crazed demand that temporarily equated the value of feathers to the price of gold. By wearing the bright feathers on their own heads, bird-brain dim-witted Homo sapiens somehow believed they'd also attract a better mate.

Elephants are facing extinction, as more are being poached than born. Their meticulously sculptured ivory tusks, hacked off their faces only to satisfy the greed of Homo-insatiable, sit on the shelves of collectors halfway around the world, increasing in value as more elephants are herded and heartlessly slaughtered. It's a win-win situation for the cold-blooded murderers of these giant, intelligent beings who love their young, because the more elephants they kill the more precious their collections of ivory become. Soon the only elephants left on the planet will be the little ivory statues of the once awe-inspiring gentle behemoths.

And let's not forget the completely senseless poaching of rhinos, whose ground up nine-pound horns, for horny old men, fetch over thirty-thousand-dollars a pound as a snake oil cure based on the false belief in its miraculous medicinal abilities for treating hangovers and the erectile dysfunction of men with small penises and smaller minds. Researchers say the sellers are cutting the powder with Viagra to "prove" to their buyers that their product is truly priceless.

And the largest Diamond ever discovered yielded a whopping pear-shaped diamond that is set in Queen Elizabeth's dildo scepter. At five-hundred-and-thirty carats I hope it gives her a lot of pleasure. Kudos to the Black slaves (viewed as subhuman until Megan Markel showed up for dinner) exploited by the British Empire so that the Queen Mum can now wave her egotistical half-billion-dollar wand at her adoring White idiot, commoner subjects whenever a fairytale coronation takes place.

An utterly boring ritual with minute details of flawless procedure and vomit-inducing etiquette that have no inherent meaning other than a declaration of "we have what you proles don't" (a bullshit title and looted old money wealth); eventually completed under a canopy and hidden from public view in order to give the new monarch a few moments to meditate on their own oh-so important "duties" while panicking about the BLM protests a mile from the protection of their Royal Guards. *#We're not that fascinated with your fucking fascinators.*

This stupidity is given legitimacy with the anointment of scented "holy oil," whose procedure is plagiarized straight out of the Old Testament, to mitigate the stench of the British Empire's never-setting-sun of slave trading and merciless military conquests, spewed with a philosophical arrogance that colonialism is the "proper" answer to civilize hundreds of millions of barbarians who were in dire need of manners and perfume. The largest empire the world has ever known earned a tidy profit while flogging, starving, and executing anyone that dared to be so rude as to stand in their way. *Don't forget how to "properly" drink your tea.*

At one point the British Empire controlled a quarter of the world's population while draining the natural resources of a quarter of the planet's entire land surface. Like Ancient Rome, they eventually grew too big for their britches.

Mankind will one day understand that allowing the merciless slaughter of animals, for food or ivory, is as barbaric as killing and trading humans for their forced labor to mine gems or harvest cotton. We will also one day realize that issuing Orders of Protection during a divorce, based on the obviously dubious testimony of an angry wife, is more insane than accepting the testimony of "witnesses" during the Salem Witch trials, who saw nothing but merely dreamt that a neighbor harmed them while they experienced REM sleep. At least everyone in Salem believe in witchcraft. And after living on Mariner Way in Monsey, I honestly don't blame them.

Unfortunately, humanity will also probably become extinct before they reach a conclusion that does not necessitate enlightenment. It's obvious to any ten-year-old. But by age twenty we just shrug our shoulders.

The pile of cash (like the Order of Protection) is an illusion. The mirage witnessed by the eyes of a greedy diamond dealer, insane ex wife, fat and shameful Jewish Kapo divorce lawyer, or vicious Victor Alfieri judge, will never be tall enough. Other than in my memory, I wonder if a gem will ever again be unearthed that was as alluring an Intense-Vivid as the one my cutter friend disemboweled. In truth, it wasn't merely one-of-a-kind. It. Was. Beautiful.

I always felt that the cutter stole five million dollars from his Middle Eastern client. He wangled the GIA protocols (possibly through bribing a few gemologists — an issue the GIA has had to deal with many times in its past) by basically plagiarizing a contrived GIA certificate for a recut diamond that only he and I knew was not a true Intense. It was pure manipulation. Allah knows the truth. And if the children of that hoodwinked Middle Eastern client ever resubmit their inherited diamond for an updated certificate from the GIA, they will discover that which only Allah and I now know. Contrary to Gordon Gekko's famous *Wall Street* rant, "Greed is not good."

Speaking of greed, the manipulatively controlled syndicated release of "ethical" white diamonds by De Beers is what props the illusion that white diamonds are a rare commodity. A company whose bloody history literally, and even figuratively, as the word is expressed by those who live on the "other side of the pond," allowed it to hoard unfathomable wealth that was created by the back-breaking labor of exploited Black Africans.

De Beers firmly controls the market after mercilessly creating chaos and civil wars for decades throughout much of the continent, and by creating private prisons and armies of forced labor provided by "guilty until proven innocent" laws in order to build the "financially sophisticated" empire they now own. The Democratic Republic of the Congo still contains incredible wealth due to its natural resources. Yet they are the second poorest country in the world.

The atrocities committed by King Leopold as he slaughtered ten million people during a forty-four-year genocide, that included hacking off the limbs of even women and children as a warning for not meeting his quota for rubber, equates him Hitlerian status for cruelty.

That genocide continued well into the late twentieth century as limbs were still being hacked off by rebels who wanted to control the supply chain of diamonds to De Beers. It's all about 'dem Benjamins. Diamond's might be a girl's best friend, as Marilyn Monroe demurely teased while singing the merits of "a chunk of coal that did well under pressure" (according to Henry Kissinger). But they are a Black man's worst enemy.

Meanwhile, Lil Uzi Vert, is sporting a ten carat, twenty-four-million-dollar pink diamond set in "mindless forehead skin." And find me a rapper that isn't sporting his hip-hop net worth bling while wearing a gold and diamond grill as he smiles on Instagram while displaying the fleet of cars in which he "rolls," and I'll probably be saying "Shalom!" to our own *Unzereh* Jewish rapper, Nissim Black.

De Beers Group sells its diamonds through many secretive channels to this day. They also have a retail division to sell the clear coal that is much more abundant than any engaged woman could ever imagine as she screeches in joy over her "He put a ring on it!" finger.

The covert monopoly fought those pesky anti-trust laws in the United States for a decade and eventually agreed to plead "guilty" to the charge of criminal price fixing while facing a fine of no more than ten million dollars, instantly clearing a path to sell their stones via "expert brand ambassadors." De Beers easily earns ten million dollars on a quiet day. Scientists claim thar our planet contains around four thousand distinct minerals. Diamonds are the hardest one of all. But they are soft when compared to the heart of De Beers.

Humans are similar to diamonds in that almost twenty percent of the human body is composed of carbon. A second similarity is that, like snowflakes, no two diamonds or humans are exactly alike. Those teachers of mine that affectionately described the good little boy of my youth as "a diamond," were telling the literal truth.

And like humans, all diamonds have flaws. There is no such thing as a flawless diamond. It doesn't exist. The GIA merely grants a diamond a "flawless" grade if the flaws that it contains are invisible under a 10X loupe. Merely twisting the microscope dial to 11X or 100X will quickly reveal major fissures that look like a shifting tectonic plate. And being married to a gem like my wife will reveal major issues that, like an earthquake, will shake and jolt the ground you walk on.

Likewise, there are no flawless humans. Twisting the dial past makeup, eyeliner, veneers, and a boob-job quickly reveals the inner personality of the person your hormones once throbbed for. The dial turns more easily as you age and your own hormones stop creating illusions in your young chemically enhanced mind. Like humans, no two diamonds are carbon copies. Just as small differences in a gems hue or clarity can mean hundreds of thousands of dollars in its value; a minute difference in a human's DNA and brain connections will result in personalities as diverse as Madame Curie versus a Jeffery Dahmer. Or, as in my divorce case, between a Mr. Lewinson and Mrs. Lewinson.

I have no question that Mrs. Lewinson's sleep-deprived and emotionally frigid brain contains fissures that researchers like Dr. Robert Sapolsky will one day marvel at upon close scientific examination. I don't believe the shortcomings are in her soul. When I did, I kept talking. And talking. And therapy. And more talking. When I sadly understood that no one was home, I finally served papers. Or one could say, I took the advice of Rabbi Nekritz to "wrap it up already."

I swear that I am not saying the above with any animosity whatsoever. But the only way I can describe my wife is by comparing her to a wonderfully programed artificial intelligence robot whose creator forgot to tighten a few tiny screws. It's almost frightening, but something elusive and subtle is sorely missing. Something human.

It took me almost two decades of placing blame for our rocky marriage on my very successful diamond business when things were going well or my poor business acumen when things went south. I'd blame my absence from my family as I constantly raced to Brooklyn to study with Rabbi Nekritz three times a week. I'd blame our busy work schedules, financial stresses, and parenting almost a half-dozen children. Or I'd blame my wife's postpartum blues and her menopausal years as the "not who she really is" tired working mother that just needs to rest, and that "Shabbos is just a day away." And so I kept insisting to myself that what ailed our relationship was always "just temporary." Meanwhile the years flew by.

I sorely suffered a lack of sleep, withheld to rehash endless nights of nasty comments spewed by my wife as we both took refuge on our lonely king-size-bed islands. My wife would eventually fall asleep during a lull of frozen silence and I'd often wind up spending the remaining scant hours of desperately needed sleep staring out the huge dining room bay window watching the sun slowly rise, while my heart raced, as I contemplated the "D" word, balanced against the love that restrained me to endure and persevere for the sake of my children. But eventually, sheer logic forced me to finally conclude that, like God's invention of death and disease, there was no explanation.

There never had been. Other than my realization that how could my marriage have been anything but a rocky one? After all, I had been married to a living lithopedion wife.

I realized that the circular logic, shameless boldfaced lies, and endless manipulations would never end. Like the out-of-left-field screaming at me in front of my shocked kids for adding salt to watery Dachau-diet-chicken soup during a Friday night Sabbath meal, as my wife insisted that skimping on a five-dollar bag of the main ingredient (chicken bones) was her way of "saving money." I looked up and queried, "If you're so worried about my blood pressure why don't you scream a little louder?" At least she wasn't throwing plates.

My wife's sudden outbursts had me on constant red alert; her seething anger at my forgetting to "save the receipt!" for a three-dollar purchase, whereas I calmly responded with, "Don't worry, there's more where that came from," when my airhead wife tossed seven-thousand-dollars in cash into the mailbox. I had asked her to watch the envelope while I went out for a long jog. My wife could alternate between being brilliant and dimwitted as quickly as the flashing of a short-circuited bulb. Fortunately for me her automaton side displayed itself during our divorce, which served me well. Mrs. Hyde had always been unable to read me.

My wife's faulty wiring mostly revealed itself by her total incompetence at reading my body language or hearing the cadence and rhythm of my voice, which supposedly accounts for ninety percent of all communication, whenever we spoke. She really didn't "hear a word" of anything I ever said. For three decades.

Forget about "going in one ear and out the other." My wife's apathetic brain was more like a simple abacus compared to the AI ability of a normal sentient emotional psyche that is capable of discerning subtle nuances in facial expressions and voice patterns. Mrs. Hyde was the same way when it came to sex. Mechanical. Just slide her arm to the right, move the bottom disc over a bit to the left ... but sadly, the results always equaled the frustrating sum of zero.

More painful than any of the above was that when my hand reached for hers, she nastily pulled it away whenever she was "annoyed" at me. Knowing I loved holding hands as much as I loved pussy, yanking her hand from mine was the biggest "Fuck you!" of all. I could live with a sexless marriage, but not holding hands is surely grounds for divorce in my book.

My wife remembered how romantic I had been upon our becoming engaged. And she knew how to manipulate any intimate emotion that I shared with her to control me at a later date. I took a wide antique 18K yellow gold wedding band that I purchased in an estate and had it sawed into two separate wedding bands. I then had them polished and seized to fit our ring fingers. After our wedding ceremony, in a tearful declaration of my eternal love, I lovingly slipped her band onto her ring finger and assured my Vybie that the original band would always remain "one" because we would hold hands forever.

Little did I imagine that those beautiful wedding bands would morph into a pair of fucking chromium handcuffs that would clasp my wrists more tightly with every cherub that the stork delivered for the next twenty-five years!

And it wasn't the bitching, whining, or nagging that I am complaining about. I understand that women like to get things done. It was the endless list of contradictions that I was constantly being rushed to deal with simultaneously, and somehow complete, that exhausted me while giving me anxiety. I'd receive a directive such as, "Zev we have to save more," while brazenly lying to me about how little savings we had, and in the next breath insist that the family really "needs" to take a vacation (a twenty-thousand-dollar trip to Israel). And I could live a life of "Yes, Dear," but not when I was yelled at upon returning home as to why I had "allowed" the trip.

My wife had me hopping. And running. And somersaulting. She'd suddenly decide that I should be home more often during the evening like so and so. "You learn enough, Ze'ev!" Or she'd insist that I work harder because I should have been as wealthy as so and so — who recently had a stroke. And why wasn't I a scholar on the level of Rabbi Nekritz, who literally studied a minimum of ten hours a day his entire life upon being born into Talmudical Royalty (besides his being a genius)? Like the dancing plague described by Paracelsus, my *Vybie* had me constantly dancing maniacally at three weddings simultaneously. And once again, trying to take on more personalities than the "Three Faces of Eve," I was the ten-year-old little boy trying to impress a wire-monkey female so that she'd love me.

I'd even be screamed at for arriving home too close to the start of Shabbat on Friday night, and its possible desecration, and be accused of being a "terrible example to our children." "You should be home a full hour before I light candles!" my righteous wife would snap. This precautionary sagacious counsel from a lunatic who would one day call the police on Shabbat morning without the slightest hesitation at desecrating the holiest of days (the Sabbath is even more holy than Yom Kippur) while lying profusely about a "dangerous!" man that she constantly called "the nicest guy in the world."

I don't believe my wife is "evil" or some kind of straying sinner. Biblical exhortations are, far too often, shallow and crude ancient descriptions attempting to define the almost endless depth of the human psyche. My wife has done far too many wonderful things to be branded with such a simple label. Six pregnancies and thirty years in an operating room is quite a resume for an *Eishet Chayil*. But what good is icing on a cake that consists of spiritually stale non-kosher half-baked (as in "crazy") crumbs?

A woman, even a scorned one, eventually tires. They realize they got carried away, and they eventually calm down. A little yelling here. A bit of revenge there. Maybe even a slap in the face. But the fiery anger fizzles out. I was ready to take quite a few punches and even a kick in the balls without striking back. I'm an ardent believer in much of the wisdom attributed to Confucius who is credited with having stated, "Before you embark on a journey of revenge, dig two graves."

My intention was to back away and move on. I had hoped to remain friends with my wife post-divorce. With five children, and two grandchildren, I figured we would amicably continue to play "house" together for their sake — even if it was from two different locations. But like a fire ant mechanically ripping its enemy to shreds, my wife grabbed onto me with her mandible-emails and instantly began to suck the life out of me the moment she was handed my motion for divorce by the female process server that knocked on our door as I was leaving with Ester to drive her to school that morning.

I had no idea of how destructive my ninety-pound wife could be, as the fallout of the detonation, sparked upon the simple handoff exchange of a piece of paper from the process server to the hand of my wife, erupted into an Armageddon Divorce as WWIII began in the foyer of my home that served as ground zero.

ESTHER ZARRA

Jewelry on the Internet: Rocks in a Hard Place

Jun 1, 2001 3:22 PM By Monica Toriello

Ice.com may never become an e-tailing giant, but companies like it — nimble, committed, focused on business basics — stand a good chance of being around for the long haul. CyberDiamond.com and Buyarock.com are two other companies that have proceeded with caution, quietly watching from the sidelines and learning from the mistakes of others. CyberDiamond's CEO Zev Lewinson has been tinkering with the site for two years.

"Those e-tailers that went belly-up so quickly were stock market fantasies," Lewinson asserted. "Their goal was basically a quick IPO, and not catering to the consumer. We never felt the need to run with the pack. We are in business because we don't live beyond our budget." Lewinson has raised close to $300,000 from private investors and is looking to raise another $500,000.

How does one explain the actions of such a diabolical mind? Revenge? Anger? Would those answers justify such a vicious and relentless assault against a man, with whom one peacefully raised five children for almost three decades, merely because he finally filed for divorce to escape a marriage in which he found himself depressingly miserable?

What normal woman spends a quarter of a million dollars to inflict actual incarceration based upon fictional accusations and then files perjured criminal charges of sexual assault and "threatened wrathful violence" against a man she previously called "the nicest guy in the world." *Are you out of your fucking sheitel-covered mind!*

Does anger justify trying to incarcerate an innocent husband, that you gave your password to, as a criminal for computer hacking? Is revenge a reason for taking out false protection orders and labeling the father of your children as a child molester who spends time "under the covers" with his own daughters? Whose fucking Da'as Torah did you follow, Mrs. Sharen Hyde, while torturing me for four months in family court where I embarrassingly sat as "the defendant" with a yarmulke on my head while being forced to endure a trial that could have resulted in my being labeled a sexual predator for life?

Does having to pay a little maintenance justify using our daughters to verbally assault Rabbi Nekritz, a world-renowned scholar, mentor, and family friend for thirty years as "a piece of shit" in front of his wife and neighbors? And what purpose did it serve to slam the door in the face of the process server that delivered the motion for divorce papers? I accepted over a half-dozen false protection orders and four summonses for criminal and familial complaints, all obtained through perjury, and gently closed the door after I dejectedly signed the receipts. How's that for flawless *Middot*?

What are the words that could possibly defend the behavior of a Jewish Orthodox wife and justify her serial email assault while spending a quarter of a million dollars to maliciously prosecute my existence through three court systems, while spreading false gossip that I'm a pedophile who comments on the development and maturation of his daughter's body through an immature rhyme of "Esty's breasties?" How does your brain even create such insane prose?

And so I ask my wife, "Into how many grisly bloody pieces can you hack our family to death because I filed for a simple divorce that would have resulted in your paying some maintenance, Sharen?! And why am I even asking? There I go again! I'm talking to a wall of ice.

And the only reason my wife stopped her assault was because she ran out of funds. It wasn't because she ran out of energy to incessantly repeat and invent more fantastical accusations. My wife will forever remain on fire with the same degree temperature as the day she slammed the door in the face of that polite, cute woman that served her my Notice for Divorce. I don't remember her name, but she certainly had a sense of humor as she texted: *8:05 Just delivered motion of divorce to your crazy bitch. Good luck!*

Society allows anyone who can drive a car and hold a job while paying their bills and taxes to be automatically labeled as "normal." Meanwhile the police, prosecutors, neuroscientists, secret government agencies, historians and the media are busy spending our tax dollars as they try to define the motives (as if they are dealing with rational minds) of serial killers and despots who commit gruesome atrocities and world wars with the same thrill and impartiality as a four-year-old licking an ice cream cone. They are only starting to realize that there is no real "motive" in the normal sense of the term. There is no true "justice being served." And there is no revenge or closure. *There is only emptiness.*

In hindsight, I realize that I didn't divorce my wife because of any one thing, or dozens of things, that she did. I kept forgiving the outbursts, lies, flip-flop promises, manipulations, and constant insults about my being "so creative" and entrepreneurial. I was "lucky in business" when I achieved success and a "harebrained bamboozler" when the internet craze imploded or when Wall Street devoured the mortgage industry.

Meanwhile my wife loved the fact that I was Mr. Mom to Ester, and she would occasionally thank me for patiently doing homework with her and for taking such good care of her. And so I stayed positive and I often smiled within at my wife's quirky lunacies. Like when she got caught pilfering plastic cutlery at her hospital. I treated her as patiently as I treated my children. I simply saw her as rushed and ditzy. And cute.

And that is why it took me years to follow through after repetitively explaining that I could not go on this way. I finally divorced my wife, not because of what she did, but because of what she *didn't do*. I divorced my wife because of her lacking emotion. Sincere emotion. Humanity. Warmth. Empathy.

I divorced my wife because I realized she didn't love me.

I realized she couldn't love me. But she sure could hate me. I honestly believe it's not her fault. Sharen's love was never anything more than an illusion. She had been mimicking love since I first held her in that stairwell in Manhattan. Her inability to love revealed itself mostly during intimacy. There was a mechanical klutziness about her. There was never any bonding between us. I was never emotionally attached to her. And I didn't understand why. Because I didn't know how to listen to my heart. I never missed her when we were apart. I now understand that there was no one to miss.

I tried to love my wife, but I now realize I chose her as nothing more than a business partner to raise a nice Jewish family. If I had really loved her, I would never have sought out anyone's "Da'as Torah" but my own. And yet, I liked being married. I loved raising children. I loved watching her nurse them. And that's what kept our dead marriage half-alive — like a fish out of water — for so long.

And like a fish out of water that is slowly suffocating and dying, yet furiously jumping around while gasping for air, my morbid marriage seemed full of life because I was so busy raising five children. Throw in Shabbat and a bunch of warm Jewish holidays (almost a hundred days a year) and things look very beautiful from the outside looking in.

I thought long and hard for fifteen years before finally admitting that I had no other choice than to end my marriage. It was literally a "divorce or die" decision. I still liked my robotic wife (I like technology — when it doesn't overtake your life) and I would have maintained a friendship for the sake of our children even post-divorce. But the synapses in her brain instantly insisted that she needed to destroy the stranger she could no longer manipulate and control the second he served her papers. In short, faulty wiring short-circuited my marriage of twenty-eight years.

And what better or more solid evidence do I need to prove that I made the correct decision than my wife's own behavior and actions, that shouted louder than the words she'd scream whenever exhibiting her narcissistic rage, upon my finally filing for divorce? Who would self-destruct their own life but a fire-ant that continues to build a colony even as it is being roasted alive, engulfed in flames, and yet totally able to ignore the incineration of its robotic-like exoskeleton body? The instincts of an ant have no "off" button. Neither does my wife.

I always felt that human behavior falls into three categories. Good. Evil. Eccentric. But there are a billion shades in each category. And that is why it is so difficult to judge people. Appraising a human takes much more than a loupe. Or a nasty Yenta's opinion. Or even an electronic microscope staring at soulless synapses. You must look very closely. Like a great detective or meticulous Talmudical research scholar you need exhaustive patience and a discerning eye. And having their password is a huge eye-opener. Above all, you need to suffer.

First impressions are lasting. And staring into a gorgeous pair of dark-blue eyes can be very misleading. Especially when you're only in your twenties. My wife has the immediate charm and warmth of a fairytale medieval castle seen from the distance. But try buying one, renovating the entire ancient structure, and then living in it. You'll quickly understand why it stood cold and empty for several centuries. Nobody's home.

Beauty really is only skin deep. The character of a person, their moral foundation and empathetic heart, reveals so much more. You really do have to live with someone merely to even begin to understand who they are. And even then, you can be easily manipulated. Their actions will speak to you loud and clear. Unfortunately, "deaf" and deluded victims of abuse are typically emotionally exhausted, which leads to their ignoring the thunder of merciless actions while groping and searching to rationalize the behavior of their abusers.

They'll blame themselves till they run out of excuses trying to define the impossible. "Evil" is a desperate misguided spiritual word that has no intrinsic meaning or value. It's a completely subjective term. Insanity can never be explained as logical behavior. No amount of words will ever explain heartless and mindless cruelty.

A normal person does not behead a wife who burns their dinner. A wife who instantly concocts, upon being served divorce papers, that her Mr. Mom husband of twenty-eight years is a pedophile full of "wrath" who is obsessed with feces, as she races to obtain protection orders that scream his need to STAY AWAY FROM MINOR CHILD is not evil. Neither is her Orthodox Jewish lawyer or the lunatic judge that mendaciously joined the fray. It is impossible to make sense out of that which is senseless. And exhausting oneself while trying to logically define screwy brain tissue will cause one to go out of their own mind — or to finally file for divorce.

Trust me, upon divorcing them (or merely trying to), abusers will rapidly reveal themselves as they double-down on their torture techniques. I don't know precisely how, but I've experienced enough manipulation to know that for some strange reason it's all about control.

It seems that those who get furiously angry and constantly "annoyed" with you (quite the opposite of those who are enlightened, free, and unattached to any drama) are the most likely to violently control you. And emotionless cyborgs who lack empathy and are disinterested in politics, world news, or global warming — or anything that doesn't insert itself into their personal sphere and "all about me" infantile focus — go berserk when they sense they are losing control.

What is more controlling than a Protection Order steel wall placed between you and the young minor daughter you love? At least you can speak with your child when standing behind a steel wall. What is more violent and embarrassing than two fully armed policemen coming, sirens blazing, to remove you from your own home sweet home in front of your little girl and all your prying nosey neighbors on your holy Day of Rest?

Actions, especially cruel ones, speak louder than words. Our hearts tell us when someone's actions are wrong. Not listening can result in a heart attack. At first the heart whispers, then it talks, and finally it screams. I waited till my heart shrieked its fucking aorta off. Someone up there must really love me. I'm still trying to figure out who.

The Talmud says there are three actions by which a person reveals himself and can easily be judged. They rhyme in Aramaic. *Kah'so. Key'so. Koh'so.* Translated into English they are: *Anger. Wallet. Cup*. How easily one is angered, how stingy or charitable they are with money, and how they behave when having one too many drinks, are the three self-revelatory means by which a person is unmasked as they instantly share with the world the type of individual they really are. One lie rots a thousand truths. One bite erases a thousand kisses. One Yenta-word besmirches the fine reputation of a phenomenal father, teacher, and scholar.

I can easily add a fourth rhyming Aramaic word to the above Talmudical dictum. *Keh'risus. Divorce*. How spouses treat each other, as they wind down their marriage, speaks volumes about a parting couple. It's too bad I couldn't divorce my wife before I agreed to marry her.

And so, to the Dr. Jekyll split-personality side of the sweet, cute wife I once loved, whose Mrs. Hyde alter-ego side never allowed me to have the closure of even saying a simple "Goodbye" after twenty-eight years of intimacy, and who will never allow me to speak to her for eternity, I sincerely address these final parting words:

Dear Sharen,

I'm sorry I had no choice but to divorce you. It would have been so wonderful and picturesque to watch our many grandchildren playing on our backyard lawn as we held hands sitting on rocking chairs as we grew old together, like the characters Beverly and Wilbur that I created in *The Hippo That Flew* (2010, etc.). But I now easily comprehend the anxiety my heart felt thirty-five years ago. We were obviously never *bashert*.

I honestly tried to love you. I never had to do that with any of the other women I dated. But I chose to marry you "by the book." You were the one time I decided to use my brain instead of my penis in a relationship. After all, I was making a very important decision: *Who would make the best mother for our future progeny?* And so, checking off the squares of "The Perfect Wife" list, you passed the test with flying colors. But that punch-list never contained a tiny box that listed the trait of "normal."

I believed I was being introspective and rational when I agreed that "nothing was gonna change" if I married you. You were more adorable than the four-year-old kindergarteners who instructed me to just sit and hold my toy cup as they poured my imaginary tea. I hesitated but listened to everyone's opinion that I had found the flawless version of what a man looks for in a wife. (The opposite of my mother.) I convinced myself that I was happy, but in truth I was an emotional cripple resting on the brittle foundation of an adverse childhood despite my ability to effortlessly jog over fifty miles of highway asphalt and mountainous trails a week from Parsippany, through Short Hills, Livingston, and West Orange.

I believed I was being flawlessly logical. I weighed all the pros and cons a thousand times while jogging, and you looked great on paper, Sharen. How was I to imagine that the paper would one day morph into multiple Orders of Protection? But in truth, like so many women entering their third decade of existence, my biological cock (no typo there) was ticking. I was painfully throbbing for the family I never had.

As when I played "house" with those adorable preschoolers back in kindergarten, I wanted to start a family with the cutest Barnard graduate I ever met. How was I to know that I was still playing nothing more than "make-believe?" When I shared with you how much I love children and that I wanted to have as many as possible, you sweetly smiled while flashing your baby blues as you coyly whispered that you agreed. That was all I needed to hear.

Amazingly enough, you delivered. Literally. Although lazy and almost frigid in bed, you were an Amazon female-warrior in the delivery room. You were the equivalent of a ninety-pound Russian peasant birthing baby after beautiful baby, despite multiple C-sections, for a straight decade, while fearlessly wielding your scalpel harvesting vein in the O.R. fields — which gave me the willpower to stay married to you for a second decade to raise our half-minyan of righteous children long after I subliminally inferred, but refused to acknowledge, that our marriage was over.

I once believed we'd be holding hands and taking slow walks together in our nineties (or at least late eighties for me). But you compelled me to use my loupe. Doing so exposed that you are flawed and ill. Your public persona on a shallow level is a flawless affectation of decorous well-mannered civility that masks your volcanic temper and camouflages how explosively unstable you sadly are. But your emails are a dead giveaway.

Your exterior personality makes quite an adorable first impression. But at best, your Jewish Orthodox devotion, Ivy League education, and poised personality are nothing more than a pastiche imitation mimicking the heroines that our society admires. You also mimic emotions. That's how you get away with so much sin. I use the word "sin" in a religious sense because of my background. But that connotes the ability to discern right from wrong. Free will. Which I honestly don't believe you have.

You're nothing more than a mindless, controlling, manipulative and delusional narcissist. You were perfectly created and flawlessly programmed for our scandalous systemically-diseased criminal and divorce court system's financial gain. Like a plague sent from God, your self-existence makes no sense. You don't like to do anything but shop for organizers. You don't even like to read. Or even sleep! You keep moving. Drive. Work. Shop. Call Jodie. Shut down. Boot up. Eat. Have babies. You even run in and race out of the bathroom to move your bowels. Drive. Work. Shop. Call Vittie. Eat. Shut down. You are a whirring robotic machine.

When we first married, I was convinced that you were a flawless diamond. In truth, the only thing you and a diamond share is that you are hard. Ruthless, in fact. My mind was too rushed to notice how empty my "feelings" felt about you. I should have gone deeper, and I take ownership for allowing myself to be manipulated as I ignored my anxious emotions that kept warning me to take a little more time. Time that would have led to more introspection and our eventual breaking up thirty-five years ago. Just like I broke up with you forty years ago when you raced to marry Dr. Leon Gilner on the rebound.

I saw stars when I met you the second time around, Sharen, but the heavenly effulgent display was never anything more than illusionary fireworks consisting of suffocating potassium nitrate and sulfur — a shallow pleasure of momentary childish entertainment that in reality was nothing more than deceptive wizardry that caused me to choke and anxiously gasp for air the closer I got to its asphyxiating source. I was now more religious and dating to find a wife, and you were definitely "the perfect wife" material.

A brilliant Yiddish proverb comes to mind as I now look back at how meticulously logical I tried to be upon choosing an eternal wife: *"Der mentsch tracht un Gott lacht."* (A man thinks, as he plans and calculates, while God laughs). Ha-ha. Que será, será.

You are obviously not the inspiring young muse I held in my arms in a Manhattan stairwell the first time we kissed more than forty years ago. And the record of our divorce, piled high in the basement of the Rockland County Courthouse, clearly proves "she" never existed. That stack of evidence certainly appraises the "real" you better than any GIA gemologist looking through a microscope ever could. A detective would marvel at the trove of evidence he had stumbled upon.

But if a gemologist were to appraise our personalities, your certificate would unfortunately read: Internally Flawed/Amoral Drama Queen. Mine would probably read: Romantic Schmuck/ Loving Father. The little note that the gemologists sometimes insert into the plastic sleeve holding the certificate, to advise diamond cutters with an added illustration and diagram along with instructions as to how they might further recut and polish their stones, would read as follows for both of our personas: Needs Improvement.

The improvement I need would probably advise me to be a tad less "creative" and a bit more practical in life. It would most likely be of an entrepreneurial nature, cautioning me to hoard a larger stash of money before launching a brilliant online diamond or streamlined internet mortgage business. Or upon filing for divorce. And the advice would certainly admonish me to assess the full risks that a new venture might encounter upon my enthusiastically rushing to market ahead of my dazed competition and leaving eventual large unpaid lines of credit at the bank as the Chapter 7 collateral damage fallout of my well intentioned, admittedly underfunded, ideas.

Somehow, I should have foreseen terrorists purchasing a one-way first-class ticket and flying into the Twin Towers that would burst the internet bubble while blasting our economy and three-thousand lives to shreds.

On the other hand, those giving me cautionary advice most likely never earned a hundred-thousand-dollars inside of one month, as clients dropped in almost magically, like manna from the sky, from a new dimension called cyberspace.

It's hard to ignore experienced investors lining up to give you hundreds of thousands of dollars and blank checks while *The Rapaport Report* is interviewing you about your company and the top family-owned jeweler in New York ("since 1910") is negotiating with you and almost begging permission to print CyberDiamond.Com on their front glass doors, just beneath their "H.L. Gross & Bro." golden-lettered signage as your brick-and-mortar partner. Would you care for one of the over one thousand bottles of jewelry cleaner labeled *CyberDiamond.Com* that still sits in their basement? Do you really believe it was all "just a fluke," Sharen? Or was our "Bashert" marriage the "fluke?"

"Hope for the best, prepare for the worst," has always been my positive mantra in my entrepreneurial endeavors. Yet, I do admit that there's room for improvement in my perhaps too-positive outlook of seeing a glass with negligible condensation as overflowing.

And while I admit to being, financially speaking, a bit unchaste by nature, I rejoice that I wasn't the one God chose to create as a "Mad Hatter" deranged cute lunatic disguised in a sheitel and oversized green surgical scrubs wearing binocular loupes.

Psychiatric hit-or-miss care is still mostly the Wild West, and not yet subject to any trial-and-error lab evaluation that could immediately improve the lives of those who suffer from certain mental ailments. True success stories are rare. "Management" is still the most efficient method of "healing" most minds at present. And hallucinogens and psychedelic drugs are only now being discovered as an amazing alternative to treat anxiety. *Maybe I'll try a few mushrooms for my PTSD.*

We've barely inched forward from the great minds of thinkers like Aristotle who labeled mental illness as "badness of spirit." Biology is still pretty much a stranger to psychiatry, where too many lunatics who are Board Certified (i.e. basically achieved through submitting three letters of recommendation and two passport-size photographs, along with being no less ethical than Dominic Ferro) are certifiably mad themselves. Perhaps not as strange as the relationship I had with you, but at least as distant as that of a prostitute and Hasid.

The improvement your brain warrants, Sharen, is beyond the ability of the common man, husband, or two-bit court-appointed bottom-feeder pathological forensic psychiatrist to fathom. It would take the painstaking research and medical talents of the best neurological scientists in the world (an army of geniuses like Leah Krubitzer and Robert Sapolsky) to describe your issues. I am not a scientist, but I'd be happy to provide them with a voluminous cache of research material toward their being awarded a Nobel prize on the subject of insanity. Tatie5521.

What did I ever do ... or even say to you during our entire twenty-eight-year marriage that could elicit such cruel and cold-hearted wanton behavior from an earthly yet-alien life-form with a beating heart? Who are you? What fucking specie are you, Sharen? Are you truly human? You said so many hurtful, debasing, and ugly things to me during our marriage and divorce. I never responded in kind.

And then, for the "sin" of finally seeking my freedom, you demolished my reputation and almost destroyed my life. Together with Alfieri and Schwartz, you metastasized into a group of cold-blooded child traffickers, trading away the most important years of my innocent daughter's life while raping her away from her father. Had I not recalled your ten-year-old password you would have torpedoed me out of existence.

You enlisted a gang of bestial oinking Mariner Way Yentas, family members, paid-off rabbi's, and overpaid lowlife lawyers to stress-whip a kind and gentle father with a frenzy of merciless inhumanity. You insulted one of the greatest Talmudical scholars of the century. You repeatedly desecrated the Sabbath along with destroying our daughters' chances of getting married to anyone half-normal one day.

Like a pit bull, you dug your teeth deep into my reputation upon my filing for divorce and refused to release my good name for almost three full years. Beating you off and blunting your yenta-fangs by exposing your emails and true nature, barely slowed you down to take a breather as you continued to destroy my name and Ester's life.

You are almost a twin sister to Lawerence Ray, who is now being charged with the incredibly bizarre extortion and sex trafficking of his daughter's Sarah Lawrence College roommates. Like you, he was a master manipulator for years. As crafty as he is deranged. I shuddered when I read "your" psychological profile of his personality in the *New York Times* and *New York* magazine. My eyes surely looked like flying saucers as they slowly scanned line after line of your brain matter described in pixels of ink.

New York magazine quotes a psychological evaluation submitted to the court during Ray's own divorce that characterized Ray as "literally impossible to evaluate" because he "is able to manipulate and control almost any situation in which he finds himself, including a psychological interview with a forensic examiner, no matter how experienced that examiner may be. Mr. Ray is very good at what he does." Big surprise.

The report further explained that Mr. Ray "can be utterly charming and one can be disarmed by his childlike simplicity and smile. But Mr. Ray is no child; he is a calculating, manipulative, and hostile man." If that doesn't describe you perfectly Sharen, what does?

So much money, time, and energy wasted in an almost fanatical Crusade to avoid paying a paltry amount of maintenance. And like many of the crusaders that sought riches and plunder, you wound up going bankrupt. Great lesson for Ester to learn about honesty, empathy, and compassion.

The Talmud calls evil gossipmongers "dead" even while they are living because their words wreak havoc and death. You are the living dead, Sharen. I see maggots crawling out of your hazel-blue staring dead eyes.

Like the biblical spies who maliciously gossiped while scouting out the Land of Milk and Honey, I easily visualize the Talmud's gruesome graphic description of their punishment as they were choked to death by hordes of worms and swarms of insects representing their tale-bearing words, that crawled out of their throats and marched into their navels (the umbilical source of life) and again out of their mouths, suffocating them to death, as God quaintly illustrated how "deadly" words (and emails) can be. You had better drink some insecticide, or inhale some Zyklon-B gas, quickly!

I see your verbal-insects as they continue their march-of-death trail, as they slither into your cute reshaped "outie" belly button and then pour out the throat of your open-mouthed corpse as they exit. I see you choking to death, gasping for air, while trying to grab your inhalers, as you still try to scream, "Obsessed with feces! I fear his wrath! Esti's breasties! Under the covers!" You are the poster-girl of evil speech (Lashon Hara), the epitome of those who craftily create and manufacture evil-intentioned, manipulative false gossip. And what did you even gain after all was said and done?

You are a modern-day version of Haman, the evil antagonist in The Book of Ester, described in the Talmud as the most oratorically gifted "Master of Lashon Hara" that ever lived.

Haman, the Prime Minister of the mighty Persian Empire around the year 357 BCE, and the second most powerful man on the planet at that time, was hung (literally) by his own words, and surely emails had the internet been invented, spoken against a very loyal Jewish citizenship and their spiritual leader Mordecai. In the original version of Hitler's future *Final Solution*, SS Officer Haman was plotting the complete annihilation of the entire Jewish race, and he would have been successful if not for the heroic efforts of Queen Ester. And like Haman and the Nazis, you also deemed that this Jew was "unworthy of life," as you attempted to exterminate any memory of the man you orgasmed for during the three decades that you bore and raised five children with him.

Words from which there was absolutely nothing to gain cost Haman his life and the lives of his ten wicked sons, along with the loss of what he valued most — his breathtaking wealth. *It's all about control.* And the old Jewish scholar, who Haman was so desperate to frame and execute as a traitor, was appointed as the new Grand Vizier the moment Haman was executed. Mordechai instantly inherited the entire estates of Haman and his ten politically powerful protege sons.

Two and a half millenniums have passed and Ester is still revered as the beautiful Queen who ruled with wisdom and integrity when Persia was the greatest empire of the entire ancient world. Mordechai and Ester are still national heroes, buried and honored in modern-day Iran.

It is nothing short of miraculous that pilgrims of all religious backgrounds (Muslim, Jewish and Christian) pray alongside each other at the Islamic Shrine, in a country whose leaders finance terrorism and still refuse to even recognize Israel's right to exist, where women place colorful cloths on the tombs of the Jewish saints as they pray for righteous children — who hopefully won't start killing each other when they grow up.

You are a twin to the serpent in the Garden of Eden who caused the downfall of mankind by committing the sin of evil speech. According to the Midrash the snake was originally a beautiful biped that could even speak. He ruled the animal kingdom but set his jealous eyes upon the most beautiful woman who ever lived, the gorgeous Mother Eve, and his plan was to cleverly cause the death of Adam, leaving Eve for himself to take as a wife. The Midrash goes so far as to say that the original serpent cleverly seduced Eve and slept with her. God punished the serpent by declaring: "On your belly you shall crawl (Genesis 3:14)." The Almighty instantly eliminated the snake's arms and legs, making him the lowest ranking member of the animal kingdom. To this day Orthodox Jews believe that snakes slither because of their ancestor's original sin. God also removed their power of speech. I now understand why you always moved like a quadriplegic in bed.

"Zev is destroying me!" you foamed at the mouth as you cried to every Yenta, Rabbi, and neighbor in town. But you found the time to waste almost three years of your life tormenting the man who gave you love, respect, a small mansion, and lots of money and jewelry during the first seventeen years of our marriage — along with five beautiful children raised by the husband you accoladed as the best Mr. Mom in the world.

By the way, Ester's wonderful principal, Mrs. Zaks, agrees with you about what a wonderful father I was. She told me how you shamelessly sent our own daughters to beg that she rescind the beautiful letter she and her husband wrote on my behalf to the court when they heard about your pernicious protection orders. She berated our girls and sent them scurrying back to mama rat.

As the refined exceptional educators of over five hundred students at their Ultra-Orthodox all-girls school, they broke their own cardinal rule of never getting involved in the details of divorcing school parents and insisted on writing a letter on my behalf to Judge Alfieri because they knew me so well and were outraged at the way you lied about me.

Like the Director of the 1984 Orwellian Ministry of Truth, you wanted to erase any possible documentation that a researching historian might one day possibly discover that described your ex-husband as the wonderful parent and father that he had always been. First Lonna, and then Mrs. Zaks. You are an ogre with beautiful eyes, Ms. Haman.

And while we're on the subject of history, I'll share a little footnote with you. The Zak's were incensed at what you were doing to me. Their original first-draft letter not only described me as an incredible and loving parent, but also psychoanalyzed you flawlessly. They emailed the letter and asked me to review it along with granting my final permission before they printed it out and signed a final draft on their Bais Yakov Chofetz Chaim (BYCC) stationery.

Believe it or not (and they were quite surprised), I asked them to leave out their completely accurate, very negative description of your cold non-maternal Mrs. Hyde personality as they described me as the primary caregiver and loving father that Ester happily ran to greet for almost a decade when I picked her up after school. They also called you a manipulator and shameless liar.

"I don't want Ester to read this," I explained to her shocked educators. Ester was only eleven years old at the time and believed that I'm "killing" you because you had to pay the mortgage. I knew how she was awestruck by Rabbi and Mrs. Zaks and that it would serve me well for her to see what her "other parents" thought about Mommy and Tatie. But I wanted Ester to have at least one parent. At eleven years old even a crazy parent is better than no parent at all. Trust me. I know. I decided to edit their letter, leaving out much of their flawless description of your perverse, warped personality. The final one, submitted to the court on BYCC stationary, was the merciful version edited by your husband.

"I can't afford it!" you protested to Alfieri upon his insistence that you pay the temporary maintenance he ordered. But you could afford a legal tab of $250-thousand dollars. We both know our divorce was never about what you could afford. Given your propensity for spreadsheets, receipt hoarding, and forensic accounting for eighty-cent Slurpee's, you obviously understood that you were paying Schwartz more than triple the amount that Alfieri was asking you to pay me.

You could have simply paid me the first month of temporary maintenance and I would have been completely out of the house. Clothes. Books. Weights. And even my leather heavy bag. I would have picked up my vast library collection at a later date. One month, Sharen. One measly month — Schwartz's weekly salary — and it wouldn't have been necessary "to toss Zev [me] out of the house."

But you preferred borrowing $80,000-dollars from your future inheritance money to pay a grotesque slob a small fortune in order to avoid paying me a red cent. And your insane family backed you up. Meanwhile for half the amount of what it cost you to bribe your canine Rabbi Schabes service dog, whose gossip-fangs were dripping my bloodied reputation as he constantly hounded Rabbi Nekritz, I would have gladly moved out.

But you kept me in the house, refusing to pay even one month of maintenance, so that you could self-destruct and make the most of the order of protection you fabricated to "protect" yourself and THE MINOR CHILD. The anxiety those three words trigger in my mind still sends me into mild shock. Loving bargains, you figured, "Why pay one month's maintenance when I can totally fuck him for free?" You called the police the very next day to throw me out of the house your way, celebrating the Sabbath the best way you knew how. By putting me through fucking Hell.

It was a brilliant cunning plan. After all, what's a little desecration of the Sabbath compared to saving $3,400 dollars for the next sixty months? And calling the police on Shabbos certainly "proved" that your life was in extreme danger. Everyone knows that an Orthodox Jewish woman would never pick up the phone on Shabbos unless her life was really in imminent peril. It's amazing how quickly you composed yourself after such a frantic "Come now!" call to the police as you delicately kissed the mezuzah and daintily stepped into the synagogue that morning.

I can only imagine how our neighbor's phones blew up on Mariner Way after the sun set that day. "Can you imagine! Her husband must be so violent! She was so scared of him that she called the police! On Shabbos!"

You weren't happy with Alfieri ordering you to pay $3,400.00 and instructing me to leave. You chose to follow Schwartz's compassionate email "long shot" instructions of "time to throw Zev out of the house" to a T. Your drama-driven life never ends. And your compelling authoritative need to control others was finally outmatched by your absolute adamant refusal to allow anyone (including Alfieri ordering you to pay some maintenance) to ever control you. You acted like a caged rat. It was truly a miracle that the police didn't take me away that morning.

I then gave you outrageous favorable offers early-on for an uncontested divorce if only to stop the pain and damage you were inflicting on Ester. I wanted to get her back on schedule. I was dying to see her and wanted those scathing iron-maiden piled-on protection orders removed so that I'd be allowed to drive her to school and be her Tatie again. I was even ready to accept half the maintenance the judge was ordering you to pay.

Boy was I in la-la-land. Your Sodomite lawyer was merely warming up as he turned around and outrageously demanded that I pay your full legal fees and that I should pay you maintenance. Although your tax returns screamed that you were the moneyed spouse, Alfieri took the time to burn up three months merely to entertain, and obviously deny, Schwartz's demented counteroffer. Kapo Schwartz constantly laughed with you in your sadistic love-letter emails, with the two of you gleefully imagining in exultant joy your sick desire of "if only we could see Zev's expression" when I read the counter offers. Ha-ha. My expression, by the way, was one of total disgust at having to deal with two sadistic Nazi barbarians.

You missed your calling in life, Sharen. You would have made a great drug lord. You are extremely well organized. You have a real knack for spread sheets. You have an almost savant ability to yank a needle from a haystack of "clutter." And you are as beguiling as you are ruthless and cruel. You respect absolutely no one, including God, and you completely lack empathy. You are also as cocky and fearless as you are manipulative and merciless.

Ensconced in a sheitel and ninety-pound frail body, you're the perfect example of a narcissistic sociopath, who are masters of manipulation and incredibly clever when it comes to convincing others to do their bidding. Like a narcissistic sociopath, you certainly love-bombed me at the start of our relationship. With endless attention and compliments, along with driving from Long Island to Parsippany every night, even if only to see me for a quickie, you insisted that you didn't mind the two-hour trip each way because you missed me so much (too bad you couldn't perform a quickie divorce). And I thought I was devoted to Rebbi Nekritz.

The only thing preventing you from assuming the title of the world's most famous drug lord, known as the ruthless "El Yenta," is love for your own "familia." Oh! One more thing. Be sure to use encryption to protect your emails if you ever do choose to embark on a career in the narco trade. The government will always have you under surveillance. Stop rushing. Just change your password every few weeks.

I have no question that when the FBI finally kicks in the door to one of your many "clutter-filled" safe-houses, which will surely be protected by a mezuzah, they'll find you sitting on your bed, chirping with your thin lying lips from your little prayer book. I can already hear you yelling at the men wearing reflective SWAT jackets, "I didn't do it! I didn't do it!"

Dostoevsky once wrote: "Nothing is easier than to denounce the evil doer; nothing more difficult than understanding him." Fyodor, in his literary-genius ability to psychoanalyze the impossible, is describing the helter-skelter mind of my wife dead-on. Just substitute the pronoun "her" in place of "him."

The reason it is so difficult to "understand" the evil doer is because there are no words of logic to describe their wildly senseless actions. The motives of a Hitler or Bundy can never be revealed because they never had any to uncover. Their existence defies logic and makes no sense. Period. Ted Bundy was as polite and charming as my wife. Several of Ted's college psychology professors wrote wonderful letters of recommendation to help Ted gain acceptance into law school. Like my wife, Ted absolutely loved psychology. He studied psychology before embarking on a law career. How can one understand a mind that is incomprehensible?

For two and a half years I dozed off listening to nearby wailing police sirens as my ears calculated if the patrol cars they were mounted on were approaching 19 Mariner Way. Thankful, as I heard their blare weaken as they faded into the distance, I tossed and turned as my mind raced, much slower than the speed at which you, in the bedroom above mine, typed out the next gauntlet you would force me to traverse.

And after a few hours of deprived by anxiety sleep, I'd groggily wake up, and my mind would instantly jump, forced once again into its fight or flight stress response as I wondered what nightmare your treachery-du-jour menu would serve up that day.

Mornings we'd meet with Alfieri always released dangerously high toxic dosages of severe dread and cortisol-induced stress symptoms. And meeting our daughter Sara in court to face charges of "being under the covers" and "threatening her with physical violence" still leaves me wondering to this day if the opposite fragrance of the Garden of Eden is the stench that surely must emanate from your mother's vagina. I'd pray for your soul, Sharen. But I'd be uttering God's name in vain (Exodus 20:7).

You have this urgent way of talking that makes it appear as if the world will come to an abrupt nuclear Armageddon end if your urgent pleas are not attended to the moment you turn on your deranged mind to destroy.

Eleven-year-old Ester is (suddenly) in danger! Twenty-year-old Sara (suddenly) found herself "under the covers" with her father who (suddenly) threatened to "mush her head!" Who came up with that childish "mush my head" accusation anyway? You? Or our learning-disabled child?

And the most horrifying scream of all, causing even my own hypocritical relatives to quickly turn their backs on me; "Zev won't go to Beit Din!" My refusal to attend a jerk-off circle of clowns had you screaming as if I was banging a prostitute on the parchment of a holy Torah scroll, open to the verse you will never comprehend: "Love Thy Neighbor as Thyself." (Leviticus 19:18). As I always told my Talmud honors class, "Look it up yourself. God rewards effort and he will store the memory of the verse in your brain." There are many beautiful commentaries explaining why the next three words in that verse read, "I am God." I'm sorry I'll never get to share them with you.

I don't want to imagine how much people must have feared me after you described how "violent" I am. No wonder they wouldn't even make eye contact with me when I saw them on the street. You fucking exhausted me, Sharen. A woman with zero positions in the bedroom attacked from angles that the world's fiercest warriors probably never imagined they could strike from. I can just imagine your MMA nickname as you'd climb into the octagon. "Sharen, the Mesuggeneh Yenta!" Kudos.

You, of all people, knew the exact results of how my being tasered could possibly have killed me or further damaged my already slightly-leaking valve when you emitted your, "Come now! He's dangerous!" Oscar-winning-cry into your cell phone that early Shabbat morning. You watched my blood spurt back into its chamber at Dr. Goldberg's office during a nuclear stress test I took a few years ago. I can still see you staring at the screen that showed some of the deoxygenated blood spurting right back into the mix of my freshly oxygenated blood. I can still hear how you gasped, "Wow!"

I also recall how calm, confident, and relaxed you looked the moment after you hung up the phone that Shabbat morning after you called the police. I'm pretty fearless for a "nice Jewish boy." But I must admit that the way you coldly stared at me, while smiling that Mona Lisa tight-lipped smile, scared the shit out of me. The sheer confidence displayed in your dark-blue eyes spoke volumes. You don't play. You calmly thought you had it all wrapped up as the police sped to our house, sirens blaring.

You have this instinctive knack in getting people to instantly jump based on whatever swirls and swooshes around the mildly rusted cogs and un-oiled gears of your brain and then exits your tiny mouth. You're just as effective when firing off email instructions to your Yenta assassins. You have this aura of believability about you. People call it confidence. I know it is nothing more than true insanity.

No one would have ever believed one word of this entire book had the memory bank hardware of your A.I. faulty-wired brain reminded you that you shared your Tatie5521 password with me ten years before you began your email assaults. You would have made minced meat out of me. Tender meat with clogged arteries. Because I already had experienced more than enough of your dramatic shenanigans for twenty-eight years.

For three years your mouth spewed whatever insane shit your batty brain came up with. Now I've taken three years to respond to your filth. I've taken the liberty to speak the truth and say what needed to be said. And that's the difference between us. You and your Yenta whores couldn't stop lying. I can't stop telling the truth.

And although some may feel that I'm completely out of control to reveal so many private and personal sexual aspects of our marriage; I know that I needed the therapy of journaling after the lengthy trauma you forced me to endure. I'm completely justified in revealing whatever needs to be exposed to explain how dangerous and truly mad you are.

That's what happens when you call a loving father of five, grandfather of two, a violent pedophile. You are the one who forced an empathetic teacher and a gentle writer of beautiful children's stories to undergo actual trials in criminal and family court to defend something more precious than his life. My reputation is priceless. You know I could never hit you. Be glad that I am only stabbing you with my pen. Like they say in the Mafia, "It's nothing personal. It's just the literary business."

Almost your entire sick family shares your acting DNA. I especially appreciate the dramatic way members of your venal family came and sat by you every time we met with Alfieri. Especially your harpy-face ugly sister, Elyce. She scares me more than Alfieri. The ingredients of beauty and cuteness that God denied her were sprinkled into your DNA strands. I guess God decided it somehow makes sense to reward you and Bundy with a face that automatically elicits trust and allows rapid manipulation and obliteration of unsuspecting prey.

One would have thought you were a victim of violent rape and that your loved ones came to encourage you and give their poor unfortunate sister emotional support, as you sat with curved hunched shoulders, intimidated by your violent husband who was full of "wrath." Where did you get that word from, by the way? No one says "wrath" anymore. You never even bothered accusing me of rape. That would have been too mild. You went right for my daughters.

You're quite a nasty piece of work. Actually, pitiful. You're as shameless as your sleazy lawyer. But then again, "shame" is one vocabulary word they obviously never taught you the definition of at Barnard. And "integrity" was obviously another word you missed during your Jewish Ethics class when you attended Bruriah High School for Girls in Elizabeth, NJ. But apparently they did teach you to always modestly kiss the mezuzah upon entering the synagogue. I'm sure God is so fucking impressed with your devotion and righteousness.

I tried to explain to several people, including my handicapped-by-laziness inept lawyer, Robert Lewis, what you were doing to Ester and what you were planning for me. I showed Robert the 3 A.M. emails of your horrific conversations with your 24/7 constantly agitated, obviously sexually frustrated (always overreacting negatively and substituting food as a stand-in for sex), sister-in-law Jodi Mailman and BFF bitch Vittie Blech. And I shared with Robert your late (too late as far as I am concerned) brother's vile advice to say I hit you, along with the wild trail of Vittie's snowballing conversations with her psychiatrist and your own eventual back-peddling. I also forwarded Robert Lewis the email trail to Hell of the wonderful "trusted" Rabbi Dr. Donny Frank to you, and between you and your malevolent siblings and porcine-faced Yentas.

I even included the diabolical emails composed by Shit-Schwartz and you, but my attorney was terrified to use them, not wanting to break your legally protected lawyer-client disclosure privilege. I'm the one who came up with the plan to personally take the blame for revealing the emails in my own submission to the court and to simply staple the emails to the back of Robert's next court submission. I couldn't even use everything I had. It was just too much shit!

Those emails clearly portrayed how deranged you are. Or perhaps how abstract God's mysterious ways are for subjecting someone as kind as me to someone as destructive as you. I should have immediately been granted sole custody of Ester, along with child support and maintenance within the first four to six months of my filing for divorce. And if the Honorable Kenneth Karas had been our judge I most certainly would have.

There are daily reported cases of SDDS (sudden divorce-death syndrome) for spouses who are in the throes of divorce. I think I just invented a new name for an old disease. And there are thousands of unsolved cases (and countless near-misses) involving dead spouses who posthumously "signed-over" the house and all the bank and retirement accounts, as they conveniently "slipped" in the shower, "fell" down the stairs, abruptly "went up in flames" in a house fire, or "accidentally" got run over while their spouse was "only backing out of the driveway" during the tribulations of divorce, as their final thoughts screamed, "*I can't believe it!*" Unlike SIDS, their death was a premeditated one.

As the gorgeous young mother of two, curled up into a fetal position while the pulsating blood gushed through the neck of her nearly decapitated head, Nicole Simpson's last thoughts before bleeding out surely must have been, "*I can't believe he's killing me ... my poor kids ....*" The loving mom had stated on record, "He's going to kill me. And he's going to get away with it." And now her words fit O.J. Simpson perfectly. Like a glove.

O.J. beat his wife for many years, constantly committing the atrocity called "wife-beating" that took legislators in the USA till the early part of the twentieth century (1920) to finally label as a crime. In what century will they finally label filing false Orders of Protection a crime? The Juice had threatened to kill Nicole many times, even warning her that he'd decapitate her ex-boyfriends. He kept his word.

And when the police came out to the home of Orenthal James Simpson, for the ninth time, after Nicole called while hiding in the bushes and crying to the dispatcher that "He's going to beat the shit out of me!" they weren't greeted by a blonde girl-next-door stunner who was merely acting hysterical because she feared that she was about to be pummeled by her panther-like husband.

What the adoring football fans wearing blue police uniforms found upon their arrival at the Simpson home was an already bruised and battered, black-and-blue Nicole, with a swollen face and welted defensive arms, who needed hospitalization — not a cunning brainsick Ultra-Orthodox method-actress in a sheitel (coached by a bloviating abhorrent divorce lawyer), whose elderly husband was quietly studying the Talmud on a peaceful Shabbat morning. I can only imagine what Nicole would have looked like had O.J. beaten "the shit" out of her. Completely decapitated, I suppose.

Simpson eventually pleaded no contest to spousal abuse in 1989 to avoid the honest prosecutors who wanted to send him to jail. A fucking idiot Municipal Judge named Ronald Schoenberg overruled and, in effect, murdered Nicole by placing O.J. in a program that treats men who batter their wives. Ronald then allowed The Juice to pick his own psychiatrist and receive counseling over the phone so as not to disrupt his wonderfully busy life running through airports while sharing with his fans to "let Hertz put you in the driver's seat." Forget about The Juice climbing into the driver's seat in a Hertz commercial. O.J. should have been strapped into the electric chair.

I guess Judge Schoenberg never felt what it's like to look at his bathroom mirror and stare at the red handprint of a powerful wide receiver embedded in his face. Nor would it have been that pleasant to witness puffy black and blue eyes as he'd make the observation. Schoenberg obviously felt no empathy upon seeing the panther beast's paw-handprint on the face of Mrs. Nicole Simpson. Her calling the police nine times in a panicked, frantic voice meant nothing to the stone-hearted Alfieri clone.

I wonder if the red-stained pavement crime scene photos portraying pools of Nicole's spilled blood finally moved Schoenberg when the young mother of two was found with her neck so severely slashed that both of her carotid arteries were sliced. If that's not control, what is? The blade had even cut into Nicole's cervical vertebrae. That takes a lot of strength. And *juice*. "The Juice," in fact, had morphed into "The Blood."

Simpson's assault wasn't merely deadly. It was angry. Wildly angry. The kind of seething narcissistic rage that I saw my wife display whenever she couldn't get her way. Or when she was served divorce papers. I think I'm gonna start wearing turtleneck sweaters year-round.

Nicole's legacy sparked a revolution in the immediate granting of protection orders upon request. It was a long overdue response. And sadly, one that evolved into a golden goose source of stealthy wealth through which divorce lawyers, judges, police, and the entire ancillary staff of our Family and Divorce Court septic system were now destined to gorge unimaginable fortunes through uncaring *In God We Trust* "So Ordered" directives. And through which adorable little princesses would no longer see their knight in shining armor Tatie's.

It certainly was way past time for society to listen to the screams of battered women. Unfortunately, the frozen pendulum that had been stuck to the right in a man's world, now swung to the extreme far left in the liberated woman's one. The weakest link, no matter which direction the pendulum swings, is the snapped and shredded lives of innocent children who become instant orphans. For their sake, and for the sake of their loving parents, I can only hope that society will one day learn how to tell time flawlessly. Like Gussie. Even in the middle of the darkest of divorcing nights.

Your obese brother David's email threats of violence written in white-trash vernacular never made me blink, Sharen. I'm not Nicole. I can take care of myself. But your fusion-like energy kept me wide-eyed whenever your ninety-pound pre-nubile body stood within ten feet of me. I never knew what you might stick into my back as we stood in our kitchen once those protection orders were in place. "He came at me ... and I was preparing a salad ...."

Meanwhile I often stood right next to your baby-ballerina body to reach for something I needed, as you stood at the refrigerator door searching for some condiment among your "organized clutter" of jars, never bothering so much as to move a drop out of my way even as I politely said, "excuse me." Silly me. I forgot that I no longer existed.

So much for your "fear of my wrath," though. I could have gently kissed your winsome beastie neck as we stood so close together. The policemen also understood how terrified you were of me that Shabbat morning when you called them to "Come now!" "But Ma'am, if you have a lock on your bedroom door, and you were so afraid, how was your husband able to burst through? Wasn't it locked?" "I forgot to lock it," you responded. PAY ATTENTION TO DETAIL.

Unlike my wife, her cousin, Shele Danishefsky Covlin, may she rest in peace, constantly feared that her husband Rod "very likely" might kill her. Like Nicole, Shele was terrified and prophetically forewarned her lawyer through her emails that Rod might murder her. And like Nicole, this blonde pretty mother of two young children became an emotional wreck knowing that her life was in constant danger.

And yet, even when Shele "slipped" and died in the bathtub the very night preceding the morning she was scheduled to see her lawyer to write her estranged husband out of her will, no one on record, including the lame detectives at the scene of the crime, believed that her soon-to-be-ex killed her. So much for Orders of Protection, by the way.

The coincidental dots were screaming bloody murder to be connected, but were wiped clean by the phrase, "It's all circumstantial evidence." "Everybody fights with their wife," the detectives rightfully declared, "Doesn't prove 'beyond a reasonable doubt' that he killed her."

The bungling "finest" instantly bought Rod's story and didn't even bother testing the crime scene for fingerprints. At twenty-five dollars an hour why would they? The Keystone cops did notice that Rod's clothes were miraculously dry after supposedly pulling his wife out of the bathtub, but they had been up all night and now had paperwork to do before getting some shut-eye. Why bother with more questions?

Shele's barbarian brutish spouse would have easily gotten away with murder while leaving Crime Scene Investigators the last staged Kodak-moment grisly photos that would ever be snapped of his naked beautiful wife — soaked in her own blood as she lay flopped on her bathroom floor at the side of her bathtub filled with orange-reddish water.

Shele was destined with never being remembered as anything more than another sad SDDS statistic. It was only Rod's own narcissistic arrogant and angry mouth that finally led to his being indicted and brought to trial. The black-belt raging golem-clod bragged, one time too many, about his ability to snap anyone's neck. When madmen make threats, they follow through. Detectives know their statistics. They know that once a predator reaches the point of wrapping his hands around the throat of a woman, he rarely releases his grip.

Patricia Swenson, a stranger Covlin met online (one of over a thousand women that investigators discovered that the murderer had reached out to for sex), testified that Rod told her that he wanted to kill his wife, or have her die "some other way." I suppose "slipping in the tub" after breaking her neck is the other way. Like my wife, Rod never imagined he'd be exposed. And once again, it was all so flagrantly obvious from the very start.

Another girlfriend, Debra Oles, a mother of three, and thirteen years older than Rod — who preyed on desperate older women — with whom she was living part-time in an apartment paid for with his daughter's college fund, testified that, "His [Rod's] anger and rage was uncontrollable." Rod and my ex were as similar in personality and sudden explosive narcissistic rage as they were a mismatch in their physical size.

My wife however had much more self-control than Rod and was able to contain her anger till she reached a private room, or our car, or during a phone call (I'm still shocked as I listen to many of the recordings I saved) before detonating. She was also fiendishly clever in manipulating others to execute her dirty work for her.

I sadly imagine Shele's last heart-wrenching thoughts in those final moments during which her brain quickly shut down to an unconscious state as it instinctively tried to protect itself due to lost blood flow, forcing the defenseless, terrified victim to gasp for air as Rod grabbed the mother of his two kids and locked her in a chokehold, that served as a dam and instantly severed the flow of oxygenated blood to her brain, before easily snapping her neck: *I can't believe he's killing me ... my poor kids. ...* Dad then stone-heartedly dropped her body like a sack of potatoes to make it appear as if she had "slipped" in the tub.

Gruesome crime scene photos show his wife's long blonde hair drenched in her own blood. Like O.J. executing Nicole after she complained about his numerous affairs and eventually divorcing the beast, Rod murdered Shele for nagging about his affairs and for daring to file for divorce.

Mommy endured a horrific "love at first sight" marriage for years for the sake of her darling children. The boy toy she thought she married turned out to be a living version of "Chucky" from the movie *Child's Play*. I can almost hear Rod saying, "Hi, I'm Rod, your friend till the end."

Shele knew she had problems the moment Rod moved into her expensive apartment and began living the life. He was as lazy as she was busy and focused. She hoped having kids would help her husband grow up. Shele suffered a miscarriage of twins, but she had two beautiful cherubs that took Mommy Angel many years and a small fortune to almost miraculously conceive before her soul flew to heaven: one daughter late in life, and, relying upon a donor egg, a second lovingly anticipated son shortly thereafter. Rod would abuse Shele that she wasn't the biological mother. Narcissists never take a break.

But to Rod, more than a decade younger than his intelligent financially successful Wall Street wife, Shele was never anything more than a meal ticket to emotionally drain and a side of beef to mercilessly strangle and dump in her bathroom tub. How dare she complain and now threaten to divorce him. *Fuck it. I'll just kill her and go out for a pleasant run to cover my tracks.*

Rod, who never suffered from insomnia or a conscience, then went out for a jog at three in the morning, while making sure to wish his doorman a pleasant evening as the minutes-old cold-blooded murderer generously offered to buy the gatekeeper a cup of coffee. What a nice, thoughtful person. The doorman later stated that during all the years he lived there, Rod never even noticed him or so much as said hello.

Within days Rod had full legal control over his children, and he instantly severed all ties with their maternal relatives. Grandparents were not allowed to visit their grandchildren. Aunts and Uncles were vaporized. The kids were instantly yanked from their private Jewish day school and placed into the public-school system.

Total alienation. These actions alone portray a deranged mind. What father, after such a "tragedy," would instantly block his children from seeing their extended family? And what kind of mother would use an Order of Protection to "protect" a ten-year-old girl from seeing the father she loved the moment he filed for divorce?

Smooth operators these wackos are. Like my wife discretely videotaping me as she fumbled while slowly turning her phone to record me during court, thinking that I wasn't aware that her skills as a spy were as klutzy as her moves in bed. *Don't Quit Your Day Job*, Honey. I won't even begin to imagine what she could possibly want with videos of me. She certainly has hundreds of them from family trips and my playing with our children as they grew up. *I would have smiled for you Sharen, but I wasn't exactly in the mood.*

Problem is that too many detectives are even more bumbling than their wacko suspects. And even when they're not, prosecutors refuse taking on a case they aren't positive they will win. Unlike Divorce and Family court, one must present solid evidence in Criminal court. Or at least a bullied tampered-with flimsy eyewitness who has been granted immunity or a reduced sentence for his "professional opinion."

Prosecutors understand a jury's decision in accepting the screaming connective dots of abuse and violence that monsters like Rod and O.J. committed against their wives during their marital relationships as "only circumstantial," and therefore inadmissible, when it came to the murder trials in which each was accused of mercilessly attacking, by slicing or snapping, the necks of the soaked-in-blood blonde mothers of their kids.

Prosecutors comprehend how mercenary unethical lawyers (pardon the redundancy) like Alan Dershowtiz can twist facts and obfuscate numbers. Dershowtiz insisted, in his defense argument, that less than one in a thousand men who beat the shit out of their wives actually wind up murdering them. What Alan "forgot" to include in his math lesson was that his statistic was only true when there was no (nearly decapitated) dead body lying on the pavement. When there is a battered wife-victim that later winds up dead, the husband-abuser is the murderer more than eighty percent of the time! See how quickly we go from "less than one in a thousand" to "eighty percent." Isn't math fun!

They know how charming a sharply dressed sleazy lawyer can appear, as he slowly buttons his jacket, while respectfully approaching a panel of gullible chumps sitting in a jury box to politely share his "beyond a reasonable doubt" lecture on law. "... and yes, my client is certainly a fucking asshole, but that doesn't mean he'd murder his own wife." #forfivemilliondollars

They also understand how easily a "jury of your (simpleton) peers" can be manipulated by a facile catch-line phrase. "If it doesn't fit, you must acquit!" O.J.'s legal team later admitted they were throwing each other celebratory high-fives when they came up with that logically-derisory, yet manipulatively powerful, Ebonics rapping tag-line in their office conference room that "proved" O.J.'s innocence. The mechanical mantra worked like a miracle and became an immediate "shot heard round the world" famous soundbite the moment it was uttered to the gullible jury by a charismatic defense lawyer dressed in beautiful expensive hand-tailored suits and bright cheerful ties.

Cochran even had his "expert" forensic scientist, Dr. Henry Lee, fitted for a few fits-like-a-glove expensive suits merely to impress the jury. Years later, Lee eulogized the late Cochran during a television interview for his "generosity." O.J. surely picked up the tab for those suits in the miscellaneous column of his legal invoices.

To this day science is catching up with the "world famous" Henry Lee who is finally being questioned about several of his blood-evidence forensic testimonies that led to false convictions. A knife whose blood Lee swore under oath, insisting and identifying it as human, was proven in fact to be animal blood. Lawyers for the falsely convicted man insist that Lee, whose personality matches the description of those who are inflicted with grandiose narcissism, knew it was animal blood all along. But there is no jail time for bombastic, sloppy forensic "experts" because they always utter three magical words: "in my opinion."

"This is not a problem with science at that time. It is a one hundred percent problem with Dr.Lee [all of the time]," Darcy McGraw of the Innocence Project explained upon finally obtaining her client's freedom from jail. A freedom that was achieved only after two additional years of his life were wasted while Darcy fought with the heartless prosecutor who held up the release while demanding a "time served" plea-bargain admission to block the wrongly convicted innocent man from suing the state for millions of dollars in the future.

Like when I finally "agreed" to sign off on the illegal division of retirement funds, before divorce, to escape the threat of being held in contempt in the courtroom of The Alf, the wrongfully convicted man acquiesced and accepted the brutal "take it or leave it" harsh demand of the prosecutor. Indeed, the medieval torture wheels of justice move slowly. Especially when innocent fathers are strapped onto the breaking wheel of our systemic divorce court system of justice.

Henry Lee was also severely rebuked by the Connecticut Supreme Court who recently overturned the convictions of two men for a 1985 murder, regarding which Lee — without even contemplating one second for every year the innocent men spent in cages unfit for animals — pompously insists that he still stands behind his "scientific merit." The two men served more than thirty years in prison because Lee testified that a single drop of something on a towel that he tested was "consistent" with blood.

The Innocence Project discovered that not only was the "something" not blood, but that the renowned Dr. Lee never even bothered to test the towel. For anything! He was probably too busy being fitted for suits. The three-decade-old murder had been so violent and grisly that the splattered seventy blood samples retrieved from the murder scene had all been tested at the time. Not one of them matched either of the suspects blood types.

But Dr. Lee knew the entire case would collapse without his sworn delusional testimony. He then incarcerated both men with his renowned magical "scientific merit" credentials and an imaginary drop of "blood" on a towel. A towel that the weird wizard never even took the trouble to test. In a twenty-three-page decision Justice Richard Palmer basically called Lee (the male version of Margaret Smith) a fucking lazy idiot. He was being too kind. Had the Innocence Project not taken the case pro bono the two men would still be in jail.

So much for the merit of "forensic" evidence calmly presented by a well-dressed putz in a fancy suit, who still boasts about his forensic credentials. Or from a shabbily dressed forensic psychiatrist who angrily submits "professional" evaluations full of typos and fabricated conversations while working out of his basement for the Rockland County Courts.

Like a prosecutor, Henry Lee faces no recrimination for his stupidity or arrogance, and no jail time for his reckless disregard for human life. Because the pompous bastard was merely sharing his "professional opinion." Lee can't even be forced to apologize. Too bad. "I'm sorry for destroying your lives," might have brought some closure to the men who remained locked in tiny cages for over three decades.

Judges, prosecutors, and forensic "experts" like Lee have total immunity. It's a good thing too. Because if the barbarians were incarcerated for their arrogance, heartlessness, and stupidity, a great majority of them would probably be jerking off in jail instead of from behind the bench.

And so with a mere seven words Johnnie Cochran, backed by "one of the world's foremost renowned forensic scientists," instantly decimated years of desperate 911 calls by a battered Nicolle, a (probable) confession to Rosey Grier, a raging O.J. breaking through a back door of his house, a heartbreaking letter from Nicole describing her "wonderful" life with The Juice, and mountains of rock-solid evidence that included the prior prosecutor's demands for the incarceration of defendant Orenthal James Simpson based on photos and hospital charts of the horrifically bruised gorgeous face of Mrs. Nicole Simpson. It's all circumstantial evidence.

The vile breath of Cochran's pathetic prose instantly evaporated sixty-one drops of scattered blood consisting of infallible solid DNA forensic evidence that was cross-checked by three separate labs. The memory of O.J.'s attempted escape drive along the L.A. highway while flanked by dozens of police cruisers and several helicopters, that was witnessed on television by almost a hundred million people on the very day that murder charges were finally filed against the football legend, became a case of mass retrograde amnesia due to Cochran's nursery rhyme. Meanwhile Domino's Pizza will never forget that June 17, 1994 was the busiest day they had ever experienced up to that time.

The murder suspect defendant's fancy size-twelve Bruno Magli bloody shoe print that matched his size-twelve foot "like a glove," and his actual blood-shrunken glove that was "proven" too tight to belong to O.J. thanks to his pitiful acting abilities as he "forced" his latex-gloved hand into it while faking a painful and anguished look on his face just in case the jury couldn't quite grasp how "tight" it felt, meant absolutely nothing to the unintelligent and confused panel. It would almost seem comical if not for the ghastly images of the nearly severed heads of Ron Goldman and Nicole that bled out on the sidewalk of her Los Angeles home.

It's only circumstantial evidence. "Just because he beat her, doesn't prove he killed her," the detectives chirped. True, it does not prove, beyond a shadow of doubt, that Rod murdered his wife. But at least allow the jury to see the obvious pattern of abuse. Our court system is too preoccupied with issuing guilty-till-proven-innocent protection orders against completely innocent fathers while self-righteously chirping "innocent till proven guilty" mantras that protect those who are obviously guilty of murder.

I guess Rod Covlin was in such a rush to get his claws on his wife's five million in savings, along with her multi-million dollar life insurance policies, that he had to instantly drop her body on the spot in order to free up his hands. He anticipated receiving the money that quickly. Shele's family spent years, and millions of dollars in legal fees, to bring him to justice. And a lawyered-up Rod, financed by a portion of the small fortune the wife he murdered "bequeathed" to him, eventually came within literal days of collecting his wife's entire estate.

Fortunately, his own fucking big angry mouth finally ensnared him. Just like my wife's own crazily concocted verbose emails illuminated more about her soul than the most advanced MRI scans of her brain could ever possibly reveal regarding her deviant behavior.

Rod's erratically wild schemes were beyond outrageous. He wreaked total havoc (Sharen, did you give him lessons?) while desperately trying to grab his deceased wife's money. First, he encouraged his two-year-old son, Myles, to claim that Shele molested him. Covlin carefully coached his tabula rasa son to complain that he was being sexually abused by mommy, executing the exact deranged future efforts of my twisted wife who coaxed our tabula rasa daughter to claim that I went "under the covers" with her.

Rod took his innocent clean-slate miraculously-conceived son to Columbia Presbyterian on July 8, 2009, six months before killing mommy, to falsely insist that his child was being sexually abused. Exactly like my shrewd shrew (*no typo there*) drove our gullible daughter to the police on Saturday night May 10, 2014 — twelve hours after her daddy's fictitious angry threat to assault Sara occurred. I guess Sara's life wasn't as important as Ester's and so my wife found it unnecessary to desecrate the Sabbath for a change.

I'm just glad I didn't sleep with my *Vybie* that Shabbat. If she was as creative as Tessa, she would have gathered some of my sperm, upon sitting on the toilet and letting it drip out the way she always used to do after I came inside her hellhole, and smeared it into Sara's vagina. My life would have been over. *Save that idea for your next frustrated schmuck.*

Rod wanted to spend a wonderful, memorable summer day of visitation with his two children. Being as unbridled as my wife, he saw no downside in making a preposterous claim that Shele was abusing their toddler son. Just like my wife suddenly decided, after twenty-eight years of marriage, that I was a dangerous pedophile who molested my own daughters.

Visitation day that Wednesday ended at 8 P.M. and several hours later, when Rod refused to answer the frantic texts of the future murder victim with whom he was in the midst of a bitter divorce, Shele called the cops. Officer Crystallee Vargas later testified that Shele was panic-stricken and crying uncontrollably, "Oh my God, I'm so scared! I'm so scared." Danishefsky even told Vargas that she was terrified Covlin would kill her — a full six months before she accidentally "slipped" in the bathtub. But all these events combined are nothing more than circumstantial evidence.

Rod then conspired to kill his own parents to get to Shele's funds. Finally, he hatched a plan to kidnap and sell his young twelve-year-old daughter as a bride in Mexico (don't even ask) so that he could grab some of Shele's estate. Just like Sharen, Rod would fling insane "Grobe Luge" accusations of sexual assault against a wonderful spouse and do anything, including murdering anyone that got in his way, for a fucking dollar.

Upon discovering that he couldn't pull that one off, Rod synchronized an Apple note that he wrote in his daughter's own words, as if she were admitting to "what really happened" that night (similar to O.J.'s "If I Did It" book). He then clicked the "send" button from his daughter's own email account, launching an off-the-wall frame-up of his minor daughter as a murderess who accidentally shoved her mom during an argument.

Covlin's insanity, like my wife's, goes on and on. These wackos never sleep. Their racing deranged brains keep sparking electrical impulses. And their fingers keep tapping and clawing their computer keyboards at all hours — when they're not busy choking out their spouses or dialing 911 on Shabbat.

And all Rod had to do was wait one more day — not even a full twenty-four hours — for his wife to meet with her attorney. Shele was absolutely terrified of Rob. She was going to request an amicable uncontested divorce (sound familiar?) along with offering a very generous sum of money for the sake of their kids and in the hopes of moving on with her life. In essence, she was offering Czechoslovakia to Hitler. And like Hitler, Rod had already decided to launch a deadly blitzkrieg attack.

Shele was going out of her way to try and keep her children's father *in* their lives while Rod was planning to remove her from theirs. Sound familiar? Like my wife, Rod wanted every penny. One spouse thinks only about the kids, while the other could care less about their own children and instantly heads for the warpath and a bloody battle. Once again, history repeats.

What do these idiots not understand about emails being traced and exposed? But then again, they're so much smarter than everyone else. So if they decide that they won't be discovered, who are we to argue? And even when they get caught, they incessantly rant, "That's not what I meant! I didn't do it! It wasn't me!"

Trust me. I could write a book about the murder of Shele Danishevsky. I'd probably title it, *Numb Blonde*. Because that is how one winds up when spending years with a manipulative abusive cyborg. Emotionally exhausted. Wracked with PTSD. Or in a body bag. In short, wackos do not sleep. You have to kill them, jail them, or divorce them. I was simply luckier than Shele because I had the password to my spouse's email account. Also, I didn't think my wife "might" kill me. I knew for certain that she would destroy me.

Everyone consoled Rod at Shele's funeral the following day as he sat on an uncomfortable mourner's chair. Faking sorrow while trying hard to feign emotion (he's not nearly as talented an actor as my ex), Rod tried to look sad, while happy thoughts of five million dollars jumped between the synapses of his caca-brain, as he received the long line of consoling relatives and friends that did their best to comfort the heartless murderer, while his two young children sat quietly to his right and left.

Hundreds of people, from Shele's huge family to stunned coworkers at UBS, where the smart blonde worked as a wealth manager, expressed their grief and shock. Except me. I couldn't walk over to him. I *knew* he did it. I just stared at him. It was all I could do not to scream "Murderer!" in front of hundreds of guests. Especially as I stared at those two dazed, sad little faces. Like my own engagement, I numbed my heart and refused to trust my gut instincts.

I kept thinking, but what if Shele really did "slip." I kept looking at those two small faces, weighing the possible results of my causing a scene. Is my outburst of protest a memory I want two freshly orphaned children to take away from their mom's funeral? Let them heal and experience the embrace of love from their remaining family and friends. I figured Rod would never hurt his own kids. How was I to imagine he'd try to marry off his minor daughter and then try to frame her for the murder he committed? My marriage had conditioned me well.

I restrained my emotions (while plotzing to roar and scream!) and remained in oh-so-fucking-painful silence. But I clearly couldn't contain myself that morning. Insisting to my wife — as we dressed in black in our master bedroom walk-in closet and during the entire long drive to the funeral home on an icy winter day — that Shele had been murdered. I couldn't stop repeating, "He killed her! He fucking killed her! I know it! I want to call the detectives! That piece of shit killed her!"

I was furious. My wife kept screaming at me, "Stop it already! Stop it, Ze'ev! You don't know! You can't prove it! You're speaking *Loshon Hara* (evil gossip)!" This righteous advice from a maniac who in the future would launch a smear campaign with an audacity that even a deranged devil like Joseph Goebbels would hesitate to pursue. When it came to evil gossip in our divorce, my wife sprayed lies like an ant sprays acid to immobilize its prey before decapitating its head and ripping off its limbs.

It was only after Shele was later exhumed, and her frozen (fortunate circumstance for the coroner) young body underwent an autopsy which revealed an intentionally broken neck, that her husband was finally a suspect and eventually arrested after years of incompetency by the DA.

Upon hearing the extremely rare news of an Orthodox Jewish soul being unearthed, I envisioned Shele's apparition hovering next to her naked broken body as it was sliced open upon the pathologist making a Y-shaped incision across her torso as a final insult to her husband's chokehold. I imagined her hot tears flowing as she likely wished, "... if only I could enter my body again and hug my kids one more time to tell them how much mommy loves them and that they'll be fine as they are raised by Aunt Eve and Uncle Marc."

I still remember how utterly shocked everyone was upon hearing the coroner's new report regarding cause of death. Everyone finally knew what I could have sworn from the very beginning. My wife's insentient mind still couldn't admit how right I had been all along. "You guessed, Ze'ev! Stop it already! You don't need my validation! You're not a detective! Stop playing one and get a real job!" My wife really thought that I merely guessed.

And I now realize why. My wife wasn't merely being her typical nasty self. "Ma nishtana?" My Mrs. Hyde could never begin to fathom the ability of someone like me. Someone who "feels" things. I'm like a detective who can work backwards. I can sense who did it. Especially if I get to sit quietly with the suspect. I can read their body language and the small changes in the slightly moving musculature features of their facial expressions. I'm incredibly accurate. Even before being granted access and reading their private emails.

Little actions, even something as simple as avoiding eye contact, unravel the most carefully hidden lies. But my wife is unable to read people, or to feel and sense anything metaphysical in a relationship. Even if someone's literally inside of her vagina. She can orgasm, but the lover inside of her is nothing more than a warm plastic dildo. I merely need to be near someone to sense and observe the truth. What is completely intangible to her is almost solid evidence to me.

The only reason my gifts failed me when staring into the crystal eyes of my adoring fiancée was because of her Asperger ability to penetrate my own "super-vision" as she bore through and held my stare. I believed she had "nothing to hide." And I was right. There was nothing inside of her. No warmth. No soul. Just a lot of faulty wire-monkey programming by a benevolent King Kong God.

Similar to my instinctively knowing that Rod killed Shele, my empath skills came into play with my upstairs neighbor, at 3755 Henry Hudson Parkway, who allegedly pushed the mother of his young daughter out the window of their seventh-floor apartment in Riverdale twenty-three years ago. I knew within hours that he was guilty (in my opinion, Ahem!) of shoving his pretty wife out of their seventh floor apartment window.

I respectfully paid a shiva call, seven hours after his wife's untimely death, to express my condolences as I sat quietly among the many visitors and neighbors who lived in *The Imperial*. I observed the mourning husband and his profusely crying mother-in-law through my own moist eyes while contemplating how sad it was that his young wife "just fell out of a window" while helping him clean an air-conditioner.

I kept choking back my own tears as I tried not to stare at his in-laws who had lost their precious daughter and were, unlike their son-in-law, crying inconsolably. I figured he was in shock with grief over his wife.

It was then, by the sudden way our newly widowed neighbor took one big swig of whiskey from his tumbler while sighing this totally, surreal-like, artificial, sad release of air, raising one eyebrow and holding it up a little too long while feigning the loss of the mother of his child, that I knew how my pretty neighbor with beautiful big brown eyes died. It was as if a dozen boxes of forensic evidence proving her husband's guilt, packaged and signed for by crime scene investigators, were flung at my head.

I suddenly found myself screaming "You killed her!" so loud in my mind that I wondered if everyone in the living room heard me. I remember telling my wife about my shiva call and that our neighbor must have killed his wife. "People don't just fall out of windows, Sharen! They fear heights and instinctively lean back!" I wanted to call the police and speak to the detectives and discuss 'the swig' with them. But my wife talked me out of it. "You don't know, Ze'ev! Don't start up with him! We still have to live in the same building with him! Think about your family, Ze'ev!" Once again, my wife knew the magical word. Family. I let go.

It was several days later that we discovered, through a mutual friend of our deceased neighbor, that our whiskey drinking widower's wife had scheduled to meet with her lawyer to formally file for divorce. The tragic "trapeze artist" had earlier circled in her calendar the morning following the day she landed on the pavement, after years of being "circumstantially" slapped and punched by her alleged executioner, as the day she chose to initiate her freedom from a very wealthy, emotionally and physically abusive, husband.

Like my own wife, he was not going to pay any alimony and child support for the next fifteen years. One little push. As quick as slamming the iconic Staples button. Problem solved. *That was easy!* Amazingly enough — exactly like Shele a decade in the future — our "Unzereh" Riverdale neighbor (allegedly) killed his wife the day before she was scheduled to meet with her lawyer.

According to the husband (and sole witness), he had been cleaning their air conditioner when his wife returned from shopping and ran upstairs for a few minutes to put away some groceries. The young mother had instructed the valet attendant in our garage not to park her car because she was coming right back down in "one minute" — never imagining it would be by flying through the window of her seventh-floor apartment.

I can only imagine the expression of our valet the moment her body thumped in the driveway directly in front of the armchair he always sat in till a car pulled up. She tried to utter a few "last words" as the blood hemorrhaged in her dying slammed-by-concrete brain. And although her lips moved ever so slightly, no one who crowded around the dying mother was able to make out the words she most likely spoke. *I can't believe he pushed me ... My poor kid ...*

What a coincidence. "She leaned out the window a bit too far [the day before her scheduled appointment with her divorce lawyer]," her husband explained. He told the detectives that he had asked his wife for some help reaching those hard-to-dust spots on their air conditioner. I guess he wanted it cleaned before he'd be ordered to vacate their million-dollar double apartment. I wonder if the donut eaters noticed that he was at least eight inches taller than his aerial-artist wife and easily possessed a much longer reach. I wonder if they asked why a woman who was coming back down in "one minute" suddenly found the time to help the man — she was afraid of and about to divorce — clean their air conditioner.

I wasn't "playing" detective, Sharen. His one glaringly overt fucking fake sigh gave it all away. More than a written confession. Actually, just like your email confessions revealed your true feelings about Rabbi Nekritz and your husband of twenty-eight years.

I also remembered walking by his wife in our building hallway almost a year earlier. I barely knew her, but I had seen enough guys in the gym, and my own reflection, to recognize a bruised cheek and black eye. "I wonder what the other guy looked like," I joked while trying to respect her boundaries with simultaneously balancing my inquiry as to her welfare. "You okay?" She laughed and told me she was rushing and slammed herself into a wall. *Probably while her husband was chasing her around their apartment.*

I believed her and totally ignored the glance of a punch that slightly stirred the feelings in my gut. After all, we lived in a fancy building with a bunch of nice Jewish people. I was conditioned to believe that only *Goyim* beat their wives. Surely not *Unzereh*. But the way he took that swig screamed his guilt to my intuition. *It was a black eye after all!*

I'm able to sense what many people are thinking. We all have the ability. Their words become unimportant because their cadence and the tone of their voice speaks volumes. I'm even more intuitive if I can watch their body language or steadfastly stare into their eyes. My only weakness, when it came to my wife, was because my God announced that Sharen was my true *Bashert*. Besides the fact that she never blinked.

God ordained our marriage the moment He created the universe. How romantic is that? After all, who could ask for a more trustworthy matchmaker than God? Like the Talmud says in Tractate Sotah: Forty days before the fetus is formed, a heavenly voice calls out, "The daughter of Mr. So-and-So shall marry the son of Mr. So-and-So."

Who was I to question God? And how was I supposed to know that he added the description of "covert narcissist" preceding the word "daughter" in his divine — or should I say "extraterrestrial" — announcement? I'm now almost embarrassed to admit that I was blinded by my faith to trust the choice of my Shadchan-God. I think things would have made more sense had he commanded me to sacrifice my son.

"Playing detective" is easy. Most men, by the way, are pitifully weak at eye contact. But even women lose their ability to hold their stare. Most will blink. Female cyborgs are the one exception. It appears that they are innocent and have nothing to hide. But it's only because they feel no guilt, fear, or shame. But their terminator battery-powered arrogance always gives them away. They're as sloppy as a hoarder. Just dig through their shit. Or emails. They almost dare you to challenge them. Because, "Fuck you! It's not what I meant! I didn't sign!"

Many deranged people act weird or eccentric. Like a glitch or pause in the Matrix, something slightly askew in their behavior will scream at their being artificial. I ignored endless eccentric behavior during my years of marriage. I labeled insanity as "cute." Five kids will do that to you.

I'm sure the prosecutor knew my neighbor was allegedly guilty of pushing his wife out the window. One quick shove. That was easy! He also knew he didn't have enough evidence for a sure win. He had a body. And he had plenty of motivation on the part of a wealthy abusive man who knew he was about to be served divorce papers. But Mr. O.J. Simpson already taught prosecutors that combining two facts (or even fifty facts) only added up to "circumstantial evidence." And my testimony of how the alleged murderer took an extra long poorly-acted swig of whiskey, while holding up his eyebrow to accentuate his sadness, obviously proved nothing. I certainly could not swear under oath that our neighbor pushed his little wife out the window.

There was nothing I could do. Although our very muscular doorman, Louis, knew the alleged truth and told me that he called the alleged murderer a "fucking murderer" to his face many times. Besides, prosecutors are loath to indict a case they might lose. Especially when the accused are wealthy and can afford to lawyer-up. That is how Bill Clinton got away with rape. It is why Bill Cosby got away with serial-rape for decades. In fact, it was the arrogant rapist's own mouth during a deposition that sealed Cosby's fate.

Prosecutors' fear of deep pockets is why Harvey Weinstein got away with rape for years and is only now finally in jail. It is why Jeffery Epstein and R. Kelly got away with sex trafficking for decades. And it is how O.J. Simpson got away with murder. After all, it's so much easier squaring off against a public defender than a dream team of highly experienced, professional liars, who are paid royally to create doubt and toddler rhymes that obfuscate truth.

My wife and Rod have amazingly similar personalities. The only difference is that Covlin's crazy consciousness is housed in the body of a six foot, three-inch-tall, athletic frame. My wife however is much more dangerous, disguising her deranged personality with incredible Asperger-enhanced acting skills inside a cute size-two "defenseless" female body that causes unsuspecting bystanders to jump to her defense as she instinctively cries out for help with an incredibly soft-spoken "hurt" voice.

My wife is not evil. Evil implies a decision chosen through an expression of free will. But such a level of wickedness would suggest that my ex contemplated not acting the way she instantly chose to act upon my filing for divorce. It would infer that she possessed a possible pause-button as she weighed and measured the pros and cons of committing perjury to alienate Ester, while spending $250-thousand dollars to possibly (yet highly unlikely since she was definitely the moneyed spouse) save $50 thousand.

"Evil" would also insinuate that Sharen thought about the future of our children before she decided to accuse their father of being a pedophile full of wrath who was obsessed with feces. But insanity is not evil. Insanity is unable to make choices. And so insanity does what insanity will always do. It jumps!

Like brain waves during sleep that instantly meander the dreamer's mind from one setting to another without rhyme or reason, the minds of the insane don't just put the cart before the horse. They'll put the horse in the cart and whip it to death while screaming, "Giddy-up!" The mind of a lunatic sparks the way random lightning strikes. And like lightning, it mindlessly destroys anything in its path.

I see your smirking face Sharen. I know your mechanical mind works like that of a trapped animal and that you'll do anything your survival instincts spark inside your frontal lobe. There is no morality in the wild. It's only about existence. Not paying me a rusted red-cent of maintenance was do-or-die survival in your feline Bengal brain. I'm still amazed at the racing Ultra-Orthodox Yenta-wildebeests that you panicked into a stampeding herd to follow your stalking efforts to hunt me down the moment I filed for divorce.

I know you'll never hear a word I'm saying and that I'm talking to myself. I guess I should probably thank God that I was able to shovel your emails into your arrogant mouth — allowing me to expose your true personality. But all too often he seems as deaf as you.

I now understand that I could write a million pages and still never begin to convince you what a horrific idea it was to take out perjured orders of protection to destroy me while alienating Ester from the most important man in her life. I instantly hear your psychological-drivel response: "Sorry Ze'ev! It was Ester's choice! It was your filing for divorce that caused all of this! You owe me $250-thousand dollars!"

Who can now replace her father? The fucking liar, Rabbi Schabes? The "trusted" therapist, Rabbi Frank? The namby-pamby, Uncle Steve Smedresman who was emasculated by your sister Elyce long before he lost his virginity to his nasty, ghoulish, control-freak wife? How do these religious Jews pray to God knowing how immoral and deceitful they are?

Or will it perhaps be my wonderful, but spiritless, milksop brother-in-law, Jon Zaslow, who would literally spring in fright, like a parched gazelle at a watering hole full of crocodiles, the moment his wife's eyes appeared above the waterline. Subdued like a Dachau inmate, jumping to fulfill any directive your reptilian sister Mindy hisses before completing her next set of demands, Jon was even forced to stop studying the Talmud with me. You, of course, know all this already. Want to see your emails?

There was nothing Jon enjoyed more than delighting in the wisdom of those who sit in the fragrant Garden of Eden. "I've never known anyone that explains it all as clearly as you do," Jon often exclaimed to me in appreciation. Mindy angrily grabbed her husband's greatest pleasure away with a bullying hiss of, "He's divorcing my sister! Don't ever speak to him again!" Jon still respectfully called me one last time, in a pitifully embarrassed voice, to apologize that he wouldn't be able to study with me or call me anymore. It was a very sad call for both of us.

"But Jon, I could call you at your office," I suggested. "We can still learn over the phone." The risk of his wife's instant hellish rage easily overwhelmed the promise of a blissful eternity. Jon literally panicked. Probably worse than when my father risked his life "stealing" raw potato peels in Dachau. "But what if Mindy calls in for something and my secretary mentions I'm on a call with you?!" It almost sounds funny. But only because you never heard how intimidating my wife and her sisters sound when they hiss. Like beastly mother-in-law. Like animalistic daughters.

I love you Jon. And I miss you. I wish I could free you and study with you again. You told me you loved me more than a brother. I still believe you. You have no idea what you're missing and how much I've studied these past ten years. I'd love to share it with you. But you somehow believe that God wants you to give up your "Olam Habbah" eternity for a shitty "Shalom Bayit" mirage marriage. Sadly, you choose to follow the Da'as Torah of a bitch over that of your brother.

I hope you forgive me for saving your marriage when you wanted to divorce Mindy many years ago. I remember how Mindy cried like a toddler over the phone, begging me to talk to you, and I convinced you to stay with her. I still have the emotional email I wrote to you to convince you to remain in purgatory. I'm so sorry, Jon. I wish I could free you now. But the hardest shackles to snap are the invisible ones wrapped around your mind and testicles.

It's true that divorce destroys everything. But then you realize that "everything" was nothing. And "nothing" is freedom. And freedom is everything. Mindy doesn't love you. And sadly, you don't love yourself. If you did, you would realize that you don't need "permission" to talk to me. You would establish some boundaries and insist that my divorce from Mindy's sister has absolutely nothing to do with your relationship with me. But that could only be accomplished by seeing your own self-worth.

Your fear of Mindy has blinded you, Jon. You don't make demands on someone you love. Mommy Mindy doesn't have to "allow" baby Jon to speak with me. If Mindy loved you, she would never have deprived you of what you loved most: studying with me. And if you loved yourself, you would never have acquiesced to such an insane demand based on pure anger and hate. My love is real. And that is why I would never try to force you to do anything. I only wish you freedom, health and happiness. And a writing career too, as I recall that you write quite well!

I clearly comprehend, Sharen, that even if I were a prophet that could display a side-by-side video portrayal of a grown up thirty-year-old Ester with my having been in her life, compared to what my orphan is now destined to look like in the future, you would still refuse to go back in time and rescind those orders. If God Himself commanded you to rescind those orders, you'd instantly email Jodi that, "god's been radicalized by zev." Both of our names would be in lower-case type of course. And both God and I would be wasting our breath.

In truth, my message beseeching civility is directed at those mothers who are only half-crazed with anger: "Please, Mom! Please! Have mercy on your child! Don't launch that protection order bomb!" My real message is to legislators and society at large who need to fix our entire criminal and family court system of lawlessness.

But I do have to thank you, Sharen, for teaching me that when no one is listening — no matter how much you talk — then it's time, way past time, to listen to yourself. And so you taught me the greatest lesson of all: *Listen to your heart.* I know you have issues, Sharen, and so I'll simply wish the best for the mother of our five children. Clearly, I'm disappointed, along with being grievously exhausted by PTSD.

I'm also lonely without my child. After all, I'm only human. Unlike you, I have feelings, misgivings about what "could have been," endless thoughts about existence, and deep emotions. But I understand how animals act instinctively to survive. All I can do, at this point, is hope that the diamond wheel of life is kind to you and the children we brought into this world. I would pray for you, Sharen, but I'm too tired.

I understand that what I once saw as a gorgeous "size-two wedding dress" gem bride was never more than a lump of coal that could combust without a moment's notice. I now realize that you were a synthetic diamond that tricked the eye of a trained gemologist. I'm not upset at you, *Vybie*. I should have turned the dial to 100X. Or even simply to 11X. But you easily convinced me during our dating phase that you were flawless. And once we were married, I refused to recognize your flaws as anything more than insignificant little scratches on a worn gem that merely needs a touch-up on the diamond wheel. I still wish that we could have remained amicable post-divorce for the sake of our children and grandchildren.

But I realize that you really can't help yourself. It's not your fault. So please forgive me when I get upset. It's not directed at you. I know you are hopelessly non compos mentis. It's directed at a seemingly deranged divine God that creates critters like you — and creatures like Bundy, Covlin, Hitler, Alfieri, Schwartz, Ferro, Tomás de Torquemada, my Mother, Putin, Caligula, Dennis Rader, Kim Jong-un and a hundred million more unknown brutish insects and beasts that swarm the planet.

The world has no shortage of deranged individuals who kill heartlessly and wantonly. And world history, beginning with Cain, is nothing more than one long story of murder, war, rape, and genocide circling our globe no matter whose version of recorded insanity or "holy book" you read. I suspect I still haven't come to terms with admitting that God is possibly as fucking psychotic as you.

After all, how can he create such a beautiful world full of flora and fauna and babies, along with the capacity to love and the ability to see, while simultaneously populating it with so many inhumane and destructive humans? There is nothing as evil and destructive as man. And nothing as beautifully kind and creative. So why would a loving God that creates toddlers invent delusion, disease, greed, sexual frustration, divisiveness, ignorance, blindness, madness, depression, war, marriage, and ultimately death for all his cherubs?

Can the author of the Talmud and the Kabbalah really be psychopathic? I know I am not evil. And I'm not a sinner. I'm merely tired of taking ownership and paying for God's sins. I'm not the one who created temptation (Satan) and then held all future mankind responsible when Adam and Eve sinned upon eating from the Tree of Knowledge. What a loaded deck of cards!

I'm also not ignorant simply because I can't make sense of a bipolar God whose actions completely contradict the concept of kindness — that selfless, angelic trait, that is dogmatized in the Talmud as the fundamental essence of God's very being and the chief attribute that God claims as his glorious crowning accolade. I'm not the one who is confused. I'm simply exhausted.

It's not that I need closure, Sharen. You can't "close" what you realize was never "open." I understand that showing anger to the spongy flawed tissue that allows you to be cruel and mean-spirited would be as senseless as my being upset at a diamond for containing the natural flaws formed under intense pressure when it was still coal, ensconced deep within the recesses of molten rock and volcanic fire, long ago. You were flawed way earlier than the moment you were born on the 21st of June in the year 1955. You were probably a stardust mess even before God announced we were to be married.

In fact, our entire marriage has been one huge erroneous contract. What the Talmud calls a "Mekach Taos." You were correct in taking your time to show up for your Jewish Get. You probably didn't even need it. I'm sure if the great Rabbi Moshe Feinstein were alive he would have declared an annulment. Especially after reading your emails. After all, the word of the insane is not binding. So technically you never agreed to marry me.

I understand that just as it would be unfair of me to yell at a blind person who bumped into me, I can't yell at you — who "bumps" along without any foresight as to what you are doing. You are unable to fathom the possible, let alone see the final, results of your actions. Nor are you in the least bit embarrassed upon having been caught and exposed as a pathological liar. You'll just emit a snarky laugh and "bump" onwards.

You constantly bump! Like a cyclone! Left. Right. Bump! Bump! Bump! You're like a kid's book I'd write titled, "Sharen goes Bump!" And wherever the tornado winds of your unsound mind cause you to wind up, you rationalize you had no choice but to do it that way. In a neurological sense, you are telling the truth. Your cacophonous blithering brain seems incapable of any semblance of orderly rational and emotional thought.

And that is why I cautioned you to "think things through" when I gently informed you that I am filing for divorce. I patiently advised you not to rush and take out an Order of Protection. "Everyone knows me Sharen. It'll blow up in your face," I warned. "I'm not like that, Ze'ev! I don't think like that!" you insisted as I recorded our entire conversation on my TapeACall app. Along with your emails, what other proof would you like me to submit, aside from MRI scans of your brain, to prove that you are exactly "like that, Sha'ren!"

You are extremely manipulative and believe you are cunning and smarter than everyone. But you're really not that smart, Sharen. In fact, you honestly don't know what the hell you're doing.

You've always been illogical and defective in much of your thinking. But I wanted to have babies with you, not someone to study the Talmud with.

I treated you patiently — even after you perjured yourself and took out three instant protection orders after adamantly admitting in your own email's that I'd never harm you. I could have put you in jail if I had an angry desire for revenge. But I'm not like you. Or our vengeful God.

The best way to describe you is by comparing you to a three-dimensional deepfake technological creation. The sole purpose of those digital videos is to make people believe something is real when it is nothing more than an early Disney cartoon on CGI steroids. The latest digital revolution, produced by sophisticated artificial intelligence, can fabricate images that walk and talk as realistic as a video of real human beings.

And all too often, the purpose and greatest talent of this creation lies in its ability to manipulate the minds of others. Like you, it mimics human life. It masterfully does what you do best — subliminal manipulation and the spreading of misinformation with viral Yenta speed. The algorithms used to create deepfake videos are a subset of A.I. technology, and it's used to create talking videos that can "learn" and "make decisions" on their own. Just like you! But it's all nothing more than sophisticated computer programming. Exactly like you! And like software programs, it's not alive and it has no soul. Flawlessly like you.

Your only strength is your aggression that wears people down. You never ever give up. If O.J. had decapitated you instead of Nicole, I'm sure your severed head would have thrashed like the serpent that you are to bite his jugular and inject venom during your final moments of consciousness. He would also have wound up on the sidewalk in front of Nicole's house.

I have no doubt that you'd do our entire divorce exactly as before, in a heartbeat, if the opportunity presented itself, because you have the energy and mind-set of an ant. Maybe, just maybe, you'd slow down long enough next time to change your password. Probably to Tatie5522 in order not to waste too much time.

The aftermath of our divorce and the continued refusal of over two hundred mindless and foolish "religious" family members, friends, and neighbors to speak with me to this day — sinfully rushing to cooperate and believe any lie your sociopathic mind chirped through your cute whispering little mandible mouth — are quite a congratulatory declaration of how amazingly energetic a fire ant gossipmonger can be.

I have no doubt that you could hand this entire book to your next future-eventually-narcissistic-husband and convince him in a sarcastic sentence or two, as you'd stare at him with those Betty

Gable eyes, while whispering in a hurt, hushed voice, that you were the one who survived a bitter and acrimonious divorce. "And he even took the house from me," you'd whisper in a tone that would instantly compel compassion and belief as you'd explain while moping that you "just had to do" what you did. I can see the moisture welling up in your sorrowful eyes as you recant the tale of your heroic escape from an "abusive narcissistic husband."

And I can hear the exact decibel level you would sigh, almost to yourself but just faint enough for your next schmuck spouse to hear, as he leans in with sadness and empathy to hug you. "I don't know how he hid so much money from me while we were married," you'd meow in the voice of a wounded kitten. "He must have spent a fortune on his lawyer to destroy me in court the way he did," you'd purr as he stroked your sad little face.

I must add that your ability to convincingly scream "Fire!" as if you're standing where you belong has probably incinerated any chances of our daughters ever finding a normal husband. Why would any prospective in-laws want to risk having the DNA of a violent pedophile who is obsessed with feces in their offspring?

Who among our circle of friends, neighbors, and rigidly insular medieval community did you not warn about the deranged behavior of your violent narcissistic husband that might replicate itself in the offspring of his grandchildren? The Yentas of Monsey won't even arrange a marriage for a girl whose father isn't among the first ten to start a minyan. Do you think they'll arrange one for the daughter of a pedophile? Try explaining that you were "just angry" during a divorce.

Did I not gently warn you not to run and take out a protection order and to consider our children before I filed for divorce? Know this, Honey: Nothing you did to me during our divorce surprised me. Not merely because I had your password. Not because I still had access to your new white computer. Not even because I figured out your new husband's name (R-A-C-H-E-L-3-11) was the entry word for the lock you had installed on our bedroom door. I couldn't believe how quickly I figured that one out. Quick! Call the police! Or actually, wait till you light your holy Shabbos candles so you can really fuck me.

And even leaving me the gift of your spiral "to do" notebook on the garage floor as you rushed off to work, filling in the details of your endless perfidious efforts to destroy me, taught me nothing I didn't already understand after being married to you for such a painfully long time. Your hoarding obsession, by the way, causes you to carry way too much emotional and literal baggage.

You noted borrowing sixty thousand dollars from your mother, forty-five thousand from Elyce, along with a reminder to yourself (number 11 on your list) to "call Rachel Skydell" for funds. Your handwriting is as skewed as your unstable cognitive thought processes. I also noticed your brazen attempt to file coercion and blackmail charges against me. Blackmail? What the hell was that about!

I especially appreciated your self-reminder "issues to discuss" sticky-note regarding your weekly sessions with Rabbi Dr. Frank — who once gave us his word as he promised he would no longer continue to see either of us as clients if you or I chose to proceed to divorce. By the way, how are your "boundary sessions" with the good liar-rabbi coming along? It's men like Frank and Schabes that allow me to understand how people can hate "those sneaky clever Jews." They're not that clever. Just ruthless.

Nothing surprised me, Sharen, because after three decades of mindlessly rationalizing your behavior for the sake of our *Shalom Bayit*, I could easily read an adorable savage-like automaton beast. I knew you could act as innocent as Doris Day, speaking gently with a voice that could bewitch anyone. While twisting your scalpel in their back.

Sorry for not returning the notebook, by the way. But there were three protection orders, in screaming uppercase letters, forbidding my making any contact with you. I placed your notebook on a pile of junk in plain sight knowing you'd never notice it camouflaged among your hoarded treasures of "organized clutter." It was exactly where I left it when I returned as the sole owner of our beautiful home.

The advantages bestowed upon you by your Asperger mind, like driving the same route to work and doing the exact same repetitive surgery twice a day for forty years, along with your ability to lie without blinking (as you do in bed) as you stared straight into my eyes while screaming at me and swearing that you didn't call anyone about our divorce, smirking while denying my accusations as if I was the one who is crazy, speaks volumes about your powerful ability to deceive.

Your words are delivered with such credible force and with such urgency, that you could probably convince Rebbi Nekritz that Santa Claus was the man who stood with God on Mount Sinai for forty days and forty nights. No wonder Ester believed that I'm "killing" you by your having to pay the mortgage. Did you forget to explain to her that it's hard to pay a monthly mortgage of $3,500-dollars only because you committed yourself to the added expense of spending $10,000-dollars a month to kill her father?

Meanwhile, I stood next to my car in our driveway and listened to your ranting denials as I wore your folded email list of names in my buttoned shirt pocket, in which you wrote to your divorce coach Rabbi Dr. Donny Frank that you had spent the entire prior Friday afternoon calling your list of over forty relatives and rabbis. I was dying to show you the list. But I have a lot of patience, Sharen. I didn't mind waiting till now.

Your clever deceitful plans to put me in jail, and your broad range of prodigious natural dramatic acting skills — including your spectacular and sincere child-like innocent little girl's voice, without any affectation, that instantly convinced anyone you spoke to that I was a pedophile — were all undermined by your total inability to sense anything intuitive upon my serving you divorce papers. Bump! How can someone with so much energy be so dead-in-bed?

The late Elie Wiesel once said: "The opposite of love is not hate. It's indifference. Because of indifference one dies before one actually dies." You didn't just hate me upon being served divorce papers. Your silence and indifference spoke volumes about my death since the day we met.

Your mind sparks like electricity, Sharen. Like when you signed the $50,000-dollar note on our house only days before I filed for divorce (the third time). I sat expressionless as I watched you sign. Bump! Thank you, Honey. Did you really believe I was going to build a basement for you to hoard more shit? I can't tell you how desperate I was for those funds. It was the least you could do after I had given you a thousand dollars a week for seventeen years. It was easier than taking candy from a baby. Forgive me Sharen, but you have to fight fire ants with fire.

I later read your emails in which you adamantly denied ever signing that note as you screamed and ranted to your lawyer, "I never signed! I never signed!" Schwartz instantly believed your tirade of denial and excitedly emailed back, "this is great news Sharen and sets forth possible criminal action!" The bumbling blob was so excited. Who could possibly resist your firm, indignant, pathological refutation? I continued to stare at your repetitious angry disclaimer and Schwartz's belief that he could finally file a motion that wouldn't just waste more time. *She really believes her own lies. She really is fucking crazy.*

Several days later I logged into your email account and read Schwartz's reply: "Sharen, I checked the signatures at the courthouse, and they are definitely yours." Bump!

So let me get this straight. Slowly now. You, Sharen Lewinson, paid your own lawyer for at least a half dozen hours to research the "possible criminal action" of your husband forging your name on a note that you knew you signed. Don't your Jekyll and Hyde bi-polar personalities communicate with each other? Or does Hyde give Jekyll the silent treatment?

At his inflated-for-the-insane special rate of $450.00 an hour, Schwartz bumbled down to our town hall to carefully examine the recorded lien that you vehemently denied signing, only to have your own astonished lawyer discover and respond that it was indeed you who signed the note. Proving that you are a liar or insane.

Schwartz simply billed you for his detective work and your latest drama ended as quickly as it began. And like the machine that you are, you never even bothered to defend your insanity, pardon yourself, or respond in any way to his discovery. You obviously weren't embarrassed. You just bumped into a wall and instantly moved in another direction like those robotic vacuum cleaners that just keep going. But unlike those automated little helpers, you *leave* shit wherever you go.

You can't even turn your frenzy-frantic button off against yourself! Your half-crazed mind works like the brain of an alligator that will swing its head to bite off its own arm if only it could reach it. In your case, more like a bitch chasing its own tail as it runs in a circle. And like those reptilian dinosaurs that somehow survived extinction, you are one scary loose cannon.

You are so passionate in your desire to destroy that you can't even slow down long enough to evaluate how self-destructive you are. I'm glad Hamas didn't wire you to blow yourself up as you stood between Ester and me. You achieved your goal of pummeling my reputation and our daughter's childhood without leaving a bloody mess.

So here is the announcer's ringside summation as he stands center ring, holding the dangling microphone as the echoes of the clanging boxing bell sounds reverberate among the crowd of cackling Yentas and hypocritical Beit Din Rabbis, proclaiming the final results of our divorce after I left my hands low and at my side, refusing to hit a girl, as I weathered your wacko-a-mano fisticuffs storm of false gossip and malicious prosecution:

"Upon the final ringing of the bell ... after Plaintiff endured seemingly endless rounds of protection orders and frivolous legal motions as he searched for the face of his little girl among the crowd of booing Yenta fans ... and after a brutal fight to the finish savage beatdown by the Defendant, in which she wore hand-wraps dipped in plaster of Paris along with brass knuckles — all right in front of Referee Alfieri ... who enjoyed joining in on the merciless malicious pummel-prosecution dealt to the defenseless Plaintiff — as Alfieri removed his judicial black robe, embossed with huge gold letters stating "In God We Trust" on its back, and slipping on his own set of brass knuckles as he illegally jumped into the ring to aid the Defendant during each round ... barking at Plaintiff, "I'll hold you in contempt!" every time he winced in pain — the score is as follows:

A technical knockout has been entered against the plaintiff-father, who fought against all odds while suffering from PTSD and was illegally forced to throw his towel and daughter into the ring in defeat. The judges tally that Defendant spent half her life savings, gave Plaintiff her share of equity in their house, committed perjury every time she signed an Order of Protection as she claimed both fighters were not contesting each other in any other arena-court of law, alienated Ester from her father that was dying for visitation — all executed in a mendacious TKO, merely to waste years of Plaintiff's life while paying promotor Dan Schwartz a fortune so that she wouldn't have to pay Plaintiff a pittance of maintenance."

Good job, Sharen! Congratulations! I can see you throwing up your gloved hands (better remove them quickly so you can type your next email) in victory as the cannonade of flashing bulbs explode all around you. I see their bursting, momentarily blinding light reflecting off your unblinking sapphire eyes, while you fluoresce your Mona Lisa smile as you gaze at the crowd with your cold stare of impersonal defiance. I'm sure you could have demolished the bare-knuckle heavyweight John Sullivan, back in the day, with one arm tied behind your back. Actually, with your confident stare-down, you could have had both your hands tied behind your back.

The announcer's summation, in essence, means that a third of the thirty-eight years that you woke up at five in the morning to be in the O.R. by seven, and then stood on your feet for ten hours — driving home exhausted as you dozed off at the wheel — was wasted on paying a sleazy-slob-schlemiel to write nonsensical crap, for which a first-year law student would be expelled, merely to keep me busy and on the ropes for two and a half years of my life. I could have written better fictional legal Motions to Dismiss with one arm tied behind my back. And I would have charged you a third of what Dan charged.

And during those bizarre years you and your Stinky Pussy Posse of Yenta Meshuggenah's ran around, screaming and crying that I'm a pedophile who is obsessed with feces, along with my being dangerously violent and full of "wrath." And let's not forget to include the incredibly refined Rabbi Nekritz receiving his feces-accolade and his incessantly being called a piece of shit in front of his wife and neighbors as the echoes of "You're a piece of shit! You're a piece of shit!" reverberated throughout their long Borough Park hallway.

I'm still shocked that you sent our own daughters, Rachel and Sara, on a mission to Hell to insult such an innocent scholar merely to antagonize me. And I'm flabbergasted to think they must share your heartless DNA to carry out your directive. How do you even come up with such perverted ideas? You really are fucking insane.

Oh! And by the way, you and Schwartz (Beauty and the Beast) were so busy making shit up, wreaking havoc while flinging feces like two angry caged chimpanzees at every direction my life took, that you forgot to simply request my actual More Mortgage Inc. tax returns. You and Schwartz believed your own lies. So it makes sense that it never occurred to you to request the returns. After all, I "never worked a day in my life."

You both were so busy lying that you forgot that a concept called truth exists. I waited and waited. But no one bothered to even think of asking me for the MoreMortgage.com checkbooks that would have leveled the disparity between our two incomes.

True, they were outside the "five most recent years" guideline dictated by the divorce laws of the State of New York. But to a masturbated mind like Alfieri, that would not have mattered. If he was willing to impute fictional salary to my paltry teacher's salary, then surely he would have yelled at me to, "Go back to the mortgage business you lazy bum!"

Every time Schwartz filed yet another verbose inane motion to block maintenance, I read his pitifully feeble logic while quickly scanning his latest requests for further documentation. I figured your lawyer would surely request the *MoreMortgage* corporate tax returns for our two-day deposition. He asked me for everything else under the sun. Schwartz sent subpoenas to dozens of people and companies that had anything to do with SwordPen Publishers in a flurry of wasting your money.

Schwartz then billed you for two full eight-hour days to prepare for the very serious deposition of Gary Barnet who had invested $150 thousand dollars into SwordPen Publishers — another total waste of your money and Mr. Barnet's precious time. But the subpoena for my More Mortgage Inc. tax returns never arrived.

Here I had been on the radio in the tristate area, 24/7, for three years in the mortgage business and no one bothered to ask me for one receipt or invoice relating to all that activity. We had a website database with over three thousand clients, and a very clever billboard ad right along the West Side Highway in Manhattan, and I even appeared on the radio as the Mortgage Maven. I had been earning anywhere from twenty to thirty thousand dollars a month before the implosion of the mortgage industry.

But you and Dan were so busy lying, emailing, manipulating, spreading malicious false rumors, scheming and plotting your next assault on my pristine reputation that you seemed to have forgotten how I constantly pulled out my phone wherever we were as I professionally responded … "More Mortgage, how may I help you?"

You and Schwartz, under the incredibly inept Alfieri asshole, were all so busy "bumping," shrieking, and bellowing "Fire! Ester! Narcissist! Pedophile! I'm afraid of his wrath! Protection Order! Sushi eater! Never worked a day in his life saki-drinker!" in such an intense delirious frenzy, that you never calmed down long enough to catch your fecal breath and recall that I had done quite well in the mortgage business before the banking crises on Wall Street occurred. The cacophony of your delusional cries drowned out any possible logical thoughts that might have allowed you to pay less maintenance. The three of you really should film a rerun of *The Three Stooges*.

With the ease of Dorothy returning to Kansas, all Schwartz had to do was click his dainty red slippers and simply ask for those returns. Although slippers never fit on the feet of ugly stepsisters. They might have leveled the discrepancy in our W-2's rather equitably. And all you needed to do, my mezuzah-kissing wife, was take off a few minutes from outperforming Judy Garland while calling the police on Shabbos. But you were so focused on destroying me and alienating Ester that you overlooked the most obvious way to avoid maintenance.

I left you enough rope to hang yourself. And true to form, you wrapped the cord around that pretty neck I used to teasingly kiss and pulled it as tightly as The Alf squeezed my balls in court — while I continued to type your latest password to see what idiocy you and your callously brutal kapo were planning next.

It's amazing how you continue to pull it tightly five years after our divorce, while still trying to create a sticky spider's web to disrupt my now calm life. Next time try to remember some of the lessons we taught our young children about being honest. It really does pay. Or perhaps you should memorize the famous line, written in 1808, by Sir Walter Scott: "Oh! What a tangled web we weave when we first practice to deceive."

I was diagnosed with PTSD during and following our divorce. You generously gifted me many parting gifts. Severe anxiety. Emotional trauma. Insomnia. Constant stress. Threats of incarceration. Homelessness. Depression. Isolation. Flashbacks. Poverty. Possible loss of my job. Kudos, Sharen. You, Schwartz, and Alfieri savagely violated my existence. But it was certainly worth the price of my freedom. Our incredibly wonderful soldiers suffer much worse protecting our freedom. I was certainly willing to suffer for my own. And I did.

I Googled PTSD and my long-term exposure to your toxic protection order IED's had clearly taken its toll. Weight gain. Rising blood pressure. Anxiety. But I did exactly what my therapist prescribed. Exercise. Therapy. Sleep. Spend time with friends. I was even dating a lovely teacher before you offered me your "uncontested divorce" option. This book has been my final therapy.

Olivia Nuzzi once advised, upon the hack and release of the Democratic National Committee's twenty thousand emails (right before their convention), that one should: "Dance like no one is watching; Email like it may one day be read aloud in a deposition." Nothing like emails. They literally allow you to read people's minds.

All the tape recordings of your frantic screaming, the vicious emails between you and Schwartz, the protection orders obtained through perjury, the unabashed instructions from you and Rachel to Sara that, "you could say he's a pedophile," followed by "you're not gonna get cold feet, are you?" as she hesitated to throw a grenade at the father she once loved — along with your obliteration of Ester to "protect" her from the man who penned a humorous book for children called "*When You Gotta Go!*" all seem to vanish with time.

But the evidence that remains of your documented confidential attorney-client-privilege emails at the Rockland County Courthouse will forever scream lunacy at best, and incredible evil at worst. I don't expect someone who desecrates the Sabbath in order to throw an innocent husband into jail to believe me, but all your actions were also recorded in Heaven. I'm sure that even I don't know half of what you did or tried to do to me.

And the emails portraying your relationship with our oldest daughter Rachel were Oedipal-weird even before she became the man of the house and insisted that you promise never to remarry upon my serving you with divorce papers. Who was she saving you for? Herself? The intimate foot and back rubs you gave each other after lighting candles on Friday nights? I must admit that of all your emails, the following shocked me the most: "Promise me you'll never remarry after Tatie divorces you," Rachel wrote. I still can't even begin to wrap my head around that one.

I guess I have to look at the bright side. At least Rachel was calling me Tatie. You and she hadn't yet instructed Ester to call me "Zev." "Don't call him 'Tatie!' He's not your father anymore!" Ouch! Great maternal guidance for teaching our daughter the Fifth Commandment. And your response to Rachel's queer request was also so you. I could almost hear your reassuring voice swearing passionate fealty. "Don't worry, I'd have to really *trust* (italics are my own) someone before I ever married again." I wanted to shoot back an edited version of the email substituting the word 'control' in place of 'trust.'

I know you'll simply chuckle-snark away this revelation exactly like you did when you were behind closed doors in *Yichud* with your wonderful therapist, Rabbi Dr. Donny Frank (whose ordination I highly doubt), even after my calmly and clearly explaining to him what every five-year-old girl in Monsey knows — that Jewish Halacha does not allow such private intimacy with a single woman, and surely not with a married one (something every single Yenta in Monsey is fanatical about).

Your obedient attack-dog, Rabbi Schabes, ignored your actual biblical violation of being in private seclusion with Rabbi Donny Frank, but raced to call Rabbi Nekritz with the "urgent" directive sham that ... "who knows, maybe, possibly, long-shot, "efsher," one-in-a-million, perhaps Zev had rabbinically declared Sharen a Sotah!" What a hoax. This fucking idiot is your new Rabbi? For this boorish dolt you now insult the famous scholar with a lowercase name of "nekritz," along with your psychological babble of his "radicalization?"

"We weren't doing anything, Ze'ev!" is not a "heter" (dispensation) to override a commandment from God to Moses at Mt. Sinai — according to Jewish doctrine. And you yourself taught this law to our own daughters. I was merely pointing out to a "rabbi" that which every girl in Monsey is taught by the time she reaches the second or third grade. Frank is obviously as much of a rabbi as he is a therapist.

Your spoken words are accompanied by this uncanny intimate confidence that subliminally assures the unaware almost-hypnotized listener as to their veracity. Your beguiling credibility emulates the description of Moses upon presenting the Ten Commandments to the world, as explained in the dictum of the Talmud, that he was believed by all as if "God spoke through the throat of Moses." You could easily convert the world's most ardent atheist into a zealous mindless theist by merely whispering that God exists. They should invite you to give a TED talk. On manipulation.

I'm still amazed at your ability to convince Sara and Rachel to drive all the way to Brooklyn on a mission to Hell. As with your sending them to beg Mrs. Zaks to rescind the beautiful letter in which she and her husband described my wonderful relationship with Ester, you once again enlisted our daughters to launch another surprise attack. Knowing the specific Sunday afternoon hours I always spent studying with Rabbi Nekritz, Sara, once again doing the dirty work while her cowardly older sister sat in their getaway car, knocked on the front door of Rabbi and Mrs. Nekritz.

Banging loudly on the elderly scholar's door, Sara repeatedly screamed, "Your husband is a piece of shit! He's a piece of shit!" as his wife (the headmistress of a huge Ultra-Orthodox Jewish girls-only school) stood frozen in complete shock upon opening the door to Sara's tirade. It surely had to be the first time in her life that Mrs. Nekritz heard a Bais Yaakov girl say the word "shit." And never in an eternity could she possibly have imagined that her husband would be the recipient of such a lovely accolade. Bravo, Sharen. #braincancerawaitsyou

"He's a piece of shit! He's a piece of shit!" incessantly reverberated off the hallway walls as quiet neighbors opened their doors to hear what all the commotion was about. Sara, laughing like a lunatic, kept maniacally repeating her fecal-smear ordination into the kind face of the wisest man I have ever known. Like mother, like daughter.

Rabbi Nekritz, the holy saint you spoke to with obsequious reverence only days earlier (and for the prior thirty years), now heard your fecal-matter description as you attempted to embarrass him in public. Your daughter's actions removed your modest sheitel head-cover and revealed the uninhibited nakedness of your bizarre obsessed-with-feces brain.

But what would I want for
my Birthday?
nothing Because I have you,
THE JOHNS HOPKINS UNIVERSITY ·
OFFICE OF THE REGISTRAR
October 27, 1977
Zev Lewinson
3421 Glen Avenue
Baltimore, Maryland 21215
Dear Mr. Lewinson:
We have been advised by the Dean's Office that you have completed all requirements for your degree. Congratulations on completing your program. Your name has been forwarded to the President's Office in preparation for the public conferral ceremony which will take place at Commencement on Friday, May 26, 1978. I sincerely hope it will be possible for you to attend Commencement. Information on how you may participate will be sent to you at the above address in mid-April.
Johns Hopkins diplomas are prepared by an outside engraver just prior the May Commencement. For this reason we will not be able to have your until Commencement Day. In the interim, should you need that you have satisfactorily completed all to send you a certificate and mail it back to gree will be entered ay be issued will
me exactly as it ap- ncement Program as
hes please let me know at we can correct the
is applicable to all nces students who en- you are in either of will be sent to you gether with any other amount that aid before your diploma can be issued in May.
Again, congratulations on your accomplishment. If you have any questions about the preparation of your diploma or the Commencement procedures, Mrs. McMahon at 338-8079 will be glad to help.
Sincerely yours,
Robert E. Cyphers
Registrar

STATE OF NEW YORK
ROCKLAND COUNTY

RAMAPO

PEOPLE OF THE STATE OF NEW YORK
vs.
ALTER LEWINSON; dob: 02/21/1953, Defendant
ASE NO: 14100058

Criminal Summons

Complaint #24-07 14

lter Lewinson
Mariner Way
nsey, NY 10952

Defendants
19 Mariner
Monsey, NY

nal Charge(s)
156.05 UNAUTH USE COMP

Amended Charges(s)

Date: 10/21/2014 Time: 09:00AM

ARE HEREBY NOTIFIED that an Accusatory instrumen
d with this Court, charging you, as a Defendant
nse(s) listed above.

efore you are ordered to appear personally befo
37 ROUTE 59, SUFFERN, NY in the TOWN OF RAMAPO,
TY, NY at the above date and time for arraignme
satory instrument above mentioned. UPON YOUR FA
R AS ABOVE DIRECTED A WARRANT MAY BE ISSUED FO
T.

at : Ramapo Town Hall Route 59 Suffern, N
: October 3, 2014
2407 14
AINANT:

Hon. Alan M. Simon
Town Justice

SIRS:

PLEASE TAKE NOTICE that the withi
signed by the Hon. Victor J. Alfieri, Jr., JSC.
he office of the Clerk of the within Court on t

Dated: Chestnut Ridge, New York
September 11, 2015

DA
KA
& G
Att
747
Ch
(84

ZEV LEWINSON
Plaintiff Pro Se
19 Mariner Way
Monsey, New York 10952

For my dear בן
Zev.
From your loving
Sylvie.

"Don't move!" Rabbi Nekritz insisted in response to my angrily bursting out of my seat. "Do not go to the door!" he firmly instructed knowing how much I love and respect him. Frozen against my will, I remained seated at the dining room table strewn with holy books where we studied together for the past thirty-five years. "Your husband's a piece of shit! Your husband's a piece of shit!" continued to waft and echo throughout the long hallway of their five-bedroom Borough Park apartment.

I cringed at the debasement of this great scholar's honor as I heard my dim-witted child repeatedly cackle her blasphemy against a sensitive saint as my own daughter relentlessly accosted him in front of his shocked wife and neighbors at their front door. Without stopping to breathe, the daughter whose self-esteem I protected from birth was now acting as deranged as her mother. "Your husband's a piece of shit! Your husband's a piece of shit!" continued to bounce off the outside hallway walls as neighbors stood behind their half-opened doors.

"Batyah, close the door!" Rabbi Nekritz called out to his wife. "Just close the door!" he repeated, as we both heard, "You're a piece of shit! You're a piece of shit!" repeated and screamed, dozens of times in the background, at the brilliant man who refused to come to the door. I've never been so angry and mortified in my life. Who's next, Sharen? Are you planning on calling the Almighty "a piece of shit" in your next attack?

Great parenting Sharen. And great job in revealing how incredibly diabolical you can be. You will use anyone, including sleazy overpriced lawyers, along with our own daughters, to attack anyone I love or respect, in order to wreak havoc in my life and possibly anger me — merely to file a real Order of Protection (as if you need a reason). First Ester. Then Rabbi and Mrs. Nekritz. Who's next? Lauren? Can you help me find her?

Once again you used the mildly intellectually disabled daughter I loved and taught how to read, and flung her, like fodder, against one of the greatest scholars on the planet. Like the clever Palestinian terrorists that convince mildly retarded young men to wear a bomb vest, "because it is the will of Allah, who will surely reward you with seventy-two virgins and great honor," you swayed our sweet, gullible Sara to verbally assault Rabbi Nekritz simply to possibly anger me. Your arrogance caused you to believe you could outsmart an incredibly clever man only because he's so nonaggressive. I don't want to imagine what Allah has in store for you.

It wasn't enough to deceive and instruct our simpleton daughter Sara to take out a false Order of Protection attempting to place her own father in jail for sexual assault. You had to now use her again to strike out against the grandson of the ancient holy "piece of shit," The Alter, Harav, Hagaon Yosef Yoizel Horowitz, of blessed memory, in your relentless insanely deviant quest to destroy me.

If you suddenly experience headaches, and an eventual inoperable brain tumor, know that God loves you and is punishing you (like he punished your brother, Fred) in this world in order to spare you in the eternal one. At least that is what we were taught to believe. Good luck, Sharen. At least you have good medical insurance.

Mrs. Nekritz finally shut the door, visibly shaken, horrified, and stunned, being completely unused to any sort of drama in the life of her scholarly husband. Rabbi Nekritz, true to form, only wanted to get right back to our studies. He smiled at me angelically as he teased me with the challenge of, "Let's see if you can concentrate now," as he delved into a deep discussion in Tractate *Menachot* regarding detailed sacrificial work that was performed by the High Priest when our Holy Temple still stood.

I honestly admit I lost the challenge and couldn't hear or understand a word of what he was saying, let alone debate him in our usual "give and take" discourse. "You're a piece of shit! You're a piece of shit!" was still ringing like tinnitus in my ears and mind's eye. Along with the pounding beating of my heart against my eardrums. I can't believe how much I still love my daughters. Not as the refined souls I hoped they'd become when I raised them. It's just that I remember how endearing they were as babies and toddlers. It's too frightful to view them as adults.

I wonder if Sara kissed the mezuzah on the doorpost after insulting one of the most righteous men on the planet when Mrs. Nekritz closed the door that day. I'm sure you remembered, upon plotting your latest scheme, to patiently instruct our learning-disabled daughter to, "Always kiss the mezuzah, my sweet child, after wreaking fucking havoc upon the life of a Talmudical scholar."

I am still at a loss to describe the look on Mrs. Nekritz's face while her neighbors stared in disbelief as they listened to the verbal assault meted out to her husband in retribution for the compassion he showed you. A man who always wore a beatific smile, ensconced by his full-flowing white beard upon greeting anyone he met, never uttered one negative word about you the moment Sara finally left. Other than, "Meshugana." I'm sure he got the big picture and was referring to you.

Batyah's mouth remained half-opened, still locked in shock at the surreal scene she had witnessed at her front door, as she walked, zombie-like, almost banging into a wall, to sit down at her kitchen table and continue writing her lesson plans for the following week before having been interrupted by perhaps the most bizarre experience of her entire marriage.

Creating drama on Mariner Way and all over Monsey wasn't enough. You had to include the neighbors on Twelfth Avenue in Brooklyn. Where are you headed next? Will you soon be yanking on the legs of God's Throne of Glory to topple him off his chair because he allowed me to survive your cardiac nuclear divorce stress-test?

You charged at me like a hungry Bengal tigress. With your ten scalpel-sharp claws extended, you did your best to rip my broken heart out of my chest at the moment of impact — typically at sunset on Friday nights when most of you hunt. You stalked me for thirty-six straight months. Your instincts, like the Terminator Tigress, don't respond in terms of "Kill or be killed." Wild beasts never hesitate to think or reflect. It's "Kill and kill!" The concept of mercy doesn't exist in the mind of a hunter. Nor in yours. Your only focus is to get those sharp typing fangs into your victim's jugular veins, as fast and as deep as possible, while simultaneously shredding their internal guts and reputations with your claws.

What did Rabbi and Mrs. Nekritz ever do other than show you kindness, love, and respect? Batyah hugged you at the door when you came to visit and speak to her husband. She told you how sorry she was about our divorce. Rabbi Nekritz spoke lovingly at all our family celebrations, always praising you profusely. He listened to you patiently for hours at a time as you cried to con him into believing what a holy woman you are and how you sacrificed "*so much*" so that I could study with him all these years, and you then asked him to insist that I go back to therapy with you.

He tried, but I explained how miserable I was. You then visited again and insisted that he "has to" stop studying with me because I refused to go to Beit Din. After telling you that our relationship is for eternity (I hope!) and that he will never stop studying with me, he advised that we should divorce amicably. You, never being one to take no for an answer, kept calling him and Rabbi Nekritz finally asked me to politely request on his behalf that you not call him anymore. "She doesn't stop calling me! Please explain to Sharen that I have several hundred students and that I'm sorry, but I can't help her."

Incredibly enough Rabbi Nekritz did try, one last time, to reconcile our marriage. He cited different logical reasons as to why it might serve me well to reconsider. "She earns a good living and supports you so that you can sit and learn," he pointed out. I stared at his intelligent eyes and answered, "What good is studying the Talmud to gain Eternal life if I have to live in Hell?" Rabbi Nekritz then told me to "wrap it up." Like the Talmud instructs, he *listened* to both sides. Unlike your barking *Schabes Schweinhund,* Rabbi Nekritz never took sides.

Most people would stop there. But with you, even when it's totally over, you're only warming up. You then had to use Rabbi Nekritz (or should I say "nekritz," so you'll know who I'm referring to?) one last time to try and get me to display my "wrath." You and Rachel tag-teamed my sweet gullible, intellectually-impaired Sara to unleash vitriol against an elderly scholar to try and anger the only parent that truly loves her.

You don't care who you have to bump (or slam) into because you have no boundaries. Simply enter Tatie5521 into your Yahoo account and type away that, "nekritz has been radicalized by zev." Bump! And like those robotic vacuum cleaners, you keep on bumping as you blindly move in any direction that allows you movement. But quite the opposite of a vacuum cleaner, you dump shit, filth, empty boxes, and devastation as you destroy lives wherever you turn.

I would say that I don't know how you are able to dupe everyone and get away with such behavior. But then again, look at how you fooled me for years. Maybe it's your small body, or what Rebetzen Swiaticky (Gary Barnet's mother) described as your "adorable figurkehlah" as she ordered me not to divorce you. "You can't divorce her! Your holy grandfather would be so disappointed in you," Gary's mom kept repeating during many of our conversations over the phone.

My *TapeACall* phone app kicked in automatically in those days. Maybe I'll send Gary some of the tapes of his mom. I heard she recently passed away. He'd love to hear those tapes. You filled his mother's ears with so much nasty negativity that even she turned on me with her other son, Rabbi Mordechai Swiaticky, as they told me to leave their synagogue right in front of the entire congregation during the middle of Saturday morning prayers. After praying there for fifteen years would I have defiled the minyan had I stayed an hour longer? And needless to say, there went my relationship with Gary. It's amazing how you were able to involve everyone in the entire State of New York in your destruction of my life. Knowing you, I'm amazed I was able to get a visa when I recently visited Israel.

I'm also amazed at how quickly you swung the masses to your side. Perhaps it's the way you speak so gently, deceptively inviting the listener to lean in and pay close attention to your message of divine and urgent importance. Most likely, it's in your casting such utterly outrageous allegations with such complete conviction — the 'Grobe Luge' — that normal people just instantly assume that what you are daring to say must be true. After all, no one just makes up unhinged, crazed irrational batshit accusations out of the blue. They'd have to be out of their fucking minds. And you're a "doctor" no less. So it must be true!

I mean, after all, what kind of wife would suddenly accuse her gentle Mr. Mom husband of being a violent pedophile after twenty-eight years of marriage that mainly centered around his raising their five children? What lunatic would instruct her yeast-infected Yentas to call her husband's principal insisting that he is a dangerous and angry pedophile that needs to be fired immediately? I can almost hear the Yentas on their cell phones as they briskly march like cackling chickens during their early morning ant mill death-spiral *Lashon Hara* power-walks around Mariner Way.

"Twenty-eight years! Can you imagine? Not only his wife, but even his own daughters had to take out an Order of Protection because he was under the covers with them! She had to shlep him to Family court! Hopefully he'll wind up in jail where he belongs. That beast! And he always seemed like such a nice quiet man. And he was such a great teacher to my Yosi — even dropping off Yosi's homework assignments and books when Yosi was sick for a week. Oy vey! You just never know. It's always the quiet ones. Thank God he never touched my son. First Rabbi Bodenheimer, and now Mr. Lewinson! Who can you trust these days? Oy vey! Can you imagine!"

What kind of wife or mother would be callous enough to log in with her Tatie5521 password and premeditatedly make up and launch an email-blast rapper's rhyme of "Esty's breasties" uttered by a "pedo" father that "noticed their slight increase in size as he lovingly greeted his daughter upon her returning home from sleep-away summer camp?"

How diabolical, cruel, and sexually perverted would a wife and mother have to be to compose an imaginary scene in which said father "held up his daughters training bra" as he uttered those fictitious words while welcoming his little girl home? What woman would manipulate her best friend, Vittie Blech, who was sexually abused for years and is mentally unstable, to join a smear campaign against an innocent husband during a simple divorce. My eyes must have popped out of their sockets when I read those emails.

And because you have no "off" switch, or boundaries, you repeated your own lies as you entered the insane conversation you made up with Vile Vittie into your sworn NOTICE OF CROSS MOTION in your response to my serving you divorce papers that included my additional request to the court for full custody because you were alienating Ester. Instead of answering my evidence regarding the alienation you were inflicting on Ester, you flew past my evidence and went straight for my jugular.

Dated October 27, 2014, in your affidavit to the court, you wrote (upon penalties for perjury): "When she [Ester] returned from camp, the plaintiff looked at her and exclaimed: Look!!! You have little breasties!!!" And what are breasties, Sharen? They are called "breasts." And why the six exclamation points, Sharen? Is it because your mind is always shrieking? And who ever says "Look!!!" with three screaming exclamation points? Was the house on fire? No. Your brain was! (See? One exclamation point is enough.)

And how did we go from "lovingly greeted his daughter" in your original emails to Vittie, to my screaming "Look!!! You have little breasties!!!" by the time you typed your concocted "fakakta" version of events into your NOTICE OF CROSS MOTION? Are you crazy, Sharen!!! Are you out of your fucking mind!!! (Dealing with you forces me to use six exclamation points.) Actually, I am amazed that your sparking brain didn't include ten exclamation points. Your folly-furious brain reveals how childish you are.

Twenty-eight years of Jewish-Orthodox matrimony, through which we brought five precious souls into this world together, and all your loony lexicon brain can verbalize upon my divorcing you is, "feces, breasties, wrath, under the covers with Sara, dangerous, radicalized nekritz," along with "your husband is a piece of shit" delivered by your duped messenger Sara, while screaming, "Pedophile!" as you constantly called the police to "Come now!" on the holiest of our Jewish calendar days. You really are a poor-thing to be pitied. And dissected by neuroscientists, for the sake of science, after you die.

Knowing how much I care about children, you once asked me why I spent so much time helping Agunot instead of kids. It was a great question, Sharen. A logical one too, because the order in which I'd save a family from a fire or sinking ship would be children, women, and then men. "Why don't you fight pedophiles instead of those crazy husbands?" you asked. Do you remember my answer? Of course you do. A.I. has great memory. Especially when calling on the past to use what their victim loves and respects in order to manipulate them while inflicting pain.

I confided that fighting pedophiles was the one time I'd possibly take the law into my own hands. I shared with you then that I knew first-hand how helpless a young child feels under the control of a pedophile. It's a very scary emotion. An adult authority the child trusts and obeys is suddenly appearing as an alien life form billions of light years distant from where the young child's mind comprehends. The child is so confused, shamed, and guilt-ridden because he doesn't have a clue as to what is desired of him or how to respond. "I wouldn't trust myself," I explained.

I was very fortunate to escape before anything happened. But I still remember feeling cornered, trapped, and completely helpless. Kinda like Alfieri's contemptible and malevolent courtroom. But at least in divorce court I understood that I was being fucked. But looking at an adult with his erect penis in his hand was a terrifying and traumatic experience for a nine-year-old boy who couldn't possibly describe or understand what he was feeling (other than fear), or why a grown man, who had been teaching a skinny kid our holy Torah only moments ago, would suddenly reveal a huge erect purple penis sticking out of his underpants as he slowly lifted the holy book behind which his huge blood-swelled circumcised unholy cock had been concealed moments ago.

"Do you know what this is?" he gently asked, as if he was referring to the next few lines of Aramaic Talmudical text. "Would you like to touch it?"

I was too scared to even talk. I slowly nodded my head up and down to his first question and sideways to the second one. I was almost immobile with fear. At that age I knew absolutely nothing about perverts, pedophiles, or future psychopathic wives. I couldn't even imagine why a man would get an erection over the Talmud. It wasn't *that* interesting.

Or was it me he was excited about? My mind was muddled. Why is Yosef acting so friendly with his penis in his hand? All I knew was that I really liked the girls in my fourth-grade class. Especially Judy Schwartz and Ruth Ackerman. Judy was blonde. And a head taller than I was. And she was as outgoing and gregarious as I was timid and shy. Ruth was a brunette. Quiet and pensive. And very smart. I would get a temporary erection thinking about them when I was alone. But then I'd go back to watching television or reading a book. What I would have given for a long hug from Judy or Ruth. I would have probably swooned and fallen to the floor. Actually, come to think of it, I was quite anemic as a kid.

My potential assailant didn't try to grab me. He was moving slowly. But I sensed a new kind of imminent danger. A type that I'd never experienced before. I didn't know why, but I knew that it was urgent that I escape. *"Now! Right now! Get out of there!"* It was the exact voice I refused to listen to twenty-one years later when it again screamed, *"Get out of there! Don't marry her!"* as I sat in a movie theater holding the hand of the pretty little smart lady from Barnard that I was going to marry.

I hadn't yet learned how to fight. And at seventy-three pounds it probably wouldn't have made much of a difference. The only method of survival I had back then was instinct and speed, and like a young fawn without antlers I darted out the door before the lone wolf, who sat equidistant from my escape route, pounced to grab me.

"I'm afraid as to what I might do if I was positive about someone being a pedophile," I explained. "I wouldn't trust myself." I shared with you that I'd never be able to wait for the slow-turning wheels of justice if I knew a kid was in danger. "At two hundred pounds, the last thing I'd now do is run," I continued to explain, "but once people take the law into their own hands, we become a lawless society, and people start shooting one another for stepping on each other's lawns."

You knew how much I hated pedophiles. "Pedophile" is probably the ugliest word in the English language. Who does society hate more than a child molester? The moniker easily beats "nazi." It elicits even more outrage than the label of "serial killer." And that's why it was the first appellation you flung at me — hoping it would become my epithet — the moment I filed for divorce. Like a sci-fi acidic-gossip-spewing arachnid, you went right for my G (as in gentleman) spot, trying to anger me with a label of exactly what I most despise. You are the pedophile Sharen. You manipulated and emotionally molested our trusting daughters.

I still can't imagine what kind of gargoyle-mother would pressure and enlist her feeble-minded learning-disabled daughter to claim that her father was "under the covers with her and threatened to mash her head." My blood pressure probably exploded when I first heard the late Martin Gotkin, may he rot in Hell, try to enter that claim at the start of the trial I found myself in, "versus Sara Lewinson," thanks to your deranged-beyond-belief Nazi-creative imagination.

"Who would make up such an accusation out of the blue if it wasn't true?" your Yenta army logically oinked. I agree. "Who would?" They'd have to be evil as sin. Or insane. I'm gonna-go with insane. I have to go with insane. I have no other choice. It's the only way I'm able to forgive everything you did, Sharen. Otherwise, I might finally slap you across your tiny face. Trust me. A protection order wouldn't help you. But you already know I could never hit a girl. Or even a female monster-mom.

You are the Queen of euphemisms, using indirect words with more deadly accuracy than the cunning serpent that seduced Adam and Eve to consume the forbidden fruit in the Garden of Eden. When you hiss your suggestive version of events, your distorted manipulation of what actually occurred becomes more believable than a divine voice from above. Not that your Pussy-Posse "hoes" have much intelligence to begin with. It's just that, like rock vapor, your victims are covered by the heat of your lies before they realize they're solidified in scalding lava that quickly cools. Your words combust anyone that dares to defy you.

You have this uncanny, almost primal forensic-exposé power to reveal snippets of people's personalities that trick listeners to instantly trust anything else you say — as if it were revealed to you on Mt. Sinai in front of the entire world. You then seal your false words with a knowing smirk that forces the naïve duped listener to infer that they'd have to be an idiot to disagree with what you so passionately state as such obvious fact.

You can turn a scholar that has the entire Bible and Talmud on the tip of his tongue into a radicalized non-entity simply by omitting his proper honorific title of 'Rabbi' and simultaneously subliminally forgetting to capitalize his surname. I imagine that had God planned your birth a few decades earlier than 1955, he would have announced "Shifra Frayda bat Avrahom" as the future *Bashert* of Joseph Goebbels.

Perhaps my entire marital experience has been a path towards better understanding my own profusely empathetic mind. Or perhaps enduring our relationship was my rebirthing to regain my identity and happy innocence as I finalize my liberating escape from a dysfunctional childhood followed by a marriage to a soft-spoken frenzied hellcat who manipulated a husband who had way too much love and empathy for his family. Otherwise known in Yiddish as a *Schmuck*. We were definitely an "opposites attract" relationship.

Most likely, I'm still handing you bricks because I've been groomed by God and conditioned by Rabbi Nekritz to define and explain the most difficult concepts of the Talmud, aside from burdening myself with the herculean challenge of explaining our purpose for existence. I seem to have also somehow volunteered my efforts in attempting to define the impossible. A mother like you.

All explanations aside, I will simply say that you should be thankful you're a girl. Be glad I'm old-fashioned, Sharen. Because had a man ever dare to speak the words you spoke about me regarding my children, you know I'd stop talking only long enough to hit him in his temple with my right fist and in his chin with an uppercut with my left. Not out of anger. I'd fucking floor him the first time he even insinuated such disgusting behavior on my part. He'd be apologizing to me in writing (and blood). Notarized by his attorney. Please don't ever transition into manhood.

I don't want to imagine the details of what I'd do to a man who made my beautiful father-adoring daughter a living orphan. I know it would not be a pretty sight. And I don't enjoy looking at roadkill. And that's why I stopped looking into your eyes long ago. And, yes, I admit it. He'd need something you've never seen in your life. A *real* Order of Protection.

Oh goodness! Did I just give you cause to take out yet another one? "But Officer! He explicitly threatened that if I ever chose to transition ... and actually, to be honest, I have been thinking about it ... Rachel and I have been seeing Rabbi Frank for premarital and transition therapy ... and I don't feel safe, Officer ... and so if *that's* not a threat ...!"

I can already see you holding up this page to the policeman taking your statement at the station, and his instantly jumping to your rescue after staring into your moist eyes which are about to flow with the precise dosage of tears necessary to induce him to jump out of his seat. "Don't worry Ma'am! Er ... Sir ... whatever! We'll be sending out two armed officers immediately!"

But don't worry your little head, Honey. As you stated in your Tatie5521 emails, I'd never hit a woman. Or the insane. No hard feelings. I understand that you acted exactly as I knew you would. Like dealing with some gang member out of the Bronx I expected nothing less than to be stabbed in the back and set on fire over nothing more trivial than a bag of chips or a couple of lousy dollars. I know you can't help yourself. I forgive the misfiring synapses inside your brain.

The only thing I underestimated was your atomic-like energy and fire ant ferocity. You'll have to forgive me for attempting to fight an insect like you. I need to brush up on my science. It's hard to be both a Talmudical scholar and a myrmecologist in addition to taking on the role of Mr. Mom.

Maybe I should even thank you. Just as a piece of coal transforms into a diamond through immense pressure and extreme heat, the stress of being married to you — and living with you intimately for almost three decades — has guided me to an understanding of humans and world history that very likely now approaches that of the Buddha. The enlightenment gifted through surviving an apathetic mother and stolid-in-bed wife, while steadfastly adhering to the irrational commandments of a relentlessly badgering and persecutory God, has certainly taken the fight out of me.

And that's because I finally understand the sublime teachings of that great philosopher. There is no one to fight. And nothing to fight over. Not only have I never been "obsessed with feces," but similar to what Rhett Butler said to Scarlet O' Hara in *Gone with the Wind;* "Frankly my dear Sharen, I don't give a shit!"

I should have listened to the Buddha before choosing you as the future matriarch of the now shredded remains of our disintegrated family. Long ago he said, "A family is a place where minds meet. If these minds love one another the home will be as beautiful as a flower garden. But if these minds lose harmony with one another it is like a storm that plays havoc with the garden." Living with you was like being lost at sea in the middle of the Pacific Ocean during a tsunami and trying to swim to shore. *During Noah's Great Flood.*

Negativity breeds only pain. Trying to change someone else's negativity is an excruciating form of masochism. A zany jumping and bumping angry brain full of zig-zagging fears is an impossible mind to have an intimate relationship with. You are, sadly, very ill. I know you'll find this impossible to comprehend and that you will only jeer at what I share with you. But like the Buddha, I feel compassion for you, Sharen, because I understand that you really can't help yourself. *You have no free will.*

You, Charles Cullen, and Ted Bundy, are all missing something very human in your personalities. I've spent my life studying the wisdom of the ancients and I am not scientifically or medically qualified to diagnose the probable genetic disorder that caused your mental deformity. But I see that modern neuroscience gets a little closer every day to defining exactly what makes psyches like yours tick. Wildly.

What I do know for certain is that you don't just have trust issues, as you claimed upon our reuniting after your divorce from Dr. Leon Gilner, and as you explained to Rachel in response to her basically asking for your hand in marriage. Your mind has an entire array of pathological illnesses.

I could say I've forgiven you in the religious sense and deceive myself that I now have closure. But one cannot possibly claim closure regarding the actions of someone who was born corrupted and never "open" to begin with. There is no closure when a tigress hunts. There is nature. The apex predator will eat. Killing is as mundane for her as a 1950's mother setting the table while humming a song and turning on the oven to prepare a nice family sit-down dinner of meatloaf and mashed potatoes.

Like lightning and fast moving violent tropical storms, insanity is not something that desires or beseeches forgiveness and eventual closure. It randomly strikes as mindlessly as your signature appearing on an Order of Protection. Six times.

Bundy insisted he was innocent despite the emotional testimony of three randomly chosen women, who were in the wrong place at the wrong time, who luckily survived his maniacal passion for necrophilia when he attempted to brutally murder them. Exactly like you protested your innocence as you insisted and screamed to Schwartz, "I never signed! I never signed!" even as your notarized signature sat as evidence in a cardboard box at the Rockland County Courthouse. You're not capable of understanding that you could possibly be wrong, so how could you ever request to be forgiven?

A being that is capable of empathy and remorse merits forgiveness in proportion to their sincerity and future commitment to change their behavior and never harm again. The overlapping temporal and frontal lobes that allow normal individuals to fathom the future and "think ahead" seem to have no control over your helter-skelter behavior. I know it's not your fault, Sharen.

I understand that your developmental gnome never progressed to exhibit that trait. And only God, and perhaps future evolutionary biologists, understands why. Would I need to forgive a viper or tiger that bit me because of their instincts? You are obviously totally incapable of any remorse. It's scary. And simultaneously sad.

Our divorce only ended because you finally ran out of money — proven by the fact that you went bankrupt immediately after our divorce. You didn't run out of your never-stopping-to-sleep frenetic pell-mell ant-like energy. Like Rommel, the Desert Fox, you simply ran out of gas.

I still must share what an exceptional actress you are. Whether calling the police in a panic-stricken voice as if your life is in imminent danger, or respectfully kissing a mezuzah upon modestly entering a synagogue on Shabbat, or sitting like a pitiful victim in divorce court surrounded by comforting family members, or screaming "I didn't sign! I didn't sign!" in your A.M. emails to your esquire lover — or even upon finally sitting hunchbacked like a financially and emotionally crippled, broken divorcee at your bankruptcy hearing — your body somehow instinctively knows precisely how a refined sixty-year-old woman should behave and what she should emote to manipulate people to instantly jump in response to her pleas for help.

You are a true character actor. A human chameleon that flawlessly portrays eccentricities. Like those great homespun lyrics in Buck Owens catchy song, you surely can croon with confidence, "And all I gotta do is ... act naturally."

You really should have played the role of Tessa. You would have been a natural-born star. With a lowered head, and in the most hauntingly soft-spoken and exhausted voice I've ever heard a victim whisper a description as to how she was violently assaulted, you haltingly responded, "I went through a very acrimonious divorce," in response to the trustee at your bankruptcy proceedings when he inquired how you were able to incur such a hefty legal bill upon your divorce.

Oh. My. God. Damn, you're good! My jaw dropped, Sharen. I almost fell off my chair. Bravo! Bravo! Diane Keaton, Vivian Leigh, Marlon Brando, and Laurence Olivier could all have learned a thing or two from you. I wanted to hug you, comfort you, and assure you that everything is going to be alright.

Your "woe is me" wringing hands clearly deserve to be imprinted into the cement of the Hollywood Walk of Fame (followed by cement shoes or handcuffs and a perp walk). Your ability to distort truth with such credible honesty in your voice is miraculous. I was sitting at your proceedings and even I believed you! I felt so sorry for you that I was ready to loan you money.

But then I remembered all those emails in which your attorney kept enticing you to continue to destroy me. "Ya gotta give the car gas to make it go!" your swine jurist oinked. And despite your being as stingy as you are, you certainly gave him gas. I would have too. Zyklon B.

Nevertheless, I spoke on your behalf at your proceeding — to the astonishment of your trustee. "I've never had a man defend his ex-spouse!" he chuckled as I blamed your attorney for goading you on. Not that you needed any help. But I figured the more money you have, the easier you'll be able to pay for the "horse therapy sessions" that Ester desperately now needs.

I would not even bother explaining all of this to you. But I'm hoping that my sentences are read by Ester one day since she is now an adult. I still can't believe she is now just turning twenty-one as I complete my final rewrite of this manuscript. It's not that I have a desire for revenge. I'm merely hoping to enlighten my child in the future. And I know how hard it is to resist the maniacal psychological evaluations which you state with such absolute confidence against anyone you profile and pass judgement. And fetid Zyklon B gossip-gas. You have all the terminology and disorders of the DSM down pat. Coupled with your acting voice, you could probably have God institutionalized if you chose to. Actually, if he were a human, it would be a no-brainer.

Your insisting, "Tatie's going to make us homeless with his going to court!" could have scared me — let alone an eleven-year-old little girl. Your "fears" would certainly work to penetrate the mind of an innocent child whose survival instincts for keeping a roof over her head would force her to gravitate towards the only parent legally allowed to speak to her. God bless those Orders of Protection.

The Trustee believed you. Because after all, you're more charming, calculated, and convincing than the character Hannibal Lecter. And like the good doctor, you know how to use a scalpel. I should be happy I didn't become your Friday night chicken soup! I can imagine our kids asking, "Is Tatie still learning in Shul?" as they slurp their soup spoons while you patiently caution them to eat politely and quietly sip my boiled remains.

Remember how stunned Alfieri looked, as we walked back into the courtroom five years ago, upon informing him that we had agreed to an uncontested divorce after you and he ignited a two-and-a-half-year inferno through which both of you incinerated whatever was left of our torpefied family? The Alf couldn't believe that we worked out our entire divorce during a twenty-minute break. He was hoping to bleed us while collecting overtime pay for at least two more years.

After recording the details of our (officially) Uncontested Divorce into the court records, I then surprised both you and Alfieri when I requested that the judge add to the decree that I'm willing to volunteer an additional two thousand dollars a year towards Ester's high school education if you would agree to foster her relationship with me after all the alienation you caused. I also asked that I be allowed to pay Ester's school directly in the hopes of seeing her schoolwork and once again helping Ester with her homework and school projects as I had done during her entire life.

You graciously accepted my offer and later your lawyer wrote that the payments were to go directly to you. I let it pass because I didn't want to fight with you. Like a schmuck, I once again imitated my dad and tolerated your lawyer "for the sake of the kids." And sure enough, you once again made sure I'd never even know if Ester was alive or dead — let alone how she was faring in school.

And because no good deed goes unpunished, you then surprised me and dragged me into family court on November 21, 2018, as "Flame on!" furiously-angry as the day I served you divorce papers on November 15, 2013, for my being late with tuition payments — as if we ever paid our tuition bills on time during the thirty years we were a family. Five years later and you're as incensed as ever.

But don't think I didn't notice how quickly you backed down when the judge snapped at you when you got snippy with her for granting me more time for something I had volunteered to do. Bullies really are the biggest cowards of all. And one year later you and a new lawyer tried to manipulate the high school payments into an additional four years of college payments along with an increase in child support.

Once again, you dragged me into court on October 28, 2019, demanding that I continue to pay two thousand a year for Ester's college till she turns twenty-one, claiming that I never "volunteered" for Ester's high school and that it was "imposed" by the now-retired Alfieri.

She Who Steals Plastic Cutlery and Kosher Chickens chose to spend eight thousand dollars, forcing me to spend the same merely to respond (any litigation is expensive) and again "volunteer" another eight thousand towards Ester's college tuition over the next four years. I could have spent five thousand (forcing you to spend a similar amount) on a quick trial to prove that I had, in fact, volunteered the original high school payments. It's all recorded in the court transcripts, Sharen (AKA, she who insists "I never signed!"). My lawyer would simply have had to present the evidence (billing me at $375.00 an hour) to the court.

But because I can look ahead, I saw how ridiculous it would be for me to spend five thousand dollars to not give Ester eight. Choosing to fight you would result in Ester being told about all the effort "Ze'ev" went through in order not to give her a penny. I know your modus operandi by now.

And yet, despite your sadistic attempt to destroy my life merely because I no longer wanted to share mine with yours, I somehow still feel sorry for you. It's like the pity I feel for seventy-year-old Sydney — the one toddler among the several dozen of my many brilliant cousins who spoke very early as a child, but sadly regressed by the age of two to the developmental level of perhaps a six-month-old, where he remains as mentally frozen in his life as you are emotively frost-bitten in yours. Doctors never came to a unanimous conclusion regarding the mental demise of Sydney. But one day science will hopefully determine what ails you.

Seems you have yet to attain the early-childhood stage of emotion that most two-year-olds reach long before they can begin to fathom the religious beliefs and societal philosophies that will shape and manipulate their future adamant opinions. By that cherubic age most children already possess an innate compassion, a trait which they grow more aware of around that time of their maturation: genuine empathy. A trait you obviously do not share with them. Although you most definitely have learned how to throw a doozy of a temper tantrum. But in your case, I don't know whether to nap you or give you a lethal injection.

I understand that both you and Sydney are helpless. I see both of your brains for what they are. Damaged goods. Your brain merely has a higher intelligence quotient. And most certainly a lower emotional one. After all, what's the real difference between the psyche of a serial-killer like Ted Bundy, who intimately tortured his victims as part of the murder process, refusing to relinquish control and even fornicating with their postmortem bodies, and a Charles Cullen prolific executioner who rarely even touched the victims he injected with digoxin?

Nurse Cullen simply added heart medication and insulin into the saline bags of sleeping random victims as he overdosed them into a permanent state of sleep with his only interaction with said patients being that he glanced at their charts. No one even knows exactly how many people this slender, wisp of a male, killed. Estimates range as high as four hundred. Talk about stranger-danger. Each murder was nothing more than a misfiring-synapse spark in either Cullen's or Bundy's brain. Just like yours.

Cullen was as gentle as Bundy was violent. As you go "Bump!" But Cullen probably racked up ten times the number of victims. You tried to rack up one. Besides the baby you aborted with Dr. Leon Gilner even though you were about to marry him. To this day Rachel has no idea that I spared her life as I often thought about breaking up with you during our engagement.

Don't worry. I had my share too. But we share nothing in common. Because I have mercy on children once they are born. And had I not possessed your password I could easily have wound up a convicted felon, or literally your second abortion as a result of the web of stress you and your bastard lawyer viciously wove to constrict my time-for-retirement heart. We'll simply call Ester your "fucking couldn't care less" collateral damaged roadkill. Part of your and Schwartz's, "This can all stop the moment you agree to forgo any maintenance," blitzkrieg campaign.

If Alfieri had been my judge in Family Court, instead of The Honorable Dean Richardson-Mendelson, I have no doubt that I would have been forced to register as a sex offender. Teaching career? Over. Publisher of beautiful children's books? Over. Love life? Over. And if the half-senile *Deers Head Inn* bartender had been my judge in criminal court, instead of Judge Simon, I would have unquestionably received a year in jail plus additional years of probation during which I'd be forced to profess faux remorse for a crime I never committed. I'd be a convicted felon who had painstakingly studied three quarters of the entire Talmud in detail with plenty of quiet time to complete the remaining quarter.

How much more humane is a mendacious wife than the two aforementioned serial killers? In fact, Bundy and Cullen worked quickly. You took your sweet, premeditated time. Like a brazen man-eater tigress, you stalked me repeatedly — pouncing with fangs, claws, protection orders, and criminal and sexual assault charges, as you tore my life to shreds.

You even stalked me at the Beit Midrash Elyon Yeshiva where I studied every morning — staring at me when I asked you why you came, and then driving away hastily without uttering a word. My greatest fear during our divorce was when you weren't roaring. You definitely got into my head. *She's in the shadows. When will she pounce? It's too quiet. What is she up to now?*

You forced my tired blood through old clogged-up veins, stressfully pumped through a leaky heart valve with thirty-percent blockage, at a faster speed than it flowed freely when I was a mighty

Spartan disciplined long-distance runner in my twenties and thirties. You also flayed the once-happy personality of our gorgeous feline cub. I know Ester will figure it all out one day. She's a sharp kid. Right now there are simply too many angry aunts and Yenta therapist voices roaring in her head.

You continued your premeditated widow-maker haymaker assault on the coronary artery leading to my heart for a full two and a half years. If you think I'm joking, go ask our cardiologist, Dr. Joel Goldberg, how many times he said, "She's gonna kill you!" as he flipped out while unwrapping the cuff as he took a third wide-eye reading of my blood pressure, second guessing the accuracy of his findings with a look of horror on his face.

I'm sure your Yenta Hogs told you about the two times the *Hatzoloh* ambulance came to our house. I hope Alfieri gets the stroke he deserves for assisting you in trying to give me one. Not said out of a desire for revenge, but merely to keep this Nazi away from ever "serving the public" again as he now runs for office seeking the position of District Attorney.

I wonder what your, Bundy's and Cullen's brain tissue must look like under the microscope of Robert Sapolsky. I find it interesting that you all share the commonality of a higher-than-average I.Q. score. Clearly you are a destructive trio cursed with very peculiar brain matter that prompts you to wreak havoc till you are caught or self-destruct. And all of you are obviously unaware of a concept called "boundaries." Only metal bars can contain you. Or a grave packed with six feet of heavy moist earth swarming with maggots feasting on a dead deranged banquet. Ask your brother.

Speaking of self-destruction, I see your exhausted sixty-six-year-old calcium deficient twig-boned body, Sharen, as it sleeps behind the wheel of your dark grey KIA Soul while your half-charged shrinking-with-age REM-deprived Tesla prototype soulless motor-brain drives you to work. I see you spending the next eight hours dozing off, even as you stand at the O.R. table over a patient's open chest-cavity and faintly-beating revealed heart that is tethered to a heart-bypass machine, as you blindly throw stitch after sleep-walking stitch through his harvested vein.

I visualize your drooping head while you continue to doze as your misfiring synapses pitifully beg for some sleep-reboot recharge while you try to remember which highway you're driving on, as you sit featureless and dazed at the wheel where your run-on twenty-four hour attempts to dream are constantly interrupted by your repetitively dropping bobbing-back-up head and angry blaring horns during your treacherous traffic-jammed drive home to an empty cold bed with no one to warm up your frozen cold-blooded reptilian little feet by entwining them between welcoming humane muscular warm legs.

Do you miss my calls through which I kept you awake, from killing yourself and others, as I entertained you with laughter and current events while you drove back home half-asleep? I really loved you then, despite what I labeled as your "quirkinesses." I constantly feared your dying as the result of a car accident, either because of the aggressive way you drove, or the passive way you dozed while barely seeing the road through eyes that were three quarters shut as they remained covered by sleep-deprived lids that are as heavy as you. You always thought sleep was such a waste of time. At the very least, don't ants take power naps?

I see you writing your nightly late A.M. to-do lists on the hoarded cardboards you used to save from my freshly laundered folded shirts as you doze off in bed, head once-again bobbing, looking so weary and skeletal as you lie there (you lie everywhere) with your long, sparse, wiry ghost-white disheveled hair that looks more tired than even you.

With no one to gently kiss your forehead and remove the pen from your frail limp hand, while quietly turning the knob of the overhead spotlight to slowly dim its rays to avoid the sound of a loud click and instant darkness that might startle you if the switch is snapped shut, you finally switch to sleep mode for a few paltry hours under the glaringly harsh bright rays. Your dangling jaw and half-opened mouth emits the frail light breathing of an imminent corpse as you dream how to frugally save money for a lonely retirement with Rachel in Florida.

Suddenly jarred awake from your cadaver-prone-slumber a handful of hours later by the merciless buzzing-for-an-eternity alarm clock, that tortured me for decades as I reached over your body (that seemed as if it had overdosed on propofol) to tap it shut, now forces you to stagger like a walking-dead wandering corpse into the bathroom, as you slowly boot-up into power mode, thinking while peeing, "When was the last time I showered?"

The caducity of your age forces you to dress slowly, even as your dreary mind begins to whirl. Throwing on the same colorless outfit for "you can't even remember how many days in a row," knowing it will be covered by your oversized scrubs anyway, while quickly sniffing your armpits as you spritz some deodorant, you raise your "muselmann" Dachau arms above your head to slip them into their Monsey-modest long sleeved turtleneck to keep you warm while you stand again in power mode in an operating room as cold as your heart and as sterile as your soul.

As the ultimate creation of "Robotic surgery" you will, once again, spend the humdrum day in snooze mode slicing and dissecting the fleshy leg of some middle-age Jewish Kapo divorce lawyer suffering from angina and hypertension, to mine and harvest his vein ensconced deep in sinful fat that honestly deserves to be sacrificed along with the patient's heart on an alter to some Aztec pagan god.

Granting him a few more worthless years of precious life to outrageously bill some lunatic wife while maliciously prosecuting an innocent father with protection orders and accusations of his needing anger management, along with Family Court trials for molesting what the court now calls "her children," is hardly what I would call a mitzvah.

Your still-dreaming brain relentlessly continues to fight for a few more moments of desperately needed REM sleep, even as you stand while brushing the aging slightly separating teeth in your slumped head in front of the bathroom mirror while leaning, with a spindly arm that can barely lift a scalpel, to rest your elbow on the bathroom vanity sink for support.

Clumps of straw-like white hair attaches to your brush as you quickly sweep it across your deranged cranium while staring at the deep crow's feet branching the outer edges of the windows to your dreary soul. Tired glassy light-colored sapphire A.I. shutter-eyes, whose sclera contains blood vessels begging for sleep, stare back from deep dark-circled bony sockets, as you wonder, "*When did I grow so old ... better put some makeup on those puffy dark bags while waiting out the red lights on the way to work.*"

I see you snapping on your sheitel as you shuffle out the door after hastily snatching a yogurt from the fridge, carrying so many bags and endless "to do" thoughts while trying to rush down the basement stairs, carried by tired scrawny legs, knowing that every minute you delay will cost you ten more stuck in early morning, clogged as my heart, traffic. Thoughts of "*I'll shower tonight when I come home,*" momentarily zap in your left hemisphere for a third day in a row.

I also see you sitting among the lonely old matriarchs at the never-ending weddings (till God's next holocaust or actual final Armageddon doomsday) of our fourth-generation relatives, celebrating the pre-arranged bullshit-bashert made-in-heaven rushed marriages of their exponentially-birthing children and grandchildren. All paid for in lots of earthly cash bribes to some plump, rushing ignorant matchmaker (hard to believe we're still using them in the twenty-first century) whose, "I have just the perfect boy for your daughter," everyone trusts as ordained by God only because they're desperate to marry off their aging anxious daughters, riddled with irritable bowel syndrome, who are over-the-hill and crying over their tear-stained prayer books by the time they turn twenty-one.

Take a chill pill Sharen. I know the science isn't conclusive as to what causes the symptoms, but isn't it strange how many "Monsey girls" suffer from this ailment that a "top boy" (any male with a circumcised penis) rarely suffers from?

Meanwhile, the matchmaker lies through her yellow teeth as she hastily describes the wonderful lineage of the prospective groom while bartering male for female with less attention to detail than a half minyan of young future "top boys" swapping a dozen run-of-the-mill Topps baseball cards. A tad more spiced-up yentasplaining to edify what wonderfully righteous men the unremarkable great-grandfathers were, having never missed praying with a minyan during their entire lives, seals the sham deal.

The Yenta then increases her demands on the family of the desperate bride-to-be to support the aspiring scholar-groom who is eager to go out into the world and earn a living, but has been educated in a religious school system that is horrified by the knowledge of science and the openness of the Internet. The unworldly young man is now terrified of a world he knows nothing about, and his mother insists on the bride's family supporting her little boy for at least five years post marriage before allowing God's will to finally be done.

"Don't worry about the money," the matchmaker assures the bride's parents, "What is more priceless than the eternal nachas that grandchildren will bring you for supporting such a fine young scholar?" Everyone then hugs each other during the wedding as artificially as two opposing political enemies who are suddenly running on the same ticket as President and Vice President. Mazel Tov!

As always, Sharen, you're doing a splendid job of looking happy (your acting always was impeccably flawless) among the many successful chimpanzee-businessmen, world renowned bonobo-scholar self-centered personalities, and all the professional Orthodox women whose sheitel-clad heads have broken many glass ceilings while cooking for Shabbos and birthing their half-dozen kids of which our families are composed.

Women wearing "stunning" glittering gowns and tons of luxurious jewelry, and men in wide-brimmed black hats and understated expensive Patek Philippe watches, laugh and cry as they jump along the branches of our family trees sharing miraculous ancestral anecdotes, so proud of their lineage, while repetitively braying, "Mazel Tov! Mazel Tov!"

If our families have such strong ancient roots, why are so many of the descendants so fucking insane? I see my bi-polar Aunt Shulamith crying over the recently deceased clever hypocrite, Aunt Chaya Spitz, and I hear her pathetic prophetic description of my mother "Esterkeh" who is "looking down from heaven" (Good luck with that, Mom!) who "nebbich couldn't be here." (Because she smoked nearly two packs a day for decades while fucking an army!) The invitations surely must arrive weekly. I'm sorry they are no longer addressed to Rabbi and Mrs. Lewinson.

And how can I not recall the yearly attendance at the huge Passover Seder family-gathering in

Silver Spring, where you now sit solitarily surrounded by two-dozen late-in-life divorcees and earlier-than-expected Fred-less widows who enthusiastically speak with you as they brag about the latest bargains and incredible super-sized eight-gallon ketchup containers they found at incredibly discounted prices at Costco.

The few surviving castrati "Yes, Dear" (sung in a timid falsetto voice) men, sitting quietly at the table, stare blankly as they tremble upon realizing what a rare retroactively extinct specie of demoralized-husband they are. They're actually amazed as they wonder why their wives show so much passion for shopping while displaying comatose sexuality in bed.

What an exciting evening! Do you miss my historical and Talmudical explanations of the Haggadah? Do you miss having a real man at the Seder table to recite Kiddush over the first of the traditional "four cups of wine" for you? It's okay. You can admit it. Watch me. "I miss you and the family I once thought I had." We shared many tender moments and many wonderful times as a family of seven as we acted out the story of The Exodus with our toddlers. But I wouldn't go back for a trillion dollars. To be totally honest, if it weren't for my desire to create a family, you would have never been anything more than a disappointing one-night stand.

Do you remember the scrawny homeless derelict that I mercifully handed a twenty-dollar bill to almost thirty-two years ago, as I rolled down our car window at the entrance to the Benjamin Franklin Bridge, on the way to your Aunt Gail and Uncle Herschel's Seder? I explained to her, with sincere empathy, how I wished I could have given her more but that I rarely carried cash. She immediately turned and looked at you with a smile that revealed half-rotted, crusty and missing teeth, as she enthusiastically warned, prophetically as I now look back, "Don't let this one get away, Honey! He's a good man!"

I thanked her and we both laughed as the light turned green and I rolled the window back up. I teased you then that a total stranger instantly "knew me better than my own wife." Turns out I wasn't joking. Too bad you couldn't take her visionary advice to heart. Actually, don't apologize, "Honey!" Because you didn't let a good man get away. I was never that attached to you to begin with. Or to my God, I now realize.

I understand you're ill, Sharen — eccentric on a good day and scarily evil on a bad one. I know you have no regrets, because that would entail the ability to look back at missed relationships. It would imply that you are able to display sadness or remorse about past events. It would mean you possess a brain that could fathom thoughts like, "Maybe I was wrong ...?" It would also have allowed you to whisper the three priceless single-syllable words that my mother was never capable of sharing with me. Those words might have stopped me from serving you divorce papers. But don't worry about it. I understand that your only instinct is to robotically and monotonously march and swarm over your perceived enemies.

Decisions and actions occur instantly in a brain like yours. You're like the *Energizer Bunny* with an *Eveready* battery-brain that has no real pattern other than intermittently executing repetitive chores. Yours is a brain that does not recollect the past or envision the future. It's an instant-action brain that sporadically sparks. Spark. Spark. Spark. Your mind is like the cadence of a children's book I'd pen about you. I clearly see the title, '*See Sharen Spark.*'

"Once upon a time there was an adorable little girl named Sharen. Sharen had raven dark hair. And beautiful sapphire eyes. Her mind would constantly spark. Spark! Spark! Spark! See Sharen Spark. Between her sparkly blue eyes and her mind that constantly sparked, everyone loved little Sharen. Her teachers loved her. Her parents loved her. And her husband loved her — even though her pussy never went ... Spark! Spark! Spark! Sharen always did whatever she was told to do. Spark! Spark! Spark! See Sharen Spark."

If it does well, perhaps I'll write the sequel describing how Sharen grew up and married Prince Schmuck Charming who filed for divorce, but was unable to remove his chinked not-very-shiny (or protective) ACE childhood armor, and was nearly electrocuted upon almost being tasered by the police while he studied the Talmud one early Shabbat morning while wearing his matrimony-bludgeoned rusty metal plates. "Spark! Spark! Spark! See Sharen dial. 'Die Zev die!' Hear his daughter cry. Spark! Spark! Spark! See his relationship with Ester die."

My mind is the opposite of yours, Sharen. And that is why it took me such a long time to compartmentalize my twoscore, dating from the very first time we met, relationship with you. And with God. The two of you basically forced me to write a book that allowed me to heal myself from a lifetime of PTSD. Psychotherapists are correct. Journaling, also called expressive writing, works!

As I now look back with a writer's eye at your devious Machiavellian manipulations during our marriage and divorce, even I, who experienced it all in an almost traumatic state of surreal numbness, find it hard to believe the convoluted quagmire of pure torrential shit that you unleashed and forced me to trudge through for no other reason than a few dollar bills. To be honest, like the Revolutionary and Civil wars I orderly chronicled in the third grade, I'm still not sure what you were fighting over. I only know that it can't be your having to pay me maintenance. After all, you spent triple that amount on your lawyer.

Never could I have imagined a betrayal worse than the one committed for a lousy thirty silver coins when Judas received payment in exchange for kissing Jesus, as he betrayed the Christian Savior's identity at the Last Supper. After all, Judas didn't birth and raise five children with Jesus.

Recall how many Passover Last-Supper Seders we spent together, as you then betrayed and almost crucified me for a few bucks. Judas was only a disciple. You were my *Vybie*. You should be so ashamed. Perhaps we'd still be married if only you possessed the ability to feel any emotion, such as embarrassment, let alone remorse.

I once believed I found the woman with whom I would spend eternity. But I now realize that I was searching for a mother I never knew, through a wife I never had, while trying to serve a circular-logic God that demanded my pure faith while he constantly went, "Spark! Spark! Spark!"

Maybe I'll write a third book titled, '*See God Spark!*'

"See God spark. See how His Chosen Children spark. Spark! Spark! Spark! Watch the cattle cars roll. Woo-wooo! Chuff-chuff-chuff! See the smoke from the engine's that coal powers? See the half-dead Jews entering showers? Spark! Spark! Spark! Into the ovens of Auschwitz, like coal, they are stoked. Chuff-chuff-chuff! Out of the chimneys they finally escape as smoke. Smoke! Smoke! Smoke! See God Spark! 'I think I can. I think I can. I know I can ... get away with it.' Spark! Spark! Spark! See God Spark!"

How can God, who taught the entire Talmud to Moses on Mt. Sinai, that includes the wisdom of Tractate Sanhedrin (37A) in which the Almighty is said to thunderously proclaim, "The saving of one life is considered as if one saved the entire world," turn around and mercilessly slaughter six million of his own *Am HaNivchar* "Chosen?" You and God are as hard as I am gentle. As cold as I am warm. As robotic as I am spontaneous. You are as dead, my dear Vybie, as I am alive. I'll let Nietzsche cast his own vote regarding God's mortality.

I needed time and space to distance my emotions from you, even as I obviously reveal through many pages of this book that I still often think about you. I still worry about your constant lack of sleep. I worry about your working in a hospital and coming down with the COVID-19 coronavirus disease. I worry about your brittle bones and shrinking brain.

And I worry about you dying in a car accident. And never getting to read this book. After all, you constantly boosted my confidence when I shared rave reviews from Kirkus, and effusive letters describing my "tsunami of creativity" and "real knack for writing" from Random House, famous agents, and other renowned publishers. You shared your literary criticism, despite my never witnessing your having read one book the entire time we were married, as you praised my writing talent. It's amazing how I still hear your adoring screeching voice; "You're not a real writer, Zev!"

Can you blame me for thinking about you and our family, Sharen? We had five kids together! Five precious souls that we believed we brought down from heaven, through embracing each other in an act of love, to raise as wonderful little Orthodox Jewish people. We shared a bed and the main thirty years of our lives together. Isn't it amazing that we were once *Ishto-Keh-Gufo* lovers: the Jewish concept that a man and woman become one in marriage (Genesis 2:24)?

How did such a beautiful and romantic dream end up a dystopian nightmare? Can you blame me for being sentimental about the destruction of our once beautiful family? Was the conflagration necessary? Did you have to wipe the hard drive of our now retroactively ephemeral "home sweet home" big family, along with Ester's brain, clean? Couldn't you simply delete the data from your own spark-wired faulty brain? How were you able to instantly decide to never speak with me again along with cutting me out of everyone's lives?

You knew how disrespectful it was for Ester to call me "Zev" as you instantly launched your alienation campaign. But that was nothing in comparison to your coaching her to hate me as she eventually succumbed to your willpower, while you laughed as my daughter threw dirt on my bed that she'd collected outside and then keyed my car while entering yours as she threw you a glance that sought your approval. I watched the two of you from my guest room window. I hope you enjoyed the *nachas*.

How do you outdo Big Brother, Sharen? In totalitarian Oceania they had to first erase history before rewriting it. But with some kind of nocturnal hypnotic wormhole ability to simultaneously warp time and people's minds through your typo-clever emails and "oh so hurt" sweet voice, you instantly traveled into the past, dumped our thirty-five-year relationship and wedding album on the floor of my study (Thank you, Darling!), along with the stuffed-toy moose you once loved, and reappeared as Sharen Mailman as if we had never met, let alone been married. *Were we?*

How were you able to abruptly act as if your lover, best friend, and husband — with whom you shared your tongue, a bed, and your spread Mikvah immersed cold-blooded crocodilian thighs for over thirty-five years — never existed? Who did you come for all those times? *What* did I ejaculate into? I'm actually quite nauseous, if not repulsed, at our having shared any intimacy. *Did we?*

We were together for such a long time, Sharen. Doesn't forty years mean anything to you? We dated and slept together in our mid-twenties before you married Dr. Leon Gilner. I broke up with you so gently. And, with tears welling up in your eyes, you asked if I had any intentions at all to date you even occasionally. Something about you was out of sync (besides your moves in bed) and I sadly admitted that it's probably best for both of us to just move on with our separate lives. (I was so right!)

You mentioned at the time that your professor had been asking you out relentlessly. "He's a brain surgeon!" you added. "Great!" I responded, "You'll probably marry him. The last eight women I broke up with married a doctor." "Maybe he could help me!" I chuckled, in an attempt to keep a lighter atmosphere. "He'd have to castrate you to help you!" was your clever, angry response as you drove off in your green Volkswagen Rabbit. I only realize now — four decades later — that you weren't joking that day.

Things didn't work out for the two of you and you got divorced. You were such a lady when I broke up with you the first time (aside for that clever remark). So when you sent regards I decided to give you a call. I'm still not sure why. Perhaps it's because I always get the last word (that's a joke). But I felt bad when you were so upset as you drove off four years earlier. Aside from that one nasty remark, which I thought of as funny, as I understood you were hurting, you were the epitome of someone I could trust and respect. You just sucked in bed. Or didn't. Either way, I dialed away my next thirty-five years as I rang you up.

On a more serious note, I had become more religious, and I was now thirty years old, and you had always been such a "good girl." This time I believed the timing was right, and you were Ms. Perfect. The opposite of my mother. Too good to be true. (You were.) And I agreed to marry you. How could I have imagined, in my most abstract thoughts, what a wild animal you were beneath such a ladylike surface. Even after twenty-eight years your bi-polar behavior still had me confused and running in circles. I can't thank you enough for sharing your password with me.

I still see you on that special day when I pronounced my wedding vow to "take you for my wife." You looked so beautiful and innocent. How could I have foreseen, as I stomped the glass wrapped in a cloth napkin on our wedding day, in memory of the destruction of God's Holy Temple, that my future constricting heart was inside the pretty crystal tumbler. Not in a trillion years could I have envisioned a future in which a woman I would have taken a bullet for would set me up with false Orders of Protection and insanely outrageous accusations of sexually assaulting my daughters. You're a very sick woman, my dear.

I'm the father of your five children. Six if we include fetus Chezkie. And I do. Surely your mad-hatter brain is able to recall one single memory that must evoke an atom of love or tenderness towards me that momentarily negates your narcissistic rage. I met you (the first time) as I turned twenty-five and left your Jewish divorce document at the Rabbinical Council of America as I turned sixty-five.

Four decades, Sharen. Hello? Anyone home? Fourteen-thousand and six-hundred nights. Have you no memory of watching us make love in the mirror of your antique vanity piece or hugging me close as I ejaculated inside of you while kissing your face as you tensed up and froze while enjoying your multiple orgasms? Don't you remember the trips back from the hospital as we brought home baby after adorable baby?

Share with me, for the sake of our kids and grandchildren, that it would have been unbearable for you to look into my lacking melanin light-blue eyes as I would have said, "Ha'ray Aht Meh'gureshess Lee," had I personally delivered the divorce document, dropping the scribe-written parchment from my hand directly into your open cupped hands — symbolizing that we would never touch each other again because we'd no longer be husband and wife.

After robocalling and emailing our entire extended family and many friends that I was violent and obsessed with feces, you immediately bombarded them with emails that I planned to make you an *Agunah* by abusing you with my Talmudical knowledge. I recall the email response of your cousin, Robert Matanky, Esq., as he advised you to calm down. "You've barely been served, Sharen. I'd hardly say you're already an *Aguna* [sic]." (Thank you, Bobby. I miss your Passover potato soup, by the way.) Agunot race to Beit Din to pick up their Jewish Get, Sharen. I know. Because I've accompanied many of them to pick up theirs.

It would be nice to know, now that our divorce is over, that you crumpled and demolished my Tatie-armor only because of your nasty anger and a total lack of morality, but that there is still some spark of human mensch warmth, inside of you. I'm almost begging you ... may I please "See Sharen Spark!" one atom of compassion? One proton? An electron?

We spent our entire adulthood — and it could have been eternity — together. Can't you unfocus from your silent treatment for a mere nanosecond and think of one nice thing to relate to Ester about how nice her Tatie was? Besides, "May he Rest in Peace." Come on, Sharen. Please? Pretty please, with a Jewish-Get on top? Forget about "Spark! Spark! Spark!" How about just one itsy-bitsy teeny-weeny quirky-quark flicker?

I understand you're suffering from deranged DNA, but it's hard for me to let go. I can't instantly delete the memory of embracing you in the House of Study thirty-five years ago. I can't erase the memories of thirty years of birthing and raising five children with you. You certainly took the time to teach Ester, but you never taught me, how to instantly and retroactively unperson people as if they never existed. My mind doesn't work that way. Neither do my feelings.

I still see the sparkle in your eyes as the soft light from the *Ner Tamid* reflected off their irides as you stared into my eyes. I feel your size-two body trembling as we anticipated becoming a family. Your rich black mane rested under my cheek as we embraced in what we believed would be an eternal hug — like the embracing cherubs that stood on the Holy Ark that miraculously floated on air (as we did that night) while leading the early Jewish Nation as they wandered through the Sinai desert for forty years.

And I still recall all the "Mazel Tov!" blessings of our parents and friends at our lavish wedding. We were that one couple everyone believed would surely live a "happily forever after" fairy tale life. And you were the "happiest girl in the world," and the most fervent devotee of all. What happened my love?

Responding to a Motion for Divorce does not mean simultaneously flinging your husband into divorce court trials to determine his fitness for partial custody, along with tandem criminal and family court trials to face criminal and sexual assault charges that could easily have landed him in jail. And it does not mean using your medical knowledge to dissect my heart without your scalpel. You, especially you, understand how cardiac mortality occurs as a result of stress.

Adrenaline floods the heart, drowning it with deadly continuous tsunami surges of the "fight of flight" hormones that cause weight gain, anxiety, and eventual heart attacks and strokes. Especially when one is not allowed to fight back and has nowhere safe to run. You stare at those obese hearts loaded with plaque eight hours a day while throwing in stitch after stitch to allow a steadier flow of oxygenated blood to give the intubated living corpse a few more years of life.

You know that broken relationships easily cause Broken Heart Syndrome. Divorce, protection orders, alienating Ester, homelessness, being shunned by the community, forsaken by family, plus the completely unnecessary drama of family and criminal court trials, were all well placed incisions to commit the perfect murder. You fucking carved my heart out.

You understood all of this. As well as I can dissect any folio in the Talmud. You know that loneliness is toxic to the forgotten elderly. It even causes Alzheimer's. You also know that when adrenaline and cortisol levels rise, so does one's anger. Our systemic court system, smeared by shitty appalling lawyers like Schwartz, trashy and inept judges like Alfieri, and an endless supply of bottom-feeder lackey professionals, supplied the perfect poisonous concoction to send my irregular beating heart into complete arrhythmia.

When Dr. Joel Goldberg anxiously warned me, "She's going to kill you!" upon releasing the air in the blood pressure cuff for the third time in a row, he was not being frantic. He was being completely scientific.

How did a devil like you even find the time to chirp your little morning daily prayers to God while you carried on like this in front of him for almost three years? Did you show remorse and ask forgiveness from God for all your transgressions on Yom Kippur? Did you ask God for health and happiness for our family and all the inhabitants of the world?

Did you chirp the *Yizkor* memorial prayer for your sneaky brother Fred whose emails full of scurrilous, "Say he hit you!" lies are now stored among the historical legal documentation of our divorce that sits buried, like Fred, in the Rockland County Courthouse, and surely at the court of the heavenly tribunal Fred met with upon his death, as permanent evidence and proof as to what a troublemaker passive-aggressive Fred was before God buried him?

Glad to hear they dedicated a Torah scroll in memory of Fred at *Woodside Synagogue Ahavas Torah*. Why wasn't I invited to deliver a eulogy for my deceased beloved brother-in-law? I could have spoken about how the Torah represents kindness, truth, and justice.

You almost killed me, Sharen. And your betrayal was so ferocious that there were many PTSD days that I wished you had. Like those creative Nazis who misused the most spiritual gift humans possess, to instead grotesquely torment and murder innocent souls, you were also quite "creative," and utterly revolting, when it came to clawing the reputation of the clean-handed husband you once swore to love for eternity. You had me begging you to, "Just take everything!" And you still couldn't stop. Scientists don't treat diseases the way you treated me.

Creativity is a gift from God, Sharen. "In the beginning God created ...." Having children is the closest we can ever come to emulating God. I taught you all of this. Just as God took a "spark" of himself, with nothing being lost, to create our souls — man and woman unite, while basically losing nothing of themselves, to miraculously create and "spark" new life. How were you able to twist the knife in the heart of your husband, with whom you "sparked" six children, without a quark of mercy?

You and fuckface Schwartz didn't only come close to "tossing" me into jail. You almost buried me. Literally. I still hear Dr. Goldberg warning me, as he tripled my medication inside of nine months while I put on stress-induced weight faster than a pregnant woman, "I can't keep doing this! I can't keep increasing your dosage! She's gonna kill you!" Goldberg was more scared than I was. Nothing raises blood pressure like stress. You kept me locked within a stress fight-or-flight response stage for over two and a half years.

How much shit can you fling against a man you once love-bombed and idolized? I remember how all the surgeons at work wanted to meet me because you couldn't stop raving about me. I can only imagine what you now tell them. How much pressure can you inflict upon one already-broken heart? And you sure as hell understand how the heart works. And how it doesn't. When you laughed with Schwartz to "give Zev a heart attack," you weren't really laughing. You were rejoicing.

It's ironic that had you succeeded you would have had to sit shiva for your husband according to Jewish Halacha. I can easily imagine the Tessa-tears flowing down your tear-stained cheeks as you'd softly kiss the mezuzah upon entering the synagogue, dressed in black, to hear Rabbi Nekritz deliver my eulogy. And I can see you drinking a "l'chayim" with our old neighbor on the seventh floor in Riverdale as you provide him with a sorely needed acting lesson.

You constantly barked orders. And I jumped as high as Michael Jordan. And shortly after 9/11 and the crumbling of my online *CyberDiamond.com* diamond business, along with the Twin Towers and 2,996 souls that perished that day, you yelled at me to take a "ton of diamonds" on consignment from all my suppliers and to then declare bankruptcy. "Your family, Ze'eh'ev! Everyone else does it! They did it to you! Do it to them!"

I can't tell you how pitifully small you looked at that moment. You were like a starving predatory animal. My creditors treated me with more compassion than you did. Don't think your hysterical shrieking and "fears" about money didn't tempt me, Sharen. Your repetitive nightly a.m. barrage, as I tried to doze off in our coffin-tight-with-you-there grand master bedroom, coupled with the depression of my father's recent death, wore me down. I felt like the Manchurian Candidate as you relentlessly brainwashed a husband of integrity to commit get-away-with-it theft.

And losing my ahead-of-its-time online diamond business (we were selling ten-thousand-dollar items when most people were still afraid to use their credit cards online) while undergoing the stress of having to go bankrupt, certainly swayed my moral compass.

For quite a few days, and endless sleepless nights, my grey matter wobbled inside my cranium as I considered granting your desires against what my heart screamed was pure I-can-easily-get-away-with-it theft. I tried to weather the constant storm of your vitality-draining insults to my manhood regarding my not caring about my family, but your incessant nagging voice was always louder than the racing beats of my tired heart. Especially when coupled with your anger at having to, "stand on my [your] feet in the O.R. all day," when all I had to do was follow your orders and "glom a fist full of gems ...."

I remember running up to the offices of Rick Shatz Inc. to return several stones a few days before my attorney arranged for me to declare bankruptcy. My lawyer knew the Trustee and assured me that my case was an open and shut common occurrence. "You're not the first jeweler to declare bankruptcy, Zev. All the paperwork has been filed and approved. She'll probably ask you a few questions about the diamond business and your losses and it'll be over. It won't take more than a few hours," my lawyer assured me.

Both my father's earlier demise and the shocking sudden death of my CyberDiamond dot-com business, along with many other bubble-busts on that fateful eleventh day of September were mild events compared to the stress of your amoral admonitions to steal. But I was losing it. The remaining days of Dad's life had been spent in a state of sleep enjoying a strict diet of morphine hooked up to an intravenous la-la-land drip (legal euthanasia).

I remember asking the doctor, upon seeing only one intravenous line, where the tube to feed my dying father was located. "How are you feeding him?" I wondered out loud. The doctor looked down and softly mumbled something about "we're keeping your Dad comfortable." You were driving me so crazy — pushing me like some ancient Roman senator's treacherous wife aspiring for power and wealth — that I could have used my own drip.

Ironically, my kind Dachau-Survivor-Dad died, not due to his prostate cancer. Technically speaking, he was mercifully executed by thirst and starvation fifty-five years after being liberated from the edge (literally) of his mass execution grave. The Nazis and God finally caught up with him. Dad looked like an emaciated skeleton upon his emancipation from Dachau, and like a coma-induced corpse whose eyes rapidly fluttered in their drugged-induced sedated state before finally being emancipated from his excruciatingly difficult seventy-five-year-old life.

A life that consisted of a childhood lived in constant fear, evolving into a nightmarish stint in Dachau, while almost his entire family was murdered, followed by depressed and difficult postwar years searching for his family (he located two sisters that miraculously escaped the Germans and hid behind the Iron Curtain), and a thirteen-year marriage to a cruel wife who quickly birthed three sons.

Dad then rented a single room for five very lonely years as a divorced man who was tossed out of his house upon being ordered to pay his ex-wife three-quarters of his paycheck in alimony and child support. My Tatie prepared his dinners on a hot plate and surely choked on his nightly supper while thinking about his three sons being raised by a muscular stranger, whose all-American cock was furiously sucked by their mother who surely never choked on her midnight snack.

Dad cut through boring mountains of patterned-women's stacked cloth for four decades by day. Any other man would have used his huge electric saw to bury his wife. On seven continents. Dad eventually found a few years of peace upon marrying a quiet widow and raising her son and daughter, culminating with a very painful demise delivered by a sadistic executioner called Mr. Cancer (a close relative of Mrs. Hyde) who took his time submitting his prisoner through years of endless excruciatingly painful medical procedures while slowly incinerating every cell inside the body of my sacrificial lamb-Dad.

Even my poor dad's testicles were eventually removed in the hopes of slowing down his cancer. I still remember my father crying over the phone in Yiddish that, "now the doctors want to *shnide* (hack off) my *baytzim*." I took a deep breath to hide my broken voice affected by his tears as my own eyes welled up with mercy, and I calmly explained to my father that, "They were only planning on removing the insides and that they were not going to just chop them off."

There probably wasn't that much to castrate anyway after my mother shredded them with her raucous laughter at Skip's hysterical jokes.

My business and marriage, at that time, were suffering a much slower death. Dad lasted an amazing eleven days without food or water, higher on morphine than any level of utopia I had ever attained in the wildest days of my self-medicated youth. My marriage, to be honest, along with my emaciated soul starving for love, had long been post-mortem.

Meanwhile, Rick asked me if I'd mind dropping off a stone to Mordechai Kopciel, his diamond cutter, on the way back to my office. It was an eighteen-carat natural yellow (not an "intense," and not a "vivid") square cut gem worth (*only*) around $280-thousand dollars. I never even signed for gems Rick gave me to sell. That stone alone would solve all my problems. And you were the biggest one, Sharen.

I'd merely have to claim that "it fell out of my pocket," and Rick would have been forced to make an insurance claim. He'd be mad at me for a while because his premium rates would go up. He'd also have a bunch of paperwork to deal with. After all, insurance companies keep a tighter grip before dispersing money than when Khabib Nurmagomedov locks onto the wrists of a shocked opponent. They force you to trail the transaction of the diamond being claimed lost in the hopes that it was paid for in cash and "never happened." False invoices constantly flew around 47th street faster than the police arriving at my home on a Shabbat morning. But no real serious financial loss for my friend. No big deal.

Rick was such a nice guy that he'd probably understand my situation and eventually forgive me even if he didn't completely believe me. His mind would always remain in doubt. And I could easily recut a large stone like that and sell it to clients in Boston or Miami, no-questions-asked. Who would know?

I'm so good at recutting stones, that I might even improve the color grade of the gem and sell it for more than even Rick ever imagined it to be worth. Who knows? I could very easily get away with selling it back to Rick himself once I recut it. He'd never know the recut gem was originally his. Too bad I'd never be able to share that story with other diamond dealer friends if I did it. Like you said, Vybie, "Everyone else does it. They did it to me. I'll do it to them!"

Even the legendary Louis Glick coincidently left the country coinciding with a major theft of millions of dollars worth of gems (when a million was money) at JFK Airport more than three-quarters of a century ago. He wound up in Israel for quite some time, his chief diamond cutter Hy Kessler (who sold me many gorgeous gems) explained to me, as blurry circumstantial events got sorted out by his lawyers before Louis reentered the States. Who would recall one stone once Rick's claim was settled, I rationalized as I considered the endless task of making my wife "happy." Who's more important — Rick, or my wife?

One of my own cousins pulled off a scheme like that, claiming an attaché case full of natural yellow diamonds was "stolen" as he made a two-minute call (and two million dollars) at a phone booth many years ago. He was fired from the company he worked for and opened his own firm in the same breath. Today he's known for giving charity. A real mensch.

Another cousin of mine buys hot goods and is super successful in the color stone business. He'd earn even more money if he didn't spend so much time frequenting hookers. His obese wife is drowning in gems. And depression. And surely STD's. I was the boring honest intellectual schmuck. Maybe my wife was right. Perhaps it was time for me to join the crowd of low-rollers.

I also still had $362-thousand in gems that I had on long-term consignment from a half-dozen different wealthy dealers locked in one of my deposit boxes that I was still planning to return. Sixty grand to each one of them, on average, was a drop in the bucket. And I had several hundred thousand dollars' worth of gems out on consignment to retail stores that I could easily finagle (like Abramoff's ordination) into the bankruptcy proceedings. I also had at least a hundred thousand dollars worth of estate goods from my good friend and longtime client, Michael Gross, that I could simply report as "sold" and then gem-dealersplain as "lost" as a result of a protracted tangled bankruptcy.

Michael would have no problem absorbing that loss, I rationalized. After all, he even spent an extra fifty grand with his caterer for a kosher Bar Mitzvah celebration just so that Sharen and I (his kosher-only main supplier) could attend. "I gave up lobster for you, Zev," Michael quipped as we hugged at the joyous outrageously expensive celebration. I still recall the waitresses at the event. They were so obsequious I hoped you were allowed to take one home with you along with the parting party gifts.

He's such a nice guy, he'll forgive me, I desperately tried to force my guilt-ridden Jewish mind to believe, as I heard, "Your family Ze'eh'ev!" looping repeatedly, like a broken tape recorder, in the occipital cortex of my drained brain.

I felt terrible at the thought of ripping off such a great friend with whom I conducted tens of millions of dollars worth of business along the years, and whose century-old family business would have been my brick-and-mortar location partner for CyberDiamond. But the incessant verbal pummeling of my Eishet Chayil raced like an F5 tornado through the synapses of my frontal lobe, grooving my Talmudical brain, while slowly submitting and manipulating me away from behaving like a true honest scholar, and eventually transforming me to live by the survival mode of a feral wild beast. Pounce! Claw! Eat!

"Your family, Ze'eh'ev! Everyone else does it! They did it to you! Do it to them! Your family, Ze'eh'ev! Everyone else does it! They did it to you! Do it to them! Your family, Ze'eh'ev! Everyone else does it! They did it to you! Do it to them!"

I had a million stories that I knew from thirty years of experience in the business, about companies and dealers who went bankrupt, that I could personally use to flawlessly cover myself to keep those gems. And I could easily delay my lawyer a few more days while I smiled warmly as I took another few hundred thousand in gems from unsuspecting big firms who trusted my handshake like a contract etched in stone.

My wife is right, I kept repeating to myself. I paid my dues. I'd suffered through so many dealers and retail chain stores that went bankrupt on me during my three decades in the business. And I didn't fly into the Twin Towers that burst the internet bubble craze. I'll simply tell everyone that those losses finally caught up with me. I'll take off a year, relax a little, and come back and start fresh. With the cash I'll have, I can easily build up my credit again. And diamonds are so easy to hide.

Rick himself told me how Louis Glick's own son and son-in-law took a bank for ten million as they threatened to go bankrupt and default on a loan in one of the many down-market trends in our business. Daddy walked in last minute with a fat cigar in his mouth and a fatter "take it or leave it" fuck-you check for one million.

Being the practical whores that bankers are and realizing that the kid's company had no legal financial connection to their father's company (exactly like The Donald and his dad), they never hesitated as they "made a business decision" and warmly shook the hand of Louis Glick as they accepted an offer they could not refuse. Louis didn't have to bother with butchering a racehorse's head to convince them. It was simple math. Ten cents to the dollar was better than nothing.

And although the market did indeed drop by about thirty percent at that time, the Glick's netted roughly nine million dollars, according to Rick, on that maneuver instead of paying interest and waiting for prices to adjust. It was all a drop in the bucket when compared to the billion's banks steal from consumers between derivatives and manipulated overdrawn fees, arranged so that large amounts are paid first in order to charge $35.00 on a half-dozen small items that post for payment at the exact same time. The banks pay the fines of class-action lawsuits with a smile.

Rick's own brother-in-law Marty also filed a huge bankruptcy in which he taped his bankers (long before the iPhone and apps were invented) while they admitted collusion they'd never want revealed. "We all go down together if you fight my filings," Marty calmly informed his "partners" in a slightly Israeli-accented whisper over the phone as he slowly exhaled his cigarette smoke through his nostrils and lips with a coolness that made Bogart look like a naive virgin. "Your family, Ze'eh'ev! Everyone else does it! They did it to you! Do it to them!"

Marty's bankers quickly learned that stuffed suits are no match for an Israeli-American diamantaire who flew his jet all over the world to mercifully deliver illegal transplanted organs to save lives. They handed Marty all his signed notes.

It would be so easy to make my wife happy and sell the gems later, slowly and at my leisure, all over the world ... I haven't been to Tel Aviv for quite some time ....

"Fuck everyone!" the Devil and my wretched wife screamed in unison as they tempted me with their anxious, "Your family, Ze'eh'ev! Everyone else does it!" cry. But I'm not like everyone else. For every thief in the business, I knew at least ten honest dealers. Like Greg Herdemian from Empire Diamonds. And Michael Gross from H.L. Gross & Bros.

For every thieving and conniving Howard Engle who purchased "dumped diamonds" (gems purchased from large companies by on-the-verge-of-bankruptcy desperate diamond dealers who buy the stones with a ninety-day bank note and immediately "dump" the goods for cash so that they can "buy time" and do other new profitable deals) and hot merchandise — laughing as he told me stories of almost shitting in his pants while sitting several feet away from the stolen items locked inside his office safe as he was being interviewed by clueless curious detectives — I knew five Greg's that possessed incredible integrity. And how could I ever again stare Michael in the face?

And most importantly ... how much is one's priceless honor worth?

"I can't," I replied to my friend who originally taught me the business almost thirty years ago.

"What? Why not?" Rick asked, very surprised at Mr. Nice Guy's sudden refusal to accommodate such a simple small-favor request.

"Because I'm about to declare bankruptcy and if anything happened to me between here and Kopciel's office, you'd never believe me."

Rick just stared at me, trying to fathom the words his stunned ears had just heard. "Wow," was all he could respond as he realized how close he had come to being totally fucked out of a quarter-million-dollar gem.

Rick then placed his hand on my shoulder in an appreciative half-hug and then he pressed his stone into my hand, as he respectfully honored my integrity as he whispered, "I trust you. Please drop it off." His grey eyes insisted, almost pleading, that I allow him to show me how much he still trusted me even after I admitted how fucking desperate I was.

I protected that stone in my pocket, with moist eyes, as if I was holding three-minute-old Ester in my muscular arms as I took the elevator at 580 Fifth Avenue down eighteen flights and then walked the half block to Rick's diamond cutter. I then rode the elevator up to Kopciel's office, as I already thought about the 2:00 a.m. "Your family Ze'eh'ev!" badgering pillow-talk I'd be forced to listen to again in a couple of hours. I'm glad no one tried to rob me at that moment of my life. I would have been shot over a stupid piece of fucking coal.

How ironic that two decades later, Kopciel's wife, Sarena, is a Facebook friend — a sheitel-clad body builder! — who follows SwordPen Publishers through her grandkids having received our books from Gary Barnett (their grandfather).

As I now look back, dropping off that gem to Kopciel was the moment my marriage began to spiral completely out of control and race downhill to the Rockland County courthouse. Returning that rock eventually cost me my rhinestone marriage and my relationship with Ester. It was worth it.

You became the worst enemy I have ever known, Sharen. I now realize the tender feelings we shared, that I once believed were mutual, only emanated from me. They were intense as they bounced off you and back onto me. My empathetic brain believed you loved me. I always felt you weren't "quite there," but being conditioned by my mother I was used to unreciprocated love. The two wacko-women I should have been able to completely trust and bond with, were as invisible as God. Who is closer to a man than his own mother, wife, and God? Looks like I struck out.

Even our young children sensed that they could trust me more than their own mother. They always relied on and sought comfort from my gentle maternal instincts over your strict and controlling temperament.

I still see the faces of our babies as they finished nursing and your nipple as it pops out of their milky little mouths; their heads slowly rolling in a drunken groggy stupor, as if they were saying, "I'm done." And as Mr. Mom I easily remember the stored bottles of pumped milk in the freezer, milked from an even colder emotional source, that I carefully warmed up and test-squirted on the back of my hand to make sure it wasn't too hot before I fed our half-minyan of babies.

I still see their eyes looking up at me as I gently pat their backs, after feeding them thousands of bottles of your expressed milk, while singing a gentle Yiddish lullaby, coaxing "*ah sheyne grepseleh*" burp, waiting patiently for their whimsical declarations of satiety — never knowing which musical note they will "sing" to release air from their Buddha tummies. "Burp!" So tender. So innocent. So cute! I still hear the uninhibited joyous laughter of our daughters and the cute voices of our articulate sons who spoke early as they nursed late.

But kids grow up. And I realized I couldn't possibly stay with you once they'd leave. You had been nasty, callous, and cruel to me one time too many. You dehumanized my facial features, taunting me that my nose made me look like a wildebeest. You regurgitated my loses ad infinitum while calling my "Willie Loman successes" nothing more than a "fluke" accomplished only by my ability to "bamboozle" investors. Then, upon my serving you divorce papers, you added "pedophile who is obsessed with feces," and that I suffer from "uncontrollable wrath," to your insanely abusive thesaurus. I nearly killed myself after what you put me through. Then this book could have been titled *Death of a Tatie*.

You said, "jump," and I somersaulted to impress you. "Jump higher," you demanded. And I executed moves like Simone Biles on the balance beam. Why would any man take such abuse other than because he was being held hostage by the love he felt for his children? As Ester turned eleven, I decided it was time to escape.

I still turn my head when I see a mother nursing in public. Not because I'm shy. Certainly not because I'm prudish. But I'm slightly embarrassed as the Mr. Mom memories of my nursing babies cause my eyes to well up. You knew how much I love children, Sharen. And upon receiving divorce papers you instantly turned the effusive love of a father into the raging perverted anger of a paternal pedophile. I pray that you become senile soon. Not because I'm angry. But your brain really needs to stop.

You used to make fun of me that I cried so easily. And it's true. Not many people have cried, or laughed, as much as I have. So, go ahead. Enjoy. Poke fun. I'm tougher than you ever imagined. Nazis and Gods don't scare me. I've had my share of bad days, but I've had so many good ones. Call me a softie. But you'll never comprehend that I laugh even more easily than I cry. Because I now enjoy living in a blissful state way beyond where your negativity lies. A place whose existence you are unable to even fathom. A place that is beyond description even with words penned by someone like me. Because those words would need to be read by a soul to comprehend what I'd describe. An emotionally vacuous artificially intelligent brain wouldn't "get it."

I did my best to live *Tzu lib der kinder*. But I eventually took the advice of that ten-year-old boy who told my father to divorce Mommy. I finally listened to my emotions instead of burying them.

Your emotions aren't real, Sharen. That is why you were able to go from adoring the man of your dreams and in the same breath run and take out fake protection orders a second after he served you for divorce. I wish you moved like that in bed. A stray dog taken in by a new family would remember its previous owner, who loved and fed her, much longer than the bitch I married remembered me. You're as cruel as my mother was to my father. You smile innocently as you twist your scalpel slowly. Being the persistent and habitual ant that you are, you never even thought to slow down and imagine how easily you might be exposed. You were as sloppy and inept as Alfieri. Tatie5521.

Allow me to give you a short philosophical lesson in the martial arts, Sharen. Wise warriors wait. Their greatest weapon is their mind. They stalk. They observe. They meditate. The chink in an enemy's armor will reveal itself. Opportunity will come. One spy is better than a brigade of five thousand ant soldiers. The kill is the easiest part. The amazing skills of the ancient warriors were not merely in their speed and stealth. It was in their ability to move as if time stood still. They would wash a simple bowl for many minutes which gave them the mastery to draw a bow and shoot an arrow at blinding speed. Almost as fast as you scribble your name on Orders of Protection.

Taking time is what allows me to compose a work of art like this book. Compare it to your blithering idiotic email scrawls full of childish accusations of my being a "pedophile" who is "obsessed with doody and Esti's breasties." Fools rush and pounce. Armies, like ants, march forward and blindly follow their orders to "Charge!" as they scurry to an early grave.

Rushing is why America is spending trillions of dollars to prevent acts of terrorism with a homeland security staff maned by a quarter million employees, while our soldiers are chasing Taliban fighters who wear torn sandals and live in caves. The insane rush. The wise breathe deeply.

Meanwhile, while America hunts feudal illiterate goat herders in flip-flops halfway around the world, modern-day nuclear power mighty Israel sits quietly like an enlightened oasis, even though she is surrounded by millions of medieval madmen neighbors, and a few "progressive" backward American congresswomen, whose desert culture and zealous zeitgeist religious nomadic beliefs (in killing gay men and removing clitorises) cause them to scream wildly, in their ancient nadbah war cries, for the destruction of the Land of Milk and Honey till the Mediterranean Sea runs red with the blood of all its Jews. #SayWhen #Tombstone

Like a true martial artist, Israel knows exactly what her enemies are doing at all times, and that the wars were never about a few more square miles or a la la new nation called Palestine. The founders of Israel graciously refused to use the name Palestine ("Israel" was their second choice) in the hope of sharing a new state with their Arab neighbors. All Israel ever wanted, or wants now, is peace. Name one country that defeated her neighbors, who viciously attacked her with the intent of utter destruction, and yet instantly chose to return land for a mere promise of peace.

The geographical area called Palestine, and much of the surrounding land, is more ancient than Judaism, Christianity, and surely Islam. It is the earliest place on the planet that boasted civilization (writing, government, agricultural farming, and taxation). If anything, the land probably belonged to the ancient dark-skinned Egyptians whose culture simply vanished upon the Exodus of the Jewish nation — similar to Spain becoming a mere shadow of what she once was, upon the expulsion of her Jews in 1492 that led to her economic demise as a world power.

Why do you think the Talmud relates that not one Jew was able to escape from Egypt during the entire two-hundred and ten years that they were enslaved? It is because the Jews had less melanin than their taskmasters. The exact opposite situation of Black slaves in America. The square mile size of Israel is a grain of sand compared to the wealth and resources of the continent of Muslim countries circling her.

Technically speaking modern-day "Palestinians" are mostly Jordanians. Jordan is "Palestine" and Jordan granted citizenship to many "Palestinian" refugees after the "Day of Catastrophe," known as "Nakba." The cold-blooded murderer, Yasser Arafat, a monster who won a Nobel Peace Prize for murdering innocent athletes and civilians and introducing terrorism to the world, declared it a national holiday in 1998.

Meanwhile we just spent twenty years in Afghanistan at the cost of well over a hundred-thousand lives, while bankrupting future American taxpayers who have yet to be born, only to have the ultra-religious Muslim population that believes in the literal strict interpretation of Islamic law, as commanded dogmatically by Mohammed "alayhi as-salam," resume what they were doing the day America invaded. Drink muddy coffee and praying five times a day while abusing their women.

They are only seen as radicals by our Western Civilization. But on their own spectrum they are no more radical than most Hasidim who believe that gays deserve a death of stoning, and that women can't serve as witnesses in cases that involve corporal punishment. The modern-day ancient believers reappeared as Taliban terrorist freedom fighters as they flooded right back into Kabul by simply walking through their front door.

America ran with her tail between her legs never understanding how temporary her presence had been during the entire two decades she wasted inflated dollars and the blood of her finest youth. Consulate officials barely had time to fold the stars and stripes that flew over our embassy. They probably had to stuff it into a duffel bag as they fled for their lives, leaving many Americans and "liberal" Afghanistan aides behind. I knew this would be the outcome twenty years ago. But what does an old Jewish scholar know compared to all the "best minds" and think tanks in Washington? I only know religion and some world history.

I also know that a lot of corporations made incredible fortunes these past two decades and that they will share a chump change portion of their profits with their political allies in our Congress and Senate upon their official retirement from public service so that they can work as highly paid corporate consultants while delivering speeches for which they are paid outrageous fees for keeping a straight face while droning on and on about courage and integrity.

Rushing insanely is why World War I has never really ended to this day. And it is the reason you spent a quarter of a million dollars after signing that note (that you "never signed!") funding me with fifty thousand dollars as I wrote out a check to Robert Lewis for one percent of the amount you paid Shitty Schwartz to torment me — only to sign the house over to me a few days later. How many times in our three-decade marriage did I gently tell you to stop rushing? Feel like suing me for writing this book? #SayWhen

I took my time as I collected and organized your shocking emails. I recorded hours of you raving like a lunatic on the phone and of our children clearly expressing their love for their Tatie. And that includes Sara pining to drive to Manhattan with me to help at our booth at the BEA show — even as she was taking me to Family Court on your instructions with claims of my threatening to "mush her head." She was so proud to be my daughter and speak to the librarians and buyers who asked how to order our books. Thanks for taking that away from her. What can you not destroy?

I knew how quickly you could fool people into believing anything you said. I now realize how you were able to act like the nicest person I ever met when I dated you. You never displayed one negative emotion or said one moody word. Like a robot. How could I have ever imagined your fuming narcissistic rage? I knew my pristine reputation was no match for your Asperger acting skills with which you entertained me when we dated. I laughed then at how flawlessly you imitated many movie stars, television personalities, and actresses.

But I wasn't laughing when I served you papers. I knew I'd need evidence (an unknown word in our divorce and family court systems) to clearly portray how you alienated our challenged daughter Sara and our young and innocent Ester. I waited many months as you spewed your ranting emails full of "Grobe Luge" lies till I finally stapled the emails to my lawyer's motion to the court. Even a half-honest, quasi-intelligent bumbling judge would have placed you and Schwartz in jail. I was certain that our divorce would now finally come to an end.

How could I have possibly known that Alfieri was a mendacious drunken bi-polar carnivore? An illiterate barbarian would easily have made for a better jurist. And how could I have foreseen what a lazy, irresponsible, white-trash, ignorant bleach-blond ancient bimbette Margaret Smith would turn out to be? Or what a pitifully slothful, mumbling good-for-nothing lazy lawyer Robert Lewis would be as he basically joined forces with Smith and Alfieri. With a lawyer like Robert who needs enemies.

I must thank you for trusting me with your password. I would have been lost without it. Not that I hadn't earned your trust. I always treated you gently and did whatever you wanted. Exactly like when I played with those little girls in kindergarten who ordered me around. I was content and so happy to be the "daddy" surrounded by the lovable "mommies" as they poured my tea and told me what to do next. Sure, I'd rather play ball, but I've always adored women. You gals are so charming! Being a real daddy brought me incredible happiness. So much, in fact, that it was even worth the pain of being married to you.

The only difference between you and those four-year-old preschoolers is that you are more childish. Seems you never got past your toddler anal stage of psychosexual development. Reading your immature "doody" laden emails allowed me to comprehend that I was already walking in a dangerous nocturnal dark jungle when I walked down the aisle with you, and not only, what now seems like a few minutes later, upon filing for divorce from you. I barely remember you as anything more than a "one nightmare stand" affair. A real *Eishet Chayil* would have had at least one fucking atom of mercy on a man with whom she bore five children.

Six, if we include Ezekiel. And I certainly do. Because in the short time that I held baby "Chezkie" in the palm of my right hand, after his premature expulsion from your body as he fell into the toilet on the 21st of August 1991, I loved him. We quickly bonded. For an eternity. You had instinctively scooped him up in a cup and ran out of the bathroom to get me. While you called your obstetrician in a calm state of mind, I got to know our child. And what an adorable little gentleman he was!

I gently poured our baby out of the cup and into the palm of my hand. He lay in a fetal position as I marveled at his resting comfortably while sucking his thumb. I don't even know why, but I suddenly used the pinky of my left hand to gently separate what would surely have become powerful thighs had Chezkie grown into a man. I saw the cutest penis and was so happy to discover something — anything — about my little boy! *Mazel Tov!* I wanted to know so much more. My mind raced almost as fast as Chezkie's tiny heart. A million scenarios played out in my mind as I gazed at a wonderful "if only ..." future that I knew was about to abruptly end.

Tears began to stream out of my eyes as I realized the rapid pulsating beat of Ezekiel's tiny mighty heart, drumming wildly against my palm, was slowing down, because his barely-three-inch-long body was no longer tethered to your heartless one for air. *He's dying! Do something!*

I sadly understood that science had not yet advanced to the level where it could save a twelve to fourteen-week-old fetus. Certainly not in 1991. I understood that my baby boy was about to die. It's a very painful experience for a man to outlive his son. But those few "lost in thought" minutes that Chezkie and I spent together playing ball, studying the Talmud, racing sprints, visiting The Museum of Natural History, and doing homework while laughing and having endless conversations about the meaning of life, were more real than the thirty years I spent with you. I'll cherish them forever.

I tried to kiss the fourth baby we attempted to bring into this world a gentle goodbye as his heart now beat at the pace of a slow-moving metronome. But he was so sticky I feared tearing his saran-wrap skin. I knew I was being overly demonstrative, but I understood that this would be the only chance we'd ever have for "Tatie Time" till we'd meet again in heaven. I tried to recall the Halacha. Does Chezkie have to be circumcised before burial? I couldn't tolerate losing such a precious child so quickly, and not wanting our relationship to end, thoughts of placing a stone and eulogizing my son swirled around in my mind.

I began with some religious dogma about Chezkie having achieved in seventy seconds what most men are unable to accomplish in a lifetime of seventy years. I didn't know what I was saying but I wanted to keep speaking to my son, hoping I could block God from interrupting our conversation and breaking my heart as he brought Chezkie's to a complete stop. Like most men who live a religious Jewish life, my third son had sadly been rushed through his. I stared at my beautiful dead baby boy for a long time as I wondered why God couldn't have given him a lifespan of ninety years instead of ninety seconds.

You pounded on the bathroom door and hurriedly told me the doctor wants to see you as soon as possible. He also wanted to meet Chezkie. I gently placed our aborted-by-God deceased cherub back in the cup with a little water to keep his post-mortem could-have-been-ripped body moist. I stared at his cute clavicle bone, and Chezkie reminded me of those transparent plastic human-body replica models that we studied back in high school during biology class. I then tenderly blanketed him beneath a few tissues, and we drove in silence to Dr. Trongone. I wondered if my wrapping Chezkie in tissues was some kind of karma punishment from God for all the cum I caught in tissue paper during my high school years at Ner Israel?

I attributed your quietness and lack of emotion to sadness. I now understand that even A.I. can emote. I tried to comfort you, but there really aren't any words, except for vacuous ones like "God's will" or "Hand of God" bullshit expressions and other futile illogical nonsensical clichés to describe very ugly ungodly situations. And so, I remained silent too.

I became closer to baby Ezekiel in those few moments that I felt his rapidly beating cherubic heart pulsating in the palm of my hand than I was ever able to bond with the stone one I used to sense pounding in your chest as I lay with you while breeding in captivity.

And now I understand why. Six children and twenty-eight years of marriage, and all your deranged mind could emote about a man like me was "I fear his wrath. He's obsessed with feces." I wonder if you now plan to email Vittie that, "Zev spent too much time in the bathroom with Chezkie." I can just imagine that emotional cripple instantly emailing her psychiatrist "for a friend" about a necrophile dad who spent too much time in the bathroom with his dead fetus son.

I never told you that I plan to rest near Chezkie when I pass. I bought a monument stone for his tiny grave. I knew Chezkie would never have anyone to cuddle. So I decided I'd sleep next to him when I die. If he wants to, he can throw his little arm around my neck and pull himself close to me for protection, like Ester always did when she was a baby and wanted to feel safe. And his siblings can visit him. Their names are recorded on the headstone. Along with our names. Don't worry. I used your maiden name. We were never married. Why would I etch a grotesque lie in stone for eternity?

You're a female version of the monster once revered by millions of fans as "America's Dad." Like Bill Cosby, you appear and act like the world's most perfect mom and wonderful hardworking-surgeon wife. But beneath the surface you are a manipulative and calculating, self-centered predator. Anthony Tortorici (Coca Cola's PR head in 1981) was quoted in *Black Enterprise* magazine at that time with gleefully praising their squeaky-clean Dr. Cliff Huxtable (everyone trusts doctors) spokesperson as follows: "The three most believable personalities [in the world] are God, Walter Cronkite, and Bill Cosby." You make all three look like liars.

Mary Oliver, surely a poet who lived an in-the-moment life, once wrote; "Someone I loved once gave me a box full of darkness. It took me years to understand that this too, was a gift."

I honestly appreciate the box full of darkness that someone I once loved gifted me. It took me decades, and a very traumatic PTSD experience, to comprehend what a gift it was. Thank you *Vybie*. Your jeers became cheers. Your threats became challenges. Your negativity uplifted me. Your, "You can't do that Ze'ev! You're not a *real* writer!" became, "Read these reviews from Kirkus!" Your, "You don't know how to write and produce radio ads!" became, "Listen to these MoreMortgage.com and CyberDiamond.com ads!"

And although I responded, "Watch me starve!" to your, "You can't divorce me! I'm your meal ticket, Ze'ev!" threat, I would have preferred risking my life searching for potato peels in garbage cans with my dad in Dachau over the emotional drain of staying married a minute longer to you.

But it seems that you won when it came to, "You're never taking Ester to fucking school again!" I was silenced because of bold letters typed by a "guilty till proven innocent" undemocratic divorce court furnace system, stoked with lunatic judges and court appointed idiots, that maniacally screamed DO NOT TALK TO MINOR CHILD.

Every time you dehumanized me by abruptly hanging up on me as I urgently tried to save our marriage; every time you rudely interrupted me, smirked at me, repeated yourself incessantly while I spilled my guts as I desperately tried to reason with your frigid emotions, has now become an existence of serenity. You fought like a wild animal to destroy the man you constantly called "the nicest guy in the world." Surviving your land mines, hunting traps, and lawyer-set snares has transformed me in ways you can't imagine.

The light is on. And like a scared young toddler, once the light is turned on, this sixty-nine-year-old child no longer needs the assurances of his father's promises. Or even the declarations of his Father in Heaven. This boy fears nothing. Not death. Not Ester never speaking with him again. He doesn't even fear Hell. Been there. Done that.

It took me quite a bit of time ex-*Vybie*, but I've finally found as much closure to my childhood and marriage as I could ever expect to discover till science finally reveals what God refuses to presently share. In truth, I can't recall experiencing a single deep and meaningful conversation with you since that first time I rang your apartment doorbell in Manhattan over forty years ago. It was always me talking and you laughing. You're not able to carry a conversation. Perhaps a quasi-intelligent one. Certainly not an honest one.

You compensate by sitting and politely staring. Your intense penetrating gaze makes you look like a great listener due to your ability to mimic and imitate others. Nothing like repeating the last few words someone just spoke to validate that you listened to what they said. And your memory is computer-like — whether the event occurred in reality or merely on your hard drive. But throughout all our conversations I now realize that your emotions were never involved. Not once did you show empathy. You were never there. I feel as if we got engaged and divorced in one evening. And somewhere in-between we had six children.

It's all quite amazing. I still dream about many of the diverse women I've loved, or was engaged to, in my lifetime. Some appear from almost a half century ago, and yet we still laugh and make love in my REM sleep as if we had just spent the day together. But the one I was married to for thirty years never appears. Because she never appeared, other than as a nightmare, during my waking hours.

I could call you an animal, but I'd only do so in an attempt to define you, not insult you. And because I love wild animals, I realize how poor such a comparison would be — as a quote to their defense by James Anthony Froude comes to mind. Froude explained that, "Wild animals never kill for sport. Man is the only one to whom the torture and death of his fellow-creatures is amusing in itself."

I imagine that's why idiots who love trophy-hunting, sport such wide grins as they hold up the huge head of their antler-ornamented dead male relative to compensate for the small size of their own brains and penises. It also explains why you laughed so often with Dan Schwartz in your emails as you both imagined my surprised final facial expressions while I suffered a heart attack as a result of your kindness. *Come to think of it, my head is rather large.*

I understand, Sharen, that some people's minds are sadly not wired the right way. It's not your fault. But I no longer care to investigate why a perfect God chose to create such warped imperfection and then hide "crazy" among the genome sequencing of Adam and Eve when he created the world. Bad things happen to good people. Period. God fucked up.

Nietzsche once said that if you stare too long into the abyss it begins to stare back at you. I might add that you also risk falling inside. Because, like the abyss itself, there is no end. A person will go insane, in a lifelong never-ending quest, trying to reason with or attempting to find closure from a mind such as yours. Or my mother's. And especially from God's.

And so all that's now left for me to say is that it certainly has been an enlightening experience to have made your acquaintance. I feel sympathy for you. Maybe I'm the one who is crazy, because I still love you. Pity, actually. But it's time for me to have compassion on myself. I've become too enlightened to take any of your perverted deeds personally anymore. Or even your kind deeds. I'm therefore only choosing to remember our family during the time we created baby after beautiful baby. I love children, my dear ex. And so, I will simply say: Thank you for your service. God bless you. Goodbye Sharen. Goodbye Mommy. Goodbye God.

And to you Ester, I have much to say, but it will have to wait till we one day pick up on those deep and meaningful conversations you once loved. I loved them too my daughter. Do you remember the topic of our last conversation? It was about Killer whales. Orcas. I was interrupted when Mommy came downstairs and waved those Protection Order papers in my face. I was about to tell you that whale fishermen used to call them "Whale killers." The name got flipped with the passage of time, like your mind and many obvious truths. Hence the term Killer Whale being bestowed upon the largest member of the dolphin family.

I miss those talks. And I miss you. I miss telling you that I love you. Even if the future will reveal that you inherited the brain patterns of Mommy, I'll still love you. At the very least, I'll always treasure having loved you. I'm no longer attached to the future. So, after many attempts to contact you, I leave it up to you to reach out to me. I never stopped talking to you. In fact, I'm exactly where you left me as you sulked and walked out of the kitchen as Mommy threatened to call the police. I'm still in the middle of that conversation about one of the most powerful predators on planet Earth. Not Mommy, Ester. Orcas. I wish I could hear your laughter.

The memories of raising you from birth will always remain priceless. You were a fairy tale princess from the moment you were conceived. Perhaps we bonded so closely because I became your mother and father. I love all your siblings, but in your case, it was almost as if I raised you as a single parent. In fact, because you were born when I was almost fifty years old, one could say you were raised by a gentle grandfather. Never in a billion years could I have imagined becoming estranged from you. But a Killer Whale Mommy predator flipped me like prey, flinging me through three court systems till my PTSD remains washed ashore on a lonely island with only memories to recall that I was once the father of a beautiful child.

Meanwhile I pray that you were merely pressured and alienated as an eleven-year-old and that you are not a genetic copy of your mother as you now approach your twenty-first birthday. I can't believe that ten years just flew by. I constantly ask myself, "Does she miss me as much as I miss her? Does she ever wonder, "Whatever happened to Tatie?"

You always were daddy's girl. And you even jokingly usurped title as CEO of SwordPen Publishing long ago. I still watch you laughing hysterically on video as you tell me that my services are no longer needed. Your sense of humor obviously shows that you don't just look like me. And I'm hoping that your mettle overrides the obstacles that life has placed in the path of our relationship. You always had a lot of spunk, passion, and heart. I know you'll be fine.

I still remember one of the many early times in your life when I took you to the Bronx Zoo. *Tatie-Time* (special time for just the two of us) began long before you can remember. I carried you through the entire zoo and showed you all the animals that I told you God created especially for you. You behaved with such dignity; a little princess patiently observing all the animals in her own private menagerie.

You were afraid of some of the larger animals and clung to me with your little wispy arms tightly wrapped around my neck, but you felt protected because your Samurai-Tatie bodyguard was holding you. I would have fought a tiger that escaped from its cage for you — eventually ripped to shreds but dying peacefully knowing you were safe. People would stop and stare at my beautiful princess, attempting to make eye-contact and hoping for a return smile, as they smiled at Her Royal Adorableness.

I still remember your reaction to a display that portrayed the food chain: how every predator eats the animal weaker than itself before being eaten, in turn, by the animal stronger than it. You quickly grasped the message as your eyes widened, in an almost hypnotic frozen gaze, while you stared fixedly at the picture. And before I could even begin to explain the natural violence called "survival of the fittest" in the animal (and divorce court) kingdom, you looked at me with the most innocent eyes I have ever seen, and whispered, almost to yourself, "I feel bad for them."
I laughed and cried at the same time.

I also remember a trip to Disney World, when we took a half-day to visit Gatorland, and the picture we took of the two of us sitting on an alligator. At first you were terrified of the alligator and refused to sit on the predator. I straddled the prehistoric archosaur and held the gators taped mouth in my hands as I suggested that you sit behind me and hold me around my waist.

But because of your total trust in your Super-Tatie, you suddenly fearlessly plopped down in front of me right next to its long head and snuggled between the arms that you instinctively knew would always be there to protect you. I laughed so hard at my brave little toddler that the photographer had difficulty snapping the picture because he was also laughing as he tried to hold his camera steady.

I tried to protect you from the army of predators that brought about your estrangement from me, Ester. But the society we live in let them out of their cages and gave them free rein. That expression, by the way, comes from holding the reins of your horse loosely so that it can just walk around wherever it wants to go.

Please forgive me, my child. I did my best. Trust me, your Samurai-Tatie didn't go down without a fight. My blood boiled as I battled for custody and eventually for mere visitation. I fought bravely. But the cowards used Orders of Protection and hid behind endless lies and "concerned parent" phone calls to destroy our relationship. And the judge was nothing more than a medieval simpleton court jester. I would have continued fighting the buffoon till my heart gave out. But sadly, they captured your mind long before I relinquished custody of your body. How does one rescue a captive that turns on her savior and desires to remain with her abductors?

I still watch you on tapes and I listen to your voice on the many phone recordings (your laughter is contagious!) that I would have had to play in court against Mommy if you would have testified against me. They easily prove the truth. They show how much you once loved me. I'm sorry your feelings have changed from when you said, "I want to live with you!" to the opposite end of the spectrum of not even speaking to me. I can't say I forgive you because none of this calamity was your fault. You don't need any forgiveness. Call me when you're ready.

Near the end of my divorce, Ester, I had another one of those crazy dreams that feel more real than real life. I dreamt that I came to your school to surprise you and help you with your homework. I wanted your school day to be completely over (homework included) by the time we left school that afternoon, figuring that we'd have the rest of the day to exercise at the JCC, play some basketball, and then enjoy a nice quiet dinner someplace where we could have one of our "deep and meaningful" conversations.

I was looking so forward, plotzing even in my dreams, to spending some Tatie-Time with you. I guess I'm a case study for G. Domhoff, a prominent dream researcher, who discovered that dreams mirror the concerns and thoughts of what a sleeping person thinks about during the day.

Arriving an hour early to pick you up from school, I waited by the front office and Mrs. Zaks walked over and greeted me warmly, like she always did, as she handed me a card that said: Room C-3. Mrs. Zaks then told me she sent one of the students to get you and that you would be waiting for me in that classroom. Exactly like the procedure for when I used to come to school to tutor Sara twice a week.

The next thing I knew I was walking around the school trying to find Room C-3. But every time I thought I'd find you, as I opened a classroom door that was strangely missing its room number (as I kept thinking while opening door after door, "this one definitely has to be C-3"), a student would tell me you fell, or stumbled, or ran into a wall during recess, but that you would be joining me soon.

This happened several times and I began to feel anxious as I wondered where you were. Suddenly one of your schoolmates told me, "Esti's okay, Mr. Lewinson. She just needed a few stitches. She'll be fine." But I didn't believe anyone anymore. I suddenly felt a panic attack come over me and I found myself racing around what eerily became endlessly long school hallways that seemed to lead nowhere, stretching out far into the distance, much longer than the length and width of the outside parameters of the building they were in, as I desperately flung open door after door while nervously yelling out your name as I raced through a nightmare of impossibly-long school corridor hallways opening endless classroom doors.

I finally found you lying curled-up on the floor in another impossibly long hallway, surrounded by a bunch of students and a few young teachers quietly staring down at you in complete silence. I sped down the long corridor, my actual physical heart racing in my chest as I somehow continued to dream, and I suddenly roared in frantic frustration, "What the fuck is going on here!" Everyone instantly scattered in all directions, horrified that Mr. Lewinson would use such a terrible word and utterly shocked that Ester's gentle soft-spoken Tatie could roar so loud.

I looked down at you, lying in a hallway that was suddenly as empty as my heart. I felt sheer dread. You looked bruised, beat up and pummeled to the point of death. You had scratches, cuts, swollen bruises, and light-pink welts on your innocent satin-skin face. Your forehead was slightly cracked and there was caked blood on your temple. I was so stunned I couldn't breathe. You looked greenish and pale. Like the dead bodies I used to ritually wash with Uncle Fred and immerse into the Mikvah, after wiping away any blood or feces, as we prepared the deceased, before dressing God's chosen-corpse in white shrouds, for their Jewish burial.

I felt too nauseous to even vomit and far beyond what people refer to as "sad," as you lay there with your arms wrapped around your knees. I thought you were dead. The dread I felt was unbearable. I couldn't even cry. It was as if someone had ripped my heart out of my chest. Had I been standing on a bridge, I would have just toppled myself over. Screaming in pain, roaring in anger; nothing I could do would have even begun to ease the endless emptiness I felt in my chest during that nightmare moment portraying what I endured for years during my waking hours.

But suddenly I noticed that you were breathing very shallow breaths. The same way you used to breathe in your sleep when I gently woke you up to get ready for school in the morning.

"Esti!" I barely whispered as I delicately rolled you over from your curled up fetal position. "Are you okay, Sweetie?" You looked up and gave me the most adorable, sweet smile I ever saw in my life, and your beautiful big blue sad eyes seemed to apologize and asked forgiveness as you sheepishly shared through their meek stare that, "It wasn't my fault, Tatie." You were too weak to even whisper. "I know Honey, I know," I nodded in response to the expressive gaze spoken by your eyes as tears welled up in mine. "Put your arms around my neck, *Scheifeleh*. I'll carry you to the car."

Tears of relief continued to softly flow as I walked down the long hallway, and I couldn't stop crying as I noticed how light you felt in my arms. I was amazed at how little you weighed and how defenseless you were. "You'll be fine. We're going home *Mamaleh*," I whispered, when I suddenly woke up to the real nightmare I was living in, still crying, with actual tears on my wet cheeks.

I understood how my dreaming mind had switched the gut-wrenching alienation abuse you and I both endured for years into a physical portrayal of a battered you. I felt completely drained and full of dreadful emptiness as I faced the reality that I lost you Ester, and that we would never be "going home" together again.

I realized the irony the two of us shared in losing our relationship with our father after our first decade of life. The only difference is that I now lost my daughter in my final decades. I hope you never have to go through that experience. I fought for you, Ester. But God let everyone "kick Zev outta the house." I fought City Hall. I fought Mommy. But you can't fight an invisible God. You can only leave him. An exhausted two-hundred-pound sack of sadness sat up in bed and pitifully whimpered.

The dream was so real, so emotionally exhausting, that I found it impossible to share with anyone without choking back tears. I couldn't even share it with the therapist I was seeing at the time. I would start to cry the moment I began verbalizing the dream. It's been several years and I am still forced to repress the tears that well-up in my eyes and I can only relate the dream by typing it, as I'm forced, once again, to embrace the reality that I'll probably never feel your arms around my neck again. I'm sorry my Princess. I'm so sorry. I'm still choking back tears even as I edit these paragraphs for the third time.

Euripides once said, "To a father growing old, nothing is dearer than a daughter." You, Princess Ester, were the daughter this elderly gentleman prayed for (more fervently than many forty-year-old women who never had any children) as he approached his half-century birthday. I was dying — as in plotzing! — for "Just one more baby, God! Please! I'm begging you! And if I'm not being too greedy, can you make it a girl?"

God answered me, overcoming the slim one percent odds of a woman giving birth at forty-six. The kosher-stork delivered the most gorgeous Intense-Vivid-Pink flawless little scintillating diamond in the world. But I'd never force a gem to be what it's not. The pleasure I had in raising you will last a lifetime if it must. I am not greedy. I only want you to be happy, Ester. And free! Truly free. No shame. No guilt. No manipulations. No intrusions of your boundaries. We have a lot to catch up on.

It would be dishonest of me not to admit that I was beyond shocked by your pictures that portrayed me as a green monster. I was saddened by your actions and "Die Zev!" captions during my divorce from Mommy. I'm only human. But I understand the power of alienation and conditioning my love. I still love you as much as the day I carried you on Shabbat for over a mile in the hot sun, even though I had a fever, because you were cranky and adamantly refused to walk. You were such a cute toddler!

I'm not in the least bit upset at you. Deep down, I'm not even angry at Mommy. I'm barely angry at God anymore. I merely lost my fear of questioning him. Anger just means that you're

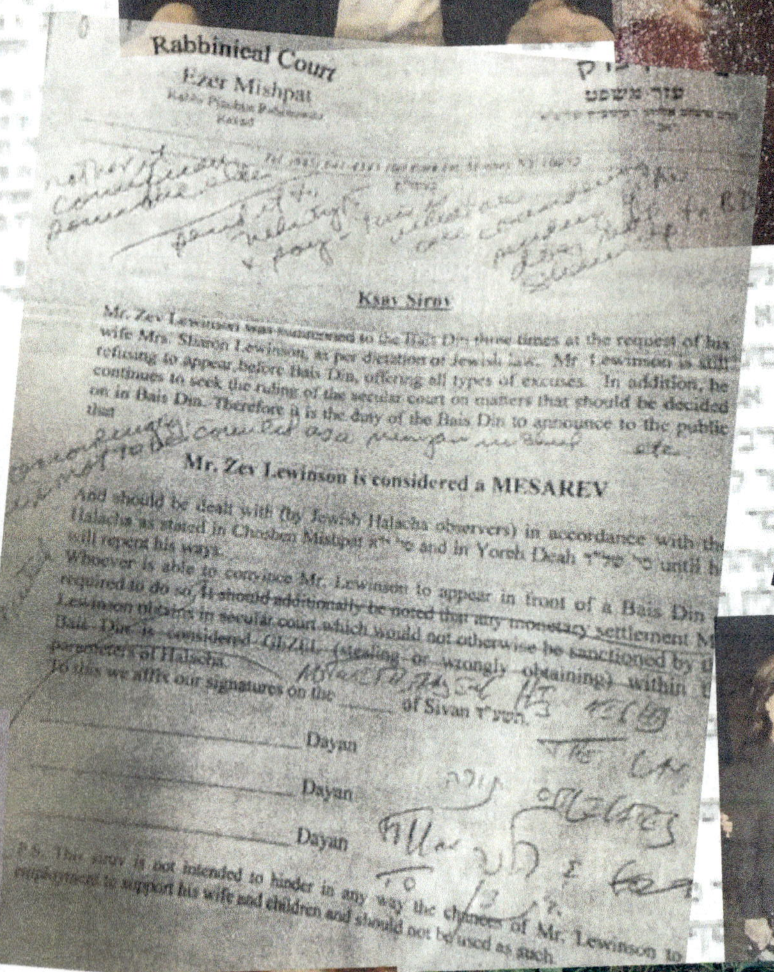

Rabbinical Court

Ezer Mishpat

Rabbi Pinchas Rabinowitz

Rosh Beis Din

עזר משפט

Ksav Sirov

Mr. Zev Lewinson was summoned to the Bais Din three times at the request of his wife Mrs. Sharon Lewinson, as per dictation of Jewish law. Mr. Lewinson is still refusing to appear before Bais Din, offering all types of excuses. In addition, he continues to seek the ruling of the secular court on matters that should be decided on in Bais Din. Therefore it is the duty of the Bais Din to announce to the public that

Mr. Zev Lewinson is considered a MESAREV

And should be dealt with (by Jewish Halacha observers) in accordance with the Halacha as stated in Choshen Mishpat סי׳ כ״ח and in Yoreh Deah סי׳ של״ד until he will repent his ways.

Whoever is able to convince Mr. Lewinson to appear in front of a Bais Din is required to do so. It should additionally be noted that any monetary settlement Mr. Lewinson obtains in secular court which would not otherwise be sanctioned by the Bais Din is considered GEZEL (stealing or wrongly obtaining) within the parameters of Halacha.

To this we affix our signatures on the _____ of Sivan תשנ״ד.

________________ Dayan

________________ Dayan

________________ Dayan

P.S. This sirov is not intended to hinder in any way the chances of Mr. Lewinson to employment to support his wife and children and should not be used as such.

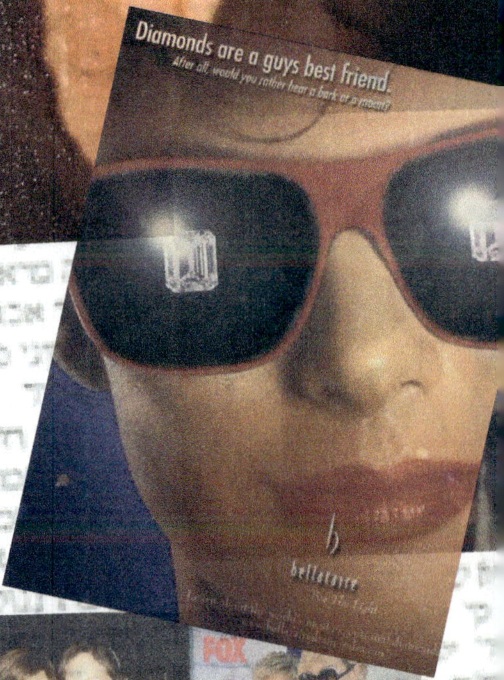

E - Exceptionally kind and caring of others.
S - Sensitive to the needs of every person and to animals.
T - Terrific at everything you do!
I - Intelligent and understanding

We are VERY proud of you on this milestone!

We wish you MUCH joy and success always!

Mazel Tov! We Love You!
Love, Grandma, the Smedresmans, Mailmans, Frids, & Zaslows

We are proud to honor **ESTI**, who has honored us!
Love,
Mom, Rachel, and Sari

punishing yourself a second time for the misdeeds committed by others. I hope your wounds heal my sweet child. Look within. Stop seeking answers from adults who lie, for truths that your heart already knows.

My only desire is for you to understand what is true and what is false. It will help you feel better if you realize what "really" happened during all those years that it became a criminal act — punishable by incarceration — for your father to merely speak to you. Yes, my sweetheart. It became a crime to have a "deep and meaningful conversation." Being silenced for years when you needed me most was the worst experience of my entire divorce. The frustration I endured from the excruciating and excoriating court-imposed pent-up silence erupted into this explosive book. I wrote it to talk to you.

And therefore, I suggest the following. Think about this. Did I ever yell or even snap at you in your entire life? Did I not always proclaim "Girlies first!" to your brothers? Did I ever lose patience while helping you with homework or when getting you ready for school? Did I ever fling pencils at you? You refused to do homework with Mommy. Did you yourself not tell me to divorce Mommy? Do you not remember laughing and saying that you wanted to live with me? Do you not recall how gently I woke you up, showing you the picture of the sleeping angel I snapped seconds earlier, to get you ready for your first day at school? You loved that picture!

I always took "first day of school" pictures of all of you. That picture, taken by eyes that radiated pure fatherly love (two years before I filed for divorce) was later used by Mommy and Dr. Ferro as "evidence" that I'm a pedophile of sorts as they desperately bestowed their "professional" psychological voyeuristic title of "weird" in place of the earlier description accoladed by Mommy of my being a "loving Mr. Mom." You just turned twenty-one and so I share these facts with you.

Ferro described you and that picture in his folly forensic, frenzy-feeding of my broken heart, evaluation as follows: "She [Ester] began to feel *scared* in the house. Father once took a picture of her while she was sleeping, which seemed *weird* (italics are my own) to her. She began sleeping in mother's bedroom, with mother and Sara, because that one had a lock on it." (The room Mommy "forgot" to lock the Shabbos morning she called the police on me.) Ferro is making it appear that the picture was so upsetting to you that it caused you to sleep in my bed. *Two years after it was taken.*

Again, here is Ferro's clinical evaluation (again, all italics are my own): "The next morning, father *burst* (this scene, an utter lie stated as fact, would be comical if not so horrific) into mothers bedroom, which had been left unlocked *inadvertently* (as if Ferro read Mommy's mind), and he *yelled* at them about the picture. Mother called the police, which Ester viewed positively, because she was *frightened* by father's behavior. (Do I need to even respond, Ester?) The police *defused* the situation."

Scared, weird, burst, inadvertently, yelled, defused, and *frightened* ... are all illusions in the sick mind of Dr. Ferro. First, if the door was constantly locked (and only *inadvertently* left open this one time), why would I even think I'd be able to *burst* through? I then love how Ferro acts as if this was the one and only time Mommy *inadvertently* forgot to lock the door. Mommy never bothered locking it. Even after her lawyer told her to install it. You all felt safer when I was home. Most of all, I am amazed at SS Ferro spewing anything his deranged mind can possibly construct to portray me as a raging lunatic as he claims that "the police" (as if a small army was employed to use tactical crowd control strategic maneuvers against a raging explosive mob) *defused* the situation.

The police report basically stated that they saw it as a sham and found it completely unnecessary to remove me from the premises. They were nice to me and warned me that I'm going to be set up again. Ferro, the Nazi Angel of Death, makes it sound like the responding police had to use a S.W.A.T. team with tasers, along with the threat of red lasers pointing from their semi-automatic assault rifles focused on my body, prancing as dancing little red dots hovering over my chest, to calm me down.

What is truly criminal about Ferro is that I calmly explained all of this to him during his "evaluation" when I met with him. I calmly shared the contents of the police report with him and offered a copy right from my iPhone. That was when he snapped, "I don't need your evidence! I can draw my own conclusions!"

In the next paragraph the heathen quack references the picture of Rebbi that sat by the Shabbat candelabra. For decades. Ferro states: "In March 2014, she [Ester] and Sara acted out their *frustration* with father by taking a picture of *his* rabbi off the wall." (Again Esti, italics are my own.)

Ferro makes it seem as if I was so cruel to you and Sara, that the two of you just couldn't take it anymore and merely took "a picture" off a wall in "frustration." Rebbi was "our" Rebbi. You admired him and you were proud that your Tatie learned with the famous man. I know that you and Sara ripped it up while laughing with Mommy. I later read Sara's diary. I don't know how you did that Ester, but I do know the power of alienation. You really should call Rebbi one day and ask his forgiveness. You'll feel better once you do, my child.

If anything, I'm the one who could claim I couldn't take it anymore after Mommy took out a protection order in her and your name, while manipulating Sara to take out her own against me. Taking that picture was a setup for the following morning when Mommy called the police and then showed them the orders "proving" that I have "anger issues." I patiently explained all of this to Ferro, and he didn't even bother to mention it in his "evaluation." I guess he was showing appreciation for the $7,500.00 check Mommy wrote out to him.

I don't know why I'm always more shocked at doctors who do evil than at regular people who are cruel. Somehow, I expect Ferro, Mengele, Cullen, and Mommy to act nicer than regular people because they swore the Oath of Hippocrates. I don't know why we fail to understand that what they really vowed was the Hypocritical Oath. I also expect Judges to be honest. I think we're both a bit too gullible, my daughter.

Don't you remember how positive and optimistic I was as I spoke to you about the fun of learning new things? For years I woke you up in the morning to patiently finish any last parts of your homework assignments as I gave you breakfast while speaking with you about any topic under the sun. Our conversation often continued as we drove to school, and sometimes even past your school because you laughed as you insisted that you wanted to keep talking. "I learn more with you than from my teachers," you cleverly posited to convince me to, "keep going!" Truth be told, I did not need to use patience when working with you. How can you lose patience with someone you truly love? I'll always have all the time in the world for you, Ester.

To be totally honest, why do I need to even ask these questions or explain myself to you? You know me! Am I telling you anything that you yourself didn't express when you said, "Don't worry Tatie, I believe you," when you called me from Aunt Mindy's house almost ten years ago? Do you not recall, from your earliest memories, how I treated you like royalty? Can you even imagine a parent more gentle than your Tatie? Actually, I wish you could have met my father who passed away six years before you were born. Do you really believe the father who came running at your slightest whim is "evil?" I couldn't even leave you at school when you cried as a toddler. What happened to you my beautiful child?

I understand the mind control you were subjected to and the constant badgering of my reputation that you must have endured as your brain rewired itself before you could ever angrily write down, "Die Zev! Die now!" It must have been very painful for you to do that my sweet child. It's called Stockholm syndrome. And it works even more powerfully when the captives are treated with kindness by their captors. So imagine how well it works when a relentless Münchausen syndrome afflicted mother can afford to give endless riding lessons to her captive daughter.

Why do you think Mommy was suddenly giving you all those endless "therapeutic" riding lessons? Do you really believe Rachel was finally allowing you to borrow her clothes and boots because she suddenly became generous? Why do you think your aunts were suddenly giving you so much attention? Your heart kept screaming that you trust your Tatie. But your manipulated mind kept debating your innocent heart. And that is why you felt so confused. And angry. But your heart will never let go Ester. You can only ignore it for as long as you are willing to suffer and endure pain. You will eventually tire. I'm waiting for your call.

The stress of Cognitive Dissonance must have been unbearable for you. Cognitive Dissonance causes the emotional exhaustion that occurs when trying to reconcile two conflicting beliefs. It will leave you spinning your wheels while racing to a circular illogical conclusion that has no end. It is a gauntlet of endless frustration. Like trying to make sense of a God that murders his own children in Auschwitz. Or having to decide between a father that you know loves you more than anything in the world, and a mother who tells you that your father is an angry pedophile who is out to destroy his family.

But that was all committed upon a child ten years ago. You're older now. I pray that you are wiser and working these thoughts out in your heart. I only share to enlighten, my child. You must think about these revelations by yourself. In a quiet place. With a quiet mind. I know I missed out on being with you half of your entire life my sweet daughter. But no one can free you. You must choose to escape. *The path begins with silence.*

Should you choose not to call me, my precious daughter, please live without regret if at some future time you sense that you made a terrible mistake. Please understand that the choice you made in the time span of your lack of awareness could not have been avoided. And don't think you hurt me. You really didn't. Because as much as I endured tremendous pain upon your becoming alienated from me, it was all merely the size of a subatomic quark compared to the amount of love I feel for you.

Please don't ever blame yourself if the opportunity to see me suddenly ends before you realize how much you miss me. It will not have been a terrible mistake. It will have been a situation that wasn't your fault any more than it was mine. I was ready to sacrifice my life for yours the moment you were born, Ester. Our separation was truly circumstances beyond our control.

If the opportunity to see me suddenly ended, my only advice at the moment of my demise would be that which I share with you now: listen to your heart; live your own life; trust yourself, my beautiful daughter. I can't leave you a better legacy than that, my love. Go for a walk in the forest or go riding on your favorite steed. Quiet your mind. Breathe. Deeply. One more time. And listen carefully to the voice that whispers from within, my sweet child. You have your Tatie's heart. Your innocent heart knows all truths. *You're such a beautiful girl.*

Don't worry about what could have been had you spent more special *Tatie Time* with me. Simply recall the awesome times we shared and the great conversations we had. And I won't pine over the missed laughter I once so enjoyed hearing from you. The pitch of your girly voice giggles still ring in my ear. You are really funny! And your facial expressions were always priceless. "Make a funny face!" I'd always coax while pointing my iPhone at the two of us wherever we were. And you sure did.

Never in a trillion years could I have imagined that my staff would crop one of those selfies of the two of us and use it to design the cover of a book about divorce and alienation. A book that began as a mere dream. I had decided long ago to only write for children and instill within them a love for books early on in their precious lives. But life, my dear child, by its very nature of endless possibilities and few probabilities, will always be full of surprises. Learn to adapt in order to survive. But never lose sight of your inner, pure and silent, beautiful self.

I never intended to write for adults. Especially a book about society, the American court system, parenting, and Orthodox Judaism; all woven throughout my own autobiography. But life rarely works out as one intends. Bad things happen to good girlies — and loving fathers. But that's yet another conversation we will hopefully share one day in the future.

For now, I'll have to be grateful with simply recalling the faint fragrant memories of your childhood as a balm to cover the cavernous hole in my heart. I know it's not enough, but I'm quite fortunate. My personality seems to let go of the painful memories while focusing on the good ones (most of the time). I hope you're like me. Actually, I realize you probably are. I hope your brain hasn't been grooved by the negativity of the cult and family that surrounds you.

One of those good fond memories I recall was handing you a surprise new manuscript I wrote called *Roy the Rainbow Boy*. Remember how I always told you how lucky you were that you get to read my stories years ahead of all the other kids on the planet? You eagerly grabbed the twelve sheets of paper and immediately started to read. I stealthily watched you from across the room as you read intently. You were sitting at the foot of my bed — as silent and still as a gorgeous sculpture — while I was knotting my tie in front of the armoire mirror while simultaneously watching your resplendent (look it up, Cutie!) frozen-in-comprehension reflection.

You suddenly jumped up in ecstatic joy and started screaming, "I love it! I love it!" You were so excited, almost beside yourself, bouncing with emotion and adorably out of control, as you begged me, "What should I do? What should I do!"

"Enjoy it Ester," I calmly responded as I laughed while marveling at your passion for such a great story. I was impressed and quite happy that a ten-year-old could display so much excitement over a beautiful story. "Read it again," I advised, "there are some great colorful metaphors and innuendoes about school and society that you should slowly savor."

By the way, it's been reworked and edited and it's more fantastic than ever. And it's waiting anxiously to be read by the pretty title-usurper of the CEO of SwordPen.

I remember you climbing fearlessly on the rope course at the Palisades Mall. I was amazed at how effortlessly my little girl, with the lithe of a ballerina, meandered gracefully through the maze of ropes and beams.

I also recall the time I taught you not to automatically believe everything you hear or read — a lesson too many adults never had the fortune to learn. You were six, perhaps seven, and you asked if I could purchase something for you on Amazon. You showed me what it was, and I assured you that I'd buy it for you, but I explained that I'd do it a bit later because I was busy with something. You then innocently and sweetly asked if I could buy it right now, assuring me (you were so cute!) you weren't plotzing, but only because the description warned, "Only three left in stock." You were unnecessarily nervous that the item would be sold out if we didn't buy it immediately.

"Watch this Ester," I calmly instructed, as I Googled "only three left," and watched your beautiful big blue eyes widen as you saw a gazillion "only three left" deceptive marketing solicitations pop up. You then flashed the most adorable "Oh My!" expression and laughed as you quickly inferred how tricky people can be. And that unfortunately includes divorcing mothers and "trusted" therapists who maliciously obumbrate (look it up!) the gullible minds of unsuspecting children. I'm sorry to say that. But you're no longer eleven years old my child. You're about to turn twenty-one as the publication of this book takes place.

There will always be many dire "only three left" beckoning siren calls throughout your life. They will arrive as the "open immediately!" (like those unimportant mass-mail offerings that we couldn't toss away fast enough) voices of politicians, marketers, clergymen, lovers, and people who you believe are close friends (simply asking for a "small" favor).

They will typically speak quickly in their attempt to proclaim urgency to hasten their access to your open heart, wallet, and every child's most susceptible Achilles' heel: their tabula rasa mind. Why do you think the advertising radio announcer speaks the "fine print" at a thousand miles an hour? He's obviously hiding what he does not want to say but is required to inform by law. So he talks super-fast to hide the truth. It's the oldest trick in the book. Everyone is aware of it. And yet it still works.

People will entice you with promises of happiness and wild profits if you'll only make a quick decision. Don't ever allow anyone to rush you. Even your mother. Actually, especially your mother! Try not to fall for their enthusiasm or their hurried, "Come now! He's dangerous!" voices. And don't become angry when you do. Learn. Move on. And next time take as much time as you need. Remember this: The faster someone speaks to you, the more you need to slow down and take your time before responding and making a decision. And please don't ever fall for, "Let's get married!"

Most people don't "think," Ester. They are "thought to." From their earliest childhood years, they are taught, told, indoctrinated, bombarded with advertisements, shamed, schooled, and conditioned by parents, teachers, religious leaders, politicians, and the media. After an assembly line lifetime of assorted indoctrinations and "only three left" lies, they are at long last granted silence as they are laid to rest.

Having died while feeling empty and incomplete, without ever understanding that they were already entombed into their polished solid-wood gleaming coffin of blind beliefs, copycat existence, foolish morals, shallow desires, idiotic allegiances, drama-driven vapid relationships, and false convictions, way before being accompanied to their graves.

They'll never so much as suspect that they raced through their "only three left" conveyer belt life on a pair of two wounded Achilles heels, as they finally rest, utterly exhausted, after limping to lie down on their death beds with "so much to do!" In their final hours they plead for a few more moments of precious time, as they wonder, just like their parents did, why they feel as if they spent their entire lives riding on a never-ending rubber loop from which they now fall off, landing in their grave.

Rare is the parent that enlightens their child. Most adults burden their babies from birth. As miserable as they are, they wind up creating more wretched and harried imperfect versions of themselves. And so most babies become people who will die having never experienced the pleasure and freedom of *being*. They were always too busy planning, conquering, worrying about, and racing towards the future while simultaneously being obsessively angry and preoccupied about something that happened in their past. *Spark! Spark! Spark! Only three seconds (of life) left!* So take your time, my Princess. Royalty does not rush. Peasants rush.

Enjoy your life, Ester. Just filling your car with gas, watching your parents go through a divorce, or having a "deep and meaningful conversation" with your future little girl one day are all priceless seconds of eternity. Enjoy! Savor them all. Because if you fully experience everything you do, you'll blossom and grow as a result of those mundane, deceitful, or exhilarating moments. Fully living through one second of time — no matter what the experience — feels like the joy of having lived for an eternity. I hope you'll find the time.

And although you will occasionally trip over the weeds sprouted from the seeds of negative experiences that destiny has already planted along the path your life will travel, your scraped knees will be a minor price to pay for the ointment of freedom. There is nothing as joyful as freedom, my child. Even though emancipation always arrives at the price of pain.

But there is no price too steep to pay for freedom. Even my losing you. Breathe deeply, while sitting quietly, and no one, including Mommy, will ever be able to deceive you again. Not even God.

So for now, remember this: Anyone who tries to rush you to make a decision — even a parent— instantly exposes themselves as not caring about *you*. A simple "Let's get married!" when you are having doubts about the relationship is a subtle and manipulative form of rushing. And becoming pregnant to "seal the deal" is a blatant one.

As you grow, you'll become aware of your own space and the boundaries you wish to set. It took me quite some time. In fact, it took me a near lifetime to understand how precious a second of time is. And that's because my mind was constantly rushing at supersonic speed. So when I finally slowed down from a hundred miles an hour to fifty, I thought I was walking slowly. In fact, I was still zooming. Learn to say, "I'll need more time to think about it." And if you're not positive about your decision, take more time. Or just say, "No."

Critical thinking is the process that allows you to overcome bias, cleverly concocted fake news headlines, and all those luring "Only three left!" manipulative seductions. There is no reward that awaits you if you'll only "Shop now!" The pot of gold at the end of the rainbow is the eternal second of life that you are living right now as you read these words.

Don't take sides quickly. Don't rush to join someone else's battle. Choose your own. Carefully. You will soon see that there aren't many, if any, to choose from. Especially when you refuse to be rushed. Think before you act. It will allow you to see the big picture before drawing pictures, and conclusions, of your own. In short, the father who loved you before you were conceived, and then diapered, fed, read, and played with you after you were born, is not a monster. Certainly not a green one that deserves to die, my love. Whatever gave you that idea?

There are times when I quietly sit completely still. I empty my thoughts from the interrupting distractions that beckon my urgent attention. My mind, free of heavy dogmas, becomes lithe and free as it travels through eons of time. I soar as I hurtle through space past galaxies and exploding stars. They're gorgeous! You'd be amazed at what you can figure out when your mind is quiet. You can't imagine the scenes you will see, hear, and remember.

The snippets of joy that I share with you now are only a few of the endless wonderful memories of the first decade of your life that I return to when I'm missing you. Let's both recall the wonderful decade we spent together full of laughter, and not anguish over the time we missed when you were manipulated into no longer speaking to your father.

Whatever you decide, I beg you to please leave your heart empty of anger, my princess, so that it can remain full of only love.

All I have to say at this point is that I'll always cherish the great times we shared. You knew them as "Tatie time." But to me, they were always "Ester time." I'll always look at the half-full part of the glass representing our relationship as overflowing. And I will always love you, Ester. I'm at peace. I only wish the same for you.

You'll always be the adorable three-year-old I tried to drop off at school as I assured you that, "Tatie's coming back." You clung to my pant leg with your tiny fist and cried your little heart out — unyielding, and absolutely refusing to let go. Parenting books, Mommy, and your teachers, told me to, "Just walk out Mr. Lewinson. She'll stop crying five minutes after you're gone." But my heart couldn't process your sweet and sincere whimpering as "manipulation."

Mommy laughed hysterically when I later called her at work and related that I brought you back home, admitting that "I couldn't do it." She called me a "manipulated wimp." That's probably the one time during our thirty-year marriage that her psychiatric evaluation was correct.

You're a woman now, and you'll have to figure things out for yourself. I know I gave you those skills by the time you turned ten. I don't own you Ester. I want nothing more than for you to be happy. I want you to be *you*.

People never "own" a diamond, Ester, no matter how much havoc they wreak to acquire them, or how much they pay to own them, or how safe a vault they lock them into. The diamond *owns* them. They'll be heading back to the earth from which they received their diamond as their diamond rolls into the hands of the next person it will temporarily own.

And parents don't own their children. Just as governments don't own their citizens. Their purpose is to serve, educate, and protect. Not manipulate, control, and endlessly tax. I don't look at you as "my" daughter. I see myself as *your* very fortunate and blessed father. Raising you and your siblings has brought out the best in me. And for that I will always be indebted to you.

As I sipped my coffee, many precious memories of Ester as a toddler, preschooler, and preteen cascaded in my still dreamy mind. Staring at the hand-painted fruit on my chipped yellow coffee cup through zoned-out eyes, my mind wandered, and I reflected and imagined the stream of lost occasions our lives would have shared during these past ten lonely years. I would have spoken so beautifully at her Bat-Mitzvah. It was a speech I began preparing as I walked home to deliver the news of her birth. And one can only imagine how much wisdom, knowledge, and laughter I could have shared with my beautiful daughter. And how much love. *I wonder if she still works out.*

It's truly a terrible misfortune. Tragic for both of us. My pretty, but chipped cup is a great metaphor representing my relationship with Ester. We both remain intact, but the damage is clearly visible. My daughter lost the most important male figure in her life. The only man on the planet who would instantly die for her was vaporized out of her life. Victor Alfieri, Dan Schwartz, and Dominic Ferro wantonly destroyed a very tender and beautiful relationship. They sorely need to memorize the following quote by Kenneth Blanchard: There is no right way to do the wrong thing. To the three greedy aforementioned pigs Ester was never anything more than a temporary cash cow. I highly doubt they've thought about her for one second once they were done torturing her father. And a split-second of time hasn't passed during which I've stopped thinking about her.

I hope their grown children read this book one day. Maybe they'll behave differently than their deplorable fathers. And I hope Ester reads it too. Maybe she'll behave more like her own father.

Siddhartha supposedly said: "There are three things that can't hide for long. The moon. The sun. The truth." The truth is always very obvious. Unfortunately, most people are quickly distracted by "only three left" marketing lies and urgent emotional pleas of, "Come now! He's dangerous!" Sabbath morning phone calls to the police.

I kept staring at the green pear, ruddy-red apple, and purple grapes on my oversized cup. I took a long, deep breath as I calmly inhaled a gallon of air while choking back tears. *I think I might still be a little fucked-up*.

I often wonder how much doublethink it must have taken for Ester to write down, "Die Zev! Die now!" "Holding two contradictory beliefs in one's mind simultaneously, and accepting both of them," is how Orwell described the ultimate power of brainwashing and eventual complete mind control. It also works flawlessly in describing the ability to believe in God. It is painful. Emotionally exhausting. As I can personally attest. Because I do it all the time as an Orthodox Jew.

Separating oneself from their abuser is the only way to begin the odyssey escape from the manipulative and bullying mind-control of individuals like my wife, Hitler, and God. Yet when it comes to Orders of Protection, escape is impossible. Because our divorce court system instantly enables and rewards the ruthless and implacable perpetrator of alienation with full legal "temporary" custody of the very child that needs to break free. An illegally-orphaned child whose already burdened-by-divorce mind our systemic court system and alienating parent will now completely brainwash and control with the full might of the police and vile anti-daddy "So ordered!" poisonous ingredients prepared by the witches and warlocks in their cauldron of boiling injustice shit — dispensed by our *In God We Trust* black robed assholes till the day the "protected" child is emancipated.

Believing in an all-loving God that inflicts pain and death is the ultimate doublethink example of accepting two contradictory beliefs simultaneously. How can a logical human be expected to sincerely worship a murderer of his own six million "chosen" children while fervently declaring their killer as all-merciful? How does one worship a God who punished the holy daughter of the patriarch Jacob, Dinah, with rape and sodomy as penance for her feminine curiosity to merely view the lifestyle and culture of the shiksas's of the land of Shechem (Genesis 34:1)? After all, there was no *Vogue* magazine in her day.

I'm in worse shape than Ester, I suddenly realize, as I comprehend that God awarded himself full custody of my life. How the fuck do I get out of here? Do I pray? What would the words of my liturgy to entreat such a God possibly entail? "Blessed art Thou, O' Lord: King of The Universe, please grant me permission and the willpower to stop believing in you."

I am unable to spend the remaining few decades of my life manipulated by irrational and abusive dogma. I'm more like an innocent child that is by nature happy and positive. Yes, I've had a few living nightmares, and my highly stressed-out Adverse Childhood Experiences resulted in my scoring a toxic 6 on the ACEs quiz (I avoided a score of 7 by the skin of my teeth as I darted out of the room while my menacer held his huge purple penis in his right hand and a Jewish commentary on the Talmud in his left), but amazingly enough I developed resilience because of that one supportive adult that bumped into my life at an early age. He gave me what even my father could not. Tough love.

Faye and Joe Levine lived on the floor above us at 256 Goldsmith Avenue in Newark. After my parents divorced, we moved about a half-mile away from where my mother abused my father. Joe was our new landlord.

Joe Levine used to take me to play paddleball with him on many Sundays. He was a tough guy, and good-looking, with a sharply chiseled angular face and a pointed nose, and he yanked me out of my extreme shyness. I was so introverted, I could barely talk to new kids, let alone adults.

"You're coming with me!" Mr. Levine insisted with a smile, as he confidently promised that he was going to help me overcome my shyness. Paddleball, and later basketball, were the first sports I became good at. Playing ball was a welcome distraction from my constant sadness. It was also a great foundation for my future racquetball career when I won first place twenty years later among over eighty contestants playing B level at the Jewish Community Center in Riverdale, NY.

By then I could see the angles the ball would ricochet off any of the four-walled glass-cage panels surrounding us and the zany direction the rubber sphere would travel the moment my opponent hit it. I often arrived early to respond with a clever placing of the ball, spinning it with the taut strings of my racquet to land and bounce awkwardly in the spot my opponent least suspected. Darting around as quickly as the ball distracted my equally fast and unhappy mind from a million questions about God, my marriage, and the purpose of existence. In those days I could have played that sport not just for hours, but forever.

By that time, I could also trash-talk as good as Michael Jordan. My playful words and torrential barbs would taunt and frustrate my opponents worse than my low, fast serves. And I'd slice the ball so that it bounced and changed course midair. My "enemies" on the court didn't know what to do and would often rush me in a desperate act of intimidation to try and limit my wind-up swing just as I stretched out my arm to smash back my response. I had no fear. I braced myself and took my full swing as I absorbed the shock of their body crashing into mine. Their foul was as obvious as their inferiority on the court. Their tactic never worked. Except when my *Eishet Chayil* used it on me whenever I tried to talk to her.

For two years the no-nonsense Mr. Levine taught me to "be a man." He told me you must always be a gentleman. That came naturally. But Joe taught me that it all started with being a man — and that meant knowing how to open your mouth. And how to clench your fists.

Joe brought me to the expensive Mens Health Club locker room at the YMYWHA on Lyons Avenue in Newark, New Jersey. My father didn't know anything about sports. Except for *Tzenter*. And Dad was off to his new life. Hanging out with Joe was "cool" (as the term was originally used in the late sixties). Joe was as loud and boisterous with the other men he knew there as I was timid. He would prance around naked, introducing me to his multiracial buddies, while cracking off-color jokes that mercilessly insulted Christians, Women, Jews, Blacks, and Italians. At least he was inclusive!

They all laughed boisterously at silly jokes that good, kind people in the tumultuous Sixties would never repeat nowadays in our frigid and faux politically correct oversensitive career-cancelling holier-than-thou world. They're no longer funny in the twenty-first century. But Dean Martin, Sammy Davis, Frank Sinatra, and Don Rickles kept households across America laughing hysterically as they watched their small television sets with alien antennas at the time. *Is there no happy medium?*

Joe would dash from the steam-room *shvitz* to the sauna, and then to the showers, constantly entertaining every guy he met; his manhood dancing as joyfully as his personality, while I bashfully hid beneath my towel and emotions as I changed and then waited for him in the quiet lounge.

I was so small and skinny I could have changed in my locker. And I was so self-conscious I could have been invisible. But I was always thinking. Always wondering. Always quietly observing Joe and his friends as if standing behind an open door while peering through the space from where it hung on its hinges. When you only weigh seventy pounds, adults never imagine that a bright never-to-be-heard child might be standing there. Especially one whose shyness begs that he not be seen.

I was still painfully diffident, but I no longer found it excruciatingly throbbing to converse. I could even look at the person speaking to me. And they could hear an actual voice instead of a timorous whisper. Being good at sports gave me a lot of confidence. Vodka and pussy completed the job a half dozen years later. Joe was a great mentor. The kind of guy who just "threw you in the water" to teach you how to swim. I almost drowned when I was five. This time I learned quickly.

Thank you, Mr. Levine. Thank you so much! Thank you for not being like Rabbi "Abusive" Tratner. Thank you for treating me with patience and respect. I understood your kind intentions. You sometimes pushed me to the point of tears. But never past. Unlike God, you knew your boundaries.

I certainly had a PTSD childhood, and a hop-skip-jump marriage, but honestly speaking, I've lived a wonderful life. I am happy despite all the bullshit drama and contradictory dogma I've lived through. I'm not an angry, vengeful, jealous little god made in the wrathful image of the big one who wishes revenge and death upon enemies in retribution for their sins. I'm happy just writing and publishing beautiful books for children.

I am one of the few thousand Americans that follows Robert Sapolsky and Steven Pinker; not that I hold anything against the hundred and fifty mindless-million who follow Kim Kardashian and the rapper 6ix9ine. I confess that I too occasionally watch a Jeffree Star or James Charles video.

Being an Orthodox Jew, I'm supposed to silently accept that all the stress, wasted time, and completely unnecessary persecution, throughout the trials and tribulations of my divorce, was somehow the "Will of God," even as my now numb heart still hears the echoes of its earlier screams when it constantly shouted in constricted frustration at the top of its oxygenated by-my-powerful-lungs voice, "This is fucking torture! Why God? Why Ester!"

I'm still looking through PTSD vision as I type these words five years after the fact. But my vision is now very clear. My wife made it too painful for Ester to love me, while our systemic legal system made it a crime for me to love Ester. And God made it impossible for me to love him.

Ernest Hemingway once wrote that, "The best way to find out if you can trust someone is to trust them." Please don't be angry God, but we've lost the most important bond that keeps a relationship strong and true. Don't take this personally, but honestly, I don't trust You.

I held my oversized mug, warming my hands, while calmly inhaling the fragrance of its Keurig Extra Bold brew. I savored the quiet enjoyment of a precious solitary moment in the welcome company of my endless thoughts. In the sublime stillness, after a life full of stormy dramas that seem to come with the territory of being a Jew and the son of a broken Holocaust survivor, a flicker of enlightenment flashed my life, and even my Afterlife, in a sudden big-bang revelation that divulged that I was still dreaming. Dreaming what will one day become nothing more than a lost and forgotten mirage as my lifetime of bricolage experiences ticks away its final few paltry lonely decades. I've never felt so at peace.

I spent most of my life fervently worshiping a God who constantly sucker-punched me with his outstretched arm while using his invisible sleight of hand as he dealt me shitty cards from his stacked deck of tarot cards that forced me to race through gauntlets of guilt and stress.
I'm exhausted.

What have I not done for Ester or God? Who more than they should know how my heart loves? If a now-mature twenty-one-year-old Ester and a huffy God given to sudden outbursts of Holocaust-anger still fail to understand how similar I am to my own gentle and clement father, then there is nothing more that I can do. Or that I am obliged to do. I never really liked card games anyway. They seem like such an utter waste of time.

Orthodox Jews firmly believe that God controls and divinely oversees even a worm crossing a congested eight-lane interstate highway. Don't forget. With narcissists and despots, it's all about control. If God ordains it, that worm will make it to the other side. Even through bumper-to-bumper traffic. Just don't bet odds on using Arnold Shapiro's protagonist, Squiggly Wiggly, as tackle if you're planning on going fishing.

Father Knows Best I've been conditioned to accept and believe by a lifetime of vigorous study. God is the one who arranges the heavenly spheres and galaxies that race throughout our entire universe — let alone supposedly orchestrating the ineptitude of a medieval inquisition kangaroo-courthouse that decrees the immolation of fathers in a modern-day, insulated from secular society, shtetl-hamlet called Monsey.

After all, according to Jewish philosophical *hashkafa* ("outlook"), God is the one who gave an amoral Asperger-ant guardianship over Ester's life while simultaneously exiling and banishing her loving father from her presence. This was all supposedly The Divine Will of God. Perhaps I should just count my blessings that I wasn't commanded to sacrifice Ester.

Were his intentions in order to make Ester a stronger person? Will God hold me accountable one day for not fighting hard enough to save her? Was I supposed to suffer an actual heart attack before tapping out? I'll make myself crazy if I try to "play God" or attempt to understand "his ways." I've finally learned to listen to my heart, and I'm not playing that game anymore. I refuse to self-crucify myself one moment longer for his Original Sin — setting up man for his own downfall and then shaming and punishing him for millenniums till the arrival of the Messiah.

Let God choose a different member of "The Chosen" to play his circular-logic "Don't you trust me?" *Tzenter* game. I refuse to play Poker with a cheating God a moment longer. Especially when he's shuffling the cards and dealing. I'm baked. Thankfully not in one of his forty-six "Arbeit Macht Frei" Auschwitz altar-ovens.

I suffered enough damage during the years I became PTSD toast in Alfieri's Armageddon. I've studied the Talmud long enough to understand that I'm supposed to say that the fires in that courtroom, along with the endless conflagrations spanning mankind's entire bloody history, were all stoked by an all-loving God.

But to be honest, all those folios of incredible wisdom, anecdotal miracles, and endless hair-splitting hypothetical what-if scenarios of judicial, puritanical, and sacrificial law just don't add up despite how intellectually entertaining and thought-provoking they are. And even the guaranteed blissful orgasmic eternal pleasure of "speaking in learning" with God for eternity, promised as a reward for a lifetime of studying the Talmud, doesn't justify the way he has behaved for as long as I've known him.

How does one even begin to question a Past-Present-Future-God who lives in multi-dimensions anyway? It's like playing an opponent infinity-dimensional chess while being confined to the two-dimensional vertical, diagonal, horizontal paths of a traditional board. How does one play "by the rules" with an extraterrestrial ruler that forbids you to so much as wonder, let alone question, why he gets to declare that he doesn't have to play by any?

And why all the savage death sentences of stoning, burning, decapitation, strangulation, and a Divine punishment of a shorter life, for gay men, blasphemers, Sabbath desecrators, Amalekites, eaters of leavened bread during Passover, and sexually frustrated horny young wives who have affairs because their husbands think their bodies are nothing more than incubators for spawning the next mindless-minyan generation of smokers and Yentas. Why not use humane lethal injection? What about repentance? Ever hear of therapy? And what's up with the thuggish forty lashes? You mad, Bro?

Confined to our three-dimensional world, I will always have endless questions for my Eternal God. Some are now quite sophisticated, but they are pretty much the same basic logical questions that have occupied my mind since that day when a skinny innocent ten-year-old birthday boy discovered a dusty, heavy, musty-smelling, old leather valise more than a half-century ago. What a thoughtful gift that was for a young, innocent, empath. "Happy Traumatic Day to Me! Happy Traumatic Day to Me!"

I suspect that even in a world that has a billion dimensions, that none of my questions will ever be answered. How does God create a Garden of Eden here on Earth and a few days later creates an Auschwitz? God is like my love-bombing, hard-working, Shabbat and Yom Tov homemaker who nursed five children, yet couldn't stop signing orders of protection in which she accused me of sexually molesting my own daughters the minute I filed for divorce. Like my spurious spouse, God is not what he purports to be. And so, in a nutshell, I'd like to ask God, face-to-face, once and for all, mano-a-mano, "Why are you so fucking cruel?"

Actually, if I (confused and seduced-by-Satan who you created), a flawed mortal, am able to love and completely forgive Ester for drawing her green monster Zev alienation-induced illustration, subtitled with orders insisting that I immediately cease to exist; then perhaps an all-loving merciful god could forgive his son for captioning, "Die God! Die Now!" beneath a picture of a terrifying, roaring god made out of fire without punishing me for transgressing the Second Commandment (Exodus 20:4).

The clergy of all the established religions claim that God hates suffering. That is why we Jews are instructed by commandments in the Bible, and by the Saints of the Talmud, to visit the sick, raise orphans, give charity, show mercy to widows, and to bury the unknown wandering traveler who was murdered by highwaymen. Nevertheless, in his infinite wisdom, God — who doesn't just know, but exists in the future, while simultaneously living in the present and past — constantly, "lovingly," tests us, while insisting that we have free will.

He then punishes us through our suffering, his greatest "*gift*," in the "*hope*" that we will repent. I cannot italicize those words with enough of an angle to display the intensity of my being in shock as to how insane those words sound no matter how firmly I press the keys on my keyboard.

In fact, aside from the F1-F12 keys, I honestly wish my computer had an F-U! key. The Nazi typewriter surprisingly had an actual SS lightning flash insignia that shared the number five key. It was simply called the swastika key. Why am I tempted to use that key when questioning God?

I've been induced to believe the circular logic that ᛋᛋ God (Whoops!) gives us the opportunity to use our free will to choose the righteous path and earn our share of an eternal life — if we fulfill the preordained destiny goal (slight contradiction there) for which God created us. A destiny that he already knew most of us would never attain before we were even created. Are you mindfucked yet?

How can the concept of "free will" coexist with an already preordained destiny — a place that already exists in the present for the all-knowing God of Mercy? An unmerciful place for the majority of us. A place where God will punish us with unimaginable torture for failing to achieve the goals he set for us.

But the problem is as follows: If God already knows (and never forgets) every single decision we will make in response to every temptation snare he will test us with during our short lifespans — eons of light years before we were even created — how dare he set us up for failure!

God was already suffocating me in utero as I nervously smoked a pack a day with my mommy, while she loved her neighbors and I (most probably) worried about getting my penis snipped. Did God blame me for being addicted to nicotine the moment I was born? Will he reward me for choosing to live a healthy tobacco-free life? Or will God say, "It wasn't really your decision, Zev. I'm the one who sent you Jack LaLanne as an inspiring role-model to watch on T.V. while Gussie hugged you in that yellow-leather chair." Once again, he gets to deal from a stacked deck.

And if someone makes, or is destined to make, really bad choices — like the evil Pharaoh who enslaved the Jews and drowned their male babies — God can "harden his heart," thus forcing said sinner to further levels of iniquity merely to prove how stubborn Pharaoh was in order to justify really kicking the shit out of him later. Is any of this making sense yet? Did you harden Hitler's heart, God, so that he could cold-heartedly slaughter your six million "Chosen" children? Who hardened yours?

I wonder if God's angelic forensic CPA's, who tally even our thoughts and emotions, remembered to keep track of all those extra ordained-by-God collateral-damage innocent Jewish babies that were drowned in the Nile River just so he could make a point.

The frenzy of Jew-hating reached levels that topped some of our own progressive American Congresswomen as the Egyptians patriotically began drowning even their own newborn male babies to preempt a single Jewish one that might have been hidden by a merciful Egyptian. Like the Nazis and Dr. Ferro, they eviscerated any chance of a Jewish father having a relationship with his child. Amazingly enough a great multitude of Egyptians left Egypt with the escaping Jewish population, whereas four-fifths of the Jewish population died during the plague of Darkness, which was a more severe Holocaust than the one which would take place in the twentieth century when "only" two-thirds of European Jewry would be extinguished like vermin.

What does "free will" even mean? Besides, how can we ever possibly "choose" a future in which God already exists in his own past? In other words, God knows our past decisions even as we face making those choices in our future — a future where he has already decided to punish us for the bad behavior we have yet to commit.

And since the all-knowing God — who somehow even knows the final digit of Pi — exists for eternity, he has actually already punished us, as he "looks back," for acts we have yet to commit. Think about that long enough and you'll probably go insane. If you are very fortunate, you will possibly become enlightened. At the very least you will have earned your Ph.D. in Physics.

I sometimes wonder if God gets bored watching reruns his whole life? Or is there a Netflix heaven that keeps regurgitating the same old Jewish theme for eternity: entice your Chosen People; watch them sin; make them suffer mercilessly; watch the few survivors repent; give them an evil character to focus on as they take revenge in your honor (instead of asking why you enabled the cruel madman to begin with); followed by a respite new holiday to celebrate with their abusive compassionate God before he slaughters the next generation of wayward Chosen.

Does God keep uploading new episodes of our millenniums of suffering existence for his sadistic enjoyment? Wasn't he already watching those shows for an eternity before he finally decided to create the world a mere 5,782 years ago? Wasn't he studying the Torah all that time? I have a commandment for God to observe: "Thou shalt not gaslight thy children." (Or gas them. Period.)

Of course, it's understood that we need to pay dearly for our sins when we fail the test that God knew in advance we were destined to flunk even as he handed out the test sheets (F-U!). Prices range, as described in the Talmud, from the most minute effort of having to reach into our pocket a second time for a different size coin than the one we first attempted to retrieve; to crying while watching the life ebb out of our twelve to fourteen-week-old male fetus lying in the palm of our hand that just fell out of our wife's womb and into the toilet moments earlier.

And if the God of Vengeance is in wrath-mode, "Sha'as ro'gez" in Kabbalah terminology, the price becomes your nursing child, as she desperately sucks the few last droplets of milk at the dry shriveled breast of your emaciated wife, before joining her mommy and *muselmann* daddy, as the three of you ascend as one big happy family of smoke to greet God via the chimney stacks of Auschwitz. Mazel Tov! Welcome to Olam HaBa!

How can God believe his Chosen People are so evil that he chooses to punish them viciously? And why always en masse? Like Topol asks in *Fiddler on the Roof,* "Sometimes, can't you choose someone else?" And, knowing the future, and that his children were predetermined to fail, isn't God himself guilty of the biblical sin that emphatically warns: "Before the blind man, do not place a stumbling block!" (Leviticus 19:14.)

What makes less sense, is that we're forced to play this sick "Better live up to your potential!" game with a flawlessly moral and spiritually pure "Source" that created and invented the very "evil" and illusionary temptations that his children then stumble over as they rebel and sin. It also makes no sense that a God, who has the power to create a billion universes for every human ever born, has to miserly dole out minuscule portions of eternal life. It's like being a multi-trillionaire and telling your two kids that if they behave perfectly their entire lives, you'll eventually give each of them a ten-dollar inheritance.

And if you, dear God, really hate suffering so much, why are you so zealous when it comes to inflicting pain? And grotesque methods of death! After imposing mortality upon mankind for the crime of "curiosity" and their eating a single fig from the tree of knowledge in their desire to be more intelligent and godlike so that they could emulate you, couldn't you just stick with your original benign method of our departing this world as described in the *Midrash*?

The holy sages explain therein that people originally died a gentle death merely upon sneezing their first (and last) time. That was the extent of the initial punishment of death that you decreed against Adam and Eve for their horrid sin of desiring knowledge that would allow them to better understand and worship their divine Father in Heaven. The soul that you blew into original man's golem nostrils exited the same way. Mercifully.

Why the later wickedly creative upgrades of Ebola, Aids, Polio, Dementia, Cancer, Progeria, Covid, Divorce, and a myriad of other hellishly sadistic and barbaric ways through which you nowadays allow the Grim Reaper to appear and slowly collect our lives and the lives of those we love? Isn't our anxiety, stress, and the daily grind of living in a universe of entropy, even in a healthy body that has to eventually waste away in atrophy, enough agony to satisfy your prerequisite for entry into Gan Eden?

Wasn't your declaration against man, "By the sweat of your brow, you will eat bread!" (Genesis 3:19), enough of a punishment as we perspire to eke out a livelihood while paying the Jew Tax? And how many women have to suffer the anguish of never being allowed the experience of childbirth and the pleasure of nursing babies, or dying during the delivery of a child they love more than themselves, thanks to your angry, "I will greatly increase your pain during childbirth!" (Ibid. 3:16) Eve enticed Adam to sin. But it was you who seduced all the participants of the very first Jewish "Greek tragedy" in literature.

Why the need for temptation and sin, followed by endless prayer and repentance? Is it really because "God loves the prayers of the righteous," as the Talmud explains, that you withheld the birth of Isaac from the remarkably virtuous Abraham and Sarah for eight full decades? Only to show off your amazing miracle of a woman delivering and nursing a baby at ninety years of age? And then, thirty-seven years later, you command Abraham to slaughter his son on an altar. Why all the fucking drama?

And if you love prayer so much, why did you demand and insist that Moses immediately stop praying, lest he move you to grant forgiveness had he tried just one more time, as the greatest prophet who ever lived begged for permission to enter the Holy Land as he stood within days of his final one hundred and twentieth birthday (Deuteronomy 3:26)? Furthermore, why didn't Abraham even attempt to pray that you accept an animal sacrifice in place of his son Isaac? I can't wait to study the Talmud with you.

Doesn't God love all humans as his children? Are we not all descendants of God's explosive ylem sperm? Talk about the ultimate "Big Bang," as we were all raped into existence. Doesn't he hear the cries of the oppressed? And the whimpers of starving bloated-bellied babies? Does God not sense the fear and dread of pummeled women whose real order of protection is utterly useless? Does he not see the tears of orphans and widows? Has he no empathy for sex slaves and rape victims?

Is God not aware of the outrageous levels of cortisol floating inside the veins and coursing through the bloodstreams of anxious PTSD divorcing fathers suddenly alienated from their daughters? Let's not forget the "kindness" of God when it comes to all the animals in nature that hunt, kill, and eat each other in fulfillment of the verse (Psalm 136:25), "He gives food to every living creature; His kindness endures forever." And mankind is a willing partner and no less guilty when it comes to trophy hunting, or mercilessly slaughtering and eating billions of their own sentient animal relatives every year — of which many seem to possess more compassion than the humans who devour them. Like father, like son.

Why does God need to force parents to watch their toddlers die from childhood leukemia, bone cancer and brain tumors, as the Angel of Death (God's very scary messenger) uses his scythe to separate the soul of their child from its tiny frail body, while they cry as they wish "If I could only trade places with my baby?" And according to the Talmud, which states there are three parents for every child born (God, who supplies the soul, and the father and mother who supply the DNA golem body of clay), surely an all-merciful God must imagine trading places too?

And the real "fun" begins after death, with a sentence in Hell (what was the life they just finished living?) that begins the moment a person is covered with shovelfuls of dirt. According to the Talmud, we still feel pain postmortem. Each bite of every single maggot is described by our holy Kabbalist commentators as "a needle in living flesh."

Hasn't God punished mankind with enough natural disasters and gruesome bioweapons of mass destruction throughout the millennia while evolving man lived a short lifespan of ignorance, serfdom, and in constant fear of eclipses, earthquakes, volcanoes, and a potpourri of angry idol gods they believed they needed to appease by sacrificing their children and many virgins? Why would the real God want to continue the onslaught after his children finally died and found some respite from their suffering?

Don't trouble yourself with answering that if we only understood how great God is, we would begin to understand how sinfully haughty and rebellious our behavior had been and that we deserve to suffer, even post-mortem, as retribution. I would simply respond that should we not expect endless compassion from such an incredibly enlightened deity instead of barbaric violent sadistic shallow revenge?

Another major contradiction in Jewish dogma is that God does not allow us to donate our bodies to science or any of our organs to those desperate for a cornea, heart, or kidney transplant.

But what greater mitzvah is there than to spend one's life studying the Torah or saving a single precious life? Imagine donating corneas to a scholar or scientist so that they can study again or find a cure for senility. Meanwhile God has no problem wasting our organ-remains in order to feed maggots. Nor is he adverse to donating the cute little toddler bodies of blue-eyed Jewish twins as lab rats to help out Mengele with his genetic research.

How can any of this make sense — especially coming from a spectacular maestro God who conducts the entire universe! I have to be honest and describe God's "music" more like the sounds of an angry punk-rock band screaming at the top of their lungs while violently playing their discordant cacophony of screeching instruments.

I've read the works of many theists (Jewish and Christian) who trip over themselves as they desperately attempt to rationalize why bad things happen to good people. Their illogical and feeble explanations are embarrassingly inept. Sadly, the pain of their doublethink headache, as they desperately desire to reconcile a belief in an all merciful-God who rules with an outstretched iron fist, blinds them to the point that they become like the abusive false idol they are trying to rationalize and defend. "Foolish people, without understanding, who have eyes but do not see, ears but they cannot hear," as described by Jeremiah (5:21).

I understand that it's their own intense sadness that forces them to grope foolishly in their own jungle-shtetl *Heart of Darkness* as they idealistically stumble and bumble while trying to make logical sense out of senseless tragedies, foreseen and left unchecked, by an imperialistic, all-powerful, brutish God.

I hope they forgive my honesty, and I pray that God doesn't punish them for making him look like a bi-polar rebellious spiritual being with supernatural abilities, or like a wayward angel who only has limited powers and is no longer interested in mankind, as they try to decipher that which is impossible for a sane and logical mind to comprehend. A God of death.

Meanwhile, there is so much pain in the world that desperate ignorant readers are buying millions of these "bestseller" moronic books. They would probably buy a morphine drip if it were legal. Anything to ease the pain of believing in a God that has been giving mankind one huge hand job with his outstretched arm, from the moment of creation, as they race around with an erection fueled by faith and a promise of one day being allowed to finally stick their holy penis into a heavenly paradise-pussy.

How can one begin to justify and explain the oceans of blood that God has continually leeched from the veins of his Chosen and the rest of mankind since the very beginning of time, when Cain killed Abel a scant handful of hours after the creation of the world? War. Famine. Disease. Slavery. Natural disasters. What is God trying to tell us? It almost seems as if God suffered from an ACE childhood in his own youth and is now angrily lashing out. The Talmud itself, in its threateningly Mafia-like way, warns us that "God has many messengers." He knows where to find you and every member of your family.

A parent must lead by example. We learn from how you behave, Dear God, not from what you preach. We learn by watching the way our Heavenly Father acts, not by the book you have given us. Please don't be like those parents who command, "Do as I say, not as I do." Stop issuing so many commandments while behaving like Sharen, Alfieri, Ferro, and Schwartz. Keep your spirituality. Try showing a little more humanity.

And why are we Jews always so willing to suffer and die? The scholars of the Talmud profusely praise Isaac, as the strong thirty-seven-year-old man quickly complied with the prophecy which only his father had heard and instantly chose to cheerfully carry the heavy wood for the altar upon which he was going to be slaughtered, roughly two thousand years before Jesus supposedly schlepped his own wooden cross. By the way, have you Catholics never heard of intellectual property?

The spiritual twin of Abraham, who looked exactly like his very handsome father, joyfully volunteered in agreement to be sacrificed as a Korban Olah (a fully immolated-offering tribute) upon being informed by his ecstatically enthusiastic old father that the absurd command to "place Isaac on the altar" was the will of God, and Abraham hastened to slaughter his only child from Sarah in response to an absolutely maniacal request had it been delivered by anyone other than God.

But none of the brilliant scholars ask God the three-letter-word question. *Why?* What possible purpose would have been served had the angel not called out to Abraham, telling him not to proceed? What lofty spiritual goal would have been achieved had Abraham continued to basically draw and quarter his son, as the Midrash describes in actual graphic detail? Would we continue to say that Abraham passed the most difficult test ever commanded by God? Wouldn't we call him a murderer?

Meanwhile the Jewish Nation has always maintained her even-in-the-face-of-death devotion to God, along with her compassionate service of Tikun Olam, even as they travelled for millenniums through parted seas of their own human sacrificial blood, while the world remained silent, till they finally arrived home (happy to have that debate) on the shores of the Mediterranean Sea in 1948.

To this day tiny Israel exists as a mighty David, with nuclear weapons in his sheath, surrounded by radical Goliath enemies screaming "Allahu Akbar!" as they blow up a bus or café, or randomly shoot missiles at completely innocent Israeli civilians, while Israeli leaders offer technology, medicine, and land for the mere promise of peace. Bereft of any historical knowledge, completely ignorant mannequin-models gooped in greasepaint makeup and push-up bras on Instagram and Twitter (their knowledge as false and shallow as their existence and eyelashes dripping in mascara), along with a few female anti-Semites in the United States Congress, mindlessly join the choir of ancient radical hate even as they themselves would instantly choose to live in liberal democratic Israel over any of the medieval nations ruled by strict Sharia law that surrounds her.

Where is the voice of these ditzy cute bimbettes regarding their brave "sisters" who are being raped and butchered by the Taliban in Afghanistan for simply protesting and requesting to be treated like humans, and not like camels? Where are the articulate statesmen of the United Nations? Where is the ex cathedra speaking Pope? Doesn't God want his divine messenger to deliver an infallible "voice of God" urgent message for world peace? Or are we once again going to experience the cowardice and silence of Pope Pius XII during The Holocaust?

It won't be long before the Taliban is recognized by the media as the new progressive government of Afghanistan, led by the very four prisoners freed by Obama in exchange for one idiot AWOL American that very likely ran to join the enemy. How badly can the politicians we keep electing fuck up our country and stupidly push policies that are destroying our very system of democracy while we continue to praise them effusively? Meanwhile the far left in our own government are allowing Iran to move full steam ahead as Iranian physicists enrich uranium while her medieval madmen "leaders" threaten to annihilate Israel the moment their scientists successfully split the atom.

We Jews are constantly being saved through miracles only to be tortured, once again, by a "Jealous God" who continues to visit the iniquity of the fathers upon their children. Even our holidays all follow the same theme and pattern: the Gentiles (unleashed by God) start exterminating the Jews as punishment for their sinful slacking in their mindless servitude; God saves a handful of them from total annihilation at the bottom of the ninth; the latest bloodied "Sh'erit ha-Pletah" (surviving remnant), a term from the Book of Ezra (9:14), once again races to "Be fruitful and multiply" in order to beef up the numbers needed to survive the next holocaust. Mazel Tov! The End.

How does one explain a Supreme Being who calmly sat on his throne, as he quietly observed tens of thousands of precious Jewish souls departing this world not so "happily ever after," while his mangled subjects dangled on their crosses with their feet nailed to the post, as they desperately tried to breathe? Jesus was one Jew among so many others. And his crucifixion, in which over two billion devoted followers fervently believe he decided to suffer to appease himself (make sense?), is in fact a very debatable event and probable delusion.

There are commentaries that claim that Jesus was never even crucified. His crucifixion was a later rewrite to hide the shame of his being executed by the Jewish Supreme Court like a common criminal for falsely claiming to be a prophet of God. Like the "Virgin" Mary. Like son. Impostors.

Furthermore, the name of God's son was not "Jesus." The first four centuries after Jesus lived are quite vague regarding any history of the man or the rules of faith regarding the religion he supposedly founded. It wasn't till the First Council of Nicaea finally convened that much of church dogma, including that Jesus was a God and not "just a man," as sung by Yvonne Elliman, was decided.

The four Gospels can't even agree upon the exact day Jesus was supposedly crucified, even though they spend over one-third of their contradictory rambling debate-delusions focused on the last week of the life of Christ known as the "Passion Narratives." Meanwhile we Jews (who have worn a crown of thorns since the birth of Isaac) know the exact birthdate of Moses who preceded

Jesus by roughly fifteen-hundred years. Matthew insists that "Jesus is the new Moses," but similar to what Lloyd Bentsen quipped to Dan Quayle in 1988, I am forced to state that, "I've studied the New Testament and the Five Books of Moses, along with the accompanying ancient Talmud, and I must insist that, 'Jesus, you are no Moses!'"

And it should come as no surprise that all the Gospels are completely in the dark even as to the year of the birth of their Savior. But again, we Jews know that Jesus died at thirty-three years of age (not thirty-five or thirty-six) whereas Moses lived exactly one hundred and twenty years. And the lengths theologians "fly through the air with the greatest of ease" to explain why the Son of God was born in a barn does not go unnoticed by modern day Lubavitcher Hasidim who simply refer to Jesus as "Der Mamzer" (said as fact, not in derision).

The original chroniclers of Christian dogma retrieved much of their material concerning the biological details of their god from the Talmud. Including the supposed name of their savior. They had no other source from which to research. The people surrounding Jesus in his lifetime were entirely illiterate. Most of his disciples were slaves, the indigent, and women (all three groups had very few rights). The earliest devotees of Christianity, gleaned from the desperate lowest rung of society, instantly fell for the simple message of Jesus. "Have faith that he is the son of God and the Messiah, and you will live for eternity!" My friend, do I have a bridge for you!

In Aramaic (the language of the Talmud), Jesus is called "Yeyshu" (pronounced *yay-shoe*). The name is actually an acronym spelling out the Hebrew letters; Yud, Shin, Vav, and Zayin. They are the first letter of each word in the disdaining four-word phrase that vociferates, "Yemach Shemo V'Zichro." Which means, "May his name and memory be erased." As it turned out, the curse of the Jewish sages worked.

To this day no one knows much about the very vague life or death of that thirty-three-year-old young man. Even his true original Jewish name that was announced in the synagogue on the eighth day of his life when he was circumcised remains erased forever. The letters *YE* became *JE* upon being translated into Latin. The *Shin* became an *S*. And the letter Vov sounded out in Hebrew is "eww," so that word ("and") became the letter *U*. The final *Z* (Zichro) became the letter *S* because Gentiles were unable to properly pronounce the Aramaic (Zah) sound.

Hence a bunch of Roman Catholics wound up worshipping a flesh and blood Orthodox Jewish god named *Jesus*, who observed Shabbos, wore fringes, and studied the Talmud. The followers of Jesus believe their god suddenly declared his infallible original testament as "old," even though in the Bible, God vehemently commands (Deuteronomy 28:14), "Do not stray right or left, from all the laws I command you this day, to follow other gods and serve them." Which is exactly what occurred upon Gentiles worshiping a "nice Jewish boy" as a god upon being advised to disregard all the laws of the Old Testament. You didn't just "stray." You fell off the deep end. But it's okay. It's not your fault. *And I still love Shiksas.*

His Catholic flock also constantly, unwittingly, insults Jesus with the acronym curse of *Yeshu*. And in the name of the Jewish Jesus, more Jewish blood has been spilled during centuries of bloody history than even God ever imagined (had he not known the future). You can't make this shit up! Or can you (once you're speaking ex cathedra)?

Speaking of "speaking ex cathedra," I find it quite amusing that the pope is considered infallible and totally incapable of being mistaken when he decides a matter of faith or belief, yet his godlike ability does not extend to scientific, historical, medical, or geographical matters. In anything but faith he's as human as the rest of us and subject to peer review. In other words, he was forced to lift his butt off his throne and provide some fucking evidence. He can no longer insist that the Sun orbits the Earth. And you thought our government sucked?

Nicholas Donin, a Kapo Jew (similar to Dan Schwartz) who converted for a fortune of earthly wealth and honor, translated many sections of the Talmud and revealed much of the above to Pope Gregory IX almost nine hundred years ago. He then used the information to bring dozens of charges of blasphemy against the Jewish nation and their Oral Law which completely undermined and butchered their New Testament, along with insulting Mary and Jesus. A guilty outcome would have been horrific for the Jews of France.

Four of the most famous Talmudical scholars in France defended the Jews and their Talmud. They conceded that *Yeshu* was indeed a name, and they even admitted that as an acronym it was a curse, but they cleverly avoided the issue of insulting a man-made god and instead made a play on the Aramaic name "Yeshu" as the name "Yehosua," which is the Hebrew name for Joshua. The root of that name is "save." The name was later translated as "The Savior."

The sages insisted that the pejorative acronym description was meant for "some other bad guy." Not hard to do when you're merely dealing with a foolish busy-with-nothing king and an ignorant kapo ex-Jewish esquire who abandoned his Talmud trophy-wife and now spent his time studying a convoluted idol-whore "New" Testament. No hard feelings (except for an erection) to my shiksa ex-girlfriends that I love. We're still friends, right?

Nevertheless, as in our own systemic court system, the Talmud itself was declared "guilty" for some other minor offenses that even the erudite scholars were unable to obfuscate. Twenty-four wagonloads of priceless handwritten manuscripts conveying the word of God to Moses during three separate forty-day and sleepless-nights of Talmudical lectures were set on fire and destroyed in the streets of Paris (right behind where the Louvre Museum sits today) as a result of Talmud being taken to court and put on trial. DO NOT STUDY THE TALMUD. DO NOT SPEAK IN LEARNING WITH FELLOW JEWISH SCHOLARS. STAY AWAY FROM JEWISH TRADITION.

The waste of time and money was very similar to my having to sit in court, enduring two trials, while facing a third, simply because I filed for divorce eight centuries after the Talmud was burned in France. Orthodox Jews are terrified to wear their Yarmulkas in public in this now tolerant country where a radical Muslim, with a rap sheet (for drug dealing and aggravated violence) as long as the Koran, can throw a nice old retired Jewish doctor out of her window while yelling "Allahu Akbar," after beating her to near death, and be found innocent of murder by the highest court in France because he had earlier smoked a joint. And like my insane wife, the first thing Kobili Traore did after the murder was pray. It didn't matter that he had been taunting Dr. Sarah Halimi with antisemitic insults and threats for over a year. What a shitty little country. Not her people. But her promises of "liberty, equality, fraternity" reek like shit.

The printing press would not be invented for another two hundred years, and the Jews cried while blaming themselves for not studying enough as they mourned the unimaginable loss of their culture and oral law, while risking their lives to hide several copies to slowly transcribe new scrolls. Thankful and content that it wasn't their families going up in smoke, the Jews did what they did best while living in exile. They survived. God would save their future furnace smokey gift from his "treasure house" for the European Jews of the twentieth century.

In truth, Jesus was forgotten. The most accurate skimpy historical record of his life remains hidden in Jewish theology. There is so much more to share, but for the sake of peace among the devoted and deluded ignorant masses, I will allow more upsetting information that I could reveal to remain buried in the past.

Ignorance is bliss. For the ignorant. Because the memory of Jesus was obliterated is why it took almost four-hundred years for the Catholic Church to basically invent, from scratch, the twenty-first century modern version of Christianity mandated by Paul that is foolishly practiced today by billions of devoted duped "faithful" sheeple.

So, we have a Pope who experiences divine revelation while speaking ex cathedra but is unable to get his God's name straight. He's also clueless regarding the lineage and historical background of the corporal God he worships despite centuries of corporate church meetings and ecumenical councils. His Holy Spirit remains clueless regarding the identity and biography of a "Yeshiva Bochur" (aspiring scholar) who simply went "Off the Derech" (off the deep end).

If some deranged fanatic killed me for writing all this, Catholics would say it was Jesus who withheld his protection. Hasidim would say Hashem lost his "endless" patience with me. And Muslims would mumble, "Allahu Akbar!" I also imagine that I won't be receiving the Eucharist anytime soon. And although I like red wine, I wouldn't want to experience the transubstantiation of the bread turning into the body of Christ inside my own body because I'm a vegan.

Meanwhile I'm simply the honest scholar speaking the truth in the hope of stopping the divisiveness that the three Abrahamic religions inflict upon the billions of ignorant people who practice their "positive" version of God's word that he commanded as the Creator of the Universe. A benign Creator who has everyone confused and killing each other.

Just for the record, Jesus observed all the 613 commandments of the Old Testament. There was no new one yet. He studied the Talmud. And he wore fringes. I also doubt that he ever ate pork. Like some Hassidim, he probably made love to a shiksa prostitute. But he certainly didn't say a Hail Mary prayer after he came. He probably raced to the nearest mikvah.

Please don't run out and kill a bunch of Jews over all this revelation. Breathe. Besides, do you really believe an all-loving God wants us to kill each other? Like the funk band, War, sang in 1975, "Why can't we be friends?" And as the beautiful Sade ponders in her adamant gorgeous voice, "Why can't we live together?! You are still my brother."

In place of jumping up in anger, why not research and read your endless convoluted Church dogma? You might learn something if you shut your iPhone and opened your mind. Or you can just trust me, because you'd probably prefer being crucified rather than being forced to read through the endless boring debates and illogical loopholes of the "truth revealed by God" guaranteed in a supposed original promise by Jesus to Peter of Papal Infallibility and a promise of ex cathedra supreme authority. It's so much easier to drown in emoji endorphins after posting, "Jesus is my Savior," on Facebook. Can I get a (blind) witness?

That supposed promise of supreme apostolic authority to Peter was not formally defined till the year 1870 by the First Vatican Council. In a vote with a tally of four-hundred and thirty-three in favor of the doctrine of infallibility and only two against— because sixty members of the council fled from Rome before the final vote as a protest of refusal in being associated with the Papal bull bullshit — an eventual separation of Church from State was sparked that we are naturally still thrilled about in the twenty-first century.

It took till 1960 to close the First Vatican Council and form the Second Vatican Council to deal with the fallout of the first council. You know how fast the Church moves. Mazel Tov!

Crucifixion was one of the most horrific forms of death ever invented by man. The Romans were said to have crucified too many Jews to count when they destroyed our Second Temple. They actually ran out of wood with which to erect more crosses. Thank you Dear, All-merciful God. With mangled hands nailed through their wrists in supplication-position to an all-loving "Father in Heaven," those who were crucified continued to pray thrice-daily with parched throats, begging for compassion, as their dislocated arms, slowly extended by several inches, hopelessly reached out in prayer beseeching mercy from the angry and deaf "Jealous God."

God eventually answered their tortured excruciating (hence the term crucify) gasping-for-air prayers for a quicker death with patient buzzards that sat on the horizontal and vertical wooden posts of the Roman "traitors." The vultures aggressively jumped to pluck out the moist dead eyes of his Chosen People the moment the weight of the flailed open-sore insect-infested bodies restricted any further exhalation of air. Releasing the final breath of life that entered the nostrils of their ancestor Adam, their souls raced, faster than the speed of light to Olam Haba. All this and more, under the watchful, merciful eyes of El Roi, He Who Sees All.

How can a sane mind even begin to formulate and then fathom an all-merciful Eternal God whose Divine Providence direction of all worldly events supervised the tumbling of his own "Chosen" children into huge mass graves as they were pelted with machine gun fire? Don't you have anything better to do with all that time on your hands, Dear God?

How does one resolve the conundrum of a Father in Heaven that blindly sees-all, but apparently feels nothing, as God stared at Mengele's finger pointing at the hungry, dazed and dehumanized nearly-frozen daily new arrivals to Auschwitz — as the good doctor barked at them to step right or left, to be the Chosen People again, to be permanently thawed out in warm ovens or cherry-picked as lab-rat patients for his post-doctoral torturous medical horror experiments.

With a deranged passion for genetic "research," Mengele treasured any twins that arrived at Auschwitz. Toddler twins suffered unimaginable nightmarish experiments that even our anything-goes society would never allow depiction of in a modern-day horror snuff-film. With toys and treats, and extra food, Mengele groomed his beloved lab vermin who gleefully shouted, "Uncle Mengele is here!" whenever the "In Doctors We Trust" monster came to visit with gifts and candy before taking them out to his ghoulish laboratory for their Kindergarten Final Solution education. I really must complete this book before I stop believing in God entirely.

Blood transfusions were made from one twin to another just to see the toxic deadly results. Sex change operations were carried out by Mengele's deranged mind, performed on little charming boys and darling girls without even stating a goal or resulting medical expectation of what he was looking to prove. Because there was no goal. Lethal germs were injected into tiny, cute bodies.

Organs and limbs were sadistically removed.

Still other Jewish lab rats were heartlessly immersed into extremely hot water followed by immediately dunking "the patient" into freezing water just to see how long it took to shock the beating of a strong, young healthy heart into arrhythmia and cardiac arrest due to the sudden extreme slowing down of the heart's rhythm. At which point the body of the sinless, innocent dead cherub was dissected to see the results of what deranged medical minds can achieve and meticulously document in the name of science. Enabler nurses helped "comfort" the tortured toddlers as they cried out for their smoke-via-chimneys mommies to come save them — similiar to their parents who completely wasted their time crying out to an invisible ghostly God.

Blue-eyed siblings, however, were the rarest of all priceless Jewish gems. A fatherly, smiling Uncle Mengele injected chemicals directly into the "windows-to-the-soul" of twins to change their color. Blue-eyed twins were a double-portion manna gift from heaven. Mengele even attempted to create Siamese twins by monstrously stitching two siblings back-to-back and connecting their blood vessels and organs. "Why?" you ask. The bigger question is why does a God who declares that his very essence is the trait of "mercy" create such devilish fiends?

All those atrocities were performed without anesthesia by Uncle Mengele upon innocent Jewish children separated from their parents. The sadistic genial doctor was as charming as Aunt Sharen, who separated blue-eyed Ester from her father. Both characters were extremely polite and soft-spoken trusted individuals in the medical field who rarely lost their temper. But when they did, you would just die not to meet them. It doesn't matter if you torture one person or hundreds. A beast is a beast.

How does one even attempt to describe the shower-gas chamber scenes of a million and a half crying and screaming parchment-skinned skeletons embracing their loved ones one last time, as their shredded lungs-on-fire screamed for mercy while suffocating like vermin due to the Zyklon B insecticide meant for their earliest evolutionary relatives? If the Germans could have stepped on the stultified Jews, and crushed them like bugs, they would have. But because the insects were the size of humans, they had to be railroaded, figuratively and literally, in cattle cars to be gassed with Zyklon B. And incinerated, post-haste, like rotting garbage.

I have more mercy on insects I find in my house, as I capture them only to release the living organism outside. I wouldn't rip a flower from the ground, let alone slaughter a chicken or cow for its leather or meat. The mighty German war machine transported the finest citizens of their cities to Hell, while those who clearly understood where their innocent neighbors were headed "purchased" mansions and priceless art for pennies on the inflated Deutschmark in a real estate market suddenly flooded with beautiful homes and profitable businesses. The descendants of the Huns refused to even use Jews as slaves. The insane goal was total extermination. Did you enjoy the show, God?

The Chosen People's "Final Solution" escape from Hell was only permitted after stripping the unsuspecting victims naked of their legal rights, self-esteem, clothes, homes, and worldly goods as they eagerly entered the "showers" after spending a week caged in a cattle car without toilet paper.

One final insult was a hastily performed postmortem dental exam to quickly yank the teeth of any corpse that had a gold cap or filling in an open mouth that had locked into position while gasping for air moments earlier. The little remaining fat of the skeletal "Chosen Corpse" was then combined with lye to make "kosher" soap.

Jewish hair was processed as stuffing for army blankets to ensconce disciplined well-trained German soldiers who dreamt of murdering more Jews. The hair of the descendants of the Biblical Patriarchs was also used to manufacture thick padded socks to keep the Aryan goose-stepping marching footsies of the Waffen-SS cozy and warm.

Approximately three thousand twins were treated infinitely worse than modern-day lab rats at the hands of Mengele in Auschwitz. Upon graduation from medical school in Frankfurt, Dr. Josef Mengele earned a Ph.D. degree in Physical Anthropology and then studied under Germany's leading expert on twins after joining the prestigious Institute for Hereditary Biology and Racial Hygiene in 1937.

All this wonderfully impressive education earned Dr. Josef Mengele his real postgraduate degree after he joined the SS and was thereupon dubbed *The Angel of Death* by the parents of the children he tortured. He certainly needed no additional training to learn to remain detached from the emotions of his patients so that he could remain level-headed during their treatment or surgery. That came naturally. As natural as my wife signing protection orders.

Angel of Death is really a half-benign name that loses much in translation because we think of angels as wonderful spiritual beings. Jewish theology teaches that there is an Angel of Life and an Angel of Death (*Malach Hamaves*). *Malach* means "messenger." Both angels dutifully carry out the mission they were instructed to complete by God. "Nothing personal, it's just business."

Malach Mengele's subhuman savage experiments proved nothing scientific other than to document the insanity of a German society at large whose entire legal system (backed by a mighty Luftwaffe) sanctioned the utterly unimportant and unscientific racial "research" and extermination of their Jewish population. Our American courts have yet to dissect the bodies of the fathers they enslave and experiment on through protection orders. Although they could certainly supply Robert Sapolsky with endless samples of cortisol infused pints of blood and tormented emotionally-mangled bodies for his research involving stress.

The Angel of Death also portrayed how ruthless God can be when he sets his mind to it. What kind of mind can even imagine such acts against humanity and then create messengers to deliver them? How were so many Germans capable of enabling such an atrocity? Even against "those Jews!"

What kind of God creates such demons? Don't doctors and Gods promise to alleviate suffering and to never inflict pain? Sharen, please explain it to me. For once, teach *me* something about God. How do minds like yours and Mengele's work?

How could you possibly accuse Ester's innocent father of being a raging pedophile? From where did you find the heartlessness to try and place me in jail as a child-molester? And upon unleashing that deranged assault on my heart and reputation, and losing in court, you instantly launched a second rocket to place me in jail for "hacking" your computer with the password you gave me. How did you twist fatherly love into rape, an award-winning kid's book into an obsession with feces, and paying a pittance of maintenance as a reason to wage a fucking Monsey World War with an army of Yentas?

What is even more incredulous is how you were instantly backed by the entire State of New York and their "Finest." Three years flew by and not one official gave a flying fuck about doing the right thing. Except for the two gentlemen who visited me on that quiet Shabbat morning as I sat down to enjoy some uninterrupted time to study a folio of the Talmud. And all they did was not jump on the opportunity to book me, fill out forms, and collect overtime like Pig Alfieri. God bless them.

As Charles de Montesquieu proclaimed, "There is no crueler tyranny than that which is perpetuated under the shield of law and in the name of justice." Charles should have concluded that pithy remark to include, "or in the name of God." Living under the tyranny of God is the most cruel existence of all.

Do you think I'm a little too obsessed with the Holocaust, Dear God? Then go ahead and punish me for trying to understand how you, of all Gods, sent my incredibly gentle father to Dachau and starved him to the point of imminent (literally days away) death. Which would have meant that I would have never been born. Come to think of it ... forget about me! I wonder how many future Einstein's never came into existence because their parents were among your Chosen, forced to execute the mitzvah of dying for your "glory" before they themselves were executed.

Surely you query, "You mad, Bro?" No. Not really. The best criminal profilers know that anger is often just a second emotion to fear, sadness, and anxiety. I'm not mad at all. Just completely outraged that you would subject your devoted son to constant fight-or-flight physiological response acute stress, pre-suicidal sadness, and PTSD depression, while forcing me to live in an incredibly anxious state for almost three years as I worried about my daughter, my finances, police visits, and Alfieri's Nazi courtroom tactics. I know I shouldn't complain. You let me off easy compared to my father and six million relatives.

Twenty percent of Nobel laureate winners are Jewish. Meanwhile Jews represent a minuscule percentage of the world's population. Imagine the inventions, discoveries, medical cures, art, literature, and potential love and humanity that poured out as smoke from the chimneys of Auschwitz as you extinguished any possibility of those Jews and their children having their own children and living productive lives.

It's amazing that only you literally saw, and only you knew what the future world would have looked like today had it been shaped by the creative descendants of the six million sacrifices that you, in your endless kindness, chose to incinerate. You understood what you were doing as you inscribed the fate of every single precious soul into your Book of Death on Rosh Hashanah during the years 1939-1945. How do you sleep? Oh! I forgot. You never sleep (Psalm 121:4). *Maybe God's sleep deprivation explains his schizophrenia.*

In your supremely enlightened state, you somehow deemed it more important to slaughter their parents and watch as the potential lives of countless millions of children, grandchildren, and great grandchildren went up in smoke. That's a lot of Yiddisheh nachas, God. Mazel Tov!

But I'm the one who is supposed to feel shame and remorse as I faithfully memorized the entire chapter of Hamafkid with the distraction of an erection and endless sharp pangs of guilt? Seriously?

And although you did promise (Numbers 13:18) "to keep in mind the iniquities of the fathers for their children, grandchildren, and great-grandchildren," as you allow the next generation to suffer for the sins of their predecessors, you simply decided to instantly wipe out three generations (and endless future ones) in one fell swoop in Auschwitz. #godisanazi Can we get this trending on Twitter?

I have no energy to even attempt a motion for God's defense. What human in one lifetime possesses the slightest amount of the impossible degree of supposed wisdom that it would take to unravel the mystery of evil, sickness, pain, depression, and ultimately a punishment in Hell for transgressing any one of 613 commandments and endless rabbinical amendments created by an all-loving perfect God?

Life is too short to even begin to ponder such a ludicrous, contradictory notion. And God created my mind to be very logical. So how could I ever possibly explain what is clearly so illogical? I'm still just trying to figure out my own divorce, let alone God's "mysterious ways."

Were you testing me, God? Knowing the future, and that I would become less religious after witnessing how hypocritical your rabbis and yentas behave over a fucking dollar (you're lucky I still keep Shabbos), what possible satisfaction did you receive while watching your scholarly CPTSD lab rat scurry through a maze of malicious prosecution as he avoided being blown apart by land mine after land mine of protection orders, court motions, threats of contempt, and policemen visiting at all hours? I understand that it was you acting like a wild dog when you disguised yourself as a merciless judge in a black robe. Victor Alfieri was nothing more than your Malach Hamaves messenger.

Was it so necessary to "test" me? Would my time not have been better spent completing three more tractates of the Talmud during those years you clogged my heart with deadly unwarranted stress? Couldn't you wait to test me in Gan Eden (Garden of Eden) on the Talmud instead of in your cardiology laboratory here on Earth in SS Alfieri's courtroom?

Did you jot down notes from Dr. Mengele on the procedure for conducting maniacal experiments as an excuse to torture blue-eyed Jewish fathers?

How many times did you deem it necessary to watch me suddenly choking on a mouth full of cereal as thoughts of Ester emerged in my mind as I stared at a bowl of floating fresh fruit, grains, and soy milk while eating my breakfast? But why am I even talking? You, of course, knew all of this before I was even born.

Who was more faithful than your humble servant? Like man's best friend I served you with every fiber of my existence. What would I not do to help talmudical scholars like Rabbi Nekritz or any of your Chosen who came calling? Who purchased two vans, donated money, raised money, and helped establish the Riverdale Yeshiva in its infancy?

Who worked tirelessly to help the Agunot you enslaved? Who studied the Talmud six to eight hours a day? And who was a better father? I wore my invisible dog collar and never imagined stepping over a line of sin. In return you kept zapping me throughout my entire lifetime. You electrocuted me during my childhood. You then increased the voltage during my marriage. And finally, you put me into the electric chair as you removed Ester from my life upon my serving her mother with divorce papers.

I don't know how I miraculously survived. But like those rare individuals who are still alive after being struck by lightning, I was also able to survive your trial by fire. I walked past that invisible electric fence. I finally articulated the thoughts that I wanted to ask my entire life. I was able to extricate myself from your leash as I removed the burden I mindlessly and foolishly carried my entire life and I placed it back where it belongs. On your galactic-sized broad shoulders. Deal with it.

Tell me the truth. Are you bored sometimes? Is that what this is all about? Talk to me, God. I feel bad for you. I almost wish I could believe Nietzsche's famous declaration about your demise. Then everything would make sense. Evolution and survival of the fittest would explain wars and deranged minds. Yet somehow (probably due to the conditioning of my youth) I still stubbornly believe in you.

I still want to believe in a God who creates babies, galaxies, kindergartners, colorful species of birds and fish, and women that love to kiss and hold hands. It's hard for me to imagine a Nazi God who allows Nazi soldiers to starve his Chosen Children in death camps where the "prisoners" needed to duck, or move away quickly to avoid being suddenly punched, kicked, or shot at "for target practice" because they were standing too close to a German citizen in uniform that suddenly walked next to them. Heil, God!

I still fathom an abracadabra God who merely spoke and those endless galaxies, striped Bengal tigers, colorful orchids, and stunning blue butterflies instantly, miraculously, sprang into existence. I like children's stories. That's why I write them too. Nevertheless, while alienating Ester from me, it seems that you've, nebech, alienated me from you.

Was all this bullshit drama really part of my "purpose for existence?" To suffer in silence and never dare question "your ways" while your invisible outstretched arm constantly constricted my heart? Couldn't you satisfy your lust for "cleansing the sins" of your Chosen People on Yom Kippur as you seal millions of Jews and Gentiles into your Book of Death?

Isn't one "Happy Holocaust Day" of bloodshed a year, decreeing the death of fifty-five million people worldwide, as you scribble into your iPad the precise karma tit-for-tat "Middah k'neged Midah" method of execution on Rosh Hashana, detailing precisely how each marked individual will be slaughtered by your Angel of Death messenger in the coming year, enough serial-killer pleasure? "*Happy Holocaust Day to you ....*"

Friedrich Nietzsche once wrote, "What really raises one's indignation against suffering, is not suffering intrinsically, but the senselessness of suffering." You forced me to endure too much senseless suffering. Do you now see that you pushed me too far? You're the sinner. Repent!

And here's the real flaw with your entire "purpose for existence" wacko-plan: it makes absolutely no sense for an all-intelligent perfect-and-kind God to act especially cruel, viciously torturing and punishing even his most devoted righteous followers for their slightest transgressions, while said God always gets to walk away scot-free after committing horrific crimes against all of humanity since the beginning of time.

When will you hold yourself accountable, surely within a hairsbreadth, for all the atrocities you've committed? Like Sharen, you can't possibly admit you're wrong. But I don't want you to go to Hell. I don't want you to suffer. I don't have it in me. Thank God. I just think it would be nice of you to apologize to Ester and the flesh and blood daddy who loves her more than you do. But why would you need to apologize when, technically speaking, you did nothing wrong?

Besides, since you taught us via Moses that you are flawless, you can plead that you have no free will. You're perfect, God. You always make the right choice. Which means you had no option but to create a world full of evil and pain that makes it appear as if you don't exist. Make any sense? Of course it doesn't! I honestly don't really look forward to "speaking in learning" with you anymore. I'd easily slaughter you in a real debate where you must abide by rules of logical consistency instead of adamantly insisting that, "You have to just trust me and have faith that I know what I'm doing!"

You now leave me no choice but to insist that you raise Ester. I pray (There I go again. Why do I bother?) that you do half as good a job as I would have. I already see what you obviously can't. Ester will never be what she was destined to become had I remained in her life. Who will replace me, God? Who will show her the love and patience of a real father? Who will you substitute in my place to have those deep and meaningful conversations with her? You? But you're a mute. And you're deaf. And so why do I continue to talk? After all, you already knew this entire conversation eons of time before the six days of creation took place. Ciào.

Perhaps because I had just spoken quite irreverently to the God of Vengeance (Psalm 94:1), I suddenly feared retribution as my lifelong conditioning kicked in and I imagined my demise followed by my entire life being condensed into a pitifully scant, sterile obituary informing the community of my passing and where Shiva will be sat: Father, Grandfather, Writer, Scholar, Pillar of the community. Faithful Schmuck.

But the gut-wrenching experience of surviving my wire-monkey motherless childhood and exiting a twenty-eight-year mirage-marriage, after living among crude quidnunc Yenta gossipmongers in a hypocritical Jewish ghetto community, has granted me a profound wisdom in my ability to understand flawed humanity. And even an imperfect God. I no longer fear him. I feel that a God should behave, at a minimum, at least as humanely as I would. The loneliness, pain, fear, and sadness of my life has ultimately rewarded me with a timeless, relaxed freedom that I could never have fathomed exists. In short; "Shit happens."

And although I'm still perplexed by a supposedly all-loving God that slaughters his "Chosen People," I am no longer consumed by negative thoughts. I've accepted that my understanding of misfiring synapses and flawed humanity is the most I could ever hope for. I no longer feel the obligation to understand — or waste my precious life a moment longer philosophizing the existence of — an inhumane "perfect" God.

How does one describe a God who gives birth to deformed babies and infects toddlers with deadly diseases, while a simple human like myself traps bees in my house and frees them outside to avoid killing them? How does one praise a God that hides behind myriads of destroying angels as he slaughters nations, while I refuse to eat meat? I no longer feel the need or experience the desire to defend him.

It would be very easy to accept Spinoza's philosophical approach of a denuded God and then claim that the brain of the Creator of the universe isn't wired right à la Robert Sapolsky. But somehow, I still imagine that God must be perfect. That is what *Unzereh* tradition (our *Mesorah*) teaches us. But after a lifetime of trying to make sense out of the impossible, I'm not going to waste any more time. I've thought about my own dying day in the next decade or two. And I've concluded that nothing is trifling. And nothing is that important. Except for one's freedom.

In short, not only was I never obsessed with feces, but I no longer give a shit. Surviving the fire-walk of my divorce and the corrupt judicial lunatics who chased me throughout the Rockland County courts like prey, coupled with the fiendish inhumanity exhibited by many of my modern-day walking-dead relatives, false friends, deceitful rabbis, and Yenta-neighbors — who all portend to pray for the imminent "speedily in our days" arrival of the Messiah while leading disgustingly back-stabbing hypocritical-holy lives, imagining that they, of all people, are God's Chosen as they anticipate a reward of Eternal life — has amazingly granted me an enlightened one. I've somehow developed an inner swagger of knowing that I am an incredibly unique and beautiful being. As the Buddhist's say, "I am awake." Even more important, I. Am. Free.

For thirty years, the invisible stainless-steel shackles of an all-loving God kept me bound to an illusionary bashert marriage. My faith, coupled with the extremely busy sleep-deprived schedule of an assembly-line, repetitive, monotonous existence — based upon a Jewish Calendar Life of kids, more kids, tuition payments, Shabbos cholent, tithing, weddings, funerals, Brit-Milah and Bar-Mitzvah celebrations, constant prayer, and more kids — had me dropping late at night and popping back up in the early morning hours to race through another rushed day of study and serving God in order to, one day, finally attain eternal days of bliss basking in the radiance of God in the afterlife. Is it any wonder that we Jews look so forward to eternal rest?

Moments of joyful "Yiddisheh nachas," celebrating the milestone events of our children, as they are molded into the next generation of religious robots, supposedly makes it all worthwhile. Jewish theology teaches that parents who raise children to observe the commandments of the Torah will continue to be rewarded for the actions of their progeny even after they themselves pass from this world. This is one reason why Orthodox Jewish people have so many children.

The converse also holds true. Murder is the ultimate sin because it removes the opportunity for the deceased victim to perform good deeds, observe mitzvot, study the Talmud, and worship God. Imagine how much punishment God deserves for sacrificing six million of his progeny along with their future descendants who would have been born into this world to worship him and complete more mitzvahs. Can he send himself to Hell?

Yiddisheh nachas occasions are the grains of spice that liven up the busy-from-birth, harried, multi-tasking, exhausting life of your average Orthodox Jew as he dozes while praying the daily *Shacharit* morning service at seven o'clock on the Monsey-bus on his way to Manhattan for forty years in order to pay expensive private school tuitions that basically serve as a baby-sitting service that teaches his half-dozen children nothing but divisiveness and intolerance — not only for Goyim, but even for the "Nisht foon Unzereh" secular Jewish crowd.

"Goyim" is not a pejorative word, by the way. It simply means "nations." As in, "Of all the nations of the world, The Jewish People are The Chosen Nation." *Goyim* has only become a derogatory word because of the cadence with which it is pronounced by too many of our own Unzereh. And the noun *Jew* describes any member of the people whose traditional religion is Judaism. It only became an offensive slur upon being pronounced with contempt by too many Goyim against a few Shylock Jews.

Rinse and repeat the prayer-process on the way back from Manhattan as our "Daf-Yomi" (Folio-a-Day) wannabe scholar looks forward to studying a few lines of Talmud in the Beit-Midrash Synagogue late at night, even as he mumbles his evening Maariv prayers while sitting on the bus with a bobbing head, repeating the Shema Yisroel ("Hear, O' Israel, Deuteronomy 6:4) prayer for a third time, because he can't remember if he warbled it correctly just moments ago. Deep breath.

For those poor souls who are living this life, please take another one to ward off your depression.

Yes, we all claim how wonderful Jewish life is, even as we joke in our sleep-deprived stupor that we'll catch up on our shut-eye, "One of these days." Or in *Olam HaBa* (Eternity). I rarely slept more than four or five hours a night the entire time I was married. The only exception was Friday night because Saturday morning prayers began at half past nine instead of seven sharp. After all, the Sabbath is a day of rest. I attended the "late" minyan whose members shuffled in at around nine-thirty.

I used to drink three cups of black coffee just to wake up in the morning. And at least five more throughout the day to stay awake. I would joke, "Who needs to sleep when you can have a cup of coffee?" But there is nothing funny about sleep deprivation. It's even used as a "soft" form of torture (a walk in the park when compared to the torment of a bad marriage). And lack of sleep also inhibits one from making correct decisions. *Why do you think my marriage lasted as long as it did?*

Meanwhile, the most important commandment in the Torah is the mitzvah to study the Talmud. *You shall deeply study it day and night* (Joshua 1:8). Yet most Orthodox Jewish men can barely begin to imagine the pleasure of dissecting, debating, and studying a single page of the Talmud in its true depth and cerebral glory. And to be honest, it's not their fault.

A scholar needs to be calm and well rested to concentrate and think clearly. Harried, tuition-paying, bus-traveling fathers lack the time and expertise to lead a scholarly life. They attended the maladroit schools they are now enrolling their half-dozen complaining children to suffer through in preparation for a "do as you are commanded" life. Talk about visiting the iniquities of the fathers upon their children to a third and fourth generation. Not knowing any science, Orthodox Jews attribute an individual's desire for sleep as "laziness." They have no clue that the brain needs to dream as much as the body needs food, water, and air.

And creative minds need to dream and imagine during the day. But creativity is a rare word in the Bible. It's only used when describing a benevolent serial killer. Of billions.

The exhausted synapses of the fried brains of Jewish Orthodox dads result in their completely lacking the peace of mind necessary for calm reflection. Mention "calm reflection" to an Orthodox Jew and he'll think you've gone off the deep end and embraced Buddhism. Lacking sleep, they typically doze off while trying to concentrate, placing their tired heads on their tomes, till a bunch of chairs scratching against the *Beit-Midrash* wooden floor alerts them that everyone is standing up for the ten o'clock evening *Maariv* final prayers of the day which are about to begin for those who work locally.

Those who already mumbled the *Maariv* evening service on the bus, to multi-task wasted prayer with wasted time sitting in traffic to spare a few precious minutes for themselves, hurriedly rush off to eat a quick dinner and grab a few hours of sleep before being interrupted by their morning shrieking yenta alarm-clock wives and God. They are forced to jump back on the hamster wheel and race through another day (living by the creative lyrics written by the late Prince) of being "busy doing something close to nothing but different than the day before." *She wore a raspberry beret …*

The majority of those who attempt to study the Talmud take the Jewish male-bonding shortcut-going-nowhere route as they race through the seven-year "Daf-Yomi" (Folio-a-Day) cycle, spending anywhere from thirty minutes to an hour each day with their friends that allows them to "complete" the entire Talmud every seven years. Once again, they are "busy doing something close to nothing but different than the day before."

I'm sorry, but who are they kidding? Surely not themselves, as they laugh nervously in admission that "it's better than nothing." In all honesty, it is a lovely pastime, and the huge cultish *Siyum HaShas* (Completion of The Talmud) sabbatical celebrations attended by several hundred thousand Jews worldwide is very touching. Yet almost sinful. Because such a shallow and rushed attempt to study the Talmud is, in truth, not much more than a placebo pill taken to assuage Jewish guilt that guarantees nothing more than eternal ignorance. It is the equivalent of substituting an intelligent trophy wife with a toothless prostitute. It is the ultimate mental masturbation. Pass the tissues, please.

In all honesty, the delusional Folio-a-day, "We finished the entire Talmud!" self-pleasuring crowd is lucky if they remember a simple parable or two, let alone any of the intricate flawlessly logical give-and-take abstract conversations — that span centuries of heated debate — of the approximately five thousand cryptic pages originally recorded in priceless scrolls. Besides, how can you "finish" something that you will study for eternity in the afterlife?

Rare is the man who has spent one hundred hours of his life on a single folio of the Talmud and all its accompanying commentaries. Rarer still is the individual who has fully comprehended that page as he humbly and slowly turns in awe to the next one. I agree it's something to die for. But I wonder why the author constantly forces those who express such a devoted sentiment to demonstrate their passion in a literal sense?

Many have heard Chaim Topol, in his role of Tevya the milkman, as he philosophically questions God in *Fiddler on the Roof,* only to break out in song, during his flawless rendition of, *If I Were A Rich Man.* "And … I'd discuss the holy books with the learned men, several hours every day," Tevya long-sufferingly wishes, praying to God, if only he could become a scholar, as he softly sighs, "… that would be the sweetest thing of all."

But like Topol, most observant Jewish men merely fantasize what it's like to experience the pleasure of traveling back in time to sit with the ancients. They'll keep wishing for that cerebral prodigious thrill till the day they die. Because they were "busy being busy," and never found the time to stop hoarding "just one more coin" and become a *real* rich man.

It was that ancient pleasure of golden Talmudical wealth that kept me alive throughout my dead marriage. The Talmud gave me all the space I needed, typically six to eight hours a day, to escape from my wife. And that didn't include many hours of travel time, while catching up on the news or listening to *Fresh Air* on NPR, to spend at least six hours a week studying with Rabbi Nekritz in Brooklyn. Ironically, I often saw my wife on the same schedule that I rarely saw my dad — Friday night dinners and on Shabbos. And like a bizarre scene straight out of the *Twilight Zone,* I became my father and Sharen basically portrayed my mother.

"I let you learn with Rebbi, Ze'ev!" was certainly perceived as a righteous act for which I constantly thanked my *devoted* wife, believing the demented demon was my *Eishet Chayil* partner. Together we would bask in the Glory of God in the World to Come where we would enjoy the eternal reward for her "taking vein," cooking, and having babies while allowing me the freedom to study the Talmud during our sojourn on Earth. We'd watch our cherubic great-great grandchildren's weddings from above and greet them with endless hugs, kisses, and tears of joy when they would reunite with us for eternity.

Once again, my wife used what I treasure most to control me. Only upon serving her for divorce did she reveal her complete disdain for "nekritz" (laughing as our daughters tore up his picture) and the Sabbath (although she was certainly rejoicing that early Saturday morning as the police arrived). I assume she also relinquished her partnership as my *Chavrusa* in the World to Come. After all, who would want to be study partners and analyze folio after folio of the Talmud with a pedophile?

In Jewish theology there are many concepts that just don't make any sense no matter how circular you are willing to reason. It eventually all comes down to blind faith when dealing with the many outlandish and irrational commandments dictated by the Torah.

A Jewish home is all about religion and instantly trusting that women are inferior to men, that gay men deserve to be stoned, and that all events, once they've occurred and no matter how horrific, were preordained by God and were retroactively unavoidable — even though we all supposedly have free will. If you are careless and not paying attention to your three-year-old child who runs into the street and is run over by a car; once she is dead, it was all predestined by God. So although we are commanded to protect life, once that life passes from this world, it was the will of God. It's always about God. It's never about you.

Ignorant Jews run to their local rabbi for an interpretation of events to explain why certain things "are happening to us." The rabbis scribble their foolish fucking fatwa explanations as they draw ridiculous circles around events that already happened and could easily be attributed to any one of a billion reasons. But they have *Da'as Torah*. Even when they argue with each other. Even if they are later proven wrong. It doesn't matter. You must listen to them. *God is testing you.*

I knew it wasn't logical, but I was also sincerely religious. So when the woman I was dating told me she "accidentally" got pregnant — after removing her I.U.D. — I blindly envisioned it as some kind of miraculous (Duh!) omen from heaven that hers was the name invoked by God as my intended bride-to-be forty days before I was created. *Crazy begets crazy.*

I shared the anxiety and hesitation I felt about marrying Sharen with my closest friends at that time of my life, as I searched for a logical reason to break the engagement, but we all agreed that Sharen was an absolute doll and that I was just a nervous ex-stud bad-boy bachelor whose time had come to settle down. *In hindsight, I now clearly see that Sharen definitely was "too good to be true."*

Even Rabbi Nekritz assuaged my fears, assuring me that Sharen is a keeper, by telling me a story about one of his world-renowned relatives who almost broke off her engagement to a saint, but was now (more than a half-century later) living happily ever after. I had such extreme faith in my rabbi that I thought I was listening to one of the hidden *Thirty-Six Righteous Ones* constantly edified in Jewish mysticism as the three-dozen individuals whose merit saves the world from instantaneous annihilation by an all-merciful God.

How was I to imagine that such a brilliant scholar — with endless holy *Da'as Torah* — could be duped into looking like a false prophet by an adorable cutie that would one day have the audacity to derisively call him "nekritz" while enlisting our mildly learning-disabled daughter to incessantly call him a "piece of shit?"

I even tried to gently explain to my fiancée during our engagement that our relationship was possibly moving along too quickly. "Perhaps we need a little more time … you're not always that easy to talk to, Honey," I meekly suggested as I attempted to request a teensy bit more space to allow myself some more time to think things through.

The crocodile tears started to flow more briskly than the flash-floods that I wrung out of my gym shirts. And like the nature of a flash flood, I was entirely caught off-guard by my future wife's manipulations which included constant attention, endless affection, and blow jobs during which she instantly gagged (at least she was willing to try). I quickly apologized and retreated. After a decade of "looking for love in all the wrong places," searching like Johnny Lee to replace the love and hugs my mother gave to total strangers over her middle son, I blamed myself for even questioning the value of the priceless diamond God was gifting me, and I assured Sharen that I was just being an insecure bachelor.

After all, "Nothing's gonna change, if you marry me, Zevie," was spoken by an angel. My darling's eyes radiated like supernova explosions whenever we met and her excitement upon embracing me was like a frisky puppy happily greeting its owner. I then allowed my split-personality love-bombing *Bashert* soul-mate, and future cell-mate, to rush me for the next twenty-eight years, trying my best to feed the barking bitch while constantly being harangued by her anxious voice echoing "*Your family Ze'ev! It's not about you!*" Relief arrived only upon her instantly ghosting me the second she was served divorce papers.

It took almost three decades, and it was worth every second, to learn to never rush. I never rush anyone. Because I try to live by the simple and flawless philosophy of Hillel the Elder. "What is distasteful to you, do not do unto others." Hillel is not merely saying to treat others as you yourself would prefer to be treated. He is advising that we examine our most minute actions, let alone the violent crime of taking out false Orders of Protection, in order not to inflict harm upon others. Nowadays, the harder someone tries to rush me, the slower I move. And at two-hundred and ten pounds they will probably tire out before I do. It was a lesson well learned. I swear, I'll even keep God waiting at this point in my life.

My wife constantly worried that I wouldn't go through with our plans for marriage. I had broken up with her once before after dating for nearly ten months. I thought she was very sweet, but she wasn't exactly awesome in the sack. That's how she wound up marrying the brain surgeon, Dr. Leon Gilner, on the rebound three months later.

Flash forward five years, and I had become quite religious again. And I had begun studying the Talmud with Rabbi Nekritz who I hadn't seen in fifteen years. Sex was no longer as important to me, as I became indoctrinated with thoughts of raising children instead of receiving great head, and I imagined that "someone like Sharen" would make an excellent future mother and spouse.

I had no idea that Sharen in the flesh was winding down her own divorce just as memories of how sweet she had been when we dated sparked between my synapses. The Lord certainly works in mysterious ways, so when Sharen sent regards through a relative of mine that she bumped into, I called her to ask if she'd like to meet for brunch.

The woman I had broken up with five years earlier remembered that I was the *Jewish Stallion,* as some of my workout tank tops whinnied in jest, but I assured her that I "had changed." My new trainer knew how to use her siren voice to delicately ease the bridle into my mouth without my bucking excessively and breaking up with her again. "*Neigh! Neigh! Neigh-ver again!*" this out-to-pasture stallion now proudly stomps in his well-deserved newfound freedom.

Many women had tried to tie me into tying the knot. But with my wife I never saw the slipknot coming. "No pressure, Zevie." The way my fiancée pronounced my name during those pre-marital love-atom-bombing days as two syllables expressed her affection. Not her utter contempt. My future bride played her hand perfectly — never revealing that she wasn't playing with a full deck.

My fiancée also knew, that as a diamond dealer, I could walk into any office on 47th street and walk out with $200 thousand in diamonds with a mere handshake. She understood what it meant in our business to "keep your word." "You're not going to break your word to me, Zevie," she'd reassure both of us many times during our tenuous engagement.

And like Tessa, she — "Whoops!" — got pregnant after having her gynecologist remove her IUD as we approached our fragile wedding date, knowing I'd never leave a baby behind. *I was now banging an IED!* My fiancée knew I was still weighing the scales. But she also knew exactly how to deceptively, and with sweet vulnerability, tip them in her favor. She never peeped during our entire engagement. I'd almost have to beg her to choose the movie we were going to see or the restaurant we'd meet at for dinner. Damn! Tessa was flawless.

"Honey, what are we going to say to your parents?" I innocently asked as an embarrassed Ultra-Orthodox young man imagining the shocked expression of his future mother-in-law. "Don't worry," Tessa calmly assured me. "The baby will be born *prematurely* six and a half months after our wedding date," she winked as she replied with flawless feigned innocence. It would be years before I learned that the sweeter she spoke, the deeper the knife in my back plunged. "Mazel Tov," I whispered as I gently kissed the sweet lying lips of my size-two pregnant *Vybie*.

I then allowed my fiancée full control and total transparent entrance into my life to assuage her fears that I might be seeing other women even though I promised her that I was not, and never would. Upon her slightest request I completely and delicately cut ties with all my female friends.

I would even hastily rush to my answering machine (the eighties) when we'd return to my apartment and I saw the red light flashing. I'd quickly erase any messages of the women who still tried to call me, to prevent my pregnant fiancée becoming upset. The last thing I wanted to do was harm "our baby." One Italian hottie bartender even tempted me with a wild threesome if my fiancée was willing. I can still hear her sultry voice. "If I can't have you to myself, Zevie, I'm willing to share." *Why do women always call me Zevie? I wonder if they still see that gentle toddler playing with the girls in kindergarten?*

Once I put a ring on it, Sharen insisted that I throw out all the pictures I had saved of my old girlfriends. I thought it was due to her insecurity since I had broken up with her five years earlier. How could I have imagined at that point of our relationship that Sharen was a hoarder who saved junk while throwing away precious memories, or that she would one day throw away our beautiful wedding album?

"Our future kids don't have to know about every shiksa you dated! You're a Talmudical scholar! Give me the pictures!" It was torture relinquishing that picture of Lauren lying on a warm rock under the hot sun in a light-blue skimpy bikini, teasing me with her gorgeous full lips, as she smiled at me seductively, while pressing her mouth against the fruit and sucking the juice out of the cold orange I peeled and handed her moments before I snapped that shot. *No wonder I love oranges.*

It was painful handing over the sweet memories of the many wonderful women that generously shared a portion of their life with mine. But, not knowing anything about the psychological concept of healthy boundaries, I allowed myself to be shiksa-shamed. After all, the Talmud insists that the highest level a marriage can attain is when husband and wife become one entity. *Ishto-Keh-Gufo*.

"If the wife's foot hurts, the husband should feel the pain in the nerve endings of his own foot." It is a beautiful concept. But heart constricting when you're married to a narcissist. Forget about a place where you end and the other person begins. Just get used to wondering why you feel anxious all the time. *I felt the pain in my wife's foot, alright. "Our" foot was killing me from constantly kicking myself in my behind.*

In truth, I should have taken the passionate advice of the sultry Roxette no later than the birth of my second child. She warned me over and over as the leaves turned orange and yellow in 1988. I considered her counsel as the weather and my marriage turned colder, but I impregnated my wife, again and again, ignoring the haunting voice of Roxette in exchange for the laughter of every cherub that followed.

In all honesty, I should have "listened to your [my] heart" years earlier and to the anxious warning cries of strewn boxes of "organized clutter" and piles of worthless junk in my fiancées apartment that tried to warn me, even tripping me to get my attention, as they screamed, "Back off! She's a hoarder! She's crazy!" My *Bashert* was terrified to bring me home to meet her parents because her own mother was more afflicted than the "organized clutter" mental illness that presented itself in my fiancée.

My wife grew up in a house that looked like a pigsty and she was mortified whenever her classmates came over. I assured her that my love for her far outweighed "a couple of messy boxes."

I believed I'd easily be able to help her once we moved into a three-bedroom co-op, never imagining that fifteen years in the future our six-foot-tall Polish Amazon nanny would flawlessly articulate, in her broken English and with sweat on her brow and upper lip, "Mr. Lewinson ... the house! It doesn't want to get empty!" as Andrea helped me carry box after box of "organized clutter" from our (now) two co-ops in Riverdale, NY to the moving van that would escort us to our brand new mini-mansion in Monsey. I had been doing my own research on hoarders by now, and I explained to my wife (pleading, actually), that moving is the perfect time to "declutter." She warned me not to jeopardize our *Shalom Bayit*. "Don't start up with me Ze'ev," she snarled, "I'll sort through it, later."

Ester was definitely the neat female of the family. She once spent three hours cleaning up her mother's office-station section of our huge kitchen because she was horrified when her friends came over to visit and play. Ester would try to greet them at the door and quickly suggest that they play outside. Her friends could see my wife's office area in the kitchen the moment they walked through the front door. History repeats.

Her mother quickly tussled Ester's orderly work repeatedly. After several rounds an exasperated nine-year-old Ester finally cried out to her mom, "How many times can I clean this! I'm so embarrassed in front of all my friends!" Sharen replied that she tolerated ***her*** own mother, so Ester would have to stop her flow of tears and just, "Deal with it! Get used to it!" her mom insisted, "It's just clutter."

The amazing part of all this was that my wife spent half her life in an O.R. where everything must be accounted for and neatly displayed. She could call out a missing clamp among hundreds of instruments after an operation (a failsafe procedure to ensure that nothing remained inside the patient post-op).

With her A.I. mind, my wife always knew where everything was. And amazingly enough, in a pile of junk, or a stack of boxes that reached to the ceiling while blocking a door from fully opening, or a messy stuffed drawer of completely unrelated random items that could barely close, my cyborg clutter-gatherer biped knew exactly where to find what she was looking for in any of the sixteen rooms of our home as she constantly, proudly declared that she was a "very well-organized person." Only a savant could pull that off.

I recall shopping for my wife as I called her because I gave up trying to locate one of the items on her list. I told her where I was standing in the store, and she directed me (as if she was watching me on the cameras in the isle) with flawless precision. "Walk down the aisle about twenty feet.

Okay, look to your left. Now look down at the fourth shelf, right next to the canned olives. See it?" I was amazed as I realized she knew, and could vividly see, the entire inventory of the store.

My *Eishet Chayil* always wore a huge fanny pack with endless different sized pouches and could instantly pull out the proverbial kitchen sink if we needed one. This was on top of schlepping a huge bag that contained countless zippers and compartments. That bag contained an entire CVS pharmacy and Sephora's total cosmetic line. It even contained a prescription pad. If some thug was shot on the street my wife could have probably stitched and patched him up on the spot.

A jeweler friend that owned a gorgeous store near her hospital once walked my wife out to her car late at night after she picked up an expensive piece that I needed the following day for another client. He later delicately suggested that I get her help upon seeing the inside of her car. "How does she even drive?" he sincerely asked, never imagining that I considered Sharen's hoarding dysfunction her most minor issue.

Roxette continued to warn me as the kosher stork delivered child number three, and all through 1989, that I should have simply told Sharen, "Goodbye." But from the time of my own arrival to this one of a trillion planets ejaculating through space, seemingly searching for something divine, I never had a family. The television was my mother. Books replaced my father. And as I turned thirty my soft-spoken fiancée appeared at the right time, at the right place. Pedigree Jewish lineage. Ivy League college. Sweet little Jewish lady.

My *Vybie* was beyond polite and proper. A real catch. If I had doubts with such a beautiful résumé during our engagement, then imagine adding the miracle of birthing and nursing three kids to that CV as I frequently pondered about divorcing a woman that I still sincerely believed was my *Bashert*. Chezkie was already floating around in my wife's womb even as she was nursing baby number three. Yes, that's rare. But like any disease, my wife was great at replicating itself.

Even though I understood my wife had "issues" as we approached the birth of our next child, I still fervently believed in my heavenly ordained marriage. If Moses himself had appeared at that time of my life and was to prophesy that my blue-blooded fiancée would one day serve me two fistfuls of perjuristically-obtained protection orders, I would have questioned his soothsaying vision and respectfully suggested that he adjust his spiritual channels to God.

I continued to convince myself that I had married a divine angel. And even if she was a slob, at least she was a cute one. Being completely honest with myself would have meant seeing my kids on Tuesday nights and every other weekend.

Besides, at thirty-five years of age, even with three kids, I was still like an old-maid Jewish Orthodox woman; primed and constantly plotzing for more kids and that idyllic white-picket kosher-fence lifestyle that keeps the Gentile world out and your half-minyan of children in (the dark). I never imagined that I was heading deeper into an Iron Maiden with each cherub, as God further seduced me into subservience while he lured me deeper into a marriage hell, till he slammed it shut upon the birth of Ester. And I could never have envisioned that I would emerge, three decades in the future, more at peace than at any other time of my storm-tossed-soul scarred-for-life existence.

This planet of ours has become a tiny zoo of sorts in my mind's eye. I see almost the entire human species, participants of all the diverse cultures and civilizations of the last six millennium of recorded history, as having evolved into indentured forty-year-workforce minimum-waged serf-slaves tethered to false ideologies and emasculating beliefs.

Whether earning a salary of fifty thousand or one billion dollars a year, they remain boorish menial peasants bartering their priceless blink-of-an-eye lifetimes for worthless currency and sheetrock. Whether sitting in their cubicle-partitioned tiny cages or penthouse twelve-foot ceiling glass offices with panoramic views, they are nothing more than human broken workhorses pulling heavy plows.

Whether defecating while sitting on a designer toilet made of 24 karat gold or squatting over an open hole dug in the earth, humans still haven't evolved from much more than an army of erect penises and overstuffed bowels of marching shit, urine, and semen who worships a God that created them with such shameful needs and the urgent desire to rid themselves of those "coming and going" lifelong nagging forceful fluids that gush out when we're young and can barely exit when we're old.

The seven and three-quarter billion people on Spaceship Earth eat, shit, fuck, and sleep believing they are individuals simply because their piffling existence is demarcated by conquests obtained through bloodshed and imaginary lines called borders. The divisive boundaries force them to remain segregated due to their ironclad mind-manipulating illusionary cultural beliefs, skin pigmentation, and invisible deities obtained through "my God is bigger than your God" religious wars and ridiculously illogical dogma bequeathed by ignorant and superstitious barbaric forefathers.

Upon accepting their personal faux "meaning of existence" philosophy they swarm to accomplish "something close to nothing," based on accumulating cryptocurrency digital keyboard-wealth and experiencing shallow multimedia Tinder relationships with their "seen one, seen them all"

AFFIDAVIT OF CONFESSION OF JUDGMENT

SUPREME COURT STATE OF NEW YORK
COUNTY OF ROCKLAND

ROCKLAND COUNTY DEPARTMENT OF SOCIAL SERVICES, Index No.

Against

Plaintiff AFFIDAVIT OF CONFESSION OF JUDGMENT

Walter Lewinson

Defendant(s)

STATE OF NEW YORK)
COUNTY OF ROCKLAND) ss.:
Walter Lewinson

ROCKLAND
COUNTY TIMES
Complaints against Judge
lfieri rack up
y dskriloff on December 10, 2015 · Comments
3Y MICHAEL VOLPE
Several more litigants have stepped
forward to complain about State Supreme
Court Judge Victor Alfieri's handling of
their cases after an open letter written by
B DIVISIO
RACQUETBALL L
1ST PLACE

lip-pouting women twerking in G-string thong bikinis, eventually settling down with a Match or eharmony solution for their loneliness, and occasionally praying to their own absurd version of an invisible silent god.

Like silverback gorillas, the more financially-evolved deluded bipeds parade independence from the troop by flaunting their sinewy well-tailored bodies hugged by classic Burberry blazers, while flailing their college diplomas and W-2's for lack of truly refined E.Q.'s, in the hopes of grabbing a silicon infused happy-hour Prozac-popping female wearing a double-padded push-up bra and tons of warpaint makeup to copulate with, while she marvels at his Rolex-wristed fist beating his hard-muscled chest concealing an unempathetic heart. *"May I buy you a drink?"*

Grunts and barks by the well-dressed lightly scented uncouth testosterone-infused male specie *Homo erection*, standing at the Upper West Side watering hole with stained glass windows from Tiffany's while quipping well-rehearsed one-liner pick-ups, are further inducements to stimulate the chilly libido of a discriminating, yet unfortunately, rapidly-aging pretty female who cares more about the balance in his bank account than the size of his swollen penis.

Her instincts and limited childbearing years rush her to protect, yet achieve insemination of, the paltry number of eggs a wordsmith God — who is obviously weak at math — gave her, while endowing the one-track mind mindless-male many frivolous decades and almost endless sperm to breed a future AA member, upon mommy handing his daddy an Order of Protection twenty years in the future.

If mommy's time runs out because daddy refuses to pop the question in fear of her future "special delivery" Order of Protection, she can always resort to being impregnated through artificial insemination while anxiously trying to believe her own bold but frustrated declaration of, "I don't need a ring to get a crib." I suppose it's (even the uncomfortable push-up bra) all part of God's cursing Eve: "In pain you will bring forth children (Genesis 3:16)." *"No thank you. The house will do."*

The mindless inhabitants of this planet are all running, brachiating, and scurrying about, aimlessly foraging for food, shelter, attention, and sex — as simple minded as any self-reproducing single-celled organism — while enthusiastically rooting for a blue uniformed team that can kick or throw a child's toy ball with more skill than the club wearing red, or salivating as they watch the vacuous lifestyles of the *Secret Lives of the Super Rich*.

Some aborigines eat mud cakes in Haiti. They and three billion other people on the planet, almost half of all mankind, pitifully live on less than two and a half dollars a day in the twenty-first century. Other "civilized" aborigines hoard shiny pebbles, crystals, treasury bonds, Bitcoin, deeds, and priceless art in their bank vaults and digital wallets, as they fly from continent to continent, enjoying fashion shows in Paris where human mannequins with impassive faces strut in bizarre clothing that even Lady Gaga wouldn't be caught dead in.

After viewing the latest exciting width of men's ties, they fly off to private parties in Dubai, voyeuristically feasting on sushi adorned with gold leaf off the Saran-Wrapped naked bodies of mannequin models who pose as tables, while gorging on small mountains of white powder. Glad to hear you "made it."

"Life is wonderful, darlings," till they wind up in a hospice, sooner than they ever imagined, shocked at how they squandered their primitive-sophisticated lives, fearing imminent death and their eventual passing from this world like the inert gold leaf that had zero nutritional value (basically valueless; like their lives) passed through their bodies, as they morph into mud cakes, while contemplating yet still failing to visualize where the time went and what their worthless lives, "might have been."

Then there are those primeval faithful worshipers who calmly drift off to an eternal sleep, believing they have lived a righteous life, free from sin because they never accidentally ate a bug or missed praying with a minyan. They are certain that they are heading to a "better place," after having suffered through a lifetime of boring rituals and repetitive incantations fervently prayed to a seemingly deaf mad-hatter, wildly vengeful, Supreme Being who brought about all their suffering, in spite of their dedicated service, "for their own good."

Still others never experience any depressed final self-appraisal of their lives, spared by their dementia-stricken brains that shrunk and shriveled up long ago — wiped clean of a lifetime of now forgotten meme-memories whose contents, like a lost black-box at sea, will never be revealed.

I see the entire human race confined in a circus of conditioned-from-birth existence, angrily roaring their political and religious opinions while racing on a frenzied dating-mating-spawning-divorcing deity-worshiping rat-wheel, that culminates with exhausted mummified products who are hastily mourned and boxed into coffins to be escorted ceremoniously by motorcade and deposited into eternal dungeon-graves to decompose back into the few scant elements from which they originated.

Everyone thinks they are the epicenter focus of everyone else's couldn't-give-a-shit short attention span as they freely move about under the bright lights of Center Ring hoping for their fifteen minutes of fame, while being chained at the ankle, like a six-ton elephant, by societal norms. Their sequined costumes and expensive Armani suits are nothing more than orange-colored made-in-prison conforming jump-suits.

Humanity (the "luckier" ones on the planet) senselessly flies through the air with the greatest of ease, while their racing distracted-by-Facebook-pings minds are weighed down by self-scrolling sponsored ads, political pitches, archaic dictums, endless silly memes, and YouTube viral videos of twerking Brazilian-butt-bimbettes whose teasing tongues dangle from swollen, herpes infected, Botox-infused promiscuous lips, brightly colored in *Promiscuous Pink* lipstick, that fervently pray to Jesus that their *OnlyFans* content with a penis in each opening of their body, goes viral.

The little remaining RAM space left on their human hard drives is ultimately brainwashed by Big Brother government calling for their patriotic allegiance with promises of reform and social programs guaranteeing their secure retirement, invisibly anchoring their vapid values and primitive beliefs with patriotic flags, marching parades, pillared edifices, and endless taxation.

The State then sacrifices their barely adult sons to the Big Oil gods and arms-producing corporations like Lockheed and Raytheon to wage worthless wars to feed their gargantuan appetites for endless profits; while local gorillas in black robes bare their teeth while beating their chest as they issue protection orders and grab the minor children of broken-hearted fathers during divorce. Meanwhile *We the People* are constantly threatened with jail for the slightest evasion of excessive taxation while billion-dollar corporations pay nothing.

This is all endured by being embraced and fortified with heavenly commandments and silly vacuous traditions based on superstitious beliefs in an eternal life of unimaginable pleasure promised by ex cathedra and Da'as Torah individuals who masturbated during their own youth. The sheeple never dare to imagine that the declarations of their religious leaders need skeptical questioning or defining. They are too rushed to question imperfect man, so how could they ever slow down long enough to contemplate and question their "perfect" Gods? How I write all this while still believing in God escapes me.

The circus troupe of society's brainwashed members then bequeath their ongoing circular loop of rushed ball-and-chain illusions to the next generation of slumbering mindless imitators who merely increase the pace of the frenzied out-of-control spiral with the help of technology, as they slubber through *their* lives, while birthing yet another mimicking gene-pool-without-direction swarm of rushing, beeping, traffic-jammed bird-flipping, cubicle-contained frustrated, angry hooting chimpanzees. Catch your breath and read that run-on sentence again. I'm not the crazy one.

Let's face it. Whether you are picking rice in ancient China, hanging on a cross in Roman-occupied Jerusalem, ploughing fields as a serf in Russia during the middle ages, or paying one quarter of your earnings towards your mortgage and local government taxes while giving away one full third of your six figure annual techie salary to the U.S. government in the year 2021, you are not much more than an indentured slave whose every move and spending habit is sorted, tracked, and taxed.

Even your "likes" on Facebook (to which you respond like a salivating Pavlov's dog) are recorded so that advertisers can feed off your mindlessness with laser-precision ads to grab whatever money remains after your well-paid government officials, who have secured excellent benefits and medical care for themselves, sucked you dry and left you homeless. And if not for a temporary moratorium on evictions during Covid-19 you would have had many more friends with whom to share your "outdoor dining" experience.

Angry citizens, and actual relatives, almost war with one another over a Republican versus Democratic ruling body of selfish *Animal Farm* piggish Orwellian leaders "chosen" by duped voters groveling for the wise solutions of "snake oil politicians" (mostly sleazy lawyers and unintelligent former actors) as to how their hard-earned tax dollars should be spent.

Congressional kingpins feign slugging it out, like two divorce lawyers winking at each other over the heads of their opposing clients, while they gorge on decades of future tax dollars, deceitfully spending the honestly earned money of others, while delaying and postponing giving "The People" a lousy six-hundred dollar feeble financial-inoculation during a year-long worldwide pandemic.

A simple rebate Monopoly-money check whose value deflated during the long year that it took our "public servants" to finally "agree" on, so that those who swore to serve their constituents in good faith could stuff their quid-pro-quo five-thousand and five-hundred page delayed "stimulus" *package* (great metaphor since we are getting "dicked") with endless special-interest pork-barrel legislation.

A nine-month legalese abortion morphed into a hastily crafted last-minute *urgent* cumbersome-as-it-is-cruel bill that was birthed in excruciating pain by a handful of congressional representatives who can barely comprehend its opaque fine print. It was passed in the nick of time so that our government would not (God forbid!) shut down before the drama queens left for their long holiday vacation. A bill so expensive that it will take years before anyone can figure out its actual true, inflated, cost. *God bless America.*

The modern-day-slave does receive a little more pie thanks to technology and advanced scientific discoveries. But he's still carrying much more than his fair share of the burden in a millennium where faster than ever, especially at the near speed of light that information travels, "The rich get richer, and the poor get poorer."

The belly of the constituent is obese. His infertile mind is complimented by his infertile testicles, whose sperm count and freedom of expression has declined by over fifty percent during the past five decades. His religious opioid beliefs, however, remain steadfast and ironclad. "Keep America Great." *Great for politicians and corporations*.

Our modern-day world still contains over a billion people who are completely destitute, ignorant, and hungry. They live on a dollar and twenty-five cents a day. They earn fifteen cents an hour compared to the $4,475,885.00 hourly wage of Jeff Bezos. The poorest five percent of Americans are wealthier than seventy percent of the world's inhabitants.

If the top five thousand corporations in the world donated five percent of their revenue (money they will never spend) to the one billion poorest people on the planet, who are still shlepping diseased water twice a day in the twenty first century, they could literally change the world overnight. The stock prices of these mega companies often fluctuate by two percent within hours of a single day as their financially-obese CEO's purchase back their retail stock to inflate their retirement portfolios.

Speaking of obese, it's not like I'm asking everyone on the globe to instantly change the carbon imprint of our planet, along with their own health and longevity, by giving up meat. I don't expect greedy corporate board members to stop their deforestation of tropical forests when they can trade "worthless" trees for cotton paper that proclaims, "In God We Trust." Nor can I imagine livestock and poultry cannibalism to stop overnight. The enlightenment and compassion necessary to make such a wonderful decision would be difficult for artery-hardened minds, that are not that much more intelligent than the life they are eating, to fathom.

Let's admit the sad truth. We are empty-headed carnivores who prefer to swap precious air, pristine water, miraculous coral reefs, and thousands of gorgeous species of flora and fauna (many of which will become extinct before they are even discovered) for cruelly slaughtered virus-laden salmonella-infested constipation-inducing gut-wrenching horror-hamburgers.

Things have not really changed all that much since Upton Sinclair's novel. The only difference is that instead of men falling into the meat grinder, they die a slower death by eating the antibiotic-infused meat that USDA inspectors, and angelic mothers, in advertisements portraying burning logs in the fireplace, describe as "wholesome."

It's hard to believe that we descended from Adam and Eve who were originally herbivores. We evolved, after the Great Flood (according to the Talmud), into a flesh-eating wealthy nation of half-wits where approximately a quarter of the population suffers from chronic constipation and probably deserves the affliction as karma payback for the perpetual holocaust we inflict upon sentient life. Time for a little fun math. Is a dollar burger worth the price of our existence?

I see the buzzing mindless masses of busy-bee drones who spend forty years of their lives worrying about health insurance that covers less and costs more annually, while continuing to wearily work at a job that they hate merely to have subpar health care coverage that they despise, while praying that their fine-print policy, in difficult to read light-grey text, will somehow cover their end-of-life care. They really needn't worry so much about palliative care because hospital errors are the third leading cause of death in the United States.

If they somehow survive all the above and have assets and savings as their memory banks weaken, they'll still have to watch out for that court appointed guardian who will suddenly have more control over their lives than a mother holding her newborn baby to her breast.

And every four years the mindless masses momentarily turn away from their dumb lives and smart phones, as they once again confidently flip a lever in a booth after arguing with their next-door neighbors about their choice for POTUS. It's amazing how the sheeple sincerely believe that *this* time the pandering liberal and conservative candidates espousing family and religious values along with their promises to "bring our boys home," coupled with visionary prophecies of "a better tomorrow for our children" as they kiss any sweet baby in the crowd, really means it.

Forget about George H. W. Bush. Read *my* lips: you're getting fucked no matter who you vote for. At my age, after experiencing more than a half-century of broken promises and outright lies by our presidents and politicians, I believe their thinly veiled emotionally-pled vacuous patriotic vows with about as much fervor as my belief in Santa Claus and the Virgin Mary copulating in ecstasy.

Upon a victorious outcome, the shameless politician immediately obsequiously panders for re-election funds from "independent" political groups and wealthy corporate board members and then unabashedly votes and passes legislation that is solely in the interests of the corporate giants that produce genetically engineered foods, Volkswagen diesel engines with falsified emission standards, cigarettes, vape pens, and addictive deadly drugs, while kissing the smelly ass of any CEO in that crowd, as he continues to bombastically parrot the words *integrity, transparency, patriotism, family, country*, and of course, *God Almighty.*

The twenty-seven letters of the alphabet are perpetually recycled as a depressed Generation X escapes their sadness while visiting the same tavern that their Generation A grandparents frequented to imbibe their ancient sorrows five-hundred years ago. The only difference between the two Happy Hour drove of customers is in the width of the lapels of the inebriated guest's dinner jackets, the exorbitant price per-square-foot leases of the modern-day bar, the slight change in the establishment's décor, and in the STD's they are likely to catch in the new millennium as opposed to the venereal diseases that infected their ancestors during the Dark Ages.

Even those exceptionally rare and wonderful individuals, gifted with intelligence, creativity, and wealth, who spend their empathetic lives toiling to make the world a better place, fail to answer the question that will ultimately be asked upon their achieving mankind's long-awaited goal of a world without war, illness, ignorance, or poverty: what now?

What will *Homo-frenzyman* now rush to conquer or exploit during his priceless short lifetime? With what delusions will he distract his conditioned goal-oriented busy mind once this world enters a state of technological nirvana? After taking care of everyone else's problems he'll ultimately have some time to look within. What will he see? Will he finally understand the true purpose of existence? Will he comprehend that there was never a need to search?

As the wisest of all men proclaims in Ecclesiastes regarding the monotony of life, after pursuing, achieving, and experiencing all the pleasures, treasures, knowledge, and wisdom that the universe has to offer (in that logical order of childish egotistical avocations): "That which has been, shall be done again; a generation goes, and a generation comes: There is nothing new under the sun." *King Solomon was bored.*

One of the greatest challenges we face as a specie is not merely preventing the physical destruction and pollution of our planet and the entropy of our own mortal lives. Uploading our brains into a computer is the easy part. Saving our priceless right to speak and think freely, our actual minds, will take a bit more effort.

The Fahrenheit 451 brigade never had to use fire to extinguish words. Google, Facebook, and Twitter are all privately owned companies that literally choose what we supposedly want to read. Even as they stream the articles that they know will keep us hooked to their platforms and endless streaming of advertisements. Exacerbating the situation are outdated laws, that apply to a relic called "television," that allows these tech giants to addict our children into becoming the next generation of must-have "only three left" shoppers. Meanwhile they publish only the posts they deem worthy of being labeled as truth, so that after "shopping till they drop" the Sheeple can swallow their sorrow during Happy Hour for stupidly maxing out their credit cards.

The "Big Five" (Amazon, Apple, Facebook, Google, and Microsoft) have the legal right, clearly explained in their Terms of Service contracts, that users acknowledge and sign with a click of their mouse, to totally ignore or ban major news events or political comments of any senator or president they despise. Or they can use a more insidious form of inhibiting free speech by simply "shadow banning" users they choose to muzzle while promising transparency and more meaningful personal control over our own data. *Please pass the barf bag.*

Meanwhile, more than half of U.S. adults now get their news from skewed social media. Facebook has more power to choose our next president and influence our decision in taking the Covid booster shot than the most articulate, enlightened, erudite Renaissance Man who ever lived. He would instantly be angrily shouted down by half of the lonely social media addicts who are busy posting selfies in desperate need of an emoji fix.

Further exacerbating the situation, our universities and schools are pumping out mindless versions of 1984 apolitical Proles, who instantly believe their pontificating professors as they chirp like parrots that Israel is an apartheid state. Meanwhile in Yemen, Jordan, Egypt, Lebanon, Iran, Syria, and Saudi Arabia, the discrimination against women, homosexuals, and many minorities is mind-boggling in the twenty-first century. And don't even begin to imagine that there is any freedom of expression. But the collegiate toddler minds in mature bodies do their little campus protest against Israel and then rush off to their "Girls Gone Wild" spring break of vomit, cum, booze, and STDs.

Intellectual stimulation for too many of these "Marketing" majors is achieved by watching *Love Is Blind* or *The Jerry Springer Show*. Their grandparents merely had to deal with the rare frigid school librarian who banned *Fahrenheit 451* when they walked to high school in six feet of snow. The guardians of wisdom considered the books "vulgar" because the Lord's name was spoken in vain.

Rather than understand that we have entered the geologic Anthropocene period of extinction and the devastating global food shortage crisis that is about to reshape our planet, the "best minds" prefer to ejaculate and orgasm just one more time as the next man-made Great Flood drowns this planet. I am not a ranting "old man." I am an enlightened one. "I once was young and now am old (Psalm 37:25)," but one thing I learned with age is that I know nothing for certain. Sadly, too many college kids major in stupidity while thinking they know it all. Many are serious about their studies and my hope for the future lies with them. I'm sure that, with time, they'll all learn how little we all know.

What I do know, however, is that religious beliefs, political ideologies, technological inventions, scientific discoveries, artistic expression, subtle philosophies, comprehensive Halachic decisions of Talmudical law, and the discovery of galaxies distant light years from our own, all began as faint thoughts that formed into vague ideas that were further refined, and finally expressed through spoken and written words. I am a sculptor of words that began as vague thoughts.

The earliest dialogue and superstitions of mankind were eventually polished through trial-and-error sincere debate based on a desire for true knowledge and wisdom. Those thoughts and early conversations eventually evolved into a system of logical Socratic debate and trial and error scientific procedure. The only delay to success has been politics, religion, and governments vying for more control over our bodies and minds. Self introspection and years of rewriting a non-fiction literary work like the one you are reading at this very moment can only exist in a world of free speech. And that world, along with our physical one, is suffocating.

Censoring the words needed to refine fetal ideas and dreams of what the future could be — with gaveling idiots threatening to, "Put you in jail!" for the crime of being logical, coupled with ad hominem attacks and instant labels of narcissism, along with societal barks and grunts of anger, and cancel culture shunning and ostracism — forces the inhibited mind to abort itself of any thoughts as it grows accustomed to living in a stunted myopic world. Or Monsey, New York.

Mankind regresses from their once-curious state and ceases to imagine and question. The individual is shut down and dies. Try and escape, and you'll soon experience what it feels like to be an excommunicated pariah. One becomes an Orthodox Jew.

In a perfect world where everyone has health, food, shelter, DNA enhanced designer blue-eyed uber-babies, 3D printers spewing out five-star chef-prepared meals, and A.I. self-driving cars in abundance — a world in which there will no longer be a need for war to hasten the quick transference of wealth and natural resources — it is only our thoughts, our words, that will entertain, liberate, and bestow true meaning and passion to our short-lived existence. Banning books is as violent as smashing someone in the head with a sledgehammer. It's simply a more subtle form of "brain damage." Why do you think Monsey rabbis equate surfing the Internet to falling into Gehinnom?

Thoughts can only be clarified and refined when expressed through completely calm, uninhibited and unencumbered free speech. An exchange of ideas can only occur when both sides are sincerely listening. It doesn't take an "open mind" to hear someone else's point of view. It takes an open heart.

Enslave the intellect of an individual, by controlling what he reads and thereby thinks, and his zombie body will surely follow. Frustrating someone by hanging up the phone on them, humiliating them with ad hominem attacks as they try to formulate a sincere thought, or smirking upon banging a contemptuous gavel in court when the litigant is flawlessly logical, is abominable. Shaming is another cruel tactic used by society and religion to ensure that the sheep follow the shepherd who is fleecing and fucking his flock.

Subliminal marketing is just one more method by which to manipulate and maneuver the individual to waste his money and life. Why else would a young man in love morph into a middle-aged man in debt as he foolishly accepts the three months' salary guideline rule when buying a diamond?

Originally established by DeBeers in the 1930's as one month's salary to "prove your love," it doubled in the 80's, and later tripled to three months, probably due to inflation of the dollar and the distension of your fiancée's silicone implants. The slick marketers brainwashed every young man to finance a "rare gem" that would take years of monthly payments to pay off. After proving your love and "putting a ring on it," at the direction of Madison Avenue; in essence wasting your life financing a piece of coal, the contempt bred by familiarity, cleverly stated by Chaucer will probably kick in early due to the stress of your monthly payments. The twenty-two thousand and five-hundred dollars you calculated, based on your ninety grand a year salary, would have been better spent as a down payment on a house, or tossing the funds into your Coinbase account. Meanwhile you should have based your three month guideline on your salary after taxes and spent only sixteen-thousand financing a piece of coal. *Testosterone clouds the mind.*

I likewise wonder why God had to hold Mt. Sinai over the heads of his Chosen Ones, according to the Midrash, threatening them and their children with being buried alive and instant extinction, when they had just experienced rapturous Divine Revelation. "We will observe, and we will listen," they miraculously responded in unison, instantly forfeiting their First Amendment rights and their freedom to question God. *Maybe they had something important to say? Why all the drama?*

Intimidation and threats only increase the emotional frustration that builds with every held-back word upon which the victim chokes. After twenty-eight years of strangulation by a wife and God who I was never permitted to question, I now see how prophetic I was the night I said, "Perhaps we need a little more time ... you're not always that easy to talk to, Honey." *Never imagining that I was also speaking to God.*

The gorgeous sapphire eyes of my fiancée, half immersed in tears, melted away my faint thoughts and fears of marriage faster than warm rain washes away a delicately sprinkled veneer of freshly fallen pristine snow. I had nothing more to say. And that's how things remained for the next twenty-eight years till I served my Vybie her divorce papers.

A person can only free their mind by being allowed to think calmly without being pressured or rushed. One needs quiet contemplation to reflect. Free from a slogan-shouting *Uncle Sam Wants You!* society. Free from a "Your family, Ze'ev!" shouting spouse. And free from a constantly demanding slave-master Deity who forces his subjects to account for every second of how they spent their day. Nothing sucks as much as wasting time filling out a picayune timesheet. Especially when you are already working yourself to death. *Overtime!*

Tranquil meditation, and peacefully thinking things through, allows a person to realize they should never be forced to share the same opinion as everyone that surrounds them. Even the opinion of their God. Especially an all-merciful God (who constantly threatens their life in this world and the next). After all, what purpose does it serve to punish and torture someone after they are dead? *Or while they are living for that matter?*

Once a church, government, or society tells you what you are "permitted" to say, or publish, your freedom and independence are completely lost. It's almost humorous that every religion bans the holy books of other religions. And God is the most intolerant of all — threatening to punish for mere thoughts. At the very least, why shouldn't an individual be allowed to question the completely illogical acts of a God who created him with a mind that is curious and logical from birth? Am I asking for too much? I can almost hear a Dr. Seuss jingle quipping, *"The more you read, the more you'll know; the further from religion you'll go!"*

Shaming or prosecuting a person as "evil" for their beliefs and opinions is the easiest way to strip away their humanity. Incarcerating them for sharing information (thoughts) with others, "leaked" through the New York Times of all places, is beyond vile. Edward Snowden and Julian Assange deserve a joint Nobel Peace Prize. Snowden deserves sainthood.

I could write a book explaining why. But simply put, there will never be peace on this planet without transparent and honest uninhibited communication. There will only be continued ignorance, fear mongering, manipulation, divisiveness, and control. Just look at China. Maoism is back.

Every lawn will eventually become a national border. And our United States Printing Office will be spewing out new legislation after every session of Congress as the idiots, with fake teeth and counterfeit souls, pass new laws inhibiting any speech that makes anyone "uncomfortable," along with proclaiming their sole solution of "more taxes!" enforced by hiring a hundred thousand new IRS employees to maintain control over everyone's money, mouth, pen, and keyboard. Public trust in the federal government has fallen from over seventy percent in the late 1950's to under twenty percent today. The fact that it's even as high as twenty percent surprises me. And scandalous state governments are completely despised. The only purpose they seem to serve is as newspaper fodder to sell advertising.

Just look at North Korea where free-thinking is scarcer than food. Look at our politicians screaming that Snowden is a "selfish traitor" because he shared the corruption of our government with "The People." And look at Monsey, New York. It's such a shame that this book will surely be banned where it's most needed. Especially when I very likely gave up my eternal portion in the World to Come to write it. *Easy come, easy go.*

As far as I'm concerned, the First Amendment should preempt the Ten Commandments. How could God carve them with fire onto flawless sapphire without free speech? Redacting the expression of a single word is as vile as inhibiting the thinking of thoughts. Those sincere thoughts must be allowed expression — even the questioning of the Ten Commandments themselves. Otherwise, we all might as well pronounce ourselves as brain dead and pull the plug on civilization. *Besides, doesn't the Talmud endlessly question everything?*

Jewish mysticism teaches that it was only through God blowing a soul into the nostrils of Adam, that speech (for prayer, study, and kind words) was able to materialize. Amazingly enough, the tongue is the one physical organ that never tires (*ask the women I've dated*).

The wise men of the Kabbalah considered the tongue an almost spiritual appendage that reveals there is an incorporeal soul in a physical body. It is the one time where the earthly dimension meets the eternal one. We hear words through a person's vocal cords and voice. But the sounds that vibrate off our eardrums are all sourced to a soul that first thought to articulate them inside a conscious mind. In truth, Shakespeare could have said that both the eyes and tongue are a window to the soul.

I believe the ultimate sin is in manipulating tabula rasa innocent young minds to follow like mindless sheep without allowing them to think. They become the walking dead. They've been figuratively lobotomized. It is of little wonder that Monsey yeshiva schools strictly prohibit children and their parents from accessing the Internet. Special dispensations are given by rabbis who place extremely restrictive filters on the computers of the adult parents they deem "trustworthy" (i.e. brainwashed).

I once tried one and suddenly found that I couldn't access my New York Times subscription. I removed the filter and discovered a front-page article about *Breast* Cancer! Just imagine how horny I became upon removing the filter and reading an article that might save a woman's life one day.

The insanity is never ending. Even an innocent visit to the local library is completely verboten unless accompanied by a "responsible" (i.e. brainwashed) adult. It's beyond insane.

The parents themselves are unaware that they are destroying their own children by forcing them to remain locked away and completely out of touch with a world where scientific and technological innovations are moving at the speed of light. They somehow believe it's much more important for their devout Jewish children to carry the emotional burden of a trauma-inducing history that includes millenniums of crusades, pogroms and Holocaust punishments inflicted by an all-loving God of kindness who is always on the alert to instantly slaughter his Chosen PTSD People for driving on Saturday or masturbating a few times a week.

Visit any of the dozens of cookie-cutter private grade schools in Monsey and you will see happy nursery school children playing, laughing, and singing. Then walk from grade to grade and observe through the small windows in the center of each classroom door as the life ebbs out of the adorable personalities of the successive first-through-eighth graders as each older flock of indoctrinated sheep loses more of their passion for life with every soul-shearing year that follows.

They all baa in cheerful unison upon escaping every June, only to return eight weeks later to submissively sit, as if shackled to their desks, as another year of what should have been a joyous part of their free-spirited middle-childhood is shorn and stripped away. Why don't parents believe their children when told how much they, "hate school!" Why are parents in such shock when their children leave the fold? *Why was my wife surprised when I filed for divorce?*

"My, how you've grown!" I would greet my students every Autumn upon seeing them after a mere eight weeks. "More depressed," I might have added, as the apathetic young lady with the neutered septum pellucidum (the "joy center" bundle of nerves in the brain that connects its right hemisphere to the left one) progresses nervously towards "graduation," and the gauntlet of an almost digital examination by the flickering tongues of roly-poly Yenta "sex-slave traders," before being allowed to proceed to the labyrinthine hurdle of "finding a 'top' boy." In medical jargon we call it a lobotomy. In Jewish circles we praise it as *"tznius"* and "*mentch'lach'kite"* (modesty and civility) and "never being late!" In lay terminology it's often referred to as, "Fucked over."

Like the deceptive gorgeous colorful leaves of Autumn that are, in reality, on the throes of death due to starvation as the frost and shorter days lacking sunlight of winter approaches; the cheerful sparkle in the eyes of the returning new-school-year playful cherubic children, descendants of Mengele lab-rat ancestors who returned from hell, diminishes as their souls turn numb due to the underlying cold-cult permafrost layers of strict colitis-inducing illogical take-it-or-leave-it dogma. Dressed in their school uniforms (emphasis on the 1984 concept of "uniform"), they slowly lose their individuality as their minds enter a state of permanent hibernation; eventually emerging from their insular-from-the-Gentile-world caves as breeding, hunter-gatherers upon becoming full-grown stunted adults.

Upon graduation and a final year of more brainwashing in a seminary for young women in Israel — while their Gentile peers attend the best Party School listed in The Princeton Review to earn their prestigious degrees in licentiousness and the consumption of booze — the uniformed virgins pray that they'll "hurriedly find their Bashert" as they speed to breed the next generation of potential lab-rats who will also "hate school," and eventually morph into hunter-gatherer shoppers who cook and "make Shabbos," or doze off for the next forty years on the Monsey Bus on their way to Manhattan (depending on their genitalia), as they, in turn, give birth to a minyan of kids and many dozens of grandchildren in our warm one-mind-fits-all Stepford Jewish Orthodox community.

And the saddest part of this tragedy is that, although saving their daughters from the horrific statistic of becoming one in four college women who experience sexual assault or rape, in their "not as bad as" fallacy proclamation, it's the mothers who are wrecking their daughters lives as they push them into future Yenta destinies, delivering their young virgins to the whining Old Yentas who are destroying the Jewish religion in their faux zealousness to impress everyone with how observant they are, as they ask their same perfidious collection of obnoxious questions to anyone desperately seeking to marry off their sons and daughters.

"Who's your Da'as Torah? Which school did your daughter attend? Did she get into "BJJ" (the elite Beth Jacob Jerusalem girls seminary) for a year in Israel post high school? Did she ever wet her bed once she potty-trained? Was she ever late to school? Can she fake a multiple orgasm if a "top boy" ejaculates prematurely? What size dress is she? Does she wear padded bras? Did she ever take medication for depression?" Soon enough they'll ask, "Did she ever give anyone a BJ? Does she gag when giving head?" How could these innocent young maidens not be depressed!

Like blabbering dolts, the Torah-tongues of the jabbering-jewesses tingle with orgasmic delight as they ask the same idiotic questions as if one ewe is somehow different than the rest of the flock as they quickly scan the copy and paste resume that was email blasted to three-dozen Yentas who all ask, in the same nasal voice, "So, what type of boy is your daughter looking for? A 'learner' (one who will study five years post marriage) or an 'earner' (a boy who will go to work immediately after the wedding)?" "Anyone with a circumcised dick," would be the most honest response.

Mothers sacrifice their shidduch-triggered daughters on the marriage alter to the Yenta Unzereh Gods who make the Buddha look skinny. "I don't care if she is a 'top girl!' How much does her father earn a year? Does he 'daven' with a minyan?" (Asked in that order of importance.) "Is anyone in the 'fehmaly,' going back three generations, even through marriage, on any medications for depression? Do any of the relatives, going back ten generations, use a smart phone? Will any future generation ever, God help us, use a smart phone or need medications for depression?"

"Is there any Goyish'eh DNA in the 'fehmaly' as a result of rapes that Hashem subjected his daughters to as they were ravished by Khmelnytsky and his rioting Cossack butchers? Are there any divorced ancestors in the 'fehmaly?' Any siblings off the Derech? Is there anyone who is (spelled out in a whispered hush, lest pronouncing the word lead to contagious contamination and becoming one) "G-A-Y?" I need to get my Shadchon Gelt!"

But it's okay if the girl's father served time in Otisville for some white-collar Wall Street crime. After all, he was "set up by the Gentile prosecutor." It will actually enhance his daughter's prospects for a great Shidduch if the felon was able to save a few million dollars of his, "It's not so bad to steal from a Goy," ill-begotten gains. She might even land a real 'top boy learner' because Tatie can now easily afford the mitzvah to support his scholarly son-in-law.

And the most ridiculous aspect of this entire emperor's new clothes fantasy, woven by uneducated nursery-school level Yentas rhyming, "eeny, meeny, miny, moe," as they perform their matchmaking magic, is that everyone believes the delusion that it was all preordained by the amazing hand of God, who orchestrated the entire miraculous "match made in heaven."

After all, God always knew the couple was meant to be, even before he invented time — finally announcing his own Bashert, "eeny, meeny, miny, moe," Shidduch proclamation to his angelic entourage forty days before the birth of the bridegroom, and two-decades before the Shadchan prophetically cast her profitable spell in her revelation of God's will. *"Oy! Do I have a top-boy-bridge for you!"*

Upon the young lassie being assured that she "found" her Bashert, after spending forty minutes with her "top boy" (the first boy she ever dated) in her parents living room, everyone marvels how God works in mysterious ways. What divine fortune that her mother's shopping cart bumped into the Yenta's cart amid the blaring music at the artery hardening Glatt Geshmak Deli section of Evergreen Supermarket. *Mazel Tov!*

Is it any wonder that the Mishnah in Tractate Pe'ah declares the singular sin of evil speech equal to the combined sins of idolatry, murder, and forbidden sexual relationships? Sounds pretty harsh. But not if you consider that the Yentas are killing the unborn babies of many wonderful potential mothers (simply because they are not a size two dress) as they inhibit them from ever having sex, because they worship the commission fees they receive for servicing the wealthier families in town.

I'm still amazed that a community that prides itself on being so holy and righteous, instantly spills its guts faster than a Mafioso turncoat when it comes to making a Shidduch or destroying an already broken family that undergoes a divorce. I would be sad, but hardly surprised, if God blasted the 2.3 square mile 10952 zip code with a giant asteroid one day.

In Israel the situation has gotten so out of hand that a young brilliant, gorgeous Jewish girl, with a flawless reputation, is destined for instant spinsterhood if her father is unable to purchase an apartment as part of the dowry she needs to even begin negotiating a marriage. Is it any surprise that real estate prices are always soaring in the 2.7 square mile city of Bnei Brak and the five-thousand-year-old city of Jerusalem?

It's all part-and-parcel of living in the modern-day 1984 "wonderful day in the Yiddisheh neighborhood" where everyone knows everyone else's business. *But sadly, not their own.*

No one understands that they are entitled to their own individual opinion regarding how they choose to live their life, along with declaring their personal safe boundaries that don't have to include the entire Monsey constrained community in their bedroom. That's why I call the Orthodox Jewish lifestyle "Death by a thousand Yenta Cuts." *You have no idea how much self-control it took not to commit a typo as I typed the last word of the previous sentence.*

Take any four-year-old and try to logically explain the concept of war or hell. Try explaining the slaughtering of Amalekite babies and the stoning of gay people upon the arrival of "the anointed one." You wouldn't get past your second sentence as she would keep asking, "Why? But why?"

Explain to clean slate little minds that some people think other people with dark skin or slanted eyes are "different." They'll never understand. We shouldn't either. Try to teach your toddler that they are "born in sin" and destined to pay for the transgression of Adam and Eve eating a fig. "But what about my doctor and my babysitter?" her ingénue mind will wonder, "What about mommy and daddy? Were they born that way too?"

In the absence of preconceived ideas, she'd just stare at you wide-eyed waiting for you to explain your insanity. Her innocent heart knows you are wrong and that what you are saying makes absolutely no sense, but the indoctrination of her mind by the parents she instinctively depends on for love, validation and survival would quickly take over her instincts.

Now tell her that she will suffer in hell if she kisses and arouses a boy. Especially if she has not immersed in a mikva to cleanse her menstrual blood. She would not even feel pressure to conform before racing to the nearest one. Having no concept of other cultures or beliefs to compare that which she is being manipulated to mindlessly accept, she would instantly believe whatever she is told. *Even celebrating the removal of her beautiful sensitive clitoris. For a lollipop.*

I'm also conditioned. That's why I asked my liberal Barnard "Yiddishe baby mama" if she would have any objection going to the Mikvah while we dated so that I could avoid the death penalty of *Kareth*. I laughed as I said, "Let's practice safe sex," even though I never wore a condom in my life. To this day I still believe that one's life is cut short for having intercourse with a woman who hasn't immersed in a pool of rainwater after menstruating. Please don't call me an idiot, Dr. Robert Sapolsky. It's not necessary because I agree with you. But, as you probably understand better than most, I have no free will due to a lifetime of indoctrination.

I knew my request was a bit medieval, but I had studied enough while at "Ner" to know that I was playing with eternal fire. My Touro College valedictorian, who majored in Biology at Barnard, knew I didn't view blood as "dirty." I've withdrawn a limp smeared-in-blood happy penis from menstruating women dozens of times in my life. But why risk a penalty of death when your date can just skinny-dip for a few seconds?

Sharen also clearly understood the concept that menstrual blood contains some kind of invisible mystical spiritual impurity, punishable with death by the "Hand (job) of Heaven," thanks to her expensive private school Jewish education. "Sure," her gorgeous eye winked, as I handed her a wedding band so that the Mikvah Lady wouldn't suspect any hanky-panky.

I'd discreetly drop off my kosher-concubine around the corner of the West Side Mikvah and watch my partner-in-crime fiancée from the distance till she nonchalantly entered the townhouse to pull off my request. I'd park my car and wait at a nearby restaurant, non-kosher (we'd have fish and salad) so we wouldn't bump into anyone we knew. I'd sit at the bar sipping a few vodka martinis for the next hour or so till Sharen arrived all relaxed and more eager than a geisha.

"I'm kosher!" she'd whisper breathlessly in my ear (that missed Lauren's warm tongue, I now realize) as Sharen joined me at the bar. "Then I'll be eating you shortly," I'd tease back. "Can I keep the band?" she quipped. "After you prove that you're *Glatt* (totally unblemished meat) *Kosher*." Yes, we become that crazy after a childhood of indoctrination. Even when flagrantly bending the rules. I basically lowered our level of transgression from a biblical sin to a mere rabbinical one. *Thank you, Ner Israel Rabbinical College, for a wonderful education!*

An ignorant mind, without the ability to compare contrasting information, is the easiest consciousness to feed false and biased information to without the data ever being questioned, let alone rejected. It is also a dangerous mind. Since it holds only one belief, it is certain that said belief is the only possibility, and hence, the absolute truth. A truth they are quickly willing to sacrifice or blow up their life for. *Allahu Akbar!*

Scientists, marketers, and politicians know that it's only necessary to convince five percent of a group to get the other ninety-five percent to follow mindlessly. People respond emotionally, not rationally. They just start walking with the crowd, believing there's safety in numbers — as they head towards the cliff. That is why the White House is constantly occupied by alternating Republican and Democratic presidents. Nothing changes because the frustrated and angry sheeple, like alienated young children during a divorce, are so easily duped.

An individual with a sophisticated mind will compare all information fed to it against a thousand other thoughts, ideas, situations, conversations, articles, and books that it previously experienced and read, before jumping like a Yenta imbecile to a hasty conclusion. Like Dr. Seuss said, "The more that you read, the more things you will know. The more that you learn, the more places you'll go."

Children are basically born wondering and learning. They are constantly asking the most important question in the world ... *"Why?"* They are full of wonder and freshly curious about everything they see. They can barely wait for an answer to their first question before repeating the next *"Why?"* question they will ask during their childhood.

The best way a parent can raise their kid to become a lifelong learner is by nurturing their curiosity and instilling within their child's young heart a passion for reading. A passion to know. That is the reason I chose to publish stories for children. Babies are born to wonder and learn. To imagine and dream. School crushes those instincts. Society even more so. This book was written by a gifted sixty-nine-year-old curious child. A mature adult would never take off three years of his life, devouring his sheetrock and savings, to write a book. Adults just drive to work and kiss the butt of their boss. Aside from a couple of superstitious religious holidays and vacations, they're always in survival mode. Like marching ants.

The moment a child stops being inquisitive or is intimidated and shamed not to question and to "just listen!" and be seen and not heard, is the moment they lose their sense of wonderfully innocent curiosity for all that the universe has to offer. This usually occurs upon entering school where they are taught to line up and shut up and do as they are told — and to stop asking questions and looking out the window while daydreaming, so that one day they'll become good little robot-citizens who drive to work and kiss butt. *Albert Einstein constantly daydreamed.*

But most likely, depending on their family, they stopped asking questions a long time ago. We all did. Because worse than going to school, most of us attended a house of worship. A place of unquestioning silence. A locus of, "We will do, and we will obey (Exodus 24:7)," mindless butt-kissing subservience and adherence to any commandment uttered by a maniacal Boss-God, whose directives, as viewed from a human perspective, are insane. After all, can you imagine a loving and ethical Abraham commanding his son Isaac to sacrifice any of the twelve tribes just to prove his devotion?

How is one to understand what they are not allowed to even question? It is tantamount to placing a person's brain in solitary confinement. I know. I stayed silent for twenty-eight years. *"Why?"* Because I wanted a family.

Evelyn Beatrice Hall wrote, "I may disapprove of what you say, but I will defend to the death your right to say it." Not being allowed to speak is death. Hall was stating that she would rather die than be forced to live a life of forced silence. The frustration becomes unbearable at first and eventually turns into an artificial mind-numbing, Stepford-conforming, bimbo existence. For most of the planet this is already their reality.

Having your spoken or written words inhibited or banned is like experiencing a forced lobotomy. At first, you'll kick and scream. But once the procedure is completed, your shrunken mind has withered, and you are now sadly intellectually incapacitated. The burning of books is the mass extermination of minds. Ideas that took millennia to conceive, centuries to debate, and decades to transcribe, become ashes overnight; blowing in the wind. The Thought-Police Church burned priceless handwritten scrolls of the Talmud. The Fahrenheit 451 Nazis burned mind-expanding books. Then they burned their Jews. Think it's a coincidence?

Jews never give up their books. They are known as The People of the Book. It's nothing short of a miracle that we still exist. We should number in the billions. But thanks to our inability to flawlessly obey the fanatical precepts of an all-loving merciful God, we are a paltry fifteen-million scattered souls whose opinions range from liberal ultra-left atheistic Marxist ideologies to far-right radically religious, Messianic beliefs. I'm honestly amazed when I hear people say, "I hate Jews." I don't have the ability to define my own personal spectrum of Judaism. How do these idiots lump such a diverse group of people into one melting pot as they pour in their chief ingredients of hate and ignorance?

"Editing" earlier classical works of literature by world renowned authors is nothing less than a sly subliminal burning of the actual books themselves. It's a procedure that I call "thought castration," and it makes the impotent reader less of a person.

Yes, the Talmud does explain the actual court procedure regarding conducting a trial, along with the punitive execution process that may include the defendant standing in actual shit, in fulfillment of the violent Biblical homophobic commandment to stone gay men (Leviticus 20:13). But must we ruthlessly burn the ancient academic tomes along with the Old Testament? Or should we just tear out a few pages? Or perhaps simply edit out a couple of words? Trust me, it won't be long till nothing is left.

We'll also have to dump the New Testament since the sagacity contained therein is based on the leftover morsels gleaned from the wisdom of the ancients in the "Old" Testament. Come to think of it, Paul basically dumped the Old Testament in his Epistle to the Galatians, forever leaving the followers of the observant Orthodox Jewish Jesus in a bit of a conundrum. For eternity.

Paul easily won the supposed debate against Peter, regarding eating only kosher and not cooking on the Sabbath, by assuring his followers that they would no longer need to risk infection upon circumcising their "Peters." This was an offer that was too good to refuse. Because although Jesus supposedly walked on water, his future revelation of antibiotics wasn't about to occur for another three thousand years. Six-hundred and thirteen Mosaic intrinsic laws were miraculously abolished, and Paul taught his duped pitifully ignorant lowest-level-of-society followers that through having mere "faith in Jesus Christ," along with a baby bath, one can enter Paradise. Forgot about the Jewish "two for the price of one." It's all free!

No need to worry about any glaring contradictions between the Old and the New Testaments ever again. And it would now be unnecessary to study the complicated three-thousand folios of the Talmud that explains the Old Testament. After all, "He has risen!" Aren't you excited? Once you've enjoyed the complete rapture of the now singular commandment to "believe that Jesus died for your sins," along with being ensconced in the Holy Spirit, you'll instantly have it all figured out because the Holy Ghost has entered you.

Boo! You'll now believe anything. You'll even be able to heal the sick. And, most important, if you speak, mumble, and grunt quickly enough, you'll make an awesome lot of money. I once wondered what the preacher was rambling as he babbled furiously from his innermost being as he spoke in tongues. When I slowed down the video it seemed he was saying, "Fools! Give me your money!"

Mark Twain's characters spoke in the vernacular of their day. Surely we must edit all old literature that uses the word negro. It's offensive and way outdated. Perhaps we should simply go back in time and rewrite history? As a matter of fact, let's start from scratch and ask God to recreate the world. According to the Midrash, God created many worlds before this messy one. Why not one more? On the other hand, why would a God need so many chances to get it *wrong*?

Why delete thesaurus-filled fine-tuned words that help describe specific details and refined pure logical truths? Remove descriptive words, and one's thoughts, emotions, and conversations remain childish. With a mind that is stuck and restrained with the smaller amount of vocabulary it possesses, the constrained speaker or writer can no longer express what they once desired to sincerely share. Have you never said, "Hold on, I'm trying to get my thoughts out?" Destroy vocabulary and see if that helps you.

Removing words would be similar to shutting out the ability to see vivid colors through our eyes and forcing everyone to live with Achromatopsia (complete color blindness), where one can only see in bland shades of black, white and gray. Color without a trace of red, orange, yellow, green, blue, indigo, and violet is not very colorful. Think how much you'd enjoy eating a gray orange or an off-white banana. Or biting into a steel-colored apple. All the different species of flowers and fish would now only appear unique in their shapes. Feathers and scales would look so similar. Imagine looking at your little girl with her white hair and dull-gray eyes. Kind of scary. Articulate words are like shades of brilliant colors. It would be quite frightful to live in a world without them. Even with them we're heading towards using caveman clubs and cancel-culture threats to impose our point of view instead of discussing and describing why we believe in the foolish ideas we are prepared to go to war over, and why we feel such intense emotions regarding vacuous competition between two different teams of men throwing a funny shaped ball.

The Founding Fathers were men. Not gods. They grappled with the slavery issue of their day. And sadly, they came up very short because of a lack of humanity coupled with pure economics and political expediency. And so did Abraham Lincoln who took way too long to emancipate Blacks. Lincoln was much more concerned with preserving the Union than with ending slavery; and he also chose a racist Vice President to appease the defeated Confederacy — which set Blacks back a hundred years when Honest Abe was later assassinated a mere six weeks into his second term.

John F. Kennedy continued to grapple with the same segregation issues as our sixteenth president. The dehumanization of "negroes" as inferior "Colored People" that "need not apply" for a job or school in the South, eventually evolved, along with modern-White-man, into the civil rights movement struggle for true equality for Blacks, and ultimately morphed into the inaugural celebration of America's first Black President.

A presidency that was won in a bitter contest against a White, very powerful, formidable, influential, and obviously politically connected, former two-term First Lady. Senator Hillary Clinton lost the Democratic Primary match as proud Black Americans, and many White people, overwhelmingly cast their precious votes which jettisoned Barack Obama into the White House for two full terms. It was the shock of her life till she met up with The Donald only to get an even larger jolt of reality. Hillary wanted the presidency more than Haman ever desired to rule over Ancient Persia and the entire world of yore.

But even Kennedy refused full confrontation with belligerent Confederate southern governors like George Wallace and Lindsay Almond who still viewed Blacks as n-words when I celebrated my tenth birthday in 1963 as I opened my own Pandora PTSD gift from God. And it took till 1964 and Lyndon Johnson's signing of the Civil Rights Act to finally enforce — with National Guardsmen — what Blacks were promised a century earlier upon the reconstruction of this country when the Civil War ended.

Why try to recall that the original n-word (with only one letter 'g') meant nothing more than "Black" in Latin. It took till the 1800's and thousands of white-trash folk spewing hate and ignorance to turn the n-word into a nasty derogatory description that epitomized laziness and beings capable of executing only demeaning simple mindless tasks while running as fast as Jesse Owens because of all the practice they had, running for their lives from KKK police, in their youth to avoid being lynched by a mob of Church worshiping Goyim. Amazingly enough, we've come full circle and we're back to the Latin word originally used to describe Black people. Black!

With the endless times I've heard the word "Jew" angrily hissed by some members of Congress, and a few Presbyterian jewelers and Catholic real estate agents whose commissions were, "Jewed down," I can easily imagine that one day the word by which I'm proud to be called will be enunciated as "the j-word."

Why study the accomplishments and maturity of a nation that elected its first Black President before its first female POTUS. Yes, there's so much more to improve and correct, but it's obviously much easier to mindlessly scream that all White people are racists while destroying inner cities to grab a pair of Nike sneakers along with a few angry votes.

Forget about all the White abolitionists and liberal Jews like Henry Moscowitz who helped found the NAACP. Ignore the fact that for several years the organization founded in 1909 was headed by a Jew. How many hate mongers are even aware that in the first half of the twentieth century forty percent of Black people educated in the South attended schools and colleges funded by the Jewish philanthropist Julius Rosenwald? His efforts and generosity were legendary. The many colleges and high schools he created became known as "The Rosenwald Schools." But why bring up the past? Especially when it's positive and encouraging. Go ahead and deny that Abraham Heschel marched side-by-side with Martin Luther King. Ignore that Jules Browde, a Jewish lawyer and founding member of "Lawyers for Human Rights," was the man Nelson Mandela trusted with his life to represent him in court. The list is quite endless.

Let's forget it all and simply throw away our entire history and hand over the wealth, industry, and technological progress of this country to the American Indians. After all, they got screwed first. But wait. Which Indian tribe should receive our atomic weapons, scientific inventions, and the keys to Fort Knox? The later tribes killed off the earlier extinct ones. And where will the rest of us go? Back to ancient Africa where men began walking upright? But my roots originated in the Garden of Eden. Let's all head back there as one happy family.

Modern-day civilization was built upon earth soaked with the blood of billions of people and slaves. Within hours of the moment that God first blew life into the nostrils of Adam, Cain lifted the first weapon ever invented, and smashed his brother in the head. We've been killing and enslaving each other mercilessly from day one. White Israelites were enslaved by dark skinned Egyptians for two-hundred and ten years till their miraculous exodus took place. The Roman Empire was built by slaves. As was Persia.

Estimates are that a third of the ancient world was enslaved. Pick your version of the history of death. How far back in time do you wish to travel? Modern man simply introduced the concept of mass destruction. But nothing has really changed other than our speed and skill to heal or kill.

Too many of us are still uncouth, simple-minded Facebook posting barbarians who are unable to carry a logical conversation for more than thirty seconds without getting angry, triggered, distracted, or upset. With huge egos fueled by tiny brains, most Americans of any political affiliation would scoot to a safe space refuge because they wouldn't last three minutes if their lives ever depended on their ability to remain logical for the time it takes to boil an egg.

Most of us make life and death decisions based on slick political marketing slogans and catchy deceptive news headlines; or upon listening to calm angelic voices in pharmaceutical advertisements espousing medical magic while quickly warning of the possible deadly side effects, as our doctor (who has "determined" that the benefits outweigh the possible side effects) is simultaneously bombarded with incentives to push the new drugs hastily approved by the FDA.

We spend our hard-earned money on a whim, put poisonous modified shit into our mouths without reading the label, and fuck as easily as quickly swiping right or left because Prince crooned his permission, that "it was Saturday night, I guess that makes it all right," as we then wonder, when looking back three decades later, why we remained stuck in a toxic relationship with a cold-hearted wife and an angry jealous God for a major part of our lives. And when it comes to political issues, we're positive that we know all the answers.

I don't want Dachau razed to the ground. I want to celebrate the miracle of my father walking out alive. Surviving the ordeal of what he endured was something he was proud of. My father was not ashamed that he was called a "pig-dog" and "dirty Jew" thousands of times. He was not embarrassed that he was forced to play "Tzenter" with maniacal laughing guards. My dad missed his mother and was focused on his family. As an eighteen-year-old, all he wanted was his freedom. His life. He wanted me. Boy, did I make him happy. Now I understand why my father constantly stared at me with so much love.

As I look back in time, my dad seemed to be staring at a miracle whenever he looked at me. I guess that explains why my Tatie often just started crying out of nowhere. Who could possibly imagine what PTSD was back in 1957 when I was a four-year-old child? But I can still clearly see my dad's sad face as he slowly began to cry. Considering that I'm alive because the "Tzenter" countdown never began nine "prisoners" away from my dad, I surely must be a miracle. Surviving my divorce proves it. I might have a few emotional scars and stress-induced added weight, but I'm gorgeous. Dad said so. And he never lied.

I'm actually a double miracle because, on my mother's side, my great-grandfather was almost killed by Cossacks. They were literally at his door and had already killed many Jews in the neighborhood. But other Gentiles explained to the invaders that my mother's grandfather was the mayor of the tiny hamlet that was soon to be erased by the first World War and one of the only literate people in town. They pleaded for his life and explained that my ancestor was a kind man who kept honest land and birth records for everyone. His life and family were spared. And so was mine. Do you believe in miracles God? Why didn't you save the other Jewish families that day?

I don't blame modern day Germans for what their parents or grandparents did seventy-five years ago. I don't have a desire to erase German history or an angry passionate emotion of revenge that incites me to destroy their culture. Their beautiful country has changed. Just as ours has. Of course some German skinheads espouse hate and some Klansmen still march in our country. But they only have that right because both nations' humanity has evolved and we guarantee freedom of assembly. I don't believe the Germans are Amalekites, or that modern-day Germans "owe" me a penny. I don't believe in the tribal concept of children paying for the sins of their fathers. I'd be happy to dominate a German dominatrix along with listening to her barking accent as she imitates my ex-wife. "Your family, Ze'eff!"

I don't want to wipe out and "Utterly obliterate (lit. "erase" in Hebrew) Amalek from under Heaven (Deuteronomy 25:19)" because of what their ancestors supposedly did to my Israelite relatives in the desert, attacking them from behind as they miraculously left Egypt and crossed the Red Sea (Exodus 17:14) after Moses parted the flowing waters almost three-thousand and five-hundred years ago. Talk about emotional baggage. I prefer to study the past. I don't need to live there.

Boundaries restricting speech are worse than iron bars. An incarcerated body knows it's in jail, but a confined mind doesn't realize how ignorant and helpless it is. It doesn't understand that it can choose or decide for itself. Look at the starving population of North Korea. Their minds are emptier than their bellies. Through their malnutrition-fogged brains, they worship their demented thuggish leader as a god instead of overthrowing him. And in our meat-nourished wits, we worship a God who acts like their assassin thug.

Think about that. Talk about it too. This was the exact message of George Orwell. Take away an individual's freedom to communicate and you will easily control his mind. Obliterate his dictionary and he becomes a robot. Or an eventual divorcing Dad-zombie. DO NOT TALK TO MINOR CHILD also meant that the minor child was forbidden to speak to me. Fuck! Sorry for that sudden outburst, but I still get triggered as I continue to suffer the very brutal and inhumane punishment I endured for loving the most adorable little girl I raised from birth. I realize I'm damaged goods. My consciousness has been scarred for eternity. Thank you, God.

Even if Ester called me tomorrow, how could we recreate the lost memories of an entire alienated decade? A decade that consisted of half of Ester's entire lifespan. As articulate as I am, I wouldn't know what to say or where to begin. It would be like being introduced to a new young lady I'd be meeting for the first time. I better stop describing this before I depress myself any further. Thank you Sharen. Thank you for sharing how sadly deranged you are. Everything makes sense now. When will you be as generous as my ex-wife, Dear God? Would you mind sharing your email password with me?

Why do you think Monsey rabbis are controlling the Internet and what their congregants read? It is the exact method through which The Church was so easily able to control the illiterate masses while serving as both their government and spiritual guide during the Dark Ages. The barbarians and serfs were, excuse my pun, in the dark.

And this was the precise method China used to shut down any possible faint memory of the Tiananmen Square massacre. Few thirty-year-olds can imagine the resulting death toll of a peaceful student-led hunger strike that was responded to with their being mercilessly slaughtered as unarmed students and many innocent bystanders were murdered in cold blood. Foreign journalists were immediately expelled from the country. Thousands of people were killed and not one word of the mini holocaust appears anywhere in print. Even remembering the massacre is now a crime in 1984 China.

More than a half-century ago Malcom X explained, "The media's the most powerful entity on Earth. They have the power to make the innocent guilty and to make the guilty innocent, and that's power. Because they control the minds of the masses." The media is more powerful than ever in our present day world where conglomerates like Google, Walt Disney, Comcast, Facebook, Bertelsmann, Viacom, CBS, and Twitter dominate over ninety percent of the information they permit you to read. Any dissent to their political views and beliefs is simply shut down. They can instantly close the account of any user for failure to comply with their standards. Even a president who was voted into power by more than half the voting population. And, like Malcom said, "That's power!" It took my controlled psyche almost a lifetime to escape "authority," and to become my own person and finally live by another pearl of wisdom stated by Malcom X. "Nobody can give you freedom. Nobody can give you equality or justice or anything. If you're a man, you take it." I love you, Malcom.

I didn't even have to "take it." As a White man I had to just stop accepting the shit everyone shoveled me. Of all the digital user-friendly wizardry that my iPhone offers, surely the simple "Block this Caller" option is my favorite. *I can't wait till Apple invents "Block this God."*

A combination of greed, ignorance, and fear cut short the life of a man who could have been POTUS had he lived three more decades, as Malcolm X was violently assassinated on my twelfth birthday. At a tad older than half my present age, the thirty-nine-year-old notoriously feared articulate young visionary was destined to become a world-renowned leader of Black and White men had the maverick word-slinger lived to further mature his views.

Even before reaching middle age Malcolm was described (sadly, posthumously) by the *NY Times* as having, "a gift of bitter eloquence against what he considered [the] white exploitation of Negroes." Sadly, like many other visionaries, he was silenced for speaking the truth. And the freedom of Blacks, along with the evolution of Whites, was set back a probable century. The State rejoiced.

I rapaciously read the posthumously published biography of Brother Malcolm a few months later — a story that portrayed incredible personal growth in the face of all odds. Malcom would have accomplished in years what six decades without his guidance has still not achieved. The future had planned possible enlightenment to soothe Malcom's justified rage, that was just beginning to subside, had God granted him a few more decades of life along with a true mentor instead of the false, conniving poop-prophet, Elijah Muhammad.

Fifty years later it's still difficult for me to fully celebrate my own birthday as I recall the day this eloquent legend, who was as famous as he was misunderstood, was murdered by his ignorant zealous Muslim "brothers" who were duped by the stupor of religion espoused by a clever thug. The Nation of Islam leader, Elijah Muhammad, insisted that his followers lead puritanical lives as he pocketed millions while cavorting with a bunch of young secretaries. While siring over a dozen illegitimate children that he refused to acknowledge, his devoted followers gunned down Malcolm, who was riddled with bullets, right in front of his own pregnant wife and three young daughters.

The charade and stench of Elijah continues with the hate and ignorance of the arrogant Hitlerian, Louis Farrakhan. God took away a diamond and replaced it with pure shitty coal as Farrakhan replaced Malcom as the national spokesman of the Nation of Islam after (allegedly) basically inciting the men who murdered Malcom. The anti-Semitic Farrakhan, who adored Hitler, describing him as "a very great man," eventually broke away from the group in 1978 as he stole their name. Fake Farrak-kaka-han has enjoyed a long life. The monster is approaching his ninetieth birthday. God certainly works in mysterious ways. What can he not fuck up?

I wish I could recite the Mourner's Kaddish in memory of Malcom X. Perhaps I could call him Moshe X. *Maybe that's why God made it so easy for me to remember the Yahrzeit of Brother Malcom. May his memory be a blessing.*

I think every child should pledge allegiance reciting the words of Evelyn Beatrice Hall before they begin their daily studies. Our flag supposedly represents freedom, but freedom can only be achieved through fearless, articulate language and intellectual honesty. We must uninhibitedly share our innermost thoughts and examine the veracity or falsehood of our opinions and beliefs to acquire world peace.

But "all-inclusive" does not mean Hitler, Sharen, Arafat, and Farrakhan get an invitation to the negotiating table that Churchill, Malcom X and Yitzhak Rabin should have been sitting at. You can't negotiate with people whose word means absolute shit. Been there. Done that. We have to be candid. It won't be easy. But it's a beautiful beginning. It's time we stopped yelling, shaming, insulting, and culture canceling anyone who doesn't share our exact point of view. On the other hand, we must realize that negotiation is impossible with serial killers disguised as "World leaders" just because they seized power. As the late, hysterically honest, Joan Rivers constantly asked, "Can we talk?"

The hazy delusional urgency by which I had lived my own multi-tasking fast-paced life of car-pooling mornings and afternoons, overdrawn-at-the-bank days, diamond-dealing sleepless nights, torturous tax withholding years, and post-dated tuition-paying decades, while turning folio after folio of the Talmud to keep pace with Rabbi Nekrtiz, sped through my memory as I continued to slowly enjoy my morning elixir.

I help my warm oversized cup in both hands as I peacefully sipped a brew that resurrected me from a miracle called sleep during which my evolved brain, rested on a pillow, ridding itself of toxic relationships while storing new information, as it spun in a solar system contained in a galaxy that was falling through space at a million and three-hundred miles per hour.

I recalled how I also barreled through my days to earn the stacks of cash I paid for the convenience of live-in maids, doormen, and nannies so that I could run even faster, while dressing beautifully to trade diamonds, so that I could donate charity to great scholars and Jewish institutions of higher learning. I ran faster every day, but for some reason, I could never catch up to my klutzy stupid and greedy fevered holy thoughts of how a carrot-dangler God might choose to define me one day as I stood trembling before him in judgment, while groveling for my heavenly reward in the afterlife.

My Orthodox Jewish lifestyle, financed by jumbo mortgages and huge lines of credit while paying outrageous property taxes on a beautiful six-bedroom hoarder's storage-facility, as I simultaneously donated charity to anyone who asked, exhausted me. I get tired just describing it.

The intensely crazy-busy Jewish life I once led, devoted in blind servitude to a cult-culture, Yenta-controlled society, and mentally ill wife, while trekking thrice-weekly to cram folio after folio of Talmudical law with Rabbi Nekritz in Brooklyn, now crystalized in my mental vision as I continued to slowly sip my coffee while quietly gazing into my frenzied evanescing past that suddenly seems to stand as still as a marble statue.

I stare at the apparition of my enchanting "till death do us part" *Eishet Chayil* as she sits across the aisle from me in my mind's eye at the Rockland county kangaroo courtroom several years ago.

I slowly scan the entire important looking woodworked room that once portrayed order in the court but was nothing more than a dysfunctional and unbridled insane asylum without any staff or oversight. The bustle of ungoverned and harebrained directives under the aegis of a huffy mildly stroked-out abhorrent, black-robed chimpanzee, who never exhibited much logic or empathy in his chimp youth, and the angry beadledom display of his constantly pounding "I'll-hold-you-in-contempt!" gavel against its sounding block become eerily silent as I travel back in time.

I'm amazed at my ability to see everyone so clearly: the annoyed frantic-looking Alfieri with his bloated ego and shriveled frontal cortex, my anxious world-coming-to-an-end wily wife, Dan Schwartz with his heartless chest and big belly strapped with lawyer-suspenders that supported the illusion that he is one, the sheitel-clad court stenographer with her disheveled wig always askew, mindlessly typing yet another sloppy never-to-be-read court-proceedings fully portraying the occluded synapses of a stroked-out judge constantly yelling "Strike that!" every time I "had a problem with authority" because I pointed out the illogical decisions he kept rendering while a mere few months away from forced retirement and surely millimeters away from his final stroke. And I see the wandering, meandering, robotic court clerk.

I also see the rows of estranged spouses waiting for their divorce-decree paperwork to catch up to the reality of their long ago reneged "through good times and bad" promises of "I do," along with their once joyously proclaimed "as long as we both shall live" raddled vows that now forever exclaim, "They don't!" and finally, the lost meandering bailiffs that never seemed to know where to stand.

My recollection of the entire judiciary cast of wasted humanity now presents itself as witless sleepwalkers as they reappear in my memory as what they truly were: unexpressive, cold-hearted, compassionately stunted, couldn't-care-less, semi-opaque haunting specters rushing about as if they were doing something of immense value, whose worthless efforts are dubbed by our oblivious society as "Justice being served."

The scene of intense frantic effort by somnambulistic paper-shuffling zombies over so many obfuscated petitions, trashy protection orders, and unread documents; "officially" and pompously stamped with a seal of faux might and handed off to someone of feigned importance who will file the piffling proceedings into oblivion — in its now slow-motion version — reveals that the emperor and his entourage were not merely naked.

Like my erratic Lilliputian wife and bizarre marriage, along with the vague memories of my loveless and tumultuous childhood, they seem to have never existed. I can barely believe that this scene — and my marriage — once seemed so real to me. *So did my God.*

Several of the actors in this lamentable tragedy have since ceased to exist, passing from this universe, leaving a bi-polar legacy of praying and practicing religious good deeds while simultaneously inflicting great harm on a wonderful brother-in-law. One email during his short voyage in *Olam Hazeh* (*This World* as opposed to the eternal *Olam Haba*), while riding this polluted-by-gossipmongers rock hurtling through space, revealed the true essence of the soul of Fred "the liar" Mailman. Like insensitive sister. Like sneaky backstabbing brother.

I often think about my wife's esquire brother who advised her to lie and claim that I hit her. Had Fred known that he had so little time left as his brain cancer relentlessly wrapped itself around his amoral cerebral tissue would he have rushed from Silver Spring to spend Shabbos in Monsey, the week after I filed for divorce, to create a scene in my synagogue about my unwillingness to go to Beit Din? Would he have yelled at his daughter in front of her cousins not to partake of my unholy Kiddush wine as if it were poison (because my blessing over the wine polluted it)? Would he have shown some mercy and not wasted his time in joining the ferocious fray to destroy my life?

And I wonder about my other brother-in-law, David, who repaid my kindness, after I patiently taught him the mortgage business and gave him a job, by sending a short and crude *Thank you!* email — that served no purpose other than imitating the potty-mind accolades of his older sister — to call me a "piece-of-shit" upon my filing for divorce, further clogging his multi-stented cruel heart ensconced in deadly fat, unwarranted hate, and anger. I have no doubt he'll be joining Fred shortly.

I recall the emails between my wife and David in which he angrily wished to spend, "just ten minutes alone in a room with Zev." I doubt if David realizes that the life expectancy of his super-obese body tenuously exits on borrowed time and that there are better things for a fifty-four-year-old tantrum-throwing child to do (like visiting the dentist to fix his rotting teeth) than fantasize about a sophomoric karate fight with his sixty-four-year-old (at the time) ex brother-in-law who simply desired an amicable divorce.

Without the Ivy League education of his sister to camouflage his stunted emotional growth, it's easy to see the true white-trash DNA strands that evolved from his Pit Bull bitch mother. And I suspect David's Shodan black belt sash will serve no other purpose than to tie his Extra-Large size shrouds when he'll be wrapped up to join his brother Fred.

Where does all the unceasing hate, perpetual anger, and negativity in this family come from, I wonder. No wonder half of the earlier generation family tree members didn't speak to the other half. I now easily comprehend why my wonderful father-in-law checked out early. It was the only way he could escape the never-ending clampdown bite of a huffy Pit Bull in lipstick. I was thrilled to reap the same benefit as my wonderful father-in-law upon filing for divorce. I was able to throw a goodbye kiss to my Monster Matriarch mother-in-law. Mwah! XOX

Evil, like beauty, is skin deep. It doesn't take much to expose the true personality hidden beneath some makeup and dark-blue eyes. A woman that I thought of as an enigma was nothing more than a high-functioning Asperger lunatic. Sharen Mailman's Tatie5521 password was certainly a priceless eye-opening gift to me. That password revealed the inner-workings of her frontal lobe and exposed most of her family's full-frontal psychopathy while sparing me from pedophilic-charged email booby traps that backfired in her cute tiny lying face.

Talk about a money-shot. Sharen's treachery cost her a treasure of cash and the deed to our home that she signed over to me. A little traffic jam here, a little serving of divorce papers there, will quickly reveal an individual's true personality. It's amazing what people will do to save a dollar. Or steal a few. They'll waste priceless precious time and squander their reputations for worthless currency that they could have easily acquired by simply working for it at half the effort. Without hurting anyone.

After all, that seems to be the battlefront of any divorce case. It's surely all that our divorce was ever about in my wife's mind. She certainly was not thinking about our children. Or the man she slept with for thirty years to conceive them. "Your family, Sha'ren!"

All that money, and wasted years stretching out a simple divorce, merely to inflict mandible shredding red-ant aggression to perpetuate a conflagration of full-blown venom-spewed lies, dispensed at four-hundred and fifty dollars an hour by the lowest ranking kapo Jewish member of the bloody-shoe firm of Kantrowitz, Goldhamer, & Graifman.

Their malicious illegal dump of defecated legalese defamation, shitted on my flawless Mr. Mom, scholar, writer, and teacher reputation, dissipated as quickly as I could type Tatie5521 into the password bar of my wife's Yahoo email account. It was only due to an ungoverned fucked-up legal system that the Zyklon B (as in "Bullshit!") smoke screen, farted out by a Jewish law firm of devils, lasted longer than a day.

Savings of four-hundred-thousand dollars plus four-hundred-thousand in sheet rock equity simply had to be divided by the number two. That first-grade math took almost three years for The Honorable Alfieri to "figure out." *In God We Trust*. In other words, when you walk into a divorce courtroom expect the illogical wrath of God.

Aleksandr Solzyehenitsyn described his relationship with the authorities he once believed in, and thereby my own divorce experience surviving a wife and her genocidal law firm team known for massacring the reputations of divorcing husbands by burying them alive in mountains of deceptive shit, as follows: "We know they are lying. They know they are lying. They know we know they are lying. We know they know we know they are lying. But they are still lying."

Some people might wonder how I could describe a wife, a mother, a grandmother, with such naked truth. How can a husband reveal what the woman who gave birth to his five children was like in bed, sharing such intimate moments, along with many other private and personal details of their twenty-eight-year mirage marriage?

But for three full PTSD infused years my wife mercilessly kept lying and spewing whatever insane nonsense her batty mind could conjure up, in a horror-thriller divorce bloodbath sending my blood pressure skyrocketing till it almost reached boiling point. The onslaught was delivered by the Yenta crows and ravens of Hitchcock's famous film, as Sharen alienated the child I raised, loved, and would have donated any of my body parts for, on the turn of a dime.

The sweet wife I once trusted with my life, a spouse I handed a thousand dollars a week in cash for over fifteen years to "run our home," stuffed in a clean white envelope with a love note, was now spending a fortune on financing a law firm known for nothing more than their willingness and audacity to fling shit. Read the mission statement on their website stating the "Ten Commandments of Divorce."

Between Kantrowitz, Goldhamer, & Graifman's fanatical observance of their perverse version of the Ten Commandments, along with my wife's faux observance on the holy Sabbath as she screamed, "Come now!" to the cops, coupled with Alfieri playing God in his hellish courtroom, it's a miracle I didn't blow my brains out with a stroke, let alone a bullet.

Post-divorce, it became my turn to spend three years writing the truth to dispel their lying, because, like Solzhenitsyn explained, they knew that I knew they were lying. And they continued to lie. And they are still lying. And so I'll keep writing. And I'll continue to write. *Wanna sue me?*

I am entitled to the therapy of chronicling and sharing the details of what I endured. And it was necessary for me to describe every facet of my wife's personality. Her hoarding. Her emotional frigidity. Her narcissistic anger when she finally volcanically explodes. I had to explain my "real" wife. Because if you met the one who gives an incredible first impression performance, you'd absolutely adore her. She's a flawless gem. Until you use a loupe. And so, I had no choice. I was also going to explode. And die. Or put my pen to paper. I had to bleed ink or blood. I chose to live. Writing my story brought me back to life. "Hi!"

That's what happens when you call a Mr. Mom, father of five, grandfather of who knows how many grandchildren by now, a raging pedophile. That's what happens when you force a writer of beautiful children's stories to undergo a PTSD trial defending something more precious than his life in criminal and family court. My wife understood the reputation I spent my lifetime earning meant the world to me. She treated it like shit. Literally.

My wife almost dissected my aorta as I took the witness stand in family court, with my heart pounding inside of my sixty-two-year-old chest, as I faced accusations that I sexually molested my own weak-minded daughter Sara. Casting duped Sara as fodder, after manipulating her to sign charges of physical and sexual abuse against the father she constantly called, "The best Tatie in the World," in front of all her friends, must surely rank among the most vile and depraved inhumane acts I could have ever imagined even from my wife. It would have made more sense had Sharen hired a hitman to kill me.

Sara felt like an idiot in court because she couldn't fully comprehend her own charges against me. And that was because my gullible daughter didn't have me sitting next to her breaking it down and explaining everything in a whisper as I always did when we sat among family and friends. That experience, of having to balance the love I felt for my daughter and not wanting to embarrass my slow-witted child as a liar and idiot, while being forced to fight for my life and reputation, annihilated me. The thought of now facing similar charges while being "judged" by Nazi Fuckface Alfieri, as I stared at an eleven-year-old sweet Ester sitting in the witness stand, was excruciating. I would have honestly preferred the odds of playing "Tzenter."

The trauma I endured extricating myself from the intricately woven web of Sharen's mercenary gold-digger law firm (suitably named Goldhamer in description of their avaricious appetite for material wealth at all costs) resulted in the dream that led to my writing this book. It became my turn to finally share the truth with my Princess Ester. And with Sara too, if someone helps her to read this book that I wrote without experiencing a nanosecond of writer's block the entire three years it took me to write my story. And that's because every pent-up word that was muzzled by the Orders of Protection blasted out of my pen. Everything in this book, along with the revelation of what goes on behind the hypocritical warm facade of our Unzereh community, is fucking fallout from the initial Big Bang Protection Order blast that vaporized my relationship with Ester.

And that is the beauty of truth. Like a ray of light illuminating pitch-black darkness, my wife's own emails instantly revealed the masked interior mind of *what* I had been married to all along. One grain of unrestrained truth utterly crushed the concealed mountains of manipulative siren-calls and black lies (along with every other color and shade of the rainbow) spoken by the Jewish Orthodox White-Trash Chosen People that I once sincerely called "family."

Robert Sapolsky shouldn't limit his research tracking the shrinking neurons of baboons due to stress. I think he'd learn a great deal by scanning the grey matter of mandrill-lawyers, in colorful ties, like Schwartz, joker-judges like Alfieri, and histrionic theatrical tantrum-throwing women like my ex-wife. And while Dr. Sapolsky is at it, he could scan my interesting brain to see the effects of long-term smothering PTSD inflicted by God. I'm not writing this in anger or as a joke. I write in the interests of psychopathology and neuropsychology.

There are a lot of crazy people out there. And their brains need to be studied. Not by pathological quacks like Dr. Ferro who use psychological hypothetical drivel to "draw their own conclusions" in circular evaluations around the bullseye hole. But by real medical neuroscientists.

Tyrants and despots still control with ease much of the land mass on the planet, along with the people confined within their borders who fear tear gas, jails, plutonium spiked cocktails, plastic and lead bullets, along with the carnage their taskmaster can inflict merely upon waking up on the wrong side of their bed. And religious people are the easiest targets to manipulate because they are used to not thinking for themselves. They ceased making decisions long ago. Most of them, upon birth. They are constantly seeking instruction and asking permission from their leaders regarding the will of God, without even imagining that they already know the often simple and obvious answers.

Orthodox Jews aren't exactly "born to be wild." They are birthed to live under someone else's constant ironclad authority and live in a world of guilt and shame, horrified at the thought of what their Rabbi or some Yenta in the community might be saying about them. They are constantly second-guessing the purity of their own intentions, motives, and actions. The self-infliction is exacerbated by an all-seeing God who can read their thoughts, as they rush through their daily prayers worrying that The All-merciful Creator knows they are bored with their lives and wives, as they mumble their monotonous daily liturgy with forced feigned devotion.

Worse than their fear of God, they are terrified of the flesh and blood pussy-army of sniper-chirping Yentas who seem to orgasm only when excitedly speaking gossip. These sheitel-helmeted bitches can destroy a father's reputation, along with his daughter's future chance of finding her Bashert, faster than the second it takes them to hit the auto-dial key of their kosher internet-blocked cell phones while they power walk, and power talk, every morning except Shabbat, clucking like Dodo birds and spewing "doo-doo" two-note pigeon-like sounds, and a lot of other shit.

Is it any wonder that, living in a world of total cognitive dissonance, the inhabitants of Monsey have very little confidence in making their own decisions? Especially when the punitive price they'll pay for doing something radical, like thinking for themselves, will entail being shunned, shamed, and ultimately sentenced to an eventual sojourn in Hell.

In the Ultra-Orthodox world, approximately two percent leave the fold. Their leaders claim that the number is very low. "Proof!" they insist, that the community is a warm and welcoming one. And it is. Till the moment an "individual" (an abstract concept in Judaism) decides to leave. Then it's scoldingly scathing. One is instantly labeled a drug addict and "ah meshuggenah." Or in my case, "a pedophile full of wrath."

I have no scientific data, but I imagine that the two percent number would easily quintuple based on the amount of utterly miserable people I know who would love to escape if not for their half-dozen children who need an eventual Shidduch, aside from their own fears triggered by the thought of living in the "outside world." I put off my own divorce for a full decade because I wanted to "be there" for my four children as they grew up. I then stayed an additional decade when my forty-six-year-old wife said, "Oops!"

The overfed, undersexed, automatons spend their lives in an insular, organized world of constant prayer and mitzvot, where one's life, schooling, section-eight housing, healthcare, future spouse for their kids, free loan societies, and even eventual burial are all "arranged" for by a Tzibur community that would do anything for their Unzereh. Give birth and your half-minyan of kids will be cared for by your neighbors. You won't cook for an entire month.

It 'Takes a Jewish Village' to raise a robot. Is it any wonder that very few dare to use the pistons in their legs to escape the loving shtetl gulag? Most religious Jews believe they are already here for their second or third reincarnation because they "fucked up" the last time they were raped into existence to earn their afterlife from their all-giving God. Who knows? Maybe they stared at some porn on a caveman wall and masturbated? Three strikes and they'll never get into Heaven.

But the Internet has entirely transformed our entire planet into a world that can be traveled in the palm of one's hand. And Blockchain, along with quantum computers, will make our present day computers look as obsolete as prehistoric cavemen drawings compared to writing. It is instinctive of man's nature to explore.

Tap your phone and you can stare closely at the cracks in the warped wooden panel portrait of the Mona Lisa hanging in The Louvre in the second it takes you to surf the web to France. Once there, simply expand your screen while moving Lisa Gherardini in any direction with your cursor. Her warm expressive eyes, full nose and subtle smile reminds me of Ester. Just down the hall you can visit the statue of the Greek beauty, Venus de Milo. Careful! Staring at her very firm marble breasts might lead to wicked thoughts and a nocturnal emission. "Oops!"

Wikipedia has become every straying Hasid's Old Testament, with Reddit and the search engine Google serving as Talmudical commentary. Most Hasidim fear drowning in the flames of hell if they surf the net. They don't believe it was created by Al Gore, who never implied anything more than that he allowed its creation, but they credit its creation to an even more outrageous ridiculous claimant known as The Satan. Nevertheless, many of them are curious and are leading double lives while carrying two cell phones. A smart one. And a muzzled internet-blocked dumb one.

Fear is also the reason 1984 Big Brother Orthodox Jewish leaders forbid smart phones and the Internet more strictly than the Bible forbids the eating of pork. I am not exaggerating. Eating pork is just one sin. So is going to a Shiksa prostitute. But one can repent. The Internet, however, is an abyss that leads directly to hell, completely exposing the online sinner's mind and soul to the spiritual cancer of the "outside world" where he will turn into ... Oy vey! A Goy!

Unzereh Jews are very confused about the outside world that surrounds and threatens to engulf them. They can hardly be blamed for fearing a world that shed their blood for thousands of years. Vaccines, science, evolution, GPT-3 technology (i.e. my ex wife), the Internet, the likelihood of extraterrestrial life, and smartphones are all viewed as threatening siren calls from the Yetzer Hara (the impulsive desire to act selfishly evil and to wantonly fling Orders of Protection upon being served divorce papers) that God injected into their consciousness at birth. Many Orthodox Jews live in a bubble of blind faith that imprisons them to ignore the reality of viruses, mental health, individualism, exercise, eating healthy, and getting a good night's sleep. Instead, they constantly sigh in exhaustion, "Goht Velt Unzerah Helfen (God will help us)."

Orthodox Jews are terrified about what they, and especially the eyes of their children, might be exposed to on the Internet. God forbid! They are strictly forbidden to search for answers that might lead to their becoming an "Apikores" (a heretical thinker)! They exist in a mindless sanctuary-haven safe place from sin. Independent self-introspection by any member of the synagogue would be viewed by their Da'as Torah Rabbi as if the rebellious congregant suddenly adopted a wild bohemian lifestyle.

The world is six thousand years old. Period. "What about archeological discoveries and carbon dating?" they wonder. "Don't worry about that," their Da'as Torah rabbi assures them, "God is just testing you. He made things look old. It's a big sin to think like a Goy!"

Orthodox Jews remain childlike simpleton sheeple even as they become adults. They are unable to fathom concepts of even respecting their spouses or their children's boundaries because they were never taught the right to set their own by an all-seeing God who commands everyone to constantly admonish each other to serve him like flawless angels.

Likewise, their children are raised unable to think for themselves, and so Mommy and Tatie will decide who they will marry. Most Hasid children meet their spouse-to-be one time for fifteen minutes to a half hour before they meet again on their wedding night. *"That was easy!"*

A minute past a half hour might insinuate that the match is not obviously *Bashert* since the beginning of time. They then drink a *lechayim* with their parents, celebrating that the ten minutes of work that the Yenta matchmaker took to pick a boy's name out of a streimel, and a girl's name out of an upside down sheitel, "proves" they were destined for each other since the moment their souls were created during the six days that God created the world. *Oy vey! Have I got a bridge for you!*

Forget about speed dating. Hasidim invented speed mating. Problem is that the blessed couple doesn't even know how to copulate — let alone what an orgasm feels like. But nine months later, they are a full-fledged Tatie and Mommy — ready to spawn a dozen more mindless devotees who will blindly follow the Torah wisdom of their local Rabbi. *Mazel Tov!*

Eighteen years later, they have become carbon copies of their clueless medieval-minded parents. And once again, *they* know zero about dating. On the other hand, during those early twentysomething years that their Goyim peers are busy drinking, fucking, getting herpes and other lovely STD's while popping ecstasy pills during concerts and competing in wet T-shirt contests during Spring break, the young Hasidim are already planning on marrying off their kids as soon as a third-generation Yenta assures them "It's all Bashert!"

While the thirty-seven-year-old Reddit Socratic philosopher king living in his mom's basement masturbates because he despises the concept of marriage and raping a conscious being into a universe in which it begins dying the moment it is born; doing a side-gig while trying to hoard some Ethereum as he complains about his personal trauma of having been raped into existence without his consent, while whining that his cruel parents owe him "big time" and forever; his Hasidic counterparts are already paying a Shadchan so that their "Yiddisheh nachas" grandchildren can be raped into existence. *Mazel Tov!*

Flawless logical declarations of, "Do you think my bumping into his mother at the grocery store (the only one in town that was selling 'two-for-one chicken's feet' that week) was an accident?"

quickly proves the Yenta Shadchon's point. Followed by, "Can't you see how *Hashem* has already arranged that you should drink a *lechayim* with his parents? Does next Sunday at three in the afternoon work for a *Bahzetsen?"*

A *Bahzetsen* is a "sit-down" date where the prospective bride and groom meet one time, where (all bets are on) they agree they're retroactively Bashert for each other since time began. They won't meet again till they stand under the Chuppah, followed by climbing into bed for a one-night stand (that will hopefully endure for many nights with the help of God and Hasidic social pressure) with a stranger they know almost nothing about. Although the conditioned-for-eternity duo most certainly share the commonality of fervently worshiping the same present-day Rebbie who inherited his royal dynasty imperial position because he was also raped into existence.

Once they clink "Lechayim!" the Bashert couple no longer meets and barely speaks on the phone till they meet again on their wedding day. I've been more intimate and shared deeper, and more honest conversations with prostitutes during a one-night stand at some out-of-town motel than these strangers ever open up to each other after ten years of marriage, or ten kids. Whichever comes first.

Women are completely obsequious to their husbands. They emulate Mother Eve and call their spouse, "Rebbi," like the Midrash relates regarding the title with which Eve addressed Adam. Women are a "help-mate" to their husbands. Eve is designated by God as an "Ezer Kenegdo" to Adam (Genesis 2:18). Don't worry, I'm fully aware of the commentaries that try to equate women to men. But the Talmud has a general guiding rule that a verse never abandons its literal simple explicit verbiage. Besides, if a woman is not inferior, why the need for all those erudite scholars to try and equate her to a man? It's contrived and forced due to the obvious following concrete Jewish laws: Why is a woman disqualified from being a witness in a Jewish court of law where the defendant is facing a penalty of death? Why does she not have the same obligation to study the Talmud as a man does? Does her lacking (and licking) two testicles mean that her brain is inferior? And why, to this day, are women not allowed to be the witnesses when a man marries a woman? Why can't she be the tenth man in the quorum that allows a minyan to pray the Kaddish? And why is it the man who always "takes" a woman in marriage and divorces her when he decides to terminate the relationship (Deuteronomy 24:1)? And why can a Jewish man have several wives, whereas a Jewish woman is stuck with just one Jewish schmuck? I can easily list two dozen more examples of a woman's patent inferiority in Judaism.

The Jewish community system, like governments, needs to control their sheeple, and wants to make sure the young couple yearn for each other during their engagement. Seems like the rabbis of yore understood hormones. Typically, the young man writes letters to the father of the prospective bride, thanking his future father-in-law while praising the righteous daughter he raised. Often the young men beseech writers like me to compose the letters they copy in their own handwriting onto beautiful stationary. Mommy adds a stamp and mails it for her little boy. *What the heck? One size fits all. It's all Bashert anyway!*

Forget about ever knowing what scientific carbon dating is. Orthodox Jews practice carbon-copy-mindless-mating. Tatie later pays the blackmail money to acquire the Jewish Get for his "righteous" daughter, as his Da'as Torah Rabbi wrings his "Oy vey!" hands while throwing an invocation neither of them believe.

"I give you a blessing that you should find your daughter's true Bashert in the near future!"

The father then obsequiously inquires his *Da'as Torah* Rabbi to enlighten him with his profound wisdom.

"But Rabbi, wasn't my daughter's first marriage 'truly' Bashert?"

"Of course it was! Everything is Bashert!"

Tatie then wonders, quite nervously since his innocent inquiry might lead his spiritual conduit to God's will to infer that a boorish, upset father is questioning the wisdom of an almighty deity who tolerates the sinful actions of a son-in-law, who is now demanding a quarter of a million-dollar bribe before delivering the Jewish Get to his *Agunah* daughter so that she can have a *Bahzetsen* with her next Bashert potential blackmailer guy who will once again withhold the Jewish Get as ransom if things go sour.

"Even my paying his outrageous demand!" the extorted father cries out, as his heart constricts, while realizing that *he* is the real prisoner.

"Yes!" his Rabbi responds, "Everything is Bashert! Once it happens, it was all the will of God."

"But Rebbi," the emotionally exhausted father now asks in complete exasperation, "how can my son-in-law have free will, as he chooses to sin, and yet you tell me that his freely-chosen decision to sin was Bashert!"

"God's ways are just too deep for us to understand," the Rabbi replies. Sadder than this entire circular conversation is that, as an Orthodox Jew, you are commanded to believe him. Your mind is basically comatose anyway, so it's not that difficult a task.

The more stressful their situation, the more our *Unzereh* believe God is "just testing" their devotion. And their tolerance for pain. If a kid gets run over by some Yenta speedily backing out of her parking spot as she rushes around to a half-dozen stores for bargains to "make Shabbos," the parents aren't supposed to grieve past the timelines prescribed by Jewish Halacha in the Talmud: "Aninut, Shiva, Shloshim, and Yud Beit Chodesh."

Aninut; the moment the parent hears of the death till their child is buried. Shiva; the seven days of mourning. Shloshim; the specific thirty days of laws on a more mild level of mourning, such as not cutting one's hair. Yud Beit Chodesh; the twelve-month period, only upon the loss of a parent, regarding not attending parties, not listening to music, and not buying any new clothes.

Especially bargains! Because you're Jewish. And what is more satisfying than a bargain you found and can boast about to another Yenta bimbette in a snood? Any lengthier amount of mourning would insinuate a lack of faith in God's decision to escort their toddler into Gan Eden with two gorgeous angels holding his hands as they skip merrily into eternity.

Orthodox Jews believe that God never tests the recipient with a situation they can't endure. Even watching their kids pouring out as smoke from a chimney in Auschwitz. Resisting the temptation to question God, they will be rewarded with Eternal Life and hugging their adorable toddler again in Gan Eden. If they fail the test, and question God, as I obviously have, they will be punished for daring to question authority and shamed forever. The "temporary" pain of those who pass God's sadistic, "This will only hurt a little," Mengele game, will be offset by the eternal bliss of basking in the presence of God's glorious *Shèchinah.*

In the interim, no matter what God or his messengers do to us, we should basically "turn the other cheek," since it's for our good. I will never give my enemy my other cheek. Except perhaps my butt to kiss. And I will never "love my enemies." That is the most ridiculous sadistic advice ever given to mankind. It's a total perversion of moral theology. Jesus may have been a masochist. And perhaps I was too. But I finally decided to file for divorce. Although I must admit that during the process there were nights where killing myself sounded like a pretty good idea.

With such instruction, it's easy to comprehend why no one turns their cheek like a Jew does. After all, it was a nice Jewish boy who coined the phrase. Jesus supposedly proclaimed in his Sermon on the Mount, "If anyone slaps you, turn to him the other cheek. And if he takes your tunic, give him your cloak as well." No wonder we tolerate everyone, God included, fucking us! But it does make a lot of sense from someone who believes that he had to crucify himself to himself to save mankind from himself.

"Turn the other cheek," would be like telling a raped woman to now offer her rapist oral sex, or similiar to telling Jewish Holocaust survivors, "If the Nazis take your parents, give them your children as well. If they take your wealth, give them your jewelry, art, and mansions. If they throw you into a fiery furnace, give them your gold fillings." I'll never love Hitler, Titus, Alfieri, Ferro and Schwartz. I would never turn my cheek to Mengele and Arafat. I'd grab an Uzi. I don't hate them. There is no reason or logic to self-immolate in anger and hate. But I will never love such ruthless enemies. I no longer even love God. I only fear him. An Uzi won't work against him. Because he's like an A.I. Terminator.

The "more pain-more gain" mentality is a recipe for self-awareness destruction and netherworld marital misery. The saintly genius, Rabbi Yisrael Meir Kagan (renowned by world Jewry as the *Chofetz Chaim,* after the title of one of his most famous books on ethics), upon being asked how he was feeling, would respond, "Thank God, a little bit worse." This holy angel's pithy response implied that he welcomed God testing him and "turning up the heat," so to speak, so that he would merit more eternal reward in Paradise.

The man was so refined, that I won't dare question his logic. He was an amazing saint and extremely kind. I will never understand why or how he was able to view himself as a sinner. Unless he believed he was being held accountable for being anything less than flawless. A human god. But I do wonder about the needy relationship of a Roman God who constantly intimidates his Chosen People to follow orders. A God who needs to be assured of the blind allegiance of his devoted subjects, loyal servants like Rabbi Yisrael Meir Kagan, who are commanded to sacrifice their lives, and the lives of their children, in sanctification of his name.

The mind-numbing frustration of living a boring, repetitive, circular-logic life is further exacerbated by their "wise" rabbi, supposedly blessed with divine *Da'as Torah*, who assures them that their suffering is priceless, and that this world is completely worthless. If it's all so worthless, why does the rabbi want your tithing money so badly? On the other hand, perhaps he does deserve a full-time salary for micromanaging every second of the tedious humdrum life you spend battling the voices of temptation.

Life in this temporal world is described in the *Pirkei Avot* (Chapters of the Fathers) section of the Talmud as a short seventy-year (Psalm 90:10) walk through a long-convoluted corridor test-track full of lifetime potholes, fog-ahead nighttime driving, married horny women, and insane road-rage babbling Yenta-beeping drivers on the wrong side of the road, along with, "The world is coming to an end! Ze'ev won't go to my Beit Din! Come now!" screaming deer that jump out from nowhere handing you Orders of Protection and summonses to Family and Criminal court, to make you swerve. As far as I'm concerned, you could be Mario Andretti and you're still going to crash.

The dirt-road corridor, after an exhausting, bumpy and sleepless ride — whose highway is landmined with endless flashing red lights and police sirens interrupting you to earn a living, birth and raise children, pay taxes and *Make America Great*; along with gigantic billboards selling you on the concept of eternal life for performing endless good deeds, as the huge Jewish-tradition-advertisements remind you to tithe and donate charity while observing hundreds of commandments and dozens of Jewish holidays, as you turn folio after folio of the endless Talmud that you must study day and night; and then leaving your house upon serving your wife divorce papers and being reciprocated with Protection Orders and Family Court trials for the sexual molestation of your daughters, after which you spend four years of your life chronicling your PTSD lifetime into an emotional literary non-fiction novel — leads, as all roads do, to death, and a supposedly magical, magnificent celestial Disney fairytale palace, where the individual finally gets to put their feet up and rest their bloodshot eyes, to enjoy spiritual bliss, along with celebrating in the festive Leviathan banquet feast. Too emotionally and physically spent to eat.

We are warned not to be distracted from our studies. Why waste time pursuing any of the siren calls of this mortal world for honor, pleasure, fame, or wealth? That would be as silly as an adult spending his lifetime playing like a child with plastic toys and blocks in Nursery School. After all, who decorates a hallway with furniture, beds, pictures, and expensive artwork anyway? And even if the corridor stroll is through a cruel gauntlet of misery, the final destiny is certainly worth the price of a fleeting seventy-year excursion on board an earthly Titanic cruise ship predestined to sink in an ocean called Outer Space.

From the perspective of Gan Eden, the outing will barely be remembered. Our over-before-it-began lifespan, like that of my son Chezkie, will seem more like a rainy-day two-hour picnic with a lot of annoying insects and outdoor bathrooms with overflowing septic tanks compared to the ecstasy we will now experience for eternity. And whether we recall the buzzing sound of mosquitos or the final choking screams of our children in an Auschwitz gas-shower, the memory will somehow be appreciated now that we finally comprehend God's will. "The tears of this world will turn into laughter in the eternal one" (Psalm 126:5). *I'll be laughing hysterically that I never got to speak to Ester again. Ha-ha.*

Orthodox Haredi Jews think it's a sign of righteousness to mindlessly ask their local synagogue kid-rabbi to decide even the most minute details of their lives. The name "Haredi" says it all. It's a translation from Isaiah (66:2) and connotes one who constantly "trembles" before God and is terrified at the thought of sin or wasting a moment of their precious life when they could have been serving the Eternal One.

We have been taught to trust our modern-day sages even when they admit they are not sure of their own decisions. Because even their "Maybe? Who knows? I think so," is considered divine revelation and the culmination of accumulated sleep-deprived years of ceaseless study and total devotion. Their sagacity-state of doubtfulness is deemed to be more ex-cathedra-reliable than trusting a professional Jewish sheeple who is positive they are correct upon reaching the opposite conclusion of the rabbi. It doesn't matter. If their leader suddenly declared the Earth is flat, they would instantly become flat-earthers and fear falling off if they traveled too far.

It should come as little surprise that many of us no longer seek the ecumenical advice and smothering regulation of our rabbis only regarding life's major milestones. It's gotten to the point where many mindless Unzerah's are texting, "Rabbi, should I order chocolate or vanilla for my ice cream sundae?" as they worry that perhaps they are enjoying Olam Hazeh (this transient world) a bit too much, and thereby using up some of their reward in the afterlife of Olam HaBa (the world to come). They hypothesize, in theory, that if they order the flavor they least desire they will not have any eternal joy subtracted from the eternal-life column in their Excel spreadsheet by a bean-counter God.

Meanwhile their Yenta wives are spewing evil gossip faster than their kids ejaculating upon sneaking mommy's iPhone out of her handbag for a few minutes. *God doesn't need to send Goyim to kill us. We're constantly fucking with our own minds.*

In Eternity there will be time to order and enjoy their preferred choice (Chocolate!) from the stingy measure-for-measure God who proclaims that this temporal world was created for spiritual growth only and was not created for childish personal pastime pleasures like ice cream or sex. Surely not a combination of both. *Oy vey!*

Unless your sole intention is the observance of God's commandments while leading a flawless holy life whose existence sanctifies His name, you are sin-shamed for enjoying physical pleasures. Why would you waste time enjoying anything in this world anyway, when the Leviathan banquet awaits your royal presence in the future?

I experienced a lot of angst till I finally stood up to the class bully as a skinny ten-year-old kid. I still remember the sharp pain as Reggie bent my arm way behind my back, possibly a lot further than most MMA fighters have ever experienced (but nothing comparable to the way God twisted it during my divorce), for no other reason than to entertain himself and a few laughing future judges and divorce attorney friends. Reggie chuckled as he insisted that I say, "Uncle!"

I literally saw stars, refusing to say the five-letter common noun, as I winced from the torment of my shoulder joint being stretched toward an angle God never intended when he created me, to the point where I could no longer even remember what exactly it was that Reggie wanted me to say, as tears welled up in my eyes. My arm dangled at my side when The Honorable Reggie Alfieri (not his real surname) couldn't move it any further and finally released it after causing me excruciating pain.

But that pain was nothing compared to the satisfied smirk that I watched spread across his face when he finally let go. I stared at Reggie, trying to understand how a kid (or future wife) could be so mean, and I suddenly swung at him with my good arm, hitting him in the head, as I yelled that if he ever did that again I'd sneak up on him with a baseball bat. Reggie had no clue that I still couldn't move my left arm when I threw my right fist. He would have pummeled me had he known I only had one arm. But I didn't care. Amazingly enough, it was not the pain in my shoulder that finally angered me enough to respond. It was the smirk that I would see on my future wife's face.

Reggie obviously believed me because he never touched me again. That was in the fourth grade. He hurt me many times till I finally fought back. It was probably the best lesson I ever learned at school: don't let someone start a fight that *you* are not willing to finish. I'm not obsessed with feces, but I amaze myself with how much shit I'll still take till I fight back. I never saw that smirk again. Not till I met up with my wife and Victor Alfieri. Or till I finally reflected deeply about God. *Could it possibly be that he is the biggest bully of all?*

Vicious Vic also enjoyed inflicting pain. SS Alfieri's smirk appeared slowly, almost as if he was fighting himself and struggling not to burst out in sinister laughter at the fun he was having garroting my throat while receiving a pension based on his overtime pay for torturing a Jew during his final years in office. And hopefully his final years of life, that I pray he spends in a wheelchair as a stroke victim. Not that I really care. I just hope the demon is immobilized so that he'll be unable to inflict further harm upon innocent fathers. Alfieri has obviously been neurologically impaired and deprived of feeling empathy his entire life. Now I just pray that God makes his mouth droop so that he can no longer yell, "I'm the law in this courtroom!"

Knowing he held all the cards gave The Alf's face this sickening look through which he seemed to dare you to challenge him. Fear is more powerful than the fight itself because it paralyzes the victim from taking action. The PTSD kicks in because you are unable to respond to the instinctive intense physiological "fight or flight" bodily demand to escape danger. Both options are off the table. Fighting is against the law. You can't punch or kill a judge. Running away is a crime. Besides, your driver's license and passport will be revoked within an hour. You therefore experience the third physiological option: "fucked." I was literally terrified to open my mouth as I watched Alfieri, Schwartz, Ferro, and my wife psychologically gang-rape the daughter

I loved.

Normal people want peace at all costs, whereas the insane are ready to go to war if someone steps on their lawn or unknowingly pulls into their intended parking spot at the mall. They instantly scream "I saw it first!" with a ferocity that convinces you they surely must have. And they use the same confident cadence as my wife when she whimpered, "I fear his wrath" to the police. It worked so well that she used those exact words as she sat calmly and filled out her next six Orders of Protection and Criminal Complaints.

Weaker, normal personalities are easily mauled by manipulative maniacs and shrieking despots. Look at Hitler and Stalin. I can't count how many times I also thought *it's just not worth it* as I silently caved into my wife's frenetic demands. Like my father, I allowed my arm to be pinned during my marriage for the sake of my children. As I look back, it was a huge mistake. I too had chosen the path of least resistance, while foolishly declaring "Peace for our time," as Schmuck Chamberlain did upon signing the Munich Agreement.

And like the gentlemanly trustful Putz Chamberlain, I was also duped and never had a moment's peace. Perhaps an imaginary truce during which I told myself that "she's happy now," till the next outburst and demand insisted that I empty the ocean with a spoon full of holes. But never peace. My frantic mind forgot the wisdom my elders taught me: *mit a lefl men dem yam nit oys' shepn*. (You can't empty the ocean with a spoon.)

I now take full ownership for being weak. I was bullied. Trust me. I am not a wimp, but it was a benign, almost subliminal bullying. Somehow, like the religious indoctrination of an innocent unquestioning child, it crept up on me. Like the Talmud's explanation of the sinful deeds of the clever generation of thieves, who lived in the time of Noah, that led to the punishment of the Great Flood. That early generation stole "only one half-penny" at a time, rationalizing that no harm was done, till their victims died due to slow starvation. Like those duped ancient casualties, I also slowly handed over my weekly paycheck and subdued soul to my wife.

The wonderful women with whom I tenderly shared sincere and romantic love; the brilliant professors and rabbis with whom I deeply discussed and debated history, politics, religion, and the Talmud; the tens of thousands of miles I covered as a long-distance runner in my youth; the millions of dollars' worth of glittering diamond estates I purchased with complete honesty from Michael Gross of H.L. Gross & Bro. and many other legendary high-end jewelers, now seem to have taken place during a dream in which one can never see themselves. *Was I really there?*

The diamond and mortgage ads I created; the dozens of children's books I wrote; the years of patiently teaching children ELA and History; the time among so many other happy moments raising beautiful children when I couldn't contain myself a second longer as I burst out laughing in the hallway of our home where I had remained hidden in plain sight, suspended from the ceiling above, as three glorious little faces, who finally admitted they "give up," stared upwards in surprised awe at their Tatie who used the sheer strength of his arms and legs in a parkour stunt to scale the walls while playing hide and seek with them; all seem to have occurred in a different dimension.

Memories of early evening dinners, as I sang while feeding my babies and then read cardboard books to them slowly, as I cuddled my cherubs into an adorable night's sleep after whispering "I love you" for the hundredth time, spoken as passionately as the first time I ever told them the most important words a child could ever hope to hear, while their cute little mommy took vein in the operating room, now seems to have taken place many centuries ago.

My joyous laughter at their inquisitive expressions of impeccant wonder, as I observed each new life I created with a woman I once loved, as the tabula rasa slowly began to observe and marvel at the miracles of the world in which the curious conscious life now found itself, has now been silenced into fleeting thoughts of, "How quickly they all grew up!" in some ephemeral parallel universe that pops in and out of existence in the neurons of my brain, faster than two dancing, imploding, neutron stars.

The busy history of my entire life, including the degrees I attained, the weddings at which I was best man at the momentous events of brides and grooms whose names I can now barely remember, along with spending three decades of my life raising five children, was instantly scorched and erased, and utterly disregarded by a dystopian-during-divorce system of law the moment my wife signed one piece of paper claiming that she "feared my wrath" upon my formally serving her with a Notice of Divorce.

All those once-in-a-lifetime never-to-be forgotten intensely experienced days of my past, that seemed so important to me then, pop up nowadays only as occasional memories that drop by and appear as faint apparitions of individuals I haven't even thought about in decades. Like a flash of lighting on a balmy summer afternoon, they show up as sudden random thoughts in fleeting dreams, or as unexpected dinner guests as I stare at my plate while enjoying lonely meals, and they leave as quickly as someone jolted awake by the nonstop ringing of a screaming alarm clock face that's flailing its long and short arms, shrieking, "You're an hour and a half late for work!"

Isn't our perception of time itself ironic? We look at any future moment as something so urgent and precious — a not-to-be-wasted gem of sorts — that we yell, "Don't waste my time!" as we hang up on a telemarketer, or curse at forces beyond our control while staring at red break-lights, sitting stuck in traffic because some robotic dolt got into an accident while texting his boss that he'd be a few minutes late.

We then panic about punching the clock (great metaphor) ourselves while thinking "I'm late!" as we text our own *manager* (I really despise that word used to describe the profession of a person who wastes his time telling us how to spend ours) that we're caught up in a traffic jam. *God is the worst piddling and petty manager of all.*

Yet the nanosecond that the unknown priceless future morphs into the past, it transforms into the least precious item in the universe. The "anything is possible" exciting future flips into the dull "ho-hum, what next?" boring and forgotten past. The eagerly anticipated about-to-happen "once in a lifetime" event is instantly mutated into a bygone relic, as if never having existed.

An incredible Olympic gold-medal victory instantly transforms from "record breaking" to a rusty record that is now expected to be *broken*. The scene of an exciting night-game football field, flooded with crowds of adoring people cheering athletic young muscular men who are willing to damage their brains for multimillion dollar contacts, amid powerful lights that make it appear as busy and bright as day, turns deafeningly silent and pitch black the moment the sound of that last clicking light switch is heard by the janitor.

And our entire traffic-jammed oh-so-busy lives, spent hoarding invisible electrical digital "coins," while snobbishly bragging about six mansions on three continents and "private collections" of rocks and colorful canvas paints flung by some tantrum-throwing artist, are no different upon the "Lights-out!" declaration of our final heartbeat.

Generation after generation, we continue to live in a mind-fuck-moment of constant fear and angst; preparing, conquering, hoarding, and worrying about a time that can never arrive. Because it becomes ancient history the moment we get there. Our racing minds are unable to slow down long enough to grasp and comprehend that simple thought. *You won't even take a moment to read these few paragraphs, that took me an hour to compose, a second time.*

And so we anxiously race towards a "sky's the limit" precious, invisible destination that doesn't exist, never daring to look back at the ancient deceased archeological past of a mere moment ago. After all, looking back at what was once priceless time would now be such an utter fucking waste of time. Only one in a hundred million people can slow down long enough to enjoy the eternity of the moment in which they exist this very second. *Once again, you can't even spare the time to read this extremely important message a second time. Because you don't have any.*

Many of us live for that limitless sky itself, a heaven in which we'll finally supposedly find peace. After being judged as rebellious, wayward, stiff-necked sinners (for not praying with a quorum of ten men) by a Viking God who gasses his own children while commanding his favorite one to slaughter the patriarch Isaac, we will ultimately be humiliated as masturbating serial murderers, and then tortured and shamed for eternity by an all-loving compassionate God. *Sorry God, but I still like Viking shiksas.*

We continue to anxiously press forward, sacrificing precious sleep and eating constipating "fast food," worrying endlessly about finally "getting organized," while multitasking in order not to waste any more valuable time ever again — never stopping to enjoy the treasure of spending one flawless diamond day of uninterrupted, completely calm, quiet. Similar to ants, we just keep marching.

Like a desperate addicted lottery ticket player who protects his dollar-dream as if it was worth a million dollars, but then rips his delusional "you never know" investment in disgust the moment the drawn numbers prove that he's still a born-loser — even as he stands in line to purchase a dozen more tickets; we also imagine the future is priceless while spitting in admission of how worthless it becomes the moment we look back at the reality of our foraging-for-food existence as we bark our dog-food order while driving through the assembly-line take-out lane at McDonald's.

All that rushing, because our minds are riddled with religious or societal angst and marred by self-delusional expectations of serenity in some perfect "only three more vacancies remaining" future retirement place that distracts us from the beauty of life itself. We have turned this once upon a time Garden of Eden planet into a gigantic garbage dump, reeking fumes, that has destroyed the quality of the sweet air we once breathed as children a mere half-century ago, while we boast about traveling to some other uninhabitable planet light years from our own front lawn, full of insecticides, to victimize and colonize.

We race to the next woman we temporarily hold and the next meal we anticipate eating, without having truly embraced or properly digesting the previous "dish" or dish. We are so tense and wound up that we speak only of unwinding because we are unable to even imagine what it would feel like to be completely unwound. *Is God laughing at us?*

Most lives are now lived as shallow and vapid as the Instagram pages that portray their flesh and blood one-dimensional digital existence. Instagram "dolls" are asking surgeons to make them look like their filtered selfies. And selfie sticks have become one of the most popular holiday gifts. So have the self-pleasuring "selfie sticks," that I imagine many women are purchasing after taking out bogus protection orders as parting gifts to the father of *their* children.

Bat Mitzvah celebrations, family vacations, births, graduations, prom nights, last night's supper, and the all-time favorite (with over fifty million "likes") record holding picture of an egg — along with trillions of photoshopped and videotaped bouncing-buttocks selfies — are the essence of everyone's obsessed-with-social-media attention. Having a hundred million Instagram followers, or acquiring rock-star status as a billion YouTube "views" rocket you to viral "here today, gone tomorrow" fame, is considered more blissful than having achieved boring Nirvana.

Facebook and Twitter completely control (while blatantly blocking voices and views they oppose) the manipulating headline news their algorithms recommend to your video-watching anesthetized brain as you quickly scroll through, and instantly trust, whatever you "choose" to read. You are alerted if the post is suspect, real, or fake, because you're obviously too ignorant to figure things out for yourself. That would take time. And yours is too precious to waste. After all, you're incredibly busy posting your augmented buttocks on six social media platforms while "I Like Big Butts" plays in the background.

Orwell himself could never have foreseen how easy it would become to control the masses, just a few scant years past 1984, due to technology. When was the last time you sat with someone you cared about and had a thoughtful ten-minute calm and uninterrupted conversation in which you paused to contemplate before speaking? Can you even imagine a quiet conversation without a notification ping or buzz as you glance toward your phone that is interrupting your train of thought? *How fast are you reading this wonderful book? What's the rush?*

Everyone is taking selfies or pictures of the remote places they visit. We are now living a snapshot existence, facing *away from* the places we have traveled so far to experience close-up. People travel thousands of miles to barely glance at the seven wonders of the ancient world, racing to snap a selfie while standing in front of a once in a lifetime opportunity to go back in time.

Harried travelers, feeling strained because there's "so much to do," experience nothing more than a few quick premature iPhone snapshot-ejaculation moments of remote places like Machu Picchu, The Blue Lagoon, Stonehenge, or the Great Pyramid of Giza. They pause momentarily, only for the purpose of taking a few pictures, to prove that they were there in their pixel-flesh. People talk too fast, eat on the run, and make love while checking their iPhones. Forget about wasting precious time sleeping. Or thinking.

Whether I live thirty more years or three-hundred-thousand more centuries, I know it won't feel like three seconds the moment I gaze into the past. Unlike the wife of Lot, I imagine that I will not be transformed into a pillar of salt. My memory of her stinginess and the tit-for-tat

CERTIFICATION
SELLER SIGNATURE
11/22/16
BUYER SIGNATURE
Lewinson
Zev
845
300-6127
19
Mariner
Monsey
BUYER'S ATTORNEY

punishment she received for refusing to serve salt to her guests — along with my faith in a chintzy God miserly rewarding his children with eternal life based on delicate scales that measure even one's thoughts — will one day be swallowed by the black hole of my eventual death.

Perhaps "It ain't over till it's over," as rustically stated by Yogi Berra and seductively sung by Lenny Kravitz, but once it's over, it's so emphatically over. We are all destined to become the past in the very near future. So where is everyone rushing to?

I can almost envision God as a stand-up comic. "What's the difference between a premature mortal like Chezkie who has sixty seconds left to live and a newborn that has a thousand-year exciting future lifespan lying ahead?" "Nothing," he responds in his heavenly deadpan voice. Ha-ha.

All the trauma, drama, and passion of my childhood and bachelor life, along with all the tragic intimacy of my married life to an *Eishet Chayil* wife, with whom I once believed I'd share a "happily forever oneness" that would continue for eternity, seems to have vaporized. I vaguely remember the names of the many women I was once tempted to marry, and I realize I never met the stranger I did.

All the endorphin-releasing halcyon Kodak-moments of birthing and raising five beautiful children over almost three decades: bottle-feeding and burping sleepy cherubs in the middle of the night, babies' first teeth, adorably uttered first words, enthusiastically cheered first steps, their splashing water in the baby pool, Prayer Book Day at school celebrating their having learned the holy Hebrew Aleph-bet letters, placing coins under their pillows as the Jewish-Tooth-Fairy, PTA meetings full of thankful pride, moving day to our four-thousand-square-foot newly built six-bedroom home; now seem as hazy as a slow drive through dense fog.

The diamonds I manufactured, books that I published, graduation days of our kids, years that I taught school, holiday celebrations, visitation days at camp, trips to the emergency room, and weddings of our children, have all become hazy memories.

Trips to Israel, the Bronx Zoo and Disneyland, births of our grandchildren, mortgages I signed for on properties that I bought, charities and rabbis I donated money to, fun-filled hours of doing homework while having endlessly long conversations with my kids about life, the funerals of our parents, and four decades of studying the Talmud with Rabbi Nekritz, now seem as if they occurred many millenniums ago.

The twenty-four-thousand helter-skelter vomited-days encapsulating my harried existence now appear like a soup of leftover scraps being stirred in an iron cauldron over an open flame by a warlock named "God." Like a blurred montage of unmemorable lost-count drug-fueled wild-orgy nights lived through a drunken stupor, I can barely recall the birthdays of my six children, let alone the chronological order of the women I dated. Life, even after all the knowledge and wisdom I've acquired, is still as messy as God's primordial ylem sperm the moment it ejaculated and impregnated the universe. *Was he jerking off?*

All of my memories now seem to consist of nothing more than a specter fistful of clumped crinkled pages representing fuzzy bygone half-forgotten days, hastily torn from my page-a-day calendar in a sudden spontaneous rash attempt to maintain its neatness, initiated by my wishful desire for a fresh start and thereby catching up to the present clean, once-again "sky's the limit" new day, as I wonder, "W*hat happened to all those other fresh-start clean new days that are now crumpled in my fist?"*

I think it's time for me to catch my own breath. For too long my mind has jumped between universes, circular-logic fallacious beliefs, and history timetables spanning millenniums. For every diamond I bought, I wanted to purchase two more. For every woman I slept with, I wanted to make love to five more. And for every drink I drank, I anesthetized myself with ten more. *So much I wanted to know, study, and experience, but never finding time to say a simple hello to myself.*

I can't believe how much, and incredibly, how little I've lived these past sixty-nine years. Everything seemed as urgent, rushed and so imminently important then, as it feels entirely insignificant now — an indiscernible illusion, a flurry of years vanishing before my aging weak-vision-eyes — almost as if never having occurred.

My entire divorce, and Sharen's abysmally Mephistophelian alienation of Ester, was merely a bad dream, I calmly reassure myself. It happened a thousand years ago. I'm awake now. The light is on. I'm okay Tatie. You don't have to swear that I'm not going to die. I'm no longer afraid.

I feel so at peace. So relaxed. I no longer care what anyone thinks about me. Even God. Like a newborn nursing happily, unaware and without a care as to how she'll find more milk when she's hungry again — because she doesn't even realize hunger exists — I continue to slowly nurse my coffee as I stretch out on my sofa, like a wise old man lying peacefully on his deathbed, whose years are full, as he passes serenely from this world without desire or regret. I've never felt more in the moment, I realize. Deep calm breath. Have I missed anything for which I wish my soul to experience reincarnation? Not really. I'm finally having such a nice day that I don't need another tomorrow.

Nothing really happening here anyway, I realize. Why not enjoy the beauty of life itself? There is so much art to observe, nature to admire, literature to read, books to write, kind people to meet, stars to gaze at throughout the night, beautiful women to love and cuddle, endless faraway places to visit … wonderful days full of absolutely nothing-to-do and fresh air to breathe. Have a nice day.

Most people spend the majority of their existence in front of alter ego computer monitors and smartphone screens, posting silly selfies, while dressed in clothes wired to be "smart," shackled at their wrists with gadgetry that measures their emotionless heartbeats while counting their steps that lead nowhere.

They jog in sneakers that measures the stress on their knees, while internally armored with stents that quickly cake with their emotional stress, after sitting stuck in daily traffic on tombstone highways for years while rotting away in self-driving cars, videotaped wherever they move on the planet.

They hurriedly gulp down genetically modified obesity causing fast-food as they multi-task a text to their secretary, while angrily engaged in a Facebook posted debate endlessly regurgitating centuries-old political issues over their latest VoIP app, believing they are being sincerely represented by "elected officials" who are nothing more than self-enriching selfish and corrupt catchphrase-spewing pay-to-play politicians ejaculating mouthfuls of vomit on both sides of the isle.

They can't possibly fathom that a simple walk on two strong legs through a silent forest, or along a beach blanketed by delicious salty air, is priceless and all that they really need. *Or ever wanted.* I'll take a powerful heart and healthy lungs inhaling a fragrant mountain breeze over choking on mired-in-pollution rancid city air any day.

Why is everyone rushing? Why do they crowd themselves like rats, with whom they share their abode, to live listless lives in stagnant polluted cities, whose boutique-lined Madison Avenue pavement reeks of the urine peed from the denied-bathroom-facilities homeless living in the stench-filled moribund shadows of so much wealth? Where does their pride originate from, as they Google the net worth of everyone they meet, feeling so proud of themselves simply because their tiny, overpriced cockroach infested apartment sits one level atop their neighbors in a man-made squished beehive called a skyscraper? Kudos to the linguist who invented that word. She certainly helped a lot of builders create the illusion of fantastical mountains out of internment molehills, where all the Manhattanites burrow throughout five boroughs. *It would be nice if the elevators inside some of the buildings on Billionaires' Row actually worked. Poor things.*

Such an arrogant, misleading word, deluding the sluggish, air-deprived, dazed minds of the Zoloft and Prozac medicated but-still-depressed worker-bees buzzing inside, who are much closer to being six-feet-under fodder-for-maggots than they'll ever come to nearly-touching the sky — *or even taking a moment to glance at it.* They can't even see the sky with all the light pollution blocking their vision. No wonder they pop their latest dosage of Zovirax while fucking more often than bonobo monkeys. It's their only temporary escape from depression — because they're jealous thinking about the busily-buzzing person residing in the tad more expensive apartment above theirs, who is jealous of the guy in the studio apartment directly facing his own cocoon because his neighbor gets longer bathroom breaks at work even though they have the same job.

Where is everyone going? And why are they constantly posting the same worthless information about their having taken a shit or birthing a baby on six social platforms? Even upon crashing through the glass ceiling and being crowned "Queen Bee," elevated to reside in the penthouse triplex of the mile-high skyscraper that technology will eventually allow us to build, the dizzy inhabitant therein will only be forced to take a stronger dosage of her medications. Living on top of the world is a precarious pinnacle from which it is so easy to slip or be toppled. *Or jump.*

People snappily battle-cry about goals, deadlines and legacies, warring against their fellowman, as they madly race through their lives in a survival of the fittest competition merely to add a few extra artificially inflated shares to their manipulated-by-CFO's stock portfolio, while never so much as pausing to contemplate how quickly the finish line jumps ahead of all of them the faster the "winner" runs. In truth, the finish line they imagine crossing can never be reached. And rare is the man who understands that it can only be crossed when one entirely stops moving.

At the very least, take a moment to memorize the poignant words of John Steinbeck, who wisely observed, "Socialism never took root in America because the poor see themselves not as an exploited proletariat but as temporarily embarrassed millionaires."

There is no such thing as "going down in history." Where are you "going" if you're gone? The future will always be *over there* somewhere. And the past, although important to study, no longer exists. "It's history," means that it is *gone*.

Just because someone knows what people did in the past does not mean they miraculously revived the dead. Besides, who will revive the historian once *she* passes? Her encyclopedic knowledge of history, soon to be whitewashed and rewritten by the next conqueror, will barely be acknowledged other than by the accolade of "historian" in the three-line *NY Times* obituary that will tersely recap her having spent an entire lifetime reading and researching endless historical accounts of ancient long-forgotten societies and mighty civilizations that no one has time to read because they are too busy scrolling false news on Facebook.

And who bothers to truly study the past? Why trouble yourself to understand the events that brought us to this moment in time when it's so much easier to angrily lash out and protest what you are too lazy to understand. Think it was really Wilbur and Orville who invented the airplane a century ago? Yet you shriek with certainty, like a screaming chimpanzee, that the 2020 Election was rigged. And perhaps it was. But rest assured that your religious and societal beliefs are manipulated.

Man's busyness is a sad and pitifully shallow attempt to exist within a deluded society, externally rushing to know everyone else's business, gossip, financial net-worth, tweets, colleges their friend's kids got into through bribes, donations, or affirmative action, along with endless sport-team data (while feigning total indifference to it all), lest they find themselves with a minute to spare. A minute of contemplation that could change their lives if they were to discover the thrill of looking deeply within, that allows the rare, very fortunate, individual to live in the present. In truth, I see how terrifyingly lonely they all are. *And I have never been happier than when I'm alone.*

We speak of emotional hygiene while rotting to the core of our faux public "I got this!" persona; more PTSD fragile, cracked, and certifiable than Humpty-Dumpty after all the shrinks, shrooms, politicians, and rip-off pharmaceutical companies couldn't put him back together again.

The ignored inner-self is mind-blowing eternally blissful as the "stay-focused!" outer-self busily takes selfies, texts, posts, multitasks, scrolls through feeds, and works weekends to hide from the emptiness of the mutilating void it feels inside. Rushing to escape their own hazy confusion and gnawing feelings of internal lonely isolation, they never pause long enough to realize that they are running away from their own nirvana selves that gently admonishes them to take their time.

But there is nowhere to hide my friend — no matter how many times you complain that there aren't enough hours in a day. And trying to fill the void-within with *busyness* and a manufactured "oh-so-busy, look-at-me, I'm-so-jammed-up" facade, is as futile as extinguishing a fire with rocket fuel. The more on-fire your Daily Planner calendar-pages rage, the more you will pine for some empty whitespace therein.

Stand within a crowd of ten thousand screaming fans at a rock concert and try to comprehend that, in truth, you are the sole inhabitant on a deserted island. Now stand on that island and imagine you are at a rock concert. Can't you see that there is no difference? Keep screaming and dancing while popping those ecstasy pills you sadly need. *To feel loved.*

Most people fear seeing the present. And, more frightening, they are terrified at seeing nothing. Because "nothing" to them means no attachment to the already out of style possessions and conditioned from birth ideological blind beliefs that define them. It means having no indoctrinated preconceived Gods to fervently worship and violently die for; no relationships filled with silly drama, no fame or legacy to preserve, nor any political ideologies to rant against. And worst of all, it means having no favorite seasonal baseball, basketball, or football team to mindlessly cheer for to distract their fearful minds.

But *nothing* is the most beautiful sight of all. *Close your eyes and you will see*. It is a serene oasis from which to quench your parched soul of the dreary lifelong drought suffered by harried humanity. *Nothing* is a place from which you suddenly see and feel *everything*. And best of all, it's a place that allows you to remain completely calm, relaxed, and utterly silent upon grasping the seemingly imperceptible answer to that age-old *"Why?"* question. Because you have nothing to do.

There is no one as special as you. And so you, an enlightened maverick no one will ever know, inhale a deep calm breath as you enjoy the symphony of silence, sipping your third morning cup of coffee from your favorite chipped mug, while conforming bipeds around the globe scurry to create empires that rise and fall almost as fast as the insect-colony hundred-million year old civilizations they mimic.

The once-mighty, now obese, United States of America is fading and waning rapidly. Like the mighty British, Roman, Persian, Greek, and Egyptian empires of yesteryear, the out-of-control cancer of corruption-politics is festering from within its judicially withered body and overburdened, financed, stroke-causing diseased-debt. Fort Knox is as depleted as your worthless lifetime savings as you face hyperinflation upon retirement because your representatives are passing multiple "trillion-dollar budgets" (that's a one-liner for a comedian if I ever heard one) that are so huge, that the interest payments alone increases more rapidly than the Bureau of Engraving and Printing is able to print money fast enough to ever repay.

The rushing sheeple, trapped in a thirty-year conventional life, mortgage, and dead-end marriage (complete with prenup Protection Orders), work overtime, popping blood-pressure and anti-depressant meds, while gasping for air like their fish-cousins, caught in nets filled with plastic credit cards and disposable relationships as they are yanked from their homes upon receiving a Notice for Divorce from a lawyer, an Order of Protection from their wives, and a pink slip from their kids.

Their racing good-as-dead air-deprived minds keep them somersaulting, jostling, competing, warring, and marching — while sounding their *You-Got-This!* battle cry — towards an imaginary cool oasis into which their sweaty bodies desperately yearn to dive upon achieving their fantastical goal of an early retirement. A location at which they foolishly imagine they will *finally* have time to inhale a calm, relaxed, deep, and full breath of fresh air; at the doctor's office while lying on a gurney as they undergo a coronary angioplasty procedure.

Like a fish abruptly yanked out of serene waters that desperately jumps, flips, and bounces about to return to its source of life; mankind is also violently ejected from the tranquil amniotic fluid filled uterus in which they peacefully floated, to frantically rush and thrust, to and fro, acting so arrogantly important, alive, and urgent, as they pathologically proclaim to know their purpose for existence, while in essence living the exact same hunter-gatherer nihilistic reality as their early oceanic primitive ancestors. As Shakespeare entertained us with an eloquent conversation between two men: "Master, I marvel how the fishes live in the sea. Why, as men do a-land—the great ones eat up the little ones."

Like fish, like son. "Big fish eat little fish." With their delusional indoctrinated twenty-first century sophistication (or should I say *sofishtication*) they ultimately mimic the hunt-eat-fuck-sleep-spawn routine movements of their fishy ancestors, living a second-hand existence of hand-me-down antiquated beliefs, while hopelessly trying to survive and catch their own breath as their ebbing mortal life ticks away.

The steady measured beats of the second hand they stared at as they slowly learned to tell time as a child now morphs, almost overnight, like their own accelerated lives, into the fast sporadic intermittent beeps of their hospital monitor till the moving angular announcement of their impending death slowly flatlines. Beep .... Do. Not. Resuscitate.

For most people, it's all about a race to some vermicular and meandering finish line. And that journey's end, often heralded by an elongated-beep-flatline (that like your life, goes nowhere while seeming to race forward), often includes the loss of your bladder and bowel, and your semi-conscious senile mind trying to recall all the things you yearn and still feel the need to do; as you finally arrive at the edge of a six-foot grave where you will be eulogized in minutes; followed by your closest relatives rushing off to split your bottom-line portfolio of properties and off-shore bank accounts; as they then gather to share a final toast to your memory at dinner, where little fish will now celebrate eating the spoils and remains of big fish. *So why exactly is everyone rushing?*

The best closure-medication is *truth*. Even if it takes a twenty-eight-year marriage and trial-separation or divorce from God to discover. No price is too much to pay for truth. I once believed that my wife and God loved me and would never hurt me. Surely not Ester. Sharen's emails, and God's apathy (at best), completely revealed the truth. And I admit the truth hurts. But only initially. Because, as Jesus supposedly said, "The truth shall set you free." Truth, meditative silence, and freedom are synonymous in my lexicon.

The older I get, the quieter I become. The Talmud quotes many wonderful ancient Folk Wisdom sayings from the townspeople among whom the codifiers of our ancient Jewish law lived. "If a word is worth a gold coin, then silence is worth two." This is quite a profound aphorism. The Talmud does not simply mean "any" word. It does not mean the instigating goading words of a Trump Twitter or the deadly *Lashon Hara* of a treacherous pack of overfed and undersexed gossip-mongering staccato-yelping cackling hyena Yentas.

What the Talmud is saying, is that *even* a wise word, a precious word, the most clever words ever spoken ... will never be worth more than *half* the value of reflective silence. Silence is not merely golden. It is the most precious gem of all.

Most words are worthless. But even the best words are semi-precious compared to priceless silence. Without silence, it is impossible to formulate and verbalize the resulting rare wisdom that originated in the thought processes of a silent mind. Without calm introspection, it is impossible to hear and internalize the wise words that are finally spoken. *Or eventually written. Ahem.*

Modern man's brain is so on fire that it rushes through a priceless golden expression like the pithy maxim that I am describing, while hurriedly thinking, "Alright already! I got it! Give me the short version!" Their impatient exasperation at having to take a moment to comprehend a four-word Aramaic ("Milah b'selah, shh'tikah b'train") sagacity, instead of instantly tapping "like" in response to an emoji, only proves how badly they need some silence in their own lives.

Silence is easily worth two. It's worth a billion gold coins. And that's why I swear I'll say, "Stop boring me!" if you dare bring out yet one more shiny latest version of the iPhone through which you unceasingly interrupt my life with a promise of my "saving time" and the seduction that my life will be so much *easier* — after brainwashing me to pay a week's salary for something I never needed the second version of. And so I'll pass on your latest "instant recharger" model. I'm happy to put down my phone and let it, and myself, recharge slowly.

All this and more, as you alert me with endless updates, while I'm constantly being mauled by a noise-pollution cacophony of different pings, rings, zings, chimes, and buzzing app sounds interrupting my sanity. Sounds you carefully researched, whose repetitive alerts condition me to jump like Pavlov's dog to simultaneously catch my friend's latest Facebook post that she hurries to repost on Twitter, Instagram, LinkedIn, and a half-dozen more up-and-coming media sites, while I check my email and text my exercise coach as I tap "like" and "love" on recipes, restaurants, and museums posted from seven continents, while writing my own latest two-cents'-worth post that no one will read if it's more than three words.

Then I can save the string of TED Talks, science videos, mindless memes, favorite songs, talent shows, "Ten-great-bars-that-friends-met-for-drinks-last-night" articles, pictures of my editor's huge Pit bull licking the face of his newborn baby girl, strewn on a cloud of servers that bounces back my age, gender, behavior and lifestyle that alerts advertisers to promote the services I might be interested in purchasing — earning billions, and even swaying elections, while suggesting endless must-have products or services that feed through sponsored posts on my social media pages, or through articles I read in my online *NY Times* and Washington Post subscriptions.

Your clamorous "only three left in stock!" constant invasive blitz and your unabashed instant-response Facebook pop-up boxes, prompting me to join the fray of bouncing emoji shallow reactions before I can even read what you are rushing me to respond to, forces me to write long-winded run-on sentences merely to describe, let alone keep up with, your relentless download of "Breaking News!" interruptions into my once-primeval simple life. *How I miss the good old days.*

Quite honestly, like my marriage, your digital wizardry no longer has any appeal or hold on me. I am no longer fooled by the twentieth century zeitgeist siren promise of "having it all" and "being in control." To my ears it's the barking of a dog. Or the booming commanding voice of an immortal God.

The only true way to "have it all" is to realize *there isn't anything to have.* But that takes more insight than almost the entire population of this planet will ever slow down long enough to begin to fathom. Isn't it ironic that we live in a time where everyone on the planet has the latest iPhone, and yet no one has time for a real conversation?

I'm wise enough to know that no one can ever "have it all." Simply observe the most powerful elite on the planet. Why are they, of all people, constantly buying homes around the globe and selling them after they barely lived there? Why are they paying Virgin Galactic a quarter of a million dollars for a ticket to be flown to the edge of space for a mere three minutes of weightlessness? Do a few jumping jacks and donate the money to charity.

The wealthy play out their frantic *You-got-this!* life while building super-yachts with multiple helipads, after landing on the "One hundred million and above" Patron's list of the world's biggest research hospitals, having purchased the honor through donating a king's ransom to pose for pictures at must-be-seen-at events — after popping a Prozac to stave off their inner sadness (and boredom) along with a Zovirax for their genital herpes delivered by the third spouse with whom they are in the middle of a scandalous divorce in which she claims retroactive sexual emotional abuse and that she was groomed and manipulated (by million dollar gifts) into marrying the man more than twice her age. Why are they smiling artificial smiles through teeth covered with the whitest veneers?

Could it be because their fleeting enjoyment is derived from the fact that we don't have what they have? If everyone drove a Rolls Royce, no one would be impressed. Wealth does not make a person special. The shallowness of the masses who observe the wealthy minority deludes all involved that there is what to be admired. Yet, the ultimate destiny of even the most privileged and powerful chimpanzees who jump and swing from tree to tree on any of the continents circling our globe, will conclude with a few days of their shitting into golden-trimmed Adult Diapers, while their loved ones greedily look forward to a bountiful inheritance.

Like us, they know their ultimate destiny will be the challenge of trying to track the numbers on their Bingo cards with a hazy mind as they excitedly anticipate the number about to be called out by the nursing home staff member who will then serve them ... drum roll ... a jello snack of their favorite color! Yeh ... yeh ... yellow!

Meanwhile the CFO of the assisted living conglomerate chain is busy tallying how many beds became available overnight in order to receive the next batch of toothless jello-loving centenarian toddlers before he himself is rolled out on a gurney through the back door.

Even Omnipotent God doesn't seem to have it all. If he did, why the constant anger? Why is he surprised when his creations sin? And why exhort us not to sin? He already knows that we are not going to obey. And how can theologians insist that we have free will? Free will clearly means that we can *choose* to do things that are *against* the will of God.

And if God "has it all," then why did the Almighty suddenly feel the "need" to create a universe in which his most radical and faithful adherents have been killing each other (in his name) since the beginning of time? If he had it all, then what was missing in his life that caused him to suddenly go into creation mode? And how can God have free will if he already knows what he will choose to do in the future — a future in which he already exists for eternity?

What could God, who "has it all," possibly gain upon creating Adam and Eve, since he had already observed their lives and the immediate murder of their son Abel, followed by millenniums of his own future bright-red artwork displaying merciless bloodletting, rape, and torture. God already witnessed the throngs of devoted future Christian and Muslim servants slaughtering his favorite "Chosen People" eons of time before he even invented light-years when he finally proclaimed, "Let there be light!" Think about this deeply and you will go insane. The Talmud itself agrees with me and prohibits deep introspection and contemplation of this very subject. But don't worry. Few of you face any danger.

I imagine that God very likely *watched* the entire Holocaust as a pulp-fiction movie-trailer preview while his entourage of accompanying angels probably ate manna-popcorn, and then numinously decided to launch the real-life sequel even though he already knew the "Final Solution" ending.

God was also in control, upon deciding to create the world as he stirred the primordial "soup" ingredients of the universe which we humans are the result of (eventually baking some of us in the ovens of Auschwitz), while he watched the snuff-film Rape of Nanking and the ten-mile high mushroom clouds over Hiroshima and Nagasaki six thousand years before directing and allowing the real-life events to take place.

God also watched, and controlled, four centuries of slave ship transports, stuffed with men, women, and children, created in his image, that were packed like sardines, as twelve-million suffocating individuals were brought to build the New World, where many of their descendants are still living a modern-day slave existence as extremely low-paid workers in federal and state politically created corporate gulags called prisons.

Speaking of total control, how can the Midrash and Talmud constantly proclaim that "God looked into the future," if he is, was, and always will already have been there? Isn't God staring into a real Infinity Mirror before making all his decisions? And why does someone who already knows everything need to *decide* anything? Let's be honest. Does this make any sense? *(Why am I still religious?)*

Er ... what exactly was God missing in his perfect life that caused him to suddenly create a world of suffering, poverty, ignorance, war, sickness and ultimately being devoured by maggots in death, to be endured by every single one of its human and animal inhabitants? Was he bored and missing entertainment? How many snuff films can one God watch? And since he has total control, by the way, why isn't he intervening and stopping the constant bloodshed of the mankind he created?

No lightning bolts please, Dear God. I'm genuinely confused and am asking an innocent question as I try to resolve your own confounding game-plan with the pitifully simplistic human mind that you so-graciously placed inside the skull of your son. Perhaps next time you'll add a little more quantum cerebral horsepower so that I can do more than spend my life asking obvious questions that any bright ten-year-old would ask about the way you run and oversee the world.

I know that your thoughts are not the thoughts of man, and that your ways are not the ways of man (Isaiah 55:8), and that in place of thorns a sweet myrtle will come forth in the future. But did you have to abuse us with so many prickly briars for so many millenniums to eventually give us the promised cypress? Allow me to express all this in layman's terms; *Why the fuck do you have to torture us in order to finally grant eternal life?*

Only a boorish arrogant fool, or a person possessed by an insane mind, would attempt to answer or debate in your defense. From the three-dimensional perspective of a rational mind, it is impossible to make any sense of how you "move" in endlessly-dimensional schizophrenic "mysterious ways," as described in a poem by William Cowper (one of the most popular poets of the eighteenth century) after he attempted suicide three times and was sent to an asylum to recover. I'll try and continue to wait for you to explain why bad things happen to good people, but I seem to have run out of patience. After all, I am only human.

I'm sorry, but I honestly wouldn't use Rabbi Harold Kushner's circular-logic lucky-beyond-imagination best-seller (in red *redneck* states where the bumpkins proclaimed, "Thank you Rabbi

Kushner! Now I understand why the Lord caused me to suffer!") placebo publication as toilet paper. But, like Cowper, Kushner was also experiencing insane emotional pain as he tried to make sense of his beautiful son dying at age fourteen due to progeria. Meanwhile, here's my own explanation for why bad things happen to good people (in a world created by God): *they shouldn't!*

I took another sip of my tepid coffee and inhaled a long, deep, calm breath to slow down my thoughts as I realized that simply swallowing some lukewarm liquid while breathing fresh air early this morning has already proven to be a more productive day than my mindlessly having set out at dawn, rushing to conquer the seven continents of this planet and acquiring all of its revenue and riches by sunset, studying the entire Talmud by midnight, and then making love to one thousand Playboy Playmates that includes a threesome with Sade and Lisa Stansfield (hopefully they'll be able to still sing a few bars after I exhaust them) in my newly built harem till sunrise. Like watching the slow stream of tears running down Ester's cherubic flushed face as she stood in the dimly lit hallway of my nocturnal imagination ... it's all a dream.

When I was a young man, like a metaphor reflecting my ACE childhood life, cloudy skies and rainy cold weather severely depressed me. It wasn't till my mother handed me that one-way ticket to Ner Israel on a cloudy day that I discovered the beauty of life. As I stared at the steel-colored dark gray skies, while sitting in an oversized first-class seat for a skinny five-foot, four-inches tall fifteen-year-old, I kept barely whispering "no thank you" every five minutes in response to the pretty stewardess who kept asking before takeoff, "Honey, can I get you something?"

I was so shy I almost started crying as she kept attempting to serve me, almost fainting when she crouched down and met me eye to eye, as she praised my "beautiful blue eyes." "Thank you," I nervously whispered in near tears. Suddenly the pilot announced the plane was about to take off. The sweet young stewardess, in her tight skirt, daintily rushed to her little seat and the plane took off.

I would have given a year off my lifespan, and sacrificed my left testicle to relieve my right one, just to spend one blissful night with the petite first-class beauty. In our sexually repressed puritanical society, where it took till the dawn of the twenty-first century to decriminalize breastfeeding in public, she would have been convicted of rape and forced to spend twenty years in jail for taking me to heaven. My thoughts of cupping her tight butt in my hands while lying on top of her, and her then lying on top of me while I tenderly fondled her breasts, faded away quickly because I couldn't even find the courage to talk to her. *Could she tell that I masturbated when she looked into my eyes? I'm so embarrassed!*

As the plane soared higher, it suddenly burst through the seemingly impenetrable clouds and I was almost blinded by the beautiful light of our sun. I laughed at myself as my "bad mood" changed instantly and I experienced a moment of enlightenment as I recognized that it's always a "sunny day." It was in that one moment that I realized to always look past the ashen-colored stormy clouds that gathered before flooding my life with pain. What appeared solid, permanent, dark, and foreboding a moment ago was nothing more than my imagination and Mother Nature clumping water vapor into raindrops to nurture the earth.

It took me another five decades to look past our sun, societal norms, cultish beliefs, and our entire solar system, as my mind now blissfully observes billions, perhaps trillions, of galaxies in possible multi-universes as I imagine light waves from distances too far to fathom and too bright to see. Like the leaden clouds of my youth, I now understand that the "bad" weather, toxic relationships, angry finger-pointing gossiping sheeple and fanatical ignorant people, along with most of what had ever saddened or depressed me during my entire life, were never anything more than an external illusion of mist.

And so after enduring more than a half-century odyssey of abusive maternal, stepdad, spousal, divinely orchestrated dysfunctional relationships, including the most emotionally scurrilous one of all that I continue to barely endure with *The Source* that declared me as his lucky "Chosen," I finally found myself. I am silent. I am happy. I am at peace.

I guess some people would describe that experience as being reborn. I must admit that I am blessed as I breathe slowly and deeply for the first time in my born-again life. Silence is worth two billion gold coins.

I really must send my ex some flowers and mint chocolates (her favorite). Perhaps I'll even invite her to meet me for dinner at a nice quiet Italian restaurant, with soft music playing in the background, to whisper my final adieu as I hand my Ameca ex-robot, designed to exhibit human-like facial expressions, an autographed copy of my book *(To my loving Vybie, Shalom! Love, Zevie),* as I shed a few tears of joy thanking her for the half-dozen children she gave birth to while remaining an emotionally frigid size-two since the day we first met. Robotic wives wired with Artificial Intelligence can't gain weight, I realize.

After discretely placing a single thornless black rose on her white dinner plate as we're being seated to an intimate dinner for two, I'll order an expensive dry red (my wife always was so cute when she got a bit tipsy), cautiously keeping an open eye, but never again staring into hers, as I guard the bottle from the insertion of potassium meds that slow down a bypass patient's heart. My *Eishet Chayil* force-enlightened me, I suddenly realize. She was a good wife. Like Charles Cullen was *The Good Nurse. Thank you Sharen! XOXO*

Criminal Justice Reform has finally become a hot topic. Many arcane legal doctrines, like the draconian Felony Murder rule, which is about as barbaric as that literal "Eye for an eye" commandment, have been deleted from the law codes of every country on our planet. Except the United States. New methods of rehabilitation, imported from countries like Norway and Paraguay, are enlightening many refined minds as society moves away from allowing inhumane authoritarian despotic judges like Alfieri and punitive ruthless prosecutors (too many to mention) free reign to destroy individuals and their families.

Medicine, science, physics, and neuroscience are speeding along at a pace that strikes fear in the hearts of sloth-like deadweight beings called managers and bureaucrats. Ethicists are doing a good job in convincing politicians and the religious right to calm down and that it's completely moral, and logical, to conduct fetal tissue research in the quest of discovering the next vaccine that will save the human race.

Improvement is certainly only a matter of time. Mankind has thankfully evolved from their enjoyment of gladiator blood sports and watching public burnings of wayward Marranos and is now content with football and MMA. And our courts, although still proclaiming their trust in God, no longer burns witches at the stake and merely enables perjured protection orders being issued against innocent husbands during a divorce.

The wealthy and powerful minority will always take advantage of the weak, the tired, and the poor majority. But the masses are waking up thanks to the speed at which information travels today.

Fortunately, Freedom of the Press grows ever stronger thanks to the internet and endless apps — even as reporters are tortured and murdered in countries like Iraq and Mexico or strangled and hacked to pieces inside the safe perimeter of the Saudi consulate itself. There is always a lull in free speech due to the initial message of intimidation and violence instilled by the despots trying to protect their image and stolen wealth. Putin is a master at this. *(Please make my plutonium cocktail a double. On ice. "Stirred. Not shaken." Don't want it to blow up.)* But it's always eventually replaced by the woken individual's ferocity and the collective willpower and passionate desire of "The People" for freedom of expression.

Assange and Snowden are the human sacrifices delivered up to the ungodly pagan bastards who rule the planet. Exactly like my marriage and (what was inevitable from day one) divorce. I was slaughtered in divorce court by a monster that idol-worshiped his overtime paycheck and a cute gargoyle wife who insisted that our 401K's and beautiful house belonged to her. My Divorce

Decree became my freedom papers of emancipation. *Free at last! Free at last!*

That freedom was paid for by surviving counterfeit Orders of Protection. Ironically, instead of sacrificing myself to save the life of my daughter, her life wound up as an offering to secure my freedom. Yes, false protection orders are terrible. But at least Ester and I have a chance, no matter how unlikely, to perhaps one day resume our once-awesome father-daughter relationship. Our courts that instantly grant custody to a mother, due to their antiquated assumption that the bond between mother and child is stronger than that between a father and his child, will one day figure out what psychologists know and what fathers have always known.

And while too much of what our penal system has to offer is certainly a nightmare for the hundreds of thousands of basically innocent and poorly represented (and hence excessively punished) masses who wind up sitting in jail suffering unimaginable life-ebbing stress and physical brutality, but at least they are not being castrated, lynched, disemboweled, and drawn and quartered. But even their chances at being exonerated exists because of forensic DNA and new technologies that can pick up and read the slightest impression of half-century old fingerprints.

Society is slowly becoming aware that many "prisoners" have low intelligence and already face horrific odds at acquiring an education or future job while forming as a fetus in utero, let alone upon birth. Science now proves that these chaotic-from-conception "criminal" cherubs are essentially born behind bars, and more likely to lead a life of crime than young Baron Trump leading a life of fortune and fame.

On a more futuristic note, we are living during an impossible to fathom moment of time. The industrial revolution will look like a match held up in front of the atomic power of the sun as we enter the Quantum Age. Most people are unable to perceive that the processing "toys" we are so excited about today are like babies who are just beginning to learn how to babble their first cute words. The biological and scientific inventions that the accelerated superconducting extraterrestrial-like computers are destined to create will appear as the hands-on handiwork of God. In fact, they will cure much of what God ails us. All in all, I'm excitedly optimistic about the future. Whether I'm here or not. I do pray that Alan Turing can see all this from heaven. *Hopefully God has become more tolerant and allowed Alan entrance through his Pearly Gates.*

Government and religion will never more than temporarily crush the free spirit and curious minds of their followers. Modern-day communication, delivered at the speed of light when traveling through the vacuum of space, hastens their demise. It's harder than ever to control the Edward Snowden's of the planet. Even if Big Brother hoards every Facebook post as a permanent record of your behavior, along with using the latest facial recognition technology to record your constant whereabouts, The State will never control the evolving enlightenment of mankind.

And blind faith in an All-Merciful perfect God, who invented confusion and temptation by allowing the silent voice of the evil-inclination Satan *(the Yetzer Hara)* into the minds and hearts of men, while keeping his "lucky" Chosen People insanely busy observing endless mindless regulations and punishing them for being unable to stomach the detailed minutiae of nonsensical laws, is becoming too tough a dogmatic pill for far too many intelligent people to swallow. If you think becoming a member of the Yakuza is tough, try some genital-mutilation circumcision upon converting to Judaism. And many women are tired of deluding themselves that they are not second-class, contaminating menstruating incubators who cause a divine decree of death upon their husbands if they fail to first immerse in a mikvah, as dictated by Jewish law.

Like every single Egyptian home that was plagued by death the night before the famous Exodus of the Jewish Nation, there is barely a house in Monsey that has not been smitten with a child who has left the fold. *I can't believe I'm writing this knowing I'm going to burn in Hell.*

Before the invention of the printing press the minds of Europeans were subject to the ideas and belief systems of the few zealots in the entire world who could read Latin. Or read, period. Books were extremely rare. Knowledge was scarcer. The Church was the sovereign authority through which God bestowed truth upon the devoted faithful ignorant, duped flock. Superstition and illiteracy coupled with a "trial by fire" system of jurisprudence was the norm of the world. (Like Alfieri's modern-day courtroom.) It was against the law to read the Bible on your own, even if you had some education, because you might interpret its message incorrectly. Like translating "maiden" as "virgin." Or "rays of light" as "horns." Trial by error was unheard of and verifiable truth was almost non-existent. Higher education and science (the slither that existed) were completely controlled by the Church.

Scientists who discovered anything in nature that opposed the Gospel "truth" of Matthew, Luke, and bi-polar Paul, were accused of heresy and blasphemy. Great thinkers and brave observers of nature were declared heretics, and hence traitors, and were burned at the stake or hung in human-shaped cages. Galileo's life was spared only because he accepted a plea bargain deal to remain under life-long house arrest when he copped a guilty plea. The Apostles all contradict one another, but somehow the Church spun and spewed a combination of dogma and threats to declare that it all made sense after all. If the Church controlled science and education in the twenty-first century we would still be drawing stick figures in caves. If you think I am joking, please explain why blasphemy is still punished by death in Afghanistan, Iran, Pakistan, and

Saudi Arabia. But keep protesting against Israel.

The Church decided that Mary was a virgin. Jesus was declared the Messiah from the House of David (even while admitting Joseph was not his true biological father). Jesus was then promoted to God status. He commanded 'Thou Shalt Not Kill,' but then decided he needed to serve himself up as a fleshy, bloody, human sacrifice. To himself. Shall I go on? Or can you comprehend how abysmally absurd this is? It was the empirical observations of mortal man that surely had to be mistaken. After all, they were merely sinful mortals who dared to question sacred doctrine, whereas the Holy See spoke ex cathedra. Lifespans were short and people thirsted for food and drink. Not for knowledge.

We are at the start of the year 2022 and Israel recently won its thirteenth Nobel prize. Almost a quarter of all Nobel award recipients are Jewish. Not only have we miraculously survived unimaginable persecution for thousands of years, but even after facing near extinction in the twentieth century, we arose from the ashes of Auschwitz and thrived like the mythical Phoenix, gifting a treasure of medicine, economics, technology, literature, art, science, and dare I say, religion to an indifferent cold-hearted world that observed our near genocide in apathetic silence. Christians and Muslims would still be worshiping polytheistic pagan gods in nature and sacrificing their virgin children to some angry volcanic monster if it wasn't for our patriarch Abraham. The first *Jew*.

We didn't merely turn our cheek, we gave you our gold teeth, hair, children-lab-rats, and whatever little fat remained on our skeletal bodies. *Can I get a witness?* (Certainly not on any college campus, or from many imbecilic Congresswomen.) Meanwhile medieval Muslims are removing the clitorises of young girls on several continents based on an archaic interpretation of a possible religious legal opinion that was espoused and commanded by a misogynist lunatic. Another major debate among these refined scholars is just how much of the female genitalia needs to be hacked away to fulfill their tradition of exerting complete dominance over the sexuality of young Muslim females.

Amazingly, the restrictive abortion laws in many Muslim countries are now more tolerant than in several of our Bible Belt states, such as Alabama and Georgia. Meanwhile, abortion is basically free in The Holy Land where the command "Thou Shalt Not Kill" was first proclaimed. *Isn't history fun?* Israel is ranked in the top five most innovative countries in the world and the life expectancy there is a tad more than three years longer than for citizens living in the United States. Is it any surprise that hardly any Palestinians living in Israel want a Palestinian passport when a two-state solution is finally reached?

Many practitioners of FGM (female genital mutilation) believe the clitoris implies maleness and that it is ugly and dirty. *What's a dick? Especially a yucky-gucky Goyim one!* The religious fanatical parents believe their little girl's G spot (and too many additional letters) must be sliced off to enhance the beauty and femininity of their young woman (typically age seven, or younger). "Mutilation" is actually a benign word to describe the searing pain (just to pee) and lifetime medical issues most of the women endure once they've suffered this ghastly procedure. Most Muslim women are very religious and refuse to discuss the religious barbaric crucifixion of their pussy, (Why am I suddenly hearing the powerful voice of Tom Jones singing "What's New Pussycat!" in my brain?) The subject matter of anything sexual is taboo in their society and the assault is underreported. It should be called a "clitorisfixion!" If a radical religious Muslim can remove the clitoris of his own daughter, how much effort do you think it would take him to slit the throat of an infidel Jew?

A mere century ago the population of the entire planet was only one quarter of what it is today. And at the time of the Black Plague, the census of the entire world was roughly the same figure as the present population of the United States. And people, whose lifespan was still hovering at around four decades at the close of the nineteenth century, were even more illiterate *(hard to imagine)* than today's texting-and-sexting American citizenry. Forget about imagining the right or notion of thinking, speaking, or a belief based on their own logic and personal introspection.

After all, in a world where merely questioning a king or pope could quickly lead to being burned at the stake or drawn and quartered as a traitor, how could one even begin to imagine a need for verification? Who even knew what science was, let alone understood the scientific method of "rinse and repeat" empirical observation (and falsifiability) followed by endless peer criticism and review?

For having the audacity to state that the earth revolves around the sun, Galileo was ordered to appear before the Holy Office to stand trial, in a court as kangaroo as Alfieri's future hellhole, for his "heretical belief." *I can only imagine what the Holy Office would have done to Einstein. How do you execute a Jew twice?*

It took three hundred and fifty-nine years for the Vatican to admit Galileo was right. And it took four hundred years (a near half-millenium) for the Vicar of Christ to apologize and fucking-feebly state that the Catholic Church "regretted resorting to violence" when it burned the brilliant philosopher Giordano Bruno at the stake after stripping him naked and hanging him upside down, for questioning the virginity of Mary and for theorizing that stars were infinitely distant suns that were surrounded by their own circling planets. *Why do I love Shiksas!*

The total insincerity of Pope John Paul II in the year 2000, after admitting regret for the earthly hell inflicted upon Giordono Bruno, was revealed when the morally blind ruler of the Holy See still insisted that the brilliant mathematician and brave freethinker, whose tongue was literally gagged to prevent his logical replies to Cardinal Roberto Bellarmino (who was canonized in

1930), was nevertheless still a heretic (i.e. "We're never letting him into heaven!") whose writings were still "incompatible with Christian thinking" and remain on the Index *Librorum Prohibitorum* list of banned books. If the Pope had any real prophetic prowess, or a real set of balls, he would have bestowed Bruno with sainthood and placed the canonized Bellarmino in the garbage can.

Fortunately, no one can gag my tongue. My First Amendment rights allow me to share my own divorce experience with millions of similar victims; the parents of over one million suffering American children a year whose entire lives are forever upended, altered, and permanently damaged because of punitive-putz judges like Alfieri who destroy their relationship with their parents. But the truth is that I always had the right to express myself. Way before any governing group of wealthy slave-owning old White men, sporting smelly powdered wigs full of parasites, scratched their permission on a piece of parchment.

And that is why I believe that the pen is truly mightier than the sword. Swords destroy. They wipe out civilizations and force the will of the despotic few upon the deluded and manipulated masses. The sword (fear of its violence) is all about control. Words create. They slowly shape history. They build civilizations, libraries, and institutions of higher learning. Words are what separates the genteel man from the wild beast. They are the spiritual breath of life that allows the soul to express its innermost thoughts, passions, and ideas. Gently.

Words are the air that we breathe, live, and use to express love. Words allow us to share many beautiful artistic concepts, ideas, literature and poetry with all of humanity. Words obliterate ignorance, fear, religion, and the silly man-made borders that the wealthy use to create an illusion of a country with an army that will "protect you," while endlessly taxing and maintaining control over their own populations. In a peaceful war of ideas, words are exchanged in place of missiles to determine the winner of a sincere debate. A feat that can only be accomplished when both sides share the same desire for ultimate truth and peace, and not by carving up journalists or spicing cocktails with plutonium. Words are beautiful. They reveal how ugly and barbaric governments and religions are.

That is why I believe the First Amendment is more holy than the Ten Commandments. Words allow us to question a God who "spoke" and created the universe. Remove words from men and they become nothing more than bickering politicians. Grunting animals. Go ahead and extradite Assange, for nothing more than handing over a treasure trove of documents to the New York Times for publication, and dig the grave of our democracy deeper.

Is it of any surprise that public trust in our despicable government in Washington remains at a disgraceful low rate of under twenty percent? Makes an awful lot of sense when you match that paltry rate with the twenty-one percent of the adults in our country who are functionally illiterate. And yes, thank God that I live in a democracy where I can write this, and not under the control of the Vatican where I would probably be stripped and hung upside down and burned at the stake for heresy.

I speak of freedom of expression appreciatively because there are so many barbaric places on this planet where it is still illegal to speak freely. China no longer even pretends to allow free speech and they are further tightening the muzzle on Hong Kong as I write this paragraph. Many countries technically allow freedom of the press, but then arrest their journalists on trumped up charges of "hooliganism" and "tax evasion." As if the bad-boy thug, Emperor Putin, ever paid a kopek in taxes. And many South American countries allow freedom of the press, but their journalists risk having their decapitated head sitting on a spike, or their naked, mutilated bodies hanging in public display off some bridge in Acapulco. Their executioners strike with impunity because too many of the publicly elected officials are being financially rewarded not to investigate.

The pantomath Renaissance man, Joseph de Maistre wrote, "Every country has the government it deserves." But I honestly believe we deserve better. Much better. *We The People*, were already guaranteed our First Amendment rights on the 15th of December in 1791. I am not a traitor when I claim that a complete overhaul of our government is long overdue. The average taxpayer is not as gullible as our politicians believe. He is simply scrounging to make ends meet and busy paying child support, while our politicians are busy with insider trading, pork-barreling at work, vacationing on their yachts, and partying with celebrities and models.

Like dealing with a dead marriage, we're just exhausted and slowly relinquishing our autonomy. As a matter of fact, the signs of a dead marriage are exactly the same symptoms we experience as citizens. We don't trust our partner. We are lonely. We don't even think about sex. We're depressed. We overcompensate by spending way too much time on social media because we fear our abusive partner (who we know will run to take out Orders of Protection, or file for our extradition). And the most obvious one: we are worried about our finances. This would almost be funny if not for the fact that we're too weak to laugh.

Things must change. And anything we wind up with will be better than the government we have now. *We should probably try to establish a democracy. In theory, they seem to work beautifully.*

The battle for freedom never ends. The earliest casualties are the brave, heroic minority who are the first to finally protest the injustice of The State, and are mercilessly slaughtered as sacrificial lambs. Next in line are the fierce warrior journalists who are intimidated, jailed, and silenced (the worst death of all). But the desire for freedom never dies. Man's instinctive and inalienable right to live free only intensifies in the face of cruelty and injustice.

Malcolm X beautifully expressed the natural existence of man as a free being when he stated, "It is only when the freedom fighter realizes that he needs to stop asking for freedom, stop demanding freedom, stop trying to even take his freedom ... that he understands that he was already born free." He might sit in jail for ten years. But he is free in his mind and heart. Now it's only a matter of some iron bars. Or the serving of divorce papers. *Or the walking away from one's God.*

Man never needed permission to be free. All he had to do was be willing to die for his freedom. Yes. It was that simple all along. *Like Dorothy clicking her red slippers and waking up, as she realized she had always been home.* What most people fail to realize is that without their precious freedom they are already dead. So why should they not risk dying to avoid certain death? I now realize I have always been free. My only prison was that I trusted the voices outside my head and allowed them to enter my mind and eventually clog and enslave my heart. *I'm an innocent child once again. A happy child. I think I'll go outside and play.*

At least God didn't create me during the eighteenth-century Puritan witch hunts or the era of the Spanish Inquisition. Surviving my unhinged *Eishet Chayil-Torquemada* was more than enough torture for me. Mankind has no choice but to figure out how to clean up the mess that an all-powerful all-knowing God created "in order to test them."

And so, to God:

The experiences of the life you forced me to live through has somehow provided me with the unique ability to calmly see through the transparent lives of most people. I even see through you. And at the risk of sounding a bit rebellious, I must be honest and say that nothing you do makes any sense. *Nothing*.

I see a God who refuses to be seen or comprehended. A hidden God that purports to being extremely kind yet presents himself as diabolically evil. The five books of Moses are full of threats and prophetic curses, many of which were carried out. Being a religious Jew almost forces one to suffer from PTSD while developing OCD.

We are supposed to be perfect, down to our thoughts, even as you supervise and promote a holocaust worse than any nightmare a human could ever dream up. We are supposed to cry out "Shema Yisrael!" as we enter the gas chambers with our children under the presence of your all-seeing eye.

How you, dear God, observe the world you created without taking ownership for so much destruction, torture, famine, incarceration, illness, and emotional pain is beyond me. You blame the children you created for *their* sinning — knowing exactly what the future held in store for them as you tempted and ensnared them to sin. You then punish them in this world, holding them accountable for their iniquities, and eventually send them off for a stint in Hell.

You create monsters like Titus, Tomás de Torquemada, Hitler, and Stalin, and then have them ruthlessly execute millions of Your Chosen throughout the centuries for "sins" such as wearing linen and wool woven together, kindling a fire on the Sabbath, or eating bread during Passover. *I suppose the absence of parents in your life has afflicted you with many negative adverse childhood experiences.*

You created my wife knowing that she would waste thirty years of my life. I even sought the opinion of the man who I believed had the most *Da'as Torah* of all before I agreed to marry her. Why did you punish me? Aren't my few paltry moments of existence important to you? Why did you send wild beasts like Alfieri, Schwartz, and Ferro to devour Ester's adolescence and future relationships with men, along with so many years of my life? *She was such a happy child. You judge like Alfieri.*

Surely you knew the exact number of folios of Talmud I could have studied in depth during those years in which my life was wasted sitting in a kangaroo court and shortened through stress. Worst of all, your utter lack of mercy or compassion for Ester proves that you are very ungodly.

You know how I suffered watching Ester as she received a lobotomy that restructured her brain to hate the father who prayed to you with so much sincerity that her soul take shape inside the form of a blue-eyed cherub. You know how my heart twisted itself into knots as I clutched my chest in shock while staring at those "Die Zev! Die now!" green-monster regressed-child drawings. You know the dread I felt as I sat in court, trying so desperately to get some visitation, as I watched your messengers from fucking Hell destroy my daughter. How does a God even *think* of creating a place like Hell?

You spent hours listening to my prayers begging for Ester to be born healthy. And you know I stayed married only because of her. You know how I pleaded with Sharen not to submit to an amniocentesis test because I was terrified of a possible miscarriage, or Ester being harmed if her blood mixed with her mother's icy lifeblood. (Meanwhile it was the mother who is abnormal and probably genetically insane from birth.) And then you took her away from the only person who really cared about her. You mercilessly fed her to wild dogs. Like a heartless Nazi.

You know how gently I spoke to Ester from the moment she was born. You saw how tenderly I held her in my arms, and how I lovingly stared at her as I smelled her brand-new faint baby-breath. You saw the tears in my eyes as you listened to me whisper, "Thank you Hashem. Thank you!" So please forgive me, but like I wonder about the darling wife I once had, "Are you fucking insane! How could you be so cruel?" *Where is your Da'as Torah, God?*

Where has your empathy been since the beginning of time? And what's so amazing is that I'm one of the luckiest people on the planet. So please don't think I'm complaining. All in all, I've had a wonderful "been there-done that" life. But that's my exact point. If my pain-filled traumatized, white-privileged lonely life is one of the luckier ones, then I can only pity the unlucky lives of the majority of the seven and a half billion people on the planet.

How were you able to watch oceans of Jewish and Gentile blood flowing for millenniums and not cry over the horrific mess you made? Man has lived in darkness from the moment Adam opened his eyes upon your blowing a soul into his nostrils as you turned a mound of dirt into the patriarch of all mankind. Cool trick, but couldn't you enlighten him a bit while you were at it?

You dispense "justice" as recklessly as Alfieri while you probably sit in front of a plaque that reads, "In Myself I Trust." *I no longer do.* I have prayed enough. I worshiped you faithfully. I was once a true *Eved Hashem* who believed that anyone abusing me was somehow a messenger delivering "God's will" and that I deserved to suffer in silence.

I'm sorry God, but I can't sincerely thank you for the pain. *Because it was too painful.* My heart tells me the truth. I didn't deserve it. And don't tell me it's payment for things I've done during past lifetimes I've lived. Especially when you claim that you punish "measure for measure." How is that even possible since you never inform the recipient exactly what it is that he's being punished for? *How could I possibly rectify things I've done in another lifetime that I no longer remember?*

I can only tell you what I feel. I'm sorry, but you are the one who has sinned. You hurt me repeatedly from the moment I began smoking in my mother's uterus. I suppose that I should thank you for not smoking me out of an Auschwitz chimney. Or did you? Did I die there in a prior lifetime? Did you reawaken my scorched soul because I failed to complete the spiritual mission that I was completely unaware of in my past life? And how am I supposed to know what my present mission is when you reincarnate me as a helpless Raggedy Ann tabula rasa baby placed into the foster care of a certifiable bonobo-fucking wire-monkey mommy? See how crazy you make me?

You owe me an apology. I'm not expecting one, because, like Sharen, you think you're perfect. But I will now live my life. I am aware that there is no such thing as "letting go of the past." It becomes a part of you. It winds up in your present, becomes engraved in your synapses, and hence it remains as part of your future. But I've learned to embrace the past and to appreciate the lessons my experiences taught me. I suffered as I turned into rust. And I healed through silence and became polished 24K gold.

I now share my advice. Suffer, and heal. But do not take revenge. Vengeance is for fools. You will become like those who deserve the punishment you wish to inflict. Besides, you will literally die trying. Because abusers have a much higher tolerance for pain (due to their inability to *feel*) than you ever imagined. They enjoy fighting and inflicting agony. An eye for an eye? Why not? As long as they can gouge out yours in exchange for the pleasure they receive while continuing to stare at the empty socket in your face with their remaining one. *Wanna try again!* Do you really believe they will ever understand the real message you so desperately desire to teach them? A lesson that every three-year-old toddler already knows. *"Be nice."*

Alfieri will always believe he is the world's greatest judge. "What's one less dad?" Schwartz thinks he deserves a "Super Lawyers Rising Star" rating. "What's one less husband?" Bundy went to his grave convinced that he never did anything wrong, and that "pornography" was the cause of his murderous killing sprees. "What's a couple of lives worth in the big scheme of things?" Putin believes he is completely justified in attacking and destroying a sovereign country based on his delusion that the paper dragon NATO is arming itself to attack Russia. He probably considers himself a generous benevolent ruler as he withholds from nuking Ukraine. "Who is going to miss a few million people anyway?" And my mezuzah kissing ex-wife would swear she has always lived a life of flawless moral perfection while calling the police to drive me to jail on Shabbat and sending our daughters to call Rabbi Nekritz a piece of shit. "Who are nekritz and zev?"

Whether you quote "Revenge is mine, I will repay (Romans 12:19)," or "Lord is the God of vengeance (Psalm 94:1)," he obviously needs anger management. And eventual enlightenment. A human being should never venture into such hellish territory. And don't ever bother looking for "closure" or "justice being served." You will become mired in the dark negative past. I have too little time in front of me to harp about, or live in, the past. I only go there to cry a little and sort things out in order to live more peacefully in the present. Mostly, I travel there to recall many of the beautiful memories of the wonderful people who will forever remain part of my consciousness.

I finally realized that I don't have to figure everything out. A logical mind will never be capable of explaining an irrational wife and God. And a kind soul can't possibly give sincere thanks to a murderer of innocent children. Nor should I be expected to fix a flawed world that a supposedly perfect God created. It's enough that I raised a family of five, gave charity, studied the Talmud, and published gorgeous books for kids. If I die tomorrow, I die in peace. Ciào.

The best closure is to comprehend that closure doesn't exist. What happened, happened. It doesn't always have to make sense. The universe is what it is. Breathe. Deeply. And laugh. Laugh, laugh again. Eventually you'll be able to laugh beyond your imagination. I have never been so happy or viewed the world as so marvelously beautiful as when I ceased looking for closure. I stopped groveling and obsequiously begging God for answers. I've learned to look within. My heart knows the truth. I am not a sinner. And God, who seems to be living inside an insane asylum, and surely not in a transparent glass house, should certainly not be casting any stones.

As I look back, all those lonely years, spent suffering in silent subconscious-simmering rage, were a small price to pay for the most valuable gift a man could ever wish to receive. Freedom. Pure, enlightened, unimaginable freedom! I'm so happy, I could scream. But I'm experiencing it now on a level so deep, that I'm only able to express my soothing freedom-joy balm through the more precious two-gold-coin way. And so I simply "feel" it. Do you think I am crazy? *Sit with me in silence.*

Like my father before me, I no longer fear anything. *"Kill them vit kindness,"* my dad used to say. I. Am. Free. Go ahead, Yentas. Talk about me. Ostracize me. I sincerely appreciate the quiet.

Your shunning has given me the space to finally look within to understand how truly unique I am. Only now, after sixty-nine years, as I approach my final ones, am I finally meeting the gentleman I ignored my entire life. I am asking myself forgiveness for allowing myself to be silenced for so long. And I take ownership for allowing myself to be manipulated, distracted, and controlled by others for these past nearly seven decades. *And all I ever wanted to do was play and wander. And wonder.*

Silence is golden. And so you blabbermouths are handing me more priceless coins — more moments of silence to discover who I am. Go ahead, God. Threaten me with the flames of Hell if I sleep late and neglect praying with a minyan or for admiring a beautiful woman. Keep bullying me. You can even kill me. But you can no longer take away the freedom I now feel. You are the one who set me free. Against my will. You can even stop loving me. It's okay, God. Because I now love myself. Henry Thoreau wrote, "Things do not change. We change." I. Am. Beautiful.

It's true. Nothing around me has changed. Exhausting myself, and having no direction left to turn after examining every angle of the circular-logic dystopian merry-go-round-life I rode till I became nauseous and dizzy, I finally erupted in a PTSD explosion and violently puked out the pain (having had a lot of practice) and became enlightened to finally look within.

And in place of the guilt-ridden Jew who constantly beseeched forgiveness through boring repetitive prayer for the tinniest of transgressions imaginable, while accepting responsibility for the incomprehensible original sins of Adam and Eve who lived thousands of years before my time, I discovered a unique and beautiful human being. *Glad to meet you!*

I found *myself.* I found the innocent child that, like a puppy, loved everyone he met — and everyone he ever slept with. I found the curious toddler that had a million questions about the world. *That he is allowed to ask!* I discovered the second most-gentle father in the world. And I even realized it's okay to binge-watch Netflix. *Although I still feel guilty.* My best discovery was unearthing an old wise man, who feels only love, after divorcing himself from all things negative and finally finding peace.

God, if you don't know or realize by now how special I am, how much I love and want to help all of your children — *Unzereh* and *Nisht-Unzereh, all colors and all genders* — and how badly I'd love to clean up the destruction you wreaked, and cleanse the blood curdling world history you knew would unfold upon your creation of the world, then I honestly have nothing more to say. Even to you.

Like a truly enlightened Buddhist monk, which I do not claim to be, I am no longer attached. Not simply because I've attained the obvious realization that there is nothing permanent to be attached to. But I have come to understand that the only true treasure we can ever "own" is *love.*

I've learned that "love" is not something physical that you can secure and lock away in a safe deposit box or immerse yourself and fall "into." Love is not a quid pro quo Jewish Monsey marriage based on Jewish law where you are commanded to satisfy your wife, or finally get laid on "Mikva Night" because your wife feels she has to perform a mitzvah. Love is not a relationship with a picayune God weighing every word, thought, and action you speak, think, or do, on a set of delicate scales that measures a hairsbreadth of sin and punishes micro-aggression emotions accordingly. And love is definitely not a "gift" of pain and suffering that forces repentance.

Love does not measure and dole itself out like a weighed portion of scooped-up mashed potatoes that God slaps onto your Leviathan dinner plate. Love is not something you "give." Love is something you can't withhold. It blazes and explodes from your heart and is something you can't control. Love is the first time I saw Ester and held her in my arms.

You don't *love* a good steak, or you wouldn't kill the cow providing it. Eating a steak is cannibalistic hate. Eating an intelligent tortured-for-profit piglet or chicken proves you are the biggest hog and birdbrain of all. How can a sensitive being eat warm-blooded sentient life? The life you are cannibalizing in your amoral deluded mind, as you swallow the flesh of a warm-blooded being that feels pain and emotions, very likely had more empathy than you will ever have.

Calling flesh, a "burger" is Marketing 101. A franchise named *Flesh King* might work among the M催orai tribe in Papua, New Guinea who still may be practicing cannibalism. Coupled with Burger King's old tag line of *"Have It Your Way"* as they eat a "biped-burger" with ketchup, pickles, and a slice of cheese, many of them believe they would be consuming the soul of their deceased relative along with some protein.

Western civilization is also quite deluded, believing they are somehow more enlightened than their aborigine relatives simply because the chemically infused and tortured sickly flesh, processed in cruel factory farms, upon which they gorge and stuff feces-infected-meat (that was raised on hooves, skin, blood, hair, feathers, drugs, plastics, chemicals, manure, euthanized horses, and roadkill, lovingly sprinkled into large amounts of grain in order to deliver a "dollar burger" that inflates faster than the meat they eat) into their obese constipated bodies is "normal" simply because the victim is served in nice plastic containers. With clever new *"Be Your Way"* taglines that proclaim their "woke" individuality, the marketers of "fresh, never frozen" shit successfully destroy our planet while the assembly-line family eats their assembly-line deadly "Happy Meal" as their kids become addicted to a lifetime of obesity. Bon Appétit!

And if we Jews are truly worried about *Tikun Olam* we should feel worse about eating Gefilte Fish and Chicken Soup on Friday night than driving on the Sabbath. Think about it. Who are we really hurting by burning some fossil fuel? The massive colonies of dead bacteria who supplied that energy source are long gone. But we Jews are blessing God and thanking him in the twenty-first century, as we run an extremely sharp blade across the throat of a frightened wide-eyed cow that stumbles for many minutes as it gushes blood till it loses consciousness and finally dies.

How can we Jews claim to be "spiritual" when we sing warm beautiful Zemiros on Shabbos, as we're about to dive into a heavy plate of chopped liver and dead delicious slow-cooked cholent meat and potatoes? And please don't tell me you're eating liver for the iron. Try a little spinach.

True love is timeless. Eternal love between heartfelt lovers would never result in arguments over budgets, credit card charges, forced commitment, hidden retirement accounts, where to vacation, or who to vote for in an upcoming election. A genuine lover could never issue a false protection order, frame you in family court, subject you to criminal court, or deny visitation with your own child. Only a devil could do that.

And a kind Father in Heaven would never issue commandments that force your behavior to sacrifice your child. He would never insist on your lack of sleep (especially assuming that he knows a little science) so that you could constantly study his holy words. Especially when he could just give you more years to live. And a generous God would not ask you to tithe. He would instantly give you food and health, without your constantly having to beg and grovel in prayer. And why would a compassionate God ask you to constantly slaughter animals every day of the year to atone for the sins he set you up to commit? What did the animals do to deserve such torturous treatment? And the last thing a loving God would ever do is request your martyrdom. And if you failed in any of the above, a gracious father would never sentence their child to damnation.

Love does not punch numbers like an accountant. It does not use a delicate diamond scale to weigh an individual's every minuscule act in a heartless "measure for measure" Day of Atonement tally of their devotion while constantly threatening affliction in this world and purgatory in the eternal one for the slightest transgression. Love doesn't send people to Hell. Love is merciful and compassionate. It is wise and forgiving. Love is generous. Love does not force, punish, execute, or seek revenge. And don't tell me it's God's version of "tough love." It is nothing more than violent hate.

Love is that which gushes deep from within and explodes like a newly birthed universe, instantly casting warmth and light wherever it reaches. It only increases as it continues to flow. It does not wax and wane. My warm tears gently fell and baptized Ester with love the moment she was born. That love and devotion only increased every single day of her life. Imagine what I endured till the well of tears drained and became parched. And it only ran dry because I would have drowned had I continued to weep the love I cried for my sweet child. Is it any wonder that I'm as fucked up as I am enlightened? Warning: Do not try this at home. You'll wind up spontaneously crying and laughing at all hours like the dark characters exceptionally portrayed by Joaquin Phoenix.

For almost two full years I'd roam around my four-thousand square foot house that barely contained a stitch of furniture post-divorce because my wife emptied it upon the instructions of the judge to leave me half the contents. But that's not why it felt empty. I once believed that the house I received post-divorce was a home that was warmed by a hearth of love. But now, stripped naked of its contents and family by an insane wretch and hellish divorce, it was revealed to have been nothing more than a dank cold dungeon.

At all hours of the night, I'd walk into the five empty bedrooms of my children and see apparitions of their toddler souls laughing in the past, as we played, read stories, or carried on beautiful conversations while I sat on the edge of their beds as they drifted off to sleep. I now stood over where their beds used to be, and I envisioned events of the decades I spent there with six individuals in relationships that I once believed would continue for eternity. I saw myself as a young father as I'd gently kiss their foreheads and quietly tiptoe out of their room. I'd suddenly start sobbing uncontrollably. Those tears flowed into the ink that became this book.

I'd wind up back in my master bedroom, sitting for hours on the edge of my bed and life, watching the earliest faint rays of the dawn sun heralding the arrival of another very lonely CPTSD day without a penny or friend, as I held a shiny midnight-blue revolver in either of my ambidextrous hands while ironically thinking how easy it would be for me to blow my brains out with either hand. "Have you lost your fucking mind! Do you really want to blow out all those beautiful memories and hard-earned folios of studied Talmud and splatter them like some wasted ejaculate on the wall?" I'd take a very deep breath; slowly open my dresser drawer and gently place the loaded gun down with its muzzle pointing away from the direction of my pillow. I had a book to finish for my daughter.

True love is an act of admiration, wonder, respect, passion, and a selfless desire for the object of one's love to continue to exist. Freely. Happily. Unconditionally. Simply because you love them. What kind of lunatic God would send murderers to forcibly convert or execute Jewish parents, threatening to kidnap their toddlers and place them in Catholic orphanages to grow up worshipping a different deity, while commanding those Chosen Parents to die in order to sanctify his name? *I know. I know. It's a test that he knew they could pass.*

True love does not coerce and control that which it claims to love. It is natural and innocent. Like Ester's breath the minute she was born. Love is Lauren's hand hovering out of thin air to reach for mine as I delicately snuggled my fingers between hers, unaware of our suddenly clasped hands. Even when I broke up with her, all Lauren had to say was, "I'll always love you, Zevie."

I have no doubt that if I bumped into Lauren on a Manhattan sidewalk tomorrow, her sixty-five-year-old hand would find its way into mine in the same exact clasping embrace (her fingers between mine) as forty years ago. *Why can't God and Sharen be as nice as a Shiksa?*

The Talmud, among the final folios of Tractate Brachot, explains (not very clearly) that any negative experience which we perceive as pain, illness, and even death, throughout the history of mankind, will ultimately be understood, upon the arrival of the Messiah, Son of David, as always having been nothing more than a dream; an illusion of sorts, because it was really an act of kindness, an act of pure love by a perfect God who is only capable of committing flawless kind deeds. *Just wait.*

I can't imagine, but the prophet King David insists, that we will then finally comprehend, rejoicing in actual laughter (Psalm 126:2), how an omniscient God could act like a deranged Nazi beast — inflicting death, disease, torture, old age, starvation, war, depression, and a host of "natural causes" and barbaric atrocities, as acts of loving kindness since the beginning of time; while holding puny man accountable for a wet dream or missing out on praying with a minyan. God can commit the most unimaginable of cruel crimes while pounding his heavenly gavel against mortal man's head for not behaving like a perfect robotic angel.

Talk about double-standards. *Good* can't possibly be *evil*. It's not logical. It takes a dystopian mind to truly believe in God. Perhaps that's why religious people accept being dehumanized so easily. We've been conditioned to take ownership even when we're completely innocent.

God has given our psyches plenty of time to practice our oxymoronic Jewish dogmatic beliefs from the moment Adam and Eve committed a sin within hours of their creation that was no worse than innocent children reaching for a candy jar after being seduced by the temptation of sugar.

And since, as Alfred Lord Tennyson proclaimed, "... ours is not to reason why, ours is but to do and die ...," we quickly grow up among our *Unzereh Da'as Torah*, myopic as they are confident, cultish authorities who obliterate and shame any questions we might have expressed as a child, proudly marching as adult soldiers of God, ready to spill our blood for his honor. We are not *The Chosen*. We are *The Abused*.

Hate and the infliction of physical or emotional pain from someone who claims to love you, proves that their love never existed in the first place. That is why jilted lovers scream in frustration, "But I thought you loved me!" Love is not something that can be undone. That is why it is the rare parent who hates their child or pulls down their pants. That is why Lauren and I, and the many women I've loved, always parted as lovers. Forty years later many of them found and friended me on Facebook. *Don't bother, God. You're blocked!*

"Don't you love me, Zevie?" Lauren innocently whispered as I tried to calmly explain our illogical love, and that our cultures were too disparate, and that perhaps she should move on with her life if she wanted a family. "What will our kids celebrate, Hanukkah or Christmas?" I wondered helplessly as I tried to delineate to the lady I loved as to why God decreed that we weren't *Bashert*. "Both?" Lauren sadly attempted as a compromise to her lover (and his racist God) who grew up being told that thousands of Jews were murdered throughout the millenniums on Christmas Day. *Merry Christmas!*

Those descendants of a Jewish Beit Din Sanhedrin, that supposedly committed deicide as they handed Jesus over to Pontius Pilate who ordered his crucifixion, never got the chance to rap the rhymes of Biggie Smalls who boastfully pattered, "Wonder why Christmas missed us." Because Christmas didn't "miss" the terrified ghetto Jews when mobs of drunken Goyim avenged their Jewish God (who taught the entire Talmud to Moses) after hearing an angry sermon describing how the Jews killed Christ. Too bad their wonderful divinely-inspired priest, repeating the supposed dogma of an ex-cathedra ex-Jew apostle, never slowed down for the nanosecond of time it would have taken to explain that it would be easier for a man to soar through space in his own body at the speed of light than to ever kill a God. But when it comes to religion and divorce, who expects anyone (yentas or priests) to pause for a moment to actually think? Supposedly, Pilate kept wavering "to and fro" in his decision to condemn and execute Jesus. Does that mean that God, who was able to harden the heart of Pharaoh, decided to harden Pilate's too?

I suffered the most withdrawal I've ever known upon Lauren's ladylike acquiescence to my unenlightened advice. And that's because, aside from toe-curling, muscle-cramping, drenched-in-sweat fucking-awesome sex, I was *not* addicted to her body. I had enjoyed great lovemaking with many smart and independent women. I was addicted to Lauren's kind shiksa soul. It was as hot as my wife's spirit was frigid. Lauren was as gracious as my wife was cruel. Lauren also didn't know how to read Aramaic. But she was definitely a hotter Yiddishe Mama than my ex ever was.

But God shamed me, through The Oral Law he taught Moses for forty days and forty nights, for loving "an animal." *Actually, she was pretty wild.* God threatened me, via the prophetic powers of Moses, with the death suffered by Zimri, a direct descendant of Jacob, who banged the beautiful shiksa Midianite Princess Cozbi (several hundred times during one session, according to the Talmud) if I continued to sleep with Lauren.

Actual visions of Phinehas son of Eleazar, throwing a spear that pierced through our genitalia while we embraced making love entangled in positions that would defy the logic of a mathematician, crystallized as the folios of the Talmud in Tractate Sanhedrin (82A) raced through my mind, as they described the gory and savage miraculous punishments of Zimri and Cozbi, while Lauren breathlessly whispered in the middle of moaning and climaxing multiple times, "Je veux avoir ton bebe!" That French sentence sure is one program for preventing premature ejaculation. "*Yes, Lauren, of course I love you.*"

Love is that which wells up deep from within our primal life-source, spilling over in endless uninhibited generosity onto all that is contained in the universe; splashing like cascading waves in a wondrous baptismal purification, washing mercifully upon those who are truly blessed to absorb love, as they eventually overflow and bless others. Love is the moment my eyes stare into the eyes of babies and toddlers, and rare women like Lauren, who ask for nothing but love. Love is extremely delicate and sensitive. Sadly, it is easily wounded. *That is why many of us suddenly cry "out of nowhere."*

Love is the collective soul of all consciousness. Close your eyes and you will see. Shut your ears and you will hear. Silence your mind and you will sense that love is the clearest imagery in your consciousness. Love is the original man before sin and shame. It is all that the heart feels, and can only feel, before becoming contaminated by the poisonous fangs of the Satan snake, divisive beliefs, religions, politics, and trickle-down let-them-eat-cake economics inflicted through the clamoring mind. *Love is the innocent, playful, happily jumping, child that was once you.*

Love is the puppy running to play and the toddler laughing. Over nothing. It is the moment unaware lovers reach out for affection in the middle of the night or for each other's hand while walking in the gentle spring breeze. Love is a mother gently directing her painfully engorged breast to the tiny beseeching mouth of her baby as it instinctively gravitates and forages to latch onto its nipple. Love is my eyes staring at Ester the moment her tiny lungs gasped their first breath of life, as I prayed that she would soon enjoy inhaling her second.

Love is the combined serenity, laughter, creativity, and joy of all that was, is, and will ever be. It is not something you command someone to do. Love is something you can't help but feel. *Thou shalt love the Lord your God with all your heart* (Deuteronomy 6:5) makes no sense.

Love overflows when there is no longer any strangulating hate in your heart. Love is calm. Love is warm. Love is forgiving. Love is Gussie wrapping her flabby arm around me, squishing me while we watched television together. Love is my father's rare laughter as he listened to the astute observations of his nine-year-old son.

Love is Lauren insisting that she wants to cook dinner for me, merely to show off her culinary skills (while I displayed my cunnilingus ones). I ate her meal. Then I ate her for dessert. Both were delicious. Love is beautiful. At times it looks like tears as it flows from my eyes. But those tears are merely cleansing any residue sadness acquired by my having lived in a world created by God.

I had spent enough of my life full of negative thoughts since the first time I innocently opened that Pandora's box in my basement and saw mounds of dead people. *How could people be so evil? How could they be so cruel? How could God sit on his throne and watch such barbarism?* I was consumed with negative thoughts against those whose minds contained nothing more than twisted wires. The God of Vengeance planted the seeds of hate and sadness into my young buoyantly optimistic heart.

I hated sex traffickers. I hated Rabbi Tratner for pulling down my pants. I hated the murderous Ku Klux Klan mobs in the south of our country that lynched and castrated innocent men because they had a darker shade of skin. I hated Nazis and their SS Einsatzgruppen paramilitary death squads that shot Jewish babies tossed into the air for target practice, and later in life, like too many merciless prosecutors and judges, retired to collect hefty pensions for their efforts.

And I hated the armies of polite, refined German and Polish citizens that couldn't wait to legally grab the houses, priceless art, bank accounts, businesses, and hard-earned property of their German Jewish neighbors as they waved goodbye to them on railroad cattle-cars. Gold jewelry and precious diamonds, hidden by being sewn into the clothing of those who were used to traveling first-class, were later traded for stale bread and putrid water to quiet the thirst and hunger pangs of their crying once-pampered children. I hated Alfieri. And I hated Schwartz.

I even, sort of, hated the Amalekites, against whom we Jews are commanded to annihilate at some future date. We have a final-revenge mitzvah (one of the 613 commandments in the Bible) to then perpetuate a holocaust of collective punishment, that will include their infants, cattle, Teslas and Beemers. Yes. Even their property. We are to execute an Orwellian total erasure of their ever having existed. Never permitted to even mention the name "Amalek" again. Basically, what my wife did to me. *Does she think I'm from Amalek?*

I was commanded by the All-Merciful to look forward to "erasing the name Amalek from under the heavens above (Deuteronomy 25:19)," but I honestly couldn't imagine the ethnic cleansing of innocent children. *I wonder how that commandment could ever be executed since it would entail erasing words from the Bible itself. After all, we'd have to erase the name of the people we're supposed to utterly annihilate*. I hated the Holy Crusaders. And I hated the Church and their Inquisition. I hated Cain for killing his brother. I did my best not to hate the mother who tormented my wonderful father. And it took a lot of effort, and an acrobatic circular-thinking exhausted mind, to excuse a God who was constantly pulling off my pants while telling me he loved me.

I exhausted myself by my endlessly questioning God's ways. And the only logical answer I could come up with was imagining God's repetitive bored voice inside my head that kept insisting "you're going to have to just trust me." I forced myself to believe that when God suddenly created an ex-nihilo universe roughly six thousand years ago (i.e. basically yesterday, according to Jewish beliefs), I had to trust that the resulting chaos was the result of his best efforts. After all, a perfect God would never have to undertake trial by error experimentation.

A sudden world, whose six-thousand-year (according to most Kabbalists) nanosecond of popping in and out of existence in the eternal scheme of things, containing a history of oceans of blood, horrific diseases, ignorance, torture, starvation, slavery, endless wars over nothing, and constant physical and emotional pain, is all supposedly the creative result of a perfect God that we are commanded to trust. *Forgive me, but how can he expect me to be so foolish?*

We're in the twenty first century and half of all U.S. adults are still unable to read a book written on an eighth-grade level. It took till the later part of the nineteenth century for a simple case of appendicitis to no longer be diagnosed as an automatic death sentence. *Is that all you got?* Three-fourths of the history of the earth's surface is covered with blood. Forget about being the Blue Planet. We're the true "Red Planet."

It's not that I wanted revenge. But I wanted answers. I needed answers. Almost as much as I needed love. I exhausted myself thinking how I could make the world a better place. From schools to governments and hospitals, I thought how fair I would be to everyone. It was not grandiose thoughts of ruling supreme that I experienced, but the desire for a chance to exert some common sense into the mad scheme of things.

But the more I thought about it, the more I realized that I did not create this world. I did not create pain and suffering. I didn't create Alfieri, or my wife. It no longer matters to me if their deranged lives were created by a God or because of a Big Bang explosion followed by evolution. It's above my pay grade to worry about. The one thing I am sure of is that I am not the one who created this messy evil-without-direction world. I'm simply the one who exhausted himself trying to make sense of the bloody world I found myself raped into.

My anger and frustration slowly dissipated and all that was left when the negativity and hangovers were gone was love. I had spent almost my entire life searching for a mother, a wife, and a God, before realizing that there was no one there that would, or could, listen. I wanted all three of them to love me, no strings attached, exactly like I once loved them.

I almost killed myself trying. I finally stopped talking. And I even stopped praying — or should I say "begging."

I finally listened to my own beautiful heart. It soothed and comforted me. It made me laugh. And it made me cry. It taught me to simply observe, breathe deep, and be silent. It taught me to, once again, love the innocent child within myself. *Silence is golden.*

Love can't inflict pain or cause destruction. True love doesn't even know how to inflict pain. Innocent babies cry for their needs when they are upset. They don't think about going on a vengeful killing spree. They instantly reflect love and warm smiles when you smile at them, and they instinctively desire to be loved. Probably the cruelest act we commit as human beings is that we give birth to happy innocent children and then "raise" them (through conditioning and shame) into guilt-ridden angry adults. *We're your babies, God. Aren't we adorable enough for you?*

How could any person with a soul, or a God without one, watch another human — shackled like a wild beast as he stands naked on an auction block, severed from his stripped naked wife and young children who are being sold nearby — as he is sold into a life of slavery, forever wondering what happened to his beautiful family?

How could a God, or any man believing he was created in God's image, not comfort a crying toddler? How could a White human being listen to the cries of a Black baby and not be moved to gently pick her up and kiss her? How the hell were our great Founding Fathers capable of slavery? Slavery! Just yesterday. How hypocritical! Did they really believe they owned the people they stole? Yes. Stole! If there were no buyers, there would have been no slave traders importing kidnapped, shackled human life from the entire continent of Africa. For centuries.

Surely the Founding Fathers understood their "property" had feelings. And that is probably why the U.S. Constitution never mentions the word "slavery" outright. But in a permanent blood stain on that precious document proclaiming that "All men are created equal," Voltaire's original writings were instantly contradicted a few lines later in a Judas bribe of political compromise to the Slave States (by many of our slave-owning Founding Fathers) as it declared that "persons held to service of labour crossing state lines, be returned to their rightful owners to whom he owes his services in the slave state."

By what rights was the enslavement of black people considered *legal*, that our wonderful Founding Fathers of the United States then declared that runaway *property* was to be returned to "their rightful owners" to complete their service of labor? How can property *owe* anything to anyone? *I'm not your property, God.*

The orphaned-for-profit children, like too many of their modern foster care descendants, would soon become subservient and obsequious, subdued to a life of slavery that they would never question or imagine escaping from for many generations. For most of them, being declared a *House Negro* would be the equivalent of entering the Garden of Eden. The process of their becoming an indentured zombie was almost as fast as an Order of Protection issued against an unsuspecting father during a divorce. And like an Order of Protection, it was all backed up by the government of the United States of America.

And so Thomas Jefferson never raped the fourteen-year-old pretty black girl named Sally Hemings, who was less than one third of the *rapist* widower's age, because he *owned* her. Literally and figuratively. She remained his cum-dumpster for the next thirty-two years, bearing six children (several of whom were whipped mercilessly by plantation overseers), till Jefferson died in 1826, on the Fourth of July.

It was truly a day of celebration for the emancipated children of Sally Hemings (*God bless America!*) — the *only* slaves among six hundred that Jefferson finally freed upon his death. It is quite remarkable that Thomas Jefferson, who is best known for his belief that the main purpose of government is to protect the rights of the people who give their implicit *consent* that allows government to serve, never even imagined needing the consent of people who had a little "extra" melanin in their skin. Sadly, Blacks were obviously not people in his eyes. Even though he was sexually aroused by some of them.

Jefferson wrote that he suspected that Blacks are inferior to Whites and unable to take care of themselves. Although very wealthy, he took out mortgages on his slaves to finance his very majestic lifestyle. Jefferson is everyone's hero, but he often reminds me of the very likable Jell-O spokesperson, Bill Cosby, whose *true colors* were exposed when he was found guilty as a serial rapist and imprisoned for heavily drugging and then raping the women who trusted and admired America's Favorite Dad.

Like Jefferson, Cosby raped young ladies. The women trusted the charming monster and viewed Bill as a mentor and as a grandfatherly open-hearted family friend. Bill feigned a sincere interest in their modeling or acting careers, always smiling, as he groomed them patiently. Then he fucked them violently. After they passed out. The victims of Dr. Huxtable could have easily choked and suffocated to death on their own vomit while they lay semi-comatose. Other drugged young women barely remember how they drove home and could easily have died while crashing their car in their medicated stupor state.

Like the adored by millions personality he portrayed as Dr. Cliff Huxtable, the gentle OB/GYN physician who ran a family practice from his home office, Dr. Bill Cosby-Hyde also medicated his patients whose pussy he wanted to penetrate and examine. With his penis.

The manipulative serial rapist planned his violent sexual assaults months in advance, generously giving constant attention, patient career advice, tickets to his shows, gifts, and dinners in fancy restaurants — as his awed young, manipulated female "friends" sat with Bill's famous ones, never suspecting they were about to become a new form of floppy Jell-O as Cosby's desert.

How could they not trust those genial eyes and captivating smiles that could instantly charm anyone's heart? Cosby easily gained their trust as he eventually spoke those cheerful famous last-rite words that uprooted the young lives of unsuspecting fans and launched their existence into a fragile PTSD tailspin, as he asked permission to, "Let me get you something to drink ..."

"America's Dad," was born, like my amicable wife, with a natural acting ability that quickly jettisoned him from class clown to unimaginable fame as a world-renowned celebrity. This cold-hearted lizard could flash his colors as a stand-up comic, actor, and pitchman faster than any chameleon. But unlike a chameleon, who changed colors to avoid predators, America's Dad flashed his *true colors* revealing that he was the most dangerous predator of all. Cosby (again, like my wife) could mimic so many funny and friendly jovial faces. All of them nothing more than facade's that hid the Mr. Hyde callous monster that lurked beneath; a sexual predator that manipulated, raped, and then boldly challenged any of his victims who dared imagine they could hold him accountable.

Dr. Huxtable melted hearts across the continent into warm jello, while inspiring confidence and immediately gaining the trust of beguiled mothers who purchased more than one billion Jell-O cups a year. He even befriended the parents (often younger than him) of the daughters he later raped. Cosby was earning millions pitching a protein made from the skins and bones of cows and pigs *(which is probably how he viewed his victims).* Meanwhile I can just imagine how Bill constantly practiced his famous ad-pitch tagline in his deranged mind as he handed two 714's to his next victim: "There's always room for quaaludes."

Forty years ago, I gave two 714's to Howard Engle, who must weigh at least two-hundred and forty pounds. Within a half hour he fell flat on his face on the sidewalk of 47th Street and chipped two front teeth. He stood up laughing at how funny he looked. At less than half the weight of my diamond dealer associate, I don't want to imagine what Cosby's victims looked like. I'm sure it wasn't funny.

The Devil, like my wife, never bothered to imagine that he might get caught. His attitude would merely be to keep repeating, "I didn't do it! I didn't do it!" And he'd have a literal army of enablers (lawyers, staff, business agents and PR firms) protecting him. *He could have saved a lot of money had he known what Yentas are.* To this very day Cosby is still claiming that the jury was a bunch of " imposters" and that his trial was a "political thing." The Messiah will arrive before my wife or Bill Cosby ever issues an authentic apology.

The reputation of a man whose squeaky-clean Dr. Cliff Huxtable character depended on his being seen as trustworthy; the celebrated prominence that earned Cosby hundreds of millions of dollars, was apparently completely worthless to Mr. Hyde once blood began to flow into his penis. None of this could have succeeded so effortlessly without the goose-stepping enablers (including the ruthless Mrs. Cosby) who followed their orders and allowed the violent predator to practice decades of overdosing and then sexually assaulting beautiful young women. It's a miracle that none of his victims died.

And although less than one percent of rapes lead to a felony conviction, Bill couldn't control his wise-guy arrogance (even during a deposition) and admitted, on record, that his intention was to use the quaaludes he acquired through his enabler doctor to drug women that he wanted to have sex with. Answering the question, "Was it in your mind that you were going to use these Quaaludes for young women that you wanted to have sex with," Cosby honestly replied, "Yes."

Cosby's enabler doctor never asked questions other than "How's your back?" as he served as Dr. Huxtable's personal pharmacy, writing out *years* of prescriptions for Cosby's date-rape addiction trysts. Always "consensual" of course.

Bill was a good sharer. He always gave his victims two. Without even informing them what they were ingesting. He might as well have hit them over their heads with a sledgehammer. No wonder they passed out. Coupled with the alcohol he served them they probably almost needed to be intubated. With their strong young hearts, they were lucky to vomit out the "love" *America's Favorite Dad* displayed towards them.

Cosby, enabled by his super-expensive dream team of lawyers who could have filed and appealed for decades, would never have seen a day in jail had his own big (no longer smiling) mouth not betrayed him. Rod Covlin's angry mouth was also the source of his betrayal. Likewise, the attestation provided by my wife's Tatie5521 password and her maniacal pedophile-laced prattling emails shoved both of her petite feet into her tiny mandible-mouth.

Bill walked himself into the Montgomery County Correctional Facility insisting he was innocent. Rod cried that he was innocent as he donned his prison jumpsuit. And Donna Dippolito finally went to prison in 2017 still insisting "I didn't do it! I didn't do it!" after an amazing eight year odyssey that included a house arrest, three trials, and endless appeals. My ex-wife's brain sits in its own correctional facility inside her skull, where it is locked away still believing that Mrs. Hyde did nothing wrong. The poet Thomas Moore wrote, "It is only through mystery and madness that the soul is revealed." *Pleasure to have met you, Sharen.*

The forensic psychologist, J. Reid Meloy, explains how a man like Cosby could be so cavalier as he went about raping, denying, intimidating, settling out of court, raping again, denying again, etc. ... in an exhaustive and expensive repetitive pattern of groom, drug, rape and deny for decades. The sheer effort to commit and cover up his crimes through PR obfuscation, out-of-court settlement agreements and intimidation is mind-blowing.

Instead of paying an army of enablers, Cosby could have gotten off cheaper stocking a private legal harem of gorgeous personal escorts. But, once again, it's all about manipulation and control. It obviously wasn't sex or love that thrilled Bill. Unless I'm missing something, I don't understand how anyone could enjoy making love to a sleeping comatose near-corpse. But Bill never made love. He made "control." Cosby not only risked his reputation for nothing but wound up in jail as an utterly destroyed monster who sincerely and insanely still insists that he merely "dated" the dozens of women he raped. Nothing they will ever plead, cry, or even scream will ever convince Bill that he needed their consent.

And this non-fiction book that took three years of my life to research and write will be deemed as complete fiction by my ex who spent three years of her life as a coward who wrote private emails, full of fictional shit, at all hours of the night, to destroy my life simply because I dared to file for divorce. To this day, and forever, Jack Abramoff, Cosby and Sharen believe that they are completely innocent. They will be lowered into their graves believing fervently that everything they have ever done during their entire lives was justified.

And "Casino Jack" is in the news once again for Bitcoin fraud, corruption, and dealing from Alfieri's deck of cards by falsely claiming he was a lobbyist again and ripping off investors to the tune of over five million dollars.

Like I said, only bars or the earth can contain the wild psycho dystopian synapses of these deranged creatures created by Jack's "Almighty" moral god. I can almost envision a tearful Abramoff once again expressing his, "profound regret and sorrow for the multitude of mistakes and harm I have caused," while pleading forgiveness — as he did sixteen years ago in front of God and Judge Ellen Segal Huvelle, as Jack groveled for a lighter sentence — from "the Almighty and from those I have wronged and caused to suffer." *Only bars or a grave.*

Cosby spent millions of dollars in legal fees and private settlements to fuel his passion for control. My Vybie, on her level, spent a quarter of a million dollars and three full years of her life committing fraud and perjury, while leaving a rancid trail of emails with which to impress the Jewish God she worships; to then settle down and offer me an uncontested divorce banged out in literally twenty minutes. Give her a call and she will convince you that she is completely innocent. *She could probably even convince me.*

Dr. Meloy explains that, "Individuals with personalities of narcissism and psychopathy, because of their sense of entitlement, often feel they are above the law. The Achilles heel of such personalities is their sense of impunity, which typically leads them to take greater risks, and eventually leads to their downfall."

They also believe they are smarter than everyone else. And they will continually blame their victims — never ever accepting an atom of ownership or responsibility for the havoc they cause. My thespian gifted ex-lizard-wife could easily have played the role of Dr. Huxtable. She already perfectly matches his real-life persona.

To this day, the eighty-two-year-old "America's Dad," convicted on three charges of "felony aggravated indecent assault" and classified as a "sexually violent predator," continues to claim that he'd rather serve ten more years in prison than admit guilt or show remorse. Like my wife, Bill will forever insist, "I didn't do it! I didn't do it!" Cosby will continue to claim "it was all a set-up" even as shovelfuls of dirt pour upon his casket.

Thomas Jefferson didn't even need drugs. And he never troubled himself with denying or affirming the sexual intimacy he shared with his human chattel named Sally. He simply ignored the accusations of his political opponents along with the innuendos of the newspaper press of his day. Jefferson's denials were fortified by enabler-historians for the next one hundred and fifty years. They loved relating the passionate "never to remarry" promise that Thomas proclaimed to Martha as she lay dying.

Science finally revealed the truth in 1998 and settled the matter, once and for all, through a simple Y Chromosome DNA analysis. Sally Hemings most definitely gave birth to the founding father's children. *Mazel Tov!*

Nevertheless, it still took another two decades, during the summer warmth of 2018, for the Thomas Jefferson Foundation to come up with a phrase that frigidly conceded, in flawless Orwellian huffy prose, that the Jefferson-Hemings controversy is a "settled historical matter." *"Duh!"* In layman's terms, "He did it! He raped her!

Thomas Jefferson, our third president, was a philosopher, lawyer, diplomat, previous vice-president, and probably the most famous Founding Father of our country. He was also a child-molester that would have been registered as a Level One sex offender had he lived in our day. I think it is a wonderful display of enlightenment on the part of society to finally honor and retroactively pardon innocent men like Alan Turing for "crimes" of homosexuality. Unfortunately, we are seldom honest enough to do the reverse. After all, President Thomas Jefferson never broke any laws. *Because the laws in place were broken.*

As a consolation prize, and in a politically correct effort to finagle the lifetime raping of a fourteen-year-old female slave into a fantasy love affair, to ease the consciousness of Whites, while attempting to defuse the anger of Blacks, the Jefferson Foundation opened an exhibit dedicated to our First Raped Lady of the United States. *FRLOTUS*. Martha Skelton Jefferson was the woman who sat for an oil portrait as the wife of the third President of the United States. Sadly, not a single image exists of the concubine who shared a bed with the gifted statesman for four decades, and the *FRLOTUS* was never officially granted her freedom, let alone invited to sit for her own portrait.

Jefferson never had to groom or intimidate his victim. Sally arrived at his plantation as a tabula rasa baby. She was one of those "lucky" light-skinned slaves who had the fortune of being designated as a House Negro and thereby avoided having to spend twelve hours a day working in the broiling fields. But her relationship with Thomas was not exactly a romantic love story. It was illegal for a slave to refuse her master's commands. There were no flowers (unless you call cotton a flower). No foreplay. No kissing. Just a whip for the slightest disobedience.

Jefferson would simply descend to Sally's hidden slave quarters when the need for relief stirred inside his gentlemanly statesman trousers. If you are going to destroy statues and plaques, you might as well go to the original source and tear our hypocritical Constitution to shreds. But if you really want to attack the root of the problem we might as well burn the Old Testament (Genesis 9:25-27). And if you desire to entirely fix the problem you would need to debate the God who dictated those words to Moses, and demand that he amend the triple-curse that Noah invoked against his son Ham.

Like a horse, a slave could be whipped without mercy for not moving fast enough. Or for not picking enough cotton. And he could be castrated if he bucked a bit too much. A black man had zero worth as an individual. He was often treated worse than a horse. Especially when he refused to be "broken" and tamed as a possession of wealth that was purchased or mortgaged, to be branded and listed in a column of his master's ledger.

Nothing more descriptive than the slave's job description and how much the valuable chattel ate, along with a probable birth date, were recorded into the ledger of his master; alongside the next few, more important columns that estimated the expectation of excellent profits and future offspring the property was expected to yield. The final column of rows most likely recorded actual realized profits. I imagine the birth of twins resulted in a hearty "Mazel Tov!"

A good specimen was usually bred to a sturdy female whose offspring was often sold faster than the quick fortunes that were made at the expense of their humanity. Who can imagine what Sally did to keep most of her children with her?

Sadly, we try to rewrite (i.e. erase) all that horrific history instead of studying and learning from it. As if the Old World, that was not that quaint after all, never existed. Books are no longer burned. They are simply called out and canceled. A mere whimper of "I'm feeling anxious!" can instantly block any book from being published, while century old classics are yanked off the shelves of libraries nationwide.

Instead of replying, "Then don't read it," contracts are being terminated faster than the heads of journalists are decapitated, as publishers make a mad dash to display how tolerant they are upon the slightest accusation of imaginary Islamophobia or homophobic innuendo being cast at many great writers and thinkers. The years spent researching and organizing their thoughts into flawless prose are discarded as trash because of a misinterpreted Twitter comment made two decades earlier.

The authors have so much to say but are silenced faster than the receiver was slammed back into its cradle every time I poured my heart out to my ex-wife. I imagine publishers will soon be selling blank books with "safe" pens containing invisible ink, and reviews on the back covers that excitedly proclaim "no book left behind," with instructions to "the reader" to "write whatever makes you comfortable." The book with no words at all will surely win a Nobel Prize. *For Shiterature*.

A baby begins life as an emperor, continues as a prince, and evolves into a serf who spends the final years of his workaholic life half-alert and visiting doctors. He is then forgotten within hours of the last shovelful of earth being tossed on his grave. It doesn't really take the wisest of all men to figure out that, "All is vanity." *Life sucks.* Like Roberta Flack and Donny Hathaway beautifully sang in the early seventies, I often wondered, "Where is the love?" *Then I looked within.*

Real love has no expectations. No commandments. No frustrations. No goals. It has no desire. It simply *is*. Love is not something you control, make demands of, barter with, try to hoard and own, or satiate your lust with. Love is open and has no boundaries.

Love is a two-year-old Ester happily screeching *"Tatie!"* as her father walks through the front door to her instantly outstretched arms as she excitedly runs to him to be scooped up and hugged after his being away for a mere couple of hours.

And love is an adorable three-year-old Ester, crying profusely, upon realizing that *her* Tatie is *married* to Mommy — and not to *her!* "Oh! My! God!" (as spoken by Janice and company 1,069 times on *Friends*). Ester threw a doozy of a passion-fueled tantrum, insisting that *she* wanted to be the one married to Tatie! The wrath of her jealously was to die for. I couldn't stop laughing inside as I swore my allegiance to Her Highness.

Nothing I said, including that I love her the most, would die for her, or that I loved her more than I love myself, could calm Princess Ester down. She screamed, kicked, and cried, almost to the point of hyperventilating, refusing all of my logical explanations about family, parents, children, and siblings.

Running out of logic, and desperate to quell her tears, I finally came up with the explanation that a Tatie could divorce a Mommy (quite prophetic), but that Ester would be my daughter forever (false prophecy that time). "A daughter is better, Ester," I reassured my Princess.

"Really?" my emotionally spent, now-way-past-bedtime cherub asked through her tear-stained face.

"Yes Ester, really," I gently whispered in my fatigued avowal of infinite love, "you can't divorce a daughter."

"Okay," Ester whispered as she threw her little arm around my neck and snuggled her tiny face next to my size-seven head as she instantly fell asleep, totally exhausted after throwing the most adorable Oedipus Complex display of undying love you could ever imagine. Freud had to be rolling in laughter. I literally laughed until the tears mizzled, like fine drops of rain, in my eyes and slowly began to flow at her display of such pure innocent love.

That three-year-old Ester will always be my daughter. *Forever*. Just like I promised her. Even when she's ninety. It's too painful for me to imagine the manipulated and alienated pre-teen as the real version. I don't care how many libelous protection orders I had to respond to, or how many scurrilous emails I had to enter into the court records.

I don't care how many sad drawings displaying nothing more artistic than a pitiful portrayal of Ester's alienation I had to stare at in shock or how many dreams my mind continues to create as a form of therapeutic visitation in order for me to occasionally "see" Ester again. I don't even care if she's the seventy-pound lightweight who finally broke a two-hundred-pound heavyweight upon her willingness to take the stand and lie. I will always love my daughter.

The alien alienated twelve-year-old who threw dirt on my bed and drew angry childish green-monster pictures of a stranger in her life named "*Zev,*" was the conditioned result of the relentless efforts of a furious divorcing cyborg wire-mother gorilla that feels no emotional pain. Not even for the precious life she gave birth to. Nothing gets in her way. Not Shabbat. Not court ordered directives. Not Rabbi Nekritz. Not God. Not being exposed as an Ivy League liar through her own perfidious feces-laden emails. Goose-stepping Nazi Ants never stop marching.

The drastically manipulated young lady who clearly knew the truth pre-divorce when she sweetly avowed, "Don't worry Tatie, I believe you," as she proclaimed her trust to a bodyguard-father that adored her and couldn't find the willpower to leave his crying princess at nursery school, is the true version of the child I named after Queen Ester.

My freedom now flows through my entire being because I am no longer attached to the sadness that results when someone I love or something I treasure ceases to exist. Because I no longer exist in an illusion called "time." And so, my relationship with Ester now consists of only the happy memories of the one decade of her life that we spent together laughing, doing homework, playing basketball, and having priceless spontaneous "deep and meaningful conversations."

Through the incredible sadness of becoming estranged from my miracle baby and the searing mental anguish I've felt for humanity since the creation of the universe, I've somehow become "cleansed" of feeling anything negative. I no longer experience fear. I no longer feel sadness. I no longer desire wealth or fame. My only desire is that of a young baby. Like a young child, I want everyone to be happy. I just want to play.

It's difficult for most people to grasp but experiencing even a single second of totally-in-the-moment pure love and admiration for anything, living or inanimate, creates an eternal bond. Most people want to *own* the person or object that they love or admire — never getting the chance to fully experience a pure relationship for even one entire second. And the harder they try to permanently grasp the object of their desire, the more ephemeral it becomes. You can't own someone's soul any more than uprooting a beautiful flower and clenching it in your tightened fist as you declare ownership while it slowly dies. *Do you hear me, God?*

One's obsessiveness, insecurity, negativity, or greediness to own and control the object of their love completely diminishes and ultimately destroys everyone involved. Like Leslie Gore hauntingly insisted as she sang in the early sixties, "You Don't Own Me." You can't own me. *"I can go out with any shiksa ... and don't tell me what to do ...!"* And the more one attempts to own and control someone else, the further they inhibit their own experience to express or receive true love.

In truth, they only love themselves while inhibiting the love that the recipient of their "love" wishes to display. And I am simply describing the manipulative destruction that people call "parenting" and "marriage." And religion. Throw in a few wire-monkey mothers, kangaroo-court judges, Ultra-Orthodox Yentas, and an "all-loving" God, and all hell breaks loose. *In this world and the next.*

By letting go of all things negative, I have come to possess riches beyond my wildest imagination. I am so free, that I have nothing more to say. I am now laughing so hard internally that I scarcely have the strength to smile externally. I barely exist. I've become a god. *The nice version.*

I never had a desire to own that GIA vivid-intense canary-yellow oval gem before it was whipped and crucified into an emerald-cut shape so many years ago. But I did enjoy and appreciate her beauty more than her diamond-plantation owner ever did. And I never wanted to own my children or any of the women I loved. I wanted them to be *free*.

How can "here today, gone tomorrow" man own anything? Why would he want to? Why would God threaten the figurative wife-nation he married moments ago with instant death, holding Mount Sinai over their heads (as stated in the Midrash) if they refused to obey him? Didn't he love them? Did he not understand that you can't own people? *Even if you created them.* There is no such thing as a slave or an "*Eved Hashem*" (*Slave of God*). There is only a slave mentality.

My brief complete intimacy with that gorgeous sun-drenched gem, as I caressed her in my hand when she was a passionate, uninhibited post-pubescent virgin, will forever be more memorable than the relationship of the boorish slave-owner diamond dealer who was obsessed with nothing more than the money-shot-profit she provided.

Truth be told, he never even "owned" that diamond. Like Thomas Jefferson, greedy domination of an object granted him the legal rights to "pleasure himself" and earn a faux-fortune through exploitation and the issuance of a GIA certificate slave-document on a purposely poorly-graded whipped gem by a few bribed overseer plantation enabler gemologists.

He then diamond-trafficked the flogged raped-recut, emotionally-frigid, scarred for life, diamond-wheel-assaulted beauty; eventually hoodwinking his Middle Eastern private-collector client who sealed the traumatized stunner in his dark impenetrable vault of harem-stored rare gems to live a life of solitary confinement, occasionally displaying her marred beauty in order to enjoy braggadocio ownership rites. *But I knew her when.*

I respectfully treasured her youthful personality and can still clearly see her intense true colorful disposition as I recall how she sparkled when allowed to live her life freely, in the shape Mother Nature so lovingly intended. And I will always remember the girly giggles and gasping-for-air laughter of my little girl as I gave her a head-start when we ran races through which my fatherly intention was to strengthen her young thighs while teaching her soul to persevere when things got tough. *Thank you, Mr. Levine.*

And I will never forget the warmth of toddler Ester's flushed skin, as her little vivid-pink tear-stained face rested beside mine. And I will always recall the smell of her sweet breath, as she dropped her tantrum-exhausted sweaty little head matted with a moist crown of gorgeous golden-blond tresses on the pillow.

And I will forever feel Ester's arm listlessly wrapping itself around my neck to pull me closer, as I stared into her baby-blue eyes sparkling with tears as she gazed directly into mine, dozing off like an exhausted angel as she whispered, "Okay," eighteen years ago. Before she was greedily molested and recut for profit. *I knew her when.* I meant to divorce my wife. Not my daughter.

I no longer wonder why an all-loving God created a world in which he knew the downfall of man would occur at the very instant of creation. I will no longer waste my precious existence wondering why God invented depression, cancer, torture, war, anxiety, stress, divorce, poverty, starvation, sickness, and, last but not least, a rotting death as maggots devour our bodies (that still feel pain post-mortem according to the Talmud) as a punishment for Adam and Eve eating from the Tree of Knowledge. And what's wrong with knowledge? What teacher would punish a child for seeking knowledge? And knowing we were going to "sin" and fail, wouldn't a couple of days in the Sahara Desert suffice as punishment coming from a compassionate God?

Why would God, who has free will, choose to create a world in which its inhabitants devour each other and other living animals? And since God exists in the future, then he already knew what all of us (including himself) were going to do in the future. And if so, how can he claim that any of us (including God) possess free will? *Everything will always remain in the past, and so blissfully easy for a real God to see and then easily choose to act wisely and compassionately.*

I experienced enough negativity to last a lifetime. To last for an eternity! I paid my dues. And I've come to understand how utterly worthless it is to inflict pain — and the revenge it seeks through anger — upon others. Hell makes absolutely no sense. Do I believe I'll somehow find some form of satisfaction or solace in watching Hitler, Alfieri, or Schwartz standing in smoldering shit (according to the Talmud) while burning in Hell one day? I am too enlightened to fall for that shit.

I've gained the wisdom to comprehend how priceless a second of love *feels*. So, I choose to love. I don't want to punish, force, take revenge, or inflict pain. I am not an "all-loving" God that has an agenda. I'm simply a human who loves all. I now understand the world. And the religious beliefs and systems of governments among its bickering and warring inhabitants seem childish to me. The modern-day civil war of blue states versus red states looks as foolish to me as children declaring "It's mine!" while fighting over toy soldiers and plastic tanks. The constant bickering over history and statues honoring imperfect men that society once called "heroes," is a waste of my time. *And I have so much of nothing to do!* I can only emit love and compassion. It's all I feel. *Silence is golden.*

The sound of a child's uninhibited laughter. The embrace of a lover. The companionship of a faithful dog. Making love to an intelligent, kind woman. The innocent smile of a child. The taste of red wine. The feel of hugging a great book you just read (for the third time). The breathtaking scene of a blazing star-filled night sky. Patiently watching an eagle soar because both of you have nothing to do. Smelling a flower as you slowly fill your lungs to capacity. Clasping hands with someone you love while gazing deeply into their eyes over a cup of strong coffee in the morning. Gently kissing their lips for no reason. Jogging nowhere. Making eye contact with a gorgeous ebony-colored baby, whose mother is distracted and busy wheeling her around in a shopping cart while tossing in groceries, and making her giggle. Even just looking in the mirror and appreciating the person you see in its reflection. These are the things that set one free. My love is the completely uninhibited lightheartedness of total *freedom*.

I hope to share it with all mankind.

It's amazing how free we suddenly become when we stop trying to be.

The answer to Hamlet's soliloquy has always been "not to be." There are no goals. There is no such thing as accumulation. Of coin or good deeds. One winds up spending their entire life counting and reckoning (and taking revenge). Governments and religions instruct mankind to become a hoarder. I was married to one. It is an illness. A crippling disease.

The human eye is the second most important earthly asset we own. Who would want to insert that GIA vivid-intense canary-yellow oval gem into their eye socket in exchange for their eyeball?

We can see planets and distant stars with our delicate eyes. What a superpower! Yet, most moments of our lives are wasted looking no farther than a screen or a few yards of asphalt road. Our mind's eye, intellect, imagination, and thoughts are our most priceless possessions of all. They are incredible treasures that enable us to see much further than the distance of our universe. They allow us to see the future. And when we close them, they allow us to see the truth.

We are capable of conceptualizing ideas that most of mankind will probably not even begin to comprehend, let alone conceive, until many millennia have faded into the distant past. Yet we rarely use our intelligence for much more than observing men riding tormented bulls that jump up and down, or teams of athletes displaying unique talents with balls of different sizes and shapes. Why do we derive pleasure from observing men and women punching each other in a UFC "cage" (how apropos) and drivers going up in flames while speeding bumper to bumper around a boring racetrack? Calm your mind and breathe deeply. You will laugh at how silly we must look to advanced possible intelligent life on other planets who are pleased to live safely many distant light years from us, and would no sooner contact us than we would have a desire to contact an ant scurrying to war with another of its kind.

I drank the last cold sip as I stared into my now-empty oversized coffee cup as if I were staring into a crystal ball, looking deep into the moment, five billion light years into nothingness, and I felt like light traveling faster than time. Thankful for my health. Blissfully at peace. In love with a beautiful universe we honestly know almost nothing about. So happy to be alive. Thrilled to be so incredibly free.

I no longer wonder, "*Whatever happened to Ester?*"

February 21, 2022

EPILOGUE

My story is unique in that it's not. It is a story about *Everyman*. In literature, the definition of the term "everyman" has evolved to describe an ordinary individual with whom the general audience or reader can easily identify. *Everyman* has no magnificent or impressive talents, cerebral gifts, or superpowers. An everyman "hero" is typically your Average Joe who is placed into extraordinary circumstances, and acts with surprising heroic qualities. Sometimes his heroism is achieved merely by surviving the ordeal into which powers beyond his control have placed him. Or in my instance — flung him. I guess you can say that for a nice Jewish boy, I sure can take a punch.

My own *Everyman* story was not intended to be autobiographical. I'm the last person who ever imagined writing about his own personal life. I've been quiet, bashful, and introspective for most of my adult life. I love writing beautiful stories for children. I have a company called SwordPen Publishers where I write fictional stories about giant mice, flying hippos, and young female ants with an attitude who refuse to stay in line. Never did I foresee my penning a bestseller novel on alienation, Jewish life, and divorce. I'm way too shy for that.

I was no superhero. Except perhaps in fighting a sinister judge and an outrageously maleficent mom as I tried to protect my daughter from the devastating effects of alienation — a condition I had only faintly heard about (and barely comprehended) before I filed for divorce, never imagining it to be a powerful psychological brainwashing assault that could ever possibly be perpetrated upon *my* daughter. Especially a daughter that I raised as a stay-at-home Mr. Mom for the first two years of her adorable life.

I was an *Everyman* dad. I'm now an elderly gentleman with a dad bod who filed for divorce upon reaching the ripe old age of sixty-two. I'm often tired and, at my present age of sixty-nine, I nap when I can. I didn't choose to be a character in a story that would almost read as fiction if not for the emails and stamped court documentation that prove the events described herein actually occurred.

I certainly never imagined myself as the protagonist of any story. This story chose me. Karma planted the seeds that sprouted into this book. Luckily, she insisted on a writer, for only a writer could patiently reconstruct a lifetime of bricolage events and piece together the torn shreds of a life shrouded in traumatic shameful loneliness and weave them into a tapestry that describes what I myself still can't believe happened. Mary Angelou wrote that there is no greater agony than bearing an untold story inside of you. What I had inside of me was too much anguish to release in the form of tears. It would have been a flood in which I would have drowned.

I had no choice but to release my tears slowly. One word at a time. The ink trickled down my cheeks and flowed out of my pen. My hand didn't pick up a pen because I wanted to write. I picked up a pen so that I wouldn't pick up a gun and end my life. I also refused to hate, and unlike a God that inflicts pain, I chose to love.

Ultimately my story also focused on God. The more I thought about my life and the God I idolized in my youth, the more I realized that he is the one responsible for all events that have occurred in the universe since the moment he supposedly created it.

I know most people have suffered a much more tragic life than my White privileged one. But a perfect God can't claim an illogical and fallacious "not so bad" argument in response to my questioning the way he decided to create and then oversee this world.

It's true that I never went to bed hungry. And I wasn't raped or forced to work in a garbage dump looking for morsels of food. I never had to carry heavy pails of impotable water for many miles in the hot sun so that my family would have water. But for years I starved to death for love. I had a roof over my head. But the home I lived in was more like being locked inside of a cage with a wild animal who constantly smoked. I did not only suffer from secondhand smoke, however. Watching the way my mom treated my dad caused me to suffer secondhand abuse.

Having experienced the flash-bang effects of protection orders and severe malicious prosecution during my Diamond Divorce, as the new demographic of divorcing older couples has come to be known, I write for the millions of "presumed innocent" men, and sadly many women, who never had the option of escaping our criminal system of injustice before becoming indentured servants. They pay dearly to see their kids rarely, if at all.

Our justice system is monetized to generate profits for those who slither and crawl along the entrails of its hallways and chambers. From judges who are as arrogant as they are inept, along with immoral prosecutors, lazy court-appointed psychologists and sleazy lawyers who bill by the amount of shit they dump; our courts are almost flawlessly set up to fail those they are supposed to serve while enriching the lawless bastards who claim an "In God We Trust" status of immunity. It destroys, to some degree, almost everyone it touches.

I portray my own divorce court judge as a bumbling vicious drunken idiot, but he is unfortunately a solid example of the unbridled power handed over to too many inadequate lawyers who can't find clients in the outside world and become deficient and defective judges collecting a secure paycheck and State government pension.

When I say that The Honorable Victor Alfieri was an alcoholic, I don't mean that I followed him into an AA meeting and saw him stand up and cry in regret as he explained how he destroyed my life because he was a drunkard. But he certainly seemed drunk (on a good day) when he judged my case. And based on stories I heard from my own inept lawyer, Victor Alfieri had quite a reputation for booze and boobs in his twenties and thirties. The malicious and skewed decisions he vomited while yelling at me in court certainly reeked of drunken behavior. They were sickening and made me nauseous.

I wrote my story for *Everyman* who has their own nightmare to tell but are not emotionally articulate, or calm enough, to sort out and share. There are no political movements for the millions of men who have been raped in prison or fucked during divorce court proceedings. Men don't protest or march in pink penis hats. They never "share their feelings." Male rape is the most under-reported crime in the world. And yet one out of ten rapes that occur are perpetrated upon a man. Men rarely talk. And admitting they were raped is an experience they will never reveal. Not even on their deathbed. And they hardly ever seek professional help.

Emotional displays are completely taboo for most men. Men are loners, like male lions, while women travel in packs, like lionesses in a pride. Raped men will never admit they were treated like a helpless woman. They don't talk. They can't talk. Every movie they've watched since they were children portray macho male heroes with gigantic guns and even bigger iron testicles.

The big screen constantly freezes in on men with thick skin who laugh while being interrogated and tortured by eight guys who he then kills. Men who walk away from deafening explosions without looking back. Men who never flinch in a gunfight or show emotion in their facial expressions as they "stare down" their beastly opponent. Men are never praised for being articulate and refined. They are honored with medallions for being warriors and idolized when extremely gifted at using their fists to bloody the face of someone almost as talented. In so many repetitive movies "trouble just seems to find them."

Try admitting you are a raped man with those images of how you were supposed to behave when you were attacked by three guys. And so men take a hot shower and move on. Or they hang themselves in their jail cell. As silent in death as when they yet lived. Divorced men are raped men. I'm the rare "pussy-boy" who was able to admit he was fucked.

Correctional Supervision (jail or probation) has *one out of every thirty-eight people* in this country locked in a vice-grip system set up to destroy their lives. What was conceived as a method for rehabilitation has instead become a dysfunctional and punitive gang-infested hellhole. And I'm just talking about the judge's chambers. Wait till you're greeted by the hardened prisoners and guards.

There are more than six and a half million people in jail or on parole in this country. That number portrays a pandemic of injustice that literally results in actual or stress-related death. One out of every thirty-eight adults are entwined in the U.S. Correctional System. Welcome to the land of opportunity.

Add the roughly seven million men a year, in their quest to exit a marriage from their "for better or for worse" spouse in our modern-day outrageously corrupt divorce and family court systems of justice, and that horrendous statistic doubles! More than ninety-five percent of dads lose (or relinquish) custody of their kids during a divorce. They are then slammed into a merciless system that automatically obligates them to pay alimony and child support.

Failing to support their spouse and children instantly transforms them into the status of a convicted criminal. After all, it's obvious that they "broke" the law. In their prior life these men could catch up on tuition bills or carry a balance at their mechanic's garage. The State has zero tolerance for "the unexpected."

Tracking these fathers who pay child support and severely punishing them the moment they fail, is accomplished by adding their name and social security number to the same system that tracks criminals. Combine these potential criminals (loving dads who miss their kids) with alleged or convicted criminals, and there are now more than thirteen and a half million people churning through the U.S. Correctional System.

Two out of every thirty-eight adults are now in the penal system. One out of nineteen men in this country are virtual prisoners whose finances are constantly being tracked by Big Brother. My paycheck has been automatically garnished for years. Thirty-eight percent of my earnings is deducted for child support and taxes. A paltry three percent is deposited into my 401K. And I "got off easy" because my wife was the "moneyed spouse" whose yearly salary was five times more than my part-time income.

Is it any wonder that one in four retirees work part-time? I have six more months till I'll be released from the penal system two months after I will have celebrated my sixty-ninth birthday. Many men are a paycheck away from landing behind bars. A simple, "Sorry, you're no longer a fit for this company," can easily translate to, "Put on this jump suit."

The Child Support Enforcement System tracks the lives of one out of every thirty-six fathers who must pay roughly a third of their salary towards child support. I'm all for child support, but the system we have now, in a century during which we are analyzing canyons on Mars and studying the history of water on that planet, is a medieval Inquisition. Dads are treated with utter contempt.

Simply losing their jobs and missing a few payments can turn a loving father into an instant deadbeat-dad criminal. Men only know about "losing the house" if they file for divorce. They have no idea how quickly they can land in jail based on a wildly flung protection order and the mood swings of a vicious tantruming gavel-banging imbecilic judge.

The punishment for losing your job can include losing your professional license (there are thousands of them — such as a mortgage originator license or a medical license), having your driver's license and passport revoked, or spending some "rehabilitation" time in jail (while your child support payments accrue). The manpower, logistics, and money needed to enslave and control thirteen and a half million people is mind boggling. It could very well cost nearly as much as the child support money itself. Welcome to the land of the free!

A third of those lucky fathers get to see their kids once a week. *Once a week!* The second third sees them less than four times a month. And the remaining third have no contact at all. I still can't believe that I — of all people — became part of that last-third statistic.

I wrote this story for the myriad of innocent fathers who continue to lose their children as a result of alienation. I am not alone. Most are *Everyman.* They've stifled their feelings their entire lives. Their families always came first. As little boys they already learned the "Women and children first" code of conduct from their own decent fathers.

I am thrilled there is a #metoo movement. Women have to be treated with dignity and respect. Religion, and eventually The State, has treated women like cattle for too many millenniums. It took till the dawn of the twentieth century for men to finally admit that women have a brain and the right to vote.

Most men instinctively realize that women are not as physically powerful as men (aside from the exceptional ability of women like Amanda Nunes who could kick the shit out of them), and most men will instantly defend a woman in distress. They have wives, mothers, sisters, and daughters they love. They want women to feel safe. At home and at work. But there is no question that too many innocent men are also suffering needlessly. And the "asshole" in their case is not some individual boss or co-worker jerk. It's the full force of the judicial branch of the U.S. court system and its army of overpaid enforcers.

The mistreatment I discuss in this book is when the tables are turned. When it comes to divorce it is typically the man who suffers abuse. And they suffer in silence. They man-up while they shut down. Women are now the abusers when it comes to divorce. Please remember that it's your husbands, fathers, brothers, and sons who are now the abused.

Men are also the least likely sector of society to seek therapy, let alone to contemplate the trauma, wasted finances, and lost years of life consumed by their divorce and its post-traumatic fallout — and to then place pen to paper to painstakingly describe their experience. Most men simply wave their hand in disgust and defeat when trying to discuss their divorce. I'm not sure if it's because of the trauma of the experience or their inability to communicate emotionally. Or maybe both. I was such an emotional wreck during my divorce that my therapist recommended a PTSD service dog. I told her that any service dog that sensed the agony, sadness and depressing emotions going on inside my brain would need its own personal service dog and I couldn't be that cruel to a living animal.

Let's face it. Guys are the weaker sex. They really are. Perhaps not physically. But they die younger. They don't take proper care of their teeth. They fail to visit their doctors for checkups. They commit suicide more often than females. And in most marriages, they typically avoid confrontation. Especially when they are young and need sex. Men really aren't as tough as they think they are. A little whining in round one and it's over.

I am a rare man. I love to talk and write. And although I enjoy hitting the heavy bag at the gym, I much prefer studying and doing library readings for children and sharing my passion for reading with them. Women can undoubtedly go through horrific divorces as well, and while I recognize that my efforts to share my story and describe my lived experiences during divorce are from a dad's perspective, I hope that everyone can benefit from the information herein. After all, I'm writing for the sake of children and their relationship with their divorced parents.

And so this story isn't only about the alienation of my sweet little girl. It's a story about millions of children who will no longer be seeing their father (or mother) once their parent files for divorce. This is not a fascinating story about one father's nightmare journey through the netherworld of divorce court. It's a repetitious ongoing story that millions of *Everyman* dads unfortunately share. And it's all the more gruesome when you're part of a religious cult and subject to shaming, excommunication, and worst of all — yapping Jewish Modern Orthodox Yentas!

Most men are not used to talking. So how can they be expected to write? They are more likely to pour some whiskey and man-up when things become too difficult to bear. After all, they heard the expression, "Be a man!" since they were little boys. Far too often, no one even imagined anything was wrong in their life till they finally announced it with a bullet to their own skull. After all, it's so "wimpy" to admit to having any mental health issues. Ever see a grown man cry? They don't. They choke.

Most men couldn't begin to explain what having emotional issues even means. In their minds only the sex that experiences menopause has emotional issues. Men like to believe they are "tough guys." They can be ninety years old, moving slowly as they carefully plant their walker a few inches in front of themselves to cautiously take their next baby step, while telling you how they once scored three touchdowns in one game playing football in college as if it were yesterday. But they never really talk about *themselves*. In truth, most men have never contemplated or even been introduced to their inner selves. They've never uttered their first baby words or taken a baby step in *that* direction.

Roughly half of all people will suffer emotionally and psychologically as a result of one traumatic event in their life. Sometimes it takes seconds or minutes (as in a car crash or rape). Other times it may take many months of being exposed to explosives and the real possibility of being blown up while on tour in Afghanistan or Iraq. The trauma may also arrive because of traumatic exposure to a cruel judge wearing a legal Nazi insignia that reads "In God We Trust," and being blown apart in three different court systems for three years while trying to divorce a wife. It may also fester after many anxious years of an adverse childhood that will have devastating lifelong effects.

Many people suffer PTSD as the result of a typical divorce, let alone enduring malicious prosecution and a lunatic judge constantly ranting, "I'll hold you in contempt!" during a stretched-out divorce. Multiply the already devastating effects of PTSD exponentially when the child you love is being alienated during the most difficult and exacting ordeal you will probably ever face, and it should come as no surprise that divorced men not only lose their finances, but even their actual identities, which makes them much more susceptible to experiencing a stroke or heart attack.

Divorce doesn't end with the Divorce Decree as you climb out of the rubble after barely surviving a bomb blast (a description I borrowed with the permission of my friend Dan Fernandez). That's when the fun starts. That decree — especially when children are involved — will restrain you more securely than a pillory till the day your youngest child reaches emancipation. If stress doesn't kill you, your own trigger finger will certainly finish the job. Divorced men are nine times more likely to commit suicide than divorced women. They don't use pills. They typically use bullets.

That shocking statistic, recently published by the Journal of Epidemiology and Community Health, is astonishing. The authors suggest that the unfairness of the way society and our court system treats divorcing men is quite possibly the reason they pull the trigger. Basically, men lose everything in a divorce — their wives, their kids, their money, their house, their reputation, and most of their friends. And when the woman your remaining friend is trying to fix you up with hears the word "divorced," her first thought is, "he's angry and has no money." Everything they worked for is gone. They justifiably feel that "life is not worth living."

Men are too quick to take ownership. And too slow to seek a mental health specialist. Because, as the title of Bruce Feirstein's best-seller quipped, *Real Men Don't Eat Quiche*. They eat shit. They don't know how to "share their feelings." But as a writer, I do. I reached deep into my Mr. Mom metrosexual personality to share my divorce experience from a man's honest "not such a tough-guy after all" perspective.

It's extremely rare for a man to write a book as maternally transparent as this one. A book that began as a dream, bled out of my pen as I woke up one morning (several years after my divorce and severe PTSD) and eventually became woke. The dream felt so real that I quickly scribbled a dozen pages in fast-moving cursive writing through moist eyes, while choking on the tears I tried to hold back, within seconds of realizing that I had been dreaming only moments ago. My bladder was bursting, but not nearly as much as my emotions. I didn't want to forget my dream, and so I basically outlined a five-hundred-page non-fiction novel while still half-asleep and holding in my pee. *It's a good thing I don't take Flowmax or this book might have never been written.*

I later shared the tear-stained pages with one of my favorite editors, who was the Senior Editor of Columbia Magazine before they dumbed down even that prestigious periodical. Having gone through his own turbulent divorce in another Jewish community in Clifton, NJ, only three years prior to my own debacle, my sensitive friend, who had his own mild PTSD that included three of his four children no longer speaking with him (accomplished without the aid of protection orders) immediately started crying. "Forget about submitting this to the *New Yorker*," he advised, "I think you have the outline of an incredible book here. Write it, and I'll edit your run-on sentences," he teased.

Indeed, the vast majority of books on divorce are written by women from their perspective. They are typically justified as they express anger at their powerful famous husbands. This is not that kind of book. Quite the opposite. None of the characters are famous. Unless being a small press publisher with great reviews by Kirkus and other major publishers marks me as famous, this book remains an *Everyman* story.

The age-old presumption during divorce in the 1950's, proclaiming that "it's in the best interests of the child to stay with their primary caregiver (i.e. Mommy)" still exists as we close upon the first quarter of this now twenty-first century. If no longer on the books — thanks to what modern-day psychology has taught us about the importance of dad being involved in their children's everyday lives — then surely the concept still sits firmly in the minds of society and the courts. Throw in windfall profits for everyone that hands dad a bill during his divorce and things are not about to change for another seventy-five years.

It should come as no surprise that Mother's Day became an official holiday in 1914, whereas Father's Day remained unofficial and was rejected by our nation till Richard Nixon finally equated dad to mom and officially proclaimed the holiday celebration in appreciation of fathers in 1972.

Let's face it. History repeats. God cursed Adam that "through painful toil you will eat from the fruits of the ground." God damned Eve with a punishment that she would experience "pain during childbirth." Seems that the ancient biblical punishments proclaimed upon the fall of humanity and the mendacious modern-day court decrees upon filing for a divorce are in synch. She gets to raise the kids. He pays the bills.

Speaking of the Original Sin, I smile at the image of the serpent depicted as a woman at the entrance to the Notre Dame in Paris. (It could just as well have been a divorce lawyer forcing divorced-man to spend eternity in limbo.) With firm naked breasts displayed in the top half of her yet-without-shame body, while her half-serpent bottom half is entwined around the Tree of Knowledge, she stands between Adam and Eve, watching as they eat the forbidden fruit.

All that's missing from the hand of the seductress-snake, I imagine, is a poisonous Order of Protection to hand Eve along with the forbidden fruit she hissed at her to feed her soon-to-be-mortal garnished-paycheck "banned from the house" husband, who relinquished custody of his sons to the woman who curtailed his lifespan from eternity to a paltry nine-hundred and thirty years.

And that is why taking out a few orders of protection and alienating a child from her dad during a divorce is possibly viewed by most judges as nothing more than a woman expressing a bit of anger while fulfilling God's will. Husbands will experience what it's like to be squeezed by Serpent wives as they try to catch their breath while trying to free an arm to hug their child if they are lucky enough to get some visitation.

Seems that God forgot to tell Adam that he would also suffer painfully as a result of childbirth (upon seeking a divorce). There is on average one divorce in America every thirteen seconds. That's 277 per hour, and 6,646 per day. Couple that number with the above statistic of nearly all mothers receiving custody and it's easy to understand the incredulous statistic that forty-three percent of children in the United States are being raised without their father's attention and love. Basically, half the kids in this country are living orphans.

Ester Lewinson, my youngest child who I raised from birth as a Mr. Mom — a baby I fed, diapered, napped, gently burped, sang to, carried on long walks, and played with, while my wife worked ten hour days, four days a week, at Northshore University Hospital (often sleeping there when an operation ran very late) — became a living orphan the nanosecond my wife was served with my Summons for Divorce Complaint. My wife ran to the police to file an Order of Protection after birthing five children with a quiet scholarly, "Yes Dear" husband during a twenty-eight year marriage. I haven't seen Ester in ten years. She just celebrated her twenty-first birthday.

The events recorded within this novel are utterly shocking because they happened to a man whose life was so mundane. I don't think I've had a parking ticket in twenty-five years. I wove the story against a Jewish backdrop only because I am a Jew, and because the colorfully rich tapestry of the Judaism I've studied for many decades is such an integral part of my life and world history.

I was also *shlepped* into the Jewish Beit-Din court system during my divorce in an attempt to force me to withdraw my motion from the secular court system. As an honest scholar, I made every effort to clearly explain and share with the reader the ineptness and malicious prosecution that goes on in those courts as well as in the secular ones.

I also had to deal with being excommunicated by the Jewish court and being shunned by my entire community while racing to three different court systems in the secular world. It was hard to even stay organized as I found myself carrying so many files to different scheduled court appearance locations. I raced in circles to divorce, criminal, and family court simultaneously. The policemen manning the security stations often waved me right through thinking that I was a lawyer.

This is not a story spewing rage at my ex-wife. I'm not angry at the woman I divorced. Although being human, I've had my internal moments of outrage and extreme frustration coupled with a great deal of sadness because of what she did to our minor daughter. But the calm and reflective rational side of me knows without a doubt that my bi-polar ex-wife is mentally ill. And the pedantic scholarly side of me knows that I made every attempt to salvage my marriage.

I divorced my wife because I realized that science has not yet caught up with the exact combination of medical and pharmacological help that she needs. And the spiritual side of me, after twenty-eight dispirited years, felt no further obligation to live in fight-or-flight stress and emotional unavailability simply because God "ordained" a match made in heaven.

What most religious people would call "sinful," I clearly understood as *deranged*. And so, feeling more sad than angry, even after all that she's done, I only wish her well. I'm much more upset at a legal system that watched her criminal acts and alienation tactics and intentionally turned a blind eye. All while feigning to be concerned with the "best interests of the child." It's enough to make an *Everyman* go insane — or to cause a Talmudical scholar to lose his faith in God.

Mine is a story for every individual who will ever get married and plans to bring children into our world. It is a story for men and women. And although roughly half of all match-made-in-heaven marriages wind up in divorce-hell, this story was not meant to be an *Everything You Wanted to Know About Divorce* book.

This is a story for all future parents. Mothers and Fathers. The simple message is as follows: If things don't work out — and there is a fifty percent chance that your marriage won't — *please leave your kids out of it*. And although my message will surely be ignored by selfish manipulative despotic mothers and a percentage of fathers; our legal court system of justice (the moral foundation of all civilized societies) needs to become woke. It cannot possibly continue this way.

My divorce experience is a story about our barbaric system of justice. Our criminal, family, and divorce court system of law has barely exited the Dark Ages when compared to the enlightened restorative justice systems of countries like Norway and Sweden. My own grueling experience with the law occurred as a result of filing a simple request for divorce.

What I imagined as nothing more than an uncomplicated simple division of assets and shared custody, morphed instead into an odyssey mired in psychological torture and malicious prosecution that continued for three long years. My wife was effusive about my being a great father, quipping to our eye doctor, "If he can't make a living, at least he's a great Mr. Mom." Detailed emotional letters, full of psychological terms that praised my parenting (along with descriptions of Ester's happy face when I dropped her off and picked her up every day at school for almost a decade), from the founders of the private Jewish school my daughter attended her entire life meant nothing to The Honerable Alfieri venal whore.

Our systemic court system encouraged, and certainly rewarded, any wild behavior and every outrageous accusation flung by my wife (of twenty-eight quiet marital Shalom Bayit years) and her lawyer as they wrapped their tentacles to squeeze my testicles, heart, and emotions, while choking off every lifeline and blocking any facet of human relationships in my existence. My constitutionally guaranteed protected rights were instantly dismissed as our criminal divorce court system instantly validated her perjured protection orders, her vile "client-attorney protected" (revealed and exposed in court) Final Solution emails, along with her many audacious accusations and contradictory lies. Sudden "urgent" forensic examinations were gaveled by an insane judge, and completely unnecessary costly witch trials were immediately scheduled into the fucking waste-of-your-life holy "Court Calendar" to determine if I sexually molested an older daughter and to then decide if I'm fit to receive chaperoned "Big Sister" visitation with my younger daughter. All in the "best interests of the minor child," of course. I am actually starting to feel triggered and nauseous again as I write this. I need to move on with finishing this epilogue.

In the blink of an eye, I lost my finances, my freedom, my reputation, my passport, my driver's license, my job, and my daughter. I also almost wound up spending a year in jail for, of all things, computer hacking. The only thing I did not lose was my relationship with Rabbi Nekrtiz. Although, heaven knows, they tried.

James Baldwin once wrote the following: "You think your pain and your heartbreak are unprecedented in the history of the world, but then you read." I love that quote about appreciating and experiencing the tribulations of others through reading. You realize that your toothache pales into insignificance when trussed against a mom holding her baby that is receiving pediatric chemo for a brain tumor. You sit breathless as your eyes scan words that describe a baby sucking at the shriveled breast of her emaciated mother in a concentration camp. You wonder if the words can possibly be true.

Reading allows you to feel empathy without having to undergo the ordeals of the protagonist to feel their pain. Reading teaches you how big the universe is while reminding you how small you are. It describes insane people that we believe are normal because they are a leader of many. And we honor historians who throw darts into a bullseye hole target of unimaginable atrocities, trusting the scholars to give us a clear perspective of ghastly events.

I also love how poignantly Baldwin reminds us that we are often selfishly eagle-eye focused and acutely aware of our own minor problems while oblivious to the millions of people in the world who suffer cruelties and illnesses we could not begin to fathom. There are so many horrific causes on which a person could spend their entire life trying to dent, let alone completely remedy.

Three quarters of a *billion* people worldwide don't have daily fresh potable water to drink in the year 2022. Five billion people still suffer the arduous and burdensome task of washing their clothes by hand in a plastic bin in the first quarter of the twenty-first century because they can't afford a washing machine. Dirty water is responsible for more death in the world than all forms of violence combined. Rape, hunger, murdered journalists, sex slaves, poverty, ignorance, disease, FGM, depression, terrorism, global warming, obesity generated by greedy corporations that know they are slowly committing "murder" (sue me, fuckers!), and the constant threat of nuclear war, are surely priorities that deserve our attention rather than focusing on a few (million) people that serve false orders of protection while alienating their kids. *So why did I choose to write about alienation and divorce?*

I only wrote about my divorce and the heartbreak of losing my daughter because it is what I have personally experienced and because it was so utterly senseless. It's not that I'm selfish or that I lack empathy for global issues that make my experience look trivial. Losing my daughter was a walk in the park compared to the pain of a parent that puts out after-school milk and cookies for a toddler who arrives home in a small blue body bag after being riddled with bullets from an AK-47.

I only shared the pain of my story because it should have never happened in the first place, and yet occurs hundreds of thousands of times a year because divorce lawyers, judges, and ancillary court-appointed leeches are allowed to wink at each other, over the unsuspecting heads of clueless divorcing couples who are forced into financing the very system that will *legally* and systematically drain their lifetime finances while stripping their emotions raw, as they destroy the lives of millions of innocent children. Most people won't even speak about their divorce. They "don't want to go there."

Gun violence is an aberration often inflicted by sick psyches. Slavery and illegal child labor are promoted by evil, inhumane minds that generate profits by using cheap labor because that is exactly how they value the lives of their victims. Accidental hospital deaths are *accidents*. Often clumsy and avoidable if hospital administration stopped rushing the staff and followed the angelic siren calls of voice actors assuring future victims that they are sincerely cared for (especially when they get to the billing department); and at a quarter of a million deaths per year surely intolerable by those who swear an oath of "do no harm." But nevertheless, they are accidental. Murders by psychopaths are never condoned with a shrug of "what else can we expect from a psycho?" They are committed by individuals with extremely aberrant behavior. And rape is committed as an act of violence by deviant psychos. However, every single one of these calamities are not executed systematically.

But getting a divorce — a natural and common everyday life situation of two people going their separate ways — somehow almost always turns into an extremely costly spectacle and an appalling horror story in our supposedly-healthy democratic judicial system led by assumed refined and highly-educated "moral" judges and lawyers.

All the issues I mentioned earlier are broken situations that need to be fixed. Unlike the extremely serious world-problems mentioned above, my life, and the beautiful father-daughter relationship I had with Ester, was never broken to begin with. It was a beautiful relationship. Ester was once a very happy child. The last thing she needed was "horse-therapy" and taking the witness stand to "testify" against her own father.

Ester was not hungry, ignorant, or enslaved in a North Korean re-education camp. She wasn't birthed into a life that necessitated her walking four miles twice a day to fetch contaminated, diseased water in some underdeveloped country in Africa. Her life was productive, creative, and very happy. She was such a beautiful little lady.

And I was one of the fortunate few people on the planet who was well fed, healthy, very educated, fruitful, and prosperous. I was a kind man. A God-fearing man. A family man. I was the busy Everyman who everyone turned to when they wanted to get things done. I was the guy every girl wanted to bring home to her parents. As a doting and loving Orthodox Jewish father of five, my life was happily committed to doing carpool and homework. You would have called me a boring guy. I was a scholar and a prolific writer of beautiful stories for children. I was a pillar of my community and a busy entrepreneur. And every spare minute of my day was spent studying the Talmud. DO NOT TALK TO MINOR CHILD.

The entire history of my adult life and three decades spent parenting five children — a flawless record of fifty years — disappeared the moment I signed that life away by filing a one-page document requesting a simple divorce upon serving my wife with papers. I placed my trust in our twenty-first century court system. Not because I was naive. But I thought that everything was transparent and well documented in court. I believed in a system that had an appeals process and a free press. Like mortgage lending, I thought everything is recorded and that fines, penalties, and incarceration are meted out to those who commit fraud, perjury, and submit false documentation. How was I to imagine that the lives of children have less value than sheetrock? How could I have known that tyrannical judges like Alfieri can roar, "I am the law!" as if they were a reincarnation of Genghis Khan and then stick my relationship with Ester on a spike?

I was instantly banished and catapulted out of Ester's life by outrageously false Orders of Protection that were launched with the force of a medieval trebuchet. My wife hurled email missiles accusing me of sexual abuse with my own daughters, and she flung projectiles of my supposed "obsession with shit" onto the hamlet of Monsey, NY. And her horde of Yenta-yaks faithfully rode their sure-footed mongolian horses as they raced to destroy the life of a teacher who was a better example of intelligence, honesty and kindness to their kids than they ever displayed as a parent. Like an evil sorcerer casting a spell ... "Presto!" I disappeared.

The reins controlling my life were placed into the hands of a nasty white-trash bum who barely made it through law school. Young Victor Alfieri basically took an "Ethics" course that was easier to pass than a DMV driving test and landed a cushy low-paying job granting him incredible power. He somehow just survived day-to-day as his "legal experience" granted his skanky judicial mind a wider berth and more control over the lives of anyone who stepped into his hellhole as the community grew exponentially. Forty-five years later I was one of his last "files" as Alfieri prepared for forced retirement.

Our toxic American court system "broke" me. And it will destroy you. It crushed my family and demolished my life. I spent three tearful traumatic years being humiliated, harassed, emotionally abused, and maliciously prosecuted. I literally starved and scrounged my pantry (checking the expiration dates on old cans of sardines) while waiting years for my maniacal Catch-22 judge to hold my wife in contempt for her refusal to pay his own court-ordered maintenance. And I was even forced to live homeless for a while as I bounced between friend's basements and inexpensive overnight motels where I could hear people moaning through the walls. And my "guilt" consisted of having been an amazing Mr. Mom and gentle husband for twenty-eight years who finally filed for a simple divorce.

A man that once gave hundreds of thousands of dollars to charity became a nervous PTSD riddled wreck who was forced to sponge for a place to sleep at night while begging for fifty-dollar loans during the day. One rabbi, to whom I generously donated tens of thousands of dollars with an open hand, stingily replied, "How much exactly do you need for Shabbos?" when I'd call him out of desperation on Thursday nights. He'd carve out that amount from his wallet as if he was chipping away at stone. "Rebbi, am I supposed to starve from Sunday till next Shabbos?" I asked in a quiet embarrassed voice. "Hashem will help you!" was his response, "You've helped so many others!"

Scholars (even my own dear Rabbi Nekrtiz) that I once gave dozens of envelopes stuffed with thick packets of hundred-dollar bills to pay their bills and the weddings of their many children, now looked at me with that empty Putin gaze and mercilessly stated, "Sorry, I don't have it. I'm not a businessman like you. You'll find your way," in response to my request for a small loan (as he and his wife took off for an eight week vacation that included Europe and Israel). Schools that I graciously gave twenty-five thousand dollar loans, because I knew money was tight before their yearly dinner (I was on the board and privy to their being temporarily cash-poor), returned the favor by loaning me a paltry five-hundred lousy dollars (two times) after I shamefully begged for a loan. I pray to God that I die before I'd ever subject myself to make such debasing calls ever again.

Another rabbi, for whose Yeshiva I once purchased two vans and in addition gave nearly a hundred-thousand dollars in donations (he actually kissed me at the time), agreed to help me with ten to twenty thousand in small dolled-out increments, but only if I allowed him to put a lien on my house for triple the amount of whatever I borrowed. After all, it wasn't his money, it was "holy money" that belonged to his Yeshiva. He did not take a penny of interest (that would be a sin). But if I died, he'd have to "take a lawyer" and he wanted to make sure that any exposure on his part would be easily recovered (that's not a sin, just pure fucking heartlessness to brazenly demand after all that I did for him with an open heart and a wide-open hand). I would have spit in his face if I wasn't so hungry. He then gave me his password and credit card to use in small increments. I saw that he had a $25K line of available credit. You have no idea how difficult it is to remain honest when your belly is empty, your electricity is about to be turned off, and your car is about to be impounded because you're a half year behind in payments. I rationalized that "I'll pay him back," but I couldn't spend my priceless reputation in exchange for the twenty-five thousand dollar limit of his credit card.

Other individuals, like my brother-in-law Jon Zaslow, for whom I would have happily donated one of my kidneys, before even being asked, instantly listened to the instructions of his nasty wife, via my ex, to cease all communication with me and "not to loan him [me] any money." My wife taught me a great lesson first tweeted by a racist Minnesota congresswoman. Divorce and religion are, "All about the Benjamins baby!"

The barbaric, heartless treatment meted out to me by The Chosen People displayed their true "merciful and charitable" colors during my divorce. For two full years that I wrote my book while dealing with my PTSD and living at 19 Mariner Way post-divorce, not one neighbor invited me for a Shabbat meal. Meanwhile my ex-wife constantly walked over on Shabbat to enjoy a lovely meal with my neighbors across the street who would report anything they saw during the week. If a friend came to visit, Mr. Fonfedder would sneak over to peek at the license plate in the hope that he'd have something of value to report to Ms. Mailman (my ex) on Shabbat. You would think busy Jews would have better ways of spending their time.

The transference of my wealth, and the wealth of millions of fathers, into the coffers of the court earns judges, lawyers, and court appointed officials billions of dollars by perpetuating the flawlessly broken system upon which it operates by never letting its right-handed tentacle know what its left-handed tentacle is doing. Short version: Millions of fathers are paying a fortune to never see their children again. *In God We Trust.*

Meanwhile, the creature's endless arms are all over your body. One handing you a protection order. One alienating your children from you. One squeezing your testicles. One up your anus. And the other arms hold you upside down by your ankles, shaking any loose change out of your pockets while simultaneously swiping the cash out of your wallet and frozen bank accounts. Dare to hack off one arm and two will instantly reappear.

As I said on my credential page at the outset of this book, "Mine is a non-fiction work." I did my best to speak the whole truth and nothing but the truth. To the best of my knowledge, I put forth my sincere effort, consisting (literally) of elevated blood-pressure, sweat, and tears, to painstakingly verify every single word among the more than quarter-million words in my story.

With the patience of an ancient Talmudical scholar, coupled with the modern-day lightning speed research power of Google, I fact-checked the accuracy of everything I wrote. Even Ian Fleming's famous original line of "Stirred, Not shaken," which the screenwriter of the movie inverted, for an endless number of possible reasons that the internet is always happy to inform us, forcing the portrayal of all the actors playing the role of James Bond to request the opposite way that a flawless martini is to be prepared for a sophisticated connoisseur of my favorite beverage. When it's "shaken" the ice melts too quickly and dilutes the drink. Almost like my marriage shook my soul and diluted my creativity. I, however, spent twenty-eight years being shaken and stirred.

Whenever I make any assumption I say "alleged," or I acknowledge that my empathetic and highly sensitive personality (HSP) gave me the upper hand in assuming what was later revealed in court or in emails to be true. I can't enumerate how many times in my life that I absolutely knew what people were feeling or thinking even before they shared the details of their emotions and thoughts with me. And that includes my ex wife. I had my lawyer file my request for divorce as I braced myself to be hit by a truck. The only detail my intuitive nature missed was that I didn't realize the vehicle would be loaded with insane dynamite. I also admit, more than several times, that I have no formal degree in psychology. Nevertheless, I included many scientific studies to validate my observations, and as a writer, I allowed the actions of the people in my book to speak for their own true character and I used their unabashed naked emails to portray the alternate lives they lead in public versus the hypocritical ones they lead in private.

My divorce taught me more than I ever imagined, more than I wanted to know, and more than my heart could tolerate without almost exploding. I was nevertheless happy to discover the truth about the people I once trusted and loved. The lessons I learned, and the ordeal I somehow survived, drastically changed my life for the better.

And so, this story isn't only about me. It's about you. And it's about your son who will get married one day and (very likely) divorced a few years later. It isn't a story about my adorable child. It's about your beautiful child when you decide to finally file for divorce. You'll be lucky if you even get to wave goodbye.

"Not me!" you naively believe. "There are always three sides to a story. Hers, his, and the truth!" you foolishly cluck like the extinct dodo bird (which you will become upon filing for divorce) in the belief that this could never happen to you. The endless research and statistics regarding filing protection orders during a divorce insist otherwise.

That said, divorce in the twenty-first century in America will very likely include your financial ruin, your precipitously declining health, your PTSD-wracked nervous system, the garnishment of your paycheck, along with your permanently destroyed reputation. It will also result in your early demise because divorced men suffer an astonishingly higher rate of heart attacks, strokes, cancer and heart disease than non-divorced men.

The saddest part is that it will surely include your lost relationship with your child.